D1641053

Christian Origins and the Establishment of the Early Jesus Movement

Texts and Editions for New Testament Study

Edited by

Stanley E. Porter and Wendy J. Porter

VOLUME 12

Early Christianity in Its Hellenistic Context

VOLUME 4

The titles published in this series are listed at *brill.com/tent*

Christian Origins and the Establishment of the Early Jesus Movement

Edited by

Stanley E. Porter
Andrew W. Pitts

BRILL

LEIDEN | BOSTON

Library of Congress Cataloging-in-Publication Data

Names: Porter, Stanley E., 1956- editor.
Title: Christian origins and the establishment of the early Jesus movement / edited by Stanley E. Porter, Andrew W. Pitts.
Description: Boston : Brill, 2018. | Series: Texts and editions for New Testament study, ISSN 1574-7085 ; Volume 12 | Series: Early Christianity in its Hellenistic context ; Volume 4 | Includes bibliographical references and index. |
Identifiers: LCCN 2018019157 (print) | LCCN 2018025547 (ebook) |
    ISBN 9789004372740 (e-book) | ISBN 9789004372696 (hardback : alk. paper)
Subjects: LCSH: Church history–Primitive and early church, ca. 30–600. | Bible. New Testament–Criticism, interpretation, etc. | Christianity–Origin.
Classification: LCC BS2410 (ebook) | LCC BS2410 .C48 2018 (print) |
    DDC 225.6–dc23
LC record available at https://lccn.loc.gov/2018019157

Typeface for the Latin, Greek, and Cyrillic scripts: "Brill". See and download: brill.com/brill-typeface.

ISSN 1574-7085
ISBN 978-90-04-37269-6 (hardback)
ISBN 978-90-04-37274-0 (e-book)

Copyright 2018 by Koninklijke Brill NV, Leiden, The Netherlands.
Koninklijke Brill NV incorporates the imprints Brill, Brill Hes & De Graaf, Brill Nijhoff, Brill Rodopi, Brill Sense and Hotei Publishing.
All rights reserved. No part of this publication may be reproduced, translated, stored in a retrieval system, or transmitted in any form or by any means, electronic, mechanical, photocopying, recording or otherwise, without prior written permission from the publisher.
Authorization to photocopy items for internal or personal use is granted by Koninklijke Brill NV provided that the appropriate fees are paid directly to The Copyright Clearance Center, 222 Rosewood Drive, Suite 910, Danvers, MA 01923, USA. Fees are subject to change.

This book is printed on acid-free paper and produced in a sustainable manner.

Printed by Printforce, the Netherlands

Contents

Preface IX
Abbreviations XI
List of Contributors XVI

Christian Origins and the Establishment of the Early Jesus Movement:
An Introduction 1
   Stanley E. Porter and Andrew W. Pitts

PART 1
The Formation of the Jesus Movement and Its Precursors

John the Baptist in the Fourth Gospel 11
   Clare K. Rothschild

John's Baptist in Luke's Gospel 32
   John DelHousaye

From John to Apollos to Paul: How the Baptism of John Entered the Jesus
Movement 49
   Stephen J. Patterson

Followers, Servants, and Traitors: The Representation of Disciples in the
Synoptic Gospels and in Ancient Judaism 71
   Catherine Hezser

PART 2
Production of Early Christian Gospels

The Pre-citation Fallacy in New Testament Scholarship and Sanders's
Tendencies of the Synoptic Tradition 89
   Stanley E. Porter and Andrew W. Pitts

Was Matthew a Plagiarist? Plagiarism in Greco-Roman Antiquity 108
   E. Randolph Richards

Compositional Techniques within Plutarch and the Gospel Tradition   134
    Michael R. Licona

The Narrative Perspective of the Fourth Gospel   149
    Hans Förster

Assessing the Criteria for Differentiating the Cross Gospel   172
    Stanley E. Porter and Andrew W. Pitts

PART 3
Early Christian Descriptions of the Jesus Movement

From Jesus to Lord and Other Contributions of the Early Aramaic-Speaking Congregation in Jerusalem   187
    F. Stanley Jones

Did Jesus, in the Memory of His Earliest Followers, Ever Nurse the Sick?   196
    Steven Thompson

The Kingdom of God is among You: Prospects for a Q Community   224
    Sarah E. Rollens

An Imminent Parousia and Christian Mission: Did the New Testament Writers Really Expect Jesus's Imminent Return?   242
    Mark Keown

Christian Origins and Imperial-Critical Studies of the New Testament Gospels   264
    Warren Carter

"No Stone Left upon Another": Considering Mark's Temple Motif in Narrative and History   283
    Adam Winn

The Holy Spirit as Witness of Jesus in the Canonical Gospels   311
    Judith Stack

New Exodus Traditions in Earliest Christianity   335
Nicholas Perrin

Sea Storms, Divine Rescues, and the Tribulation: The Jonah Motif in the Book of Matthew   351
Susan M. Rieske

The Parables of Jesus and Socrates   373
Adam Z. Wright

PART 4
The Jewish Mission and Its Literature

Why Have We Stopped Reading the Catholic Epistles Together? Tracing the Early Reception of a Collection   393
Darian Lockett

A Jewish Denial: 1 John and the Johannine Mission   412
Matthew Jensen

Love One Another and Love the World: The Love Command and Jewish Ethics in the Johannine Community   426
Beth M. Stovell

The New Perspective (on Paul) on Peter: Cornelius's Conversion, the Antioch Incident, and Peter's Stance towards Gentiles in the Light of the Philosophy of Historiography   459
Christoph Heilig

Tradition as Interpretation: Linguistic Structure and the Citation of Scripture in 1 Peter 2:1–10   497
Andrew W. Pitts

1 Peter and the Theological Logic of Christian Familial Imagery   517
Matthew R. Malcolm

Index of Modern Authors   535
Index of Ancient Sources   546

Preface

This volume represents the fourth in our continuing series of volumes on Early Christianity in its Hellenistic Context. The first two volumes appeared in the Texts and Editions of New Testament Study series (TENTS): Stanley E. Porter and Andrew W. Pitts, eds., *Christian Origins and Greco-Roman Culture: Social and Literary Contexts for the New Testament* (ECHC 1; TENTS 9; Leiden: Brill, 2013); and Porter and Pitts, eds., *Christian Origins and Hellenistic Judaism: Social and Literary Contexts for the New Testament* (ECHC 2; TENTS 10; Leiden: Brill, 2013). The third volume in the series, because of its emphasis upon language-related matters, appeared in a different series but still maintaining the same overall emphasis: Porter and Pitts, eds., *The Language of the New Testament: Context, History, and Development* (ECHC 3; LBS 6; Leiden: Brill, 2013). We are pleased that these volumes have been well received by the scholarly guild and have already been noted as making a contribution to the series subject. This volume now returns to the TENTS series because of its focus upon Christian origins and how the Jesus movement became established in the latter half of the first century. We thought that this subject would provide a natural and important extension of the work of the previous volumes.

Based upon the individual contributions, we believe that this volume of essays provides a commendable continuation of the series, and we are already working on subsequent volumes. The essays within this volume—though all within the ambit of the series orientation—range over a number of diverse subjects, and are organized according to four related and intertwined topics (see the table of contents). However, within each topic category, as well as among them, there is plenty of diversity of opinion to give scholars plenty to ponder.

The editors wish to thank the contributors for their willingness to contribute their essays to this collection. We appreciate their patience as we went through the editing process, a process that sometimes required more time than we were anticipating. Nevertheless, as a result of the kind of work and dedication demonstrated by the contributors, we believe that this volume makes an important contribution to the topic and advances knowledge within the field in significant ways. Our hope and desire is that a number of the essays will promote further research and deliberation over the topics that are treated here and some of the new proposals that are put forward. Many of the ideas contained here would seem to merit critical responses, whether in support of or in opposition to the proposals contained. We would like to invite contributors, both those who have contributed to this and previous volumes and those who have not yet submitted an essay for consideration, to consider submitting an essay to future volumes in this series for their well-considered ideas on our further topics regarding early Christianity and its Hellenistic context.

We as editors would like to thank our respective academic institutions, McMaster Divinity College and Arizona Christian University, for their continuing and unflagging support of our scholarly endeavors. On behalf of our contributors to this volume, we would also like to thank their respective institutions for their tangible and other support that makes contributing to volumes such as this possible.

As we have in the past, and without any sense of duty or obligation, we wish to thank those closest to us for their unwavering support of us. We realize, and never wish to forget, that they make greater sacrifices on behalf of our scholarship than we realize and, if truth be told, more than we who are directly engaged in it.

Abbreviations

AB	Anchor Bible
ABD	*Anchor Bible Dictionary.* Edited by David N. Freedman. 6 vols. New York: Doubleday, 1993
ABRL	Anchor Bible Reference Library
AJSR	*Association for Jewish Studies Review*
AmJT	*American Journal of Theology*
AnBib	Analecta biblica
ANRW	*Aufstieg und Niedergang der römischen Welt.* Berlin: de Gruyter, 1972–
ANTC	Abingdon New Testament Commentaries
ArBib	The Aramaic Bible
ATANT	Abhandlungen zur Theologie des Alten und Neuen Testaments
ATDan	Acta theologica danica
AUSS	*Andrews University Seminary Studies*
BA	*Biblical Archaeologist*
BBR	*Bulletin for Biblical Research*
BDAG	Baur, Walter, Frederick W. Danker, W.F. Arndt, and F.W. Gingrich. *Greek-English Lexicon of the New Testament and Other Early Christian Literature.* 3rd ed. Chicago: University of Chicago Press, 2000
BDF	Blass, Friedrich, and Albert Debrunner. *A Greek Grammar of the New Testament and Other Early Christian Literature.* Revised and translated by Robert W. Funk. Chicago: University of Chicago Press, 1961
BECNT	Baker Exegetical Commentary on the New Testament
BETL	Bibliotheca Ephemeridum Theologicarum Lovaniensium
Bib	*Biblica*
BibInt	*Biblical Interpretation*
BibInt	Biblical Interpretation Series
BibLeb	*Bibel und Leben*
BibS(N)	Biblische Studien (Neukirchen, 1951–)
BJRL	*Bulletin of the John Rylands Library*
BLG	Biblical Languages: Greek
BNTC	Black's New Testament Commentary
BSac	*Bibliotheca Sacra*
BTZ	*Berliner Theologische Zeitschrift*
BZAW	Beihefte zur Zeitschrift für die alttestamentliche Wissenschaft
BZ	*Biblischen Zeitschrift*
BZNW	Beihefte zur Zeitschrift für die neutestamentliche Wissenschaft
CanJTh	*Canadian Journal of Theology*

CBQ	*Catholic Biblical Quarterly*
CBQMS	Catholic Biblical Quarterly Monograph Series
ConBNT	Coniectanea biblica: New Testament Series
ConNT	Coniectanea Neotestamentica
COQG	Christian Origins and the Question of God
CPNIVC	College Press NIV Commentary
CQ	*Classical Quarterly*
CTQ	*Concordia Theological Quarterly*
CurBR	*Currents in Biblical Research*
ECHC	Early Christianity in Its Hellenistic Context
EDNT	*Exegetical Dictionary of the New Testament*. Edited by H. Balz and G. Schneider. ET. Grand Rapids: Eerdmans, 1990–1993
EEC	Evangelical Exegetical Commentary
EKKNT	Evangelische-katholischer Kommentar zum Neuen Testament
ERT	*Evangelical Review of Theology*
ETL	*Ephemerides Theologicae Lovanienses*
EuroJTh	*European Journal of Theology*
ExpTim	*The Expository Times*
FolOr	*Folia Orientalia*
FRLANT	Forschungen zur Religion und Literatur des Alten und Neuen Testaments
GCS	Die griechischen christlichen Schriftsteller der ersten [drei] Jahrhunderte
HB	Hebrew Bible
HDR	Harvard Dissertations in Religion
Herm	*Hermanthena*
HNTC	Harper's New Testament Commentaries
HNT	Handbuch zum Neuen Testament
HO	Handbuch der Orientalistik
HR	*History of Religions*
HTKNT	Herders Theologischer Kommentar zum Neuen Testament
HTR	*Harvard Theological Review*
ICC	International Critical Commentary
Int	*Interpretation*
ITQ	*Irish Theological Quarterly*
JAAR	*Journal of the American Academy of Religion*
JAC	Jahrbuch für Antike und Christentum
JBL	*Journal of Biblical Literature*
JDS	Judean Desert Studies
JECS	*Journal of Early Christian Studies*
JETS	*Journal of the Evangelical Theological Society*
JGRChJ	*Journal of Greco-Roman Christianity and Judaism*

JHS	*Journal of Hellenic Studies*
JNSL	*Journal of Northwest Semitic Languages*
JSJSup	Supplements to the Journal for the Study of Judaism
JSNT	*Journal for the Study of the New Testament*
JSNTSup	Journal for the Study of the New Testament Supplement Series
JSOT	*Journal for the Study of the Old Testament*
JSOTSup	Journal for the Study of the Old Testament Supplement Series
JSPSup	Journal for the Study of the Pseudepigrapha Supplements
JSS	*Journal of Semitic Studies*
JTI	*Journal of Theological Interpretation*
JTS	*Journal of Theological Studies*
KEK	see MeyerK
L&N	Louw, J.P., and E.A. Nida, eds. *Greek-English Lexicon of the New Testament: Based on Semantic Domains*. 2nd ed. New York: United Bible Societies, 1989
LBS	Linguistic Biblical Studies
LCL	Loeb Classical Library
LNTS	Library of New Testament Studies
LSJ	Liddell, Henry George, Robert Scott, and Henry Stuart Jones. *A Greek-English Lexicon*. 9th ed. Oxford: Clarendon, 1976
MeyerK	Kritische-exegetischer Kommentar über das Neue Testament (Meyer-Kommentar)
MNTS	McMaster New Testament Studies
MPER	Mitteilungen aus der Papyrussammlung Erzherzog Rainer
MThSt	Marburger Theologische Studien
NA27	*Novum Testamentum Graece*. 27th ed. Based on the work of Eberhard and Erwin Nestle. Edited by Barbara Aland, Kurt Aland, Johannes Karavidopoulos, Carlo M. Martini, and Bruce Metzger. Stuttgart: Deutsche Bibelgesellschaft, 2006
NA28	*Novum Testamentum Graece*. 28th ed. Based on the work of Eberhard and Erwin Nestle. Edited by Barbara Aland, Kurt Aland, Johannes Karavidopoulos, Carlo M. Martini, and Bruce Metzger. Revised under the direction of Holger Strutwolf. Stuttgart: Deutsche Bibelgesellschaft, 2013
NAC	New American Commentary
NCBC	New Century Bible commentary
Neot	*Neotestamentica*
NHC	Nag Hammadi Codex
NICNT	New International Commentary on the New Testament
NIGTC	New International Greek Testament Commentary
NIV	New International Version
NovT	*Novum Testamentum*

NovTSup	Supplements to Novum Testamentum
NRSV	New Revised Standard Version
NTD	Das Neue Testament Deutsch
NTL	New Testament Library
NTS	*New Testament Studies*
NTT	New Testament Theology
NTTSD	New Testament Tools, Studies and Documents
NTTS	New Testament Tools and Studies
ÖBS	Österreichische biblische Studien
OTP	*Old Testament Pseudepigrapha*. Edited by J.H. Charlesworth. 2 vols. New York: Doubleday, 1983
PAST	Pauline Studies
PRSt	*Perspectives in Religious Studies*
RAC	*Reallexikon für Antike und Christentum*. Edited by T. Kluser et al. Stuttgart: Teubner, 1950–
RB	*Revue Biblique*
RevExp	*Review and Expositor*
RevQ	*Revue de Qumran*
RNT	Regensburger Neues Testament
RSR	*Recherches de science religieuse*
SBG	Studies in Biblical Greek
SBLDS	Society of Biblical Literature Dissertation Series
SBL	Society of Biblical Literature
SBT	Studies in Biblical Theology
SC	Sources chrétiennes. Paris: Cerf, 1943–
SDSSRL	Studies in Dead Sea Scrolls and Related Literature
SHBC	Smyth & Helwys Bible Commentary
SNTSMS	Society for New Testament Studies Monograph Series
SNTW	Studies of the New Testament and its World
SP	Sacra Pagina
STDJ	Studies in the Texts of the Desert of Judah
StPB	Studia post-biblica
ST	*Studia theologica*
StudLit	*Studia Liturgica*
SwJT	*Southwestern Journal of Theology*
TB	Theologische Bücherei: Neudrucke und Berichte aus dem 20. Jahrhundert
TCGNT²	Bruce Manning Metzger, *A Textual Commentary on the Greek New Testament: A Companion Volume to the United Bible Societies' Greek New Testament (Fourth Revised Edition)*. 2nd ed. Stuttgart: Deutsche Bibelgesellschaft /United Bible Society, 2012

TDNT	*Theological Dictionary of the New Testament*. 10 vols. Edited by Gerhard Kittel and Gerhard Friedrich. Translated by Geoffrey W. Bromiley. Grand Rapids: Eerdmans, 1964–1976
TDOT	*Theological Dictionary of the Old Testament*. Edited by G.J. Botterweck and H. Ringgren. Translated by J.T. Willis, G.W. Bromiley, and D.E. Green. 8 vols. Grand Rapids: Eerdmans, 1974–
TENTS	Texts and Editions for New Testament Study
ThT	*Theologisch tijdschrift*
TJ	*Trinity Journal*
TLG	*Thesaurus Linguae Graecae*
TQ	*Theologische Quartalschrift*
TRu	*Theologische Rundschau*
TSAJ	Texte und Studien zum antiken Judentum
TS	*Theological Studies*
TU	Texte und Untersuchungen
TynBul	*Tyndale Bulletin*
TZ	*Theologische Zeitschrift*
UBSHS	United Bible Societies Handbook Series
UTb	Uni-Taschenbücher
UUA	*Uppsala Universitetsårskrift*
VCSup	Vigiliae Christianae Supplements
WBC	Word Biblical Commentary
WTJ	*Westminster Theological Journal*
WUNT	Wissenschaftliche Untersuchungen zum Neuen Testament
WW	*Word and World*
ZAC	*Zeitschrift für Antikes Christentum*
ZBK	Zürcher Bibelkommentare
ZECNT	Zondervan Exegetical Commentary on the New Testament
ZNW	*Zeitschrift für die neutestamentliche Wissenschaft und die Kunde der älteren Kirche*
ZTK	*Zeitschrift für Theologie und Kirche*

List of Contributors

Warren Carter
Brite Divinity School at Texas Christian University, Fort Worth, TX

John DelHousaye
Phoenix Seminary, AZ

Hans Förster
Univerisity of Vienna

Christoph Heilig
University of Zürich

Catherine Hezser
SOAS, University of London

Matthew Jensen
Sydney University

F. Stanley Jones
California State University, Long Beach, CA

Mark Keown
Laidlaw College, Auckland, New Zealand

Michael R. Licona
Houston Baptist University, TX

Darian Lockett
Talbot School of Theology, Biola University, La Mirada, CA

Matthew R. Malcolm
Universitas Pelita Harapan, Indonesia

Stephen J. Patterson
Willamette University, Salem, OR

Nicholas Perrin
Wheaton Graduate School, Wheaton, IL

Andrew W. Pitts
Independent scholar

Stanley E. Porter
McMaster Divinity College, Hamilton, ON, Canada

E. Randolph Richards
Palm Beach Atlantic University, West Palm Beach, FL

Susan M. Rieske
Wheaton College, Wheaton, IL

Sarah E. Rollens
Rhodes College, Memphis, TN

Clare K. Rothschild
Lewis University, Chicago, IL

Judith Stack
Augsburg University, Minneapolis, MN

Beth M. Stovell
Ambrose Seminary of Ambrose University, Calgary, AB, Canada

Steven Thompson
Avondale College of Higher Education, Cooranbong, NSW, Australia

Adam Winn
University of Mary Hardin-Baylor, Waco, TX

Adam Z. Wright
College of Emmanuel and St. Chad, Saskatoon, SK, Canada

Christian Origins and the Establishment of the Early Jesus Movement: An Introduction

Stanley E. Porter and Andrew W. Pitts

This book continues a series of volumes we have been editing related to Christian Origins and its earliest contexts within the Hellenistic world of the Roman empire. The first two volumes provided a number of studies that situated Christian origins in relation to Greco-Roman culture and Hellenistic Judaism respectively. The third volume focused on the sociolinguistic contexts for the emergence of early Christianity and its literature.[1] The range of topics discussed in all of these volumes is evidenced by the fact that the third volume appeared in a different series than did the first two. This fourth volume turns to further sociological questions in probing the relation of Christian origins to the establishment of the early Jesus movement, although it does so from a less linguistic and more social-cultural perspective. By the establishment-period for the 'Jesus movement,' we refer to the time from the formation of Jesus's earliest followers into some types of recognizable groups to sometime around the beginnings of the Antioch church. The fundamental question we wish to consider is this: How did this early phase of Christianity propel its literary and social momentum into the first century? The task of answering this question will involve our contributors in several avenues of research, ranging from the role of John the Baptist in the development of the Jesus sect to the establishment of the Jewish mission and its literature. As a result, the volume is divided into four parts: (1) The Formation of the Jesus Movement and its Precursors; (2) Production of Early Christian Gospels; (3) Early Christian Descriptions of the Jesus Movement; and (4) The Jewish Mission and its Literature.

We begin with a set of four articles devoted to exploring the formation of the Jesus movement and its precursors. Clare K. Rothschild's initiatory chapter, "John the Baptist in the Fourth Gospel," addresses how the Baptizer

---

[1] Stanley E. Porter and Andrew W. Pitts, eds., *Christian Origins and Greco-Roman Culture: Literary and Social Contexts for the New Testament* (ECHC 1; TENTS 9; Leiden: Brill, 2013); Stanley E. Porter and Andrew W. Pitts, eds., *Christian Origins and Hellenistic Judaism: Literary and Social Contexts for the New Testament* (ECHC 2; TENTS 10; Leiden: Brill, 2013); Stanley E. Porter and Andrew W. Pitts, eds., The *Language of the New Testament: Context, History, and Development* (ECHC 3; LBS 6; Leiden: Brill, 2013).

traditions in the Fourth Gospel serve the author's wider agenda. It presents the Johannine portrait of John the Baptist by stressing points of continuity and discontinuity with the Synoptic descriptions. Rothschild argues that the Fourth Gospel's presentation of John the Baptist deliberately duplicates, omits, supplements, adapts, and corrects the Synoptic Baptist traditions. This strategy underlines the author's effort to supplant the seemingly contradictory picture of John and Jesus that emerges in the Synoptics with a more consistent portrait that weaves together its various threads into a unified account of the Baptizer.

Continuing the theme of the Baptizer in John's Gospel, in the next chapter, John DelHousaye focuses upon the potential Lukan appropriation of the Fourth Gospel's Baptist in its departure from the Markan tradition. Proceeding from Mark Matson's close reading approach, DelHousaye compares the beginnings of the Fourth and Third Gospels. Assessment of verbal overlap, harmonization, and shared omissions with the Fourth Gospel leads DelHousaye to conclude that Luke likely used a form of John's Gospel not unlike its canonical form.

In his chapter, Stephen J. Patterson widens the frame of the discussion with his study of the entrance of the baptism ritual into earliest Christianity, especially in connection with some of the more perplexing Pauline traditions. Patterson points to three pictures of baptism within the Jesus movement. He stresses the tendency of the John the Baptist traditions to connect the ritual with a transformation conveyed by the Holy Spirit. Second, in his analysis of the pre-Pauline formula in Gal 3:26–28, Patterson discovers evidence of baptism as an initiation rite for entrance into an egalitarian community where issues of class, gender, and ethnicity challenge group cohesion. Paul represents a third and final position. In his deployment of baptism in Rom 6:3–11 as a metaphor for the dying and rising Christ, unrelated to accompanying Spirit traditions, Paul represents a departure from the pneumatologically driven baptism traditions that cluster around John the Baptizer.

Catherine Hezser explores the master-student relationship in Palestinian rabbinic texts to better understand how Jesus's disciples and sympathizers are depicted in her paper on "Followers, Servants and Traitors." Just as Jesus's disciples functioned as the tradents of the Jesus tradition, the disciples of sages functioned as tradents of traditions for their rabbinic masters. In the rabbinic tradition, the later compilers/editors of sage traditions remained anonymous and focused instead upon the authoritative sayings of the Rabbi and their known disciples as tradents of this tradition. The tendency of later rabbinic editors was to remain anonymous in order to focus upon and elevate the authority of their sources. Hezser suggests a potential connection with the Gospel tradition here, where only a select number of disciples are emphasized by the Gospel authors while the authors themselves remain anonymous.

Section 2 of this book explores the production of early Christian Gospels as a byproduct of the early Jesus movement. The first chapter in this section, by Stanley E. Porter and Andrew W. Pitts, identifies what they refer to as the pre-citation fallacy in scholars' reception of and response to E.P. Sanders's research on Synoptic tendencies and their transmission. Some scholars completely ignore Sanders's work. Some take it into serious consideration, whether developing or responding to it in some way, while a third group curiously refers to Sanders but then undertakes analysis inconsistent with his conclusions (i.e. the pre-citation fallacy). Porter and Pitts reassert the importance of Sanders's work and contend that merely referencing his research is not enough to bypass its significant implications for form-critical methodology.

Was Matthew a plagiarist? E. Randolph Richards seeks to answer this question through a study of pseudonymity and related practices in the ancient world. Richards commends many aspects of Bart Ehrman's analysis of ancient forgery and plagiarism, especially his critique of so-called innocent apostolic pseudepigrapha. However, Richards argues for a more nuanced account of intellectual property in the ancient world, in which literary borrowing does not necessarily count as literary theft. Although correct on many accounts, the situation—at least with respect to Matthew's Gospel—seems to be less duplicitous than Ehrman imagines.

In the next chapter, Michael Licona examines two sets of texts, Plutarch's *Lives* and the canonical Gospels, in an effort to compare how the authors narrate the same stories differently. He proposes five compositional devices used in two or more of Plutarch's *Lives* and argues for the deployment of similar strategies in the composition of the Synoptic tradition. Licona concludes that Plutarch's methods for documenting parallel accounts *via* distinct literary strategies reflect patterns employed by the Synoptic authors, resolving a number of traditional Gospel discrepancies without forcing the issue of harmonization.

Hans Förster's chapter explores "The Narrative Perspective of the Fourth Gospel." The first part of the paper lays out the narrative perspective and literary genre of the Fourth Gospel in comparison to Luke and Acts. He then argues for the possibility that the Gospel of John includes a self-attestation to its literary form—a non-fiction narrative based on eyewitness tradition. Proceeding from this analysis, Förster probes the range of consequences a possible self-assignment of a literary genre might entail for the interpretation of the Fourth Gospel. Among some of the most important implications, Förster notes that his proposed Johannine literary self-assignment may function as internal evidence in support of the long ending for John's Gospel.

In their chapter, Stanley E. Porter and Andrew W. Pitts assess John Dominic Crossan's most recent study of the so-called Cross Gospel. Despite Crossan's attempt to reestablish his argument for the early, independent status of the Cross Gospel within the larger Gospel of Peter, Porter and Pitts seek to show that whether considered separately or together, the two documents reflect a later account, derived from the canonical Gospels, and possibly other canonical material. In particular, they argue that the failure to differentiate friends and enemies as a source-critical criterion, the dependent nature of the execution account, the clear indicators of later developed Christology, the failure to incorporate the resurrection account in the canonical Gospels, and the lack of support for the transitionary units all indicate that the Cross Gospel is derivative and later than the canonical sources.

From the production of early Christian Gospels, in the third part we move on to early Christian descriptions of the Jesus movement. This section leads off with a chapter by F. Stanley Jones on the early Aramaic-speaking congregation in Jerusalem. He responds to the tendency of scholars to discuss the movement "from Jesus to Christ," arguing that such reconstructions overlook an initial first step in the process of how Jesus became "Lord." Jones argues that the understanding of Jesus as "Lord" or *mareya* has roots in the Aramaic tradition of the early Jesus movement rather than in later developments within urbanized Christianity. He then seeks to qualify a few further significant elements of the terminology of the early Aramaic-speaking community in Jerusalem.

In his chapter, Steven Thompson asks, "Did Jesus, in the Memory of his Earliest Followers, ever Nurse the Sick?" By reframing the question of Jesus's healing narratives in this broadly medical context, Thompson attempts to avoid the dichotomy created by asking whether Jesus performed his healings "miraculously" or "naturally." Instead, Thompson argues that Jesus did indeed, at times, provide basic nursing care for the sick—an answer that at least partially avoids this common bifurcation.

Sarah E. Rollens accentuates the failure of the Q community thesis in the next chapter. She argues that the evidence from Q itself is too thin to reconstruct a group who employed the text as a template for its identity. She insists that the theoretical grounds for interest in such a community remains highly problematic; in particular, she questions the ability to extract the concept of a "unified" community from a very limited set of data. Instead of a single author for Q, Rollens explores the possibility of a network of interested intellectuals, involved in constructing and engaging with the text. In this way, she encourages scholars to move beyond simplistic reconstructions that see "Christian" communities looming behind the scenes of all Jesus-centered texts.

In the following chapter, Mark Keown adopts the position that while some Christians likely held to the notion of an imminent Parousia (especially in certain communities that Paul addresses), it is unlikely that Mark or Paul's writings support this view. Keown offers three new lines of evidence: (1) Mark and Paul believed that Christ would be proclaimed to the nations before the Parousia; (2) it seems unlikely that Mark or Paul thought this mission would end in a generation, given its magnitude; and (3) several large geographical regions remain untouched by the mission at the end of the first century.

Warren Carter proceeds from the claim that any version of the origins of the early Jesus movement must account for its negotiations with the Roman imperial world. This chapter is both explanatory and evaluative. Carter begins by examining a range of potential contributing factors that gave rise to imperial-critical studies of the Gospels in the last two decades or so. He focuses mainly on methodological developments but also points to several potential implications for New Testament interpretation, rounding his essay out with projections for future imperial Gospels research.

Adam Winn's chapter combines emphases from traditional redaction-critical understandings of Mark (especially its historical setting) with recent narrative approaches. Redaction criticism enables a historical reconstruction that sheds light on Mark's narratival treatment of the temple institution and the question of an underlying Markan community. However, narrative critics have rightly emphasized the tentative nature of such historical reconstructions. Yet a purely narrative approach leaves Mark in a historical vacuum. In order to curtail the limitations of each method, Winn gives attention to both redaction- and narrative-critical models to support Mark's anti-imperial reading of the Markan temple narrative.

Judith Stack investigates the role of the "The Holy Spirit as Witness of Jesus in the Canonical Gospels" in her chapter, drawing attention to issues of unity and diversity in Gospel accounts of the Spirit. She argues for distinct perceptions of the Spirit in each Gospel. This may reflect either the differing perspectives of the Gospel communities or unique authorial/reactional accounts. The most consistent point of continuity among the canonical Gospels, however, seems to be the perception of the Holy Spirit as an agent of witness to Jesus.

In the next chapter, Nicholas Perrin asks whether the alleged linkage between *kerygma* and Exodus is unique to Paul. The chapter argues that this association can indeed be traced to early kerygmatic traditions seemingly unconnected to Paul. Perrin points in particular to the collocation of the Feeding of the 5,000 and Jesus Walking on Water in both the pre-Markan and pre-Johannine traditions as suggestive of this connection at a very early point in the church's history.

Susan M. Rieske turns our attention to Matthew's deployment of the Jonah-complex in the narratives about the stilling of the storm (8:23–27), the sign of Jonah (12:38–42; 16:1–4) and the confession of Peter, the "Son of Jonah" (16:13–20). She argues that Matthew's use of Jonah is unified by a theme that was also central in the reception of Jonah within Judaism—tribulation. Rieske insists that it is not a general sense of tribulation that Matthew alludes to but a specific period of intense distress and suffering that was to come at the eschaton. Since this period of tribulation coincided with the advent of the messiah, it seems directly tied to the end of the exile as the climactic point of Israel's suffering. This fact is important, Rieske argues, since Jonah's own tribulation was also tied to Israel's suffering in exile.

Finally for this section, Adam Z. Wright compares the parables of Jesus with those of Socrates. Wright suggests that thinking about the Parable of the Sower in philosophical terms may be helpful since the most prominent features of the parable are concerned with knowledge and ignorance. The parable seems to function as an attempt by Jesus to qualify the nature of true knowledge and the avenues by which one comes to a position of knowledge. Wright argues that this kind of dialectic was common in the ancient world, and first-century readers of the parable would have made a number of connections with other dialectics concerning the same topic. Wright does not wish to make the stronger claim that the Synoptic tradition is directly indebted to Plato. He does suggest, however, that by focusing on the same topic, the Synoptic tradition is in communication with similar dialectic traditions.

The fourth and final section of this volume investigates the Jewish mission and its literature. Darian Lockett opens this section by asking "Why Have We Stopped Reading the Catholic Epistles Together?" In an attempt to reinstate the unity of the tradition in its reception history, Lockett draws attention to several considerations not usually in view when assessing the reception of James, Peter, John, and Jude. Although each text has its own story, the unified function of the Catholic Epistles as a collection within the eventual New Testament canon underlines the tight relationship of these documents early on in their reception history. Lockett's analysis confirms the picture of canonical development outlined by Adolf Harnack and Jens Schröter, suggesting that, by the end of the canonical process, the Catholic Epistles operated as a collection in tandem with the book of Acts. Lockett also seeks to clarify the terminology of "Catholic" and/or "General" epistles, preferring the former in concert with the earliest descriptions of the collection in its reception history.

In his chapter, Matthew Jensen studies the relationship between 1 John and the Johannine mission. Jensen begins by exploring what is said about John's mission in Irenaeus, Revelation, Acts, and Paul. He then attempts to reconstruct the audience of the mission in 1 John, assessing the impact John's message would have had on its readers. The chapter concludes with an attempt to situate 1 John within the larger trajectory of the Johannine mission.

Beth Stovell's chapter continues the focus upon the Johannine letters with her treatment of the love command. She argues that an application of emotion theory establishes continuity with Jewish conceptions of emotions associated with love in the Second Temple period. The idea of love as a new "command" and the need to obey this command suggest coherence between notions of law and love implicit in the Johannine community. The major conceptions of love in the Second Temple period offer a highly likely antecedent to the Johannine presentation of love. According to Stovell, exploring conceptions of love in this relation provides a new basis for examining the Johannine community.

In "The New Perspective (on Paul) on Peter," Christoph Heilig turns toward Peter some of the gaze previously reserved for Paul in the New Perspective, asking whether the changed perspective on Paul has implications for how we understand Peter as well. Heilig focuses upon the Antioch incident in Gal 2:11–21. After a thorough analysis, he sees that Peter's reaction, even as depicted by Paul, is consistent with what we know of Peter from Acts 10–11 and his engagement with Cornelius. Heilig suggests that the New Perspective has not been fully appreciated for the insights that it has to offer into Peter's role in Gentile relations within the early church.

Andrew W. Pitts turns attention to the Petrine corpus with an analysis of linguistic structure and the use of Scripture in 1 Pet 2:1–10. Pitts argues that, as with other uses of the Old Testament in 1 Peter, 2:1–10 employs Scripture in the service of developing/supporting communal motifs and/or exhortations issued in connection with them. In addition to making a new argument for the linguistic unity of 1 Pet 2:1–10, he departs from traditional pesher-like or Jewish midrash readings of the function of Scripture in 1 Pet 2:1–10 and argues instead for a position initially suggested by Ernest Best—that this passage (as well as the letter more broadly) likely frames its hermeneutic in light of primitive Christian traditional material rather than ancient Jewish methodologies.

The concluding essay, by Matthew R. Malcolm, likewise addresses themes in 1 Peter. Malcolm points to the use of family imagery in early Christian literature to make the case that 1 Peter provides a window into the theological logic that consolidated the widespread adoption of such motifs. He argues for this development in three phases: (1) the essential function of familial imagery in 1 Peter; (2) the use of familial language in early Christianity across a wide range of documents; and (3) the gospel of the Son of God's renegotiation of family imagery for earliest Christianity. Malcolm concludes that familial imagery in 1 Peter, while partially explained by a number of potential backgrounds, receives logical consolidation in the light of the governing conceptualization of the Petrine gospel of God's son: believers are to conceive of their own identity as arising from that of Jesus Christ, who was "made alive" by the Father.

PART 1

The Formation of the Jesus Movement and Its Precursors

John the Baptist in the Fourth Gospel

Clare K. Rothschild

1 Introduction

This paper analyzes the depiction of John the Baptist (hereafter: JB) in the Gospel of John.[1] Scholars such as Wilhelm Baldensperger and Raymond Brown have inferred several dialectical engagements between John's Gospel and late

---

1 Since the present discussion involves the role of "John" in the Gospel of "John," to avoid confusion John will be referred to with his title, "the Baptist," although the Fourth Gospel never includes his title. Standard works on this topic include E. Bammel, "The Baptist in Early Christian Tradition," *NTS* 18 (1971–1972): 95–128; J. Becker, *Johannes der Täufer und Jesus von Nazareth* (Neukirchen-Vluyn: Neukirchener Verlag, 1972); M. Dibelius, *Die urchristliche Überlieferung von Johannes dem Täufer* (Göttingen: Vandenhoeck & Ruprecht, 1911); J. Ernst, *Johannes der Täufer: Interpretation, Geschichte, Wirkungsgeschichte* (BZNW 53; Berlin: de Gruyter, 1989); A.S. Geyser, "The Youth of John the Baptist: A Deduction from the Break in the Parallel Account of the Lucan Infancy Story," *NovT* 1 (1956): 70–75; M. Goguel, *Au seuil de l'évangile: Jean-Baptiste* (Paris: Payot, 1928); P.W. Hollenbach, "Social Aspects of John the Baptist's Preaching Mission in the Contexts of Palestinian Judaism," *ANRW* II.19.1 (1979): 850–875; C.H. Kraeling, *John the Baptist* (New York: Scribner, 1951); H. Lichtenberger, "Reflections on the History of John the Baptist's Communities," *FolOr* 25 (1988): 45–49; E. Lohmeyer, *Das Urchristentum 1: Johannes der Täufer* (Göttingen: Vandenhoeck & Ruprecht, 1932); E. Lupieri, *Giovanni Battista fra Storia e Leggenda* (Brescia: Paideia, 1988); J.P. Meier, *A Marginal Jew: Rethinking the Historical Jesus. Volume Two: Mentor, Message, and Miracles* (New York: Doubleday, 1994), 199–223; Meier, "John the Baptist in Matthew's Gospel," *JBL* 99 (1980): 383–405; J. Murphy-O'Connor, "John the Baptist and Jesus: History and Hypothesis," *NTS* 36 (1990): 359–374; J. Reumann, "The Quest for the Historical Baptist," in *Understanding the Sacred Text: Essays in Honor of Morton S. Enslin on the Hebrew Bible and Christian Beginnings* (ed. J. Reumann; Valley Forge, PA: Judson, 1972), 181–199; J. Schütz, *Johannes der Täufer* (Zürich: Zwingli, 1967); C.H.H. Scobie, *John the Baptist* (London: SCM, 1964); J. Steinmann, *Saint John the Baptist and the Desert Tradition* (New York: Harper, 1958); W.B. Tatum, *John the Baptist and Jesus: A Report of the Jesus Seminar* (Sonoma, CA: Polebridge, 1994); J. Taylor, *The Immerser: John the Baptist in Second Temple Judaism* (Grand Rapids: Eerdmans, 1997); W. Trilling, "Die Täufertradition bei Matthäus," *BZ* 3 (1959): 271–289; W. Wink, *John the Baptist in the Gospel Tradition* (Cambridge: Cambridge University Press, 1968); Wink, "Jesus' Reply to John: Matt. 11:2–6/Luke: 7:18–23," *Forum* 5 (1989): 121–128; R.L. Webb, *John the Baptizer and Prophet: A Socio-Historical Study* (JSNTSup 62; Sheffield: JSOT Press, 1991); Webb, "John the Baptist and his Relationship to Jesus," in *Studying the Historical Jesus: Evaluations of the State of Current Research* (ed. B.D. Chilton and C.A. Evans; Leiden: Brill, 1994), 214–299; Webb, "The

first- and early second-century followers of the Baptist.[2] Since all four NT Gospels feature JB at the beginning of Jesus's ministry, it seems reasonable to infer that JB was accepted as a *favorable*, possibly even flattering, association for Jesus. The evangelists would not be expected to include, let alone begin their works with, a figure who dulled, checked, or stifled the subsequent narration of Jesus. That said, the association with JB has certain undeniably negative implications. In Matthew and Mark, for example, JB's ministry is prior to Jesus's ministry and JB baptizes Jesus, indicating Jesus's inferior position as JB's student. In Luke, JB is Jesus's older cousin.[3] Gospel portraits of JB are, thus, inherently contradictory. To be sure, JB's statements in all four Gospels explicitly qualify his life and ministry as inferior to Jesus's. Based on the observable contradictions, however, these claims only heighten suspicions of special pleading.[4] The expectation of an appearance of Elijah prior to the Messiah is not sufficient to explain why JB is not simply left out of the Gospel narratives. Was JB's endorsement of Jesus unavoidable, otherwise compelling, or both? If Markan Priority is trustworthy, should the earliest evangelist bear the burden for JB's inclusion, later evangelists simply doing their best with what they were given? Returning to Raymond Brown's proposal, what internal or external circumstances—ostensibly vital to each of the different evangelists—might have compelled the first or all of the Gospel writers to begin with JB?

Not all of the possible questions concerning JB's NT portraits will be attempted in the scope of this paper. Rather, the present discussion addresses how Baptist traditions serve the agenda of the Fourth Gospel (hereafter: 4G) exclusively. The essay first presents the Johannine portrait of JB, emphasizing where it is similar to and different from the Synoptic portraits, after which it tests the hypothesis that JB's portrait in the 4G deliberately duplicates, omits, supplements, adapts, and corrects Synoptic Baptist traditions in order to

---

Activity of John the Baptist's Expected Figure at the Threshing Floor (Matthew 3.12—Luke 3.17)," *JSNT* 43 (1991): 103–111; A. Yarbro Collins, "The Origin of Christian Baptism," *StudLit* 19 (1989): 28–46.

2 W. Baldensperger, *Der Prolog des vierten Evangeliums: Sein polemisch-apologetischer Zweck* (Freiburg: Mohr, 1898); R.E. Brown, *The Gospel of John I–XII* (AB 29; New York: Doubleday, 1966), lxvii–lxx. See also C.W. Rishell, "Baldensperger's Theory of the Origin of the Fourth Gospel," *JBL* 20 (1901): 38–49.

3 Elizabeth is referred to as Mary's συγγενίς "kinswoman" in Luke 1:36.

4 Since the four Gospels, each in different ways, feature numerous reversals (e.g., reversal of the superiority of prior to latter), it is possible to ask whether JB's self-deprecating remarks are not in fact meant to be interpreted as competing with Jesus for inferiority (i.e., false humility).

replace the contradictory and perplexing presentation of the relationship between JB and Jesus in the Synoptics with a categorically negative one.

2 John the Baptist's Ministry: Actions

Baptist traditions in the 4G may be divided into two categories: actions and sayings or statements (the latter group including reports about deeds). Beginning with actions, John's ministry consisted of essentially three types: testifying, baptizing, and making disciples.

2.1 *Testifying*

Unlike the Synoptics, the 4G characterizes JB as a μάρτυς. He is a "man sent from God" (v. 6) and a witness sent to "testify to the light so that all might believe through him" (v. 7).[5] The writer qualifies that JB is not the light himself, but a witness to the light (v. 8). In 1:19, JB spells out his testimony, focusing on his identity and the significance of his baptism. He is not, he says, Elijah or the Messiah. He is Isaiah—or a prophetic voice similar to Isaiah's—a voice that, in the sixth century B.C.E., announced the reign of King Cyrus of Persia, the end of the Exile, and the Lord's reinstallation in Jerusalem. In 1:15, John amplifies his testimony with news that "the Word" which "became flesh" ranks ahead of him. In 1:29–30, he declares "the Word" to be Jesus, implying that Jesus's superior rank is the result of his status as God's lamb ("Here is the Lamb of God who takes away the sin of the world"). Of these traditions, the Synoptics include only the reference to Isa 40:3 (Matt 3:3; Mark 1:3; Luke 3:4).

John 5:33–37 also reports about JB's testimony. In 5:33, Jesus asserts that JB's testimony about him reflects the truth (ἀλήθεια), although the particular testimony to which Jesus refers is not specified. In v. 36, Jesus states that he himself has a testimony that is greater than JB's and that his works testify that God sent him. John, Jesus says, offered only human testimony (v. 34) as contrasted with the Father's *divine* testimony (v. 37). This passage also characterizes JB as a "burning and shining lamp" (contrast 1:8) in whose light the audience rejoiced for a while (ὑμεῖς δὲ ἠθελήσατε ἀγαλλιαθῆναι πρὸς ὥραν ἐν τῷ φωτὶ αὐτοῦ, v. 35).

---

5 The present essay will not address the difficult redactional questions of Baptist traditions in the 4G. The issues are acute in chs. 1, 3, and 4. Commentators on the 4G never fail to mention the intrusive quality of 1:6–8 and 15. See, e.g., Craig S. Keener, *The Gospel of John: A Commentary* (2 vols.; Peabody, MA: Hendrickson, 2003), 1:393, 419.

2.2 Baptizing

The 4G agrees with the Synoptics that John's ministry consists of baptizing.[6] Josephus too includes baptizing as a facet of JB's ministry (*Ant.* 18.116–119). Since Jesus's baptism implies his sinfulness, inferiority to JB, or both—a problem for Christian theologians as far back as the Gospel of Matthew and perhaps why the 4G omits it—the report that John baptized Jesus strikes even the most skeptical of historians as likely (i.e., criterion of embarrassment). The 4G's omission of any baptism of Jesus, let alone baptism by JB, is distinctive. In John 3:23–24, JB baptizes others (not Jesus) at Aenon near Salim. The 4G reports that JB selected this location "because water was plentiful (ὅτι ὕδατα πολλὰ ἦν ἐκεῖ)" (cf. 10:40).[7] The narrator's comment in v. 24 that JB continues to baptize because he has not yet been arrested appears to be a correction of Mark 1:14.

One additional reference to JB in John 10:40–42 characterizes him as having baptized.[8] Jesus returns to the place where John was baptizing.[9] JB is not there. The narrator does not reveal why Jesus went there or why JB no longer baptizes there. In the Synoptics, cessation of JB's baptizing ministry concurs with his imprisonment (Matt 4:12–17; Mark 1:14–15; Luke 3:18–22). According to the 4G, people visited Jesus in this place where JB had baptized people and "believed in *him* [i.e., Jesus]" (ἐπίστευσαν εἰς αὐτὸν ἐκεῖ). The people that trust or believe in Jesus in this passage also attest that John performed no sign.[10] However, as in 5:33, they affirm that what John said about Jesus *was true*.

---

6   Passages attesting JB's water baptism in the four Gospels: Mark 1:4, ἐγένετο Ἰωάννης ὁ βαπτίζων ἐν τῇ ἐρήμῳ κηρύσσων βάπτισμα μετανοίας εἰς ἄφεσιν ἁμαρτιῶν; Matt 3:11, Ἐγὼ μὲν ὑμᾶς βαπτίζω ἐν ὕδατι εἰς μετάνοιαν; Luke 3:15, Ἐγὼ μὲν ὕδατι βαπτίζω ὑμᾶς; and John 1:24 Ἐγὼ βαπτίζω ἐν ὕδατι.

7   Cf. Did. 7.

8   The Gospel of John notes John's imprisonment (3:24), but doesn't go into detail. Mark and Josephus go into a little more depth. Josephus calls John "a good man" stating that "Herod, who feared lest the great influence John had over the people might put it into his power and inclination to raise a rebellion, (for they seemed ready to do anything he should advise) thought it best, by putting him to death, to prevent any mischief he might cause" (Feldman, LCL). In the end, John met the same end as Jesus, but without the subsequent fanfare—without his own 'Paul' to spread news of his resurrection. The Book of Acts reports about JB's disciples (Acts 18:24–19:7). Was Apollos JB's 'Paul'?

9   The question arises as to whether the cult of the dead is here signified.

10   καὶ ἔλεγον ὅτι Ἰωάννης μὲν σημεῖον ἐποίησεν οὐδέν, πάντα δὲ ὅσα εἶπεν Ἰωάννης περὶ τούτου ἀληθῆ ἦν (v. 41). The text does not specify the role of σημεῖα. Apparently, they are evidentiary in some sense, but perhaps in a way different from later understandings of the Christian apostolate. Moreover, the 4G's position on the role of σημεῖα is inconsistent. On

2.3 Attracting and Maintaining Disciples

Synoptic reports of JB's baptizing ministry emphasize crowds without specifying followers or disciples,[11] apart from JB's reference to someone "coming after him" (ἔρχεται ὁ ἰσχυρότερός μου ὀπίσω μου, Mark 1:7 pars.).[12] In John 1:25, unspecified individuals question JB about his baptizing ministry;[13] the text does not qualify them as disciples. In John 3:26, however, JB is referred to with the title of ῥαββί and John 4:1 reports that through baptism Jesus attracts more disciples than JB. This rumor suggests competition between the two men, or at least simultaneity of ministries (contrast Mark 1:14–15). Within the Johannine narrative, Jesus's success must come as no surprise to JB, since only six verses earlier he predicted that he would decrease and Jesus would increase.[14] That said, according to the 4G, John's baptism serves to indicate that Jesus is God's lamb (1:29, 36). Since John's disciples understand this reference as JB's endorsement of Jesus (i.e., on hearing it they follow Jesus), readers are forced to credit JB, not just for predicting but multiplying Jesus's successes by acknowledging his own inferiority.

3 John the Baptist's Ministry: Sayings

3.1 *John the Baptist's Eleven Sayings*

In addition to testifying, baptizing, and making disciples, the 4G records eleven sayings of JB, seven of which are unique to this Gospel.[15]

---

one hand, it links faith to signs, but on the other hand, this linkage is criticized (cf. e.g., 20:8 vs. 20:9). Nevertheless, σημεῖον is an important expression for Johannine Christology, so JB's failure to perform signs depicts him unfavorably.

11 Although personal names are avoided, in Mark 6:29 John has disciples.

12 N.B. Acts 13:25, like the 4G, does not refer to John's coming one as "stronger" perhaps because the "stronger one" was obviously Paul (e.g., baptizing with the spirit) not Jesus. Also, Jesus uses δεῦτε ὀπίσω μου to call Simon and Andrew in Mark 1:17. Each case implies succession.

13 Were the unnamed priests and Levites from Jerusalem sent by Jews according to v. 19 or by Pharisees, according to v. 24; or does v. 24 qualify that the Jerusalem Jews were Pharisees? The text is unclear.

14 John 3:30 ἐκεῖνον δεῖ αὐξάνειν, ἐμὲ δὲ ἐλαττοῦσθαι. On the predictive quality of the auxiliary verb δεῖ, see C.K. Rothschild, *Luke–Acts and the Rhetoric of History* (WUNT 2.175; Tübingen: Mohr Siebeck, 2003), 185–212.

15 Italics indicate the saying is not unique (i.e., it has a Synoptic parallel).

1. Prediction of a More Powerful One to Come

   John 1:26–27: "I baptize with water. Among you stands one whom you do not know, the one who is coming after me; I am not worthy to untie the thong of his sandal."[16]

2. Proclamation of the Lamb of God

   John 1:29: "Look, the Lamb of God who takes away the sin of the world!"

   John 1:36: "Look, the Lamb of God!"

3. JB's Relationship to the Coming One

   John 1:15: "This was he of whom I said, 'He who comes after me ranks ahead of me because he was before me.'"

   John 1:30: "This is he of whom I said, 'After me[17] comes a man who ranks ahead of me, because he was before me.'"

4. Report about Vision at Jesus's Baptism

   John 1:32: "I saw the Spirit descending from heaven like a dove, and it remained on him."[18]

5. JB's Lack of Knowledge/Insight

   John 1:31: "I myself did not know him; but I came baptizing with water for this reason, that he might be revealed to Israel."

   John 1:33: "I myself did not know him, but the one who sent me to baptize with water said to me, '*He on whom you see the Spirit descend* and remain is the one who *baptizes with the Holy Spirit.*'"

---

16 Cf. Luke 3:16b–17; Mark 1:7–8; Acts 13:25.
17 Is this JB's prediction of his own death?
18 Cf. Matt 3:13–17; Mark 1:9–11; Luke 3:21–22.

6. Declaration that Jesus is Son of God

   John 1:34: "And I myself have seen and have testified that this is the Son of God."[19]

7. Denials about Himself[20]

   John 1:20–21: "I am not the Christ (ὁ Χριστός)." [Are you Elijah?] "I am not." [Are you the prophet?] "No."

   John 3:28: "You yourselves are testifying for me that I said, 'I am not the Christ (ὁ Χριστός), but I have been sent ahead of him.'"

8. JB as Wilderness Voice

   John 1:23: "I am a voice crying in the wilderness, 'Make straight the way of the Lord.'"[21]

9. Response to Popularity of Jesus's Baptism

   John 3:27: "No one can receive anything except what has been given from heaven."[22]

10. Self-Description as Bridegroom's Friend

    John 3:29: "He who has the bride is the bridegroom. But, the friend of the bridegroom, who stands and hears him, rejoices greatly at the bridegroom's voice. For this reason my joy has been fulfilled."

11. Increase–Decrease Saying

    John 3:30: "It is necessary that he increase, but I decrease."

---

19 Cf. e.g. Mark 1:1, 11; 3:11; 5:7; 9:7; 12:6; 14:61; 15:39. See 3.2.1.3 (below) concerning textual variant.
20 Cf. Mark 6:15; Matt 16:14–15; Luke 9:8.
21 Matt 3:3; Mark 1:3; Luke 3:4.
22 Cf. John 19:11.

3.2 *Analysis*

Having presented the evidence constituting the Johannine portrait of JB, this section seeks to analyze it in comparison with his Synoptic portraits. For heuristic purposes, JB's Johannine actions and sayings are divided into four positions vis-à-vis the Synoptics: (1) coherence, (2) omission, (3) augmentation, and (4) correction. Each position is treated in turn.

3.2.1 Coherence

JB's composite portrait in the 4G coheres with Synoptic sayings on at least four points related to Jesus's baptism: (a) appearance of the Spirit in the form of a dove; (b) prediction of "coming one"; (c) characterization of Jesus as ὁ υἱὸς τοῦ θεοῦ;[23] and (d) association of JB with Isa 40:3 (as noted above). However, each of these traditions is distinctive in its Johannine appropriation.

3.2.1.1 *Spirit as a Dove*

The Synoptics report the physical appearance of the Spirit in the form of a dove at Jesus's baptism. Whether JB baptizes Jesus as in Mark and Matthew (Mark 1:9–11; Matt 3:13–17) or Jesus is baptized by the Spirit (divine passive) as in Luke 3:21–22, the Spirit's appearance like a dove is a part of the event. However, in Mark and Matthew, *Jesus* sees the dove-like physical manifestation of the Spirit and hears the voice from heaven speaking to him (Mark 1:10–11; Matt 3:16–17); whereas, Luke's report is unclear as to who sees the dove and hears the voice. In the 4G, Jesus is not baptized at all and JB reports that *he* sees the physical manifestation of the Spirit, in that moment recognizing the purpose of his baptism. To be sure, omission of Jesus's baptism avoids the theological challenges of JB's priority/superiority and Jesus's need for repentance. That *Jesus* does not see the dove in the 4G, however, implies that, as Revealer, he is already enlightened (e.g., as to his mission, destiny, etc.). Signs are important only for those seeking enlightenment—and even for them they are a crutch indicating weakness (John 20:29).

Conversely, just as Jesus is enlightened and does not need a sign, JB is *not* enlightened and *does* need one. Twice JB states as much in 1:31 and 33 ("I did not know ..."), but the point is emphatic when he sees the dove. The point, then, of the dove in the 4G is that JB's stage of enlightenment is inferior to Jesus's.

---

23   Unless the variant reading ὁ ἐκλεκτὸς τοῦ θεοῦ (1:34) is correct.

3.2.1.2   Prediction of "Coming One"

Although held in common across the four Gospels, the precise appropriation of "the coming one" prediction in the Johannine account differs from the Synoptics. The report may be divided into two sections: (A¹) prediction concerning the coming one's sandal; and (A²) description of coming one's baptism. Four modifications by the 4G are significant: (1) inclusion of the crowd's inability to recognize the coming one: μέσος ὑμῶν ἕστηκεν ὃν ὑμεῖς οὐκ οἴδατε; (2) omission of ἰσχυρότερος as qualification of the coming one: ὁ ὀπίσω μου ἐρχόμενος vs. ἔρχεται ὁ ἰσχυρότερός μου ὀπίσω μου (Mark), ὁ δὲ ὀπίσω μου ἐρχόμενος ἰσχυρότερός μού ἐστιν (Matthew), or ἔρχεται δὲ ὁ ἰσχυρότερός μου (Luke); (3) the adjective, ἄξιος, replacing the Synoptic ἱκανὸς in the comment about JB's ability to untie the sandal of the coming one; and (4) exclusion of Q's fire element in the description of the coming one's baptism. The chart (below) highlights these differences.

Mark 1:7–8

A¹. Ἔρχεται ὁ ἰσχυρότερός μου ὀπίσω μου, οὗ οὐκ εἰμὶ **ἱκανὸς** κύψας λῦσαι τὸν ἱμάντα τῶν ὑποδημάτων αὐτοῦ·

A². ἐγὼ ἐβάπτισα ὑμᾶς ὕδατι, αὐτὸς δὲ βαπτίσει ὑμᾶς ἐν πνεύματι ἁγίῳ.

Matthew 3:11

A¹. ὁ δὲ ὀπίσω μου ἐρχόμενος ἰσχυρότερός μού ἐστιν, οὗ οὐκ εἰμὶ **ἱκανὸς** τὰ ὑποδήματα βαστάσαι·

A². αὐτὸς ὑμᾶς βαπτίσει ἐν πνεύματι ἁγίῳ **καὶ πυρί**.

Luke 3:15–16

A¹. ἔρχεται δὲ ὁ ἰσχυρότερός μου, οὗ οὐκ εἰμὶ **ἱκανὸς** λῦσαι τὸν ἱμάντα τῶν ὑποδημάτων αὐτοῦ·

A². αὐτὸς ὑμᾶς βαπτίσει ἐν πνεύματι ἁγίῳ **καὶ πυρί**.

John 1:24–27[24]

A¹. μέσος ὑμῶν ἕστηκεν ὃν ὑμεῖς οὐκ οἴδατε, ὁ ὀπίσω μου ἐρχόμενος, οὗ οὐκ εἰμὶ **ἄξιος** ἵνα λύσω αὐτοῦ τὸν ἱμάντα τοῦ ὑποδήματος.

---

[24] Resembling a response to Luke 3:15, John 1:25b poses the question, Τί οὖν βαπτίζεις εἰ σὺ οὐκ εἶ ὁ χριστὸς οὐδὲ Ἠλίας οὐδὲ ὁ προφήτης;

A². [John 1:33b: Ἐφ᾽ ὃν ἂν ἴδῃς τὸ πνεῦμα καταβαῖνον καὶ μένον ἐπ᾽ αὐτόν, οὗτός ἐστιν ὁ βαπτίζων ἐν πνεύματι ἁγίῳ.]

Cumulatively, these four modifications again reduce JB's stature. The crowd's inability to recognize Jesus in John 1:26 qualifies JB as attracting only the *stulti*. Furthermore, their inability implies that JB's teaching is inferior presuming that, had he taught it, at least a few would have recognized Jesus. Exclusion of the adjective with comparative suffix, ἰσχυρότερος, implies that Jesus is not *comparably* stronger than JB. Rather, he is *categorically* superior in every way, not just in strength. Ἄξιος replaces the Synoptic ἱκανός to denote unworthiness instead of mere unsuitability;[25] and, the exclusion of Q's fire element reflects the Johannine anti-eschatological *Tendenz*: apocalypticism as mythological and (hence) philosophically weak.

3.2.1.3   Son of God Declaration

John the Baptist's characterization of Jesus as ὁ υἱὸς τοῦ θεοῦ in 1:34 (cf. the same testimony by Nathanael in 1:49) involves a textual variant. Instead of υἱὸς τοῦ θεοῦ, P^{106vid} ℵ*, it[b,e,ff2*], syr[c,s], and Ambrose read "the chosen one of God" (ὁ ἐκλεκτὸς τοῦ θεοῦ). It[a, ff2c], syr[palmss], and cop[sa] read "the chosen son of God" (*electus filius*). Most commentators prefer to read "the son of God" because it is attested in older, more diverse witnesses, and matches 4G terminology (e.g., John 1:49; 3:18; 5:25; 10:36; 11:4, 27; 19:7; 20:31).[26] If one opts for "the elect one of God," then JB might have portrayed Jesus as either the Isaianic suffering servant (referred to as "chosen" in Isa 42:1) or an eschatological redeemer as in the *Similitudes of Enoch* (39:6; 40:5; 45:3, 4; 48:6; 49:2, 4; 51:3, 5; 52:6, 9; 53:6; 55:4; 61:5, 8, 10; 62:1). However, neither suffering servant nor eschatological redeemer is consistent with Johannine topics and themes. On several different grounds "the son of God" is more likely. In the 4G, "son of God" refers to Jesus's messiahship (1:49; 3:18; 5:25; 10:36; 11:4, 27; 19:7; 20:31). The title is exclusive to the Christ (3:18), Jesus claiming it for himself in 10:36. What is more, the 4G explicitly contrasts the two "voices" of JB and Jesus. Whereas Jesus's voice, as the Son of God, has the effect of raising the dead (5:25), JB's voice (more below) merely echoes in the wilderness. In the 4G, to identify Jesus as Son of God *is* to identify him as Christ—the positive restatement of JB's negative assertion that he himself is not the Christ.

---

25   LSJ, s.v ἄξιος and ἱκανός.
26   *TCGNT*², 172.

3.2.1.4 *Isaiah 40:3*

Finally, in each one of the four canonical Gospels, JB is associated with Isa 40:3. Yet, the occurrences vary. Mark 1:3 loosely associates JB with Isa 40:3 (and Exod 23:20, Mal 3:1) through a literary juxtaposition with JB's baptizing ministry. The Markan citation of Isa 40:3 locates the "crying voice" *in* the wilderness, whereas the original passage did not, most likely implying that Mark intends the figure in the passage to be understood as JB.[27] In contrast, as one of a dozen or so predictions of events in Jesus's life, Matt 3:3 appropriates Isa 40:3 as a general prophecy of JB's wilderness ministry. Similarly but with a more general thrust, Luke 3:4–6 cites Isa 40:3–5 to depict JB in line with previous expressions of hope for Israel's restoration.[28]

The 4G's presentation of Isa 40:3 offers a marked contrast to these three accounts. In the 4G, Isa 40:3 is a self-identifying statement issued by JB. In John 1:23, priests and Levites from Jerusalem ask John whether he is the Christ, Elijah, or "the prophet." Although the precise identity of ὁ προφήτης is not specified, JB nevertheless denies all three identifications. His questioners, thus ask him who he is: Τίς εἶ; To this fourth and final question, he replies by citing Isa 40:3. That is, he claims to be "a voice in the wilderness crying, 'Make straight the way of the Lord'" (φωνὴ βοῶντος ἐν τῇ ἐρήμῳ· Εὐθύνατε τὴν ὁδὸν κυρίου). The most significant difference in this appropriation of Isa 40:3 as compared with its Synoptic parallels is its appearance on the lips of JB. It is not enough to negatively identify JB as the Christ, Elijah, or the prophet. In the 4G, JB must offer his own positive identification as a φωνή. Invariably related to the Hebrew קול בת or divine voice, all but this and one other occurrence of φωνή in the 4G refers to Jesus or God.[29] Of the two exceptions, only 10:5 (sheep will not follow the voice of a stranger) really qualifies because 1:23, although about JB not Jesus, is nevertheless a manifestation of the divine voice. Since, in the history of tradition, the divine voice is often only an echo or whisper (1 Kgs 19:12–13) and invisible,[30]

---

27   Mark 1:2, φωνὴ βοῶντος ἐν τῇ ἐρήμῳ (cf. Isa 40:3, LXX is identical) locates the voice in the wilderness, whereas Isaiah locates the voice in the city but the highway God will use in the processional from Babylon to Judah in the wilderness.

28   Whereas Matt 3:3 specifies JB as the voice in the wilderness of which Isaiah speaks, the Lukan quotation formula "as it is written" only invites the association of JB's proclamation with that of Isaiah 40: καὶ ἦλθεν εἰς πᾶσαν περίχωρον τοῦ Ἰορδάνου κηρύσσων βάπτισμα μετανοίας εἰς ἄφεσιν ἁμαρτιῶν, ὡς γέγραπται ἐν βίβλῳ λόγων Ἡσαΐου τοῦ προφήτου· Φωνὴ βοῶντος ἐν τῇ ἐρήμῳ· Ἑτοιμάσατε τὴν ὁδὸν κυρίου, εὐθείας ποιεῖτε τὰς τρίβους αὐτοῦ.

29   John 1:23 [JB]; 3:29; 5:25, 28, 37; 10:3, 4, 5 [strangers], 16, 27, 11:43; 12:28, 30; 18:37. I have noted in brackets the only exceptions; all other occurrences denote either Jesus or God.

30   E.g., Deut 4:12; Job 4:16; Ezek 1:25, 28; Jer 25:30; Joel 4:16–17; Amos 1:2, and Dan 4:31.

JB's claim to be a φωνή represents his most self-effacing remark so far. With this remark, he claims to amount to nothing more than a symbolic act. In the 4G, JB does not wear clothes, a special mantel, or eat a special diet to symbolize his call, as he does in the Synoptics; in the 4G, he *himself* is the symbol, a living mirror reflecting and pointing others to Jesus.

3.2.2 Omission

Synoptic Baptist traditions omitted from the 4G also give a good sense of the 4G's distinctiveness. The most striking omission is the title, "Baptizer." Its absence may be related to the 4G's claim that John was not the only baptizer. Jesus too baptized disciples (4:1–2). Alternatively, it may wish to deny to JB any title at all. In John 3:26, JB is called rabbi, implying he had students (see above).[31] JB is evidently a rabbi although he "testifies" rather than teaches.[32] JB's two important Synoptic teachings concerning the kingdom in Matt 3:2, "Repent, for the kingdom of heaven has come near" and the announcement of judgment in Q 3:7–9, do not appear.[33] Assuming, as many scholars do, that the eschatological tenor of these sayings prompted the 4G to omit them neglects the more fundamental problem that they impute important *teachings* to a mere *witness*. In addition to the missing title, JB is also not chronologically positioned during the reign of Tiberius as he is in Luke 3:3–18 (cf. Matt 3:1–12) and has no birth narrative (cf. Luke 1–2).[34] The 4G makes no reference to his clothing or diet as in Mark 1:4–6 (cf. Matt 3:4–6).[35] If known, the 4G does not credit JB with

---

31 The 4G has seven references to Jesus as rabbi, 1:38, 49; 3:2; 4:31; 6:25; 9:2; 11:8. Geza Vermes, *Jesus the Jew: A Historian's Reading of the Gospels* (Philadelphia: Fortress, 1973), 115.

32 C.H. Dodd refers to JB as a "the first Christian confessor" in *Historical Tradition in the Fourth Gospel* (Cambridge: Cambridge University Press, 1965), 299, see comment on 1:20.

33 "Generation of vipers! Who informed you to flee from the coming wrath? Bear fruit worthy of repentance, and do not begin to say to yourselves: We have Abraham as father! For I tell you: God is able to raise up children to Abraham out of these rocks! And the ax already lies in front of the root of the trees. Then every tree not bearing good fruit will be chopped down and thrown into a fire." JB's protestation against Jesus's baptism in Matt 3:14 ("I need to be baptized by you, and do you come to me?") is unnecessary since the event is not included in the 4G.

34 "In the fifteenth year of the reign of Emperor Tiberius, when Pontius Pilate was governor of Judea, and Herod was ruler of Galilee, and his brother Philip ruler of the region of Ituraea and Trachonitis, and Lysanias ruler of Abilene, during the high priesthood of Annas and Caiaphas, the word of God came to John son of Zechariah in the wilderness."

35 "John the baptizer appeared in the wilderness, proclaiming a baptism of repentance for the forgiveness of sins. And people from the whole Judean countryside and all the people of Jerusalem were going out to him, and were baptized by him in the river Jordan, con-

a message of good news (Luke 3:18–19),[36] the teachings in Luke 3,[37] or the Lord's Prayer (Q 11:1–4).[38] In the 4G, JB also does not speak against divorce in any context, let alone as a condemnation of the king[39] and is not placed in prison such that he might pose a question to Jesus from there.[40] Although the 4G alludes to JB's imprisonment (John 3:24),[41] his arrest is not explained.[42] Finally, the 4G contains no mention of JB's death and burial (i.e., Mark 6:17–29; cf. Matt 14:1–12).[43] And Herod never views Jesus as JB *redivivus* (cf. Mark 6:16).

---

fessing their sins. Now John was clothed with camel's hair, with a leather belt around his waist, and he ate locusts and wild honey."

36 "So with many other exhortations, he [John] proclaimed the good news to the people."

37 For example, the following three sayings: (1) Luke 3:11: "Whoever has two coats must share with anyone who has none; and whoever has food must do likewise"; (2) Luke 3:13: "Collect no more than the amount prescribed for you"; and (3) Luke 3:14: "Do not extort money from anyone by threats or false accusation, and be satisfied with your wages."

38 "'Lord, teach us to pray, as John taught his disciples.' He said to them, 'When you pray, say: Father, hallowed be your name. Your kingdom come. Give us each day our daily bread. And forgive us our sins, for we ourselves forgive everyone indebted to us. And do not bring us to the time of trial.'"

39 Mark 6:18: "It is not lawful for you to have your brother's wife."

40 As in Q 7:19: "Are you the one who is to come, or are we to wait for another?"

41 Luke 3:19: "But Herod the ruler, who had been rebuked by him because of Herodias, his brother's wife, and because of all the evil things that Herod had done, added to them all by shutting up John in prison."

42 As in Luke 9:7–8 (cf. Mark 6:14–16): "Now Herod the ruler heard about all that had taken place, and he was perplexed, because it was said by some that John had been raised from the dead, by some that Elijah had appeared, and by others that one of the ancient prophets had arisen. Herod said, 'John I beheaded; but who is this about whom I hear such things?' And he tried to see him."

43 "For Herod himself had sent men who arrested John, bound him, and put him in prison on account of Herodias, his brother Philip's wife, because Herod had married her. For John had been telling Herod, 'It is not lawful for you to have your brother's wife.' And Herodias had a grudge against him, and wanted to kill him. But she could not, for Herod feared John, knowing that he was a righteous and holy man, and he protected him. When he heard him, he was greatly perplexed; and yet he liked to listen to him. But an opportunity came when Herod on his birthday gave a banquet for his courtiers and officers and for the leaders of Galilee. When his daughter Herodias came in and danced, she pleased Herod and his guests; and the king said to the girl, 'Ask me for whatever you wish, and I will give it.' And he solemnly swore to her, 'Whatever you ask me, I will give you, even half of my kingdom.' She went out and said to her mother, 'What should I ask for?' She replied, 'The head of John the baptizer.' Immediately she rushed back to the king and requested, 'I want you to give me at once the head of John the Baptist on a platter.' The king was deeply grieved; yet out of regard for his oaths and for the guests, he did not want to refuse her. Immedi-

JB becomes something like a figment of the collective imagination: a favorable sign that is at once tangible and intangible. The Johannine JB is reduced, in the words of R.H. Lightfoot about the historical Jesus, to "an echo of a whisper."[44]

3.2.3 Augmentation

The 4G also augments Synoptic traditions about JB with a unique set of self-deprecating sayings. Generally speaking these sayings express deference to Jesus, articulating JB's low self-estimation and/or his identification of Jesus as superior. Statements featuring first- and third-person (with or without the copular verb: subject complement) predominate. Some of the sayings are so self-effacing they provoke questions of irony or false humility on the part of interpreters.

> "I am not the Christ."
> "I am not [Elijah]."
> "No [I am not the prophet]."
> "He who comes after me is ahead of me because he was before me." (1:15; cf. 1:30)
> "I am not worthy to untie the thong of his sandal." (1:27)
> "Here is the Lamb of God who takes away the sin of the world!" (1:29)
> "I myself have seen and have testified that this is the Son of God." (1:34)
> "He must increase, but I must decrease." (3:30)

Raymond Brown argues that such claims about Jesus could not be historical—their uncertainty flagged by JB's assertions that he did *not* understand until illuminated by the Spirit (vv. 31, 33). Brown solves this dilemma by reasoning that, since the author of 4G was John, son of Zebedee, he knew JB's predictions to have eventually come true:

---

ately the king sent a soldier of the guard with orders to bring John's head. He went and beheaded him in the prison, brought his head on a platter, and gave it to the girl. Then the girl gave it to her mother. When his disciples heard about it, they came and took his body, and laid it in a tomb."

44 Citation from: R.H. Lightfoot, *History and Interpretation in the Gospels* (The Bampton Lectures 1934; New York: Harper and Brothers 1935), 225, first applied to JB by Reumann, "Quest for the Historical Baptist," 187.

... the statements *were* actually made by JB, but that he intended by them a meaning perfectly consonant with the Synoptic picture of his expectations of the one to come. His disciple, John son of Zebedee, remembered these statements of his master and incorporated them with slight adaptation into his Gospel; for he saw in the light of the Holy Spirit that they were even more applicable to Jesus than JB had realized.[45]

Agreeing with Brown's judgment that the historical John could not have known the things he says about Jesus (although not with Brown's attribution of the 4G to John, the son of Zebedee),[46] the question stated in this essay's introduction now arises perforce: Why not leave JB out of the tradition? Even if it could be demonstrated (and it cannot) that the *historical* JB believed that the *historical* Jesus was superior to him in some or many ways, would this have constituted such a clear emphasis of his teaching that the NT Gospels would be inclined to report?

What is more, the 4G seems even more determined than the Synoptics to convince readers that Jesus, not JB, is the Christ. It stands to reason that some first-century Jews and Gentiles were convinced JB *was* the Christ. Mark 6:16 (cf. Matt 14:2) states that Herod perceived Jesus as JB risen from the dead. As I have argued elsewhere, if Elijah represents JB in Mark's Gospel,[47] then Elijah's "appearance" (with Moses) at Jesus's so-called transfiguration signifies JB's resurrection.[48] High claims in the Gospel of Luke, such as that JB is the Davidic "horn of salvation" (Luke 1:69a) and "the dawn from on high" (Luke 1:78b), might also reflect messianic interpretations of JB's ministry. Lukan narration of Paul's encounter with followers of JB in Acts 19:1–7 seeks to imply that the movement persisted into the second century.

---

45 R.E. Brown, "Three Quotations from John the Baptist in the Gospel of John," *CBQ* 22 (1960): 292–298 (293).

46 The narrative explains that the descent and dwelling of the Spirit on Jesus enabled JB to "know" Jesus and thus reveal him to Israel as one baptizing with the Holy Spirit. Joan Taylor writes, "He cannot have come into existence in some magical way as a voice in the wilderness calling people to look towards Jesus. This is the stuff of myth. The real John was probably far more a man of his age" (*The Immerser*, 12).

47 John A.T. Robinson observed that John never used this representation of himself, even if his costume, diet, and baptizing locale in Mark and Matthew seem to suggest it. J.A.T. Robinson, "Elijah, John and Jesus: An Essay in Detection," *NTS* 4 (1958): 263–281; repr. in J.A.T. Robinson, *Twelve New Testament Studies* (London: SCM, 1962), 28–52.

48 See C.K. Rothschild, *Baptist Traditions and Q* (WUNT 190; Tübingen: Mohr Siebeck, 2005), ch. 4.

Returning to Brown's comment, I agree that JB's sayings—in particular, (1) "He who comes after me is ahead of me because he was before me" (1:15); (2) "I am not worthy to untie the thong of his sandal," (1:27); and (3) "He must increase, but I must decrease" (3:30)—are likely to be historical. I do not, however, agree that JB applied these statements to Jesus as Brown would have it, using John, son of Zebedee, as a conduit. They would have been applied by JB to a future coming one, for example, Elijah, the Messiah, the Lord, or some combination of these figures. It is unquestionable that JB would have considered himself inferior to *this* figure. JB may also have referred to this figure as God's goat or lamb, as removing the world's sins, and as Son of God. Sayings #1 and #3 (above) are unique to the 4G as are references to the figure as God's atoning goat or lamb, and Son of God. The 4G positions each with reference to Jesus. Whatever their historicity, the implications of these sayings for JB's portrait in the 4G are significant. First, as compared with the Synoptics, JB demotes himself, even to the point of subverting or negating the efficacy of his own ministry when he declares Jesus to be the lamb removing the sins of the world. This statement suggests that, in the eyes of the evangelists, JB's authority as removing sins was so formidable that he must state *himself* in no uncertain terms, multiple times, that Jesus removes sins. To be sure, the Synoptic Gospels curtail JB's ministry. The alluring sermons with which Josephus credits JB are only suggested in Luke 3:7–17. The 4G, however, takes him down yet another notch. In the 4G, he is known for a baptizing ministry, the value of which is not forgiveness of sins and the meaning of which he himself does not comprehend. What is more, he does not baptize Jesus and Jesus's baptizing ministry is more popular than his. He is known for his testimony, but requires a sign to understand what he sees and, in any case, Jesus's testimony is greater.

3.2.4 Correction

Finally, on at least the following two issues (1) the onset of Jesus's ministry and (2) JB's comprehension of Jesus as the Christ, the 4G seems to correct traditions present in the Synoptics.

Although the 4G agrees with the Synoptics that JB's ministry consists of baptizing, it differs with regard to the official onset of Jesus's ministry with respect to JB's. Whereas the Gospel of Mark presents John as locked up in prison prior to Jesus's preaching of the good news (1:14), and whereas Luke presents John as locked up prior to Jesus's baptism (3:19–22), and whereas Matthew is not clear as to the timing of the two proclamations, the Gospel of John not only presents John's and Jesus's ministries as simultaneous but indicates competition between the two groups. The result of this competition, whether staged or real, is that Jesus acquires a rival over which to triumph. This report of ministry competition over which Jesus's enjoys clear-cut victory demotes JB significantly beyond his devaluation in the Synoptics. Up to this point we had seen that, in light of Jesus, the value of JB's testimony and baptism was reduced. Now, however, JB is categorically defeated. With Jesus in view, the Johannine JB no longer effectively attracts followers. Rather than claim, with the Synoptics, that JB and Jesus did not practice ministry simultaneously (making it impossible to establish that Jesus was the superior attraction), the 4G positions them against one another to demonstrate that, in a face-off, Jesus was the clear favorite.

3.3   John and the Theme of Misunderstanding

A second correction by the 4G of the Synoptic tradition concerns JB's relationship to the Johannine theme of misunderstanding. A significant body of literature is devoted to exploring the topic of misunderstanding in the 4G. Beginning with Oscar Cullmann, the debate continues today.[49] Some arguments engage the problem of scope (i.e., what constitutes misunderstanding). H. Leroy, for example, draws narrow parameters, isolating only eleven *Rätsel* in John 2–8.[50] Others insist that a formal *pun* must be identified for the passage to qualify as misunderstanding. Still others define the theme broadly, qualifying every obscure statement as misunderstanding.[51] As noted above, JB participates in this theme insofar as initially he does not understand, only coming to understanding with the physical manifestation of the Spirit. The purpose of his lack of understanding is now explored.

3.3.1   John Does Not Understand

First, JB himself does not understand. Twice in John 1,[52] JB claims *to have lacked* (note verb tense) the adequate insight to discern Jesus's true identity:

> John 1:31: "*I myself did not know him* (κἀγὼ οὐκ ᾔδειν αὐτόν); but I came baptizing with water for this reason, that he might be revealed to Israel."

---

49 O. Cullmann, "Der johanneische Gebrauch doppeldeutigen Ausdrücke als Schlüssel zum Verständnis des vierten Evangeliums," *TZ* 4 (1948): 360–372; repr. in Cullmann, *Vorträge und Aufsätze 1925–1962* (Tübingen: Mohr; Zürich: Zwingli, 1966), 176–186.

50 John 2:19–22; 3:3–5; 4:10–15; 4:31–34; 4:32–35, 41f.; 6:51–53; 7:33–36 and 8:21f.; 8:31–33; 8:51–53; 8:56–58. H. Leroy, *Rätsel und Missverständnis: Ein Beitrag zur Formgeschichte des Johannesevangeliums* (Bonn: Hanstein, 1966). Main points summarized in the following, brief article, Leroy, "Das johanneische Missverständnis als literarische Form," *BibLeb* 9 (1968): 196–207.

51 D.W. Wead, *The Literary Devices of John's Gospel* (Basel: Reinhardt, 1970), 69–70.

52 Crucial questions of redaction are a desideratum.

John 1:33: *"I myself **did** not know him* (κἀγὼ οὐκ ᾔδειν αὐτόν), but the one who sent me to baptize with water said to me, *'He on whom you see the Spirit descend* and remain is the one who baptizes with the Holy Spirit.'"

Resembling other *dramatis personae* in the 4G (e.g., specified and unspecified Jews, 2:19–21; 3:4; 4:31–34; 6:51–52; 7:33–36; 8:21–22; 11:12; cf. 4:1–15; 6:32–35; 8:51–53, 56–58),[53] initially John does not understand the role Jesus plays in salvation history. He was, thus, not *always* able to "testify" to Jesus but had to *acquire* this ability. To be sure, JB's initial inability to recognize Jesus is perplexing since his primary role in the 4G is as μάρτυς, the hallmark characteristic of which is reliable eyewitness-based testimony.[54] Perhaps this is why Jesus declares that JB's testimony is not as valuable as his own or God's. JB's recognition of Jesus's true identity occurs when the dove lands and remains on Jesus, unrelated to Jesus's baptism.[55] Of all misunderstandings in the 4G, JB's is thus first. He is the 4G's first misunderstanding Jew.[56]

3.3.2   John the Baptist Comes to Understand

JB also, however, establishes the Johannine paradigm of *understanding* with the aid of a sign. According to John 1:29–34, at the moment that a dove alights and settles on Jesus, JB realizes the following four truths: (1) that Jesus is the person to whom JB referred as ranking ahead of him because he was before him (implying that when JB first made this announcement [v. 15] he did not know Jesus was its referent); (2) that the purpose of his baptism is to *reveal* Jesus as the first to be enlightened by the Holy Spirit and the first to enter God's king-

---

53   In one instance, a Samaritan woman misunderstands (4:10–15); in another, the disciples lack this perception (4:31–34).

54   R. Bultmann, *The Gospel of John: A Commentary* (trans. G.R. Beasley-Murray, R.W.N. Hoare, and J.K. Riches; Philadelphia: Westminster, 1971 [1964]), 50 n. 5. See also Keener, *Gospel of John*, 1:392, esp. nn. 274–284. Keener points out that in Acts 10:43 and 1 Pet 1:11–12 prophets act as "witnesses" (393).

55   Careless redaction may have obscured the order of events. Note that JB first tells "some sent from the Pharisees" that among them stands one *they* do not know. Next, he sees Jesus and declares him to be the Lamb of God, but then flashes back to his own inability to recognize Jesus until Jesus is baptized. Highly suspicious aspects of the section include repetition of sayings in vv. 15 and 30, τῇ ἐπαύριον in vv. 29 and 35 and Ἴδε ὁ ἀμνὸς τοῦ θεοῦ declarations in vv. 29 and 36. Bultmann reconstructs this passage persuasively. His reconstruction does not however bypass all difficulties. See Bultmann, *Gospel of John*, 85.

56   Perhaps John the Baptist's not achieving enlightenment but Jesus's disciples achieving it constitutes a refutation by the 4G of Mark in which Jesus's disciples utterly fail (cf. esp. John 1:48–51; 2:11, etc.).

dom to Israel (κἀγὼ οὐκ ᾔδειν αὐτόν, ἀλλ' ἵνα φανερωθῇ τῷ Ἰσραὴλ διὰ τοῦτο ἦλθον ἐγὼ ἐν ὕδατι βαπτίζων, 1:31); (3) that Jesus will baptize with the Holy Spirit; and (4) that Jesus is the Son—or chosen one of—God (ὁ ἐκλεκτὸς τοῦ θεοῦ). With the sign of the dove, JB comes to understand.

However, this pericope also sets a precedent for how and to whom enlightenment comes, a mechanism subsequently explained in chapter 3. One must be born of water and the Spirit to enter the kingdom of God (3:5). In 1:32, Jesus is born of the Spirit. Immediately prior to his departure, Jesus breathes the Holy Spirit on his disciples (20:22), suggesting that, having been born of both water and the Spirit, they may now also enter the kingdom of God with Jesus. In contrast to Jesus and the disciples, however, JB does not receive the Holy Spirit's illumination. Although he is first to *observe* the Spirit's illumination and first to correctly interpret a sign, he models the individual—a Jewish sage and prophet of substantial stature and reputation no less—who *never* receives enlightenment.

Vague grades or levels of illumination, on the model of ancient mystery cults, emerge. According to Jerome, the mysteries of Mithras were organized into a strict hierarchy of seven initiation grades: Raven (*Corax*), Bride (*Nymphus*), Soldier (*Miles*), Lion (*Leo*), Persian (*Perses*), Courier of the Sun (*Heliodromus*) and Father (*Pater*).[57] Each grade was represented by a different symbol. The trajectory, as described by Aristotle, begins with learning about (μαθεῖν) the divine, advances to seeing the divine, culminates in experiencing (παθεῖν) the divine,

---

57 Jerome, *Ep.* 107 ch. 2 (To Laeta): "… did not your own kinsman Gracchus whose name betokens his patrician origin, when a few years back he held the prefecture of the City, overthrow, break in pieces, and shake to pieces the grotto of Mithras and all the dreadful images therein? Those I mean by which the worshippers were initiated as Raven, Bridegroom, Soldier, Lion, Perseus, Sun, Crab, and Father?" The grades may have been for all initiates; alternatively, they may have applied only to priests. See M. Clauss, *The Roman Cult of Mithras: The God and His Mysteries* (trans. R. Gordon; New York: Routledge, 2000 [1990]), 131. Different ritual meals were associated with each initiation grade. The 4G may possess a version of this in its adaptation of the feeding of the five thousand, featuring a little boy with a basket (John 6:1–14). JB's middle level of initiation may have connections with a ritual meal also, although the 4G does not adopt the Synoptic tradition that JB fasted and/or subsisted on a diet of locusts and wild honey (tree sap). Jesus evidently does not eat enough since his disciples must urge him to eat (John 4:31–38). Jesus speaks to the unimportance of actual food as compared with spiritual "food" in 6:25–59. Parallels between Christian and Mithraic ritual meal practice were evidently substantial enough for Justin Martyr to remark that one of the ritual meals of the cult of Mithras was a parody of the Christian meal.

and incorporates a change of mind along the way (διατεθῆναι).[58] The 4G does not possess its own parallel discipleship hierarchy. Even most mystery cult organizations were not that structured. The 4G may, nevertheless, imply a loosely similar ranking system. In the 4G, the entry level is symbolized as πρόβατα, "cattle, flocks, herds" (sheep, John 10:2–4, 7–8, 11–13, 15–16, 27). As in the Mithraic mysteries, a bridegroom (νυμφίος) or male friend of the bridegroom (John 3:29) and a lamp (John 5:35) symbolize the second level.[59] At this level, the initiate is able to recognize the divine and testify to what s/he has seen. This initiate is *not* her/himself born of the Spirit. To rise to the second level, a sign is required. JB exemplifies this level. He receives the sign of the Holy Spirit as a dove alighting and remaining on Jesus promoting him to the second level of initiation. The third and highest level of initiation is baptism by the Spirit. The Spirit is breathed into and remains with this person and s/he enters the kingdom of God. In the 4G, only Jesus is born of the Spirit and has entered the kingdom of God. References to Jesus as lamb, shepherd, and Father[60]—as in Mithraism—symbolize the highest level of initiation. Since at the highest level of initiation the individual merges with the deity, this rank represents not just a quantifiable improvement upon the lower ranks but a new category. The 4G positions JB in a class above the populace, yet of their same category. In contrast, Jesus has been transformed from initiate to revealer; and John 20 suggests that when Jesus breathes the Spirit on his disciples, they too enter this process of divine transformation.[61]

---

58   According to Porphyry, lower-level initiates primarily attended the mysteries, whereas higher-level initiates participated in them. See W. Burkert, *Ancient Mystery Cults* (Cambridge, MA: Harvard University Press, 1987), 69, 89.

59   Firmicus Maternus, *Err prof. rel.* 19.1 records: "Hail Nymphus, hail new Light" suggesting that both a bridegroom and a light were associated with this level. See Clauss, *Roman Cult of Mithras*, 134.

60   The highest grade, *pater*, is the most common image to appear on dedications and inscriptions. The form *pater patrum* ("father of fathers") is often found, which appears to indicate the *pater* with primary status. There are several examples of persons, commonly those of higher social status, joining a Mithraeum with the status *pater*—especially in Rome during the "pagan revival" of the fourth century. It has been suggested that some Mithraea may have awarded honorary *pater* status to sympathetic dignitaries.

61   "Kingdom of God" appears only twice in the 4G at 3:3–5 and 18:36; cf. 6:15. According to Robert M. Grant, each reinterprets a Synoptic reading ("The Origin of the Fourth Gospel," *JBL* 69 [1950]: 305–322 [321]). The Beth Alpha floor mosaic may be instructional here. On the central panel is a Jewish adaptation of the Greco-Roman zodiac. Helios is at the center of the zodiac with his four-horse-drawn chariot. The northern panel depicts the Binding

Thus, JB's statements about Jesus's superior ranking (1:15, 29–30, 36) and his declarations of Jesus as lamb may be interpreted literally as references to an initiation system. Jesus ranks higher than JB because Jesus has obtained the highest level of initiation and JB has not. Jesus is a kingdom of God participant as are his disciples. JB's fate is sealed at an intermediate level; he is not illuminated by the Spirit and never enters the kingdom of God.

4 Conclusion

Whether the 4G duplicates, recontextualizes, modifies, omits, extends, or refutes a Baptist tradition, the net effect is a demonstrably less imposing portrait of JB. Without history, distinctions, and titles undercutting the value of his baptism, testimony, and teaching, the Johannine JB shrinks deep into the abyss of history. Possible explanations for JB's diminution in the 4G fall into two basic categories: historical and literary. Returning to the thesis of Raymond Brown, the attenuation of JB's portrait may suggest a *historical* community of Baptists with which the 4G is competitive. In this case, the 4G seeks not to demote JB, but have him demote himself—a much more effective means of curbing his legacy. Alternatively, the 4G may represent a *literary* riposte to one or more of the Synoptic Gospels, since each creates confusion by presenting JB as savior, light to the Gentiles, prior to Jesus, baptizing Jesus, proclaiming good news before Jesus, and/or arousing messianic suspicions.[62] The Johannine JB is not just quantifiably but categorically inferior to Jesus. This depiction of JB extinguishes the perplexing contradictions of the Synoptic Gospels, offering in its place a wholly coherent picture.

---

of Isaac (Gen 22:1–18). The southern panel depicts the Ark of the Covenant with other traditional ritual objects such as a Menorah.

62 Joan E. Taylor proposes a kind of cascade—from Mark, to Matthew, to Luke, to John—each edition more prone than the next to considering Jesus, the Messiah, JB's superior (*The Immerser*, 3–4).

John's Baptist in Luke's Gospel[*]

John DelHousaye

Bonaventure (1221–1274) approves a tradition that Luke "indicates in his prologue that other Gospels were written before his."[1] This is a natural, if not inevitable, reading from a scholastic theologian in medieval Italy. However, the Franciscan probably understands the "other Gospels" to be Matthew and Mark because of another tradition passed to Europe: John was written "last of all."[2] This may have led to the canonical order of the Gospels, which solidifies this impression.[3] What I call Johannine posteriority, the assumption that the Fourth Gospel was completed after the Synoptic Gospels, has dominated ecclesial opinion and biblical scholarship.[4] Ambiguities make certainty impossible; nevertheless, a highly plausible solution to the Synoptic Problem and John's place in that trajectory would further our understanding of Christian origins.

Source criticism was initiated by Augustine (354–430) and has been nurtured in the academy; it remains our best way for testing these opinions that have come down to us. The older, somewhat out-of-fashion discipline has been chastened for its modernist logocentrism.[5] But scholars like James Dunn, who

---

[*] An earlier draft of this paper was read at the SBL Synoptic Gospels Section on Monday November 24, 2014 at the SBL Annual Meeting in San Diego, CA.
[1] Bonaventure attributes the prologue to Jerome, but scholars identify it as part of the Monarchian prologues originally published in the late fourth or early fifth century: *Works of St. Bonaventure: St. Bonaventure's Commentary on the Gospel of Luke: Chapters 1–8* (ed. Robert J. Karris; Saint Bonaventure, NY: Franciscan Institute Publications, 2001), 14.
[2] The quotation is taken from Eusebius's note on Origen's view (Eusebius, *Hist. eccl.* 6.25.6). Irenaeus explicitly claims John is the last Gospel to be written (*Haer.* 3.1.1).
[3] See David Trobisch, *The First Edition of the New Testament* (New York: Oxford University Press, 2000), 79–80.
[4] Critical scholars are remarkably compliant, although they have challenged nearly every other patristic opinion.
[5] In my opinion, the criticism is not entirely fair. J.G. Herder (1744–1803) and J.C.L. Gieseler (1792–1854) anticipated orality studies. B.F. Westcott addressed the Synoptic Problem from this perspective: *An Introduction to the Study of the Gospels* (New York: Macmillan, 1895). See also Bo Reicke, *The Roots of the Synoptic Gospels* (Philadelphia: Fortress, 1986) and John M. Rist, *On the Independence of Matthew and Mark* (SNTSMS 32; Cambridge: Cambridge University Press, 1978).

became more sensitized to the role of orality, remain convinced of a literary relationship between at least the Synoptic Gospels.[6] This is not a claim of consensus, but it is probably fair to say that most who address the Synoptic problem recognize the appropriation of over fifty percent of Mark in Luke.[7] By "appropriation" I mean the use of a pre-existing text with little or no transformation that is nevertheless recontextualized by its place in the new work. Arguments for Markan priority cannot be reviewed here, but I see this as one of the safest conclusions from over a century of research.[8] Augustine was right about literary dependence, but wrong about Mark being an abbreviation of Matthew and Luke.[9] Rather, Mark is the point of departure for the presentations of the other Synoptics.

Luke[10] engages in what may be called *aemulatio* (ζήλωσις)—a way of composing that respects one's predecessors by updating their work, a practice common among Greco-Roman and Jewish writers:

> Classical rhetoricians felt it important to imitate authoritative texts to the best of their ability, with as little personal contribution as possible.

---

6   James Dunn appropriates Kenneth Bailey's work in oral transmission theory, which emphasizes the role of communal memory: *Jesus Remembered* (Grand Rapids: Eerdmans, 2003). Birger Gerhardsson emphasizes the role of an apostolic collegium: *The Reliability of the Gospel Tradition* (Peabody, MA: Hendrickson, 2001), 74. Both dynamics were probably at play in the early church.

7   For a recent discussion, see Donald A. Hagner, *The New Testament: A Historical and Theological Introduction* (Grand Rapids: Baker Academic, 2012), 131–192.

8   See, e.g., Peter M. Head, *Christology and the Synoptic Problem: An Argument for Markan Priority* (SNTSMS 94; Cambridge: Cambridge University Press, 1997).

9   *Harmony* 2.4. In book 4, Augustine describes Mark as a "unifier"—bringing the kingly and priestly emphases of Matthew and Luke respectively together. After modern scholars began to argue for Markan priority, it was refined as the Griesbach hypothesis. The primary work of Johann Jakob Griesbach (1745–1812) on this topic is *Synopsis Evangeliorum Matthei Marci et Lucae una cum iis Joannis pericopis: Quae historiam passionis et resurrectionis Jesu Christi complectuntu* (2nd ed.; Halle: J.J. Curtii Haeredes, 1797). William R. Farmer had championed this view more recently. See his *The Synoptic Problem* (New York: Macmillan, 1964).

10 I presume Lukan authorship of the Third Gospel. Irenaeus (d. c. 195) identifies the author of the Third Gospel as Λουκᾶς ("Luke"), "the companion of Paul" (*Haer.* 3.1.1; 3.14.1). Papyrus Bodmer 14 (P75), the earliest witness to the end of the Gospel (c. 200), originating in Egypt, uses the inscription "Gospel According to Luke." There are no alternative claims for authorship in early Christian tradition. Like Mark, he was not remembered as an eyewitness, making the invention of his involvement implausible.

Originality was esteemed less highly than copying, repeating and discovering how others thought. Ultimately, this provided the incentive for one's own thinking.[11]

Luke may appropriate Josephus (37–after 100) as a source.[12] This is suggested by their similar prefaces, the census of Quirinius, and focus on the destruction of the Second Temple of which the historian was an eyewitness. At least by the time of Origen, Christians were making explicit use of his works. There is no reason why Luke could not have been an early adopter. Steve Mason suggests he attended readings in Rome.[13]

Josephus and Luke emulate the style of sacred biblical history, a genre that originates in Ancient Israelite Scripture. For Luke, this begins immediately after the Gospel's preface—Ἐγένετο ἐν ταῖς ἡμέραις Ἡρῴδου βασιλέως τῆς Ἰουδαίας, "This happened in the days of Herod, king of Judea" (1:5)—which echoes narrative transitions like καὶ ἐγενήθη ἐν ταῖς ἡμέραις ἐκείναις (1Sam 4:1 LXX).[14] In addition to clarifying details for his non-Jewish readers, Josephus looked to precedent—the example of the high priest Eleazar in *Letter of Aristeas*. He adopted the twenty-book structure of *Roman Antiquities* by Dionysius of Halicarnassus, and dedicated his later works to a certain Epaphroditus (*Ant.* 1.8; *Life* 430; *Ag. Ap.* 1.1). For the first half of *Antiquities*, he relies primarily on Scripture, but also appropriates earlier texts and tradition like Philo's *De opificio mundi* and lore about Moses's birth (2.205). He rearranges and condenses his sources,

---

11 Jacques T.A.G. van Ruiten, "The Book of Jubilees as Paratextual Literature," in *In the Second Degree: Paratextual Literature in Ancient Near Eastern and Ancient Mediterranean Culture and Its Reflections in Medieval Literature* (ed. Philip S. Alexander, Armin Lange, and Renate J. Pillinger; Leiden: Brill, 2010), 65–95 (65). In the first and second centuries, we find "old comedies" in the style of Aristophanes; "new comedies" after Plautus and Terence. Seneca (c. 4 BC–AD 65) emulates Euripides to test the knowledge (literacy) of his audience: J.J. Gahan, "'Imitatio and Aemulatio' in Seneca's 'Phaedra,'" *Latomus* 46 (1987): 380–387 (380). Arno Reif's dissertation is often cited: "Interpretatio, Imitatio, Aemulatio: Begriff und Vorstellung literarischer Abhängigkeit bei den Römern" (Cologne, 1959). See also John W.H. Atkins, *Literary Criticism in Antiquity: A Sketch of Its Development* (2 vols.; Cambridge: Cambridge University Press, 1934); Bernard Kytzler, "Imitatio und aemulatio in der Thebais des Statius," *Hermes* 97 (1969): 209–232.

12 Francis Crawford Burkitt (1864–1935) grounds the modern argument for this scenario: *The Gospel History and its Transmission* (3rd ed.; Edinburgh: T&T Clark, 1911), 105–110. Although it is possible Josephus used Luke, this scenario seems unlikely because the historian was not part of the Christian community.

13 *Josephus and The New Testament* (2nd ed.; Peabody, MA: Hendrickson, 2003), 279.

14 See also the opening of *Letter of Aristeas* for a broad parallel.

reserving elements for a later work, and amalgamates *Kings* and *Chronicles*, eliminating the most embarrassing elements of his people's history like the golden calf and the breaking of the first tablets of the Law (3.99).[15]

Papias of Hierapolis (c. 60–130), who seems to appropriate Luke's preface, defends Mark against criticism for its lack of rhetorical arrangement (frg. 15).[16] He claims Mark simply wrote down what Peter taught about Jesus.[17] The apostolic backing secured the authority of the Second Gospel, but it was reasonable that its rough presentation would undergo refinement.

Luke also shares thirty-six units (230 verses) with Matthew. Instead of positing a shared document (Q),[18] which has been the dominant paradigm, many prefer, as I do, the option that Luke used Matthew.[19] According to Papias, Matthew "arranged" (συντάσσω) the sayings of the Lord—possibly a reference

---

[15] I derived this list from H.St.J. Thackeray's introduction to Josephus's *Antiquities* (LCL; Cambridge, MA: Harvard University Press, 1926–1965), 4.viii–xiii.

[16] For the fragments, see Michael W. Holmes, *The Apostolic Fathers: Greek Texts and English Translations* (3rd ed.; Grand Rapids: Baker Academic, 2007), 738–741. Ralph Martin claims Papias defends the apostolic authority behind Mark in response to Marcion's championing of Luke: *Mark: Evangelist and Theologian* (Grand Rapids: Zondervan, 1972), 81, 83–84. But Martin Hengel notes that Marcion's separation from the community in Rome probably took place around 144—too late for Papias's exigence: *Studies in the Gospel of Mark* (trans. John Bowden; London: SCM, 1985), 48. However, for the plausible scenario that Papias knew Luke, see Andrew Gregory, *The Reception of Luke and Acts in the Period before Irenaeus* (Tübingen: Mohr Siebeck, 2003), 35.

[17] Monte A. Shanks, *Papias and The New Testament* (Eugene, OR: Pickwick, 2013), 183–188.

[18] The Q hypothesis is a gradual development. Christian Hermann Weisse (1801–1866) speculated that Matthew and Luke followed a common source of Jesus sayings in his *Die evangelische Geschichte, kritisch und philosophisch bearbeitet* (2 vols.; Leipzig: Breitkopf und Härtel, 1838). Heinrich Julius Holtzmann (1832–1910) argues that Matthew and Luke used an *Urmarkus* ("Document A") in addition to another source ("Document B"), which is roughly equivalent to Q. Holtzmann later abandoned the *Urmarkus* hypothesis. His standard works are *Die synoptischen Evangelien: Ihr Ursprung und geschichtlicher Charakter* (Leipzig: Engelmann, 1863); *Lehrbuch der historisch-kritischen Einleitung in das Neue Testament* (Freiburg: Mohr Siebeck, 1885). Burnett Hillman Streeter (1874–1937) extends Holtzmann's classification into a four-document hypothesis: (1) Mark, (2) Q, (3) "M", and (4) "L." The latter two sources comprise material unique to Matthew and Luke. Q was written in Greek and is almost wholly preserved in Matthew and Luke, although the latter is more faithful in wording: *The Four Gospels: A Study of Origins* (London: Macmillan, 1924).

[19] James H. Ropes suggested this without offering a comprehensive argument: *The Synoptic Gospels* (Cambridge, MA: Harvard University Press, 1934). See Mark Goodacre, *The Synoptic Problem: A Way through the Maze* (London: T&T Clark, 2001), who furthers the work of Austin Farrer, "On Dispensing with Q," in *Studies in the Gospels: Essays in Memory of*

to the five discourses in his Gospel (frg. 16).[20] Yet, because of the Hebrew or Aramaic background of the teaching, some labored to understand them.[21] These difficulties—lack of arrangement and ambiguity—presumably led Papias to write his own *Expositions of the Sayings of the Lord*. The motivation does not seem to be one-upmanship but the effective communication of the Gospel.[22] The phenomena of Luke's presentation suggest that he might have had a similar stance towards his predecessors. Papias seems to be following Luke's hope for Theophilus: "that you might recognize the truth of the words by which you were taught" (1:4). If correct, these conclusions vindicate Bonaventure's tradition: nearly seventy-five percent of Luke is a reworking of Mark and Matthew into a rhetorically pleasing, pedagogically effective narrative. However, those who remain convinced of the Q hypothesis may still find the burden of this paper convincing: Luke appropriated the Fourth Gospel.

Scholars have noted overlap between Luke and John.[23] In addition to verbal parallels, the evangelists shared common themes like sympathy towards Samaritans and women.[24] Luke also appears to sharpen implications of John's presentation. Jesus cooks breakfast in John, but eats in Luke.[25] Jesus claims he must depart for the Spirit to come in the Upper Room Discourse; Luke depicts the Ascension and Pentecost. Yet, like the previous studies of triple (Matthew, Mark, Luke) and double traditions (Matthew and Luke), the reversibility of the observations failed to disturb the paradigm of Johannine posteriority.[26]

   R.H. *Lightfoot* (ed. D.E. Nineham; Oxford: Blackwell, 1955), 55–88; E.P. Sanders and Margaret Davies, *Studying the Synoptic Gospels* (London: SCM, 1989); Michael Goulder, "Is Q a Juggernaut?" *JBL* 115 (1996): 667–681.

20 The Sermon on the Mount (chs. 5–7); Mission Instructions to the Twelve (ch. 10); Parables of the Kingdom (ch. 13); Discipleship and Discipline (ch. 18); Eschatology (chs. 24–25).

21 It is not clear if this arrangement included translation from Hebrew or Aramaic or if Matthew first published a Hebrew Gospel. See George Howard, *Hebrew Gospel of Matthew* (Macon, GA: Mercer University Press, 1995).

22 F.H. Colson, "Τάξει in Papias (the Gospels and the Rhetorical Schools)," *JTS* 14 (1913): 62–69.

23 See John Amedee Bailey, *The Traditions Common to the Gospels of Luke and John* (NovTSup 7; Leiden: Brill, 1963); P. Parker, "Luke and the Fourth Evangelist," *NTS* 9 (1963): 317–336; Julius Schniewind provides an extensive list of parallels: *Parallelperikopen bei Johannes und Lukas* (Hildesheim: G. Olms, 1958).

24 Paul N. Anderson, *The Fourth Gospel and the Quest for Jesus: Modern Foundations Reconsidered* (LNTS 321; London: T&T Clark, 2006), 115.

25 Gregory, *The Reception of Luke and Acts*, 59. See also his "The Third Gospel? The Relationship of John and Luke Reconsidered," in *Challenging Perspectives on the Gospel of John* (ed. John Lierman; Tübingen: Mohr Siebeck, 2006), 109–134.

26 Anton Dauer finds Lukan redaction in John: *Johannes und Lukas: Untersuchungen zu den*

But Luke does two other things that are not easily reversed. First, his deviations from Mark's order often follow John. Mark and Matthew jump to Galilee after the resurrection, but Luke remains committed to Judea with John. Paul Anderson notes: "at least three dozen times, Luke appears to depart from Mark and to side with the Johannine rendering of an event or teaching."[27] The Fourth Gospel makes little attempt to follow the Synoptic arrangement; more likely Luke defers to Johannine order. Second, when the other Synoptics and John present similar yet different accounts of an event, Luke often conflates or harmonizes them.[28] In contrast to Mark and Matthew, but like John, Luke has only one feeding miracle. John relates a call story featuring Peter and a miraculous catch of fish at the end of his presentation, understating their initial encounter (cf. 1:40–42; 21:4–8). Immediately after Jesus's baptism and temptation, Mark relates Peter's call story (1:16–18). Without contextualization, the reader might assume Jesus says, "Follow me" to strangers. Luke seems to find a middle ground: he inverts Mark's arrangement, placing the healing of Peter's mother-in-law before his calling (cf. Luke 4:38–39; Mark 1:29–31), and adds John's miraculous catch—all perhaps to explain why he would leave everything behind and follow him (Luke 5:11).

Of course, it does not necessarily follow that Luke used the canonical form of John's Gospel. F. Lamar Cribbs, who deserves credit for disrupting the paradigm, and Anderson claim he appropriated Johannine tradition.[29] This allows a harmonization of both ecclesial traditions: Luke appropriated Mark (and possibly Matthew or Q) and Johannine tradition that had yet to reach closure as the final form of the Fourth Gospel. Perhaps Luke interviewed John or took notes from his preaching.[30] Although we cannot know, they may have known and influenced one another.

---

johanneisch-lukanischen Parallelperikopen Joh 4,46–54/Lk 7,1–10—John 12,1–8/Luke 7,36–50; 10,38–42—Joh 20,19–29/Lk 24,36–49 (Würzburg: Echter Verlag, 1972); *Die Passiongeschichte im Johannesevangelium: Eine traditions-geschichtliche und theologische Untersuchung zu Joh 18,1–19,30* (Munich: Kösel-Verlag, 1972). But he does not consider the reverse. I am grateful to Mark Matson for drawing my attention to Dauer's work.

27 *The Fourth Gospel and the Quest for Jesus*, 112. See also Gregory, "The Third Gospel?," 129.
28 Anderson, *The Fourth Gospel and the Quest for Jesus*, 114.
29 F. Lamar Cribbs, "St. Luke and the Johannine Tradition," *JBL* 90 (1971): 422–450; "A Study of the Contacts That Exist Between St. Luke and St. John," in *Society of Biblical Literature: 1973 Seminary Papers. Vol. 2* (ed. George MacRae; Cambridge, MA: SBL, 1973), 1–93; Anderson, *The Fourth Gospel and the Quest for Jesus*, 114.
30 E. Osty, "Les points de contact entre le récit de la Passion dans S. Luc et dans S. Jean," *RSR* 39 (1951): 146–154 (154).

However, the extensive overlap between Luke and John suggests a literary relationship. What led Dunn and others to a both/and concerning oral and textual sources is applicable here. Two recent monographs, independent of one another, claim Luke appropriated a pre-canonical edition of John. Barbara Shellard interprets Luke's prologue as acknowledging dependence on the other three Gospels, and Mark Matson traces a dialogue with John throughout Luke's passion narrative.[31] But they are unsure if the version Luke appropriated had the prologue (1:1–18), which, along with the epilogue, is often considered to be a later addition.[32] My aim is to tie up this loose end and hopefully extend their work by attending to how Luke appropriates John's Baptist, pointing out distinctively Johannine emphases and departures from Mark's presentation, applying Matson's close reading approach to the beginning of the Third Gospel.[33] Much of Luke's unique presentation focuses on the Baptist, particularly the opening birth narrative (1:5–2:40). Even if John proves to be a minor source, this would still cast at least a candle into the darkest corner of the Synoptic Problem.

---

31   Barbara Shellard, *New Light on Luke: Its Purpose, Sources, and Literary Context* (JSNTSup 215; London: Sheffield Academic, 2002); Mark Matson, *In Dialogue with Another Gospel? The Influence of the Fourth Gospel on the Passion Narrative of the Gospel of Luke* (SBLDS 178; Atlanta: SBL, 2001). He notes, among other things, that with John Luke does not record the flight of the disciples (Mark 14:49–52//Matt 26:55b–56) or the Barabbas exchange (Mark 15:10–11//Matt 27:17–20). In contrast to the other Synoptics, but with John, Luke relates Judas to Satan/the devil (Luke 22:3//John 13:2, 27), has Pilate declare Jesus innocent three times (Luke 23:4, 15, 22//John 18:38; 19:4, 6), and places two angels at the tomb (Luke 24:4//John 20:12).

32   Matson does not see any of John's prologue in Luke (*In Dialogue*, 447). Shellard recognizes the *synkrisis*, but attributes it to the narrative portion of the Fourth Gospel (*New Light*, 216). John A.T. Robinson claims without text-critical justification that the prologue was written to introduce the Gospel after the publication of the Johannine letters because of common terms and themes: "The Relation of the Prologue to the Gospel of St. John," *NTS* 9 (1962): 123–124.

33   I use "the Baptist" to avoid confusion: John does not refer to John as the Baptist, but does associate him with immersing others. Michael Goulder employs a similar criterion for establishing the Farrer hypothesis: "Luke's Knowledge of Matthew," in *Minor Agreements Symposium Göttingen 1991* (ed. Georg Strecker; Göttingen: Vandenhoeck & Ruprecht, 1993), 143–162 (144).

1 John 1:1–18

Some limit the opening of the Fourth Gospel to five verses, but most cut the unit at verse eighteen.[34] In any case, there is a clear transition between the fifth and sixth verses:[35]

> καὶ τὸ φῶς ἐν τῇ σκοτίᾳ φαίνει, καὶ ἡ σκοτία αὐτὸ οὐ κατέλαβεν, and the light in the darkness shines, and the darkness did not overcome [or comprehend] it.

> [6] Ἐγένετο ἄνθρωπος, ἀπεσταλμένος παρὰ θεοῦ, ὄνομα αὐτῷ Ἰωάννης· οὗτος ἦλθεν εἰς μαρτυρίαν ἵνα μαρτυρήσῃ περὶ τοῦ φωτός, ἵνα πάντες πιστεύσωσιν δι' αὐτοῦ. οὐκ ἦν ἐκεῖνος τὸ φῶς, ἀλλ' ἵνα μαρτυρήσῃ περὶ τοῦ φωτός, There came a human being [or a human came into being], sent from God. His name was John. This one [or he] came for a witness that he might witness concerning the light, that all might believe through him. That one [or he] was not the light, but [came] that he might witness concerning the light.
> John 1:5–8

In contrast to "the light," who will be identified as Jesus, God sends John as a witness. But he is emphatically not the light. John commits to this *synkrisis* (σύνκρισεις, *comparatio*) throughout his presentation of the Baptist. In his final appearance, the Baptist reinforces the metaphor of being the lesser or waning light and introduces a complement, the groom and his friend who brings the bride (3:29–30).[36] Plutarch (46–120) employs the trope in his parallel lives.[37] But the rhetoric is more like Isocrates's encomium for Evagoras (435–c. 373 BC),

---

34 J. Ramsey Michaels classifies the relatively small unit as a "preface or preamble": *The Gospel of John* (NICNT; Grand Rapids: Eerdmans, 2010), 45.

35 For a list of commentaries and translations that recognize the transition, see John McHugh, *John 1–4* (ICC; London: T&T Clark, 2009), 78–79.

36 Andrew Lincoln, *The Gospel According to Saint John* (BNTC; London: Continuum, 2005), 161.

37 Concerning Plutarch, see T.E. Duff, "Plutarchan Synkrisis: Comparisons and Contradictions," in *Rhetorical Theory and Praxis in Plutarch* (ed. L. Van der Stockt; Leuven: Peeters, 2000), 141–161; Hartmut Erbse, "Die Bedeutung der Synkrisis in der Parallelbiographien Plutarchs," *Hermes* 84 (1956): 389–424. Zeba Crook notes the absence of any attempted definition in ancient literature as if it would be stating the obvious: *Reconceptualising Conversion: Patronage, Loyalty, and Conversion in the Religions of the Ancient Mediterranean* (Berlin: de Gruyter, 2004), 118.

who is compared to Cyrus (c. 600 or 576–530 BC), the heroic paradigm of an opposing people. The Persian is great, but the Cypriot is greater (*Evag.* 37–39).[38] John's asymmetrical praise anticipates conflict from the disciples of the Baptist (3:25–30).

After refocusing on the "true light" for a stanza (John 1:9–14), John returns to the Baptist:

> Ἰωάννης μαρτυρεῖ περὶ αὐτοῦ καὶ κέκραγεν λέγων· οὗτος ἦν ὃν εἶπον· ὁ ὀπίσω μου ἐρχόμενος ἔμπροσθέν μου γέγονεν, ὅτι πρῶτός μου ἦν, John witnesses concerning him and has cried out saying, "This one [or he] was who I spoke. The one who comes after me has come before my (face) [or ranks before me][39] because he was before me."[40]

Without making any final judgments about the prologue's structure—a remarkably contested issue—there is clearly a back-and-forth between Jesus and the Baptist:

Jesus (Logos)	1:1–4
Baptist	1:5–7
Jesus (Logos)	1:8–14
Baptist	1:15
Jesus (Logos)	1:16

With each transition, Jesus increases and the Baptist decreases.

2 John 1:19–34

The following unit (1:19–28), which may open the narrative proper, unpacks the witness of the Baptist in the prologue, subdividing into a negative and positive witness:[41] The Baptist is not the Christ, Elijah, or the Prophet (vv. 19–21);

---

38 See Crook, *Reconceptualising Conversion*, 118.

39 My reading attempts to convey the spatial sense of ἔμπροσθέν—before the presence of someone or something (see Matt 5:24; 6:1; John 10:4; 12:37). As the Logos is before (πρὸς) the presence of the Father (1:1), John is before the Son.

40 It is difficult to know where the Baptist ends and John begins. If we include v. 16 as part of the Baptist's logion, there would be equal or nearly equal (depending on textual criticism) words in both subunits (vv. 6–8 and 15–16). But most place quotation marks after v. 15.

41 John uses an article before John at v. 29, which is probably referring back to the anarthrous

he is a voice crying in the wilderness (vv. 22–23).[42] The Isaiah citation (40:3) aligns with the Synoptic portrait, but the Baptist's rejection of being identified with Elijah is remarkably distinctive (cf. Mark 9:13; Matt 17:11–13).[43] After the initial witness, Jesus enters the narrative (v. 29). Instead of depicting his baptism, as we find in Mark and Matthew, John appears to present the event from the perspective of the Baptist, who is moved to testify after seeing the Holy Spirit (1:32–33).

3 Luke's Birth Narrative

François Bovon (1938–2013) has analyzed the structure of Luke's birth narrative:

A   Declaration of John's Birth (1:5–25)
A' Declaration of Jesus's Birth (1:26–38)
B   Meeting between Mary and Elizabeth (1:39–56)
C   Birth of John (1:57–80)
C' Birth of Jesus (2:1–40).[44]

Like most influential interpreters, Bovon does not consider John as one of Luke's sources.[45] Yet both introduce Jesus with the same rhetorical strategy: the Baptist is great, but Jesus is greater.[46] Gabriel claims, "For he [John] will

---

occurrences in the prologue (1:6, 15). Masanobu Endo emphasizes the thematic overlap between the prologue and narrative: *Creation and Christology: A Study on the Johannine Prologue in the Light of Early Jewish Creation Accounts* (WUNT 149; Tübingen: Mohr Siebeck, 2002), 230–247.

42   The redundant elements of the opening negative confession are especially emphatic—something like, "instead of denying, he made bold confession, I myself am not the Christ." In contrast, denials of being Elijah or the Prophet progressively shorten: I am not … No, anticipating his self-erasure (3:27–30).

43   John's citation of Isa 40:3 differs from the OG and Synoptics: instead of ἑτοιμάσατε ("prepare"), the Baptist says, εὐθύνατε ("make straight"). But this is merely a conflation of the remaining line: εὐθείας ποιεῖτε τὰς τρίβους αὐτοῦ, "Make his paths straight."

44   See now François Bovon, *Luke 1: A Commentary on the Gospel of Luke 1:1–9:50* (Hermeneia; trans. C.M. Thomas; Minneapolis: Augsburg Fortress, 2002), 29. But scholars were already using this analysis in the 1990s from his *Das Evangelium nach Lukas* (EKKNT III/1; Zürich: Benziger Verlag/Neukirchen-Vluyn: Neukirchener Verlag, 1989), 46–47. See Darrell L. Bock, *Luke. Volume 1: 1:1–9:50* (Grand Rapids: Baker, 1994), 68.

45   *Luke 1*, 6–8.

46   Bock notes, "Everything about these two chapters [1:1–2:52] shows Jesus' superiority to John" (*Luke*, 49).

be great before the Lord ... And he will be filled in the Holy Spirit, even from the womb of his mother" (1:15). But Jesus "will be great" without qualification—an attribute normally reserved for God (v. 32). Jesus is not simply "filled in the Holy Spirit," but "conceived in the Holy Spirit."

Following Bovon's analysis, Luke's structure may be described as an altarpiece between two diptychs: the emphasis falls on the meeting of John (Elizabeth) and Jesus (Mary) in utero.[47] In both Gospels, when Jesus first approaches, the Holy Spirit moves the Baptist (Luke 1:41//John 1:32–34).

These interconnections may have encouraged Tatian (c. 120–after 174) to follow John's prologue with Luke's birth narrative in his harmony.[48]

The overlap may be accidental—*synkrisis* was a common rhetorical device—but Luke appears to appropriate John's prologue in two other places. In his version of the Transfiguration, the disciples wake up and see Jesus's "glory" (δὲ εἶδον τὴν δόξαν αὐτοῦ, 9:32). Although absent in the parallels of Mark and Matthew, the wording is similar to John's "we beheld his glory" (καὶ ἐθεασάμεθα τὴν δόξαν αὐτοῦ, 1:14). Coincidence is unlikely because of the thematic similarity of the units.[49] Indeed, John may be offering his version of the Transfiguration tradition. In Acts Luke echoes John's unique presentation of the Baptist's disciples becoming followers of Jesus. Paul comes to Ephesus and explains:

> Ἰωάννης ἐβάπτισεν βάπτισμα μετανοίας τῷ λαῷ λέγων εἰς τὸν ἐρχόμενον μετ' αὐτὸν ἵνα πιστεύσωσιν, τοῦτ' ἔστιν εἰς τὸν Ἰησοῦν, John baptized with a baptism of repentance, speaking to the people concerning the one coming after him—that is, Jesus—*that they might believe.*
>
> Acts 19:4

We find the purpose in John's prologue, not Luke's earlier depiction of the Baptist in his gospel:

> οὗτος ἦλθεν εἰς μαρτυρίαν ἵνα μαρτυρήσῃ περὶ τοῦ φωτός, ἵνα πάντες πιστεύσωσιν δι' αὐτοῦ, This one came for a witness that he might witness concerning the light *that* everyone *might believe* through him.
>
> John 1:7

---

47 Bovon notes: "The scene in which Mary visits Elizabeth serves as the connecting link between the traditions about John and Jesus" (*Luke 1*, 7).

48 Carmel McCarthy, *Saint Ephrem's Commentary on Tatian's Diatessaron: An English Translation of Chester Beatty Syriac MS 709 with Introduction and Notes* (Oxford: Oxford University Press, 1993), 44.

49 Anderson, *The Fourth Gospel and the Quest for Jesus*, 113.

Again, thematic coherence suggests a dialogue with John's Gospel. (We should exercise caution when appealing to Acts because it is possibly from a different author.[50] However, tradition and most Lukan authorities hold that both works are from the same author.[51]) These allusions suggest that Luke not only appropriated John's prologue, but intended the reader to do the same. He seems to play off the ecclesial tradition that John wrote his Gospel in Ephesus.

4 Luke 3:1–3

Luke also appears to use John as a historical source, like he may do with Josephus. When Luke re-introduces the Baptist for his public ministry, he provides a political context that includes ἀρχιερέως Ἅννα καὶ Καϊάφα "the high priesthood of Annas and Caiaphas" (3:2; see also Acts 4:6). John is the only other New Testament writer to mention both high priests (18:13, 19). Luke may appropriate the name from Josephus (*Ant.* 18.2.1–2) or elsewhere, but he also seems to adopt John's emphasis of the Baptist's itinerant ministry in the same unit: ἦλθεν εἰς πᾶσαν [τὴν] περίχωρον τοῦ Ἰορδάνου, "he went into all the surrounding region of the Jordan."[52]

5 Verbal Overlap

Overlap continues in the Baptist's confession.[53] Among the Synoptics, Luke uniquely writes:

> Προσδοκῶντος δὲ τοῦ λαοῦ καὶ διαλογιζομένων πάντων ἐν ταῖς καρδίαις αὐτῶν περὶ τοῦ Ἰωάννου, μήποτε αὐτὸς εἴη ὁ Χριστός, Now while the people were waiting in expectation and all were questioning in their hearts about John, if *he* could be the Christ.
>
> Luke 3:15

---

50 See Patricia Walters, *The Assumed Authorial Unity of Luke and Acts: A Reassessment of the Evidence* (SNTSMS 145; Cambridge: Cambridge University Press, 2009).

51 I still find Robert C. Tannehill's work compelling: *The Narrative Unity of Luke–Acts: A Literary Interpretation* (Minneapolis: Fortress, 1994). See also Kenneth Wolfe, "The Chiastic Structure of Luke–Acts and Some Implications for Worship," *SwJT* 22 (1980): 60–71.

52 Cf. Luke 3:1//John 1:28; 3:23; 10:40. Noted by Anderson, *The Fourth Gospel and the Quest for Jesus*, 113.

53 Shellard, *New Light*, 217; Anderson, *The Fourth Gospel and the Quest for Jesus*, 113.

In Mark and Matthew, the Baptist's self-identification is unsolicited. John more specifically identifies the interlocutors as "priests and Levites" (1:19) than Luke's "crowds," but we find a similar phenomenon in a double tradition. Matthew has Pharisees and Sadducees coming to the Baptist for immersion (3:11). In Luke's parallel, it is "the crowds" (ὄχλοις, 3:7). Luke may be preserving the original wording of Q, but the wording begins an *inclusio*—A = the crowds, B = the tax collectors and their enforcers, then the crowds (A') again—which includes his unique material (3:7–14). The crowds, then, may reflect Luke's special theme. In John, the Baptist leads off by denying he is the ὁ Χριστός (1:20). In Luke, the people wonder if he could be ὁ Χριστός. Luke's wording then largely parallels John's:

> ἀπεκρίνατο λέγων πᾶσιν ὁ Ἰωάννης, John answered them all, saying
> Luke 3:16

> ἀπεκρίθη αὐτοῖς ὁ Ἰωάννης λέγων, John answered them, saying.[54]
> John 1:26

More of the logion occurs in Acts:

> οὐκ εἰμὶ ἐγώ· ἀλλ' ἰδοὺ ἔρχεται μετ' ἐμὲ οὗ οὐκ εἰμὶ ἄξιος τὸ ὑπόδημα τῶν ποδῶν λῦσαι, I am not (he). Yet look: he is coming after me—of whom I am not worthy to untie the sandals of his feet.
> Acts 13:25

> οὗ οὐκ εἰμὶ [ἐγὼ] ἄξιος ἵνα λύσω αὐτοῦ τὸν ἱμάντα τοῦ ὑποδήματος, of whom I am not worthy to untie the strap of his sandals.[55]
> John 1:27

6   Harmonization/Shared Omissions

Luke appears to harmonize Mark and John. Mark presents the Baptist in the dress of Elijah (1:6//1 Kgs 1:8) and has Jesus affirm the connection (9:13).[56] Luke does not include either verse in his presentation presumably because of the Baptist's denial in John:

---

54 Cribbs, "St. Luke," 432.
55 Shellard, *New Light*, 217. John and Luke use ἄξιος, not ἱκανός; the singular ὑπόδημα.
56 Mark (1:2) ensures the connection by implicitly citing Malachi (3:1) in context.

> σὺ Ἠλίας εἶ; καὶ λέγει· οὐκ εἰμί, "Are you Elijah?" And he says, "I am not."
> John 1:21

But instead of choosing one Gospel over another, he offers a harmonizing interpretation in the birth narrative: the Baptist will come "in the spirit and power of Elijah" (John 1:17).

Like John, Luke does not describe Jesus's baptism in contrast to the other Synoptics (cf. Mark 1:9–11//Matt 3:13–17; John 1:32–34). He also passes over the narrative of John's demise, allowing a summation of his arrest to suffice (3:19–20; cf. Mark 6:19–29//Matt 14:5–12). These omissions are consistent with the rhetorical purpose sketched already.

7 Implications

There is no universally accepted solution to the Synoptic Problem, and bringing John into the discussion further complicates the matter. We may only argue for degrees of plausibility. Still, previous studies have provided good reasons to maintain that Luke used Mark, Matthew, and John for his Gospel. I find Luke's Baptist in verbal overlap, harmonization, and shared omissions with the Fourth Gospel. Luke also appears to have adopted the structure and language of John's prologue. If this is correct, then Luke probably used a form of John's Gospel like its canonical form.[57]

Here I can only sketch some of the implications for our understanding of Christian origins. Luke, the most shadowy of the evangelists, emerges as the great synthesizer of the Jesus tradition, although the synthesis is asymmetrical. He probably writes in a context where Mark is an established authority because of his association with Peter.[58] Like rewritten Scripture we find in the Dead Sea Scrolls, a kind of *aemulatio*, Matthew appropriates Mark while integrating

---

57 I do not include the *Pericope Adulterae* (John 7:53–8:11).
58 According to the early form critics, like Paul Wendland (1864–1915) and Karl Ludwig Schmidt (1891–1956), the second Gospel is largely the product of anonymous contributors in the early church. But we find uniform testimony that Mark preserved Peter's memories of Jesus. In addition to Papias, already discussed above, Justin Martyr (c. 100–165) describes the second Gospel as "memories" of Peter. He presents the Gospels as "the memories of the apostles." The phrase occurs twice in *1 Apol.* (66.3; 67.3) and thirteen times in the *Dial.* (e.g. 103.8). In *Dialogue with Trypho*, he mentions "the memories of the apostles and their successors" (103.8). By way of exception, he mentions "his memories"

additional didactic tradition that was attractive to Luke's didactic interest.[59] Luke furthers this textual conversation, but also finds a modest place for John's contribution to the Jesus tradition.

Luke apparently valued John as a historical source, an eyewitness, as his preface implies, to Jesus's ministry. He may have known John or his circle, or he received the Fourth Gospel's own claim in good faith (21:24). In any case, we have a very early corroboration that John is engaged in history and theology. The general marginalization of the Fourth Gospel from the study of the historical Jesus should be reassessed.[60]

There are limits to Luke's harmonization of his predecessors. In some cases, he sides with John in contrast to Mark; in others, Mark instead of John. For example, Luke follows the other Synoptics concerning the timing of the Temple Demonstration, placing the event at the end of Jesus's ministry. This suggests he did not read John uncritically, but in a creative tension with Mark, who represented the eyewitness testimony of Peter.

Luke appropriates John for historical clarification, but there is also evidence of a careful reading, even meditation, of John's message. The persistent *synkrisis* between Jesus and the Baptist in the Fourth Gospel probably served an apologetic in Luke's social world, but also contributed to his pneumatology.

Yet, as we noted, Luke's appropriation of John is asymmetrical. Perhaps the Fourth Gospel had not reached the same level of authority as Mark and Matthew by the time Luke began his project. Although this may be possible, Luke's primary interest appears to be adding sixteen parables to the stream of rewritten Gospel. As Bovon notes, The Prodigal Son occurs at the center of his narrative.[61] After the contributions of Mark, Matthew, and his special material, there was little room left in the scroll for John's presentation. This constraint may explain why Luke passes over the Samaritan woman episode, despite his interest in Jesus's relationship with the people group.

(106.3) in reference to Peter. Justin reveals he has the second Gospel in mind when he refers to the sons of Zebedee as "Boanerges, which is 'sons of thunder'"—a clear allusion to Mark 3:16.

59 The description "rewritten Bible" is attributed to Geza Vermes. See his *The Complete Dead Sea Scrolls in English* (New York: Penguin, 1998), 429–504. I appropriate the language of Sidnie White Crawford, *Rewriting Scripture in Second Temple Times* (SDSSRL; Grand Rapids: Eerdmans, 2008). She describes the genre as "characterized by a close adherence to a recognizable and already authoritative base text ... and a recognizable degree of scribal intervention into that base text for the purpose of exegesis" (13, see also 40).

60 See Anderson, *The Fourth Gospel and the Quest for Jesus*.

61 *Luke 1*, 3.

As the final evangelist, Luke provides the archetype for what Irenaeus of Lyon (d. c. 195) calls a "tetramorph" or Fourfold Gospel: they are "fourfold in form but held together by one Spirit" (*Haer.* 3.11.8). There had to be four—and only four—Gospels like the four zones or compass points of the world, the four winds, and the four covenants with Adam, Noah, Moses, and Christ (*Haer.* 3.11.8–9). Following the Western order of the Gospels, he pairs each evangelist with a face of the tetramorph angel seen by Ezekiel:

Matthew	Human
John	Lion
Luke	Ox
Mark	Eagle[62]

This way of reading the Gospels won assent, but the referents of the allegory shifted. Jerome's (c. 347–420) order became standard:

Matthew	= Human
Mark	= Lion
Luke	= Ox
John	= Eagle

The analogies are mysterious and have invited much reflection over the centuries. In any case, the rhetorical point is that each face is distinctive yet harmonious with the others.[63] The unity of the Spirit probably alludes to Ezekiel who writes: "And each was proceeding according to its face—wherever the spirit was proceeding they were proceeding, and they were not turning" (1:12 LXX).[64] Luke's Gospel embodies something of the other three.

Irenaeus uses this view to oppose Marcion's preference for a revision of Luke's Gospel.[65] Ironically, Marcion rejected Gospels that Luke respected enough to emulate. Instead of appreciating the *aemulatio*, he took Luke out of context.

Irenaeus had lived and lectured in Rome (c. 177) and mediated a conflict between the churches in Asia Minor and Victor of Rome (d. c. 198). There, we find an earlier proponent of the Fourfold Gospel, although he does not use this

---

62 T.C. Skeat, "Irenaeus and the Four-Gospel Canon," *NovT* 34 (1992): 194–199.
63 For more discussion, see Richard A. Burridge, *Four Gospels, One Jesus? A Symbolic Reading* (Grand Rapids: Eerdmans, 2005).
64 *Haer.* 3.1.2; 3.11.8.
65 Some believe Marcion appropriated Luke's source, a "proto-Luke."

language. Justin Martyr (c. 110–165) describes the Gospels as "the memories of the apostles," but also "of those who followed them" (τῶν ἐκείνοις παρακολουθησάντων).[66] This may presume the same arrangement as Irenaeus—Matthew, John, Luke, and Mark.[67] Although some argue Justin did not know John, he presumes Jesus's discussion with Nicodemus (*1 Apol.* 61.4–5).[68] In context, Justin cites Luke (22:44, 42), who is not an apostle. Justin's student, Tatian, produced his harmony in Syria or more likely Rome.[69] He followed Matthew's arrangement, supplementing it with material from the other three Gospels, trimming nearly thirty percent through conflation and harmonization.[70] The harmony was read liturgically in the Syrian church, but was supplanted by the individual Gospels in the Peshitta in the fifth century.[71] Tatian, Justin, Irenaeus, Papias—all appear to reflect Luke's monumental project.

---

66   *Dial.* 103.56–58. The Greek text is from *S. Justini Philosophi et Martyris cum Tryphone Judaeo Dialogus* (ed. W. Trollope; Cambridge: Cambridge University Press, 1890), 2:70. The verb παρακολουθέω suggests a close relationship.

67   P[45], Old Latin, D, W. Streeter claims they "put the least important Gospel last" (*The Four Gospels*, 11). But Augustine was able to make the same point from the canonical order, viewing the eyewitnesses as holding the first and last positions (*Harmony* 3). For more discussion, see T.C. Skeat, "A Codicological Analysis of the Chester Beatty Papyrus Codex of the Gospels and Acts (P45)," *Herm* 155 (1993): 27–43; James Keith Elliott, *New Testament Textual Criticism: The Application of Thoroughgoing Principles: Essays on Manuscripts and Textual Variation* (Leiden: Brill, 2010), 616.

68   In my opinion, he also owes much to John's prologue, particularly the Logos.

69   Streeter, *The Four Gospels*, 9. Tatian does not describe his work as a *diatessaron*. Ulrich B. Schmid suggests he viewed it as an independent Gospel, although evidence is lacking: "The Diatessaron of Tatian," in *The Text of the New Testament in Contemporary Research: Essays on the Status Quaestionis* (ed. Bart D. Ehrman and Michael W. Holmes; 2nd ed.; NTTSD 42; Leiden: Brill, 2013), 115–142. For a more traditional presentation, see William L. Petersen, *Tatian's Diatessaron: Its Creation, Dissemination, Significance, and History in Scholarship* (VCSup 25; Leiden: Brill, 1994). Carmel McCarthy notes: "The fact that the Diatessaron never fell under suspicion of heresy suggests that it might have been produced in Rome before Tatian returned home to the East. Since there is no evidence of a Syriac version of the separate Gospels earlier than the Diatessaron, it might seem more logical that Tatian would have made his harmony in Rome in Greek and then taken it eastwards with him": *Saint Ephrem's Commentary on Tatian's Diatessaron*, 5.

70   McCarthy, *Saint Ephrem's Commentary*, 7.

71   Aphrahat (c. 270–c. 345) appears to quote from the *Diatessaron* in his sermons, the *Demonstrations*. Near one of the earliest church buildings to be recovered, the Dura–Europas Church (c. 235), a harmony was discovered. Its relationship to Tatian is unclear: Petersen, *Tatian's Diatessaron*, 196.

From John to Apollos to Paul: How the Baptism of John Entered the Jesus Movement

Stephen J. Patterson

There is no greater paradox in the story of how Christianity began than the origin and meaning of baptism. The ritual of baptism was the rite by which people made their association with the Jesus movement. And yet, Jesus was apparently not the source of this practice. The original baptizer was another prophet—John. In the Synoptic accounts of John's baptism, John claims to baptize with water, but the coming one, Jesus, will baptize with the Holy Spirit. Then, John baptizes Jesus with water *and* the Holy Spirit. Jesus goes forth and baptizes no one. The first mention of baptism in the New Testament is in 1 Corinthians, where it is apparently practiced by Paul's rival, Apollos, a follower of Jesus who baptized like John the Baptist (see Acts 18:25). Apollos's baptism filled his followers with the Holy Spirit, but Paul was skeptical. As for baptism, he regrets that he baptized anyone (1 Cor 1:14–16). He even goes so far as to repudiate baptism (1:17)! Later in this letter we learn that some were baptizing others on behalf of the already dead (15:29). Paul doesn't dispute this bizarre practice. In fact, he thinks it proves his point—that the dead will one day be raised! This was an idea that must have stayed with him, for when he later articulated his own understanding of baptism, it had become for him a metaphor for dying and rising with Christ (Rom 6:3–11). This appears to be a brand new idea with no obvious relationship to John the Baptist and the idea that baptism coveys the Holy Spirit. Paul never mentions the Holy Spirit in Romans 6. Also new and apparently unrelated to John the Baptist was the pre-Pauline baptismal formula embedded in Paul's letter to the Galatians (Gal 3:26–28). Where did this baptismal egalitarian manifesto come from? Paul quotes it, but he did not create it.

What are we to make of these multiple and quite varied ideas about baptism all so clearly present in the first few decades of nascent Christian activity? What story do they tell of how baptism came to be a Christian ritual in the first place? That is the subject of this essay.

I take my point of departure from two attempts to tell this story. The first is Adela Yarbro Collins's essay, "The Origin of Christian Baptism."[1] Collins understands Christian baptism to have been a continuation of John's baptism of

---

[1] In her collected essays, *Cosmology and Eschatology in Jewish and Christian Apocalypticism* (JSJSup 50; Leiden: Brill, 1996), 218–238.

repentance in the face of the approaching wrath of God, first practiced by Jesus, and then by his followers.[2] Taking her clues from Acts 2:37–42, Collins reasons that just as acceptance of John's baptism signified acceptance of his message of repentance, so also baptism in the name of Jesus signified acceptance of his message of repentance in view of the nearness of God's kingdom.[3] The second is Michael Labahn's more recent essay on the subject, "Kreative Erinnerung als nachosterliche Nachschöpfung. Der Ursprung der christliche Taufe."[4] Labahn argues that Jesus himself did not engage in baptism,[5] but agrees in turning to Acts 2 to discover, like Collins, the story of how baptism came to be a Christian rite. Labahn sees in Acts both the continuity and discontinuity with John's baptism that explains both the roots and the distinctiveness of Christian baptism. Like John's baptism, the early Christian rite signified repentance, but unlike his, Christian baptism was thought to convey the Holy Spirit.[6] When did this change occur, and why? Labahn believes that Matt 28:18–20 represents the "creative memory" of the early church, which in fact revamped baptism "in the name of Jesus" in the immediate post-Easter period, when it became the rite of initiation into the Christian community.[7]

The economy of these accounts is impressive.[8] In both, Johannine baptism is quickly and easily transformed into the rite of initiation for the newly constituted church of God. But Luke does not mention baptism on behalf of the dead. Nor does Paul in Acts ever repudiate baptism, or argue with anyone about whether or not it actually imparts the Holy Spirit. Only the oddity of Apollos survives Luke's all-powerful hand, popping up in Acts 18 as the Alexandrian who "spoke and taught accurately the things concerning Jesus, but knew only the baptism of John" (Acts 18:25). How did he miss Pentecost? In turning too soon to Luke's magnificent story of Christian origins, have we missed something of the color and texture of the process, the complexity of the

---

2   Collins, "Origin," 231.
3   Collins, "Origin," 232–233.
4   In *Ablution, Initiation, and Baptism: Late Antiquity, Early Judaism, and Early Christianity/Waschungen, Initiation und Taufe: Spätantike, Frühes Judentum und Frües Christentum* (ed. David Hellholm, Tor Vegge, Øyvind Nordeval, and Christer Hellholm; 3 vols.; BZNW 176.1–3; Berlin: de Gruyter, 2010), 1:337–376.
5   Labahn, "Kreative Erinnerung," 350–354.
6   Labahn, "Kreative Erinnerung," 347–350.
7   Labahn, "Kreative Erinnerung," 355–366.
8   A third account, impressive for its breadth and scope, is Everett Ferguson's magisterial study, *Baptism in the Early Church: History, Theology, and Liturgy in the First Five Centuries* (Grand Rapids: Eerdmans, 2009). Ferguson, however, focuses on theological questions associated with the texts, rather than the kind of historical questions I will pose here.

experimentation and argument that must have been part of the history of social formation that finally delivered baptism into the hands of nascent Christian practitioners, like Apollos and Paul? In what follows, I wish to set aside Acts, at least for the moment, and look instead at a variety of earlier sources to see if there is not a more interesting story to tell here. I will begin with another look at the apparent source of nascent Christian baptism, John the Baptist.

1   John the Baptist

Today we know little about John the Baptist, a relatively obscure religious figure of the first century—only that he is said to have baptized Jesus himself.[9] The Synoptic Gospels and their sources offer accounts of this famous first encounter.[10] But this story is not likely the first story that was told about John and Jesus. If Q had an account of the baptism of Jesus,[11] it will have been secondary to the story that is told in Q 7:18–19 and 22–30 about another (close) encounter. In this story, John sends his disciples to inquire of Jesus, "Are you the one who is to come?" It is as though they had never met on the banks of the Jordan, or anywhere else. The two figures, John and Jesus, seem to stand at the head of two different, but related and overlapping followings (see Q 7:29–30). Q 7:24–28 makes a partisan claim for Jesus and the kingdom of God, but this is tempered by Q 7:31–35, in which Jesus and John are depicted as more or less complimentary prophets working in contrasting styles. John is ascetical; Jesus is indulgent; yet both are children of Sophia, mother Wisdom.

Was Jesus, then, baptized by John? Q 7 would not necessarily preclude it. If Jesus was in fact among the crowds that came to John to be washed in the Jordan, it is unlikely that John would have taken any special notice of him. For all practical purposes, they would have remained strangers. So, conventional scholarly wisdom may be right: Jesus must have been baptized by John, or else

---

9   For the state of the question about the historical John, see Clare K. Rothschild, *Baptist Traditions and Q* (WUNT 190; Tübingen: Mohr Siebeck, 2005), 29–82; also 1–2 n. 2 for a list of standard works in the extensive literature on John.

10 Mark 1:1–13; Q 3:2–3 (Luke 3:2b–3a//Matt 3:1, 5); 3:7–9 (Luke 3:7–9//Matt 3:7–10); Q 3:16–17 (Luke 3:16–17//Matt 3:11–12); 3:21–22 (Luke 3:21–22//Matt 3:16–17); Q 4:1–4, 9–12, 5–8, 13 (Luke 4:1–13//Matt 4:1–11).

11 The International Q Project includes the episode in their critical edition of Q, but enclosed in square brackets to indicate a high degree of uncertainty. See *The Sayings Gospel Q in Greek and English, with Parallels from the Gospels of Mark and Thomas* (ed. James M. Robinson, Paul Hoffmann, and John S. Kloppenborg; Minneapolis: Fortress, 2002), 78–79.

the Gospel writers would not have created the theological embarrassment of a story in which the putative Son of God submits to John to be cleansed of sin.[12] On the other hand, one should not overlook the likelihood that John was a much better known figure than Jesus in his day. So, it is also possible that the baptism of Jesus was a legend motivated by the idea that Israel's famous prophet, John, would bow down before the Messiah, Jesus.[13] Who better to preside over the Messiah's coronation ceremony than John the Baptist, to whom the crowds went for preparation? Preparing for what, or whom? Jesus, of course.

Whether he was baptized anonymously by John, or never baptized at all, the scenes of Jesus's baptism in the Gospels were created after the fact, complete with auditions and visions and conversations with Satan in the wilderness. But some form of this story must have arisen fairly early. There is, after all, a version of it in both Mark and Q, which share the same basic features: the preaching of John; Jesus's baptism; the accompanying vision/audition; and a subsequent scene in which Jesus is tested in the desert.[14] This suggests that a cycle of stories surrounding Jesus's baptism had already developed before Mark and Q were composed. The stories in this cycle would have been based, however, on existing memories of the Baptizer. For the association to seem credible, the baptism of Jesus would have to resemble, in the main, the actual baptismal practice of John. After all, John's followers would have still been around to dispute the details and thereby discredit the claim that their hero had in fact fashioned himself the forerunner of Jesus. This may prove important for our understanding of the Baptist. For we have just one account of John actually baptizing someone, and that is the baptism of Jesus.

---

12 The theological problem was there, of course, almost from the beginning, as one can see from Matt 3:14–15. The Fourth Gospel cleverly omits any direct reference to Jesus's baptism by John (see John 1:29–34) and in the *Gospel of the Hebrews* (Jerome, *adv. Pel.* 3.2) Jesus actually denies any need to be baptized by John.

13 Rothschild, *Baptist Traditions*, 73.

14 Of these elements, the most problematic in Q is the actual baptism of Jesus. Overlap of the relevant texts (Luke 3:21–22//Matt 3:13–17) with Mark (1:9–11) and spare verbatim agreement across the texts make it difficult to tell if Q actually spoke of Jesus's baptism. The minor agreements in Luke 3:21–22//Matt 3:16–17 (esp. ἀνεῳχθῆσαν/ἀνεῳχθῆναι v. σχιζομένους Mark 1:10) are a good indication that Q held this scene, and the presence of the remaining elements of the cycle, especially the temptation in the wilderness, strongly suggest that the whole cycle, including the baptism of Jesus, was present. See Arland Jacobson, *The First Gospel: An Introduction to Q* (Sonoma, CA: Polebridge, 1992), 85–86.

2 John's Baptism

The Synoptic Gospels, their sources, the Gospel of John, and the *testimonium* in Flavius Josephus[15] all agree in describing John as a baptizing prophet. So, John's program likely involved interpreting Israel's tradition of ritual washing in terms of Israel's rich prophetic tradition of social justice and reform.[16] By the Synoptic accounts, John's baptism signified repentance; Josephus says it presupposed repentance. Either way, this interpretation of ritual washing was unusual.[17] John linked ritual purity to a change of heart, or a change in the way one thought (Q 3:3//Mark 1:4).[18] Its purpose, then, was not simply a return to purity; it also looked forward. It was transformational. John baptized like a prophet, not a priest.[19]

John's precise message, though, is not portrayed in the same way across the sources. Q's version of John's preaching is apocalyptic, speaking explicitly about the wrath that is to come (Q 3:7–9). Mark depicts John preaching about the ritual itself, that it signifies repentance and forgiveness (Mark 1:4). This is augmented with quotations from Exodus (1:2) and Isaiah (1:3), which depict John as a prophet preparing the way for Jesus. The distinctive Markan description

---

15   *Ant.* 18.117.
16   Robert L. Webb, *John the Baptizer and Prophet: A Socio-Historical Study* (JSNTSup 62; Sheffield: JSOT Press, 1991), 349–378.
17   Whether one speaks of Hellenistic religion in general, or ritual ablution in the context of Second Temple Judaism, the significance of ritual washing is almost always, more or less, cleansing. It does not signal repentance. Its purpose is simply to achieve ritual purity as prerequisite to entering the realm of the sacred, whether that be a temple or a sectarian community. See the comprehensive essays collected in David Hellholm et al., eds., *Ablution, Initiation, and Baptism/Waschungen, Initiation und Taufe*, esp. Friz Graf, "Baptism and Graeco-Roman Mystery Cults" (1:101–118); and Antje Labahn, "Aus dem Wasser kommt das Leben: Waschungen und Reinigungsriten in frühjüdischen Texten" (1:158–219).
18   Assuming, of course, that μετάνοια refers to the repentance of people, not God; see Adela Yarbro Collins, *Mark: A Commentary* (Hermeneia; Minneapolis: Fortress, 2007), 140–141; she raises doubts about Mark, but the use of the verb in Q is unambiguous.
19   With this phrasing I hope to capture the gist of Joan Taylor's excellent description of John's practice in *The Immerser: John the Baptist within Second Temple Judaism* (Grand Rapids: Eerdmans, 1997), 49–100. In Second Temple Judaism immersion signifies ritual cleansing. John does not invent something entirely new. But by linking baptism with personal (or social) change, he adds a unique dimension to the concept. See also Arthur Darby Nock, "Hellenistic Mysteries and Christian Sacraments," in Nock, *Essays on Religion and the Ancient World* (ed. Zeph Stewart; 2 vols.; Oxford: Oxford University Press, 1972), 2:803.

of John's dress (1:6) goes hand in hand with these quotations and associates John with Elijah (see Mal 3:1).[20] In the Fourth Gospel, the Baptist holds forth in typically Johannine fashion, focusing exclusively on Jesus and his true identity. Josephus says John's message was about "justice toward one another and reverence for God" (*Ant.* 18.117). So, there is variety in the sources about John's preaching. Q, Mark, and John agree, however, in attributing to John the saying about the imminent arrival of a figure greater than himself (Q 3:16; Mark 1:17; John 1:27). This idea is also built into the archaic tradition in Q 7, which antedates the cycle of stories about Jesus's baptism (see Q 7:19). So this was probably part of John's original message. It was this idea that gave the followers of Jesus a role for their master in the framework of John's message: *Jesus* was the coming one. Words about the "coming one," then, may be the earliest reliable words we have from John's preaching. John's baptism signaled a life-change in anticipation of one who was to come.

To find the cogent center to all of this we will need analogies. For ritual washing there are plenty. Most pagans and Jews washed to achieve the ritual purity necessary for proper worship of the gods. In Second Temple Judaism ritual washing was understood more or less in this way. There are possible extraordinary permutations, but we know too little about them. Bannus apparently laid particular stress on ritual ablutions, but Josephus tells us only that they signified ritual purity.[21] The Essenes assigned great importance to ritual washing, but also, apparently, for the purpose of maintaining a state of ritual purity.[22] Neither of these would capture the salient features of John's baptism and what our sources say about it. Among the many references to ritual washing in the Qumran materials, most have to do with simple ritual purity.[23] Collins, though, calls attention to one strain of thinking at Qumran that carries some of the same elements as John's baptism.[24] The relevant passage occurs in the Rule of the Community (1QS4). It is illuminating.

In the Rule, amidst the various instructions on how the communities are to conduct themselves, there is an extended mythic excursus on the "character and fate of humankind" that goes like this: When God created human beings to rule over the earth, he also created two spirits, the spirit of truth and the spirit of falsehood, or, elsewise, the spirit of light and the spirit of darkness. God ordained that these two spirits should govern every action, with the fate

---

20 Collins, *Mark*, 145.
21 *Life* 11–12.
22 Josephus, *J.W.* 2.119–161; Philo, *Prob.* 84.
23 Labahn, "Aus dem Wasser," 168–208.
24 Collins, *Mark*, 139–140.

of humankind resting in the exercise of their equal but opposite powers—all this, until the last age. Then, at the time appointed for God to come, God will destroy the spirit of darkness, of falsehood, of perversity, and allow the spirit of truth to prevail. How?

> By his truth God shall then purify all human deeds, and refine some of humanity so as to extinguish every perverse spirit from the inward parts of the flesh, cleansing from every wicked deed by a Holy Spirit. Like purifying waters, he shall sprinkle each with a Spirit of truth ... he shall give the upright insight into the knowledge of the Most High and wisdom of the angels, making wise those following the perfect way. Indeed, God has chosen them for an eternal covenant; all the glory of Adam shall be theirs alone.[25]

So, the communities that used the Rule were also engaged in a metaphoric interpretation of ritual washing. When God arrives there will be a great spiritual cleansing, effected by a Holy Spirit, the Spirit of truth. Those who receive this cleansing will be transformed intellectually and sapientially: they will receive "knowledge of the Most High," and the "wisdom of the angels." Their transformation will also be protological: the glory that Adam lost in the Garden will be restored to them. They will be transformed, made perfect, immortal, bearing once again the image of God which Adam bore at creation.[26]

The Rule offers some illuminating parallels to the Synoptic accounts of John's baptism. The Rule speaks of God's imminent arrival. Without the Christian conceit that Jesus was the coming one, this would be a straightforward reading of John's talk about the coming one as well.[27] The coming one in John's preaching was God. The Rule also speaks about a Holy Spirit that will enlighten and transform those it touches. John's baptism of Jesus, of course, features the descent of a Holy Spirit, which transforms Jesus into the Son of God. A common critical reading of this material would judge this all to be Christian adaptation of a more original story about John's simple water baptism. It reflects later

---

25   1QS 4:20–23 (Michael Wise, Martin Abegg, Jr., and Edward Cook, trans., *The Dead Sea Scrolls: A New Translation* [San Francisco: HarperSanFrancisco, 2005], 119–120).

26   For Adam's "glory" as the image of God, see Jacob Jervell, *Imago Dei: Gen 1,26f. im Spätjudentum, in der Gnosis und in den paulinischen Briefen* (FRLANT NS 58; Göttingen: Vandenhoeck & Ruprecht, 1960), esp. 101–103; on the protological speculation about Adam among the rabbis, see 96–112.

27   Collins, "Origin," 221–222.

Christian practice, not earlier Johannine practice.[28] But as we have seen, this cycle predates Mark and Q. It is therefore too early to reflect any newly constituted Christian form of baptism. This was a time when the followers of John were still around and still baptizing in the Johannine manner. They were also still mixing with followers of Jesus. It is likely, then, that the contrived scenes of Jesus's baptism in the Gospels are based, not on some new and distinct Christian baptismal practice, but on the baptismal traditions of the original baptizers, the followers of John. If we follow the story of baptism forward into our first accounts of nascent Christian baptism, we shall see this hunch confirmed. But first, a transitional question: Did Jesus baptize?

3   Did Jesus Baptize?

The next episode in the story of baptism does not belong to Jesus, for he, apparently, did not baptize. Only the fourth evangelist says that he did (John 3:22, 26; 4:1)—and then his editor corrects him (4:2).[29] Over against this evidence stands the stunning silence of the Synoptic Gospels. Neither Jesus nor his disciples are ever depicted as baptizing in the Synoptic tradition. Some have argued that Jesus nonetheless baptized, and the Synoptic authors and John's redactor sought to suppress this fact.[30] But this seems unlikely. Why would the church

---

28   Most notably, Rudolf Bultmann, *History of the Synoptic Tradition* (trans. John Marsh; rev. ed.; New York: Harper & Row, 1963), 250–253.

29   Why? Bultmann's explanation for the Johannine references is still convincing: they reflect later rivalry between the followers of John and the followers of Jesus. The correction in 4:2 would have been an editorial gloss from the ecclesiastical redactor to bring the story more in line with the Synoptics. See Rudolf Bultmann, *The Gospel According to John: A Commentary* (Philadelphia: Westminster, 1971), 167–168.

30   E.g., Joachim Jeremias, *New Testament Theology: The Proclamation of Jesus* (trans. John Bowden; London: SCM, 1971), 45–46; C.H. Dodd, *Historical Tradition in the Fourth Gospel* (Cambridge: Cambridge University Press, 1963), 279–287; Raymond E. Brown, *The Gospel According to John I–XII* (AB 29; Garden City, NY: Doubleday, 1966), 153–155; D. Moody Smith, "The Problem of History in John," in *What We Have Heard from the Beginning: The Past, Present, and Future of Johannine Studies* (ed. Tom Thatcher; Waco, TX: Baylor University Press, 2007), 317; Jürgen Becker, *Johannes der Taüfer un Jesus von Nazareth* (BibS(N) 63; Neukirchen-Vluyn: Neukirchener Verlag, 1972), 13–14; Collins, *Cosmology and Eschatology*, 230; Jens Schröter, *Jesus von Nazareth: Jude aus Galiläa—Retter der Welt* (Biblische Gestalten 15; Leipzig: Evangelische Verlagsanstalt, 2006), 138, among others. Petr Pokorný suggests he perhaps baptized in the style of John for a short while at the beginning of his ministry (*Entsthehung der Christologie: Voraussetzungen einer Theologie des Neuen*

suppress the fact that its central rite of initiation came from its founding figure, leaving the impression that it was actually created by a rival?

I am persuaded that Jesus himself probably did not baptize.[31] At first surprising, upon further reflection this apparent oddity actually makes historical sense. John was the baptizer. Jesus went to him, like everyone else, to be baptized. Everyone who was baptized by John did not go out and start baptizing. That wasn't the point. *John* was the baptizer; everyone went to him. Q 7 presupposes that John did have a close circle of disciples, who, perhaps, would also have baptized. But Jesus was not one of them. And when John was killed, there must have been successors. Indeed, other traditions that honor the Baptist name them variously—Dositheos among the Samaritans, for example.[32] But Q 7 depicts Jesus as a more distant follower, who defined himself rather differently than John. John lived as an ascetic, but Jesus indulged in life. Finally, Jesus himself did not last very long after John's demise. In the year or so that Jesus carried on after John's execution, it is unlikely that he would have sorted out his own ideas about baptism and begun to baptize in his own distinctive way. So, if Jesus baptized at all, it would have been more or less in the manner of John, *the* baptizer.[33] The salient point, then, is that the earliest baptismal practice of the nascent Christian community was not a newly invented rite, but a continuation of John's earlier rite. This is true whether Jesus never baptized anyone, or baptized for a time in the manner of John. If this is so, then the baptism that shows up in our earliest Christian sources must have been a version of the baptism of John. The earliest sources, however, do not include Acts 2. Our earliest Christian word about baptism was written not by Luke, but by Paul.

4 Christian Baptism—A First Sighting

The earliest mention of baptism in a nascent Christian context is almost always overlooked in the various attempts to tell this story. It occurs in a place that is easily missed, at the very beginning of 1 Corinthians:

Testaments [Stuttgart: Calwer Verlag, 1985], 148; also Jerome Murphy-O'Connor, "John the Baptist and Jesus: History and Hypothesis," *NTS* 36 [1990]: 359–374).

31 So Labahn, "Kreative Erinnerung," 344–347, 350–354, and the large majority of scholars.
32 See Ps-Clement, *Rec.* 2.8; *Hom.* 2.24.
33 So, plausibly, Pokorný, *Entstehung der Christologie*, 148.

> For it has been reported to me by Chloe's people that there is quarreling among you, my brothers. What I mean is that each of you says, "I belong to Paul," or "I belong to Apollos," or "I belong to Cephas," or "I belong to Christ." Is Christ divided? Was Paul crucified for you? Or, were you *baptized* in the name of Paul?
>
> 1 Cor 1:11–13

There it is, the first word about baptism in the Jesus tradition. It is not as casual a reference as it may at first seem. For Paul carries on now about baptism rather vehemently:

> I'm thankful that I baptized none of you (except Crispus and Gaius), lest anyone should say that you were baptized in my name. (Oh, I did baptize also the house of Stephanus. Beyond that I don't know if I baptized anyone else). For Christ did not send me to baptize, but to preach the gospel, and not with wisdom expressed in words, lest the cross of Christ be emptied of its power.
>
> 1 Cor 1:14–17

If we take this brief paragraph seriously, and at face value, we learn something very surprising. When Paul was in Corinth he did not do much baptizing.[34] This can only mean that in the Pauline communities baptism was not yet the universal rite of entry. Only a handful of Paul's correspondents were baptized by him. In 1:17a he actually goes so far as to renounce baptism. We know that this is hyperbole, for in the later letters, Galatians and Romans, he will appropriate various understandings of baptism to his own cause.[35] Still, Paul could not say this at all if baptism was the initiation ritual by which everyone entered his newly formed Christ communities. Baptism must have been, for Paul, as for the Corinthians, something special, something extra.

If Paul himself did baptize, why does he repudiate it here? Because it is obviously related to the dissention now appearing in the Corinthian churches in connection with the wisdom teaching to which Paul is so opposed. This is clear from 1:17, which consists of two pairs of contrasting opposites: baptism v. preaching (17a) and wisdom v. cross (17b). Paul came not to baptize but to

---

34 Cf. Hans Dieter Betz's remarks in "Transferring a Ritual: Paul's Interpretation of Baptism in Romans 6," in *Paul in His Hellenistic Context* (ed. Troels Engberg-Pedersen; Minneapolis: Fortress, 1995); repr. in H.D. Betz, *Paulinische Studien: Gesammelte Aufsäzte III* (Tübingen: Mohr Siebeck, 1994), 258–262 (citing the reprint ed.).

35 Gal 3:26–28; Rom 6:3–11.

preach; and not to preach wisdom but the cross. By contrast, whoever came to Corinth after Paul did baptize, and did teach wisdom. Who was he? His name was Apollos, whom Acts describes as a learned Alexandrian who baptized in the manner of John (Acts 18:15).[36]

The claim that Apollos was the teacher whose ideas are at issue in 1 Corinthians is no longer controversial,[37] so I will not pause for a defense of it here. More disputed is the characterization of Apollos in Acts 18:25. The doubts about this passage go back to Ernst Käsemann, who simply found the idea of this kind of John/Jesus hybrid preposterous.[38] But if Käsemann thought a half-Christian Apollos was an historical impossibility, the author of Acts clearly did not. There probably were such hybrids in Luke's own universe, as Acts 19 suggests.[39] More than that, Acts 18 and 19, together with 1 Cor 1:14–17, make very good historical sense, given the consensus about the roots of Christian baptism in Johannine practice. Jesus did not baptize, or if he did, it was to continue the practice initiated by John. Therefore, others in the Jesus movement who continued to baptize would have done so out of their continuing devotion to John, just as Acts says was true of Apollos. But not everyone in the Jesus movement— Paul, for instance—had been so influenced by John. So we must contemplate

---

36 Esp. Richard Horsley, "Wisdom of Word and Words of Wisdom in Corinth," *CBQ* 39 (1977): 231–232.

37 See esp. Gerhard Sellin, "Das 'Geheimnis' der Weisheit und das Rätsel der 'Christuspartei' (zu 1 Kor 1–4)," *ZNW* 73 (1982): 69–96; repr. in Gerhard Sellin, *Studien zu Paulus und Epheserbrief* (FRLANT 229; Göttingen: Vandenhoeck & Ruprecht, 2009), 9–36; Sellin, "Hauptprobleme des Ersten Korintherbriefes," *ANRW* II 25.4 (1987): 2940–3044. More recently, rhetorical-critical approaches to the letter have yielded the same consensus. See Joop Smit, "What is Apollos? What is Paul? In Search for the Coherence of First Corinthians 1:10–4:21," *NovT* 44 (2002): 231–251. For a history of the long discussion of this question, see John Hurd, *The Origin of I Corinthians* (repr., Macon, GA: Mercer University Press, 1983), 96–107.

38 Ernst Käsemann, "The Disciples of John in Ephesus," in Käsemann, *Essays on New Testament Themes* (SBT; Naperville: Allenson, 1962), 136–148 (orig. "Die Johannesjünger in Ephesus," *ZTK* 49 [1952]: 144–154).

39 Thus the broad consensus, prior to Käsemann, that Apollos and the mysterious disciples of 19:1–7 were, as Dibelius described them, "halb-Christen." See Martin Dibelius, *Die urchristliche Überlieferung von Johannes dem Täufer* (FRLANT 15; Göttingen: Vandenhoeck & Ruprecht, 1911), 88–89; also Hans W. Wendt, *Die Apostlegeschichte* (KEK; Göttingen: Vandenhoeck & Ruprecht, 1913), 270; E. Preuschen, *Die Apostelgeschichte* (HNT; Tübingen: Mohr Siebeck, 1912), 115; Alfred Loisy, *Les actes des apôtres* (Paris: Nourry, 1920), 719–720; Ernst Lohmeyer, *Das Urchristentum*, Bd. 1: *Johannes der Täufer* (Göttingen: Vandenhoeck & Ruprecht, 1932), 26; H. Preisker, "Apollos und die Johannesjünger in Ephesus," *ZNW* 30 (1931): 301–304; more recently, see Taylor, *The Immerser*, 72–76.

a time when some baptized and some didn't—exactly as 1 Cor 1:14–17 suggests. Apollos, a devoted follower of John, baptized; Paul, devoted only to Jesus, not so much. So Acts 18:25 and 1 Cor 1:14–17 together offer just the sort of person and the sort of situation one would expect if baptism was indeed imported from the Baptist movement: Apollos the baptizer is confronted by Paul the preacher.

But there is something about Luke's reportage in Acts 18:24–19:7 that is truly out of step with what we otherwise know about Apollos from 1 Corinthians. Together, these two stories imply that the baptism practiced by Apollos in Ephesus had nothing to do with imparting the Holy Spirit. This is highly unlikely. For if there is one thing we know about the teaching of Apollos, it is that it was all about the Spirit. Those who followed him in Corinth claimed to be "spirituals" (πνευματικοί; 1 Cor 3:1); they excelled in spiritual gifts, such as speaking in tongues and prophecy (1 Cor 12 and 14). Therefore, any baptism practiced by Apollos would most certainly have conveyed the Holy Spirit. So, how shall we understand Apollos to have baptized in the manner of John, and yet imagine that his rite somehow conveyed the Holy Spirit? To answer this we will need to look more closely at Apollos's teaching, as reflected in 1 Corinthians.

5   Apollos the Baptist in Corinth

So, what may be said about Apollos's teaching on the basis of 1 Corinthians? In what sense might we understand it as continuing and developing the ministry of John the Baptist?

John's baptism was eschatological, anticipating the "greater one who is to come." This appears to have been true for Apollos as well, but in a modified sense. For him, the coming one *had* arrived. This is an aspect of Apollos's teaching that Paul criticizes most vehemently. "Already you are filled! Already you have become rich! Without us you have begun to reign!" (1 Cor 4:8). Apparently, for Apollos, the baptism in the Holy Spirit that John had associated with the one who was to come was already at work, transforming those who had received Apollos's teaching into "spirituals" (πνευμάτικοι); they were the "perfect" (τέλειοι), no longer "children" (νήπιοι), no longer mere "mortals" (ψύχικοι, σάρκινοι).[40] This eschatological step forward is important to grasp if we are to understand how Apollos's ideas about baptism can be understood to continue

---

40 Paul nowhere else uses the terminology that crops up in chs. 2 and 3; it almost certainly derives from his opponents. See Birger Pearson, *The Pneumatikos–Psychikos Terminology in 1 Corinthians* (SBLDS 12; Missoula, MT: Scholars Press, 1973), 38–39; also, Richard Horsley,

and develop those of John. John spoke of "one who is to come," who would bring a baptism in the Holy Spirit. For Apollos, that future was now; the Holy Spirit was already doing its work.

The historical Baptist spoke of one who was to come, but he did not identify this figure with Jesus. Paul, of course, did. For him the experience of the Spirit was closely associated with the experience of the risen Christ. For him, the Spirit, the Spirit of God, and the Spirit of Christ were all one thing (Rom 8:9–17). Did Apollos share Paul's Christocentric view? Probably not. It is Paul, not Apollos, who says—and pointedly—that *Christ* is the wisdom of God (1 Cor 1:24). And when Paul rehearses, and thereby demonstrates how well he understands the Platonic conceptuality that undergirds his opponents' position (2:6–15), he very pointedly adds, "But we have the mind of Christ" (2:16), as if it were not enough to possess the "Spirit of God." And how could any of the opponents have shared his orientation and still uttered anything like ἀνάθεμα Ἰησοῦς while under the influence of the Spirit of God (12:13)? This all probably indicates that Apollos did not share Paul's focus on Christ. While his presence in the Corinthian churches must mean that Jesus played a role in his theology—as Acts 18:25 indicates—it was not the preeminent role that he played for Paul. And yet, this is probably what we should expect for someone who was a Baptist first, and a follower of Jesus second.

So, if Apollos would not have shared Paul's ideas about the Spirit as the Spirit of Christ, how did he understand the coming of the Spirit and its effects? It must have been in connection with baptism, of course. In ch. 15 Paul mentions something about the Corinthian teaching that is very revealing in this respect: the Corinthians practice something like surrogate baptism—they baptize on behalf of the dead (15:29a). This means that they saw baptism as an answer to the problem of death. Paul does not dispute this! He simply avers that if they believe this, they must grant him the point that there will indeed be a future resurrection of the dead (15:29b). His reasoning is that if surrogate baptism works, that by it the dead are made to live, then where are they? We will see them in the future—at the resurrection of the dead. But the Corinthians must have learned something different from Apollos—that there was no future resurrection of the dead (15:12), that baptism could overcome death already in the present. How? We must take our clues from the distinctive language that turns up in Paul's polemical engagement of Apollos' teaching. As

---

"Pneumatikos vs. Psychikos Distinctions of Spiritual Status among the Corinthians," *HTR* 69 (1976): 269–288; and Horsley, "'How Can Some of You Say That There Is No Resurrection of the Dead?' Spiritual Elitism in Corinth," *NovT* 20 (1978): 203–231.

Pearson, Horsely, and others have demonstrated, the distinctive *pneumatikos–psychikos* language of Paul's opponent in 1 Corinthians derives from Hellenistic Judaism, such as one finds in Philo, the great sage of Apollos' hometown, Alexandria.[41]

As is well known, Philo engaged in a Platonic exegesis of Genesis 1–2 to show that Moses knew all about Platonic anthropology. The man created from dust in Gen 2:7, he says, is mortal, "consisting of body and soul" (ἐκ σώματος καὶ ψυχῆς συνεστώς).[42] This is typical Middle-Platonic anthropology. The mortal parts of a human being are the body and the (mortal) soul.[43] Now, Philo believed that when Genesis tells of God breathing life into the mortal man, Adam (in Gen 2:7), he was imparting to him the *immortal* soul, what Plato called the "mind" (νοῦς), but which Philo calls the "divine Spirit" (πνεῦμα θεῖον).[44] This is what makes the human being immortal. The mortal human being, created from dust, was mere body and soul. He became truly alive only when God breathed the divine Spirit into him.

Was this something like what Apollos taught the Corinthians, that in baptism the Spirit enters a person and makes them immortal? It is telling that Paul's argument against them consists, finally, in an alternative exegesis of Genesis 1–2 (1 Cor 15:42–50). By his reading, "the first Adam" was alive, but mortal, as Genesis says (εἰς ψυχὴν ζῶσαν; Gen 2:7); but Christ, the "second Adam," was a "life-giving spirit" (εἰς πνεῦμα ζωοποιοῦν). Now people bear the image of the man of dust, the first Adam, but soon they *shall* bear the image of the second Adam, the "man of heaven," Christ. That "shall" is key, for while Philo, Apollos, and many Hellenistic Jews read Genesis protologically, Paul is reading Genesis eschatologically. Between now and immortality there lay, for Paul, resurrection. For the followers of Apollos, however, baptism brought immortality now, even for those already dead. They are made immortal, like the first Adam, through the gift of the divine Spirit.[45] Odd? Perhaps, but not unprecedented. Recall, baptism in a Holy Spirit at Qumran also had protological implications:

---

41 Pearson, *Pneumatikos–Psychikos Terminology*; Horsely, "Pneumatikos vs. Psychikos"; Horsely, "Words of Wisdom."
42 Philo, *Opif.* 134.
43 See, e.g., Plutarch, *Mor.* 943A.
44 *Opif.* 135.
45 For the general background of these ideas in Hellenistic Judaism, especially Philo, see J. Dupont, *Gnosis: La connaissance religieuse dans les épîtres de Saint Paul* (Paris: Gabalda, 1949), 172–180; also Pearson, *The Pneumatikos–Psychikos Terminology*, 17–23; Horsley, "Pneumatikos vs. Psychikos," 274–280.

recipients would possess once again the "glory of Adam."[46] This protological understanding of baptism would later turn up as a fairly consistent thread in a variety of early Christian texts.[47]

Finally, the baptism of Apollos was accompanied by wisdom teaching— "word wisdom" as Paul calls it (1:17, *et passim*). This also recalls what we saw in 1QS4, where baptism, understood spiritually, metaphorically, also entailed gaining "insight into the knowledge of the Most High and wisdom of the angels." In the cycle of stories about John's baptism of Jesus, the Spirit drives Jesus into the wilderness to prepare for what is to come. In Q he emerges as a wisdom teacher. Baptism inaugurates him to his calling as a prophet of wisdom, an honor he shares with John (Q 7:35). Paul characterizes Apollos's teaching as a "higher" wisdom, the "mystery of God" (1 Cor 2:1). This idea also turns up, surprisingly, in Q, where Jesus, speaking in the Holy Spirit, is heard to utter words that would have been right at home among the Corinthian "spirituals": "I praise you, Father, Lord of heaven and earth, for you have hidden these things from the wise and learned, and revealed them to children (νηπίοις)."[48]

So, the figure of Apollos, whom Paul engages in 1 Corinthians, offers a plausible scenario for how the baptism of John could have been mediated into the Jesus movement. Jesus, like John, would have been understood as a prophet of Wisdom. The Spirit of which John spoke on the banks of the Jordan was the same Spirit that drove Jesus into the wilderness and filled him with wisdom. Now that the Spirit of God had begun to act, baptism became the rite by which it was imparted. Baptism now became something more than an act of μετάνοια. It transformed one into a "spiritual"—a πνευματικός, already rich, filled, prepared to reign in the kingdom of God. Baptism in the Spirit rendered one immortal.

We may circle round now to that early story told by Mark and Q about Jesus's baptism. It turns out that it was apparently modeled on a version of John's baptism as it was adapted and mediated into some of the communities in which Jesus also now played a role. In these communities the clock had ticked one more tock forward, the Spirit had come and begun its activity of transformation. Jesus, by their lights, was its first recipient. Baptism had transformed him. He was immortal, a son of God. This, one might think, is not too far from Luke's depiction of things in Acts 2. But before jumping to the conclusion that this tells the whole story, remember that Paul didn't buy it. He was skeptical of the

---

46 1QS 4:20–23 (see discussion above).
47 See esp. Jonathan Z. Smith, "The Garments of Shame," *HR* 5 (1966): 217–238; also, Jervell, *Imago Dei*, 197–256.
48 Q 10:21, after the reconstruction of the IQP; see Robinson et al., *The Sayings Gospel Q*, 103.

Corinthians' baptismal claims and did not think that they possessed the Spirit at all. In other letters he expresses two quite different ideas about baptism, and neither has much to do with the Spirit.

6 The First Baptismal Creed (Gal 3:26–28)

By strict chronology, the next mention of baptism in a nascent Christian text comes in Paul's letter to the Galatians. This is the archaic baptismal creed Paul cites in Gal 3:26–28:

> ^{26}For you are all sons of God through faith in Christ Jesus.
> ^{27}For as many of you as were baptized into Christ have put on Christ.
> ^{28a}There is no Jew or Greek;
> ^{b}There is no slave or free;
> ^{c}There is no male and female;
> ^{d}For you are all one in Christ Jesus.

That these verses constitute something like a pre-Pauline baptismal creed is well known. The creed itself comprises vv. 26 and 28; v. 27 is Paul's commentary, but ultimately the clue to the creed's original *Sitz im Leben*. Paul has also added "through faith" in v. 26, so that the first and last lines would originally have been parallel in structure, as are the three, central oppositional clauses.[49] It is a new formulation, still, one that contains strands of earlier baptismal themes. "You are all children of God" echoes the acclamation of the heavenly voice in the Synoptic stories of Jesus's baptism, a reminder that you did not have to be the messiah to be a child of God. Such a pronouncement may have been part of the original Baptist tradition. And the third oppositional clause ("no male and female") may predate the other two.[50] This protological theme was also baptismal currency, as we have seen.[51] Evidence of protological exegesis in 1 Corinthians 15 suggests that such thinking was also part of Apollos' baptismal theology.[52]

---

49   The analysis of the creed's original form follows Hans Dieter Betz, *Galatians* (Hermeneia; Philadelphia: Fortress, 1979), 181–185.
50   Dennis R. MacDonald, *There Is No Male and Female: The Fate of a Dominical Saying in Paul and Gnosticism* (HDR; Philadelphia: Fortress, 1987).
51   See n. 47, above.
52   See n. 45, above.

The composition as a whole, however, introduces an entirely new and distinctive theory of baptism. From the days of Herodotus and Thucydides, Xenophon and Aristotle, individual identity in Hellenistic culture had been brokered in terms of severe binary thinking: Greek v. barbarian; free v. slave; male v. female. These binary oppositions created the framework by which free Greek males established themselves as superior human beings.[53] Later, the Romans would adjust it to their own perspective, as would others. It is often noted that this triad forms the basis of a common Jewish blessing in the Talmud:

> There are three blessings one must pray daily:
> Blessed art Thou, who did not make me a Gentile;
> Blessed art Thou, who did not make me a woman;
> Blessed art Thou, who did not make me an uncultured brute.
>   t. Ber. 7:18

But the roots of the idea are much deeper and broader than this.[54] Here is the same idea in Diogenes Laertius, told now of Thales:

> Hermippus, in his *Lives*, refers to Thales the story which is told by some of Socrates, namely, that he used to say there were three blessings for which he was grateful to Fortune: "first, that I was born a human being and not one of the brutes; next, that I was born a man and not a woman; thirdly, a Greek and not a barbarian".
>   *Lives* 1.33 [HICKS, LCL]

By the first century such thinking had apparently become such a cliché that someone in the Jesus movement had it playing in his or her head when it came time to express what in meant to be part of a Christ community. Could that have been Paul? This is not the first time we encounter this creed. Paul must have already known it when he wrote 1 Corinthians, for he quotes it there too:

> For by one Spirit we were all baptized into one body—Jews or Greeks, slave or free—and all were made to drink of one Spirit.
>   1 Cor 12:13

---

53 Paul Cartledge, *The Greeks: A Portrait of Self and Others* (2nd ed.; London: Oxford University Press, 2002).
54 See Betz, *Galatians*, 184–185, n. 26.

The context is an argument about how all should experience equal honor and respect in the community, regardless of one's spiritual gifts or social standing. In this sense, Paul uses the creed to good effect. Yet, it is often noted that in alluding to the creed here, Paul actually abbreviates it: no Jew or Greek, and no slave or free, but "no male and female" is missing.[55] Why? It must be because in 1 Cor 11:2–16 he had just declared himself only nominally supportive of the third proposition. So, it is unlikely that Paul himself would have composed a creed he would later mutilate, and in part, repudiate. Recall, at this time Paul did not consider himself to be a baptizer (1 Cor 1:17a).

Could Apollos have been the source for this creed? In favor of this idea is the fact that aspects of the partisans' ideology in 1 Corinthians could easily have been inspired by it. It could account for the gender-bending prophets of ch. 11; the controversy over eating meat from a pagan sacrifice—a key Jewish/Gentile issue; and the various issues touched upon in 7:17–31—ethnicity (vv. 17–20), slavery (vv. 21–24), and gender roles (vv. 25–31). And yet, the egalitarian ethos of the creed seems not to have been the main thrust of Apollos's teaching. For Apollos, baptism brought spiritual enlightenment, and with it, social elevation, not necessarily equality. This much shines through, even without Paul's caricature of his rival's position. In this creed the Spirit plays no obvious role.[56] No one is elevated; all are made equal.

So, we are left with an anonymous author to take the credit for this gem. From the formulation of the first dyadic phrase we may assume that our author was Jewish. He or she was also interested—obviously—in baptism, which means, probably, that our author was, like Apollos, someone who also revered John the Baptist. Beyond that we can only say that she or he was a poet. He or she had taken in the preaching of Jesus and decided that its meaning could be expressed in a new understanding of baptism. Baptism already signaled transformation. Our anonymous author fleshed out exactly what this meant. What did it mean to become a "son of God?" It meant that a new identity replaced the clichéd, binary "thank-god-I'm-not-that" definition of self, by which Greeks,

---

55 E.g., Elisabeth Schüssler Fiorenza, *In Memory of Her: A Feminist Theological Reconstruction of Christian origins* (New York: Crossroad, 1988), 218–219.

56 Paul does speak of the Spirit when he refers to the creed in 1 Cor 12:13: "For by one Spirit we were all baptized …" So, does Paul frame the creed in this way because of the Corinthian context (conflict over spiritual gifts), or did the creed originally go something like "For we are all sons of God in *the Spirit*"? Earlier in Galatians Paul discusses receiving the Spirit (3:1–5), and a few sentences after the creed he speaks of how the Spirit of Jesus causes people to cry out "Abba!" (4:6). So, if the creed did originally refer to the Spirit, it is not clear why Paul would alter it. The texts do not offer a clear answer to our question.

Jews, Romans, and nearly everyone else past and present has achieved a sense of self. The resulting creed was a new, but very elegant summary of the whole Jesus tradition.

But why was it created? It is often said that Jesus never intended to create a church. Indeed. But within a few years the processes of social formation had begun to work, and new, distinct communities began to emerge, some, but not all of them, created by Paul. As is evident from 1 Corinthians, baptism as John and his followers, like Apollos, practiced it, was not really conducive to community formation. It was not a community-wide initiation ritual. It was focused on individuals and probably understood as initiation into higher mysteries. But these new communities were not just about personal transformation. They were developing new communal understandings as well. Our Galatian baptismal creed is as good an indicator of this as anything we have. "You (pl.) are *all* sons of God … You are *all one* in Christ Jesus." This creed makes baptism about solidarity with others in community. The three central dyadic claims spell out the terms of that solidarity. Those things by which the human race was seen as divided in the Hellenistic world—ethnicity, class, and gender—are declared relevant no more. In this new community each would have a new self-understanding to be shared with all others in that community: children ("sons") of God. Galatians 3:26–28 signals the fact that at least in some places, baptism had now become a rite by which people entered into the Jesus movement by joining a community.

7 Dying and Rising with Christ

The other interpretation of baptism to emerge in this early period is found in Rom 6:3–11. This, too, is a familiar enough text:

> [3]Do you not know that anyone who has been baptized into Christ Jesus has been baptized into his death? [4]So, we have been buried with him through the baptism into death, so that just as Christ was raised from the dead by the glory of the Father, so also we might walk in newness of life. [5]For if we have been united with him in something like his death, we shall certainly be united with him in something like his resurrection—[6]for we know this, that our old self has been crucified with him, so that the body of sin might be destroyed, so that we might no longer be enslaved to sin. [7]For anyone who has died has been freed from sin. [8]But if we have died with Christ, we believe that we shall also live with him, [9]for we know that Christ, having been raised from the dead, dies no more. Death no longer

rules over him. ¹⁰For in dying, he died to sin, once and for all, but in living, he lives to God. ¹¹So also you, consider yourselves dead to sin but alive to God in Christ Jesus.

Here is yet another interpretation of baptism. I include it after the pre-Pauline creed in Galatians because it occurs in the later letter to the Romans, and because many believe that this represents Paul's own ideas about baptism. Of course, this is by no means a matter of consensus. Since there is no actual evidence that anyone connected baptism with Jesus's death before Romans,[57] many have argued that it comes from Paul. Paul also experiments with the idea of dying with Christ in Gal 2:20, and Betz actually argues that Paul could have developed Romans 6 on the basis of Gal 3:26–28.[58] Others have argued that Paul seems actually to correct or adjust the idea of dying and rising with Christ with an "eschatological reservation" in vv. 5 and 8. Dying and rising with Christ as a ritual transfer from mortality to immortality is a fairly straightforward idea—and one that appears unaltered in Col 2:12 and Eph 2:5–6. So, the theory goes, Colossians and Ephesians, though later, actually represent the original idea, while Romans 6 is Paul's rendering of it with modifications.[59]

Whether the whole concept of baptism as dying and rising with Christ came from Paul, or whether he simply used the concept to make his point in Romans is not a critical question for us. It is more important to notice that this, too, is a very different theory of baptism. This fact is obscured somewhat by the way Paul uses it in Romans. In Romans 6 his purpose is not really to lay out a theory of baptism, but to offer baptism as a solution to the problem of sin. Dying with Christ means freedom from the power of sin (6:7). Baptism, then, as ritual death, could be seen to break the power of sin and free one to live righteously, that is, if one chose to do so (6:12–14).[60] However, Paul's ethical exegesis of dying and rising with Christ should not obscure the original meaning of the formula, even as Paul captures it in 6:5: "For if we have been united with him in a death like his, we shall certainly be united with him in a

---

57 Rudolf Schnackenburg, *Baptism in the Thought of St. Paul: A Study in Pauline Theology* (trans. G.R. Beasley-Murray; Oxford: Blackwell/New York: Herder & Herder, 1964), 33–34.
58 Betz, "Transferring a Ritual," 264–265.
59 Rudolf Bultmann, *Theology of the New Testament* (trans. K. Grobel; New York: Scriners, 1951, 1955), 1:140–141; Ernst Käsemann, *Commentary on Romans* (trans. G.W. Bromiley; Grand Rapids: Eerdmans, 1980), 166–167.
60 Bultmann, *Theology*, 1:140–144.

resurrection like his."[61] The idea that baptism meant dying and rising with Christ was not originally about ethics. It was about salvation. Whether or not this concept *of baptism* could be found among the various cleansing rituals of the so-called mystery religions is a moot question.[62] The *soteriological* concept of associating personally with a dying/rising demi-god is certainly common, and Paul seems to have applied it to the death and resurrection of Jesus.[63] Dying and rising with Christ is another route to immortality, whether immediately, or in Paul's "eschatologically reserved" future.

It should be noted that there is no talk of the Spirit here at all. Gone is the idea that in baptism the Spirit enters and transforms one into a son of God. Paul had not forgotten that earlier idea. He expounds it most beautifully in Romans 8. But for some reason he does not chose to associate it with baptism. Recall that Paul was uncomfortable with the understanding of baptism proffered by Apollos in Corinth. Among its shortcomings was the fact that it drew focus away from the death and resurrection of Jesus. Romans 6:3–11 offers a theory of baptism that placed death and resurrection at the center and made them critical to the self-understanding he wished the baptized to adopt. Betz believes that this was Paul's attempt to create a new rite of entry for his communities.[64] If so, he will have replaced the pre-Pauline formula of Gal 3:26–28 with this new concept. They could not be more different. The Galatians formula aims to create a utopian community of equals. The Romans 6 formula aims to create an eschatological community of the saved.

8 Conclusion

By the end of the Pauline era there were at least three distinct understandings of baptism in the Jesus movement. One, which may go back to John the Baptist himself, imagined that baptism conveyed the Holy Spirit to the baptized

---

61 Cf. also 6:8–9a: "If we have died with Christ, we believe that we shall also live with him. For we know that Christ, being raised from the dead, will never die again ..."
62 Günter Wagner, *Pauline Baptism and the Pagan Mysteries: The Problem of the Pauline Doctrine of Baptism in Romans VI.1–11, in the Light of Its Religio-Historical "Parallels"* (trans. J.P. Smith; Edinburgh: Oliver and Boyd, 1967); but see Brook W.R. Pearson, "Baptism and Initiation in the Cult of Isis and Sarapis," in *Baptism, the New Testament and the Church: Historical and Contemporary Studies in Honour of R.E.O. White* (ed. Stanley E. Porter and Anthony R. Cross; JSNTSup 171; Sheffield: Sheffield Academic, 1999), 42–62.
63 Bultmann, *Theology*, 1:140; Käsemann, *Romans*, 160–171.
64 Betz, "Transferring a Ritual."

and transformed them into enlightened, immortal, children ("sons") of God, like Adam, their primordial kin. This was the idea conveyed by Apollos to the Corinthians, as well as the archaic story of Jesus's own baptism by John shared by Mark and Q. A second understood baptism as initiation into an egalitarian community in which ethnic, class, and gender differences were to be overcome. This is the interpretation of baptism reflected in the pre-Pauline baptismal formula in Gal 3:26–28. A third, perhaps created by Paul himself, imagined baptism as vicarious participation in Jesus's death and resurrection, such that the baptized would someday rise with Christ and die no more. This is the idea used by Paul in Rom 6:3–11 in his argument about sin and the Law.

All of this still leaves us somewhat short of Luke's elegant and unifying myth of origins in Acts 2. To get there we would have to traverse yet another generation at least, taking in, for example, the deutero-Pauline attempt to declare a unity to all this diversity (see Eph 4:4–6). But we have seen enough to know now that Luke's reach back into the early days of the church to define baptism for his time involved not just an act of remembering, but of choosing. It is truly peculiar that the Paulinist does not endorse Paul's preferred view of baptism from Romans 6. Did he even know about it? Nor does he showcase the baptismal creed from Gal 3:26–28. He chooses, rather, the older model of Johannine baptism—even though his hero, Paul, did not favor it. But it, among the three, involved the imparting of the Holy Spirit. That, of course, fit very well Luke's understanding of *Heilsgeschichte*. It was baptism by which the Spirit entered Jesus and directed him on his path; it was through baptism that the Spirit entered the church and now directs its path. That is Lukan *salvation* history, but it is not the whole history. The whole history of baptism is much more complicated, diverse, and interesting.

Followers, Servants, and Traitors: The Representation of Disciples in the Synoptic Gospels and in Ancient Judaism

Catherine Hezser

In a number of publications Gerd Theissen has suggested that Gospel traditions about Jesus's disciples may have had their original *Sitz im Leben* in the life of early Christian wandering charismatics: their decision to follow Jesus would have constituted a strong personal commitment to their teacher and a complete change of lifestyle.[1] From a historical point of view Jesus's relationship to his disciples and relations among the disciples themselves must have been complex. Internal hierarchies would have led to differences of opinion, competition, jealousy, and perhaps even hatred. At the same time the earliest disciples served as eyewitnesses and representatives of their master, whose traditions and remembrance they transmitted to later generations.

This study will focus on literary and tradition-historical aspects of the Gospels' presentation of Jesus's disciples. Which strategies, models, and motifs are recognizable and from which cultural contexts are they derived? The Gospel of Mark shall constitute the basis of our discussion while variants in Matthew and Luke shall be indicated if relevant. A comparison with the master–student relationship in Palestinian rabbinic texts can reveal significant similarities and differences. Since the Gospels were probably used by early Christian missionaries, strategies that are commonly used in advertizing may be informative. To better understand the role of Judas, who appears as Peter's antagonist and personifies the negative end of the scale of ambivalence toward Jesus, we shall refer to redundance theory. The following questions will be central to our discussion: How are Jesus's disciples and sympathizers depicted? Which literary models may have had an impact on this presentation? What could have been the significance and function of this presentation in the context of early Christian missionary activities?

---

1 See, e.g., Gerd Theissen, "'Wir haben alles verlassen' (Mc. x. 28): Nachfolge und soziale Entwurzelung in der jüdisch-palästinischen Gesellschaft des 1. Jahrhunderts n. Chr.," in Theissen, *Studien zur Soziologie des Urchristentums* (WUNT 19; 2nd ed.; Tübingen: Mohr Siebeck, 1983), 106. This paper is based on a presentation given at the University of Heidelberg on April 26, 2013, on the occasion of Gerd Theissen's seventieth birthday. I thank Prof. Theissen for his comments and suggestions.

1 Literary Models: The "Sons" of Prophets in the Bible and Disciples in Hellenistic Philosophy

The Hebrew Bible refers to disciples only in connection with prophets. According to Isa 8:16, Isaiah's disciples served as repositories of the revelation he received and transmitted to them: "Bind up the testimony, seal the instruction with my disciples [חתום תורה בלמדי]". By being stored in his disciples' memory the prophet's teaching is locked away and protected against falsification. In this way it can be preserved for future generations. Others can gain access to it only through the disciples' oral or written testimony. In the Hebrew Bible Isaiah's disciples remain anonymous; they serve as a mere depository of his knowledge. A creative interpretation of the received message is not expected of them and might have been considered a falsification. In the literary context of the book of Isaiah the motif of sealing the prophet's teaching serves as a guarantee for the authenticity of the textual tradition.[2]

In 1 and 2 Kings the so-called "sons of the prophets [בני הנביאים]" are mentioned as adherents of Elijah and Elisha (cf. 1 Kgs 20:35; 2 Kgs 2:3, 5, 7, 15; 4:1, 38; 5:22; 6:1; 9:1). It is noteworthy, however, that they are associated with "prophets" in the plural and with a variety of locations (Bet El: 2 Kgs 2:3; Jordan: 2 Kgs 2:7; Jericho: 2 Kgs 2:15; Gilgal: 2 Kgs 4:38; Ephraim: 2 Kgs 5:22). This means that the group was not simply identical with a particular prophet's disciples. These collectively mentioned "sons [or followers] of the prophets" (בני may indicate membership in a particular group here) are presented as a relatively large group (2 Kgs 2:7 mentions fifty men), encountered at the various locations which Elisha visited. 2 Kings, therefore, seems to imagine them as local sympathizers or less important prophets, hierarchically inferior to Elisha. In the literary context they are responsible for predicting the transfer of the prophetic spirit from Elijah to Elisha (see 2 Kgs 2:15). They serve as witnesses of the legitimacy of Elisha's succession to Elijah. Interestingly, one of them is called a "slave" of Elisha (2 Kgs 4:1: עבדך). Just as the prophet himself is a "slave" of God, his followers are "slaves" of the prophet, that is, the prophet has an intermediary role.[3]

---

2   From the perspective of historical-critical scholarship this claim has to be questioned. According to Siegmund Mowinkel, the prophet's students probably adapted the traditions of their master and proclaimed them in liturgical contexts related to the temple cult. See the discussion in Marvin A. Sweeney, "The Latter Prophets: Isaiah, Jeremiah, Ezekiel," in *The Hebrew Bible Today: An Introduction to Critical Issues* (ed. Steven L. McKenzie and Matt Patrick Graham; Louisville, KY: Westminster John Knox, 1998), 73.

3   Disciples of rabbis also appear in the role of slaves or servants of their teachers, performing servile tasks for them. On this issue, see Catherine Hezser, *Jewish Slavery in Antiquity* (Oxford:

The close relationship between Elisha and the "sons" of the prophets is expressed in narrative traditions according to which he hosts them at home (2 Kgs 4:38) and they are sitting in front of him (2 Kgs 6:1: "Behold, the place in which we sit before you is too narrow for us"). Whether the sons of the prophets are identical with the "elders" mentioned shortly afterwards remains uncertain (2 Kgs 6:32: והזקנים ישבים אתו). Although this terminology cannot be used as evidence for a school associated with Elisha, it brings up the question whether and to what extent later rabbinic traditions present the teacher-disciple relationship on the basis of biblical models (cf. the expression "sitting before" one's master).[4] The later rabbinic term תלמיד, "disciple," is not used in this sense in the Hebrew Bible, however.[5]

Biblical wisdom traditions and Hellenistic concepts seem to have inspired the teacher-student relationship as it is depicted in Jewish and Christian texts of Greco-Roman times.[6] The idea of the wise teacher surrounded by more or less small circles of students who receive his teachings and imitate his practice appears in philosophical texts of the Hellenistic period. According to literary accounts, famous philosophers had close circles of disciples as well as a broader range of sympathizers.[7] The texts point to philosophical networks spanning different locations and a number of generations. According to Edward Jay Watts, such philosophical networks may partly be an illusion, constructed by the literary sources, rather than historical reality.[8]

Oxford University Press, 2005), 174–178. The Babylonischen Talmud explicitly states that disciples have to serve sages like slaves who serve their masters (b. Ketub. 96a). These services were part of the so-called *shimush hakhamim* ("service of sages").

4 Kathleen A. Farmer, "The Wisdom Books: Job, Proverbs, Ecclesiastes," in *The Hebrew Bible Today: An Introduction to Critical Issues*, 144, thinks that this text refers to Elisha's school.

5 Michael J. Wilkins, *The Concept of Disciple in Matthew's Gospel as Reflected in the Use of the Term Μαθητής* (Leiden: Brill, 1988), 46: the term appears only in 1 Chr 25:8 to denote low status temple musicians.

6 See Catherine Hezser, *The Social Structure of the Rabbinic Movement in Roman Palestine* (TSAJ 66; Tübingen: Mohr Siebeck 1997), 130–131.

7 Glen Warren Bowersock et al., eds., *Late Antiquity: A Guide to the Postclassical World* (Cambridge, MA: Harvard University Press, 1999), 704; Edward J. Watts, *City and School in Late Antique Athens and Alexandria* (Berkeley: University of California Press, 2006), 31, with reference to Marinus, *Vita Proc.* 38.

8 Watts, *City and School*, 91 n. 61: "... the narrow network of prominent intellectuals deliberately constructed by the authors of our sources," with reference to Giovanni Ruffini, "Late Antique Pagan Networks from Athens to the Thebaid," in *Ancient Alexandria between Egypt and Greece* (ed. William V. Harris und Giovanni Ruffini; Leiden: Brill, 2004), 241–257.

Josephus seems to have imposed the Hellenistic teacher-student relationship on his biblical sources: Joshua is called a "disciple" of Moses (*Ant.* 6.5.4: τοῦ μαθητοῦ αὐτοῦ), Elisha a "disciple and servant" of Elijah (*Ant.* 8.13.7: καὶ μαθητὴς καὶ διάκονος). Josephus's account of the way in which Elijah chose Elisha as his follower is very reminiscent of Jesus's selection of his disciples in the Gospels. According to Josephus, Elijah found Elisha when the latter was carrying out agricultural work (*Ant.* 8.13.7). Following divine inspiration he nominated him to be his disciple by throwing his garment on him. After this ritual act Elisha is said to have left his field and oxen and followed Elijah until the end of his life. He became Elijah's "disciple and servant" until his teacher died. When Elijah disappeared for good (cf. *Ant.* 9.2.2: "until today no one knows of his death"), his disciple Elisha became his successor. Josephus continues to refer to Elisha "the disciple of Elijah" (cf. *Ant.* 9.3.1), that is, his legitimization as a prophet depends on his nomination by Elijah, who is said to have followed a divine command.

Josephus turns the "sons of the prophets," mentioned in 2 Kings, into Elisha's "disciples," who were sitting in front of him and listening to his teachings (*Ant.* 9.4.4). Wilkins notes: "This is typical 'school' terminology from the rabbinic model ..."[9] From a chronological point of view, Josephus can hardly have been influenced by rabbinic texts. We rather have to assume that Josephus used the Hellenistic teacher-student model before the rabbis already: he tried to explain biblical prophetic succession and hierarchy to a readership familiar with Hellenistic educational practices. According to another text, Elisha sent one of his disciples to Ramot to anoint Jehu as a king chosen by God (*Ant.* 9.6.1). The disciple appears in the role of a "servant" of Elisha here: he acts in accordance with his master's orders. Josephus imposes the teacher-student relationship on other biblical prophets as well: Baruch is presented as Jeremiah's "disciple" (*Ant.* 10.9.1, 6: "his own disciple"). In contrast to the anonymous "sons of the prophets" mentioned in the Bible, Josephus depicts named individuals as personal students of the most prominent prophets.

In Josephus's writings the same model is used in connection with Pharisees of Hellenistic-Roman times: Hyrcanus was a "disciple" of the Pharisees (*Ant.* 13.10.5); Sameas a "disciple" of the Pharisee Pollio in Herodian times (*Ant.* 15.1.1). In Josephus's *Life* Pharisees are introduced as a group with a shared disposition (αἵρεσις), similar to philosophical schools, which one could join and become a member of (cf. *Life* 38–39), just as Josephus did himself (*Life* 2) after having tried out various other such groups. As a community united on

---

9   Wilkins, *Concept of Disciple*, 114.

ideological grounds, Pharisses are compared to Stoics (*Life* 2) and juxtaposed to the "schools" of the Sadducees and Essenes (*Life* 2).

Josephus's equation of Jewish religious "denominations" with Hellenistic and Roman philosophical schools may have had both apologetic and hermeneutic reasons: Pharisees are presented as equal in significance to Greco-Roman teachers of advanced education; for readers trained in *paideia* this analogy may have been the best explanation. Whether the social organization of Pharisaic Judaism actually resembled that of contemporary philosophical schools cannot be determined on the basis of Josephus's writing.

2 The Teacher-Disciple Relationship in the Gospels and in Rabbinic Literature

On the basis of this tradition-historical background we now have to ask how following Jesus is depicted in the Gospels. What are the similarities and differences between the Gospels and rabbinic literature with regard to their presentation of the teacher-disciple relationship?

We shall start with Jesus's own following of John the Baptist. The way in which the Baptist is presented in the Gospels is reminiscent of the portrayal of Elijah in 2 Kings (cf. Mark 1:6; par. Matt 3:4 with 2 Kgs 1:8): the Baptist is depicted as an ascetic prophet.[10] He is said to have had many followers who visited him in the desert and let themselves be baptized by him (Mark 1:5; Matt 3:5). Among these followers only Jesus is mentioned by name. John is said to have followed divine inspiration when regarding Jesus as his successor who, according to the Gospels, superseded him spiritually.

The Gospels are obviously interested in emphasizing the difference between John and Jesus and in presenting Jesus as superior to his teacher (cf. Matt 3:11: "The one who comes after me is more powerful than me and I am not worthy of carrying his shoes"; cf. Luke 3:16). Here the traditional hierarchy between the prophet and "the sons of the prophet" and the teacher and his disciple is reversed: the teacher becomes the student's trailblazer, paving his way. Jesus is thereby excluded from the conventional model. This becomes even more clear by the Gospels' insistence that God declared Jesus to be his "beloved son" (Mark

---

10 According to Gerd Theissen in "Das doppelte Liebesgebot in der Jesusüberlieferung," in *Jesus als historische Gestalt: Beiträge zur Jesusforschung* (ed. Gerd Theissen and Annette Merz; Göttingen: Vandenhoeck & Ruprecht, 2003), 57–72, the Gospels may have confined John's activity to prophecy whereas in reality Jesus may also have learned ethical teachings from him.

1:11; par. Matt 3:17 and Luke 3:22). Jesus's superiority was allegedly legitimized by both his predecessor and God.

The rabbinic story about Honi the circle-drawer, transmitted in m. Ta'an. 3:8, can serve as an analogy to Jesus's designation as "son" of God. According to the narrative, Honi was asked by locals to make rain fall. In order to comply with their demand he stepped into a drawn circle and prayed to God, referring to himself as "your [i.e., God's] son" to express his particular closeness to God. Although such a self-designation was generally considered haughty, Shimon b. Shetach's reaction at the end of the story exculpates Honi. Shimon is said to have recognized Honi's charismatic power and therefore refrained from excommunicating him, "for he [God] fulfills your wish like that of a son who importunes his father and he [nevertheless] fulfills his wish. And about you Scripture says: 'Let your father and your mother be glad, and let her that bore you rejoice' [Prov 23:25]" (m. Ta'an. 3:8). The rabbinic tradents and editors of this story were obviously willing to recognize particular charismatic powers. As with Jesus, Honi is presented as an extraordinary human being, distinct from ordinary rabbinic Torah scholars and their circles of students. In later talmudic tradition Honi is "rabbinized" and turned into a Torah sage.[11]

The way in which the Gospels present Jesus's calling of his disciples resembles Josephus's depiction of Elijah's nomination of Elisha. The literary depiction follows a certain pattern: Jesus sees particular individuals at work—he invites them to follow him—they leave their work (and family) and follow him (see, e.g., Mark 1:16–20: Simon and Andrew; James; Mark 2:14: Levi). The pattern is not employed in the tradition about the collective calling of the twelve, transmitted in Mark 3:13–19 (par. Matt 10:1–4; Luke 6:12–16), which seems to stem from a different source.[12] In Matthew this tradition is better integrated into its literary context: instead of a call to discipleship the text thematizes the transfer of exorcizing powers onto an already existing group of followers.

What these two traditional strands share is Jesus's initiative in the choice of his disciples. This form of calling already appears in the biblical narratives about prophets and may have been a necessary ingredient of depictions of

---

11 On this process, see Jeffrey L. Rubenstein, *Rabbinic Stories* (Mahwah, NJ: Paulist, 2002), 128–133.

12 Mark's tradition about the calling of the twelve may have been modelled after the biblical tradition about the divine election of (the twelve tribes of) Israel. Eckhard J. Schnabel, *Urchristliche Mission* (Wuppertal: R. Brockhaus, 2002), 270, considers the number twelve symbolic of the early Christian hope for the collection of the twelve tribes of Israel at the end of times ("die Sammlung des Zwölfstämmevolkes Israel"). See also Peter Schäfer, *Jesus in the Talmud* (Princeton: Princeton University Press, 2009), 75.

spiritual following.¹³ In contrast to the calling of individual named disciples (Elijah's calling of Elisha, John's calling of Jesus, Jesus's calling of his disciples) a broader set of sympathizers is said to have approached their chosen master themselves and to have maintained a more distant relationship to him (cf. the "sons of the prophets" at the time of Elisha; Josephus' depictions).

The close circles of students associated with particular rabbis are also at least partially traced back to the prospective students' own initiative: they are said to have approached a particular rabbi in order to study with him; some of them left their families and their home towns for that purpose.¹⁴ Whether they were accepted into their chosen teacher's disciple circle would have depended on the teacher's approval, on personal affiliation and learning ability. The Gospels' depiction of charismatic succession, based on biblical prophetic models, clearly differs from the rabbinic model of intellectual succession.¹⁵ The Gospels are not so much concerned with the disciples' Torah study but rather focus on miracles, exorcisms, and healings. These practices depended on magical powers that could not be learned or acquired on the basis of one's own efforts. They could only be transmitted by someone who was in possession of these powers himself. Even though the Gospel of Matthew emphasizes Jesus's teaching more than the other Gospels, even there Jesus's actions are most significant.¹⁶

---

13   On this issue, see also Suzanne Watts Henderson, *Christology and Discipleship in the Gospel of Mark* (Cambridge: Cambridge University Press, 2008), 54. Rainer Riesner, *Jesus als Lehrer* (Tübingen: Mohr Siebeck, 1981), 228, emphasizes the Gospels' focus on Jesus's initiative.

14   According to rabbinic traditions, disciples often underwent long journeys to join a particular master. After 70 CE, pilgrimages to the temple seem to have been replaced by pilgrimages to rabbinic masters as physical repositories of the holy (Torah); see Catherine Hezser, *Jewish Travel in Antiquity* (TSAJ 144; Tübingen: Mohr Siebeck, 2011), 383–385. In order to live with a master at a location that was distant from their home town and family, disciples of sages had to leave their familiar areas of life. m. Ketub. 5:6 (cf. t. Ketub. 5:6) discusses how long disciples of sages may stay away from their wives without having to ask them for permission. In contrast to day laborers, who may stay away for one week only (cf. *t. Ket.* 5:6), disciples of sages may leave their wives and families for an entire month to study with a master. On the early Christian ethos of leaving one's family, see Peter Balla, "How Radical is Itinerant Radicalism? The Case of Luke 14:26," in *Jesus—Gestalt und Gestaltungen: Rezeptionen des Galiläers in Wissenschaft, Kirche und Gesellschaft* (ed. Petra von Gemünden, et al.; Göttingen: Vandenhoeck & Ruprecht, 2013), 51–61.

15   On charismatic succession, see Theissen, "'Wir haben alles verlassen,'" 106.

16   Therefore, the opinion of R.D. Kaylor, *Jesus the Prophet: His Vision of the Kingdom on Earth*

The education which Jesus's disciples receive consists of observing Jesus's acts and listening to his parables and proverbs. This connection between teaching and practice and the emphasis on the oral and visual also appears in rabbinic texts. Disciples of sages accompany their masters in daily life and observe their behavior.[17] Rabbis' practice was halakhically significant since it constituted an actualization of their opinions. Seemingly trivial everyday life practices obtain religious significance. The master's teaching has practical relevance. All of this is based on the idea that the Torah should be lived and fulfilled in daily life. By contrast, in the Gospels charismatic power finds expression in words and deeds. Therefore, following Jesus does not consist in Torah study and interpretation but in providing testimony of his charismatic powers and in imitating his miraculous healings (see Mark 3:14).[18]

Matthew seems to have tried to combine the two models by giving more emphasis to the biblical basis of Jesus's teaching.[19] On the other hand, he omits the reference to the "preaching of the Gospel" (Mark 3:14) in the tradition about the twelve taken over from Mark, merely stressing the transmission of magical powers—Matt 10:1: Jesus "gave them authority over unclean spirits, to cast them out and to heal any kind of disease and sickness." Magical powers cannot be acquired on one's own initiative: a person either possesses them or they are transferred on him. Therefore, the Gospels had to present Jesus's call to discipleship in a fundamentally different way than rabbinic texts. Their presentation of discipleship necessarily implied a certain amount of inequality and hierarchy (between Jesus and the disciples; among the disciples themselves), whereas rabbinic texts try to present sages as status-equal Torah scholars.

In the Gospels Jesus's followership appears in accordance with the model of concentric circles: Jesus himself is immediately surrounded by a few named disciples (especially Peter and the sons of Zebedaeus, John and James). The twelve form the next outward circle: most of these disciples are mentioned by name only once and therefore remain unknown to the readers. Eventually,

---

(Louisville, KY: Westminster John Knox, 1994), 176: "Matthew presents a view of the disciples similar to rabbinic disciples," is only partially correct.

17 The connection between teaching and practice also appears in connection with ancient philosophers and "holy men." See Garth Fowden, "The Pagan Holy Man in Late Antique Society," *JHS* 52 (1982): 33–59.

18 See also Gerd Theissen, "Wanderradikalismus: Literatursoziologische Aspekte der Überlieferung von Worten Jesu im Urchristentum," in Theissen, *Studien zur Soziologie des Urchristentums*, 91: "Jesus war der erste Wandercharismatiker. Die Tradenten seiner Worte übernahmen seine Lebensweise."

19 See especially the Sermon on the Mount in Matt 5:1–48.

there are individual "clients" and sympathizers, mentioned in narrative traditions, who benefit from Jesus but are not his disciples and do not follow him (the blind beggar Bartimaeus, son of Timaeus, is the only healed person allowed to follow Jesus, see Mark 10:46–52).[20] Finally, the outer circle is constituted by the "many," the constantly mentioned anonymous mass, which allegedly assembled wherever Jesus went.

An important aspect of the Gospels' representation of the disciples is the emphasis on their inferiority to their master. The disciples are mostly referred to collectively and remain in the background: they accompany Jesus, serve him, and function as mediators between him and the anonymous masses. Yet they also appear as eyewitnesses of his miraculous deeds and recipients of his secret messages (see, e.g., Mark 4:34). Jesus's disciples are compared with the followers of John the Baptist and the Pharisees (Mark 2:18): the disciples' behaviour is considered evidence of their master's teaching. Just as slaves were seen as an extension of their master's hand, disciples were seen as reflections of their teacher's ideology.[21]

Rabbinic sources occasionally state that a student may teach only once his teacher has given him permission to do so or if he maintains a certain distance.[22] Such rules were probably meant to prevent competition since disciples of sages aspired to become rabbis themselves. Eventually the relationship between a teacher and his students would be transformed into a relationship between colleague-friends. Therefore, rabbinic texts tend to portray the rabbinic movement as a community of status equals. Christological beliefs would have prevented a similar depiction of Jesus and his followers. The disciples could never obtain Jesus's status as messiah or son of God. Christological ideas prevented the disciples' full identification with Jesus so that the claim of succession had to remain unfulfilled. The disciples would always remain mere

---

20   The protagonists of miracle stories, example stories, and disputes usually remain anonymous, e.g., the Syrophoenician woman in Mark 7:24–30, the rich man in Mark 10:17–23, the scribe in Mark 12:28, and the poor widow in Mark 12:43. They have a merely generic function in the Gospel texts.

21   On slaves as an extension of their master's hand, see the tannaitic formula, "the hand of a slave is like the hand of his master," transmitted in y. Pe'ah 4:6, 18b and elsewhere in rabbinic sources. On the later Babylonian talmudic interpretation, see Catherine Hezser, "'The Slave of a Scholar is Like a Scholar': Stories about Rabbis and Their Slaves in the Babylonian Talmud," in *Creation and Composition: The Contribution of the Bavli Redactors (Stammaim) to the Aggadah* (ed. Jeffrey L. Rubenstein; TSAJ 114; Tübingen: Mohr Siebeck, 2005), 198–217.

22   See the discussion of references in Hezser, *Social Structure*, 108–110.

servants of Jesus, they could never obtain their master's prestige. As servants they were destined to remain status equals (cf. Mark 9:34–35: hierarchical dispute; 10:36–44: the sons of Zebedaeus want to sit at the right and left hand sides of Jesus).

Nevertheless, the Gospels occasionally reveal differences among the disciples. Sometimes it is not the anonymous twelve but two or three named disciples who accompany Jesus. Peter, James, and John are the ones who are referred to most. In the story about the daughter of the synagogue leader, whom Jesus purportedly raised from the dead, it is explicitly stated: "And he let no one follow him except for Peter and James and John, the brother of James" (Mark 5:37). These three disciples are also said to have been present at the transfiguration of Jesus (Mark 9:2). On the Mount of Olives Peter, James, and John allegedly asked Jesus privately for signs of the end of times (Mark 13:3). Jesus takes only Peter, James, and John with him to Gethsemane (Mark 14:33). Simon/Petrus, Andrew, James, and John are said to have been the first persons whom Jesus called to follow him (Mark 1:16–19). Despite the fact that James's and John's claims to superiority over the rest of the disciples are rejected (Mark 10:36–44), they are given a prominent role in the Gospel of Mark. Like Simon Peter they are given a cognomen (Mark 3:16–17: Boanerges, "sons of thunder"). Other disciples listed in Mark 3:18 (e.g., Philip, Matthew, Thomas, Bartholomew) are mentioned only once and remain mere ciphers who do not contribute to the development of the plot.[23]

In the Gospel of Mark the most positively depicted disciple is Peter, who allegedly identified Jesus as Christ (Mark 8:29) and compared him to Moses and Elijah (Mark 9:5). Peter appears as the quintessential follower who gave up everything to be Jesus's disciple (Mark 10:29).[24] By contrast, Judas has the most negative image: he is revealed as a traitor already at the beginning of the Gospel (Mark 3:19; cf. 14:10) but otherwise remains entirely colorless. Matthew has further elaborated the positive role of Peter and the negative role of Judas. Peter is called the "rock" on which the church is built (Matt 16:18). Judas, on the other hand, is portrayed as greedy and corrupt (Matt 26:14–16, 47–49). He deceived Jesus with a kiss (Mark 14:44–45; par. Matt 26:48–49; Luke 22:47–48 with variations). In antiquity, as nowadays, the kiss was associated with

---

23   According to a tannaitic tradition in the Babylonian Talmud (b. Sanh. 43a), Jesus had five disciples who were killed together with him. See Schäfer, *Jesus in the Talmud*, 75–81.

24   On the Gospels' image of Peter, see also the short treatise of Marlen Bonke, *Die ersten Jünger Jesu: Exegetische Betrachtungen zur Petrusüberlieferung und die Analyse der historisch-archäologischen Zeugnisse für Petri Martyrium in Rom* (Norderstedt: GRIN Verlag, 2010).

love and friendship. This common understanding is evident in Jesus's reaction (Matt 26:50: he addresses him as a "friend"). At the same time deceitful kisses were also not unknown.[25] References to such kisses in Greco-Roman literature and in the Hebrew Bible will have influenced the motif of Judas's kiss in the Gospels.[26]

In all likelihood members of early Christian communities evinced ambivalent attitudes toward Jesus, especially as far as christological beliefs were concerned. This ambivalence seems to have been expressed in the literary figures of the disciples and is also evident in the representation of Peter. As Kari Syreeni has already stressed in his study on Peter, this ambivalence appears especially in Jesus's rebuttal of Peter as "satan" after his confession (Mark 8:32–33; par. Matt 16:22–23; omitted by Luke).[27] Mark and Matthew present even Peter, who recognizes Jesus as Christ (Mark 8:29) and son of God (Matt 16:16), as an "obstacle" to the belief in his resurrection. The depiction of Judas constitutes the culmination of this ambivalent attitude. Judas is said to have deceived Jesus by informing the priests against him (Mark 14:10–11, 43–46; par. Matt 26:14–16). In Matthew's Gospel this deceit is already announced beforehand so that Judas, who addresses Jesus as "Rabbi" and is called "friend" and "companion" by him (see Matt 26:50), cannot be held responsible at the end (Matt 26:24–25; 49–50).

How can this shift between confession and deceit, friendship and rejection, and support and slander be explained? According to the philosophical theory of redundance, sentences that maintain that something is true are redundant, since they express a fact without providing new information.[28] It would not make any sense for someone who stands in front of a red door to say, "It is true that the door is red," since this is obvious. For the editors of the Gospels an affirmation of the "truth" of their christological beliefs would have been redundant, since they were convinced of Jesus's divinity. It is possible, however, to negate a wrong statement, but in order to do so it has to be explicitly stated. Therefore,

---

25 Peter Krapp, "Auf die Zunge beissen: Zur kannibalistischen Kommunikation," in *Verschlungene Grenzen: Anthropophagie in Literatur und Kulturwissenschaften* (ed. Annette Keck et al.; Tübingen: Gunter Narr, 1999), 346.

26 Krapp, "Auf die Zunge beissen," 346. See also Fatima Casaseca, *Judas Iskarioth im Matthäusevangelium*, Studienarbeit (Norderstedt: GRIN Verlag, 2007), 17, with reference to 2 Sam 20:9–10 (Joab).

27 Kari Syreeni, "Peter as Character and Symbol in the Gospel of Matthew," in *Characterization in the Gospels: Recovering Narrative Criticism* (ed. David Rhoads and Kari Syreeni; Sheffield: Sheffield Academic, 1999), 130–131.

28 On this theory, see Richard Schantz, *Wahrheit, Referenz und Realismus: Eine Studie zur Sprachphilosophie und Metaphysik* (Berlin: de Gruyter, 1996), 5–14.

the evangelists let disciples such as Peter and Judas doubt or deny Jesus's "true" divine nature in order to refute this denial and thereby express their christological ideas (on Peter's denial see also Mark 14:67–72; par. Matt 26:69–74 and Luke 22:56–62). In comparison with the disciples, the readers and audiences of the Gospels, who lived in post-Easter times, were expected to have advanced knowledge of Jesus's nature and destiny, which is expressed through the literary motifs of denial/affirmation and secrecy. At the same time possible doubts concerning Jesus's divinity can be taken up and neutralized in this way.

This explanation does not exclude the possibility that the disciples actually held ambivalent attitudes toward Jesus. Betrayal, denial, and abandonment may have happened among the discipleship. Celsus used the disciples' failings as an argument against Jesus.[29] His argumentation was motivated by polemics, however. Interpretations that see the negative traits of Mark's depiction of disciples as an indication of his polemics against or dissociation from earlier tradents of Jesus's teachings are not convincing.[30]

3 The "Many" Followers as a Propaganda Mechanism of Early Christian Missionary Activity

In antiquity a prominent man was assumed to have many sympathizers, disciples, and clients. Roman dignitaries served as patrons whose clients supported them in the political realm.[31] Greco-Roman philosophers had disciples and adherents among the upper strata of society who would approach them in public and listen to their words of learning.[32] Rich landowners exhibited their

---

29 See Origen, *Cels.* 2.12, referred to by John Granger Cook, *The Interpretation of the New Testament in Greco-Roman Paganism* (Tübingen: Mohr Siebeck, 2000), 48.

30 Polemics: see Theodore J. Weeden's position outlined in C. Clifton Black, *The Disciples According to Mark: Markan Redaction in Current Debate* (2nd ed.; Grand Rapids: Eerdmans, 2012), 141–177. Dissociation: Heikki Räisänen, *Messianic Secret in Mark's Gospel* (London: Bloomsbury, 1994).

31 See Andrew Wallace-Hadrill, "Patronage in Roman Society: From Republic to Empire," in *Patronage in Ancient Society* (ed. Andrew Wallace-Hadrill; London: Routledge, 1989), 63–88. Patrons would have been accompanied by their clients in the public sphere, see Susan P. Mattern, *Galen and the Rhetoric of Healing* (Baltimore: Johns Hopkins University Press, 2008), 22.

32 H. Gregory Snyder, *Teachers and Texts in the Ancient World: Philosophers, Jews, and Christians* (London: Routledge, 2000), 115: "Obviously, having an entourage composed of well-heeled and sophisticated students could only enhance one's status."

wealth by having beautiful and well-dressed slaves accompany them to bath-houses and to the forum.[33] Jesus and the rabbis, who were neither particularly wealthy nor public office holders, did not have these options. Yet later generations could not imagine them without a more or less large following because his following indicated a man's status. The larger the number of adherents and sympathizers, the greater the prestige of the man they were associated with. Therefore, the Gospels and rabbinic texts ascribe a large general audience to Jesus and prominent rabbis, to supplement the smaller disciple circles.

In comparison to the relatively small circles of students associated with rabbis, twelve disciples would have constituted a crowd. In rabbinic narratives usually only two or three students are mentioned by name, despite the fact that some general statements refer to the "many disciples" of R. Aqiva or other prominent rabbis.[34] Furthermore, local sympathizers of individual rabbis (in Tiberias, Sepphoris, Caesarea) are sometimes mentioned collectively[35] and "many" are sometimes said to have flocked to a study house to listen to the Torah interpretation of particular rabbis.[36]

The Gospels constantly mention the "many" who gathered wherever Jesus appeared (see, e.g., Mark 2:2; 6:31–32) and who followed Jesus (e.g., Mark 2:14). When he entered a synagogue, "many" are said to have been impressed by him (Mark 6:1). Jesus allegedly healed "many" (Mark 1:34; 3:10; 6:56), cast out "many" demons (Mark 1:34), and taught "many" in parables (Mark 4:2.33; cf. 6:35). Acts 10:38 states explicitly that Peter stressed in his sermon Jesus's healing of "all" those who were possessed by an evil spirit. These summary references to Jesus's activity, which allegedly affected many, were part of early Christian missionizing efforts.

The Gospels' emphasis on the large number of Jesus's adherents can be considered a recurring literary motif which must have been significant for both

---

33   William L. Westermann, *The Slave Systems of Greek and Roman Antiquity* (Philadelphia: The American Philosophical Society, 1955), 89: "... seven slaves and seven other attendants who may be slaves were a sufficient entourage for a proconsul of Syria." See also James S. Jeffers, *The Greco-Roman World of the New Testament: Exploring the Background of Early Christianity* (Downers Grove, IL: InterVarsity, 1999), 60: "A great man would be accompanied by as many slaves and free clients as he could muster since the size of the entourage proclaimed his importance."

34   See Stuart Miller, *Sages and Commoners in Late Antique 'Erez Israel* (Tübingen: Mohr Siebeck, 2006), 427, n. 100, with reference to b. Yebam. 62b.

35   See Miller, *Sages*, 160. It sometimes remains unclear whether this group of local adherents consisted of students and colleagues or (also) of lay people.

36   See, e.g., y. B.M. 2:12–13, 8d: everyone is "running" to hear R. Yochanan expound in the study house of R. Benaiah in Sepphoris.

the tradents and the editors of the texts. By referring to the "many" who followed Jesus, they confirmed and demonstrated his popularity and influence among his contemporaries. This image of a popular charismatic would have been important for Christian missionary activity: the more popular a religious teacher had proven to be, the more adherents he could gain in the future. Especially if the real number of adherents was limited, such traditions could create the image of an outstanding personality, an image which would have been perpetuated by later generations of Christians.[37]

Sociologists have pointed to the significance of the "perceived popularity" of an individual: the more popular a person is considered to be, the more friends and adherents that person can gain in the course of time.[38] Today large Facebook networks tend to expand almost by themselves this way. Similarly, the advertising industry creates a so-called "hype" to increase the sale of particular products (e.g., new iPhones). Especially if a novelty product is introduced, such a strategy is employed to prepare its launch and to create a base of potential buyers. Obviously, Jesus was not a sales product, but we may assume that early Christian missionaries would have encountered similar problems as modern advertising agencies to spread their new message among their contemporaries.

4   Discipleship and the Transmission of the Jesus Tradition

Just as disciples of sages served as tradents of traditions of and about their rabbinic masters, Jesus's disciples and later generations of followers would have been the tradents of the Jesus tradition. What is missing in the Gospels, however, are attributions and chains of transmission such as, "R. X said in the name of R. Y," which are characteristic of rabbinic transmission.[39] Nowhere do we find formulas such as, "Peter said in the name of Jesus," or "X said that John said

---

37   This consideration does not preclude the possibility that, as a charismatic healer, Jesus might have had a certain number of adherents among his Jewish contemporaries.

38   Mark Schaller, "Unintended Influence: Social-Evolutionary Influences in the Construction and Change of Culturally-Shared Beliefs," in *Social Influence: Direct and Indirect Processes* (ed. Joseph P. Forgas and Kipling D. Williams; Philadelphia: Psychology Press, 2001), 83: "All else being equal, the more popular a meme is perceived to already be, the more communicable it is, and the more likely it is to become even more widespread and remain so."

39   See Hezser, *Social Structure*, 65–66.

in the name of Jesus".[40] The Gospel editors may have attributed parables and other teachings to Jesus himself in order to create the impression of authenticity and immediacy. Although rabbinic oral tradition is ultimately traced back to Moses at Sinai, this vertical line of transmission is supplemented by a horizontal one that counteracts direct inspiration. Despite differences in the use of attributions, Jesus traditions would also have been transmitted from one generation of followers to the next.[41]

Interestingly, the later tradents decided to remain anonymous or the editors decided to withhold their names. In the rabbinic history of transmission anonymity appears at the post-amoraic editorial stage only. The so-called *stam* (anonymous Talmud) responsible for combining tannaitic and amoraic traditions and creating larger discursive units, also often commented upon, harmonized, and adapted traditional material.[42] In both cases we may assume that the anonymous editors considered themselves inferior to earlier authorities who are mentioned by name. Although they were the ones who actually created the texts that came down to us, they decided to remain hidden behind their creations. In the Gospels only the twelve disciples and a few other individuals are named and most of the Twelve (such as Thomas, Bartholomew, Philip, etc.) are mentioned by name only once (Mark 3:14–19). In all likelihood the few more often mentioned disciples—especially Simon Peter (mentioned 21 times in Mark), John, and James (mentioned 15 times; 5 times together with John), perhaps also Andrew (mentioned 4 times)—occupied a particularly important role in the Synoptic transmission history.

Both Simon Peter and Andrew, and James and John, sons of Zebedaeus, were brothers. All four are said to have been working in the fishing industry before they became Jesus's disciples (Mark 1:14–20). According to the Gospels, they were the first followers of Jesus. Would they therefore have occupied a superior status as eyewitnesses and guarantors of the Jesus tradition?[43] Did Mark

---

40   The beginnings of a Christian chain of transmission are to be found with Papias who, according to Eusebius, constructed a line of transmission from Jesus to Peter and Mark; see Eusebius, *Hist. eccl.* 3.39.15.

41   On the various contexts of transmission, see Gerd Theissen, *The Gospels in Context* (London: Continuum, 2004), 97 ff. (miracle stories), 112 ff. (apophthegmata).

42   On the anonymous editing of the Babylonian Talmud and differences to the Palestinian Talmud, see Jeffrey L. Rubenstein, *The Culture of the Babylonian Talmud* (Baltimore: Johns Hopkins University Press, 2003), 4–5; Moulie Vidas, *Tradition and the Formation of the Talmud* (Princeton: Princeton University Press, 2014), 115–149.

43   This is the view of Gottfried Rau, "Das Markusevangelium: Komposition und Intention," *ANRW* II.25.3 (1985): 2090.

decide to elevate them while other strands of transmission were linked to other eyewitnesses so that a number of (probably originally orally transmitted) transmission complexes competed with each other? Some of these corpora may have become lost over time or were integrated into other writings (e.g., the Gospel of Thomas).

Interestingly, the Q source rarely refers to disciples and never mentions their names,[44] that is, discipleship and followership seem to have been linked to the narrative literary form of the Gospels. Does this mean that the Gospels were written by and for followers of Jesus to propagate particular teachings and life styles within early Christian communities?[45] The post-Easter continuation of the practice of following Jesus is emphasized in the book of Acts,[46] but has its basis in the Synoptic Gospels. Gerd Theissen has already pointed to different types of followerships in the early communities that encompassed wandering charismatics as well as settled local Christians. This hypothesis has been elaborated by other scholars and does not require further discussion here.[47]

---

44 See also Heinz-Wolfgang Kuhn, "Jesus im Licht der Qumrangemeinde," in *Handbook for the Study of the Historical Jesus*. Vol. 2: *The Study of Jesus* (ed. Tom Holmén and Stanley E. Porter; Leiden: Brill, 2011), 1256, n. 41.

45 See Ferdinand Hahn, *Theologie des Neuen Testaments* (vol. 2; 2nd ed.; Tübingen: Mohr Siebeck 2005), 448–449; Helga Kuhlmann, *Fehlbare Vorbilder in Bibel, Christentum und Kirchen: Von Engeln, Propheten und Heiligen bis zu Päpsten und Bischöfinnen* (Münster: LIT Verlag, 2010), 147.

46 See Charles H. Talbert, *Reading Acts: A Literary and Theological Commentary on the Acts of the Apostles* (Macon, GA: Smyth & Helwys, 2005), xxv.

47 Esp. Markus Tiwald, *Wanderradikalismus: Jesu erste Jünger—Ein Anfang und was davon bleibt* (Frankfurt: Peter Lang, 2002); Thomas Schmeller, *Brechungen: Urchristliche Wandercharismatiker im Prisma soziologisch orientierter Exegese* (Stuttgart: Katholisches Bibelwerk, 1989); Hans Jürgen Milchner, *Nachfolge Jesu und Imitation Christi: Die theologische Entfaltung der Nachfolgethematik seit den Anfängen der Christenheit bis in die Zeit der devotio moderna—Unter besonderer Berücksichtigung religionspädagogischer Ansätze* (Münster: LIT Verlag, 2004), 11–15. On the development of offices in the early Christian church, see Jochen Wagner, *Die Anfänge des Amtes in der Kirche: Presbyter und Episkopen in der frühchristlichen Literatur* (Tübingen: Francke, 2011).

PART 2

Production of Early Christian Gospels

∴

The Pre-citation Fallacy in New Testament Scholarship and Sanders's Tendencies of the Synoptic Tradition

Stanley E. Porter and Andrew W. Pitts

1 Introduction

It has become customary in New Testament scholarship—and most research-based disciplines for that matter—to give a nod in the direction of important paradigm shifts or ground-breaking studies within the discipline when one is embarking upon a topic where important, widely recognized research has established something of a consensus, or at least a widely held opinion. This seems wise enough. A problem occurs, however, when the acknowledgment is merely perfunctory and does not constrain the results of the study appropriately. For example, in Michelle V. Lee's work, *Paul, the Stoics and the Body of Christ*, an entire (although small) section is devoted to "Avoiding 'parallelomania': Samuel Sandmel,"[1] referring to Sandmel's seminal insights into the tendency among biblical scholars toward discovering an abundance of similar passages as the supposed source of a later literary tradition (especially positing genetic relations). However, she goes on, we believe, to engage in precisely the kind of analysis that Sandmel warns against throughout the rest of her book. Fredrick J. Long commits a similar error in his book on Pauline rhetoric in 2 Corinthians. In the first few paragraphs of his chapter on the rhetorical "Apologetic Letters," he discusses the growing tendency among New Testament scholars to draw a distinction between epistolary and rhetorical literary categories. He even mentions the specific arguments given for maintaining this dichotomy.[2] But instead of responding to these arguments, he reduces them to a call for "ancient rhetorical critics to use ancient sources with greater care, clarity, and consistency when interpreting biblical materials."[3] This is hardly what scholars like Stanley Porter, Jeffrey Reed, R.N. Anderson, and Dennis Stamps (whom he cites) mean when they say that it confuses genres to speak about

---

[1] (SNTSMS 137; Cambridge: Cambridge University Press, 2006), 12–13, referring to Samuel Sandmel, "Parallelomania," *JBL* 18 (1962): 1–13 (see esp. p. 1, for definition).

[2] Fredrick J. Long, *Ancient Rhetoric and Paul's Apology: The Compositional Unity of 2 Corinthians* (SNTSMS 131; Cambridge: Cambridge University Press, 2004), 97–98.

[3] Long, *Ancient Rhetoric*, 98.

rhetorical (i.e. oratorical) letters. He then goes on in the rest of the chapter to simply give further exposition of the same sources that were used to establish the apologetic rhetorical letter by Hans Dieter Betz, but have now been widely called into question. Again, we may point to varying responses to this critical work on epistolography and rhetoric, ranging from absolute ignorance to informed, sustained endorsements of the research.[4]

Further examples along these lines could be multiplied. What may be observed among the scholarly responses in these cases is a frequent three-fold reaction to significant research. Some choose to ignore it. Others choose to endorse it and incorporate (or adapt/expand) the conclusions, including their implications into their research. But a third group of scholars, which we want to focus our attention on in this essay, tends to acknowledge the relevant research, but effectively ignores its implications within the body of their work.[5] They give a nod in order to show their awareness of a particular study or set of conclusions, but their analysis ends up running contrary to these acknowledgments, creating an incoherent or self-refuting argument. Their early endorsement of a specific body of research undermines their eventual conclusions. We refer to this pattern as the pre-citation fallacy in New Testament scholarship because it involves citing research to show awareness of it (usually at an early stage in the work), but then proceeding to make assertions that run contrary to it or at least to its implications. Although numerous individual instances of this fallacy could be elucidated, perhaps what is most profitable at this stage is to examine scholarly response to one work so that the fallacy, as well as the other levels of response, can be consistently developed and demonstrated. E.P. Sanders's often overlooked work on Gospel studies provides an excellent case study for exploring these levels of response and especially the pre-citation fallacy through a consideration of scholarly reaction to his critique of form criticism. It is our hope, however, not only to highlight varying levels of scholarly response to Sanders, but also to call for a greater appreciation of Sanders's research on Synoptic criticism.

---

4   For an example of ignoring this distinction, see Robert Jewett, *Romans: A Commentary* (Hermeneia; Minneapolis: Fortress, 2007), who rigorously applies ancient rhetorical categories to Paul's letter to the Romans. For an acceptance and application of the distinction, see C. Joachim Classen, "St. Paul's Epistles and Ancient Greek and Roman Rhetoric," in *The Galatians Debate* (ed. Mark D. Nanos; Peabody, MA: Hendrickson, 2002), 95–113.

5   We might mention a fourth response, criticism of the work, which could in itself lead to a paradigm shift. Here, however, we want to focus on work that has not been substantially contested.

2 Response to Sanders's Tendencies of the Synoptic Tradition

In 1969, E.P. Sanders published the first of his many important scholarly monographs, his *The Tendencies of the Synoptic Tradition*.[6] This work, a revision of his doctoral dissertation under the supervision of W.D. Davies at Union Theological Seminary, New York, was a harbinger of Sanders's future iconoclastic research conclusions, as it attacked the heart of one of the fundamental approaches to New Testament criticism, form criticism and its laws of transmission. When this work was first published, form criticism was still enjoying its position of virtually unassailed authority within especially Gospel criticism.[7] In many ways, in fact, Sanders's was one of the, if not the, first to directly call into question the fundamental assumptions of form-critical transmission, and to substantiate such claims with data.[8]

---

6 (SNTSMS 9; Cambridge: Cambridge University Press, 1969). This position is represented within in a discussion of form criticism in E.P. Sanders and Margaret Davies, *Studying the Synoptic Gospels* (London: SCM/Philadelphia: Trinity Press International, 1989), 123–137, esp. 127–128. Sanders's work also had implications for source criticism (see Sanders, *Tendencies*, 276–279), which we do not explore here.

7 Several much earlier responses to form criticism, such as by Vincent Taylor (*The Formation of the Gospel Tradition* [London: Macmillan 1933]) and E.B. Redlich (*Form Criticism: Its Value and Limitations* [Studies in Theology; London: Duckworth, 1939]), were not as critical of the Jesus tradition as were some of the early practitioners, such as Rudolf Bultmann (*History of the Synoptic Tradition* [trans. John Marsh; Oxford: Blackwell, 1963 (1921)]). Martin Dibelius (*From Tradition to Gospel* [trans. Bertram Lee Woolf; London: Ivor Nicholson & Watson, 1935 (1919)]) was never as skeptical as Bultmann. For a survey of form criticism, with bibliography, see Stanley E. Porter, *The Criteria for Authenticity in Historical-Jesus Research: Previous Discussion and New Proposals* (JSNTSup 190; Sheffield: Sheffield Academic, 2000), 63–69 and the notes, esp. n. 4.

8 According to Gerd Theissen, to whom we will return below (*The Gospels in Context: Social and Political History in the Synoptic Tradition* [trans. Linda M. Maloney; Edinburgh: T&T Clark, 1992 (1989)], 1 n. 1), the works that mark the "dissolution of the form-critical consensus" are Erhardt Güttgemanns, *Candid Questions Concerning Gospel Form Criticism: A Methodological Sketch of the Fundamental Problematics of Form and Redaction Criticism* (trans. William G. Doty; Pittsburgh: Pickwick, 1979 [1970]); Walter Schmithals, *Einleitung in die ersten drei Evangelien* (Berlin: de Gruyter, 1985); and Klaus Berger, *Formgeschichte des Neuen Testaments* (Heidelberg: Quelle & Meyer, 1984) and *Einführung in die Formgeschichte* (UTb 1444; Tübingen: Franke, 1987). We note that Theissen only cites German scholars, and does not note at this point Sanders's *Tendencies*, Humphrey Palmer's *The Logic of Gospel Criticism* (London: Macmillan, 1968), or J. Arthur Baird's *Audience Criticism and the Historical Jesus* (Philadel-

Sanders, assuming for the purposes of his study that oral and written sources follow the same principles of transmission,[9] attacked four large-scale fundamental presuppositions of form criticism regarding the transmission of tradition. Sanders examined the claims that four criteria indicated the development of the tradition: (1) increasing length, (2) increasing detail, (3) diminishing Semitisms, and (4) the (what amounts to two criteria) use of more direct discourse and the conflation of episodes. As a result of his detailed analysis, Sanders concludes: "There are no hard and fast laws of the development of the Synoptic tradition."[10] He finds through his extensive studies of the Gospels and early church tradition as recorded in the church fathers that the evidence, rather than pointing in a singular direction, is mixed. Sometimes it supports the particular assumption involved, but, on at least as many occasions as otherwise, it indicates the opposite conclusion. Therefore, *"dogmatic statements that a certain characteristic proves a certain passage to be earlier than another are never justified."*[11]

In the midst of Sanders's further research in Paul and the historical Jesus, research that still captures the imagination of most scholars, it is worthwhile considering the reception of Sanders's conclusions regarding form-critical assumptions. In this chapter, we will first examine a range of responses to Sanders's work in form-critical scholarship since publication of his *Tendencies*.[12] Then we will examine one particular form-critical study that acknowledges his significance, though does not appear to have fully appreciated the impact of his conclusions on the method and results of their study.

---

phia: Westminster, 1969), esp. 145–152, all of which precede the earliest of his works, and have damaging implications for form criticism. Sanders himself notes earlier critics (*Tendencies*, 8–29).

9   Sanders, *Tendencies*, 8. Sanders notes that this is the same assumption of Bultmann (*History*, 6), and that others also hold to this assumption. Many would no doubt wish to disagree with him on this. In any case, as Sanders states, "We investigate written tradition because that is all that is available to us" (p. 8). Some more recent linguistic research may well affect such an analysis. See Douglas Biber, *Variation across Speech and Writing* (Cambridge: Cambridge University Press, 1988).

10   Sanders, *Tendencies*, 272.

11   Sanders, *Tendencies*, 272 (italics original).

12   We do not include specific discussions of the criteria of authenticity used in historical Jesus research, although Sanders's research findings have direct significance especially for the criteria of least distinctiveness and of Semitic language and related phenomena. See Porter, *Criteria for Authenticity*, esp. 77–79, 89–99; and more recently Porter, "Criteria of Authenticity," in *Dictionary of Jesus and the Gospels* (ed. Joel B. Green, Jeannine K. Brown, and Nicholas Perrin; 2nd ed.; Downers Grove, IL: InterVarsity, 2013), 153–162.

3 Three Responses to Sanders's Work in Recent Scholarship

Since 1969, when Sanders's *Tendencies of the Synoptic Tradition* first appeared, there have been numerous major and minor responses to his work. This is not the place to attempt to survey all of them. Nevertheless, at least within predominantly English-language scholarship, we have noticed at least three distinct tendencies in the scholarly literature that merit attention because they specifically address matters related to form criticism and the transmission of tradition. These are: acceptance of Sanders's conclusions and even building upon them, ignoring of them altogether, or acknowledging but effectively neglecting them. It is from the third of these tendencies that we select one major form-critical study for further scrutiny in the last major section.

3.1 *The Acceptance of Sanders's Conclusions and Their Implications*

The first of the responses is to accept Sanders's conclusions as valid, and in several cases even to build upon them. In the light of the detailed study that Sanders performed, it is not surprising to encounter a number of scholars who find the force of his work convincing and decisive. We cite several of them. Within a decade of the appearance of Sanders's book, Ralph Martin, in a precisely outlined treatment of form criticism, noted that Sanders's work presented a challenge to one of the major axioms of form criticism, that is, that the antiquity and historical veracity of a traditional unit can be determined by definable criteria.[13] As a result of Sanders's research, William Farmer revised his four "canons of criticism" for studying the Synoptic tradition down to three, eliminating the one concerned with later traditions having increased specificity.[14] Stephen Travis, presenting a thorough case for and against form criticism, defined its axioms and major forms, before raising several questions regarding its limitations. Concerning the "main contention" of form criticism that "traditions develop from the simple to the more complex," he noted the lack of thorough analysis of these "laws of tradition." However, he noted that Sanders "has shown that in the manuscript tradition and the apocryphal gospels there are developments *both* from the simple to the more complex, *and*

---

[13] Ralph P. Martin, *New Testament Foundations: A Guide for Christian Students*. Volume 1: *The Four Gospels* (Grand Rapids: Eerdmans, 1975), 132–135, esp. 133.

[14] See William R. Farmer, *The Synoptic Problem* (New York: Macmillan, 1964), 228, changed in the second edition (Dillsboro, NC: Western North Carolina Press, 1976), 201. See C.M. Tuckett, *The Revival of the Griesbach Hypothesis: An Analysis and Appraisal* (SNTSMS 44; Cambridge: Cambridge University Press, 1983), 9–10, 190.

from the complex to the simpler."[15] Craig Blomberg has written on form criticism a number of times, each time accepting the critique offered by Sanders. In his discussion of form criticism in relation to the historical reliability of the Gospels, Blomberg rejects the so-called "laws" of transmission on the basis of Sanders's study, noting also that later, subsequent studies have demonstrated a counter-tendency to the supposed laws. Here Blomberg cites a study by Leslie Keylock, who builds upon Sanders (see below), and one by himself on the Gospel of Thomas, which indicates that detailed accounts tend toward abbreviation, condensation, and less vividness the more they are told.[16] Blomberg expands upon these comments in direct application to the parables.[17] In a major dictionary article on form criticism, Blomberg offers one of the best short definitions and treatments of form criticism. He endorses Sanders's conclusion that the "so-called law of increasing distinctness is extremely misleading." In fact, he notes that "[i]f anything, a slight tendency toward decreasing distinctness occurs with longer forms such as parables, miracle stories and other historical narratives" (he does not here name studies that endorse this tendency, but apparently means his own on the Gospel of Thomas).[18] Blomberg goes on to identify several other suspect tendencies as well, drawing upon work in the Old Testament, intertestamental writings, and rabbinic literature, such as parables ending with aphorisms, and speeches being compilations even in their earliest forms. In his fourth such study, Blomberg in his critique of form criticism simply notes that "a principle of 'decreasing distinctiveness' or abbreviation of detailed narratives was actually more common than any of the alleged laws of

---

15 Stephen H. Travis, "Form Criticism," in *New Testament Interpretation: Essays on Principles and Methods* (ed. I. Howard Marshall; Grand Rapids: Eerdmans, 1977), 153–164 (159). Travis (p. 159) also notes that regarding "folk tradition," by which he apparently means oral tradition, experts do not agree on the laws of transmission, citing Baird, *Audience Criticism*, probably 149–152.

16 Craig L. Blomberg, *The Historical Reliability of the Gospels* (Leicester: IVP, 1987), 25 and n. 3 (2nd ed., 2007, p. 54). See Leslie R. Keylock, "Bultmann's Law of Increasing Distinctness," in *Current Issues in Biblical and Patristic Interpretation* (ed. Gerald F. Hawthorne; Grand Rapids: Eerdmans, 1975), 193–210; Craig L. Blomberg, "Tradition and Redaction in the Parables of the Gospel of Thomas," in *Gospel Perspectives: The Jesus Tradition Outside the Gospels*, V (ed. David Wenham; Sheffield: JSOT Press, 1984), 177–205.

17 Craig L. Blomberg, *Interpreting the Parables* (Downers Grove, IL: InterVarsity, 1990), esp. 82–85 (2nd ed., 2012, pp. 95–98).

18 Craig L. Blomberg, "Form Criticism," in *Dictionary of Jesus and the Gospels* (ed. Joel B. Green, Scot McKnight, and I. Howard Marshall; Downers Grove, IL: InterVarsity, 1992), 243–250 (246) (the essay on form criticism in the second edition is not written by Blomberg, and so this essay is no longer so widely available).

increasing distinctness."¹⁹ In a final treatment, Blomberg again notes the tendency in the Gospels toward abbreviation as one moves from Mark to Matthew and Luke, while within the larger scope of Christian literature the tendencies are mixed.²⁰ As with Blomberg, Robert Stein in an assessment of form criticism attacks the notion of laws governing transmission of traditions. He endorses Sanders's conclusion regarding the lack of clear tendencies, if there are tendencies at all, in the written sources.²¹ Scot McKnight notes in his criticism of form criticism that Sanders has shown the laws of tradition to be "inaccurate."²² D.A. Carson, Douglas Moo, and Leon Morris endorse Sanders's finding that oral traditions do not always grow longer.²³ In another introduction to form

---

19 Craig L. Blomberg, "Historical Criticism of the New Testament," in *Foundations for Biblical Interpretation: A Complete Library of Tools and Resources* (ed. David S. Dockery, Kenneth A. Mathews, and Robert B. Sloan; Nashville: Broadman & Holman, 1994), 414–433, esp. 421–422, where he cites Keylock in support of this conclusion. But see the discussion of Keylock below.

20 Craig L. Blomberg, *Jesus and the Gospels: An Introduction and Survey* (Nashville: Broadman & Holman, 1997), 83–84 and n. 13 (2nd ed., 2009, pp. 94–95 and n. 31), citing Keylock in support of the first and Sanders for the second conclusion. But see the discussion of Keylock below. Blomberg perhaps should have cited his study of the Gospel of Thomas in support of the development of later tradition, as he does in his *Interpreting the Parables*, 84.

21 Robert H. Stein, *The Synoptic Problem: An Introduction* (Nottingham: InterVarsity, 1987), 181–182. However, Stein notes that some studies of oral tradition, as opposed to written tradition, may contradict or be mutually exclusive of patterns found in written tradition. He cites, among others, Albert B. Lord, *The Singer of Tales* (Cambridge, MA: Harvard University Press, 1960), 128, and Werner H. Kelber, *The Oral and the Written Gospel* (Philadelphia: Fortress, 1983), 14–32. In any case, he notes that "we then possess neither any clear 'laws' as to how the gospel traditions developed during the oral period, nor even any tendencies about which we can be certain!" (p. 182). In the second edition of this book, Stein (*Studying the Synoptic Gospels: Origin and Interpretation* [Grand Rapids: Baker, 2001], 191 n. 61) notes that the "disjunction between oral and written tradition suggested by Kelber, however, is itself being challenged," citing Shemaryahu Talmon, "Oral Tradition and Written Transmission, or the Heard and the Seen Word in Judaism of the Second Temple Period," in *Jesus and the Oral Gospel* (ed. Henry Wansbrough; JSNTSup 64; Sheffield: JSOT Press, 1991), 158. Kelber himself seems to have recognized this; see the "Introduction" (pp. xix–xxxi), in the reprint (Bloomington: Indiana University Press, 1997), where he notes (xxi) his "polarity of orality versus textuality," and seems to concede Joanna Dewey's criticism that "oral operations (presentation and hearing) and literary operations (reading and writing) were ... inescapably interlocked" in the ancient world (Dewey, "Textuality in an Oral Culture: A Survey of the Pauline Traditions," *Semeia* 65 [1994]: 37–65 [45]).

22 Scot McKnight, *Interpreting the Synoptic Gospels* (Grand Rapids: Baker, 1988), 77.

23 D.A. Carson, Douglas J. Moo, and Leon L. Morris, *An Introduction to the New Testament*

criticism, Darrell Bock cites Sanders against those who assumed that "accounts expanded as they got older,"[24] and summarizes these findings in a later study.[25] Finally, James Dunn recognizes that Sanders's position contradicts Bultmann's laws regarding tradition.[26] One could probably find more such studies, but these suffice to show Sanders's acceptance in a variety of sources.

There are three treatments, however, that we wish to note that expand upon and develop the findings of Sanders. The first, already mentioned above, is by Leslie Keylock. Keylock commends the work of Sanders on the postcanonical tradition and the Synoptic Gospels, as showing that Bultmann's hypotheses regarding the tendencies of the tradition cannot be substantiated. However, Keylock believes that there are a number of observational factors where Sanders can be improved. He suggests focusing exclusively upon the Synoptic Gospels and using a more refined method for examination of what constitutes a change in text that indicates increased or decreased distinctiveness. As a result, he compiles six tables: Luke being more/less precise than Mark, Matthew being more/less precise than Mark, and Matthew being more/less precise than Luke. Once he has gathered the data and attempted to explain the changes in accounts, Keylock differentiates the causes of the changes that have occurred. He believes that most changes can be accounted for simply on the basis of redaction, rather than invoking the kinds of fanciful and novelistic changes he claims Bultmann was advocating. In the end, Keylock, like Sanders, concludes that the data do "not indicate the existence of a tendency or 'law' of increasing distinctness, at least not in the form in which it is stated in the

---

(Grand Rapids: Zondervan, 1992), 25 (the second edition, by Carson and Moo, 2005, p. 84, has essentially the same statement, while correcting reference to the "criterion of authenticity" to "criterion of dissimilarity").

24   Darrell L. Bock, "Form Criticism," in *New Testament Interpretation and Criticism* (ed. David Alan Black and David S. Dockery; Grand Rapids: Zondervan, 1991), 175–196 (175) (also in the revised edition, *Interpreting the New Testament: Essays on Methods and Issues* [Nashville: Broadman & Holman, 2001], 106–127 [110]).

25   Darrell L. Bock, *Studying the Historical Jesus: A Guide to Sources and Methods* (Grand Rapids: Baker, 2002), 184.

26   James D.G. Dunn, *Jesus Remembered* (Christianity in the Making 1; Grand Rapids: Eerdmans, 2003), 194 n. 112, n. 114. However, note that Dunn minimizes Sanders's contribution for failing to distinguish between rules for oral and written tradition (p. 195 n. 118). This paper is not a discussion of the relation between oral and written tradition, but an examination of the impact of Sanders's *Tendencies*. However, Dunn states, "We certainly do not know enough about oral traditioning in the ancient world to draw from that knowledge clear guidelines for our understanding of how the Jesus tradition was passed down in its oral stage" (*Jesus Remembered*, 210). Sanders thinks the same (*Tendencies*, 18 n. 4).

writings of Rudolf Bultmann ... In no instance did we note a clear-cut case of imaginative or fanciful, 'novelistic' interest such as is apparently common in the apocryphal NT literature and other post-apostolic writings ..." With Sanders, Keylock notes that, "Instead of a single tendency of the traditions to develop definition, in fact, there appears to have been a dual tendency at work in which some materials tended to become more distinct and others tended to become less precise."[27]

The second work that develops Sanders's insights is N.T. Wright's advocacy of what he calls a "revised form-criticism."[28] Wright first reviews traditional form criticism in the light of his previous discussion of Jesus and the Gospels. He recognizes the importance of form criticism, but also notes three misunderstandings: it is not a method to investigate Jesus, but rather the early church; it is not necessarily linked with one particular theory regarding the early church and its development; and it tends to create a false disjunction between Jesus and the early church. In the light of this, Wright attempts a new set of form-critical categories, within a framework in which "traditions *both* expand *and* contract," not accepting "simplistic developmental theories either way."[29] He notes that Sanders is the one to consult "above all" on this point.[30] Wright then goes on to define his new form-critical units: prophetic acts, controversies, parables, and longer units such as Mark 13 and the so-called passion narrative. In some instances, the stories resemble traditional form-critical categories (e.g. a miracle story, Wright contends, can hardly be told any other way), while in others Wright sees more complex developed forms from inception (e.g. Mark 4:1–20).

Richard Bauckham, as a third and final extended example, has accepted and extended Sanders's work even further. In his *Jesus and the Eyewitnesses*, Bauckham notes that Bultmann endorsed the law of increasing detail, while Henry Cadbury claimed that the opposite occurred.[31] Sanders himself recognized the diversity of opinion on this particular issue, citing numerous scholars on both sides of the divide, before undertaking to examine criteria in both the post-apostolic tradition and the Gospels themselves. Sanders concludes that the "simple priority of any one Gospel to the others cannot be demonstrated by

---

27 Keylock, "Bultmann's Law," 210.
28 N.T. Wright, *The New Testament and the People of God* (London: SPCK, 1992), 427.
29 Wright, *New Testament*, 429.
30 Wright, *New Testament*, 429 n. 31.
31 Richard Bauckham, *Jesus and the Eyewitnesses: The Gospels as Eyewitness Testimony* (Grand Rapids: Eerdmans, 2006), 40–41, citing Henry J. Cadbury, *The Making of Luke–Acts* (London: Macmillan, 1927), 59.

the evidence" regarding increasing detail. Further, "we must conclude that the principal lesson to be learned from the study of details is that of caution. It is clear that the criterion of detail should not be used too quickly to establish the relative antiquity of one document to another."[32] Bauckham runs a similar test regarding names in the Gospels, other than those of the twelve disciples and public people, a specific test that Sanders did not perform. When performed, however, Bauckham concludes similarly to Sanders: "The material common to the three Synoptic Gospels therefore shows an unambiguous tendency toward the elimination of names, which refutes Bultmann's argument, so long as one accepts Markan priority, as Bultmann did." Bauckham goes on to note that most of the names that he has studied "belonged originally to the Gospel traditions in which they are found," and uses these findings to suggest that the best explanation is that these people were "well known at least in the circles in which these traditions were first transmitted."[33]

Without attempting a comprehensive study, we have found that a significant number of scholars from the beginning have endorsed Sanders's conclusions, and even built upon them, expanding the scope of his original study.

3.2 The Ignoring of Sanders's Conclusions

In the light of the thoroughness of Sanders's conclusions, it is perhaps surprising that there are those discussing form criticism who appear to ignore his conclusions altogether. Nevertheless, such is the case in a number of instances. For example, in examples chronologically arranged, Graham Stanton conducts his excellent discussion of "Form Criticism Revisited," which criticism he labels as a "stagnant discipline," without mentioning Sanders's study or its possible impact on the laws of tradition.[34] Similarly, and perhaps even more surprisingly, Earle Ellis can discuss "New Directions in Form Criticism," which involves treatment (among other topics) of both oral transmission and, on the basis of use of Greek in Palestine and by Jesus's earliest followers, early written traditions, without mentioning Sanders's work,[35] and Ellis can purport to offer a "perspective on

---

32 Sanders, *Tendencies*, 188. Sanders does note (p. 189), however, that the post-canonical tradition does become more detailed in a number of instances.

33 Bauckham, *Jesus*, 45.

34 Graham N. Stanton, "Form Criticism Revisited," in *What about the New Testament? Essays in Honor of Christopher Evans* (ed. Morna D. Hooker and Colin J. Hickling; London: SCM, 1975), 13–27 (13).

35 E. Earle Ellis, "New Directions in Form Criticism," reprinted in Ellis, *Prophecy and Hermeneutic in Early Christianity: New Testament Essays* (Grand Rapids: Eerdmans, 1978), 237–253.

the state of the art" in Gospel criticism with a similar lack of discussion.[36] Several treatments of form criticism within larger reference and related works are no better. There is no discussion of Sanders's work on the tendencies of the Synoptic tradition in, as a random sampling of works, Raymond Collins's introduction to the New Testament, Conzelmann and Lindemann's introduction to New Testament exegesis, Tom Wright's update of Stephen Neill's history of New Testament interpretation (but note above), Edgar McKnight's treatment of form criticism in *The New Testament and Its Modern Interpreters*, Robert Gundry's treatment of form criticism in his introduction, Bruce Chilton in his discussion of traditio-historical criticism, Luke Timothy Johnson in his bibliographical survey of form criticism, Klaus Berger in his dictionary survey, or Michael Burer on form criticism within narrative.[37] Even a relatively recent discussion of historical Jesus research does not treat Sanders's important research. Gerd Theissen and Annette Merz, although they treat form criticism throughout and in some detail, do not appear to mention Sanders.[38] Some works appear even to argue contrary to Sanders. Norman Perrin and Dennis Duling's introduction to the New Testament adopt Bultmann's form-critical framework and discuss the relative age of Gospel traditions on the basis of distinctive features, with no

---

36   E. Earle Ellis, "Gospels Criticism: A Perspective on the State of the Art," in *The Gospel and the Gospels* (ed. Peter Stuhlmacher; Grand Rapids: Eerdmans, 1991), 26–52.

37   Raymond F. Collins, *Introduction to the New Testament* (Garden City, NY: Doubleday, 1983), 156–195; Hans Conzelmann and Andreas Lindemann, *Interpreting the New Testament: An Introduction to the Principles and Methods of N.T. Exegesis* (trans. Siegfried S. Schatzmann; Peabody, MA: Hendrickson, 1988 [1985]), 59–82; Stephen Neill and Tom Wright, *The Interpretation of the New Testament 1861–1986* (2nd ed.; Oxford: Oxford University Press, 1988), 363, though Wright knows other works by Sanders; Edgar V. McKnight, "Form and Redaction Criticism," in *The New Testament and its Modern Interpreters* (ed. Eldon Jay Epp and George W. MacRae; Atlanta: Scholars Press, 1989), 149–174, esp. 150–152; Robert H. Gundry, *A Survey of the New Testament* (rev. ed.; Grand Rapids: Zondervan, 1981 [the first edition of 1970 probably appeared too late to take it into consideration]), 68–71 (and still not in the 4th ed., 2003, 96–101); Bruce Chilton, "Traditio-Historical Criticism and Study of Jesus," in *Hearing the New Testament: Strategies for Interpretation* (ed. Joel B. Green; Grand Rapids: Eerdmans, 1995), 37–60 (an essay not included in the second edition of 2010); Luke Timothy Johnson with Todd C. Penner, *The Writings of the New Testament: An Interpretation* (rev. ed.; Minneapolis: Fortress, 1999), 152–153; Klaus Berger, "New Testament Form Criticism," in *Methods of Biblical Interpretation* (Nashville: Abingdon, 2004 [1999]), 121–126; and Michael H. Burer, "Narrative Genre: Studying the Story," in *Interpreting the New Testament Text: Introduction to the Art and Science of Exegesis* (ed. Darrell L. Bock and Buist M. Fanning; Wheaton, IL: Crossway, 2006), 197–220, esp. 204–205.

38   Gerd Theissen and Annette Merz, *The Historical Jesus: A Comprehensive Guide* (London: SCM Press, 1998).

mention of Sanders's findings.[39] Raymond Brown also seems to be unaware of the significance of Sanders's work, as he claims that "The absence or presence of an expected feature in a particular parable or miracle story, therefore, can be studied to help determine how that parable or story was passed down in the tradition."[40]

In the light of the positive response among many scholars, it is disappointing to see the number of scholars who have apparently not come across, or who have simply chosen to ignore or not accept (though without argument), Sanders's conclusions regarding the tendencies of the Synoptic tradition.

3.3 *The Pre-citation Fallacy with Reference to Sanders's Conclusions*

The third category of responses includes those who acknowledge Sanders's work, but who, in effect, overlook it in terms of their treatment of issues related to form criticism. These scholars commit what we have above termed the pre-citation fallacy. In his well-known treatment of the disjunction between oral and written tradition, Werner Kelber, in the midst of his discussion of Bultmann, acknowledges the work of Sanders, calling it "one of the more perceptive critiques."[41] He acknowledges that Sanders perceived that Bultmann did not glean his laws of tradition from actual study of folk literature, as these types of laws are not emphasized in the study of such folk literature. Kelber is dissatisfied that Sanders failed to pursue such a study himself, but chose to study the written Gospel tradition and the post-canonical authors, believing that the tendencies of the two traditions are similar. This is the only place in his monograph that Kelber refers to Sanders's work on the Synoptic tradition. This isolated reference includes Kelber's new introduction, which acknowledges that perhaps his disjunction between oral and written tradition was too strong, or at least that he polemicized it for the sake of emphasis.[42]

In his overview of Gospel criticism, Craig Evans notes at the outset of his discussion of form criticism that "We really do not know what the practices were of first-century Christians who told and retold the sayings of and stories

---

39 Norman Perrin and Dennis C. Duling, *The New Testament: An Introduction* (2nd ed.; San Diego: Harcourt Brace Jovanovich, 1982), 401–404.

40 Raymond E. Brown, *An Introduction to the New Testament* (New York: Doubleday, 1997), 22–23.

41 Kelber, *The Oral and the Written Gospel*, 7.

42 Kelber, *The Oral and the Written Gospel*, xxi–xxiv. Many of these issues are addressed in Samuel Byrskog, *Story as History—History as Story* (WUNT 125; Tübingen: Mohr Siebeck, 2000).

about Jesus," citing Sanders's work in a footnote.[43] However, when Evans turns to an example for discussion, he treats the parable of the pounds in Luke 19:11–27 as probably a combination of two other shorter parables, one of the pounds (Luke 19:13, 15b–24) and one of the throne claimant (Luke 19:12, 14–15a, 27), from which "[m]ost of the components of these parables have been preserved and can be reconstructed."[44] He then offers a traditional interpretation of the parable and a form-critical analysis. In the form-critical interpretation, he uses as criteria, for example, christological allegorical features as being later characteristics. He also notes further details that he sees as later, as the parable was shaped from its original context in the life of Jesus to one in the early church. It appears that the findings of Sanders have not entered into this interpretive discussion. In a later treatment of form criticism, Evans does not mention Sanders at all.[45] More obvious still is David Catchpole's treatment. He notes that "debate has not ceased over the so-called tendencies of the Synoptic tradition," citing Sanders's work, but then Catchpole states that, nonetheless, "there are certain typical principles that have commended themselves widely."[46] One he cites, from the commentary by W.D. Davies and Dale Allison on Matthew, is that "the general tendency of early Christology ... was from the lesser to the greater,"[47] in other words, increase in detail, one of the very assumptions Sanders disputes. Another is that "it is easier to understand the removal than the deliberate insertion of details which might cast a shadow across the figure of Jesus."[48] He then illustrates these criteria in his treatment of several passages. For example, he

---

43 Craig A. Evans, "Source, Form and Redaction Criticism: The 'Traditional' Methods of Synoptic Interpretation," in *Approaches to New Testament Study* (ed. Stanley E. Porter and David Tombs; JSNTSup 120; Sheffield: JSOT Press, 1995), 17–45, esp. 27–32 (28).
44 Evans, "Source," 31.
45 Craig A. Evans, "Form Criticism," in *Encyclopedia of the Historical Jesus* (ed. Craig A. Evans; London: Routledge, 2007), 204–208.
46 David R. Catchpole, "Source, Form and Redaction Criticism of the New Testament," in *Handbook to Exegesis of the New Testament* (ed. Stanley E. Porter; NTTS 25; Leiden: Brill, 1997), 167–188 (171).
47 Catchpole, "Source," 171, citing W.D. Davies and Dale Allison, Jr., *The Gospel according to Saint Matthew*, I (ICC; Edinburgh: T&T Clark, 1988), 104 (which reads: "general direction," not "general tendency"). Davies and Allison present a more nuanced discussion than Catchpole summarizes, noting above that arguments for the priority of Mark over Matthew using grammatical criteria have been weakened by Sanders's work. However, it is worth observing that the example that Catchpole cites is not one of the examples cited by Davies and Allison on pp. 104–105. In fact, their types of passages are of a different type than the one cited by Catchpole.
48 Catchpole, "Source," 171.

contends, on the basis of his criteria, that "it defies credibility and demands intolerable credulity" to think that Mark had Matthew's Gospel and abbreviated Peter's confession in Matt 16:16 to Mark 8:29.[49]

There are clearly those who have not fully grasped the interpretive significance of Sanders's work on the tendencies of the Synoptic tradition. Whereas some scholars recognize that his arguments must be taken into account, clearly the traditions of form criticism remain deeply embedded in the scholarly ethos.

4   The Pre-citation Fallacy and Gerd Theissen's Social Context Theory

Gerd Theissen's treatment of the social context of the Gospels is one such study—it recognizes the significance of Sanders's work, but finds it difficult to extricate its arguments from the form-critical precedent. As noted above, Theissen recognizes that form criticism has undergone revision in the light of criticism offered by such scholars (he names) as Güttgemanns, Schmithals, and Berger, and so he sees his work as in some ways a new means of creating the "history of the synoptic tradition" without relying upon classical form criticism.[50] Theissen summarizes four common critiques of form criticism: determination of literary-critical layers of the text, including separation of primary, secondary, and tertiary textual elements, is arbitrary; it is naïve to believe in "pure forms"; the recognition has grown that reconstructing the *Sitz im Leben* for oral transmission is extremely difficult; and there are no consistent Synoptic tendencies, in which he highlights Sanders's critique of consistent tendencies in transmission of tradition.[51] Nevertheless, despite these difficulties, Theissen wishes to revive what he would contend is a more robust version of form criticism, drawing especially upon social and political historical considerations.

Theissen's model of form criticism is best explained as follows. There are three layers of tradition according to Theissen, organized around what he calls dislocations of place. The most primitive layer of tradition originated in Galilee, and spread throughout surrounding regions. The tradition is earliest, not least because Jesus was from Galilee. This layer of tradition includes "smaller" units of what is ultimately Gospel tradition, such as tradition from the sayings source (Q), the miracles stories, and apothegms. A second stage in the history of this

---

49   Catchpole, "Source," 171–172 (171).
50   Theissen, *Gospels in Context*, 2.
51   Theissen, *Gospels in Context*, 5 (we reverse the third and fourth criteria). Theissen (p. 5 n. 10) also wishes to recognize issues regarding what he calls "the conflicting character of written and oral tradition," citing Kelber, *The Oral and the Written Gospel*.

Synoptic tradition, according to Theissen, develops in and around Jerusalem. Here he has in mind two "large" units, the Markan apocalypse and the passion account. The second stage was reached as early as ten years after Jesus's death. The "core of the synoptic apocalypse dates from the Caligula crisis of 40 C.E., and the oldest Passion account could have been shaped in the 40s as well."[52] The final stage occurs outside of Jerusalem, with the writing of the Synoptic Gospels.[53] Although none of the Gospels were written in Palestine, according to Theissen, Mark reflects a "neighborhood perspective" and was probably written in Syrophonecia, just north of Palestine, a region that, according to Theissen, would have been reached by the popular stories of Jesus.[54] Matthew reflects an eastern perspective, "beyond the Jordan," whereas Luke writes from the wider world of the cities of the Mediterranean.[55] Essential to Theissen's theory, and emphasized throughout his book, is the presupposition that smaller units represent earlier material and larger units relate later developments within the Synoptic tradition. Social and political considerations are then used to support the respective dates of composition of longer and shorter units of tradition. Theissen states, "The large units are thus distinguished from the small by greater complexity, individuality, and 'literary' character. In them, the movement from oral tradition to the Gospels is already underway. Precisely for this reason, it is important for a history of the Synoptic tradition that we give a more exact account of their historical context as revealed by indications of time and place."[56] According to Theissen, what "demonstrates that we are at a second stage," as opposed to the first, is the fact that "Jesus traditions were being transmitted not merely in small units, but in longer complexes."[57]

We recognize the fact that Theissen has understood the purport of Sanders's work on the tendencies of the Synoptic tradition and wishes to take cognizance of these findings into his revised theory. We further commend Theissen for, in the light of these findings, wanting to develop a new means by which he can trace the history of the Synoptic tradition. Nevertheless, there are a number of comments that may be made in response to Theissen and his approach. The first, and most important, concerns the issues of length and detail. As Sanders concludes regarding the tendencies of the Synoptic tradition, "On all counts the tradition developed in opposite directions. It became both longer

---

52 Theissen, *Gospels in Context*, 290.
53 Theissen, *Gospels in Context*, 290; see also pp. 2–5, and throughout the book.
54 Theissen, *Gospels in Context*, 290.
55 Theissen, *Gospels in Context*, 291.
56 Theissen, *Gospels in Context*, 123–124.
57 Theissen, *Gospels in Context*, 290.

and shorter, both more and less detailed ..."[58] Sanders draws this conclusion on the basis of two major sections of investigation in his work. The first section, concerning length, applies a number of different criteria to the Gospels and the post-apostolic tradition. He examines such features as the use of Old Testament quotations, speeches, dialogues, scenes, and actions in the Gospels, as well as similar features in the post-apostolic material. Concerning the use of Old Testament quotations, speeches, and dialogues, Sanders finds that one cannot determine earlier and later traditions on the basis of their presence or absence, or variations in length. However, Mark, Sanders notes, is longer than Matthew and Luke in terms of new scenes and physical actions.[59] The second section, concerning detail, contains a wide range of linguistically based studies. The results regarding Synoptic relations are mixed, and cannot be reliably used to determine the relative temporal relations of the documents, that is, which are earlier and which later.

Theissen, however, clearly uses the criteria of length and detail as the bases for his method to recover the history of the Synoptic tradition. He uses these in two ways. In the first, he simply assumes, despite the evidence that Sanders has provided, that a shorter unit is earlier than a longer unit. For example, at the very outset, before he has even discussed Sanders's work, Theissen states that "We will also maintain the second basic postulate of form-critical investigation, namely, the notion of small, individual units," and that the Jesus tradition is the product of combining these small, individual traditional units.[60] In regard to Mark 13 specifically, as an example, Theissen states further that the mini-apocalypse assumes previous earlier sayings regarding the future of the son of man and places them within a new Gospel context. By placing them in this new context, the previous "small units" of tradition are abandoned in order to form this new, complex unit of material. As Theissen says, "this is a longer text with a complex structure. Probably it existed in written form, which means that we have to acknowledge an early transition from oral to written tradition,"[61] but still a transition from smaller units to the larger one.[62] Theissen does not counter the evidence that Sanders has marshaled in an attempt to show how he is justified in beginning from this assumption; instead, he merely invokes it as a basic postulate. Sanders has called such a postulate into serious question,

---

58 Sanders, *Tendencies*, 272.
59 Sanders, *Tendencies*, 82–83.
60 Theissen, *Gospels in Context*, 4.
61 Theissen, *Gospels in Context*, 165.
62 This hypothesis has been called into question on other grounds. See Wright, *New Testament*, 392–395; Porter, *Criteria for Authenticity*, 210–237.

to the point of anyone utilizing such a theory needing to argue for its foundation, rather than simply assuming it. Therefore, the foundation upon which Theissen rests his case is highly vulnerable.

In the second way in which he uses the criteria of length and detail, Theissen correlates small unit length with specific geographical locations. As one of the major examples that he develops, Theissen assumes that the small unit in Matt 11:7 regarding John the Baptist as the shaken reed implies a specific geographical location and with it a specific time. Theissen claims that Matt 11:7 can be located in the twenties CE because of a coin minted for only three years by Herod Antipas.[63] What we see Theissen doing here is substituting literary characteristics for linguistic characteristics. Sanders performed his studies on the basis of definable linguistic features that either were or were not expressed in the Gospels. Theissen has substituted such literary characteristics as geographical or political or social factors for such linguistic characteristics, and then argued to the same conclusion of an early date. However, if it is questionable that these linguistic characteristics are reliable for determining the relative antiquity of traditions, what reason is there for believing that geographical or other features are more reliable? Theissen does not argue for them, nor does he show how they might be reliable. His example of a reed in Matt 11:7, although it has a Synoptic parallel in Luke 7:24, is not studied by Sanders because of a lack of the linguistic features that he analyzes. However, if we consider it as an element of specific detail, we note that it may or may not indicate earlier or later tradition. If it does not, then Theissen's entire reconstruction, including location and date, does not follow. As Sanders has said, one cannot be dogmatic about drawing conclusions concerning the date of a unit of tradition based on individual characteristics of that tradition. Instead one must be cautious in drawing such conclusions.[64]

A final example from Theissen's new form-critical approach is his use of the Old Testament. Theissen claims that "all the major units [by which Theissen means large or long units] are marked by Old Testament quotations, allusions, or motifs."[65] The oldest tradition, formed in Galilee, according to Theissen, would have spread to other regions, including Jerusalem, where the next level of tradition was formed around Old Testament quotations. According to Theissen, larger units which were composed in Jerusalem as the second major stage in the history of the Synoptic tradition were, on the basis of their location, "closer" to

---

63 Theissen, *Gospels in Context*, 26–39. For pictures of the coins involved in his discussion, see p. 30.
64 Sanders, *Tendencies*, 272.
65 Theissen, *Gospels in Context*, 123.

the Scriptures and therefore utilized Old Testament quotations, allusions, and motifs more readily than did smaller units, which were located at a distance from Jerusalem. Larger units, which cite the Old Testament, so Theissen posits, reflect "a milieu in which the Scriptures were familiar," such as Jerusalem.[66] In his work, Sanders had already addressed the issue of the use of Old Testament quotations. In his study of increasing length, he notes additions or omissions of Old Testament quotations in the post-canonical tradition, and Old Testament quotations in one Gospel but not another.[67] Sanders concludes that there is no clear tendency to be observed in the use of Old Testament quotations in the various Gospels. This leaves Theissen without one of his major planks for establishing the second level of tradition.

In conclusion, Theissen, although to be commended for wishing to develop a new approach to reconstructing the history of the Synoptic tradition, is still nevertheless vulnerable in terms of three major areas. The first vulnerability is in terms of the major assumption of his study, that is, that small units precede longer units. In the light of Sanders's work, there is simply not such a platform in place as a basis for historical reconstruction. The second vulnerability is in terms of the establishment of the first major stage of his developmental hypothesis. For establishing this first major stage, Theissen relies upon establishing shorter units in particular locations as the basis of the growth of larger units in other locations. Not only is his initial assumption suspect—he never answers Sanders's work—but the basis of his first stage cannot be substantiated. Further, his use of the example of the reed in Matt 11:7 simply substitutes a literary for a linguistic characteristic, and does not substantiate the locative case that he needs to make. The third vulnerability is that the second stage of development is itself also unfounded. The evidence that Theissen wishes to use regarding Old Testament quotations has already been shown by Sanders to be at best ambiguous, and at the least insufficient to establish such a level of analysis. As we have indicated by means of our analysis above, Theissen is elusive in his formulation and development of his complex argument, so that it is difficult to note the points of logical correlation and the basis of his argument. He posits a number of suppositions that are never more fully developed. His primary interest is clearly in marshalling geographical, political, and social factors in the interest of reconstructing the history of the Synoptic tradition. However, as interesting as such information may be, it is placed upon an insecure foundation that has already been undermined by the work of Sanders. Therefore,

---

66   Theissen, *Gospels in Context*, 123.
67   Sanders, *Tendencies*, 53–54, 69–70.

Theissen's acceptance of Sanders's results in his introductory remarks (thus, it is a *pre*-citation) ends up undermining his entire argument since Sanders's analysis runs contrary to the major conclusions and assumptions of Theissen's study.

5 Conclusion

This paper has attempted to survey, both in some breadth and in some detail, responses to E.P. Sanders's *The Tendencies of the Synoptic Tradition* in the light of a common threefold pattern of scholarly response to significant research. Now that the survey has been concluded, what conclusions can we draw from it? A very clear conclusion is that there are a number of scholars who have in varying ways and to varying degrees accepted, and even expanded upon, the arguments that Sanders laid down nearly fifty years ago. However, the amount of work, so far as we have readily discovered it, that has gone well beyond Sanders is still relatively minimal compared to those who are simply content to accept his conclusions. Nevertheless, there are still those who, either through ignorance or simple defiance, have rejected Sanders's findings, and have continued to view form criticism on the basis of the work of those whom Sanders has refuted. There are even some, such as Theissen, who, while acknowledging Sanders's contribution, have found it difficult, if not impossible, to realize or incorporate the serious implications of his work into their form-critical research. We refer to this tendency as the pre-citation fallacy in New Testament scholarship. In the case of Sanders's research, what used to be basic assumptions of form criticism concerning matters of length, detail, Semitic features, use of direct discourse, and conflation have all been called into question. Before a new, improved, or future incarnation of form criticism can be unveiled, the results of Sanders's fundamental research must be taken fully into account instead of acknowledging his work in various introductory remarks but essentially ignoring it in subsequent analysis.

Was Matthew a Plagiarist? Plagiarism in Greco-Roman Antiquity

E. Randolph Richards

1   Introduction

New Testament scholars often accept as a given the assertion well stated by the Jesus Seminar: "The concept of plagiarism was unknown in the ancient world. Authors freely copied from predecessors without acknowledgment."[1] When looking at our Gospels, this assertion seems prima facie true, perhaps lending to its common acceptance. If however plagiarism was known (and condemned) in antiquity, then we are justified in asking if the Gospel of Matthew, for example, is guilty of plagiarizing the Gospel of Mark, *i.e.*, Was Matthew a plagiarist?

Introductory textbooks on Gospel studies typically note that approximately 90% of Mark is found in Matthew. It is not merely wording but also the general presentation of the Jesus story.[2] This essay is not the place to reargue the Synoptic problem. William Farmer has presented what is perhaps the best recent assertion of Matthean priority,[3] but I remain unconvinced. Markan priority will be assumed for the essay. Again, since the topic is more technically plagiarism in the Synoptic Gospels, the point would remain if we had asserted Mark plagiarized Matthew.

2   Setting the Stage

One of the best recent discussions of ancient plagiarism is found in Bart Ehrman, *Forgery and Counterforgery: The Use of Literary Deceit in Early Christian Polemics*.[4] It is a well-researched, careful scholarly work and we are

---

[1]   *The Five Gospels: The Search for the Authentic Words of Jesus* (ed. Robert Funk, Roy W. Hoover, and the Jesus Seminar; New York: Polebridge, 1993), 22.

[2]   See, e.g., Mark Strauss, *Four Portraits, One Jesus: A Survey of Jesus and the Gospels* (Grand Rapids: Zondervan, 2007), 48–52.

[3]   William R. Farmer, *The Synoptic Problem* (repr., Macon, GA: Mercer University Press, 1981).

[4]   Bart D. Ehrman, *Forgery and Counterforgery: The Use of Literary Deceit in Early Christian Polemics* (Oxford: Oxford University Press, 2012).

indebted to him.⁵ This is not a review of his book⁶ nor will I be responding to most of the book. Rather, I will be reacting to and building upon a very small section of his work where he addresses plagiarism to see if his definition requires nuancing.⁷

Ehrman's section on plagiarism reaffirms the conclusion that ancients viewed plagiarism as wrong, as thievery.⁸ He assumes the theft was of intellectual property. The question for this essay is what exactly was stolen, since this will bear upon the discussion of Matthew's use of Mark.

2.1 Definitions

Forgery and plagiarism are related issues and commonly discussed together but they are distinct ideas.

2.1.1 Forgery

Ehrman notes that some scholars object to the term forgery, preferring terms like pseudonymity or pseudepigraphy. In fact, to avoid even the use of the term pseudo-, I.H. Marshall has suggested New Testament scholars use allonymity

---

5   His discussion of my work on secretaries in Greco–Roman antiquity is gracious, but he and I will fundamentally disagree on how to conclude from the ample evidence. He states: "Somewhat less commendable are the conclusions that Richards draws, at times independently of this evidence" (Ehrman, *Forgery*, 218). I think my conclusions are merited. He notes the evidence "does indicate that a secretary would *occasionally* edit an author's letter stylistically" [emphasis is mine, not his] and asks, "Could this not explain, then, why Colossians differs so significantly (in style) from the other Pauline letters?" (219). This is the proper question and I believe the answer is yes but he concludes no. Secretaries edited more than merely "occasionally." I suspect this was one of the reasons for hiring a good secretary. This conversation, however, is for another day. See E. Randolph Richards, *The Secretary in the Letters of Paul* (WUNT 2.42; Tübingen: Mohr Siebeck, 1991); Richards, *Paul and First Century Letter Writing: Secretaries, Composition, and Collection* (Downers Grove, IL: InterVarsity, 2004); and Ehrman, *Forgery*, 218–222.

6   For a recent review, see Armin Baum, "Review of Bart D. Ehrman, *Forgery and Counterforgery*," *NovT* 56 (2014): 428–431.

7   There are some (including me) who have critiqued other, more popular, books by Bart Ehrman for (what seems to me) playing a bit loose with the facts. While popular books have the right to speak in generalities and make broad, sweeping statements, I consider some of his earlier comments to be irresponsible. He would no doubt disagree. Nonetheless, the scholarly quality of this recent work on ancient forgery differs significantly from his earlier, popular book: Bart Ehrman, *Forged: Writing in the Name of God—Why the Bible's Authors Are Not Who We Think They Are* (New York: HarperOne, 2011).

8   So Bernard Legras demonstrates in his excellent study on plagiarism: "le plagiaire est un voleur (κλέπης) et le plagiat un vol (κλοπή)"; "La sanction du plagiat littéraire en droit

and allopigraphy, since Marshall is convinced the author—not Paul—who penned the Pastorals was not intending to deceive anyone.[9] Pseudonymous writings describe all works where the author's true name is not used. This includes writings under a pen name.[10] Pseudepigrapha are more specifically writings falsely claiming to be the work of someone else who was a real author.[11] It would not include anonymous works incorrectly ascribed by others to a real author (such as Hebrews). Ehrman also introduces a new term, counterforgery, to refer to forged works designed to rebut another forgery. His added distinction is unnecessary here.

2.1.2 Plagiarism

Plagiarism can be simply defined as "taking over the work of another and claiming it as one's own ... he obviously has borrowed the work of another without acknowledgment, or as the ancient sources would put it, he has 'stolen' his work."[12] Ehrman unnecessarily nuances the definition by excluding plagiarism that occurs in a forged work. For example, he doesn't discuss as plagiarism when 2 Peter "borrowed a good deal" of Jude. His reason is that since both books are forgeries, a forger cannot commit plagiarism, since he isn't claiming the plagiarized material as his (as the real author) own words. This is an unnecessary distinction. Would Samuel Clemens be innocent of plagiarism as long as he wrote under the name Mark Twain?

---

grec et hellénistique," in *Symposion 1999* (Festschrift for Joseph Mélèze Modrzejewski; ed. E. Cantarella and G. Thür; Cologne: Böhlau, 2003), 443–461 (446).

9   I.H. Marshall, *The Pastoral Epistles* (ICC; Edinburgh: T&T Clark, 1999), 83–84. I have respectfully disagreed previously with Prof. Marshall. I agree with Ehrman's conclusion that Marshall "is precisely wrong" (*Forgery*, 33 n. 9).

10 An example is Mark Twain. Ehrman notes that even pen names are not necessarily "innocent," citing Mary Anne Evans's use of the pen name George Eliot for the benefits of a male name or Xenophon's use of Themistogenes (*Forgery*, 29–30).

11 Ehrman, *Forgery*, 29. He notes especially the distinction by Eve-Marie Becker: "Die Begriffe Pseudepigraphie und Pseudonymität wird ein fiktiver Autor gewählt, bei der Pseudepigraphie wird das Werk einem realen Autor zugeschrieben." Becker, "Von Paulus zu 'Paulus': Paulinische Pseudepigraphie-Forschung als literaturgeschichtliche Aufgabe," in *Pseudepigraphie und Verfasserfiktion in frühchristlichen Briefen* (ed. Jörg Frey, Jens Herzer, Martina Janssen, and Clare K. Rothschild; WUNT 246; Tübingen: Mohr Siebeck, 2009), 376.

12 Ehrman, *Forgery*, 55.

2.1.3 The Ancient Perception of Forgery

Ehrman has contributed significantly to our understanding of ancient forgery by defining more carefully pseudonymity and by critiquing common modern contentions for innocent pseudepigrapha.

2.1.3.1 *Drawing the Lines More Clearly*

While referring to pseudepigrapha as forgery may be deemed pejorative by many, I agree with Ehrman that it is not inaccurate.[13] Ancients refer to ψευδεπίγραφα (pseudepigrapha), commonly labeling them a lie (ψεῦδος), a bastard (νόθος), and a counterfeit (κίβδηλος).[14] A plagiarist was commonly called a thief.[15] When an ancient wished to exonerate the author of a pseudepigraphon, he clarified with a phrase like καθ' ἀγνοίαν.[16]

Ehrman does, however, assert that he is not attempting to pass judgment on those canonical works he labels forgery:

> When I call a text forged I am making a literary-historical claim about its author; I do not mean to imply any kind of value judgment concerning its content or its merit as a literary text (religious, theological, ethical, personal, or any other kind of merit). In particular, I am not claiming that it is somehow inferior in these ways to a work that is orthonymous.[17]

I find Ehrman's claim to neutrality impossible, if not disingenuous.[18] How can one insist there is no critique of a work's "ethical merit," when one has labeled it a lie, a bastard, and a counterfeit?[19] It is inappropriate for modern scholars to assert forgeries are not inferior to an orthonymous work. Elsewhere Ehrman correctly notes: "[I]t is enough to note that the books falsely claiming to be

---

13   Ehrman does nuance his definition. For example, he notes this distinction doesn't include non-polemical works. It also doesn't include literary fiction. Other than when the work was produced in an artificial environment, such as a classroom exercise in imitating Plato, I find his exclusions perhaps a bit unnecessary.
14   Ehrman, *Forgery*, 29.
15   Diogenes Laertius, *Lives* 2.62; Martial, *Epigrams* 1.66; Pliny, *N.H.* preface.23.
16   Armin Daniel Baum, *Pseudepigraphie und literarische Fälschung im frühen Christentum: Mit ausgewählten Quellentexten samt deutscher Übersetzung* (WUNT 2.138; Tübingen: Mohr Siebeck, 2001), 11–12.
17   Ehrman, *Forgery*, 7.
18   Elsewhere Ehrman describes the author of a pseudonymous work which condemned other pseudonymous works as lies as "Here a liar condemns the telling of lies" (Ehrman, *Forgery*, 16). This (rightly) judges the ethics of the pseudonymous author.
19   Ehrman, *Forgery*, 31–32.

written by Peter (for example) inside the New Testament are no different, in extending that false claim, from books that falsely claim to be written by Peter outside the New Testament."[20] While Ehrman considers many of the canonical books in the New Testament to be forgeries, I do not. Nonetheless, if 2 Peter were pseudonymous, then it is a forgery and should be regarded in the same way we regard the Gospel of Peter.

2.1.3.2 Are Innocent Apostolic Pseudepigrapha a Myth?

Some scholars have insisted that the intention to deceive is an essential element to label a pseudepigraphon as a forgery.[21] By arguing there was no intention to deceive, scholars have attempted to create space for innocent apostolic pseudepigrapha, asserting that a writer could denounce lying as a sin and do it (with a clean conscience) in a pseudepigraphal work. For example, Wolfgang Speyer argued the pseudepigrapha were inspired by God. Kurt Aland suggested they were apostolic prerogative.

Armin Baum makes the best defense of this position, building upon David Meade's assertion these pseudepigrapha were merely the reactualizations of tradition.[22] Here I must disagree with Baum. While Baum insists that ancients did not consider writings by followers who wrote in the name of their master to be forgeries, Ehrman mounts a persuasive rebuttal.[23]

A pseudepigraphon intended to deceive. As Ehrman notes, it is a theological decision to assert that a pseudepigraphic 1 Timothy wasn't intending to deceive but merely to reactualize Pauline tradition for a new situation: "Here again, this is theology, not history. Are there really *historical* grounds for claiming that 1 Timothy is pseudepigraphic Vergegenwärtigung but 3 Corinthians is a forgery?"[24] I will join my voice with Ehrman's and assert that if 1 Timothy is pseudepigraphic, then it belongs in the pile with 3 Corinthians.

There is a practice that is identified by both Ehrman and Baum as not a forgery. When a student published his notes of his master, the notes were

---

20   Ehrman, *Forgery*, 17 n. 19.
21   Ehrman defends well his use of intentionality as a criterion (*Forgery*, 30, n. 3).
22   Baum, *Pseudepigraphie*. See also David Meade's revised Ph.D. dissertation from the University of Nottingham; David Meade, *Pseudonymity and Canon: An Investigation into the Relationship of Authorship and Authority in Jewish and Earliest Christian Tradition* (repr., Grand Rapids: Eerdmans, 1985).
23   See esp., Ehrman, *Forgery*, 85–92. It is outside the scope of this work to evaluate Ehrman's critique of Baum's thesis. Ehrman describes Baum's work as "a detailed and learned study," *Forgery*, 87. Baum in a sense responds with his review, pp. 428–431.
24   Ehrman, *Forgery*, 40.

published under the master's name. To publish it as the student's words would have been viewed as plagiarism. Publishing them under the master's name would avoid plagiarism but could raise the accusation of pseudepigraphy. Ehrman and Baum argue the results were not viewed as forgery. Baum asserts the students published it under the master's name. Ehrman argues the student did not. The best example is Epictetus's *Discourses*. We note two points. First, Arrian does not publish the notes pseudonymously; they are under Arrian's name. Second, Arrian take pains to explain carefully why his work on Epictetus's discourses are not plagiarism (λογοκλοπία); he is merely presenting his notes of Epictetus's lectures:

> I have not composed these *Words of Epictetus* as one might be said to "compose" books of this kind, nor have I of my own act published them to the world; indeed, I acknowledge that I have not "composed" them at all. But whatever I heard him say I used to write down, word for word, as best I could ...²⁵

Arrian notes carefully that the words are not his and that he was not publishing them "to the world" as his. Arrian claims no honor, as we will note later. But other examples are not as clear. Quintilian refers to works published under his name (pseudonymously):

> ... two books on the art of rhetoric are at present circulating under my name, although never published by me or composed for such a purpose. One is a two-days' lecture which was taken down by the boys who were my audience. The other consists of such notes as my good pupils succeeded in taking down from a course of lectures on a somewhat more extensive scale. I appreciate their kindness, but they showed an excess of enthusiasm and a certain lack of discretion in doing my utterances the honour of publication.²⁶

---

25 Epictetus, *Disc.* 1.8: οὔτε συνέγραψα ἐγὼ τοὺς Ἐπικτήτου λόγους οὕτως ὅπως ἄν τις συγγράψειε τὰ τοιαῦτα οὔτε ἐξήνεγκα εἰς ἀνθρώπους αὐτός, ὅς γε οὐδὲ συγγράψαι φημί. ὅσα δὲ ἤκουον αὐτοῦ λέγοντος, ταῦτα αὐτὰ ἐπειράθην αὐτοῖς ὀνόμασιν ὡς οἷόν ... The contrast here between γράφω and συγγράφω is quite intentional by Arrian, in the assessment of the LCL editor; Epictetus, *The Discourses as Reported by Arrian* ed (trans. W.A. Oldfather; LCL; 2 vols.; Cambridge, MA: Harvard University Press, 1925), 1:5 n. 2.

26 Quntilian, *Inst. Proem.* 7 (trans. H.E. Butler; LCL; Cambridge, MA: Harvard University, 1920): *... duo iam sub nomine meo libri ferebantur artis rhetoricae neque editi a me neque in hoc comparati. Namque alterum sermonem per biduum habitum pueri, quibis id praestabatur,*

He does not seem pleased by the practice but he doesn't denounce them as forgeries. Ehrman concludes (based on Arrian), "it was perfectly acceptable to publish the notes of a teacher in his name; but to publish them in one's own name, as if they were one's own teachings, was seen as plagiarism."[27] Presumably, Quintilian's complaint is because the notes are not well done. It seems less certain that such a practice was commonly accepted, since Quintilian refers to the perpetrators as lacking discretion. Quintilian is careful to explain that the notes were not authorized and he published his own version.

In another example, Galen voices his opinion on books 2 and 6 of Hippocrates. Ehrman notes these books are not to be labeled plagiarism, because the books were the notes of Hippocrates published by Hippocrates's son Thessalus after his father's death.[28] Baum counters by arguing these works were acceptable pseudepigrapha because the content and ideas were Hippocrates's, even if composed by another.[29] Ehrman disputes Baum's understanding:

> It is not simply that the thoughts and ideas happen to be those of Hippocrates. What is important to note is that the books were written on the basis of papers that Hippocrates left behind. In other words, this is analogous to a student publishing the lecture notes of his teacher. The words really are the teacher's, and so should be attributed to him.[30]

This debate merits further evaluation, but for the purposes of today, whether or not a student publishing lecture notes under his master's name was commonly accepted practice (and I think it wasn't), we shall see that plagiarism was denounced.

2.2 *Honor and Shame*

This may seem a strange deviation from topic, but I believe it is very relevant. Scholars on honor/shame often assert that it lies behind much that happened in the ancient world. It is outside the scope of this essay to summarize honor/shame in antiquity. Elsewhere I have maintained that "what goes

---

  exceperant; alterum pluribus sane diebus, quantum notando consequi potuerant, interceptum boni iuvenes, sed nimium amantes mei, temerario editionis honore.

27   Ehrman, *Forgery*, 114–115.
28   Ehrman, *Forgery*, 117.
29   Baum, *Pseudepigraphie*, 58–59.
30   Ehrman, *Forgery*, 117.

without being said" are usually the most powerful shapers of a culture.[31] I suggest honor/shame is the elephant in the room when it came to plagiarism.

3   Plagiarism in Greco-Roman Antiquity

An examination of ancient texts suggests that ancients recognized and condemned plagiarism. Bernard Legras concludes, "plagiarism and forgery of literary works were considered offenses and punished."[32]

3.1   Bart Ehrman's Evidence

Ehrman assembles an impressive collection of ancient writers denouncing plagiarism.

3.1.1   The Plagiarist Heraclides Ponticus

Diogenes Laertius spends considerable time denouncing the various crimes of Heraclides, such as bribery, forgery, and other forms of deceit. For our purposes here, Heraclides's crimes included plagiarism: "Chamaeleon complains that Heraclides' treatise on the works of Homer and Hesiod was plagiarized from his own."[33]

3.1.2   The Plagiarist Aeschines

Diogenes tells us that Menedemus accused Aeschines of plagiarizing some of Socrates's dialogues: "It was said maliciously—by Menedemus of Eretria in particular—that most of the dialogues which Aeschines passed off as his own were really dialogues of Socrates obtained by him from Xanthippe."[34] Diogenes adds other accusations of plagiarism: "Moreover, Aeschines made use of the *Little Cyrus*, the *Lesser Heracles* and the *Alcibiades* of Antisthenes as well as the dialogues of other authors."[35]

---

31 E. Randolph Richards and Brandon O'Brien, *Misreading Scripture with Western Eyes* (Downers Grove, IL: InterVarsity, 2012), 12.
32 Legras, "La sanction du plagiat littéraire," 459: "... le plagiat et la forgerie d'oeuvres littéraires pouvaient être considérés comme des délits et sanctionnés."
33 Diogenes Laertius, *Lives* 5.92: Χαμαιλέων τε τὰ παρ' ἑαυτοῦ φησι κλέψαντα αὐτόν τὰ περὶ Ἡσιόδου καὶ Ὁμήρου γράψαι.
34 Diogenes Laertius, *Lives* 2.60: διεβάλλετο δ' ὁ Αἰσχίνης καὶ μάλισθ' ὑπὸ Μενεδήμου τοῦ Ἐρετριέως ὡς τοὺς πλείστουσ διαλόγους ὄντας Σωκράτους ὑποβάλλοιτο, λαμβάνων παρὰ Ξανθίππης. Xanthippe was Socrates's wife.
35 Diogenes Laertius, *Lives* 2.61: ἀλλὰ καὶ τῶν Ἀντισθένους τόν τε μικρὸν Κῦρον καὶ τὸν Ἡρακλέα

3.1.3   Martial, the Victim of Plagiarism

Martial forcibly complains about being plagiarized. He notes that it is easily (and cheaply) done for the price of having the text rewritten under a new name. Martial notes it cannot be done if the book is well known but can be accomplished rather easily if the book was unfinished (i.e., unpublished):

> You mistake, you greedy thief of my works, who think you can become a poet at no more than the cost of a transcript and a cheap papyrus roll. Applause is not acquired for six or ten sesterces. Look out for unpublished poems and unfinished studies, which one man only knows of … A well-known book cannot change its author … Whoever recites another man's work, and so woos fame, ought not to buy a book, but—silence.[36]

It will be important later in this essay to note the two conditions that Martial adds: the work was not well known and the thief was stealing Martial's fame and applause (honor).

3.1.4   Vitruvius, the Exposer of Plagiarists

In the preface to Book 7, Vitruvius honors men who preserved for us the deeds of great men such as Thales, Xenophanes, Plato, Zeno, Alexander, and Darius. He then adds there are plagiarists who must be denounced:

> … on the other hand we must censure those who plunder their works and appropriate them to themselves; writers who do not depend upon their own ideas, but in their envy boast of other men's goods whom they have robbed with violence, should not only receive censure but punishment for their impious manner of life. And this practice, as we are informed, was duly dealt with by the ancients. It is not out of place to relate these trials as they have been handed down.[37]

τὸν ἐλάσσω καὶ Ἀλκιβιάδην καὶ τοὺς τῶν ἄλλων δὲ ἐσκευώρηται. Ehrman (*Forgery*, 53) correctly adds "fraudulently" to his translation of ἐσκευώρηται. LSJ confirms this nuance.

36   Martial, *Epigrams* 1.66: *Erras, meorum fur avare librorum, fieri poetam posse qui putas tanti, scriptura quanti constet et tomus vilis: non sex paratur aut decem sophos nummis. secreta quare carmina et rudes curas quas novit unus scrinioque signatas custodit ipse virginis pater chartae, quae trita duro non inhorruit mento. mutare dominum non potest liber notus. sed pumicata fronte si quis est nondum nec umbilicis cultus atque membrane, mercare: tales habeo; nec sciet quisquam. aliena quisquis recitat et petit famam, non emere librum sed silentium debet.*

37   Vitruvius, *On Architecture* (trans. Frank Granger, 2 vols.; LCL; Cambridge, MA: Harvard University, 1934), Book 7, preface 3.

At first glance, the reference to "other men's goods" suggests property, but a close look will show themes of boasting, envy and honor. Vitruvius then recounts the fascinating story of the founding of the library at Alexandria to compete with the library at Pergamum. To augment Alexandria's library, Ptolemy "consecrated games in honour of the Muses and Apollo" to give prizes to new writers.[38] To the six chosen judges was added a seventh by the governors of the library, who commended "Aristophanes, who read each book in the library systematically day by day with comprehensive ardour and diligence."[39] Various contestants recited their works. Aristophanes accused all but one contestant of plagiarism, stating "the others recited borrowed work, whereas the judges had to deal with original compositions, not with plagiaries."[40] The King was doubtful until Aristophanes quoted the passages himself. For our purposes, it is important to note that the plagiarists weren't merely punished—although they were tried for theft—they were also required to publicly confess they were thieves.[41] We must also underscore that Vitruvius considered the shaming of plagiarists to be the required counterpoint story to his earlier stories of honoring the great writers. Plagiarists were thieves and deserved censure as well as punishment.[42]

3.1.5 Unidentified Plagiarists

Pliny the Elder describes plagiarism as a common problem in the preface to his Natural History. Whether this is rhetorical hyperbole or an accurate description of its prevalence, we still see that plagiarism was recognized and denounced:

> You will deem it a proof of this pride of mine that I have prefaced these volumes with the names of my authorities ... to own up to those who were the means of one's achievements, not to do as most of the authors to whom I have referred did. I have found that the most professedly reliable and modern writers have copied the old authors word for word, without acknowledgement.[43]

---

38   Vitruvius, *Arch.* Book 7, preface 4. Ehrman mistakenly states it was the king of Pergamum and the passage was 3 not 4. With the sheer volume of ancient texts Ehrman cites, minor mistakes like these are understandable.
39   Vitruvius, *Arch.* Book 7, preface 5.
40   Vitruvius, *Arch.* Book 7, preface 7. ... *ceteros aliena recitavisse; oportere autem iudicantes non furta* [stolen property] *sed scripta probare.*
41   Vitruvius, *Arch.* Book 7, preface 3.
42   Vitruvius, *Arch.* Book 7, preface 3.
43   Pliny, *N.H.* preface 21–22.

He goes on to compare Virgil, Cicero, and Panaetius who mention their sources. He then concludes, "Surely it marks a mean spirit and an unfortunate disposition to prefer being detected in a theft to repaying a loan,"[44] indicating Pliny considered plagiarism to be a theft.

Likewise, Polybius notes the challenge of writing events that have already "been recounted by many writers and in many different styles." He then adds:

> an author who undertakes at the present day to deal with these matters must either represent the work of others as being his own, a most disgraceful proceeding, or if he refuses to do this, must manifestly toil to no purpose [since the events] have been adequately narrated and handed down to posterity by previous authors.[45]

Polybius considers plagiarism disgraceful.

3.1.6   A Disputed Example of Plagiarism

Ehrman cites one example of plagiarism that I will need to dispute. Diogenes recounts how Empedocles was expelled from the school of Pythagorus for, as Ehrman asserts, plagiarism: "… having been convicted at that time of stealing his discourses, he was, like Plato, excluded from taking part in the discussions of the school."[46] We also note the only punishment involved banning Empedocles from participating in school discussions as had been Plato. In fact, the text goes on to state Empedocles's crime was that "Empedocles himself made them [the school's discussions] public property by his poem …"[47] Furthermore, Diogenes Laertius notes that Theophrastes thought Empedocles admired Parmenides and "imitated him in his verses."[48] Diogenes adds that Hermippus thought Empedocles actually admired Xenophanes "with whom in fact he lived and whose writing of poetry he imitated."[49] Both statements had no hint of censure. The remainder of Diogenes's description of Empedocles carries no condemnation as a thief but rather a man to be admired, such as "the inventor

---

44 Pliny, *N.H.* preface 23.
45 Polybius, *The Histories* (trans. W.R. Paton; 6 vols.; LCL; Cambridge, MA: Harvard University, 1922–1927), 9.2.1: … ἢ τὰ ἀλλότρια δεῖ λέγειν ὡς ἴδια τὸν νῦν περὶ τούτων πραγματευόμενον, ὃ πάντων ἐστὶν αἴσχιστον …
46 Diogenes Laertius, *Lives* 8.54: καταγνωσθεὶς ἐπὶ λογοκλοπίᾳ τότε, καθὰ καὶ Πλάτων, τῶν λόγων ἐκωλύθη μετέχειν.
47 Diogenes Laertius, *Lives* 8.55: ἐπεὶ δ' αὐτὸς διὰ τῆς ποιήσεως ἐδημοσίωσεν αὐτὰ κτλ.
48 Diogenes Laertius, *Lives* 8.55.
49 Diogenes Laertius, *Lives* 8.56.

of rhetoric," "powerful in diction," "great in metaphors," a writer of poems, tragedies and political discourses.[50] I think the earlier reference to "stealing his discourses" may connote not plagiarism but rather revealing school secrets.

3.2 Some Additional Texts

Beyond those cited by Ehrman, there are additional texts on plagiarism worth noting.

3.2.1 Seneca the Elder

In his later years, the Elder Seneca bemoaned the decline in literacy and rhetorical learning that he saw among the youth. He compared how well learned were the audiences when he was a youth to the much diminished skills of the audiences later:

> So assiduous (not to say carping) were audiences in those days that not even a single word could be plagiarized. Nowadays anyone can pass off the Verrines for his own without being detected.[51]

The Elder Seneca was not indifferent to plagiarism. Like other ancients he took it quite seriously. He defends another writer against a charge of plagiarism: "Porcius Latro, who cannot be suspected of plagiarism, for he both despised the Greeks and was ignorant of them ..."[52]

Likewise, Seneca noted that Ovid enjoyed a Virgilian phrase, *plena deo*.[53] More significantly, Seneca asserts that Ovid *wanted* his readers to recognize that he had borrowed the phrase from Virgil.[54] The Elder Seneca explicitly states that:

---

50   Diogenes Laertius, *Lives* 8.57–58.
51   The Elder Seneca, *Declamations* (trans. M. Winterbottom; 2 vols.; LCL; Cambridge, MA: Harvard University Press, 1974), vol. 2: *Suasoriae* 2.19: *Tam diligentes tunc auditores erant, ne dicam tam maligni, ut unum verbum surripi non posset; at nunc cuilibet orationes in Verrem tuto licet pro suis ⟨dicere⟩.*
52   The Elder Seneca, *Declamations* (trans. M. Winterbottom; 2 vols.; LCL; Cambridge, MA: Harvard University, 1974), vol. 2: *Controversiae* 10.4.21. Seneca seems to suggest that Porcius's use of a short epigram should be assumed coincidental because he was ignorant of Greek writings for he despised them. Whether or not Porcius was innocent, it is clear that Seneca was sensitive to plagiarism.
53   The same phrase he notes that his friend Gallio liked to use to ridicule overly pretentious speakers; Seneca, *Suas.* 3.6–7.
54   So Christopher Trinacty, "Like Father, Like Son? Selected Examples of Intertextuality in

Ovid had very much liked the phrase: and that as a result the poet did something he had done with many other lines of Virgil—with no thought of plagiarism, but meaning that his piece of open borrowing should be noticed.[55]

Neither Ovid nor the Elder Seneca considered this plagiarism, but rather a quotation (without our modern conventions of punctuation or citation).

3.2.2 Seneca the Younger

The Younger Seneca writes at some length about later writers imitating the work of older rhetoricians. He insisted that writing on material covered by other authors required the new writing to be recast so as not to be plagiarism. He used the metaphor of bees gathering from a variety of beautiful flowers to produce one singular delicious product, honey:

> We also, I say, ought to copy these bees, and sift whatever we have gathered from a varied course of reading ... we should so blend those several flavours into one delicious compound that, even though it betrays its origin, yet it nevertheless is clearly a different thing from that whence it came.[56]

Such a description would match our modern definition of paraphrasing our sources. Like Seneca, we see this as a means of avoiding plagiarism—a charge to which he was sensitive, putting it on the lips of Lucilius as an interlocutor:

> "What," you say, "will it not be seen whose style you are imitating, whose method of reasoning, whose pungent sayings?"[57]

Seneca the Younger and Seneca the Elder," *Phoenix* 63 (2009): 269. Trinacty conducts a fine study of intertextual echoes of the Elder in the writings of the Younger.

55   Seneca, *Suas.* 3.7: ... *non subripiendi causa, sed palam mutuandi, hoc animo ut vellet agnosci.*
56   Seneca, *Ep.* 84.5: ... *nos quoque has apes debemus imitari et quaecumque ex diversa lectione congessimus, separare, melius enim distincta servantur, deinde adhibita ingenii nostri cura et facultate in unum saporem varia illa libamenta confundere, et etiam si apparuerit, unde sumptum sit, aliud tamen esse quam unde sumptum est, appareat.*
57   Seneca, *Ep.* 84.8. Such an objection is raised over 2 Peter's use of Jude.

Seneca replies, as a chorus uses multiple voices to make one sound, so a skilled writer blends a selection of sources into something new.[58] For Seneca, the important thing was to show indebtedness and relationship but not to plagiarize:

> I think that sometimes it is impossible for it to be seen who is being imitated, if the copy is a true one; for a true copy stamps its own form upon all the features which it has drawn from what we may call the original, in such a way that they are combined into a unity.[59]

A writer should show one was shaped by the source but not steal its image:

> This is what our mind should do: it should hide away all the materials by which it has been aided, and bring to light only what it has made of them. Even if there shall appear in you a likeness to him who, by reason of your admiration, has left a deep impress upon you, I would have you resemble him as a child resembles his father, and not as a picture (*imago*) resembles its original; for a picture is a lifeless thing.[60]

Seneca insisted that the work of others should be "digested" and that what the writer "absorbed should not be allowed to remain unchanged."[61]

3.2.3 Diogenes Laertius

Diogenes notes another accusation by Aristippus that Aeschines plagiarized from Socrates:

> Aristippus among others had suspicions of the genuineness of his dialogues. At all events, as he [Aeschines] was reading one at Megara, Aristippus rallied him by asking, "Where did you get that, you thief?"[62]

---

58 Seneca, *Ep.* 84.9. It seems likely 2 Peter's use of Jude would meet Seneca's approval for "digesting" the material and giving it a "new face" (*novam faciem*) (Seneca, *Ep.* 79.6), since, for example, 2 Peter reduces the number of Jude's OT *exempli* and puts them into Tanak order; see E. Randolph Richards, "In Exile but on the Brink of Restoration: The Story of Israel in the General Epistles," in *The Story of Israel: A Biblical Theology* (ed. Marvin Pate; Downers Grove, IL: InterVarsity, 2004), 232–254 (245–248).
59 Seneca, *Ep.* 84.8.
60 Seneca, *Ep.* 84.7–8.
61 Seneca, *Ep.* 84.6–7.
62 Diogenes Laertius, *Lives* 2.62: τούτου τοὺς διαλόγους καὶ Ἀρίστιππος ὑπώπτευεν. ἐν γοῦν Μεγάροις ἀναγινώσκοντος αὐτοῦ φασι σκῶψαι εἰπόντα, "πόθεν σοι, λῃστά, ταῦτα;"

It is noteworthy that Diogenes describes not only the theft but also the *public* denunciation of Aeschines as a thief.

3.2.4 Virgil

When the Roman poet Virgil composed the *Aeneid*, his similarities to the *Iliad* and the *Odyssey* were unmistakable. As he began publishing pieces, Virgil was accused of plagiarizing Homer. Virgil is credited with retorting: "it is easier to steal a club from Hercules than a verse from Homer."[63] For Virgil, his practice was clearly not plagiarism, *for the very reason*, he argued, no one could fail to recognize the words as belonging to Homer. In Virgil's mind, no one could accuse him of claiming Homer's words as his own. No one, Virgil reasoned, could mistakenly assume Virgil was claiming to be the genius behind the borrowed metaphors and phrases.

4 Distinguishing Ancient Plagiarism from Modern Plagiarism

Ancient plagiarism, however, was not completely analogous to modern plagiarism. Certainly, the basic definition was the same: an author claimed the words of another as his or her own. Yet, there are texts that suggest at least two situations (that would constitute modern plagiarism) that were not considered plagiarism. First, when readers recognized (or could be expected to recognize) the borrowed words as belonging to another; they were part of the ancient *publica*, the common property. Everyone knew the words belonged to another. And second, when an author reused his own material in another writing, there is no suggestion this was deemed as plagiarism.

4.1 *Publica*

When discussing the imitation of older rhetoricians, Seneca nuances a point about well-known words:

> Besides, he who writes last has the best of the bargain; he finds already at hand words which, when marshaled in a different way, show a new face.

---

[63] Donat. *Vit. Verg.* 46: *facilius esse Herculi clavam quam Homero versum subripere*. Madeline Miller posted an essay with the title "Stealing Hercules' Club," possibly to avoid the same critique in her modern retelling of the story of Achilles (http://www.madelinemiller.com/stealing-hercules%E2%80%99-club/, accessed October 28, 2014); Miller, *The Song of Achilles: A Novel* (New York: HarperCollins, 2012). See also Trinacty, "Like Father, Like Son?," 265 n. 23.

And he is not pilfering them, as if they belonged to someone else, when he uses them, for they are common property.[64]

By *publica* (common property), Seneca doesn't precisely mean the equivalent of our term "public domain," where the knowledge belongs to everyone, but rather that everyone knows to whom the words belong. Seneca meant that the public[65] knew the words and who the source was. You could not claim them as your own, hence steal them. While public knowledge in modern parlance can include facts without citation, Seneca is referring to quotations one can make without citation. (Modern convention would require at least quotation marks.)

4.2 Self-plagiarism

Ancients apparently did not consider copying one's own words verbatim into another work to be plagiarism. Cicero's nephew sent a letter to both Cicero and Atticus with the same text describing an adventure. Although this is self-plagiarism by modern standards, Cicero notes it with no censure: "I am sending you young Quintus' letter … I have sent you half the letter. The other half about his adventures I think you have in duplicate."[66] Likewise, Cicero without any hint of wrongdoing repeats the same clever and witty reference to Caesar's assassination and Anthony's survival in letters to two different recipients.[67] Cicero sheepishly confesses to Atticus that he had carelessly used the same preface in two different works. The problem, according to Cicero, was that the works were too similar to allow this.[68] It was not the self-plagiarism but the literary faux pas that embarrassed the elitist Cicero. While an aristocratic author like Cicero might be embarrassed, it was not from plagiarism but from

---

64 Seneca, *Ep.* 79.6: *Praeterea condicio optima est ultimi; parata verba invenit, quae aliter instructa novam faciem habent. Nec illis manus inicit tamquam alienis. Sunt enim publica.*
65 By public, Seneca meant the intended audience. We need not assume Seneca meant the general masses knew the material.
66 Atticus wrote the same passage in letters to two different people. Unfortunately for Atticus, one of the recipients, Cicero, saw the other letter as well and commented to Atticus: "The letter contained the same passage about your sister that you wrote to me"; Cicerco, *Att.* 13.29.
67 Cicero, *Fam.* 10.28.1: "How I should like you to have invited me to that most gorgeous banquet on the Ides of March! We should have left no leavings [Anthony]," and *Fam.* 12.4.1: "I should like you to have invited me to your banquet on the Ides of March; there would have been no leavings."
68 Cicero, *Att.* 16.6. Cicero admits to keeping a notebook of prefaces from which to draw.

social factors. He might be viewed as lazy or as viewing his recipient unworthy of a fresh composition. So, why was self-plagiarism not plagiarism? I suggest because one cannot steal honor from oneself.

Although those two examples of modern plagiarism weren't considered plagiarism in antiquity, we have already seen that plagiarism was recognized and condemned in Greco-Roman antiquity. Yet, there is one more significant way that ancient plagiarism differed.

4.3 Stolen Honor

Ancients considered plagiarism to be stealing, but because of the situations in which the accusation of "Plagiarist!" was raised, these texts bring up the question of what exactly was stolen. Bernard Legras, in his excellent study on ancient plagiarism, noted that the evidence showed it was an offense. Legras talks about the "right of intellectual property," but he notes it doesn't match exactly our modern definition.[69] Ptolemaic justice required the thieves to forfeit both prize *and* honor: "En annulant le concours, la justice ptolémaïque leur faisait d'abord perdre 'les prix et distinctions' (*praemia et honores*) qu'ils devaient obtenir (un Grec penserait sans doute φιλοκέδια et φιλοτιμία)."[70] Furthermore, in his lengthy discussion of consequences of plagiarism, he notes: "A reproach may be demanded by the plaintiffs in addition to restitution."[71] He adds this sanction of the reproach (ἐπίπληξις) was well practiced in the Egypt of Ptolemy V Epiphanes as attested by a royal ordinance in a letter dated 184/183 BC.[72] When we compare the various texts indicating what was and was not considered plagiarism, I suggest an essential element was the theft of honor.

When discussing Seneca the Younger's encouragement to Lucilius, Trinacty brings out a point I would like to nuance:

> Seneca believes that Lucilius will be able to bring his own literary sensibilities to the topic, and that accounts of previous authors will help enhance his description. It is the rearrangement and redeployment of

---

69 Legras, "La sanction du plagiat littéraire," 459.
70 Legras, "La sanction du plagiat littéraire," 459.
71 Legras, "La sanction du plagiat littéraire," 458: "… ἐπίπληξις, que l'n traduit généralement par 'blame, réprimande.' L'ἐπίπληξις peut être demandée, dans les requêtes, par les plaignants en sus du dédommagement."
72 Legras, "La sanction du plagiat littéraire," 458: "Cette sanction de l'ἐπίπληξις était bien pratiquée dans l'Égypte de Ptolémée V Épiphane comme l'atteste une ordonnance addressée par le roi à l'épistate des gardes Synnomaos en 184/183 av. n.è. (*C. Ord. Ptol.* 31,1.12)."

earlier works within a new context that gives them novel meaning (*novam faciem*). One must not worry about plagiarism, because these famous poetic antecedents are now in the public domain, and a knowing reader will recognize the borrowing.[73]

Trinacty helpfully clarifies why ancients would *not* have considered this example to be theft: "a knowing reader will recognize the borrowing." Lucilius could expect his readers to recognize the material; it was "common property" (to use Seneca's words), *publica*, in the public domain, so to speak. Lucilius's use would have not been understood as stealing the honor of another by falsely claiming the words were his own. The key element seems to be the author's reasonable expectation that his readers would recognize the material as borrowed (without the modern convention of quotation marks).

The Elder Seneca was well aware that an audience could confuse *imitationes*[74] with plagiarism.[75] For him, a key factor in determining if something was plagiarism was how well-versed the audience was in literature. "Seneca the Elder often focuses on the learning of the speakers and the audience in his discussion of plagiarism."[76] Would the audience think the speaker was the source of the words or did they recognize the original source? In other words, was the speaker stealing another's honor?

When the Younger Seneca discussed imitation using the metaphor of bees and honey, his metaphor of bees was used by Macrobius. Trinacty notes the key to deciding if Macrobius had plagiarized Seneca was whether Macrobius expected his readers to know Seneca's letter:

> It is interesting that much of this letter [Seneca, *Ep.* 84] is appropriated by Macrobius in the preface to his *Saturnalia* without acknowledgement or any attempt to change the form. Does Macrobius expect his reader to recognize the material as an allusion to Seneca? Petrach castigates Macrobius for his misuse (*Seneca, De Reb. Fam.* 1.7).[77]

---

[73] Trinacty, "Like Father, Like Son?," 263.
[74] The ancient skill of *imitationes* began with the self-conscious act of analyzing, memorizing, and paraphrasing; see Elaine Fantham, "Imitation and Decline: Rhetorical Theory and Practice in the First Century after Christ," *Classical Philology* 73 (1978): 102–116, esp. 110.
[75] Trinacty, "Like Father, Like Son?," 265.
[76] Trinacty, "Like Father, Like Son?," 265 n. 23.
[77] Trinacty, "Like Father, Like Son?," 263 n. 17.

It seems noteworthy that the verdict over plagiarism was not whether the quotation was verbatim or even whether Seneca was explicitly acknowledged; rather, it hinges upon whether Macrobius was implying to his readers that he was the genius behind the metaphor. In other words, was Macrobius stealing the honor that was Seneca's?[78]

Martial describes a plagiarist as a greedy thief who "recites another man's work, and so woos fame"; he steals applause.[79] In a similar vein, Vitruvius considers just punishment (censure) of a plagiarist to require a public confession. This public shaming is the restitution of the stolen honor, making things right. It is not just the fines or the punishment but the "reproach" (ἐπίπληξις) that restores the balance. So also, Aristippus seems to require a public reproach, calling Aeschines a thief in public. Making the same point by way of contrast, Arrian's careful delineation that he was not "publishing to the world" Epictetus's discourses as his own words seem to me an attempt to insure he is not accused of stealing Epictetus' honor.

5 Matthew as a Plagiarist

Although Matthew and Luke are frequently posited as both drawing from Mark, they do not use Markan material in the same way. For example, in the Parable of the Fig Tree (Mark 13:28–31 = Matt 24:32–35 = Luke 21:29–33):

> the entire text of Mark is copied almost without change by Matthew, with several small exceptions. Meanwhile, Luke again rewrites the opening portion of this text for no apparent reason other than to render it in different language.[80]

---

78   Petrarch writing a thousand years later thought Macrobius was stealing; yet, Petrarch was not in a position to evaluate what Macrobius's readers knew (nor are we).
79   Martial, *Epigrams* 1.66.
80   Evan Powell, "Luke, the Eccentric Evangelist," in *The Synoptic Problem and Its Solution* (http://synoptic-problem.com/luke_eccentric_evangelist.html, accessed October 8, 2015). He is arguing a case against Q, but his point here is well made, "Luke exhibits a strong desire to paraphrase Mark … he manifests a need to render Mark's text in his own words, even when Mark's version does not seem to call for it." Other than a stretch of 26 verbatim words in Luke 4:34–35 (of direct discourse), Luke usually follows the "common literary practice in the Hellenistic world" to paraphrase sources when using Markan material.

Seneca would likely approve of Luke's paraphrasing of Mark's material. Matthew's nearly verbatim copying of Mark certainly seems to qualify as ancient (and modern) plagiarism. Let us take a brief look at some texts where Matthew might be accused of plagiarism. Again, the purpose of the essay is not to delineate the topic in depth, but to ask if Matthew would have been seen as a plagiarist in antiquity.[81]

5.1   Old Testament Quotations

Matthew made extensive use of the Old Testament, quoting it at least 45 times, depending upon how one distinguishes quotations from paraphrases. Usually when quoting, Matthew indicates it is a quotation. For example, we see quotations introduced, often with a formula like "what was spoken/written by," in 1:22–23; 2:5–6, 15, 17–18, 23; 3:3; 4:4, 6, 7, 10, 14–16; 5:21, 27, 31, 33, 38, 43; 8:17; 11:10; 12:40; 13:14–15, 35; 15:4, 7–9; 19:4–5, 7; 21:4–5, 13, 16, 42; 22:31–32, 36–39, 43–44; 24:15; 26:31; 27:9–10. Yet Matthew (or the Matthean Jesus) also quotes an Old

---

81   In researching this essay, I investigated the discussion of ancient epitomes, since some effort has been made to connect our Gospels to the epitome tradition; e.g., David Dungan contributed to the revival of the Griesbach hypothesis by suggesting Mark was an epitome of Matthew and Luke; Dungan, "Mark—An Abridgement of Matthew and Luke," in *Jesus and Man's Hope* (ed. D.G. Buttrick; 2 vols.; Pittsburgh: Pittsburgh Theological Seminary, 1970), 1:51–97. These writers pulled out excerpts, often verbatim, from longer literary sources. These documents called an epitome (ἐπιτομή) served as an abridgement of an older, longer work. Epitomizing (or abridging) longer works was commonly done by both Greek and Latin writers, "particularly technical treatises by Greek writers and histories by Latin writers"; Robert A. Derrenbacker, Jr., "The 'Abridgement' of Matthew and Luke: Mark as *Epitome*?" in *Resourcing New Testament Studies: Literary, Historical, and Theological Essays in Honor of David L. Dungan* (ed. Allan J. McNicol and David B. Peabody; Edinburgh: T&T Clark, 2011), 36–45 (37). (He argues against Mark as an epitome.) Opelt notes, for example, a two-volume work by Theopompus of Chios (4th c. BCE) who extracts from Herodotus's nine-volume history. Hers remains the best work on this subject; I. Opelt, "Epitome," *RAC* 5 (1962): 944–973, but see also M.S. Silk, "epitome (Greek)" and R.A. Kaster "epitome (Latin)," in *Oxford Classical Dictionary* (ed. S. Hornblower and A. Spawforth; Oxford: Oxford University Press, 1996), 549. Of the 42 epitomes Opelt lists, seven of them are anonymous. While I have not examined all the epitomes, in the ones with claimed authorship, the epitomator noted his source and usually claimed to recast the material, in much the way that Seneca argued was appropriate. For example, the epitomator in 2 Maccabees notes, "all this, which has been set forth by Jason of Cyrene in five volumes, we shall attempt to condense into a single book ... but the one who recasts the narrative should be allowed to strive for brevity of expression" (2 Mac 2:23, 31). The anonymous epitome of Athenaeus begins: "Athenaeus is the author of this book; and in it he is discoursing with Timocrates: and the name of the book is the

Testament text without any indication that it is a quotation, such as in 9:13; 10:35–36; 11:23; 12:7; 18:16; 19:18–19; 21:9; 23:39; 24:29–30; 26:64; 27:46. For example, Jesus admonishes the crowd, "Go and learn what this means, 'I desire mercy, not sacrifice.' For I have come to call not the righteous but sinners" (Matt 9:13). It seems clear Matthew is expecting his readers to recognize the quotation from Hos 6:6. (The modern reader is assisted by the addition of quotation marks.) In Matt 26:63–65, it states:

> Then the high priest said to him, "I put you under oath before the living God, tell us if you are the Messiah, the Son of God." Jesus said to him, "You have said so. But I tell you, from now on you will see the Son of Man seated at the right hand of Power and coming on the clouds of heaven." Then the high priest tore his clothes and said, "He has blasphemed! Why do we still need witnesses? You have now heard his blasphemy."

Matthew's point (and to some extent Jesus's) requires his audience to know the passage came from Scripture and were not merely Jesus's own words. If Jesus were plagiarizing (claiming the words as his own), Jesus's words might still be blasphemous, but Matthew's point of identifying Jesus with Daniel's Son of Man would have been lost. The readers (and perhaps the original leaders) needed (and were expected) to recognize the material as "borrowed" from Daniel. Likewise, in the shouts of the crowd in the Triumphal Entry or when Jesus laments over Jerusalem, "For I tell you, you will not see me again until you say, 'Blessed is the one who comes in the name of the Lord.'" (Matt 23:39), Matthew expects the readers (at least the ideal reader) to recognize the quotation from Ps 118.

5.2 Markan Excerpts

One might insist these OT lines were *publica* and hence not plagiarism, but it would be difficult to argue this for the Markan material. Matthew's reuse of Mark has long been noted. "Matthew preserves about 90 percent of the stories and passages that are found in Mark's Gospel, but he edits this

---

Deipnosophists. In this work Laurentius is introduced, a Roman, a man of distinguished fortune, giving a banquet in his own house"; Athenaeus, *The Deipnosophists or The Banquet of the Learned of Athenaeus* (trans. C.D. Yonge; London: Henry G. Bohn, 1854); http://www.perseus.tufts.edu/hopper/text?doc=Perseus:text:2013.01.0003, accessed October 3, 2015. Neither type of epitome seems to be plagiarism (ancient or modern), because the work is labeled an epitome of a specific work and the original author is cited. Epitomes do not seem relevant to our discussion of plagiarism.

material in accord with certain principles," notably reorganizing, condensing, and polishing Mark's material.[82] Much of this usage could fall under the category of acceptable use of source material as outlined by the Younger Seneca.[83] Nonetheless, there are places (such as the parable of the fig tree) where Matthew uses Mark's material verbatim in a way that meets ancient and modern standards of plagiarism. This is widely accepted,[84] so it is not necessary here to demonstrate it. Matthew plagiarizes Mark in that he takes Markan material and presents it as his own. So, why isn't Matthew a plagiarist?

5.3 Modern Plagiarism but Not Ancient Plagiarism

Ancient complaints about plagiarism noted the plagiarist had stolen the original author's applause, fame and honor. I suggest when no honor was stolen, no theft occurred. This distinction may explain why plagiarism was not condemned in all instances. Ehrman made a passing comment about the Gospels and plagiarism:

> Assuming a two-source hypothesis, Matthew and Luke both acquire considerable amounts of their material, often verbatim, from Mark and Q, without acknowledgment. But, if plagiarism is defined as taking over the work of another and claiming it as one's own, possibly the charge does not apply in these cases, as all the writings in question are anonymous. That is to say, the later Synoptic authors are not claiming anything as their own, as they do not even name themselves.[85]

Ehrman notes that the Gospels seem to be "possibly" exempt from plagiarism and connects it to anonymity. The missing link is why anonymity would excuse plagiarism. Matthew by not claiming honor (through authorship) was not

---

82 Mark Allan Powell, "Matthew's Use of Mark," http://assets.bakerpublishinggroup.com/processed/esource-assets/files/543/original/05-02.pdf?1417301746, accessed October 3, 2015.
83 Seneca, *Ep.* 85; see the discussion above.
84 Ben Witherington III, *The Gospel of Mark: A Socio-Rhetorical Commentary* (Grand Rapids: Eerdmans, 2001), 19, n. 66: "Matthew uses some 95 percent of Mark, Luke some 53 percent; but of the percent each takes over, Luke is a bit more apt to follow Mark verbatim than Matthew is." Yet Luke often paraphrases in the middle of Markan material, etc. To argue that Matthew, Mark, and Luke were all drawing independently from *publica* takes us back to the pre-critical view of the Synoptic problem.
85 Ehrman, *Forgery*, 55.

stealing anyone else's honor and thus was not a "thief," a plagiarist. Matthew was innocent of plagiarism, *not* because all ancients plagiarized, but rather because Matthew didn't steal another's honor.

6 The Canonical Gospels as Anonymous

This brings up an intriguing possibility. Why are the canonical Gospels anonymous? It is a fair (but largely ignored) question.[86] Often it is assumed on a popular level that the evangelists wrote anonymously out of modesty. While possible, this motivation fits modern sensibilities, not ancient ones. "The boasting culture of Greco-Roman antiquity—with its catalogues of achievement and virtue—was sidelined in the Western intellectual tradition." Gradually, boasting became a Western vice instead of a Roman virtue.[87] Modesty seems unlikely an ancient motivation for the Evangelists. As Mark Strauss notes, our Gospels were probably not anonymous to the original readers.[88] Certainly, Theophilus knew who wrote the third Gospel. Likely this is true of all four Gospels. The question is better worded: Why were the Gospels *published* anonymously?

6.1 Older Explanations

There have been attempts to explain the Gospels' anonymity. Eduard Meyer suggested that Xenophon's publication of *Anabasis* under the pseudonym Themistogenes provided a parallel for John.[89] A.J.M. Wedderburn argues anonymity was used to indicate that the Evangelists relied upon "tradition, rather than

---

[86] Aune notes "the subject has been almost completely neglected"; D.E. Aune, "Anonymity," in *Westminster Dictionary of New Testament and Early Christian Literature and Rhetoric* (Louisville, KY: Westminster John Knox, 2003), 35.

[87] James R. Harrison, "The Imitation of the 'Great Man' in Antiquity: Paul's Inversion of a Cultural Icon," in *Christian Origins and Greco-Roman Culture: Social and Literary Contexts for the New Testament* (ed. Stanley E. Porter and Andrew W. Pitts; ECHC 1; TENTS 8; Leiden: Brill, 2013), 213–254 (previous quotation 253). This article is an excellent scholarly discussion of Paul's inversion of "boasting." For a popular discussion, see E. Randolph Richards and Brandon O'Brien, *Paul Behaving Badly: Was the Apostle a Racist, Chauvinist Jerk?* (Downers Grove, IL: InterVarsity, 2016).

[88] Strauss questioned in a personal email, dated September 28, 2015, "Were they in fact anonymous to the original readers?" His point is well taken.

[89] Eduard Meyer, *Ursprung und Anfänge des Christentums* (3 vols.; Stuttgart: Cotta, 1925), 1:313. I am indebted for my summary of older theories to Armin D. Baum, "The Anonymity of the New Testament History Books: A Stylistic Device in the Context of Greco-Roman and Ancient Near Eastern Literature," *NovT* 50 (2008): 123–124.

on any firsthand experience."[90] Suetonius, however, felt no need to remain anonymous in his biographies of Roman leaders before his time. Michael Wolter takes a completely different, more theological, approach, arguing publishing anonymously was a distinctly Christian phenomenon. Christian writers considered Jesus the sole authority and that all human writers should remain anonymous. Gospel writers published without mentioning their names because Jesus (or the Spirit) is the true author.[91] As Baum rightly critiques, Paul did not join in this effort. Although he cites Jesus as his authority on numerous occasions, he wrote under his own name.[92] In fact, most Christian writers used their names.

6.2 Old Testament Historiography: The Baum Hypothesis

Armin Baum discusses anonymity well, noting that all the New Testament "historical books" (his term) were published anonymously.[93] He argues that the Gospel writers were imitating OT historiography. He summarizes his thesis this way:

> Unlike the Greek or Roman historian who, among other things, wanted to earn praise and glory for his literary achievements from both his contemporaries and posterity, the history writer in the Ancient Near East sought to disappear as much as possible behind the material he presented and to become its invisible mouthpiece. By adopting the stylistic device of anonymity from OT historiography the Evangelists of the NT implied that they regarded themselves as comparatively insignificant mediators of a subject matter that deserved the full attention of the readers. The anonymity of the Gospels is thus rooted in a deep conviction concerning the ultimate priority of their subject matter.[94]

While this is a commendable theory, I note two weaknesses. First, Baum must skip over contemporary Jewish historiography. Josephus was writing history and wanted his name prominent, no doubt for the same reason as the Greek

---

90 A.J.M. Wedderburn, "The 'We'-Passages in Acts: On the Horns of a Dilemma," *ZNW* 93 (2002): 96.
91 Michael Wolter, "Die anonymen Schriften des Neuen Testaments: Annäherungsversuch an ein literarisches Phänomen," *ZNW* 79 (1988): 1–16, esp. 14–15.
92 Baum, "Anonymity," 123–124.
93 Baum, "Anonymity," 120–142.
94 Baum, "Anonymity," 120.

and Roman historians, honor.[95] Second, Baum does note correctly that all canonical "historical books" (in contrast to letters) were anonymous, but this basically means the Gospels (including Acts). Since the Gospels were *bioi* and not histories and since other Christian writings weren't anonymous, Baum's appeal, skipping over contemporary models and stretching back to Old Testament historiographical practice, seems less likely if we are able to find a more contemporary explanation, a reasonable solution within Greco-Roman practice.[96]

6.3 Avoiding the Charge of Plagiarism (Stealing Honor)

It seems unlikely the customs of OT historiography *initiated* the decision to publish the Gospels anonymously, but I believe Baum is on the correct track when he contrasts OT historians with Greco-Roman ones, who wanted honor, who "wanted to earn praise and glory."[97] The desire to publish anonymously was to avoid any claims to praise and glory, and thus to avoid charges of plagiarism, of stealing honor, and not some vague theological motive like giving Jesus the credit as author.

Baum may be correct in finding parallels to OT historiography. These parallels may have *reinforced* the practice, keeping the Gospels anonymous for awhile, even though it was known who authored them. As need arose in the church to identify the authors (for authority), it seems to me the authorship claims continued to be nuanced. Rather than state that Mark was the author, Papias tells us, "The Elder used to say: Mark, in his capacity as Peter's interpreter [ἑρμηνευτής], wrote down accurately as many things as he recalled from memory."[98] Likewise, the earliest titles for the Gospels used the odd κατά construction, "according to Mark."[99] These provide the early church with the required

---

95 Josephus seems unwilling to share any glory with his assistants in the writing process; *Ag. Ap.* 1.50.

96 In fairness to Baum, he notes contemporary Jewish writers (Josephus and Jason of Cyrene) and even Jewish writers from the previous century (Eupolomus, Artapanus, Cleodemus Malchus, and Theophilus) didn't write anonymously. He notes that they wrote "in accordance with Greco-Roman practice"; Baum, "Anonymity," 126.

97 Baum, "Anonymity," 120.

98 Eusebius, *Hist. eccl.* 3.39.15–16. The translation is from Richard Bauckham, *Jesus and the Eyewitnesses: The Gospels as Eyewitness Testimony* (Grand Rapids: Eerdmans, 2006), 203.

99 For John's Gospel, source criticism is rarely done. If the writer of the Fourth Gospel (perhaps John) reworked a book of signs from the Beloved Disciple (not John) and a passion narrative from accepted tradition, then the risk of plagiarism could be raised, unless it was published anonymously. I hope to argue this in a forthcoming commentary; see E. Randolph Richards, *John* (WBC; 2 vols.; Grand Rapids: Zondervan, forthcoming).

apostolic authority but still remove our Gospel writers a step from normal authorship. Both constructions I would contend prevent the author from being seen as claiming the *honor* of authorship.

7 Conclusion: Matthew and Plagiarism

There is still research to be done, but I suggest the precipitating factor for Matthew to write anonymously was to avoid being labeled a plagiarist. It would have been a reasonable accusation. The real and present danger from the charge of plagiarism, rendering the author dishonored as a thief, kept our Gospel writers from claiming authorship (and honor). By claiming no honor, they stole nothing. Lastly, we might muse why the earliest pseudonymous gospels, such as the Gospel of Peter or the Gospel of Thomas, do not plagiarize material. Their writers know the canonical Gospels. Is it because they are not anonymous?

In summary, Ehrman has assisted scholarship by clarifying what constituted forgery and plagiarism in the ancient Greco-Roman world. Furthermore, he contributes significantly to the critique of the common scholarly assertion about innocent apostolic pseudepigrapha. Although several of us have previously insisted pseudepigrapha were never innocent but were written to deceive, Ehrman has given the most comprehensive treatment on the subject. I disagree with his contention that many of the New Testament writings are forgeries, but he has helped clarify the ancient view of pseudepigraphy.

With respect to his brief discussion on plagiarism, Ehrman rightly critiques the position among many modern scholars that ancients had no concept of plagiarism. Rather, Ehrman demonstrates well that plagiarism was recognized and condemned by ancient Romans. While Ehrman argues it was condemned as the theft of intellectual property, I hope to have nuanced the ancient concept of plagiarism.

Compositional Techniques within Plutarch and the Gospel Tradition

Michael R. Licona

Most Gospel specialists agree that the canonical Gospels share much in common with Greco-Roman biography and that this genre allowed a degree of flexibility in the way events were reported. But little work has focused on identifying specific compositional devices of ancient biographers. In this essay, I focus on two sets of texts, Plutarch's *Lives* and the canonical Gospels, and compare how the authors can narrate the same story differently. I then infer five compositional devices employed by Plutarch by examining a number of pericopes that appear two or more times in his *Lives* and where the evangelists appear to be employing similar devices.

There are nearly one hundred extant biographies written within roughly 150 years on each side of the life of Jesus. Of these, Plutarch is responsible for writing fifty. We are indebted to Plutarch, since much of what we know of the Greco-Roman world derives from what he reported.[1] Upon concluding my first read of Plutarch's *Lives*, I noticed that nine of them featured characters who had lived at the same time and had known one another. Sertorius, Lucullus, Caesar, Cicero, Pompey, Crassus, Younger Cato, Brutus and Antony were involved in seminal events that led to the decline of the Roman Republic.

One can with benefit compare how multiple historians of that time reported the same event. Craig Keener has compared how Tacitus, Suetonius and Plutarch reported the suicide of the Roman emperor Otho in 69 C.E..[2] It is interesting to observe that their stories contain many differences that are quite similar to what we observe between the Gospels. There are numerous reasons why these differences occur, such as, slips of memory, the authors are using different sources, the elasticity of oral tradition, redaction, and the authors the employment of a variety of compositional devices. We can often make a good guess pertaining to why one text differs from another. But there are limits.

Plutarch provides modern historians with a rare opportunity. Because so many of his prominent characters knew one another and participated in many

---

[1] See D.A. Russell, "Plutarch," in *The Oxford Classical Dictionary* (ed. S. Hornblower, A. Spawforth, and E. Eidinow; 4th ed.; Oxford: Oxford University Press, 2012), 1165–1166, esp. 1165.

[2] C.S. Keener, "Otho: A Targeted Comparison of Suetonius' Biography and Tacitus' History, with Implications for the Gospels' Historical Reliability," *BBR* 21 (2011): 331–355.

of the same events, Plutarch will often tell the same story in several *Lives*. For example, Plutarch reports Caesar's assassination in his Lives of *Caesar, Cicero, Antony* and *Brutus*. So, rather than comparing how three authors told the same story, we are able to compare how the same author told the same story on multiple occasions and quite often using the same sources. Many differences appear when we do this. And when the same type of difference recurs repeatedly, this suggests intentionality on Plutarch's part and that the difference resulted from a compositional device he was employing.

While extremely promising, this work is not without its landmines. As one may surmise, it took some time for Plutarch to write the more than sixty biographies of which fifty have survived. In fact, it took him more than two decades. So, when reading the different Lives, we must consider the possibility that Plutarch later discovered more accurate information than he had available to him when he wrote an earlier Life involving the same characters and that this led to a number of differences. Moreover, some of these differences may be the result of flawed memory or a careless inattention to detail on Plutarch's part. Unfortunately, we will never know why some of his accounts differ. So, we must resist the temptation to see a compositional device lurking behind every difference.

The relative chronology in which Plutarch penned his extant *Lives* is difficult to establish.[3] However, the challenge is not prohibitive, since our present research focuses on only nine of Plutarch's fifty Lives. Christopher Pelling is perhaps today's leading Plutarch scholar. Pelling argues that of the nine Lives we are considering, *Lucullus* and *Cicero* were written first, *Sertorius* may have been written last, and the other six were written closely in time and as a set between the earlier and later Lives.[4] Although Plutarch may have discovered more reliable data that he used when writing the set of six than what he had before him years earlier when writing his *Life of Cicero*, we are able to detect compositional devices with a greater confidence when identifying how Plutarch tells the same pericope differently within the set of six Lives.

I will proceed with caution, looking for recurring differences that appear to form a pattern within the nine parallel Lives and give special attention to the set of six, in order to identify various compositional devices employed by Plutarch. Pelling has conducted some initial work in this matter. In an essay titled "Plutarch's Adaptation of His Source-Material," Pelling notes six

---

3   Russell, "Plutarch," 1165.
4   C. Pelling, *Plutarch and History: Eighteen Studies* (Swansea: Classical Press of Wales, 2002), 11, 35 n. 68.

"compositional devices" he observes Plutarch employing.⁵ In personal correspondence with Pelling, I learned that his list of six is by no means exhaustive and that he examined only a few pericopes for his essay. Notwithstanding, Pelling's work provides a very nice springboard into our present research.

1   Biography and Character

Before visiting Plutarch's *Lives*, I want to briefly discuss the genre of the Gospels. In the middle of the twentieth century, most NT scholars thought the Gospels were *sui generis*. Beginning in the 1970s, Charles Talbert among others proposed that the Gospels belong to the genre of Greco-Roman biography.⁶ Richard Burridge objected and set out to demonstrate that the Gospels were *sui generis*. He discovered instead that the Gospels did indeed belong to Greco-Roman biography, and his resulting book, *What Are the Gospels?* has become the definitive treatment on the subject.⁷ Today, a growing majority of scholars regard the Gospels as Greco-Roman biography.

One may ask why the genre is Greco-Roman rather than Jewish biography. The Gospels contain many of the same traits as Greco-Roman biography. And we know of no Jewish biographies of sages written in Jesus's day. The closest we come is Philo's *Life of Moses*, which is not regarded as biography by most scholars. Burridge wrote, "Philip Alexander concludes his study of 'Rabbinic Biography and the Biography of Jesus' thus: 'there are no Rabbinic parallels to the Gospels as such. This is by far the most important single conclusion to emerge from this paper ... There is not a trace of an ancient biography of any of the Sages ... This is a profound enigma.'"⁸ Jacob Neusner similarly wrote, "There is no sustained biography of any [Jewish] sage."⁹

---

5 Pelling, *Plutarch and History*, 91–115. See also Plutarch, *The Life of Cicero* (trans. J.L. Moles; Classical Texts; Warminster, Wiltshire: Aris & Phillips, 1988), 36–39.
6 C.H. Talbert, *What Is a Gospel? The Genre of the Canonical Gospels* (Philadelphia: Fortress, 1977); D.E. Aune, *The New Testament in Its Literary Environment* (Philadelphia: Westminster, 1987).
7 R.A. Burridge, *What Are the Gospels? A Comparison with Graeco-Roman Biography* (2nd ed.; Grand Rapids: Eerdmans, 2004 [1992]).
8 Burridge, *What Are the Gospels?*, 301. Phillip Alexander's quotation is from P.S. Alexander, "Rabbinic Biography and the Biography of Jesus: A Survey of the Evidence," in *Synoptic Studies: The Ampleforth Conferences of 1982 and 1983* (ed. C.M. Tuckett; JSNTSup 7; Sheffield: JSOT Press, 1984), 19–50 (40).
9 J. Neusner, *The Incarnation of God: The Character of Divinity in Formative Judaism* (Philadelphia: Fortress, 1988), 213, quoted in Burridge, *What Are the Gospels?*, 302.

The objective of Greco-Roman biography was to reveal the character of the subject through the person's sayings and deeds. Writing around the same time as some of the Gospels were written, Plutarch provided a statement concerning the objective of such biography in his *Life of Alexander*:

> For it is not Histories that I am writing, but Lives; and in the most illustrious deeds there is not always a manifestation of virtue or vice, nay, a slight thing like a phrase or a jest often makes a greater revelation of character than battles where thousands fall, or the greatest armaments, or sieges of cities. Accordingly, just as painters get the likenesses in their portraits from the face and the expression of the eyes, wherein the character shows itself, but make very little account of the other parts of the body, so I must be permitted to devote myself rather to the signs of the soul in men, and by means of these to portray the life of each, leaving to others the description of their great contests.[10]
> PLUTARCH, *Alex.* 1.2–3 [PERRIN, LCL]

Plutarch makes similar statements in his *Life of Pompey* (*Pomp.* 8.7) and *Life of Nicias* (*Nic.* 1.5). The tone of his statements suggests he was following the existing objective of biography rather than amending or even inventing it.

2   Compositional Devices in Plutarch and in the Gospels

So, the primary objective of biography was to reveal the character of the biography's subject. And we are about to see that Plutarch often employed compositional devices to assist him in achieving this objective. In what follows, I will describe five compositional devices, the first three were also observed by Pelling whereas the latter two break new ground. I will also provide corresponding examples from the Gospels where similar compositional devices may be in view.

2.1   *Compression*
When an author knowingly portrays events over a shorter period of time than the actual time it took for those events to occur, the author has compressed the story. In 66 B.C.E., the command for the war against Mithridates and Tigranes is transferred to Pompey from Lucullus who returned to Rome. Although

---

10   The Loeb reference numbering is used for Plutarch throughout this essay.

Lucullus requests a triumph for his contribution to the war, his request is initially blocked by Gaius Memmius who charges him with needlessly protracting war in his region and diverting the spoils of war for his own use. However, leading citizens intervene on Lucullus's behalf and persuade the people to award him a triumph in 63 C.E.. This is how Plutarch tells the story in his *Life of Lucullus* (*Luc.* 37.1–4). However, since Lucullus is not the primary character in Plutarch's *Life of Cato Minor*, he compresses the story and merely states that Lucullus *almost* lost his triumph (*Cato Min.* 29.3–4). He does not mention that Memmius's attempts were initially successful.

The idea that the evangelists used compression is not new to New Testament scholars. There are three very clear examples of compression in the Gospels: the raising of Jairus's daughter (Matt 9:18–26; par. Mark 5:21–43; Luke 8:40–56), Jesus's cursing the fig tree (Matt 21:18–22; par. Mark 11:11–14, 19–25), and Luke's account of Jesus's resurrection appearances and ascension. Perhaps the very clearest of these is the story of Jesus's raising Jairus's daughter.

In Mark 5:21–43, Jairus approaches Jesus and asks Him to come and heal his daughter *who is about to die*. Jesus agrees and they head toward Jairus's home. On their way a woman touches Jesus and is healed. Shortly afterward, some servants from Jairus's house meet him with the news that his daughter has just died. Jesus tells Jairus not to worry. They then proceed to Jairus's home and Jesus raises his daughter from the dead. Matthew tells the story differently. In Matt 9:18–26, Jairus approaches Jesus and asks Him to come and heal his daughter *who has just died*. Jesus agrees to heal Jairus's daughter and they head toward his home. On their way a woman touches Jesus and is healed. They then proceed to Jairus's home and Jesus raises his daughter from the dead. Matthew has compressed the story by portraying the girl as already dead when Jairus approaches Jesus.

The resurrection narratives have conflicting reports in terms of how long Jesus remained with his disciples after his resurrection. Matthew has Jesus instructing the women on Easter to tell his disciples to meet him in Galilee, a journey of several days (Matt 28). Mark implies such a journey (Mark 16:1–8). And John has Jesus appearing to ten of his twelve disciples on Easter. Eight days later he again appears to them, but this time Thomas is present. Then some time later he appears to his disciples while they are fishing in Galilee (John 20–21). None of the Gospels specify the period of time in which Jesus remained, although Mark, Matthew, and John are clear that it was no less than several days, if not weeks. On the other hand, Luke reports that Jesus's resurrection, all of the appearances of Jesus to his disciples, and his ascension had occurred on Easter (Luke 24). It is clear that Luke has compressed his account, since the same author elsewhere reports that Jesus remained with his disciples for a period of forty days before ascending (Acts 1:1–11). Because Luke has compressed his resurrection narrative, he must place all of the postresurrection appearances in Jerusalem.

2.2 Transferal

When an author knowingly attributes words or deeds to a person that actually belonged to another person, the author has transferred the words or deeds. In 52 B.C.E., Rome was in chaos and Caesar was quickly becoming a threat to the Republic. So, the drastic measure of electing Pompey sole-consul was affected. Pompey established a number of new laws to bring about order. One law stated that encomiums could not be read on behalf of a defendant at his trial. Plutarch reports that Pompey broke the very law he had established when he had an encomium read at the trial of Plancus (*Cato. Min.* 48.4). In that account, Pompey writes the encomium and has it read at the trial but is not present. This is confirmed by other historians (Cassius Dio 40.55.1–4; Valerius Maximus 6.2.5).[11] Therefore, it is interesting to observe that in *Pomp.* 55.5, Plutarch reports that Pompey himself appeared in court and delivered his encomium. If the event had been videotaped and we were viewing it, we most likely would have seen an emissary sent by Pompey read the encomium at the trial. In his *Life of Pompey*, Plutarch merely brushes the emissary out of the story and has Pompey himself read the encomium at the trial, since he was certainly behind it.

An example of transferal in the Gospels is the centurion who asks Jesus to heal his male servant. In Luke 7:1–10, the centurion sends some Jewish elders to ask Jesus to heal his male servant. Jesus agrees and they begin their journey to the home of the centurion. When the centurion learns that Jesus is approaching, he sends some friends to Jesus to communicate on his behalf that he is unworthy to have Jesus enter his home and that Jesus only needs to say the word and his servant will be healed. Jesus then praises the centurion for his faith and pronounces that his servant is healed. When the same story is reported in Matt 8:5–13, the centurion himself comes to Jesus and makes his request. Matthew transfers the request for healing from the mouth of the Jewish elders, whom the evangelist has brushed out of the story along with the centurion's friends, to the mouth of the centurion,[12] thereby also compressing the story a little.

---

11 I am grateful to John Ramsey for alerting me to these references.

12 E. Earle Ellis refers to this technique as *shaliaḥ* in E.E. Ellis, *The Making of the New Testament Documents* (BibInt 39; Leiden: Brill, 1999), 342. However, it is more appropriate for the technique to carry a generic (non-Hebrew) name, since Plutarch, a Greco-Roman author employed it.

Another example of transferal may be observed in Mark. In Matthew, the mother of James and John approach Jesus with her two sons and requests that one sit on his right hand and one on his left when he establishes his kingdom. In Mark, however, it is James and John who come to Jesus and make the request while no mention is made of their mother being present (Matt 20:20–28; Mark 10:35–45).

It is obvious that Matthew or Mark has redacted the story. Perhaps Mark knew the mother had made the request with her two sons present. But he transferred the request to James and John, since they were ultimately behind it.

2.3 Displacement

When an author knowingly removes an event from a context and transplants it in another, that author has displaced the event. In his *Life of Caesar*, Plutarch reports that a group of senators approached Caesar to honor him. When Caesar in turn refused to stand in respect, the senators left humiliated and the crowd frowned on Caesar's act. When Caesar realized his gaffe he pulled back his toga, exposing his neck, and invited anyone who wished to strike and kill him (*Caes.* 60.3–5). On a different occasion, Caesar was seated at the Lupercalia festival when a number of men who had just completed the traditional race lifted up Antony who then attempted to place a diadem on Caesar's head, a gesture suggesting Caesar should be made king. When only a few applauded Antony's act, Caesar declined the wreath, pushing it away. This elicited a robust applause from the crowd. Antony again offered the diadem to Caesar, which was again met by weak applause. Once more, Caesar declined to allow Antony to place it on his head and pushed it away. And, once more, this was met by hardy applause. At this, Caesar left the event greatly disappointed (*Caes.* 61.1–5).

Both events are described in Plutarch's *Life of Caesar*. But in his *Life of Antony*, Plutarch omits the first event. However, he likes the story of Caesar's act of baring his neck. So, he displaces it from its original context and transplants it to the running event at the Lupercalia festival (*Ant.* 12.6).

The evangelists often displaced events. An example that immediately presents itself is the pericope of Jesus overturning tables in the temple. In John, the event occurred at the beginning of Jesus's ministry, whereas in the Synoptics it occurred at its end, on Palm Sunday (John 2:13–22; Mark 11:15–19; Matt 21:12–17; Luke 19:45–48). While it is possible Jesus performed the act twice, it is also possible that John displaced the event from its original context and transplanted it at the beginning of Jesus's ministry.

A more certain example of displacement occurs elsewhere in John's Gospel. Mark, Matthew, and John report Mary's anointing of Jesus with costly perfume before his crucifixion (Mark 14:3–9; Matt 26:6–13; John 12:1–8). Luke provides a similar report. But he is either reporting a different event or has adapted this one significantly (Luke 7:36–50).[13] Mark and Matthew are clear that the event occurred two days before the Passover, whereas John says it occurred six days before the Passover. Mark and Matthew report that the anointing occurred after Jesus's triumphal entry on Palm Sunday, whereas John reports that it occurred beforehand.

One may wish to resolve the difference by suggesting that John is reporting a different event. After all, only in John is the woman identified as Mary, whereas she is anonymous in Matthew and Mark. However, those inclined to take this route should consider the following:

- In all three accounts, the plot of the Jewish leaders to arrest Jesus immediately precedes the woman's anointing of Jesus.
- In all three accounts, the anointing occurs in Bethany.
- In all three accounts, the woman pours costly perfume on Jesus.
- In all three accounts, the perfume is worth around 300 denarii.
- In all three accounts, one or more of those present are indignant.
- In all three accounts, Jesus's response is the same. He tells the objectors to leave the woman alone, that she did a beautiful thing, that they will always have the poor with them, and that she has anointed him for burial.

These similarities suggest that John is referring to the same event as Matthew and Mark. Accordingly, it seems more likely that John is doing what Plutarch does on numerous occasions, dislocating the event from its original context

---

13   The following elements suggest that Luke is either providing his readers with a different story or has adapted it: (a) The story appears in a different context in Luke's Gospel with no apparent reason for displacing it. (b) The conversation in the story is different in Luke. (c) Luke mentions Mary later in 10:38–42 but does not link her to the woman in 7:36–50 by describing her as "the woman who had earlier anointed Jesus." (d) Simon is indignant for a different reason than those in the accounts provided by Matt, Mark, and John. (e) In John, Mary is known by Jesus (John 11:1–2), whereas the woman appears to be unknown by him in Luke. (In Matt and Mark, the woman could be known by Jesus.)

Despite these elements, there are interesting similarities (Luke 7:36–50; par. Matt 26:6–13; Mark 14:3–9; John 12:1–8): (1) In Matthew, Mark, and Luke, the event occurs in the house of Simon. In Matthew and Mark, the host is Simon the leper, whereas in Luke he is Simon the Pharisee. (Since Simon was the most popular name among male Judean Jews of the first century, there is no need to require that this is the same Simon.) (2) In Matthew, Mark, and Luke, the woman pours the perfume from an alabaster flask.

and transplanting it in another. But why would John dislocate the story? Lucian of Samosata, the 2nd-cent. AD Greek writer, may provide us with the answer in one of the precious few extant ancient treatments concerning the writing of history. He asserts that when an author writes a narrative, he should link his topics together like a chain, using common matter that overlaps (*How to Write History* 55).

So this leads us to ask, is a link present in the pericope of Mary anointing Jesus? Matthew and Mark's accounts of the anointing are the only appearance of this woman in their Gospels. And she is not mentioned by name in either. However, in John's Gospel, the pericope of Jesus raising Lazarus and his interactions with Martha and the same Mary has just been told in the previous chapter. So, perhaps John is thinking, "Since I have just mentioned Mary, this would be a very good time to tell the story of her anointing Jesus." And so, he does. Mary is the overlapping material that links the two stories. John places the story of the anointing directly after the raising of Lazarus, even chronologically, in order to link together two stories involving Mary and to keep the narrative flowing smoothly, although he perhaps knew the event had actually occurred two days prior to the Passover rather than six. And in the two verses that follow (12:9–10), John continues the chain by adding that when others learned that Jesus was in Bethany, they came to see him and Lazarus whom Jesus had raised and that the Jewish leaders were now planning to put Lazarus to death.

Another possible example of displacement in the Gospels concerns the day and time on which Jesus was crucified. The Passover meal was distinct from other meals eaten during the week of that feast. According to Exodus 12, the Feast of Unleavened Bread lasted seven days and the Passover meal was to be eaten on the first evening. Any food left over from that meal was to be burned the next morning. In other words, there were no leftovers when it came to the Passover meal.

According to all three Synoptics, Jesus was crucified after the Passover meal had been eaten (Matt 26:17–20; cf. Mark 14:12–18; Luke 22:7–15). However, John's Gospel creates a tension. Jesus eats his last meal with his disciples where he tells them that one of them is about to betray him, just as the Synoptics report. He identifies Judas as the betrayer, who then leaves and the rest is history (John 13:1–30). So, this is the same event reported as the Passover meal in the Synoptics. However, there is nothing in John's account suggesting that it was the Passover meal. In fact, the Last Supper in John's Gospel could not have been the Passover meal, since it is introduced in 13:1–2 with the words, "Now before the Feast of the Passover ..."

Later, in John 18, the meal is over and Jesus has been arrested. John reports, "Then they led Jesus from the house of Caiaphas to the praetorium. It was early. They themselves did not enter the praetorium, so that they might not be defiled, but might eat the Passover" (v. 28). Pilate then proceeds to condemn and execute Jesus. So, while the Synoptics report that Jesus was crucified after the Passover meal, John reports that he was crucified prior to the Passover meal.

Craig Keener proposes a solution that takes into account the flexibility of ancient biography. He notes the teaching in the Mishnah that when the Passover fell on the eve of a Sabbath, the evening burnt-offering would be moved back two hours and the paschal lamb was slaughtered afterward. Since burnt offerings were normally slaughtered around 2:30 in the afternoon, they would be moved back to around noon.[14] It is, therefore, of additional interest that John reports Pilate delivering Jesus over to be crucified around the sixth hour, i.e., noon (John 19:14), whereas Mark reports that it was the third hour or 9:00 in the morning (Mark 15:25). Pliny the Elder informs us that Roman priests and magistrates recognized a day to begin and end at midnight (*N.H.* 2.79 [77]). While this proposal is possible, it does not account for the different days. Keener's proposal accounts for both the day and time of Jesus's crucifixion by suggesting that John may have altered them, thus displacing the event, in order to make a theological point, one that Paul had recognized decades earlier: Jesus is our Passover Lamb and the burnt offering for our sins (see Rom 8:3 and 1 Cor 5:7; cf. Eph 5:2. See also Heb 10:10, 14; 13:11–12).

2.4 *Spotlighting*

During a theatrical performance, the lighting crew sometimes will shine a spotlight on an actor and draw such attention to the person in the spotlight that others who are present in the scene are not really visible to the audience. *When an author focuses attention on a person so the person's involvement in a scene is clearly described whereas mention of others who were likewise involved is neglected, the author has shined his literary spotlight on that person.* Thus far in

---

14 See C.S. Keener, *The Gospel of John: A Commentary* (2 vols.; Peabody, MA: Hendrickson, 2003), 2:1129–1131. The Mishna reference provided by Keener is m. Pesaḥ. 5:1. For an alternative view that the Jews of Jesus's day did not all agree on the proper day on which the Passover fell and that Jesus celebrated the Passover on a different day than the Jewish leadership, see D. Instone-Brewer, *Traditions of the Rabbis from the Era of the New Testament*. Vol. 2A: *Feasts and Sabbaths; Passover and Atonement* (Grand Rapids: Eerdmans, 2011), 115–200. I find Keener's hypothesis preferable to Instone-Brewer's, since the former also accounts for the different times given by Mark and John at which Jesus was crucified. Moreover, John appears to have been intentional in erasing signs that the Last Supper was a Passover meal.

my research, spotlighting appears with greater frequency than other compositional devices in the nine Lives written by Plutarch under consideration. Space allows only a few examples.

In the autumn of 63 C.E. and at the height of the Catilinarian conspiracy, Marcus Crassus received late at night some letters addressed to him and many of the senators informing them of the impending violence to the city planned by Catiline. In Plutarch's *Life of Cicero*, Crassus, Marcellus, and Metellus together go to the home of Cicero, who is one of the consuls, and deliver the letters to him (*Cic.* 15.1–4). However, in his *Life of Crassus*, Plutarch mentions only Crassus in the visit to Cicero (*Crass.* 13.3). Although Plutarch does not say Crassus was alone, that is the impression his account gives. Plutarch is spotlighting.

On the following morning, Cicero calls the senate together to reveal the conspiracy, and Catiline is asked to leave Rome. However, he has friends in the city who were intending to carry out the rebellion. When these friends in turn are discovered and arrested, Cicero once again calls the senate to discuss the fate of the conspirators. At first, many opine that they should be executed. However, Caesar contends that they should instead be imprisoned until they can be properly tried. In his *Life of Caesar* and *Life of Cicero*, Plutarch reports that Catulus and Cato opposed Caesar and persuaded the rest of the senate to execute the conspirators (*Caes.* 7.4–8.2; *Cic.* 20.3–21.4). However, in his *Life of Cato Minor*, Plutarch mentions only Cato's opposition, and the reader receives the impression that it was Cato alone who opposed Caesar and persuaded the senate to execute the conspirators (*Cato. Min.* 22.3–23.3). Plutarch is shining his literary spotlight on Cato.

There are several candidates in the Gospels where the evangelists may be shining their literary spotlight. How many women went to the tomb on Easter morning? The Synoptics mention multiple women (Matt 28:1; Mark 16:1–2; Luke 23:55–24:3). However, John's account says Mary Magdalene went to the tomb early in the morning and discovered it empty (John 20:1). John makes no mention of others accompanying her. It is quite plausible that John knows of the other women but neglects to mention them in order to focus on a single figure, Mary Magdalene. This suspicion is virtually confirmed by the second verse of John 20:

> She ran and came to Simon Peter and to the other disciple whom Jesus loved, and said to them, "They took the Lord out of the tomb, and *we* do not know where they laid him".
>
> John 20:2; emphasis added

Who is the "we" to whom Mary Magdalene's words refers? It seems highly likely that it is the other women.

John is not the only evangelist to mention the primary person while neglecting to mention others who are present. In Luke's resurrection narrative, when the women return from the empty tomb and inform the disciples that Jesus has been raised and that angels had announced this to them, Peter gets up, runs to the tomb and finds it empty (Luke 24:1–12). This differs from John's narrative which says Peter and the beloved disciple run together to the tomb and find it empty (John 20:1–10). But one need read only twelve verses further in Luke 24 to see what Luke has done. Jesus is conversing with the disciples walking to Emmaus who are kept from recognizing him. He asks why they are troubled, and they relate the story to him: "We thought Jesus was the Messiah. But he was crucified on Friday. Then something strange happened this morning. Our women folk went to the tomb and discovered it empty. They also informed us they had seen angels there who told them Jesus had risen from the dead. Then *some of our own* went to the tomb and discovered it empty as the women had claimed" (Luke 24:21–24a; emphasis added).

In v. 12, Luke mentions only the lead disciple, Peter, running to the tomb. But the "some of our own" in v. 24 suggests that Luke may know of at least one other who had accompanied Peter. In these examples, both Luke and John appear to employ spotlighting. On occasion, they mention only the chief person involved, although they appear to be aware of others who were present and who are mentioned by another evangelist. Perhaps spotlighting may be why Matthew and Mark mention a single angel at the empty tomb, whereas Luke and John mention two. Matthew and Mark may be focusing on the angel announcing the news to the women that Jesus had risen from the dead.

2.5 *Simplification*[15]

When an author adapts material by omitting details that may complicate the literary portrait of the person being described, the author has simplified the story. Of the nine primary characters in the nine Lives we are examining, one of the finest moral characters is Brutus, the man at whose sight Caesar is said to have given up his struggle when he was being assassinated. Plutarch's Brutus is a lover of the Roman people, a loving husband, and a man who is fair and moderate in his dealings with others, especially when compared with other Roman leaders, who were often brutal and stopped at nothing to achieve their objective of supremacy.

---

15   I am grateful to my friend Udo Karsten for suggesting this term.

In 48 B.C.E., Caesar had defeated Pompey who had fled to Egypt when the young king Ptolemy XIII, brother of the famous queen Cleopatra, took the advice of his advisors, betrayed Pompey, and put him to death. When Caesar arrived in Egypt and learned of the betrayal and inglorious death suffered by Pompey, he seized and executed those who had been involved. However, the king escaped, as did his counselor Theodotus who had advised him to have Pompey killed. Brutus later discovered Theodotus while in Asia.

In the *Life of Pompey*, Plutarch says Brutus puts Theodotus to death using every sort of torture (*Pomp.* 80.5–6).[16] But in the *Life of Brutus*, Plutarch reports that when Brutus discovers Theodotus, he punishes him (*Brut.* 33.4). And no mention is made of the brutal manner in which the punishment is carried out.

In the previous chapter of *Brutus* (32), Plutarch tells a story of how a city surrenders to Brutus, knowing he is a man of great moderation and justice. Plutarch adds that the people's hopes are met and even exceeded. Then, a few chapters later (35), Brutus again emerges as a highly principled man. Therefore, it is understandable that Plutarch would omit the detail that Brutus had punished Theodotus in a most cruel manner, since this would have complicated the portrait he is painting of him as a kind and moderate leader. Plutarch also omits the story in which Brutus exerts his political influence by permitting a loan to be made to Cyprus at 48 percent, an interest rate that will cripple the city. Including this incident likewise would have complicated his portrait of the fair and highly principled Brutus (see Cicero, *Att.* 5.21).[17] Plutarch simplifies his *Life of Brutus* in order to present an accurate representation of Brutus to his readers. But his portrait is obviously not an exhaustive account, which would have to include a number of details liable to distract readers from seeing the true Brutus.

When we come to the Gospels, a compelling case can be made that John has simplified his passion narrative.

In the Synoptics, Jesus struggles mightily over his impending suffering. Mark 14:33–36 reports the following:

> And [Jesus] took with him Peter and James and John, and began to be alarmed and greatly troubled. And he said to them, "My soul is grieved to the point of death. Remain here and keep watch." And going a little farther, he fell on the ground and prayed that, if it were possible, the hour

---

16   In *Caes.* 48.2, Plutarch says that Caesar receives Pompey's head and signet ring from Theodotus and does not mention Caesar's attempt to capture him.

17   I thank John Ramsey for the example from Cicero's letters.

might pass from him. And was saying, "Abba, Father, all things are possible for you. Take this cup away from me. Yet not what I will, but what you will."

Mark mentions Jesus praying that the hour might pass from him. All of the Synoptics portray Jesus in the garden praying fervently, asking God to remove the cup from him, if possible (see also Matt 26:38–44; Luke 22:40–42).

John portrays Jesus differently. Throughout John's Gospel, Jesus is in total control of his fate and has no hesitation regarding it. In 10:18, Jesus says that no one takes his life from him, but by his own choice he lays it down. He has the authority to lay it down and to take it up. In 12:27, Jesus says, "Now my soul is troubled. And what will I say? 'Father, save me from this hour'? But it was for this purpose that I have come to this hour."

In John, Jesus is confident and resolved in the garden (John 18:1–12). There is little indication he is grieving and struggling. When Peter cuts off the ear of the high priest's servant, Jesus instructs him, "Put your sword into its sheath; the cup that the Father has given me; will I not now drink it?" (v. 11). Instead of requesting that the Father save him from the hour (in Mark) and remove the cup of suffering so that he may not drink it (as reported in the Synoptics), in John, Jesus says he refuses to ask the Father to save him from the hour and remove the cup, since he came into the world to drink this cup in this hour.

It is clear that John has omitted some details and has employed simplification in writing his biography of Jesus. He suppresses almost all detail pertaining to Jesus's struggle in the garden because it would have complicated the literary portrait he is painting of Jesus as divine. Perhaps John knows that many of his readers may struggle given John's high Christology on the one hand and a Jesus who wrestles with thoughts of the torture and death that mere humans were about to inflict on him on the other. It also appears that John has altered Jesus's words so that he could more clearly portray the course of action Jesus took. No questions are left in the minds of John's readers: Jesus willingly suffered and died for them. Similar to how Plutarch simplifies his portrait of Brutus, John is simplifying his portrait of Jesus in order to reveal more clearly who Jesus really is.

3   Conclusion

Most New Testament scholars now agree that the canonical Gospels bear close affinities with Greco-Roman biography and that this genre permitted some flexibility in the manner events were reported that is rare in modern biographical literature. Classical scholars have identified a number of compositional devices they suspect authors employed. Since the canonical Gospels bear close affinities with Greco-Roman biography, we could anticipate that their authors would employ similar devices. In this brief analysis, we have observed how both Plutarch and the evangelists reported the same events differently and inferred five compositional devices they appear to have employed: compression, transferal, displacement, spotlighting, and simplification. Our findings may have implications pertaining to how some of the discrepancies often observed between the canonical Gospels originated.

The Narrative Perspective of the Fourth Gospel

*Hans Förster**

The Fourth Gospel is in many ways different from the other three canonical Gospels. Therefore, the other three canonical Gospels are also called Synoptic Gospels, since they share many common features concerning material, narrative structure, and the like. There exists not even a consensus concerning the relationship between the Fourth Gospel and the three other Gospels,[1] even if the so called Leuven hypothesis has shaped the discussion for quite some time.[2] There seems, however, a consensus that there is no difference concerning the narrative perspective and the genre between the four canonical Gospels. The common features between the four canonical Gospels seem to be so strong that they even have been seen as *one* genre separate from other genres in Greco-Roman literature.[3] Within this context the statement of the "eyewitness" in John 21:24–25 is mostly seen as an addition by the anonymous author in order to give credibility to the story.[4] The decision to use the final form of the text and not a hypothetically reconstructed "original" does not presuppose any final decision as to the actual literary history of the text at hand. It is a rather pragmatic approach using the observation that the text as it is used today is

---

* The author of the article is currently preparing a critical edition of the Sahidic version of the Gospel of John (FWF-project 25082 / funded by the Austrian Science Fund).

1 Cf. K. Haldiman and H. Weder, "Aus der Literatur zum Johannesevangelium 1985–1994. Erster Teil: Historische Sicherung und diachrone Analysen II," *TRu* 67 (2002): 425–456 (452).

2 For this hypothesis, cf. Michael Labahn, "Scripture Talks because Jesus Talks: The Narrative Rhetoric of Persuading and Creativity in John's Use of Scripture," in *The Fourth Gospel in First-Century Media Culture* (ed. Anthony Le Donne and Tom Thatcher; LNTS 426; London: T&T Clark International, 2011), 133–154 (133); cf. also Gilbert van Belle, "Tradition, Exegetical Formation, and the Leuven Hypothesis," in *What We Have Heard from the Beginning: The Past, Present, and Future of Johannine Studies* (ed. Tom Thatcher; Waco: Baylor University Press, 2007), 325–337.

3 For a recent discussion of this opinion, cf. Andreas J. Köstenberger, "The Genre of the Fourth Gospel and Greco-Roman Literary Conventions," in *Christian Origins and Greco-Roman Culture: Social and Literary Contexts for the New Testament* (ed. Stanley E. Porter and Andrew W. Pitts; ECHC 1; TENTS 9; Leiden: Brill, 2013), 435–462 (438–440) and literature.

4 Köstenberger, "Genre," 462: "Finally, the Gospel claims to be the work of an eyewitness and first-hand source. In a Greco-Roman context, this was generally considered to provide a more reliable recounting of events."

preserved in the Greek manuscript tradition.⁵ There exists no known Greek manuscript attesting a Gospel of John ending with ch. 20.⁶

In order to discuss a possible self-assignment of a literary genre and the consequences of this self-assignment as to the narrative perspective of the Gospel⁷ of John a comparison is necessary. The text of the Gospel of John *as circulated*⁸ in antiquity (thus, seeing the text as literary unit⁹) will be compared with two other narrative texts from the New Testament that attest an explicit self-assignment of a literary genre (and thereby implicitly give an indication of an intended narrative perspective). The first part will set forth the narrative perspective and literary genre (in most general terms) of these two texts. The second part will discuss a possible self-assignment of a literary genre in the

---

5   This does not preclude some minor problems of the textual tradition like the possibly in the original text missing verse John 5:4 or the probably missing pericopa of the adulteress (John 7:53–8:11).

6   As opposed to the secondary ending to the Gospel of Mark, there is no extant Greek manuscript attesting to a Gospel of John ending with ch. 20; the "private Textabschrift" (Gesa Schenke, "Das Erscheinen Jesu vor den Jüngern und der ungläubige Thomas, Johannes 20,19–31," in *Coptica—Gnostica—Manichaica: Melanges offerts a Wolf-Peter Funk* [ed. Louis Painchaud and Paul-Hubert Poirier; Bibliotheque Copte de Nag Hammadi; Section Études 7; Leuven: Peeters, 2006], 893) on a single leaf of papyrus in the Sahidic dialect containing John 20:19–31, does not constitute enough proof to argue even for a "sahidische Vorlage" without ch. 21; cf. for the edition of the papyrus fragment Schenke, "Das Erscheinen Jesu," 893–904.

7   It is not possible in the constricted space of the article to discuss the question as to what a "Gospel" may be.

8   For a comparable approach, cf. also Hartwig Thyen, *Das Johannesevangelium* (HNT 6; Tübingen: Mohr Siebeck, 2005), 1: "Da die handschriftlichen Zeugen weder für die vielfach vorgeschlagenen Umstellungen von Teiltexten noch für eine nachträgliche Bearbeitung eines vorliegenden Evangeliums durch einen *kirchlichen Redaktor* irgendwelche ernstzunehmenden Indizien bieten, dürfte unser Evangelium *öffentlich* nie anders als in seiner überlieferten kanonischen Gestalt existiert haben. Darum haben wir hier auf die Erörterung aller Fragen nach der vermeintlichen *Genese* unseres Evangeliums, nach seinen mutmaßlichen *Quellen* oder gar nach einem bereits literarisch verfaßten Vorläufer (*Predecessor*, Fortna), sowie nach seiner vermeintlich sekundären Bearbeitung durch eine 'kirchliche Redaktion' (Bultmann, Becker u.a.) verzichtet."

9   Cf. Tom Thatcher, "The Rejected Prophet and the Royal Official (John 4,43–54): A Case Study in the Relationship Between John and the Synoptics," in *Studies in the Gospel of John and its Christology: Festschrift Gilbert van Belle* (ed. Joseph Verheyden et al.; BETL 265; Leuven: Peeters, 2014), 119–148 (145): "[...] Van Belle's reading does not stand or fall on the claim that John used the Synoptics as sources; the genius of his exegesis stands, rather, on his decision to read FG as a unified composition alongside other extant witnesses, without recourse to putative sources or complex developmental theories."

Gospel of John and the third part will raise the question whether a possible self-assignment of a literary genre might have consequences for the interpretation of the Gospel of John. The Gospel of John is usually seen as a text which might have a somewhat defective narrative: "[...] the so-called *aporias* in the Gospel of John—abrupt changes in the flow of the narrative, artificial transitions, inconsistencies in grammar or logical sequence—are also important considerations in assessing the relationship between literary unity (and literary criticism) and historical reliability."[10] It may, however, well be that the very narrative perspective, which might be different from the narrative perspective of the other canonical Gospels, has contributed to the perception of the so-called *aporias*. Thus, it is well possible that the perceived inconsistencies might be more due to the way how the text is read (i.e. as the narrative of an omniscient author) and less the result of a defective narrative.

1 Two Narrative Texts in the New Testament and Their Self-assigned Literary Genres

Among the five narrative texts in the New Testament—besides the four Gospels the Acts of the Apostles also belong to the narrative texts of the New Testament—two define the basic literary genre in their preface: the Gospel of Luke and Acts of Apostles. Both of them are probably from the same author, and, therefore, can be dealt with together.

The Gospel of Luke uses a key term to describe the intention of its narrative and thereby the literary genre of the text: διήγησις[11] occurs in the first verse of Luke's Gospel describing the literary genre of other Gospels known to the author/narrator[12] and of the text he intends to produce. A definition of διήγησις in rhetoric in antiquity is: "the διήγησις is the setting forth of a deed which had happened or as if happened."[13] This "setting forth of events" is then further described by the author/narrator as "written down carefully" after a thorough

---

[10] Van Belle, "Tradition," 335.
[11] Luke 1:1: ἐπειδήπερ πολλοὶ ἐπεχείρησαν ἀνατάξασθαι διήγησιν περὶ τῶν πεπληροφορημένων ἐν ἡμῖν πραγμάτων.
[12] It is in this context irrelevant whether the first person used in Luke 1:3 represents the narrator or whether it can be interpreted as authorial comment. It is possible to argue that every author becomes a narrator if comments are made within the text.
[13] *Rhetorica Anonyma* (ed. C. Walz; Osnabrück: Otto Zeller, 1968), 3:664, 24–25: διήγησίς ἐστιν ἔκθεσις πράγματος γεγονότος ἢ ὡς γεγονότος.

inquiry.[14] Thus, the definition of διήγησις as quoted is in line with the description of the research by the author/narrator[15] of the Gospel of Luke before writing his text.

It is important to note that this definition does not distinguish between hypothetical events and actual events. The definition focuses rather on the question that facts are reported as happened or as if happened. This definition of διήγησις does implicitly take into consideration that there is no possible way for the person who is reading a text to decide whether the convincingly narrated events[16] are set forth correctly or incorrectly. And, in case that the facts are set forth incorrectly, there is also no way to discern whether this is done deliberately or erroneously. Thus, the διήγησις is a way of describing events whether historical or hypothetical. And one of its central characteristics of this way of describing facts is the verisimilitude.[17] Thus, by opening the text of the Gospel of Luke in such a way the author/narrator assigns the text to "historical non-fiction" as literary genre using as narrative perspective the perspective of the "objective" and "omniscient" narrator.[18]

The same happens in the Acts of Apostles. There, the word λόγος is used to describe the content of both, Gospel and Acts.[19] Λόγος (a word with deep theological implications in many cases) is—in this context—the "account," the "orderly setting forth" of "what happened".[20] By using this word the author/

---

14   Luke 1:3: ἔδοξεν κἀμοὶ παρηκολουθηκότι ἄνωθεν πᾶσιν ἀκριβῶς καθεξῆς σοι γράψαι.
15   In the terminology of Irene J.F. de Jong, this would be the external narrator; cf. Irene J.F. de Jong, "Introduction: Narratologial Theory on Narrators, Narratees and Narrative," in *Narrators, Narratees and Narratives in Ancient Greek Literature: Studies in Ancient Greek Narrative, Volume One* (ed. Irene J.F. de Jong et al.; Leiden: Brill, 2004), 1–10.
16   This is not the place to discuss the problem that inconsistencies in the testimony of a witness are used to call the testimony into question during cross-examination. Such a witness is not any more convincing. However, the "cross-examination" of the Gospel of John (perceived as "historical narrative") discovers literary inconsistencies which might be connected to its very literary genre of a subjective account.
17   The paper does not intend to discuss whether the text of Luke's Gospel has verisimilitude for today's readers. The question is the self-definition as presented in the text.
18   This is in contradistinction to how e.g. Andrew T. Lincoln sees the eyewitness; cf. Andrew T. Lincoln, "The Beloved Disciple as Eyewitness and the Fourth Gospel as Witness," *JSNT* 24 (2002): 3–26 (15): "They might well now be encouraged to identify that omniscient narrator as the Beloved Disciple."
19   Acts 1:1: τὸν μὲν πρῶτον λόγον ἐποιησάμην περὶ πάντων, ὦ Θεόφιλε, ὧν ἤρξατο ὁ Ἰησοῦς ποιεῖν τε καὶ διδάσκειν.
20   For this word and its meaning in the preface of another literary text cf. Hans Förster, "Zur Bedeutung von ΛΟΓΟΣ im Prolog des Judasevangeliums," *ZAC* 14 (2010): 487–495.

narrator shows the intention to describe facts as they happened—or as they are perceived/supposed to have happened.

Thus, the self-assignment of the literary genre of the two works connected with the name Luke makes these texts orderly accounts of things which happened or which are narrated as if happened. In this case the intention is for both texts to be narrative non-fiction. This is, however, not the place to reopen the discussion whether e.g. Acts of the Apostles actually conform to the literary prerequisites of the literary genre "historical account" with arguments for[21] and against[22] their conformity to this literary genre. This discussion is not important within the current context. It is important that the self-assignment of the literary genre of these two narrative texts from the New Testament shows the intention that they are written in a way as to belong to the genre of narrative non-fiction. This genre is further qualified by the fact that they are written by an author who was not present when these things happened but who did extensive research and used sources to create his account of what happened. Thus, the very intention of the narrative is to make it a (more or less exhaustive) description of historical events as given by a historian also for other historical events.[23]

---

21 Cf. e.g. Martin Hengel, "Zur urchristlichen Geschichtsschreibung," in *Studien zum Urchristentum: Kleine Schriften VI* (eds. Martin Hengel and Claus-Jürgen Thornton; WUNT 234; Tübingen: Mohr, 2008), 1–104 (48–49): "Hinter *anderen antiken Geschichtsschreibern* steht Lukas an Vertrauenswürdigkeit nicht zurück. Man hat ihm großes Unrecht getan, wenn man ihn in die Nähe der erbaulichen, weitgehend fiktiven, romanhaften Schriftstellerei im Stile der späteren Apostelakten rückte, die Fakten je nach Bedarf und Belieben frei erfindet. [...] Er ist nicht bloßer 'Erbauungsschriftsteller', sondern ernstzunehmender Historiker und Theologe zugleich. Seine Berichterstattung hält sich durchaus im Rahmen dessen, was für die Antike als zuverlässig galt."

22 Cf. e.g. Loveday C.A. Alexander, *Acts in its Ancient Literary Context: A Classicist Looks at the Acts of the Apostles* (JSNTSup 289; London: T&T Clark, 2005), 157: "The narrative of Acts, in particular, inhabits many of the spaces allocated to 'fiction' on the Greco-Roman cultural map."

23 There is no need to discuss the question further whether these texts fully comply to the narrative conventions of ancient historiography since—in principle—the differences might arise less from deliberate deviation than from shortcomings of the (anonymous) author; and the question at hand is the *intended* narrative genre and perspective which does not need any judgement as to how far the author succeeded.

2 The Narrative Genre Assigned to the Gospel of John

In contrast to the two texts from the New Testament mentioned above, it seems to be obvious that the Gospel of John is taking a different approach—if it is taken as a literary unity. The so-called second ending—it is quite often seen as later addition to the text[24]—states that the text has been written by an eyewitness.[25] One may add that this actually repeats in different words what is already mentioned in other places; it might well be that he is to be identified with the unnamed disciple accompanying Andrew (John 1:35–40) and he is mentioned throughout the Gospel.[26] Thus, it seems probable that the "beloved Disciple would [...] be in a position to be an eyewitness of all the events from 1.19 to 21.23."[27] It might be important to note that the wording of John 21:24 uses phraseology which occurs also in Greek documentary texts from antiquity to stress the interdependence between the facts described and the actual historical events reported: the anonymous author intends this to be a narrative which closely adheres to facts. Almost all terms used there occur in judicial contexts.[28] The witnesses (μαρτυρέω, μαρτυρία) are used in documentary texts as

---

24   Felix S. Just, "Combining Key Methodologies in Johannine Studies," in *What We Have Heard from the Beginning* (ed. Tom Thatcher; Waco: Baylor, 2007), 355–358 (356): "All but a small minority of readers today accept the proposal that the Fourth Gospel was not written all at once by only one author. The double endings at John 20:30–31 and 21:25, along with the third-person reference in John 21:24 to the Beloved Disciple as the author of the (main portion) of the Gospel, make it virtually indisputable that the text was edited and expanded at least once, if not numerous times." For the narrative in the third person, cf. also D. Wyrwa, "Augustins geistliche Auslegung des Johannesevangeliums," in *Christliche Exegese zwischen Nicaea und Chalcedon* (ed. J. van Oort and U. Wickert; Kampen: Kok Pharos, 1992), 185–216 (189): "Daß dieser sich übrigens hier wie auch sonst nicht direkt nennt, sondern von sich in der 3. Person spricht, erklärt Augustin als eine Gepflogenheit biblischer Autoren, die auch bei Matthäus, Mose und Paulus zu beobachten sei, und die der Überheblichkeit vorbeugen soll."
25   John 21:24: οὗτός ἐστιν ὁ μαθητὴς ὁ μαρτυρῶν περὶ τούτων καὶ ὁ γράψας ταῦτα, καὶ οἴδαμεν ὅτι ἀληθὴς αὐτοῦ ἡ μαρτυρία ἐστίν.
26   As to the question whether John 19:35 refers to the Beloved Disciple or to another person, cf. Andrew T. Lincoln, "The Beloved Disciple as Eyewitness and the Fourth Gospel as Witness," *JSNT* 24 (2002): 3–26 (12–15).
27   Lincoln, "Beloved Disciple," 15–16.
28   It may well be that also the use of the term σημεῖον (used also John 20:30) within the Gospel of John might derive partially from documentary use; this is, however, not the scope of the discussion of the narrative genre of John's Gospel.

guarantee for the validity (ἀληθινός[29]) of a text as written (γράφω).[30] It is further to be noted that the judicial terminology used in John 21:24 (μαρτυρέω[31] and μαρτυρία[32]) occurs well throughout the Gospel of John while the Synoptics do not show any preponderance for these two words.[33] This can be called a proclivity for forensic terminology—and forensic terminology is something quite common to judicial literature,[34] which albeit is different from historical literature. Common to both types of literature is their intention as to its character as "non-fiction": judicial literature as well as historical accounts are to be understood *as written*. Thus, by means of the "second ending" as well as on a semantic level it seems that the anonymous author of the Gospel of John declares his intention to give a report of facts as (if) they happened in this way and as if they were reported by an eyewitness. In this case the narrative strives—in the very manner in which it is reported—for verisimilitude,[35] albeit in a manner quite different from the Synoptic Gospels.

It is further to note that there is one remarkable feature within John 21:24, which needs to be commented on and which might not have received proper attention. The very nature of a "witness" who usually appears at the end of a documentary text seems to be in contradistinction to the "witness" of the Gospel. Witnesses are known persons and are usually even described as "respectable" (the Greek term ἐλεύθερος can be used for this in Coptic documentary texts) and "trustworthy"[36] and always sign with their names. The "normal"

---

29 For ἀληθινός as "trustworthy," cf. Friedrich G. Preisigke, *Wörterbuch der griechischen Papyrusurkunden mit Einschluß der Griechischen Inschriften, Aufschriften, Ostraka, Mumienschilder usw. aus Ägypten*. Bd. 1 (Berlin: Eigenverlag, 1925), 55.

30 The phrase ὡς γέγραπται is widely attested in legal documents and γράφω may refer to legal documents or even the law; this might well be an additional semantic implication for γραφή in the Gospel of John since the text alternates between γραφή and νόμος; for the use in documentary texts, cf. Preisigke, *Wörterbuch*. Bd. 1, 308–313.

31 John 1:7, 8, 15, 32, 34; 2:25; 3:11, 26, 28, 32; 4:39, 44; 5:31, 32, 33, 36, 37, 39; 7:7; 8:13, 14, 18; 10:25; 12:17; 13:21; 15:26, 27; 18:23, 37; 19:35; 21:24.

32 John 1:7, 19; 3:11, 32, 33; 5:31, 32, 34, 36; 8:13, 14, 17; 19:35; 21:24.

33 Matthew: μαρτυρέω: 23:31; μαρτυρία: not used; Mark: μαρτυρέω: not used; μαρτυρία: 14:55, 56, 59; Luke μαρτυρέω: 4:22; μαρτυρία: 22:71.

34 The use of this terminology might even be an argument in favour of the unity of the Gospel, however, this is not the question at hand.

35 The term "eyewitness" is put within quotation marks to indicate that the term is used as defined within the narrative of the Gospel. There is no possible means—as with the διήγησις—to discern whether facts or fictitious events are detailed in the report.

36 Cf. Hans Förster, *Wörterbuch der griechischen Wörter in den koptischen dokumentarischen Texten* (TU 148; Berlin: de Gruyter, 2002), s.v. ἀξιόπιστος and ἐλεύθερος.

witness is a (very often prominent and) identifiable person. In opposition to this description the very "witness" of the Gospel of John stays anonymous and is, therefore, unknown. Thus, the witness is not what a person from antiquity would expect a witness to be: an authoritative figure who is well known within his local society.[37] This seems to be also an important difference to texts like the Gospel of Thomas or the Gospel of Judas[38] or the Protevangelium of James—all three claim to derive their authority from the persons mentioned already in the title and either at the beginning or the end of the text. Thus, they might be pseudonymous but they are not anonymous.

It seems, therefore, necessary to raise the question as to how much credibility an *anonymous* witness would have in antiquity;[39] and in case that the *anonymous* witness seems to be rather witless concerning the function of giving credibility to a text,[40] self-assignment as eyewitness might imply a different

---

37 Cf., however, Richard Bauckham, *Jesus and the Eyewitnesses: The Gospels as Eyewitness Testimony* (Grand Rapids: Eerdmans, 2006), 5: "There can be good reasons for trusting or distrusting a witness, but these are precisely reasons for *trusting or distrusting*. Trusting testimony is not an irrational act of faith that leaves critical rationality aside; it is, on the contrary, the rationally appropriate way of responding to authentic testimony. Gospels understood as testimony are the entirely appropriate means of access to the historical reality of Jesus. [...] We need to recognize that, historically speaking, testimony is a unique and uniquely valuable means of access to historical reality." One is tempted to add that, judicially speaking, knowing the witness is one precondition for trusting the testimony; this is a proper remark since Bauckham (p. 385) adds with reference to "witness," "testify," and "testimony": "The word-group has a primarily legal meaning and, when used outside a literal courtroom context, constitutes a legal metaphor."

38 For these compare now also Hans Förster, "Geheime Schriften und geheime Lehren? Zur Selbstbezeichnung von Texten aus dem Umfeld der frühchristlichen Gnosis unter Verwendung des Begriffs ἀπόκρυφος (bzw. ϩⲏⲡ)," *ZNW* 104 (2013): 118–145.

39 The additional question might be raised; why should the author as "beloved disciple" stay anonymous if he was even not well known; cf., however, Bauckham, *Jesus and the Eyewitnesses*, 407: "It seems that the Beloved Disciple was not a well-known disciple. He was not completely unknown; otherwise the rumor that he would not die (21:23) could not have existed, but he was not well-known, especially not as a character in Gospel traditions. [...] As a character in the Gospel traditions his readers or hearers are not likely to have heard of him—certainly not from Mark's Gospel, which he probably assumes they know, and probably not from whatever other Gospel traditions they may have known. His claim to be qualified to write a Gospel from his own eyewitness testimony is therefore not easy to advance [...]." It is even harder since he stays the "beloved disciple" without revealing a name.

40 Cf. however James H. Charlesworth, *The Beloved Disciple: Whose Witness Validates the Gospel of John?* (Valley Forge, PA: Trinity Press, 1995), 47: "The thrust of the final word

intention of the author as to its function in the narrative. The answer to the first question seems obvious: since "witnesses" to documents are always named and guarantee with their "name" to the validity of the document to use an anonymous witness is in legal matters problematic, or even witless. And, if the commonly accepted date for the "final redaction" of the Gospel of John may be presupposed in this context—the end of the first/beginning of the second century—the use of an anonymous attestation to a narrative becomes even more problematic. In his letter to Pliny the Younger, the Emperor Trajan states explicitly that anonymous charges are not to be accepted.[41] This can be seen as evidence that the Roman empire at that time was a well ordered and comparatively humane empire.[42] Thus, the Gospel might well have been written during a time when anonymous charges were frowned upon and finally outlawed. This does not help to strengthen the credibility of the anonymous testimony at the end of the Gospel of John (in this context, it might well be better to phrase "commonly associated with the name of John" since there is nothing that intrinsically connects this text with a person named John as author). It seems that even written testimony was regarded as inferior to oral testimony in judicial procedure[43] (and the Gospel of John uses judicial language)—however, these

---

about the Beloved Disciple is the answer to any who would challenge his authority: 'and we know that his witness is true' (21:24). Such words are exceptional; there must have been an extreme need to support the trustworthiness of the Johannine tradition." The question, however, is whether an anonymous testimony would receive much attention—if the anonymity was meant to evoke credibility.

41 Cf. Pliny the Younger, *Ep.* 10.97.2: *Sine auctore vero propositi libelli in nullo crimine locum habere debent. Nam et pessimi exempli nec nostri saeculi est.* Cf. Georg Glonner, *Zur Bildersprache des Johannes von Patmos: Untersuchungen der Johannesapokalypse anhand einer um Elemente der Bildinterpretation erweiterten historisch-kritischen Methode* (Neutestamentliche Abhandlungen; Neue Folge 34; Münster: Aschendorff, 1999), 42 and on 129: "Die Korrespondenz des Plinius bescheinigt dem Kaiser (Trajan) eine eher zurückhaltende Position. Das Denunziantentum bedurfte aber offensichtlich einer staatlichen Eindämmung." Cf. also Bernd Wander, *Gottesfürchtige und Sympathisanten: Studien zum heidnischen Umfeld von Diasporasynagogen* (WUNT 104; Tübingen: Mohr, 1998), 179.

42 Cf. Martin Hengel, *Juden, Griechen und Barbaren. Aspekte der Hellenisierung des Judentums in vorchristlicher Zeit* (Stuttgarter Bibelstudien 76; Stuttgart: KBW, 1976), 74: "Plutarch zeichnet dieses ideale Bild unter dem Eindruck der stoischen Weltbürgeridee und auf dem Hintergrund des befriedeten und relativ human gewordenen römischen Imperiums, das noch nicht von den Krisen des 3. Jahrhunderts n. Chr. geschüttelt wurde."

43 Cf. Michael Durst, "Christen als römische Magistrate um 200: Das Zeugnis des Kaisers Septimius Severus für Christen aus dem Senatorenstand (Tertullian, Ad Scapulam 4,6)," *JAC* 31 (1988): 91–126, 106: "Der Regelfall war das mündliche Zeugnis vor Gericht; daneben gibt es auch schriftliche Zeugnisse, die jedoch den mündlichen an Beweiskraft nachstehen."

testimonies were signed and dated. And the problem of the written testimony was that it was impossible to ask the witness in order to clarify problems. This problem became obvious during the time of Hadrian; it is one of his rescripts that deals with this matter and stresses the importance of the witness over the testimony.[44] Thus, claiming that a trustworthy witness gives testimony without revealing the name of the witness would be unacceptable at a court of law during the first/second century in Roman society.

Thus, the second question, the function of the self-assignment as "testimony of an eyewitness" (albeit anonymous), comes into the focus. Given that this "second ending" might not be connected with the "credibility" of the anonymous author, other reasons for this statement to have been inserted at the end of the narrative must be discussed. One possible reason for adding this statement to the text might be to give the reader at the very end a clue as to how the book must be read: as if written by an eyewitness. This phrase "as if written by an eyewitness" must be stressed in order to prevent possible misunderstandings: The focus of this discussion is the *narrative perspective* and not the question of the historical reliability of the text. However, it seems to be a matter of fact that there are differences in the narrative perspective of the narratives of the same event given either by a (seemingly omniscient) "historian" and by an eyewitness who relates (only) what he has seen. The first is a comprehensive account; the second must be selective. This identification of the narrative perspective as differing from the narrative perspective of the three Synoptic Gospels, makes it possible to revisit some of the *aporia* in order to raise the question as to how they might function within the narrative strategies of an account of an "eyewitness."

---

44 Cf. Digestes 222.5.3 § 3.4: *Idem divus hadrianus iunio rufino proconsuli macedoniae rescripsit testibus se, non testimoniis crediturum. verba epistulae ad hanc partem pertinentia haec sunt: "quod crimina obiecerit apud me alexander apro et quia non probabat nec testes producebat, sed testimoniis uti volebat, quibus apud me locus non est (nam ipsos interrogare soleo), quem remisi ad provinciae praesidem, ut is de fide testium quaereret et nisi implesset quod intenderat, relegaretur"* (The Divine Hadrian also stated in a Rescript to Julius Rufinus, Proconsul of Macedonia, that he must pay more attention to the witnesses than to their evidence. The words of the Rescript on this point are as follows: "Alexander accused Aper of certain crimes before me, but he did not prove them, or produce any witnesses; but he desired to use evidence which I am unwilling to admit, for I am accustomed to examine witnesses, and I have sent him back to the Governor of the province that he may make inquiry with reference to the credibility of the witnesses, and unless he proves what he alleges, he shall be sent into exile"). For the translation, cf. S.P. Scott, *Corpus Juris Civilis: The Civil Law V* (New York: AMS, 1932). Cf. also Digestes 3.2.21. where written testimony is summarily rejected in a judicial proceeding.

3   The Narrative of John's Gospel: As If Reported by an Eyewitness

As argued the self-description of the text as "report of an eyewitness" is in accordance with aspects of the judicial vocabulary used by the author. The judicial language seems to underline the fact that the Gospel of John is an account of a (faithful albeit anonymous) witness who gives his statement of the events as subjectively perceived and "as witnessed." The next question to be addressed is the problem of the literary characteristics of such a report of an eyewitness as compared with the Synoptic Gospels and their narrative genre as "historical accounts." If the self-assignment of the Gospel of John is compared with the self-assignment in the Gospel of Luke one important difference is obvious. The author/narrator of the Gospel of Luke describes his task quite differently from the self-assignment in the Gospel of John. The description in the prologue of the Gospel of Luke stresses the fact that the text is written by a person who was no eyewitness and who researched his sources carefully in order to give a well-structured account of what happened. Thus, most of the facts reported in the Gospel of Luke would be perceived in a judicial context as hearsay. In 21:24–25, the account of John's Gospel is described as a report of an eyewitness. And eyewitnesses are not supposed to include hearsay into their narratives.

Therefore, it seems quite obvious that differences should be expected in the narratives of the Gospel of Luke and of the Gospel of John due to the different character of the two reports. A report of a historian who has researched historical events and who has compiled them into a well-ordered account reports differently from an eyewitness. The first report would be an "objective" account giving the pertinent facts in suitable order. The second report would be a "subjective" account giving the facts as *perceived* and as *seen*; and (with some exceptions) only those facts *that* have been seen. Thus, the account of an eyewitness seems to be different in at least two aspects of its narrative due to the perspective of the narrator. And this seems to set it apart for the account of a historian. The first characteristic would be that an eyewitness reports only what has been witnessed. This is in contradistinction to the historian who reports things which he never saw but which he researched carefully. After careful research the best sources available for the report are selected by a historian. This is described in the beginning of the Gospel of Luke. Compared to this an eyewitness would seem to be eclectic: the report of an eyewitness would primarily include what has been witnessed and not report on those things where the eyewitness was not present; thus, on principle an eyewitness might be forced to omit things deemed by others important for the larger context of a narrative or might hint at things connected to the narrative but not part of his testimony.

This has important implications for the narrative of an eyewitness: in consequence the report of an eyewitness might seem incomplete if compared to the report of a historian who covers the same event—or might be perceived as incomplete if taken to be the report of a historian. An eyewitness might also include a few things, which are usually called hearsay. These elements of a narrative are, however, only at the very borders of what can be narrated. The second characteristic would be that an eyewitness reports the facts and events as perceived—and might even expect his audience to draw conclusions from his testimony. Further, there might be some detail which is (seemingly) irrelevant but which (for whatever reason) has stuck in the memory of a witness. One would, therefore, expect an eyewitness to include details into an account that a detached historian does not deem necessary for a well-ordered description of events. To summarize these two characteristics of an eyewitness, one should take into consideration that an eyewitness may be selective (or even forced to be selective) as concerning the "larger picture," while he may go into great detail in the description of the events witnessed. And, if the narrative of John's Gospel intends to be perceived as the faithful account of an eyewitness, one would expect it to show (or at least not be surprised to discover) some traits in its narrative, which are typical for the account of an eyewitness.[45]

3.1 An "Incomplete" Report in the Gospel of John

It is obvious that the selectivity of the narrative—or its "incompleteness"—has puzzled scholars of John's Gospel. One important example for seemingly "missing information" or an "incomplete narrative" is the information given concerning John the Baptist. The Gospel of John mentions explicitly that "John had not yet been thrown into prison."[46] If seen from the point of view of a reader of a well-ordered narrative written by a historian, this seems to imply that there will be also an account of what happened to John the Baptist in prison. However, the fate of John the Baptist is not reported in the Gospel of John and, therefore, this omission can be counted among those puzzling things in the Gospel of John which are called *aporia*. Seen from the perspective of the account of a *historian* the information given seems to be either incomplete or superfluous[47]

---

45 The discussion of the characteristics in the following two parts is not intended to be exhaustive.
46 John 3:24: οὔπω γὰρ ἦν βεβλημένος εἰς τὴν φυλακὴν ὁ Ἰωάννης.
47 Josef Ernst, *Johannes der Täufer: Interpretation—Geschichte—Wirkungsgeschichte* (BZNW 53; Berlin: de Gruyter, 1989), 207: "Die Feststellung, Johannes sei noch nicht gefangengesetzt, ist nach dem ungehinderten und freien Wirken in Änon überflüssig."

or even witless,⁴⁸ and despite this the fact seems to be important enough (to the author of the Gospel) that it is mentioned.⁴⁹

The rationale for including this information is not obvious. One possible assumption is that the intended reader knew about the fate of John the Baptist.⁵⁰ The knowledge might derive from other sources, the most obvious being the Synoptic Gospels.⁵¹ However, one counterargument is that the note seems too short and too incomplete to function as recourse to the Synoptic Gospels,⁵² even if it is assumed that the reader was expected to know the Synoptic Gospels.⁵³ There are some discrepancies between the chronology of the ministry of Jesus and John the Baptist as presented by the Synoptic Gospels and by the Gospel of John respectively.⁵⁴ This makes it possible to perceive this

---

48   Cf. Thyen, *Johannesevangelium*, 228: "Abgesehen von seiner möglichen *intertextuellen* Bedeutung ist dieser kurze Satz für unsere Erzählung nicht nur überflüssig, sondern absolut sinnlos. Denn daß einer, der in einer quellenreichen Gegend (Judäas?) regelmäßig Leute tauft, nicht gleichzeitig im Kerker des Antipas sitzen kann—und das dazu womöglich noch in der Festung Machairos im fernen Peräa (Josephus, Ant. XVIII/116 ff)—, versteht sich ja wohl von selbst."

49   Ernst, *Johannes der Täufer*, 206–207: "Der Evangelist erwähnt ausdrücklich, Johannes sei noch nicht ins Gefängnis geworfen—offenbar war ihm diese Feststellung besonders wichtig."

50   Leon Morris, *The Gospel according to John* (2nd ed.; Grand Rapids: Eerdmans, 1995), 210: "Apparently he regarded this as so well known that he had no need to do other than simply mention it."

51   Andrew T. Lincoln, *The Gospel according to Saint John* (BNTC 4; London: Continuum, 2005), 159: "The apparently superfluous note—for John had not yet been thrown into prison—is best seen as underscoring, for those familiar with the Synoptic tradition where Jesus is portrayed as only beginning his own ministry after John's imprisonment (cf. Mark 1.14; Matt. 4.12; Luke 3.20), that the present story has to be set in an earlier period in which the two figures were operating concurrently."

52   Cf. Thyen, *Johannesevangelium*, 228: "Denn wirklich *sinnvoll* wäre der Satz ja nur dann, wenn er sich intertextuell auf einen *konkreten* Prätext, wie etwa Lk 7,17 ff, bezöge."

53   William Hendriksen, *The Gospel According to John*, vol. 1 (18th ed.; Grand Rapids: Baker, 2002), 147: "[...] evidently taking for granted that believers in Asia Minor at this relatively late date had read the earlier Gospels (see pp. 31, 32), the author corrects a possible misunderstanding, and shows that between Matt. 4:11 and 4:12 (or between Mark 1:13 and 1:14; or between Luke 4:13 and 4:14; i.e., between Christ's temptation and the arrest of John the Baptist) there was a considerable period of time during which Jesus and John were engaged in a parallel ministry."

54   Andreas J. Köstenberger, *John* (BECNT; Grand Rapids: Baker, 2004), 136: "But the evangelist is concerned that those familiar with, say, the Gospel of Mark will see a contradiction between Mark's account (which does not record any Galilean ministry on the part of

comment as a correction of the events as presented in the Gospel of Mark,[55] or as a possible infringement of the trustworthiness of the Gospel of John.[56] This tension is solved by the suggestion that the report in the Gospel of John concerns a time which is not covered by the narrative of the Synoptic Gospels.[57] John 3:24 can also be seen in the context of literary criticism as a later insertion in the text.[58]

Jesus prior to John's imprisonment) and his own narrative (which does). In fact, a reading of the Synoptics seems to suggest that Jesus began his Galilean ministry *after* John's arrest (Mark 1:14; Matt. 4:12); only from the present Gospel do we learn that there was an interim period during which the Baptist's and Jesus's ministries overlapped." Cf. also Ulrich Wilckens, *Das Evangelium nach Johannes* (18th ed.; NTD 4; Göttingen: Vandenhoeck & Ruprecht, 2000), 75–76: "Die Angabe einer parallelen Taufwirksamkeit von Johannes und Jesus widerspricht dem Zeitschema der synoptischen Tradition, nach der Jesu Wirksamkeit erst nach der Gefangennahme des Täufers begonnen hat (Mk 1,14f.; Lk 3,19 f. 23; Mt 11,2–6). Die Bemerkung v. 24 will diesen Widerspruch durch zeitliche Vorordnung ausgleichen und ist ein Wink des Joh.evangelisten an seine Leser, daß er die synoptische Chronologie sehr wohl kennt." Cf. also Ernst Haenchen, *Das Johannesevangelium: Ein Kommentar aus den nachgelassenen Manuskripten* (ed. Ulrich Busse; Tübingen: Mohr, 1980), 231.

55 Christian Dietzfelbinger, *Das Evangelium nach Johannes. Teilband 1: Johannes 1–12* (2nd ed.; ZBK; Zürich: Theologischer Verlag, 2004), 91: "Die Notiz, daß Johannes noch nicht ins Gefängnis geworfen worden war, widerspricht Mk. 1,14a. Die Korrektur ist bewußt vorgenommen worden." Cf. also Siegfried Schulz, *Das Evangelium nach Johannes* (16th ed.; NTD 4; Göttingen: Vandenhoeck & Ruprecht, 1987), 65; see further Ludger Schenke, *Johannes Kommentar* (Düsseldorf: Patmos, 1998), 79: "Der *Autorkommentar* 3,24 macht einerseits klar, daß das gewaltsame Ende des Täuferwirkens unmittelbar bevorsteht, und will andererseits möglicherweise den Synoptikern (vgl. Mk 1,14) direkt widersprechen und den Widerspruch sogar betonen."

56 D.A. Carson, *The Gospel According to John* (Leicester, UK: Inter-Varsity, 1991), 210: "The Synoptics adopt the stance of Mark 1:14, which places the opening of Jesus's *Galilean* ministry in the period *after* John the Baptist had been arrested, without reporting any earlier *Judean* ministry. Apparently the Evangelist is aware that such a construction had circulated widely, and he does not want his credibility diminished by failing to explain the apparent discrepancy."

57 Georges Zevini, *Commentaire spirituel de l'Évangile de Jean 1* (Montréal: Médiaspaul, 1995), 97: "L'insistance du verset 24, 'Jean, en effet, n'avait pas encore été jeté en prison' montre que l'évangéliste connaissait cette tradition et loin d'en atténuer l'importance, il la met en valeur en relatant des événements antérieurs aux premiers faits rapportés par l'évangile de Marc."

58 Martin Stowasser, *Johannes der Täufer im Vierten Evangelium: Eine Untersuchung zu seiner Bedeutung für die johanneische Gemeinde* (ÖBS 12; Klosterneuburg: Bibelwerk, 1992), 192:

With the hypothesis that the Gospel of John might share characteristic elements with accounts of eyewitnesses, the seemingly superfluous or incomplete reference to the imprisonment of John the Baptist can be interpreted differently: the very fact that there is no mention of the actual imprisonment of John[59] might in light of the comments above be interpreted as hinting at an event which was not witnessed by the eyewitness of this narrative. The expected conclusion to be drawn by the intended reader would be that the imprisonment is not narrated since such an account would be hearsay. Thus, within the narrative world of an account by an eyewitness, John 3:24 might be a comment which the intended reader perceives not as an inconsistency of a well-ordered narrative but as proof of the accuracy of the account given by an eyewitness. This eyewitness mentions that John the Baptist is not yet in prison but does not recount the entire story of the imprisonment and death since he did not witness the events.

3.2 Inclusion of Hearsay

It is, however, also obvious that the narrator who describes himself as an eyewitness in John 21:24 was not present at all of the events which are reported in the Gospel of John. "These include, for example, the conversation between Jesus and the Samaritan woman in the absence of the disciples (4.7–26), what happens to the man born blind in the absence of Jesus (9.8–34), the interrogation before the high priest (18.19–24), the trial before Pilate (18.28–19.16a) and the appearance to Mary Magdalene (20.11–18)."[60] Thus, he seems to include these in his account and this seems to contradict the concept of the report of an eyewitness. In these cases the report is deviating from the very nature of the account of an eyewitness.

3.2.1   The Appearances to the Samaritan Woman and to Mary Magdalene and the Man Born Blind

Two outstanding events where exclusive hearsay is included in the narrative and which are dealt with together since they share common features are obviously the discourse between Jesus and the Samaritan woman at the well (John 4:4–42) and the encounter between Jesus and Mary Magdalene within the story

---

"Im Gegensatz zu 3,23 wird 3,24 allgemein als spätere Einfügung gewertet, durch welche eine Angleichung an die synoptische Chronologie erreicht werden sollte."

59   Cf. also Barnabas Lindars, *The Gospel of John* (NCBC; London: Oliphants, 1977), 165: "A parenthetical explanation, perhaps an editorial note, to account for the discrepancy with the Synoptic record. The Baptist's imprisonment is not referred to elsewhere by John."

60   Lincoln, "Beloved Disciple," 16.

of the empty tomb (John 20:11–18). The events are reported as if witnessed. It is, however, obvious that Jesus was alone at the well with the Samaritan woman—at least for some time—and was also alone with Mary Magdalene at the empty tomb. Despite this the conversation between the two is reported in detail: according to the narrative all of his disciples had left to buy edibles and would only return later. The absence of the disciples is even crucial for the events to evolve as they did: Jesus is forced to ask the woman for water to drink[61] since his disciples are absent (who, by inference, might have carried water with themselves or might have been able to take water from the deep well).[62] This is the beginning of a longer conversation. After their return the disciples are astonished that Jesus actually talks with a Samaritan woman,[63] highlighting the fact that it is uncommon for Jews to be in closer contact with Samaritans.[64] Thus, without the absence of the disciples the story would not have evolved as it did; however, there was nobody to witness the conversation between Jesus and the woman at the well.

The same holds true for the story of the empty tomb. The narrative states explicitly that Peter, the Beloved Disciple, and Mary go to the empty tomb after Mary announces to the disciples that she found the tomb empty. However, after the two men have checked the story of Mary Magdalene they leave again. Therefore, Mary is alone when she encounters him whom she perceives as the gardener.[65] Thus, these two encounters of women with Jesus were witnessed by nobody and still reported in the Gospel of John.

It seems, however, possible that answers to this problem might be provided within the narrative. It seems that in both cases the meeting is described to

---

61   Cf. Susan Miller, "The Woman at the Well: John's Portrayal of the Samaritan Mission," in *John, Jesus, and History*. Vol. 2: *Aspects of Historicity in the Fourth Gospel* (ed. Paul N. Anderson, Felix Just, and Tom Thatcher; Atlanta: SBL, 2009), 73–81 (75): "This translation is supported by the woman's comments that Jesus has no bucket, and he must rely on her water jar in order to drink some water (4:11)."

62   John 4:8: οἱ γὰρ μαθηταὶ αὐτοῦ ἀπεληλύθεισαν εἰς τὴν πόλιν ἵνα τροφὰς ἀγοράσωσιν.

63   John 4:27a: Καὶ ἐπὶ τούτῳ ἦλθαν οἱ μαθηταὶ αὐτοῦ καὶ ἐθαύμαζον ὅτι μετὰ γυναικὸς ἐλάλει.

64   Cf. John 4:9c: οὐ γὰρ συγχρῶνται Ἰουδαῖοι Σαμαρίταις. Even if no full agreement exists as to exact meaning of συγχράομαι in this context, it is indisputable that this comment underscores a distance between Jews and Samaritans; cf. Schulz, *Evangelium nach Johannes*, 73: "Die Pointe wird unüberhörbar in v.9 ausgesprochen: Jesus wendet sich als Jude den verhaßten Samaritanern zu und durchbricht damit demonstrativ die Schranken der pharisäisch geführten Synagoge!"

65   For this encounter cf. also Hans Förster, "'… damit ich dir deinen Lohn gebe'—Eine etwas andere Begegnung am leeren Grab (Joh 20,15) in einer koptischen liturgischen Handschrift," *Mitteilungen zur Christlichen Archäologie* 18 (2012): 91–100.

others: the Samaritan woman reports on her encounter with Jesus[66] and makes it thereby common knowledge and part of the story and Mary Magdalene is told by Jesus to tell the disciples whom she has seen.[67] The encounter at the empty tomb makes it abundantly clear that the hearsay is included not by a whim of the author but rather following a directive of Jesus. He orders Mary to go to the disciples and to tell them about the encounter.[68] The next sentence just is the fulfilment of this order: she goes and tells them.[69] Since the order of Jesus resembles the order to the apostles and since the verb ἀγγέλλω has theological implications the passage is the source for the honorific title *apostola apostolorum*.[70] In the narrative world of the account of an eyewitness the order to narrate the events and the confirmation that Mary Magdalene followed orders are means of explaining to the implied reader as to why the narrator is privy to the events which he could not witness. However, instead of describing the entire scene as indirect speech of Mary, the events are narrated as if witnessed and at the end the fact is established that these events have been told the disciples. For the modern mind this might seem a rather liberal view of how an eyewitness should or can report.[71] The (either silent or explicit) stipulation in such cases is that the report can use direct speech and

---

66   John 4:28–29.
67   John 20:17–18.
68   John 20:17: λέγει αὐτῇ Ἰησοῦς· μή μου ἅπτου, οὔπω γὰρ ἀναβέβηκα πρὸς τὸν πατέρα· πορεύου δὲ πρὸς τοὺς ἀδελφούς μου καὶ εἰπὲ αὐτοῖς· ἀναβαίνω πρὸς τὸν πατέρα μου καὶ πατέρα ὑμῶν καὶ θεόν μου καὶ θεὸν ὑμῶν.
69   John 20:18: ἔρχεται Μαριὰμ ἡ Μαγδαληνὴ ἀγγέλλουσα τοῖς μαθηταῖς ὅτι ἑώρακα τὸν κύριον, καὶ ταῦτα εἶπεν αὐτῇ.
70   Cf. for example Eva Maria Synek, *Heilige Frauen der frühen Christenheit: Zu den Frauenbildern in hagiographischen Texten des christlichen Ostens* (ÖC NF 43; Würzburg: Augustinus, 1994), 32; Peter Dschulnigg, *Jesus begegnen: Personen und ihre Bedeutung im Johannesevangelium* (Theologie 30; Münster: Lit, 2000), 302–303: "Maria von Magdala [...] wird zwar nicht ausdrücklich als Apostel bezeichnet, hat aber sachlich gesehen dennoch eine 'quasi apostolische Rolle'. Diese wurde von den Kommentatoren auch schon früh wahrgenommen, welche sie als 'apostola apostolorum', als 'Apostelin der Apostel' bezeichneten." Cf. also Silke Petersen, *"Zerstört die Werke der Weiblichkeit!": Maria Magdalena, Salome und andere Jüngerinnen Jesu in christlich-gnostischen Schriften* (Leiden: Brill, 1999), 99–100; Erika Mohri, *Maria Magdalena: Frauenbilder in Evangelientexten des 1. bis 3. Jahrhunderts* (MThSt 63; Marburg: Elwert, 2000), 129–152; and Andrea Taschl-Erber, *Maria Magdalena—erste Apostolin? Joh 20,1–18: Tradition und Relecture* (Herders Biblische Studien 51; Freiburg: Herder, 2007).
71   However, it does seem undisputable that a narrative which reports an entire encounter including the dialogue as indirect speech is rather clumsy.

describe the events as if witnessed. And this stipulation is made explicit in Jesus telling Mary to tell the apostles and then mentioning that she told the apostles. Thus, instead of reporting this as indirect speech this is reported as a scene "as if witnessed." The text of the Gospel rephrases in this case the report of the women as a narrative of an impartial observer, including, however, subjective judgements of the person: it is explicitly mentioned that Mary presumes the person to be the gardener. The implication is that the narrator is privy even to the personal thoughts of Mary which is explained by John 20:18: Mary did report her encounter in detail. And this statement has an interesting textual aspect: depending on which textual tradition is used for the translation, either the entire speech of Mary or the second half of the speech are indirect speech. Thus, the narrator distances himself from the testimony given by Mary Magdalene by the very fact that the content of the report is described as indirect speech.

The situation is somewhat different with the man born blind but the account follows however the same narrative patterns. First the story is told as to what happened to the man born blind in the absence of Jesus (John 9:8–34). And the connecting sentence mentions explicitly that Jesus hears what befell this man born blind after he had been healed.[72] Thus, it is made explicitly clear that hearsay has been included into the narrative and why it had been included.

3.2.2 The Interrogation before the High Priest and the Trial before Pontius Pilate

These two passages are open to interpretation. In John 18:19–24 it depends on how one is to understand the Greek word αὐλή. According to the dictionary of Bauer-Aland in the English translation of Danker this word means "enclosed open space, courtyard."[73] Thus, the NIV and the NRSV translate "high priest's courtyard" and the KJV "palace of the high priest." In both cases the fire is supposed to be somewhere either outside or at least not at the same place as where Jesus is interrogated by the high priest. This is in contradiction to the use of the same term in the Gospel of Matthew. Peter enters the αὐλή in order to be "in the know."[74] And the wording is rather interesting, there (Matt 26:58) as well as a bit later (Matt 26:69) Peter sits "outside within the courtyard."[75] The situation is quite obvious: the (semi-) official building has an enclosed open space

---

72 John 9:35a: ἤκουσεν Ἰησοῦς ὅτι ἐξέβαλον αὐτὸν ἔξω καὶ εὑρὼν αὐτὸν εἶπεν.
73 BDAG, 150.
74 Mt 26:58: ὁ δὲ Πέτρος ἠκολούθει αὐτῷ ἀπὸ μακρόθεν ἕως τῆς αὐλῆς τοῦ ἀρχιερέως καὶ εἰσελθὼν ἔσω ἐκάθητο μετὰ τῶν ὑπηρετῶν ἰδεῖν τὸ τέλος.
75 Matt. 26:69: ὁ δὲ Πέτρος ἐκάθητο ἔξω ἐν τῇ αὐλῇ.

which has probably the form of a quadrangle and is surrounded by a portico. The dealings between Jesus and the high priest take place somewhere under the portico and those in the middle are "outside" of the portico but take part in the proceedings and can witness what is spoken. Thus, it seems highly probable, that the high priest holds semi-open court and that all those around the fire can listen to what happens. If this were the case the Beloved Disciple would be an eyewitness.

The story of the interrogation by Pontius Pilate seems to be well known to all those who entered with Pontius Pilate—we have to assume that the building looks like described above (which, actually, would be a rather common structure of many if not most of the Roman buildings of upper class people). And it is explicitly mentioned that "these who lead him there did not go in in order not to become unclean."[76] Thus, there is no reason to assume that the disciples (including the Beloved Disciple) did not enter. They were not among those who held Jesus prisoner and brought him to Pontius Pilate. And the very fact that they could have entered if they had not feared to become unclean seems to point strongly to the interpretation that it was a public interrogation. Thus, also these passages, which are usually reckoned among the passages where there was no recorded witness, might well be part of a narrative world where the Beloved Disciple had been present.

3.2.3 Highly Detailed Reports

It is also one of the characteristic traits of the Gospel of John that detailed information is given. One example would be the wedding at Cana. The jars are not only mentioned, but rather described in detail concerning their content ("water jars"), their number ("six"), their material ("stone"), their capacity ("two to three measures") and their religious function in the household ("for purification according to Jewish custom").[77] This can be seen as a large amount of information. However, there are no indicators within the text that give an indication of the rationale for including all this information into the narrative. Thus, different interpretations have evolved. The metric measures given[78] have been interpreted as "eschatological amount of wine," which shows an abundance of generosity. It seems, however, that modern concepts of wine

---

76 John 18:28: ἄγουσιν οὖν τὸν Ἰησοῦν ἀπὸ τοῦ Καϊάφα εἰς τὸ πραιτώριον· ἦν δὲ πρωΐ· καὶ αὐτοὶ οὐκ εἰσῆλθον εἰς τὸ πραιτώριον, ἵνα μὴ μιανθῶσιν ἀλλὰ φάγωσιν τὸ πάσχα.

77 John 2:6: ἦσαν δὲ ἐκεῖ λίθιναι ὑδρίαι ἓξ κατὰ τὸν καθαρισμὸν τῶν Ἰουδαίων κείμεναι, χωροῦσαι ἀνὰ μετρητὰς δύο ἢ τρεῖς.

78 The six jars would have held between 480 and 720 litres of water changed into wine.

consumption do not fit antiquity. Thus, the abundance is probably not mentioned since the amount was not perceived as inordinately much.[79] The jars of water have been interpreted as a symbol for the law which is abolished; this can be connected to the fact that six jars are mentioned.[80] There is, however, neither an indication that the jars are destroyed (as in the allegory of the new wine in old wine skins[81]) nor that a seventh jar is added[82] making this interpretation at least problematic (and implicitly anti-Judaic). This explains probably why the number six, usually a symbol of something incomplete,[83] has even been taken as an indicator for completion;[84] however, this is usually the function of the number seven in biblical texts. In addition, it is possible to see the fact that information is given concerning the use in a specific context ("according to the purification of the Jews") as an indicator for readers, who do not know much about Jewish customs.

This all might be an overinterpretation if the main purpose of the narrative is to convince the implied reader that the report is given by an eyewitness. In this case the number is not important for its actual value and the symbolic implications but for the fact that the jars have been counted. The implied message would be that the narrator is a reliable witness, since details are mentioned. This hypothesis seems supported by the fact that not only the number but also the capacity and the material are mentioned. An attentive observer notes these things especially if some implications of the observations might be of importance for the narrative. In the case that the jars are just as they are described and had exactly the functions as mentioned; there was never anything else in them besides water (this is their specific purpose in ritual purification) and there could nothing have been added to color the water (since they have been filled to the brim).[85] This would make the narrator an attentive observer, giving details which make it possible for the reader to decide that there was no room for trickery. There are other elements within the narrative frames of the signs in John's Gospel that seem to imply that the signs follow a dynamic,

---

79 Cf. Förster, "Perikope."
80 Raymond F. Collins, "Cana (Jn. 2:1–12)—The First of his Signs or the Key to his Signs?" *ITQ* 47 (1980): 79–95 (89) or Morris, *John*, 155.
81 Mark 2:22.
82 Carson, *John*, 174.
83 Köstenberger, *John*, 96; Moloney, *Belief in the Word*, 85; Charles Kingsley Barrett, *Das Evangelium nach Johannes* (KEK; Göttingen: Vandenhoeck & Ruprecht, 1990), 215.
84 Michael Theobald, *Das Evangelium nach Johannes: Kapitel 1–12* (RNT; Regensburg: Friedrich Pustet, 2009), 214.
85 John 2:7: λέγει αὐτοῖς ὁ Ἰησοῦς· γεμίσατε τὰς ὑδρίας ὕδατος. καὶ ἐγέμισαν αὐτὰς ἕως ἄνω.

starting with the smallest and ending with the most miraculous. This conclusion, drawn from the elements of the narrative, is, however, in contradistinction to the usual perception of the signs in John's Gospel. They are seen to be much more miraculous than most of the miracles in the Synoptic Gospels. Thus, the attempt to reconstruct the "original" text by means of an exchange of chs. 5 and 6 might destroy the narrative structure of the text which seems to contain a dynamic.[86] If the signs actually seem to be described in a way as to start from a small event, the miracle at the Wedding at Cana,[87] and to proceed to the greatest sign,[88] the resurrection of Lazarus,[89] the exchange of two signs has as consequence a destruction of this dynamic.

4   Conclusion

The starting point of the discussion of some literary problems in the Gospel of John has been that there is no textual witness (among the Greek manuscripts of the Gospel of John) that would attest a "short" text of the Gospel with the "first ending" in John 20:31 as the final sentence of John's Gospel (and thus missing ch. 21). Thus, it is safe to assume that a possible earlier state of the redaction of this Gospel without the "second ending" never circulated (or, if it ever circulated, circulated in such closed quarters that no manuscript survived). The consequences for the self-assignment of the narrative genre of the text are obvious: if the final form of the text of the Gospel of John as attested in manuscripts is used to understand as to how this text intends to be perceived by the intended

---

[86] Rudolf Schnackenburg, *Das Johannesevangelium II. Teil: Kommentar zu Kap. 5–12* (4th ed.; HTKNT 4/2; Freiburg: Herder, 1985), 10; he comments concerning the chs. 5 and 6: "Die äußeren literarkritischen Gründe sind härter und sicherer als solche Überlegungen zur theologischen Gestaltung."

[87] The suggestion that this is a "massives Wunder" does not take into consideration wine consumption in antiquity; cf. Hans Förster, "Die Perikope von der Hochzeit zu Kana (Joh 2:1–11) im Kontext der Spätantike," *NovT* 55 (2013): 103–126.

[88] The article uses the word "sign" to denote the miracles that took place publicly and which have been assigned to the so called signs source; for a discussion concerning this hypothetical source, cf. Udo Schnelle, "Aus der Literatur zum Johannesevangelium 1994–2010. Erster Teil: Die Kommentare als Seismographen der Forschung," *TRu* 75 (2010): 265–303 (289): "Innerhalb der letzten 30 Jahre hat sich auch hier die Forschungslage grundlegend geändert, denn auf internationaler Ebene bezweifelt heute eine deutliche Mehrheit der Exegeten die Existenz dieser 'Semeia-Quelle'."

[89] Hans Förster, "Die johanneischen Zeichen und Joh 2:11 als möglicher hermeneutischer Schlüssel," *NovT* 56 (2014): 1–23.

reader, John 21:24 might be one of the key elements providing a clue as to how the text is to be read. Since the text is written by an anonymous witness[90] the trustworthiness of the witness cannot have been the rationale for including this: if this were the case there is no reason why the witness could not have been mentioned by name. Just contrary: since documents are signed by known witnesses giving their name there must be a reason for the narrative element of the "anonymous" witness. One possible solution is that the text should be perceived in its narrative characteristics as comparable to the account of an eyewitness. Thus, the literary genre can be described as "narrative non-fiction with attention to detail and negligence concerning the completeness of the narrative" (i.e. account written as if by an eyewitness).

It seems that the assumption that the text of John's Gospel might contain narrative strategies that are similar to the account of an eyewitness (and thereby dissimilar to those used in the Synoptic Gospels) makes possible the following suggestion: a literal interpretation for some passages that causes hermeneutical problems if the text is presupposed to function like a well-ordered narrative of a historian might be what is called for in case it is written from the perspective of an eyewitness. Further, this hypothesis implies also the possibility that seemingly superfluous details might have been included into the narrative of an eyewitness. In case that the text is intended to be perceived as if written by an eyewitness, it might well be the case that the facts reported might just be the facts as an eyewitness would report them. Therefore, the proposed hypothesis seems to change the perception of the text of the Gospel of John quite fundamentally and might have implications for the interpretation of the entire text. It might well be that also other passages with information concerning various details are meant literally in order to create the impression of verisimilitude. Thus, for example in the case of the interpretation of the "six jars" at the wedding at Cana no interpretation seems to be necessary if the "eyewitness" is just an observer with attention to detail. In light of the often anti-Judaic interpretations given to these jars this seems to be progress.

Two remarks at the end seem to be necessary: the hypothesis that the narrative perspective might be different from the other canonical Gospels does not solve all *aporia* created by the narrative style of the Gospel. It might, however,

---

90   For the way the Gospel of John deals with the identity of the Beloved Disciple, cf. also Charlesworth, *Beloved Disciple*, 30: "We must also remember that the Beloved Disciple appears anonymously (at least initially). Nowhere does an author or editor of the GosJn clearly and unambiguosly identify the disciple with a named disciple in the GosJn; [...]."

prevent too fast a tendency to "correct" narrative "errors" that might be actually part of the narrative strategy. Further, the narrative perspective of an "eyewitness" is part of the narrative world of a text. Thus, the hypothesis of such a perspective is not able to shed light on the question of how "trustworthy" the text is: it is narrated as if seen by a witness who is careful to avoid the inclusion of hearsay and, at least in the two cases of the dialogues between Jesus and the Samaritan woman and between Jesus and Mary Magdalene, the author declares within the narrative how he came to know what happened there.[91] Thus, the hypothesis of the "anonymous witness" as indicator for a narrative perspective deals only with the narrative world of the Gospel of John and its consequences for different aspects of the narrative.[92]

---

91 This is not necessary if the "historian" states that the text is based on well researched sources, a statement to be found at the beginning of Luke's Gospel.

92 Thus, the "series of gaps" may not be dynamic but rather result of the perspective; cf., however, John Ashton, "Second Thoughts on the Fourth Gospel," in *What We Have Heard from the Beginning: The Past, Present, and Future of Johannine Studies* (ed. Tom Thatcher; Waco: Baylor University Press, 2007), 1–18 (9): "The suggestion of 'a dynamic series of gaps' [...] is clearly an invitation to the implied readers of the Gospel to fill the gaps in for themselves. But how? In accordance with 'the perceived strategies and ploys' not, be it noted, of the real author, who guards his independence, but rather of the implied author, always at the beck and call of his inventor, the narrative critic who has designed and constructed him? I cannot take this seriously."

Assessing the Criteria for Differentiating the Cross Gospel

Stanley E. Porter and Andrew W. Pitts

1 Introduction

One of John Dominic Crossan's most noteworthy, and in many ways most significant, contributions to discussion of the Gospels is his positing of a source for the Gospel passion and resurrection accounts, which he labels the Cross Gospel. The Cross Gospel, according to Crossan, comprises a portion of the Gospel of Peter. His theory regarding the so-called Cross Gospel was first proposed in his *The Cross that Spoke: The Origins of the Passion Narrative*,[1] and has been articulated several times since.[2] Most recently, he has repeated the latest form of his argument in a volume dedicated specifically to discussion of the Gospel of Peter.[3] In this chapter, in which Crossan focuses upon views of the relation between the Gospel of Peter and our canonical Gospels in scholarship from the United States, Crossan distinguishes his position from two other major positions. The first position, represented by Helmut Koester,[4] argues that the Gospel of Peter is independent of our canonical Gospels, and the account of the passion and resurrection found in the Gospel of Peter is very early. The second position, represented by Raymond Brown,[5] argues that the account of the

---

[1] John Dominic Crossan, *The Cross that Spoke: The Origins of the Passion Narrative* (San Francisco: Harper & Row, 1988).

[2] See, e.g., John Dominic Crossan, *The Historical Jesus: The Life of a Mediterranean Jewish Peasant* (San Francisco: HarperSanFrancisco, 1991); Crossan, *Who Killed Jesus? Exposing the Roots of Anti-Semitism in the Gospel Story of the Death of Jesus* (San Francisco: HarperSanFrancisco, 1995).

[3] John Dominic Crossan, "The *Gospel of Peter* and the Canonical Gospels," in *Das Evangelium nach Petrus: Text, Kontexte, Intertexte* (ed. Thomas J. Kraus and Tobias Nicklas; TU 158; Berlin: de Gruyter, 2007), 117–134.

[4] E.g. Helmut Koester, "Apocryphal and Canonical Gospels," HTR 73 (1980): 105–130, esp. 126; Koester, *Ancient Christian Gospels: Their History and Development* (London: SCM, 1990), cited in Crossan, "*Gospel of Peter*," 118–119, esp. 118 n. 8, 119 n. 13.

[5] E.g. Raymond E. Brown, "The Gospel of Peter and Canonical Gospel Priority," NTS 33 (1987): 321–343, esp. 335–336; Brown, *The Death of the Messiah: From Gethsemane to the Grave: A Commentary on the Passion Narratives in the Four Gospels* (ABRL; New York: Doubleday, 1994), cited in Crossan, "*Gospel of Peter*," 119–121, esp. 119 n. 14, 120 n. 15.

passion and resurrection in the Gospel of Peter is dependent upon the canonical Gospels. The third position, to which Crossan holds, is that there are both independent and dependent elements within the Gospel of Peter in relation to the canonical Gospels.[6]

The Gospel of Peter, somewhat recently brought again to the fore in New Testament study with proposals such as those by Koester and Crossan, among others, has been subject to growing critical examination. The Akhmim codex (P.Cairo 10759), fairly recently re-edited, contains both the Gospel of Peter and the Apocalypse of Peter and, in its current form, is dated by its latest editors to the sixth or seventh century.[7] On the basis of how the manuscript begins mid-episode, it appears clear that this is a portion of a larger work, with this manuscript a later copy of an earlier document.[8] As a result, in some instances it is difficult to determine the specific changes from earlier versions, though they no doubt have been made by successive copying.[9] The issue of the reliability of the copy that we do have has been compounded by discussion of whether we are in possession of other portions or fragments of this ancient text. P.Oxy. XLI 2949, which was originally published as a fragment of an unknown gospel, now appears to be a second- or third-century fragment of an earlier recension of the Gospel of Peter.[10] The text, though not identical, overlaps at a number of significant places. However, two other documents that have on occasion been proposed as part of the Gospel of Peter, including P.Oxy. LX 4009 and P.Vindob. G 2325, the so-called Fayyum Fragment, are not likely parts of the Gospel of Peter.[11] P.Oxy. LX 4009 does not have any mention of Peter and no other wording that overlaps with the Gospel of Peter as found in the Akhmim codex. P.Vindob.

---

6 Crossan, "*Gospel of Peter*," 121–133.

7 *Das Petrusevangelium und die Petrusapokalypse: Die griechischen Fragmente mit deutscher und englischer Übersetzung* (ed. Thomas Kraus and Tobias Nicklas; Berlin: de Gruyter, 2004), 29. Earlier dating was to the ninth century. This is an issue that clearly requires further study.

8 See Peter van Minnen, "The Akhmîm Gospel of Peter," in Kraus and Nicklas, eds., *Evangelium nach Petrus*, 53–60 for a description of the codex.

9 See Paul Foster, "The Discovery and Initial Reaction to the So-called Gospel of Peter," in Kraus and Nicklas, eds., *Evangelium nach Petrus*, 9–51 for the history of reception of the Gospel of Peter.

10 Republished in Kraus and Nicklas, eds., *Petrusevangelium*, 55–58.

11 See Kraus and Nicklas, eds., *Petrusevangelium*, 59–63 and 65–68. The leading advocate of such a position is Dieter Lührmann, for example in his and E. Schlarb's *Fragmente apokryph gewordener Evangelien in griechischer und lateinischer Sprache* (Marburg: Elwert, 2000), 78–81. A cogent response is Paul Foster, "Are There Any Early Fragments of the So-Called Gospel of Peter?" *NTS* 52 (2006): 1–28.

G 2325, though it has a *nomen sacrum* for Peter in red lettering, has no other overlapping wording and is instead a combined text from Mark 14:26–30 and Matt 26:30–34.[12] There are clearly some unresolved critical issues regarding the Gospel of Peter in the Akhmim codex; nevertheless, this text provides the basis for Crossan's reconstruction of the Cross Gospel and will be used here in the discussion.[13]

2   The Arguments for the Cross Gospel

Crossan has provided the latest statement on his reconstruction of the Cross Gospel, and it is this statement that we will evaluate here. He claims that the "purpose or function of the Gospel of Peter was to conflate together two quite divergent versions of the passion-resurrection narrative," a process that he dates to the second century.[14] He calls this an "apologetic harmonization," by which he means that "the author/redactor is aware of problems with having two very divergent accounts of the passion-resurrection narrative."[15] Rather than choosing between the two contradictory narratives, the author or redactor harmonized the two accounts into a single narrative, but a narrative that, according to Crossan, still reveals the attempt at unifying the two conflicting narratives. The differentiation of "whether enemies or friends are involved in terms of the burial and resurrection" is the major criterion for differentiating the two versions used in the Gospel of Peter.[16]

On this basis, Crossan repeats the content of the two versions (labeled as versions I and II), as he has outlined them before:

Version I: (a)   *Execution*: Jesus is tried and crucified by his enemies (Gos. Pet. 1:1–2 & 2:5b–6:22)

(b)   *Tomb*: Jesus is buried and his tomb guarded by his enemies (Gos. Pet. 7:25 & 8:28–9:34)

---

12   For recent discussion, see Stanley E. Porter and Wendy J. Porter, *New Testament Greek Papyri and Parchments: New Editions: Texts* (MPER 29; Berlin: de Gruyter, 2008), 291–294 (no. 62).
13   We use the edition of Kraus and Nicklas, eds., *Petrusevangelium*, 32–53, with English translation.
14   Crossan, "*Gospel of Peter*," 129.
15   Crossan, "*Gospel of Peter*," 129.
16   Crossan, "*Gospel of Peter*," 129.

Version II:
- (c) *Resurrection*: Jesus rises and appears to his enemies (Gos. Pet. 9:35–10:42 & 11:45–49)
- (a) *Execution*: Jesus is tried and crucified by his enemies
- (b) *Tomb*: Jesus is buried and his tomb visited by his friends (Gos. Pet. 6:23–24 & 12:50–13:57)
- (c) *Resurrection*: Jesus rises and appears to his friends (Gos. Pet. 14:60)[17]

Crossan contends that version I, the privileged version, provides the frame for the integration of version II. Version II reflects what is now found in the canonical Gospels. The execution account from version I is used in the Gospel of Peter, with no indication in the Gospel of Peter, so Crossan believes, of use of the canonical Gospel account. Version I also reflects the various enemies of Jesus, including the Jewish leaders and, at least initially, the Jewish people. In version II, according to Crossan, Jesus's enemies would have included the Jewish leaders, the Jewish people, and the Roman soldiers. In order to make these conflicting stories into a harmonized account, transitionary sections were added, including a request for the burial of Jesus in Gos. Pet. 2:3–5a, actions taken by the disciples in Gos. Pet. 7:26–27 and 14:58–59, and the arrival of the young man in Gos. Pet. 11:43–44—all as preparation for the sections in version II on Jesus's friends. Lastly, Crossan notes that there was a redactional element that stylized the account to fit a second-century context.[18]

3 Assessing Crossan's Arguments

Much rides on the ability to differentiate these two versions in Crossan's reconstruction of the development of the passion and resurrection accounts. This includes his ability to differentiate version I as the Cross Gospel that is not reflective of material found in the canonical Gospels, and his chronological reconstruction of the Cross Gospel as earliest of the Gospel accounts because of its description of the Jewish people as becoming good, something not found in any of the supposed later Gospel accounts.[19]

There are a number of questions, however, that might be raised in relation to this pattern of reconstruction. We will not here enter into text-critical issues

---

17 Crossan, "*Gospel of Peter*," 129–130.
18 Crossan, "*Gospel of Peter*," 130.
19 Crossan, "*Gospel of Peter*," 127. Crossan adopts this from Brown, *Death of the Messiah*, 1421–1423.

specifically regarding the Gospel of Peter or translational issues regarding the text, but wish instead to raise questions regarding the development proposed in Crossan's argument.

3.1 Friends and Enemies

The first question to raise concerns the differentiation of the sources on the basis of whether friends or enemies are involved. Let us say, for the sake of argument here, that Crossan is correct that version II, reflective of the canonical Gospels, has an execution section in which Jesus is put to death by his enemies and he is buried and visited by friends and rises and then appears to friends. It appears that version I, the material related to enemies, is simply the material that is left when the "friends" portion is removed. However, this is not entirely satisfactory, as version II, by Crossan's admission, has the execution section, as in the canonical Gospels, attributed to enemies. Crossan himself admits and here indicates that there is a possible crossover between friends and enemies material in the versions. There is nothing to say that this could not have occurred at other places, and this thus dilutes the notion of the type of coherent Cross Gospel that Crossan wishes to reconstruct. One might perhaps just as well believe that a later account would expand upon the depiction of the tomb and resurrection accounts involving Jesus's friends with a realization that depiction of the reaction of his enemies was equally if not more appropriate, and thus duly added. If this were true, then the Cross Gospel would not be a unitary source, but simply a part of a later expanded version of the canonical Gospel account as found in version II, one that attempts to be inclusive by providing not only for Jesus's friends but for his enemies as well.

There is the further difficulty of necessarily positing that the material that does not fit within version II is therefore not only a separate coherent source, but an earlier source. Crossan bases this argument on his supposition that version I had sections in which the Jewish people are depicted as repenting of their actions (e.g. Gos. Pet. 7:25; 8:28). According to Brown, who is here followed by Crossan, there is increasing "anti-Judaism" in the sources, and this developmental criterion may be used to determine the relative chronology of sources. There are a number of questions that might be raised first regarding Crossan's depiction of the canonical Gospels and their degree of and type of anti-Judaism.[20] This aside, there is the further problem of ascribing such a "law" to the transmission. E.P. Sanders has shown that one must be very cautious about attributing firm tendencies to the canonical Gospels and the early

---

20   See Crossan, "*Gospel of Peter*," 127.

church tradition, since there are no predictable patterns, and by almost any reckoning the various trends that sometimes can be identified move in diametrically opposed patterns.[21] By this recknoning, even if we assume that Crossan's characterizaton and identification of the Cross Gospel is correct, its tendency with regard to depicting the Jewish people may or may not be earlier than the canonical Gospel material. Crossan's criterion is also asked to be able to differentiate the hypothetical Cross Gospel from the canonical Gospels. However, in discussing the canonical Gospels, Crossan paints them with a much broader brush than he does the Cross Gospel, claiming that Mark depicts the Jewish authorities as bad and the Jewish "crowd" as bad, while Luke/Acts and Matthew depict the Jewish authorities as bad and the Jewish people as bad. One might have expected a more nuanced differentiating function with known sources, when the same criterion is being asked to formulate clear distinctions for a hypothesized source.

3.2   *Execution Account and Use of the Canonical Gospels*

Crossan contends that the execution account of version II is not found in the Gospel of Peter. As he states, "I see no secure indication there of material from the passion accounts of the canonical gospels."[22] He goes on to note that "The reason is that both versions agree that, of course, the execution was conducted by Jesus's enemies in both versions."[23] Crossan seems to want to have the situation both ways with this argument. Either the Gospel of Peter does or does not reflect the canonical Gospels. That Jesus was executed by his enemies is certainly a feature of the canonical Gospels, and so, according to Crossan, it is in the Gospel of Peter. In that sense, the execution account from version II is, in fact, found in the Gospel of Peter, as it is similar to the one found in version I. This is further evidence of blurring of the categories between the two versions, and further reason to question whether one can differentiate the Cross Gospel so clearly.

There are other indications of knowledge and reflection of the canonical Gospels, or later Christian thought, in the supposed Cross Gospel account, however. One of these is the historical situation of Pilate and Herod. Crossan apparently contends that the situation depicted in the Gospel of Peter of camaraderie between Pilate and Herod (Gos. Pet. 1:1–2) does not reflect the canonical Gospel account, because there is no such scene in the Gospels. Indeed there

---

21   E.P. Sanders, *The Tendencies of the Synoptic Tradition* (SNTSMS 9; Cambridge: Cambridge University Press, 1969), e.g. 272.
22   Crossan, "*Gospel of Peter*," 130.
23   Crossan, "*Gospel of Peter*," 130.

is not. However, Luke 23 records Pilate as enquiring, when Jesus is delivered to him, whether he is a Galilean, and then, upon learning that he is, sending him to Herod, who interrogates him. Upon Jesus's return to Pilate, Luke states that "Herod and Pilate became friends with one another that very day" (Luke 23:12). It appears that the Gospel of Peter goes one step further and wants to show what that friendship must have looked like by placing Pilate and Herod together in the same room, with them making their decisions together. There is the further difficulty that the Gospel of Peter appears to depict Herod as having significant jurisdiction over Jesus and even authority to execute him in Jerusalem, something that is anachronistic and further evidence for the Cross Gospel not being early but reflecting a later situation than at least Luke's Gospel.[24]

There are a number of other details that are depicted in the Cross Gospel that reflect the canonical Gospels as well and indicate later developments. For example, in the execution portion, the following details seem to reflect the canonical documents: recognition of Jesus's death taking place in relation to the feast of unleavened bread (Gos. Pet. 2:5; Mark 14:1; Matt 26:2; Luke 22:1), clothing Jesus in a purple robe (Gos. Pet. 3:7; Mark 15:17; Matt 27:28), crowning him with a crown of thorns (Gos. Pet. 3:8; Mark 15:17; Matt 27:29), physically abusing him (Gos. Pet. 3:9; Mark 14:65; 15:19; Matt 26:67; 27:30), crucifying him between two criminals (Gos. Pet. 3:10; Mark 15:27; Matt 27:38; Luke 23:33, 39–40), putting a sign up on the cross (Gos. Pet. 4:11; Mark 15:26; Matt 27:37; Luke 23:38; John 19:19), casting lots for Jesus's garments (Gos. Pet. 4:12; Mark 15:24; Matt 27:35; Luke 23:34; John 19:24), one of the criminals admitting his guilt (Gos. Pet. 4:13; Luke 23:40–41),[25] the breaking of the legs of some criminals being discussed (Gos. Pet. 4:14; John 19:32–33), the darkness coming upon the earth at the time of Jesus's death (Gos. Pet. 5:15, 18; Mark 15:33; Matt 27:45; Luke 23:44), giving Jesus a drink of vinegar (Gos. Pet. 5:16; Mark 15:36; Matt 27:48; John 19:29), his calling something out at his death (Gos. Pet. 5:19; Mark 15:34; Matt 27:46),[26]

---

24 James H. Charlesworth and Craig A. Evans, "Jesus in the Agrapha and Apocryphal Gospels," in *Studying the Historical Jesus: Evaluations of the State of Current Research* (ed. Bruce Chilton and Craig A. Evans; NTTS 19; Leiden: Brill, 1994), 479–533 (506–507).

25 There is some apparent confusion in the Cross Gospel (Gospel of Peter) in 4:13 regarding the action of the criminal, who rebukes those who are crucifying Jesus and casting lots for his garments, rather than rebuking the other criminal. This arguably reflects a later time when there is an attempt to bring the two separate stories together into a single one but at the expense of coherence.

26 What Jesus calls out in the Gospel of Peter—"My power, power, you have forsaken me"— would also arguably reflect a later attempt to smooth over the possible appearance of despair in Jesus's words of the canonical Gospels. In fact, there is a chance that these words reflect a docetic strain of thought. Cf. Charlesworth and Evans, "Agrapha," 507. On the issue

and the tearing of the temple veil (Gos. Pet. 5:20; Mark 15:38; Matt 27:51). Such features are found in the rest of the Cross Gospel as well. These include the attestation of the crowd regarding how righteous Jesus was (Gos. Pet. 8:28; Luke 23:4),[27] erecting of a guard at the tomb (Gos. Pet. 8:30, 32; 9:35; Matt 27:65), the large stone placed at the tomb (Gos. Pet. 8:32; Mark 15:46; 16:3–4; Matt 27:60), "men" watching over the tomb (Gos. Pet. 9:36; Mark 16:5; Matt 28:5; Luke 24:4), their descending from heaven and appearance being bright (Gos. Pet. 9:36; Matt 28:2–3; cf. Mark 16:5; Luke 24:4), the tomb being opened and the stone rolling away (Gos. Pet. 9:37; Mark 16:4; Luke 24:2; John 20:1), reporting back what had happened (Gos. Pet. 11:45; Matt 28:11), acclamation of Jesus as "Son of God" by those associated with a centurion (Gos. Pet. 11:45; Mark 15:39; Matt 27:54; cf. Luke 23:47),[28] and efforts to suppress what had been seen (Gos. Pet. 11:47; Matt 28:13). The question asked from heaven to those emerging from the tomb, regarding preaching to those who sleep (Gos. Pet. 10:41), itself seems to reflect 1 Pet 3:19 and Jesus's preaching to those in prison. Crossan addresses some of these parallels elsewhere, depicting them as "prophetic allusions" that he says are "now buried under the narrative surface."[29] They are hardly buried under the surface of either the Gospel of Peter or the canonical Gospels' accounts, but there are a number of clear and distinct parallels throughout the entire account. They indicate that the author of the Cross Gospel was familiar with probably all of the canonical Gospels and perhaps more of the canonical New Testament.

3.3   *Later Elements of the Cross Gospel*

The Cross Gospel has a number of other later features that should be noted. Besides the anachronistic depiction of Herod, probably included because of lack of later information on the scope of his authority and physical location, there are a number of other clear later elements to note. One feature is how Jesus is addressed throughout both the Cross Gospel and the entire Gospel of Peter. In the Cross Gospel, Jesus is drug away and referred to as the "Son of God" (Gos. Pet. 3:6). When those who drug Jesus away were beating him, they addressed him as the "King of Israel" (Gos. Pet. 3:7), not King of the Jews, a more pejorative term. Later in the beating, this same group addresses Jesus as "Son of

---

of Jesus's despair, as reflected in his own dying words (or not), see Stanley E. Porter, *Sacred Tradition in the New Testament: Tracing Old Testament Themes in the Gospels and Epistles* (Grand Rapids: Baker, 2016), 153–177.

27   Charlesworth and Evans, "Agrapha," 510.
28   Charlesworth and Evans ("Agrapha," 511) believe this reflects direct Matthean influence.
29   Crossan, *Historical Jesus*, 386.

God" (Gos. Pet. 3:9). The statement erected on the cross addresses Jesus as the "King of Israel" (Gos. Pet. 3:11). Finally, Pilate says that he is guilty of the blood of the "son of God" (Gos. Pet. 11:46). Elsewhere Crossan addresses such instances and states that these were part of the "accusations" that were "lost but residually indicated."[30] This use of clear and overt christological titles is unparalleled in the canonical Gospels and reflective of a high Christology, one that is not easily (or early!) placed in the mouths of those who are abusing and about to crucify Jesus. Crossan could contend that they reflect the kinds of accusations brought against Jesus, in which case one or possibly two instances might be understandable. However, one of the major forms of address of Jesus in the Cross Gospel is by means of these christological titles. Crossan could further contend that these reflect later redactional changes to elevate the theology of the text. The text as it reads clearly does have an elevated Christology. However, such an appeal to redaction becomes circular and makes it difficult to prove one's case for an early and coherent Cross Gospel, if clearly contradictory evidence is simply dismissed because it is inconvenient or, worse, counter to the hypothesis.

Similar evidence is found in the use of the term "Lord" in reference to Jesus. The term "Lord" is used of Jesus in Gos. Pet. 1:2, 2:3 (2×), 3:6, 4:10, 5:19, 6:21, 6:24, 12:50; and the term "Lord's day" is found in Gos. Pet. 9:35; 12:50. This term, "Lord"—rather than Jesus, which is not used at all in the Gospel of Peter—is found in both versions I and II of Crossan's dissection of the Gospel of Peter. Rather than reflecting the early independence of the Cross Gospel, this exclusive use of the term "Lord," rather than Jesus, reflects a later form of theological address of Jesus, and it serves as a unifying factor for the entire narrative. The use of the term "Lord's day" is also clearly anachronistic. Charlesworth and Evans have also noted a number of other indicators of late date for the Cross Gospel in relation to the canonical Gospels. These include passages in the Gospel of Peter where Jesus appears to feel no pain from his beating and crucifixion (Gos. Pet. 4:10) or is said to be taken up at the time of his death (Gos. Pet. 5:19), which they think may well reflect later docetic influence.[31] Further, Charlesworth and Evans note that the criminal who defends Jesus states that Jesus "has become the savior of men" (Gos. Pet. 4:13).[32] Crossan might well contend that much of this reflects the later second-century redaction. It well might, but the fact that "Jesus" and other terminology used in the canonical Gospels

---

30   Crossan, *Historical Jesus*, 386.
31   Charlesworth and Evans, "Agrapha," 508.
32   Charlesworth and Evans, "Agrapha," 508. The scholars who have found later elements in the Gospel of Peter are summarized in Charlesworth and Evans, "Agrapha," 512–513.

is not found and that the christological language is used as consistently as it is in the Gospel of Peter certainly does not help the case for an independent and early Cross Gospel.

3.4   Resurrection Accounts

Crossan maintains that, concerning the passion and resurrection, "Matthew and Luke do not know an alternative to Mark and, at least in this area, John is, in my judgment, dependent on the synoptic versions."[33] Furthermore, he states that "All four gospels are in remarkable general agreement until Mark ends at the empty tomb in 16:8, but when Mark stops they all go their very separate ways."[34] As a result, he asks the question: "What happened to history remembered when Mark stopped and left the others on their own?" A more pertinent question might well be what happened to the "prophecy historicized" (Crossan's term) of the Cross Gospel's resurrection account? Crossan agrees with Koester that there was a passion-resurrection source that preceded the canonical Gospels.[35] Although he appears to be more cautious and guarded in his statements regarding the relation between the Cross Gospel and the Synoptic Gospel accounts of the passion and resurrection than he was earlier,[36] Crossan still seems to contend that the Cross Gospel was the source for the passion and resurrection accounts behind the canonical Gospels.[37] He goes into some detail to argue for the passion account, but, as Charlesworth and Evans have enquired, "How are we to explain why [Mark] made use only of the [Cross Gospel's] passion account, but not its resurrection account?"[38]

There are a number of issues raised by this question. One concerns the account of the resurrection found in Crossan's Cross Gospel. In the Cross Gospel (according to Crossan's version 1), as the soldiers were keeping watch at the tomb, the heavens are opened and two men come down to the tomb. The tomb stone rolls away, and the two young men enter. Three men come out of the tomb, with two supporting the third, and a cross following, with all three having their heads reaching into heaven. A voice from heaven asks, "Have you preached to those who sleep?" and a voice answers "Yes." There are two major difficulties with this account. One is the fact that it seems to be dependent upon

---

33   Crossan, "*Gospel of Peter*," 128.
34   Crossan, "*Gospel of Peter*," 128.
35   Crossan, "*Gospel of Peter*," 118, 128.
36   Cf. Crossan, *Cross that Spoke*, 404.
37   Crossan, "*Gospel of Peter*," 134.
38   Charlesworth and Evans, "Agrapha," 513.

earlier canonical sources, including especially the canonical Gospels, but also 1 Pet 3:19, as noted above. A second is its inherent implausibility as an early (the earliest?!) resurrection account. Perhaps, one might respond, that is the reason why Mark and the subsequent Gospel authors did not use the account. That, however, is an admission that, though the account may have been early, it was thought implausible. Rather than looking to prophecy historicized, the canonical authors were looking for "history remembered" (Crossan's term), the opposite tendency to the one posited by Crossan. In fact, the canonical Gospel authors apparently would rather exclude an implausible account than perpetuate one that they thought unbelievable. Of course, the easier solution is that the Cross Gospel resurrection account is simply later and derivative from the canonical Gospels, which would account for why it is not found in the canonical Gospels. As Charlesworth and Evans have suggested, perhaps, to use the framework of Crossan's scenario,

> Just as Matthew and Luke, who are dependent upon Mark, follow the evangelist's account of the passion right up to the discovery of the empty tomb (Mark 16:1–8), then go their separate ways because there is no more Mark to follow, so the *Gospel of Peter* follows Mark (and the other two Synoptics). The *Gospel of Peter* breaks away from the Marcan narrative here for the same reason that Matthew and Luke break away: There is no Marcan resurrection narrative to follow.[39]

The lack of use of the Cross Gospel's resurrection account by the canonical Gospels is not easily accounted for.

3.5 Transitionary Sections

Crossan states that these transitionary statements were used to harmonize the two versions, rather than simply place the accounts together.

The first of these supposed units (Gos. Pet. 2:3–5a) relates how Joseph, who was a friend of Pilate and of the "Lord," asks about the body of the "Lord," and Pilate enquires of Herod regarding it. Although the communication between Pilate and Herod is not found in the canonical Gospels (see above for a possible explanation), this appears to be a unit that expands upon the canonical Gospel account of Joseph asking for the body of Jesus (Mark 15:43; Matt 27:57–58; Luke 23:50–52; John 19:38). In the Gospel of Peter, he asks in advance of Jesus's execution, while he asks after in the canonical Gospels. While Crossan

---

39 Charlesworth and Evans, "Agrapha," 513.

claims that this section supposedly prepares the reader for the friends being involved in Jesus's burial,[40] on the basis of what has been said above regarding putting Pilate and Herod in contact, and the use of language of "Lord," there is no reason to see this unit as transitionary but it could just as easily have been placed in the Cross Gospel.

The second of the transitionary units (Gos. Pet. 7:26–27 and 14:58–59) concerns actions of the disciples. In the first instance, Peter is depicted as saying that he, along with others, mourned, while trying to hide from those who were after them. Crossan says that this section prepares for Jesus to appear to his friends in 14:60.[41] However, there is little on the surface to distinguish this unit from its being in version II, as the unit seems to be an expansion of the canonical Gospels, where Peter regrets his actions and the disciples are in hiding (Mark 14:72; Matt 26:75; Luke 22:62; Acts 1:13; 2:1). In the second instance, the twelve disciples are said to have grieved for what had happened and have gone home (see Luke 24:12). The tomb account of version II ends with material that is reflective of Mark 16:1–8, with Gos. Pet. 13:57 having the women fearful and fleeing (see Mark 16:8). This supposedly transitional unit then continues the story for the disciples, with them also fearful. There is a further link to version I, however, in reference to the day of unleavened bread in Gos. Pet. 14:58 and 2:5b.

The third of the transitionary units (Gos. Pet. 11:43–44) mentions the arrival of the youths and, according to Crossan, prepares for the tomb being visited by friends in Gos. Pet. 12:50–13:57.[42] This unit, however, also reflects the canonical Gospels in the opening of heaven and the men descending (Matt 28:2), as is found in Gos. Pet. 9:36, a passage found in version I.

In all three instances, rather than there being clear reasons for creation of the transitionary passages, it appears that they are as integral to the Gospel of Peter as are other passages, and often overlap with either version I or II or the canonical Gospels, or some combination of these. This does not strengthen the argument for these passages as clear independent units created to aid in unifying the disparate narrative.

---

40   Crossan, *"Gospel of Peter,"* 130.
41   Crossan, *"Gospel of Peter,"* 130.
42   Crossan, *"Gospel of Peter,"* 130.

4   Conclusion

We can be thankful that Crossan has continued to articulate and refine his position regarding the Gospel of Peter and in particular the Cross Gospel that he posits as forming one of two important passion-resurrection accounts within that document. Despite Crossan's most recent attempt to re-articulate and bolster his argument for the early, independent status of the Cross Gospel within the larger Gospel of Peter, there are still a number of factors that point to not only the Gospel of Peter as a whole, but the Cross Gospel in particular, as being a later account, derived from the canonical Gospels and possibly other canonical material. The failure of the differentiation of friends and enemies as a source-critical criterion, the dependent nature of the execution account, the clear indicators of later developed Christology, the failure to incorporate the resurrection account in the canonical Gospels, and the lack of support for the transitionary units all indicate that the Cross Gospel is derivative and later than the canonical sources. Crossan's case for distinguishing his Cross Gospel within the Gospel of Peter, though still not adequately made, has continued to raise questions regarding the relationship between this particular apocryphal text and the canonical New Testament and to provoke useful debate. No doubt the discussion will continue.

PART 3

Early Christian Descriptions of the Jesus Movement

From Jesus to Lord and Other Contributions of the Early Aramaic-Speaking Congregation in Jerusalem

F. Stanley Jones

While recent scholars and popular forums have pondered the question of "From Jesus to Christ,"[1] I believe an initial first step in this process has been neglected, namely, the question of how Jesus became "Lord." The following finds its point of departure in the understanding of Jesus as "Lord," or *mareya* in Aramaic, and then attempts to circumscribe some further elements of the Aramaic terminology of the early Aramaic-speaking community in Jerusalem. A couple of preliminary comments are perhaps in order.

First, it has been repeatedly stated in the last generation of scholarship that the earliest Christians, particularly those in Jerusalem, were not Christians at all, but were rather Jews. Terminologically, there can be no doubt that the community in Jerusalem did not call themselves "Christians." The writings found near the Dead Sea, the Dead Sea Scrolls, do provide a warning, however, that it was not impossible for some Jews to distance themselves spiritually from other Jews to the point of dissociation. The authors and adherents of these documents separated themselves spiritually and physically as the sons of light from the sons of darkness, including "the multitude of the people" (4Q397 14–21 7;[2] 1QS 5:1–2; 3:20–21). For early followers of Jesus, this instance helps to clarify that it is indeed possible that they separated themselves out as a special group with respect to others who also called themselves Jews. The fact that the early

---

[1] This was the title of a 1988 book by Paula Fredriksen, *From Jesus to Christ: The Origins of the New Testament Images of Jesus* (New Haven: Yale University Press, 1988), which has appeared in a second edition, 2000, and then was used as the title for a FRONTLINE documentary television series (*From Jesus to Christ: The First Christians*) about the early Christians written and produced by Marilyn Mellowes (United Productions, 1998). Earlier the title is found in the English translation of Rudolf Steiner, *Von Jesus zu Christus* (Berlin, 1912), *From Jesus to Christ* (London: H. Collison, 1930).

[2] The standard reconstruction of this line has been questioned by Elitzur A. Bar-Asher Siegal, "Who Separated from Whom and Why? A Philological Study of 4QMMT," *RevQ* 25 (2011): 229–256, but even if the proposed reconstruction for this line of the manuscript is accepted, the separatist stance of the community behind the scrolls is apparent. See, e.g., Albert I. Baumgarten, *The Flourishing of Jewish Sects in the Maccabean Era: An Interpretation* (JSJSup 55; Leiden: Brill, 1997), 12–13.

followers of Jesus remained in Jerusalem may indicate that they were not as radically distinctive Jewish as the adherents of the Dead Sea Scrolls, but not even this conclusion is assured; while issues of calendar, doctrine, and purity kept the Qumran inhabitants apart from Jerusalem in the desert, early followers of Jesus apparently held other views, though that does not necessarily mean that they were any less radically discrete as a group. For historical research, the Dead Sea Scrolls have, in any event, supplied an important historical frame of reference to evaluate what seems to be evidence for a distinctive group of followers of Jesus in Jerusalem.

Second, I do hold to the historical conclusion that Aramaic was the primary language of Jesus, his earliest followers, and the community in Jerusalem. The fairly recently recovered and quite relevant Babatha documents, for example, demonstrate that: "Although Greek was the *lingua franca* of government and business in the whole eastern Mediterranean area, it was not the mother tongue of the parties and the scribes of the Babatha documents."[3] These Palestinian Jews from the later first and early second centuries spoke Aramaic among themselves, and so did Jesus and his associates. Stories in Acts do not convince me that Peter was bilingual or that Paul was bilingual:[4] why else would Paul never cite the Hebrew Bible, but only its Greek translation? Whoever spoke some Greek among the earliest followers of Jesus, the main community in Jerusalem conducted itself in Aramaic, and it is this Aramaic that needs to be reconstructed in historical studies—the topic is sorely neglected, but it should not be.

As a final preliminary comment, I wish to point out that the study of Palestinian Aramaic of the first century has advanced considerably and substantially since the time of Gustav Dalman, who admirably attempted to triangulate in on Jesus's dialect from the sources available to him.[5] Most significantly, we

---

3 *The Documents from the Bar Kokhba Period in the Cave of Letters: Greek Papyri* (ed. Naphtali Lewis; JDS 2; Jerusalem: Israel Exploration Society, 1989), 13.

4 Acts' account of a bilingual Paul (Acts 21:17–22) is apparently accepted as historical by Fergus Millar, *The Roman Near East 31 BC–AD 337* (Cambridge, MA: Harvard University Press, 1993), 364–365, whom Sang-Il Lee, *Jesus and Gospel Traditions in Bilingual Context: A Study in the Interdirectionality of Language* (BZNW 186; Berlin: de Gruyter, 2012), 129 n. 67, cites in support of his bald assertion that "Paul seems to have been bilingual, also being very capable in Aramaic and Greek" (127). Indeed, Lee thinks that "Paul's matrix language was Aramaic" (127). Lee's case for a bilingual Peter is made on pp. 117–118 n. 29.

5 Gustaf Dalman, *Die Worte Jesu*. Vol. 1: *Einleitung und wichtige Begriffe* (2nd ed.; Leipzig: Hinrichs, 1930), 63–72; *The Words of Jesus*. Vol. 1: *Introduction and Fundamental Ideas* (trans. D.M. Kay; Edinburgh: T&T Clark, 1902), 79–88.

have now recovered Aramaic manuscripts and papyri from the time; this data has revolutionized the field and has finally given historical reconstructions something solid to build upon. We are emerging out of the realm of pure speculation, but there are virtually no scholars around to rewrite history accordingly.

The designation of Jesus as "Lord" (*mareya*) is a fine place to begin because a number of indices coincide to show that this was an early and dominant designation for Jesus in the earliest community. First, one reads *maranatha*, which has generally been considered early. Second, there is the Semitic-colored phrase of baptism "into the name of the Lord," *leshum mareya*. Third, there is early documentation for the term "the day of the Lord." Fourth, and related, there is early evidence for the expression the "Lord's day." Fifth and sixth, there are early references to the "Lord's meal" that is carried out "in memory of the Lord." Seventh, there is the early designation the "brothers of the Lord." Virtually all of these usages are found in our earliest preserved source, Paul's letters, and they are often also witnessed in other early sources.

While each of these items deserves independent analysis, it must be said at the outset that unless there was a massive highjacking of the tradition—which is perhaps not to be excluded in principle—the designation "Lord" must go way back. Most would agree. One fairly common way to undermine the significance of this insight for understanding the early followers of Jesus in Jerusalem is to push the designation "Lord" further back into the life of Jesus, where it supposedly meant not much more than "sir." For lack of contemporary evidence, in the past there has been some confusion about the usage of the word "Lord" during the lifetime of Jesus. With the papyri from Nahal Hever, it has now become even clearer that unless Jesus was the owner of a large tract of land with attendant employees or otherwise a powerful figure such as a judge or ruler,[6] it is not likely that he would have been called "Lord" during his lifetime.[7] Thus, the

---

6 Ada Yardeni, *Textbook of Aramaic, Hebrew and Nabataean Documentary Texts from the Judaean Desert and Related Material* (2 vols.; Jerusalem: The Hebrew University, 2000), 2:102 lists the passages where "Lord" occurs; the clear references are to the king of Nabataea and to Caesar. Siegfried Schulz, "Maranatha und Kyrios Jesus," ZNW 53 (1962): 125–144, esp. 134–137, reviews the other Aramaic evidence and concludes: "Beherrschend ist in seinem Verständnisbereich ist seine richterliche Würde: Mara ist Richter über Leben und Tod der ihm Untergebenen. Immer also, wenn es im aramäischen Sprachgebiet darum ging, eine königliche, militärische, administrative, lehrmäßige oder göttliche Richter-Autorität und -Macht zu bezeichnen oder anzureden ..." (137).

7 See Philipp Vielhauer, *Aufsätze zum Neuen Testament* (TB 31; Munich: Chr. Kaiser, 1965), 153–157, for an argument from internal New Testament evidence that this was the case, in

supposition that *marē'* was just a usual designation of respect, such as "sir,"[8] has been exposed as incorrect.[9] Consequently, the usage of the term by the early followers of Jesus has been liberated to unveil some actual substance in its early usage. This new evidence has thus permitted a significant advance in scholarship that carries consequences in several areas of research, as the following hopes to highlight.

The evidence from the Christian tradition indicates that the origin of the designation of Jesus as "Lord" was in the time after his death, in the eschatological context as found particularly in the expression "day of the Lord." In Paul's letters, scholarship has observed a clear association of the title "Lord" with the notion of the parousia.[10] The cry *maranatha*[11] is also a pillar of support for this view of the eschatological origin of the application of the title "Lord."

Movement from a Hebrew Bible "day of God [or Adonai]"[12] to a "day of the Lord [*mareya*]" was, however, not quite as simple as it sounds in English. Two main factors enabled it.

One the one hand, there was a softening of the "day of God" to a day of God's representative, something like a "day of the Elect One" as found in 1 En. 61:5 or a day of the Servant or Son in 4 Ezra 13:52.[13] On the other hand, the concept of a post-mortem assumption of the righteous was connected with the notion that these righteous would be involved with the final judgment.[14] Q parables of an absent and returning "lord" (Q 12:42–46; 19:12–26) reveal the combination of the secular usage (wealthy landowner) with the religious usage, found in Q 6:46 ("Why do you call me Lord, Lord?"), precisely in the context of the eschatological judgment.[15] For the early followers of Jesus in Jerusalem, Jesus had been

---

refutation of Ferdinand Hahn (see n. 8). See also Joseph A. Fitzmyer, *A Wandering Aramaean: Collected Aramaic Essays* (Missoula, MT: Scholars Press, 1979), 127–128.

8   Werner Kramer, *Christos Kyrios Gottessohn* (ATANT 44; Zurich: Zwingli, 1963), 175; *Christ, Lord, Son of God* (SBT 50; trans. Brian Hardy; London: SCM, 1966), 177; Ferdinand Hahn, *Christologische Hoheitstitel* (5th ed., exp.; UTB 1873; Göttingen: Vandenhoeck & Ruprecht, 1995), 81–82, cf. 463.

9   Cf. also Fitzmyer, *A Wandering Aramaean*, 133 n. 16.

10 Kramer, *Christos Kyrios Gottessohn*, 172–174; *Christ, Lord, Son of God*, 173–176.

11 1 Cor 16:21; Did. 10:6; cf. Rev 22:20.

12 Reference are found in Gerhard von Rad, "ἡμέρα," *TDNT* 2:943–947, esp. 944–947.

13 Cf. Gerhard Delling, "ἡμέρα," *TDNT* 2:947–953, esp. 951.

14 See, for example, the recent overview of "Assumption in Jewish Literature" in Daniel A. Smith, *The Post-Mortem Vindication of Jesus in the Sayings Gospel Q* (LNTS 338; London: T&T Clark, 2006), 66–85, where further literature is listed.

15 Christopher M. Tuckett, *Q and the History of Early Christianity* (Edinburgh: T&T Clark, 1996), 214–218, in argument with David R. Catchpole, *The Quest for Q* (Edinburgh: T&T

assumed and would reappear as the face of the "day of God" on the "day of the Lord." Q can thus possibly use the formulation "day of the Son of Man" (Q 17:24, 26, 30).

But why did they call him "Lord, Lord" (*mareya*)? Qumran documents have again provided the critical evidence that *mareya*, with or without possessive suffixes, could be used of God.[16] Nevertheless, the struggle to find this evidence is likely a tell-tale sign that this word was not the usual way of speaking of God.[17] *Mareya* was rather most common for the human context; it dominantly indicated someone with judgmental power.[18] Thus, I suggest, the early followers of Jesus could readily adopt the term for the one they thought would soon become apparent as the representative of God in judgment.[19]

So Jesus became "Lord" via assumption as a righteous one. His main function as "Lord" is in the coming judgment. Other phrases with "Lord" (*mareya*) seem to have made up some of the central vocabulary of the early community. "Brother of the Lord"[20] suggests that the Lord will take particular care of his family at his return as judge. The "day of the Lord" early took on weekly significance to signify when the "meal of the Lord" should be held.[21] Doubtless, this weekly "Lord's day" was derivative and still closely connected with the eschatological "day of the Lord," just as Paul indicates that, as he received the tradition, the meal should be held in memory of the Lord, until he should come (1 Cor 11:25–26), and as Paul again intimates when he connects this meal thoroughly with judgment (1 Cor 11:27–34), not least the Last Judgment (1 Cor 11:32).[22]

Proposal of the presence of these rituals and institutions for the early Jerusalem community may seem bold, but this is where the evidence leads: back to

---

Clark), 99–100, attempts to deny the connection between these passages to conclude that "Lord" was not a term of great christological significance for Q. Cf., furthermore, Q 13:25.

16 See the texts printed in Fitzmyer, *A Wandering Aramaean*, 124.
17 See Schulz, "Maranatha und Kyrios Jesus," 133–134, 137. On p. 136, Schulz correctly notes that the address in the *Genesis Apocryphon* 1Q20 22: 32 ("my Lord, God") demonstrates that "Lord" is not equivalent to "God."
18 Schulz, "Maranatha und Kyrios Jesus," 137.
19 Similar: Schulz, "Maranatha und Kyrios Jesus," 138.
20 Gal 1:19; 1 Cor 9:5.
21 1 Cor 11:20; Did. 14:1. Cf. the expression "Lord's day" also in Gos. Pet. 9:35; Ign. *Magn.* 9:1; and Didascalia Apostolorum 13 (2.59.2).
22 From the perspective of contemporary Greek usage, Amphilochios Papathomas, *Juristische Begriffe im ersten Korintherbrief des Paulus* (TYCHE Supplementband 7; Vienna: Holzhausen, 2009), 166–172, identifies clearly the pervasive juristic and forensic terminology in this passage, though the reference is not mainly to signing a new contract with the apostle (contra p. 168).

the early Aramaic-speaking Jerusalem community. Surprisingly strong support for such postulation comes from consideration of the possibility of early baptism by this community. It is widely held that Paul implies that he himself was baptized when he states in 1 Cor 12:13, "We were all baptized into one body."[23] Paul's own baptism thus seems to have occurred when he changed his mind about the movement he states he had been persecuting (he calls it "the church of God"; 1 Cor 15:9 and Gal 1:13), and this baptism will have taken place only a few years after Jesus's death. The formula for early baptism into this group of believers has been carefully studied and found to contain a Semiticism, namely, the phrase "into the name," which is widely thought to reflect an original Aramaic *leshum*. Hartman concluded that the oldest phrasing was "into the name of the Lord Jesus" (*leshum mareya Yeshu*).[24] While one can debate the exact meaning of this phrase, the presence of "the Lord" here again surely anchors its eschatological relevance.[25]

In recent times, it seems to have been forgotten that the Mandaeans are also attested to have performed certain cultic actions "into the name of ..." (*leshum* ...).[26] It is from this larger perspective that the question of the Aramaic name for baptism by the early Jerusalem community can be raised. To this I now turn.

In the voluminous literature on John the Baptist, there is, surprisingly, little discussion of the Aramaic behind the sobriquet "the Baptist." One can search high and low in most of the monographs on John without finding any mention of Aramaic whatsoever, though surely these studies assume that Aramaic was the language of John's proclamation. In the few instances where Aramaic

---

23 Lars Hartman, *"Into the Name of the Lord Jesus": Baptism in the Early Church* (SNTW; Edinburgh: T&T Clark, 1997), 29.
24 Hartman, *"Into the Name of the Lord Jesus,"* 43.
25 Cf. Gerhard Lohfink, "Der Ursprung der christlichen Taufe," *TQ* 156 (1976): 35–54, esp. 47–48, who proposes eschatological relevance of earliest baptism without seeing the indicator in the naming of the "Lord." In his many studies, Lars Hartman has not clearly recognized the term "the Lord" as central for the early interpretation of the ritual. The title of his early article "'Into the Name of Jesus': A Suggestion concerning the Earliest Meaning of the Phrase," *NTS* 20 (1973–1974): 432–440, reveals that Hartman only later came to an awareness, at all, that "Lord" belonged to the earliest formula. The simple "into the name of the Lord" is found in the Did. 9:5 and Herm. *Vis.* 3.7.3; "Jesus" is found additionally in Acts 8:16 and 19:5.
26 Noted and discussed by August Johann Heinrich Wilhelm Brandt, *Die mandäische Religion* (Utrecht: C.J.G. Repelius, 1889), 106 n. 2. It is noteworthy that in the one instance cited by Brandt in which the phrase is used in reference to baptism, the reference is to Christian baptism. The standard Mandaean baptismal formula uses "on the name of ..." (*'l shum* ...) and arranges for names to be pronounced "on" (*'l*) baptismal candidates.

terminology is found, it is usually assumed without question that John's baptism involved the Semitic root *tbl*. Joan Taylor, in her *The Immerser*, states baldly that *tebilah* is the Hebrew word equivalent to *baptisma*.[27] Such security perhaps derives from the influence of Joachim Jeremias's *New Testament Theology*, where he stated that the Greek passive verb corresponds to the intransitive active qal *tebal*.[28] Jeremias followed the uncomfortable and often forgotten conclusion that Jesus immersed himself, and that "John the Baptist had the function of a witness, as in proselyte baptism."[29] For philological support in connection with the root *tbl*, Jeremias referred to Harald Sahlin's more extensive presentation.[30]

Searching around, one finds that Brandt, Dalman, Merx, Easton, Billerbeck, and Dahl have also pronounced in favor of the root *tbl*.[31] Occasionally, one finds here the further specification that the Aramaic word for "baptizer" was *matbelana*.[32] Dalman noted that the Christian Palestinian version of the Gospels used *masbeana*, but he declared it "inapt" *ex cathedra*.[33] Evidence has actually mounted that the root *sba* might not be quite so inapt. If it was noted back in the days of Brandt that Mandaeans and Christian Palestinians used this root to speak of baptism,[34] Kurt Rudolph ventured to state, taking into consideration the Sobiai connected with Elchasai[35] and the Masbothaeans mentioned in Hegesippus,[36] that the verb *sba* unites the heretical Jewish baptizers.[37] One

---

27 Joan E. Taylor, *The Immerser: John the Baptist within Second Temple Judaism* (Grand Rapids: Eerdmans, 1997), 50.
28 Joachim Jeremias, *New Testament Theology* (trans. John Bowden; New York: Scribners, 1971), 51.
29 Jeremias, *New Testament Theology*, 51.
30 Harald Sahlin, *Studien zum dritten Kapitel des Lukasevangeliums* (UUA 1949.2; Uppsala: A.-B. Lundequistka, 1949), 130–133.
31 Wilhelm Brandt, "'Ονομα en de doopsformule in het Nieuwe Testament," *ThT* (1891): 565–610, esp. 599; Adalbert Merx, *Das Evangelium Matthaeus* (part 2, 1st half of *Die vier kanonischen Evangelien nach ihrem ältesten bekannten Texte*; Berlin: Georg Reimer, 1902), 38–39; Dalman, *Einleitung und wichtige Begriffe*, 115; *Introduction and Fundamental Ideas*, 141; Str-B 1:102; Burton Scott Easton, "Self-Baptism," *AmJT* 24 (1920): 513–518; Nils A. Dahl, "The Origin of Baptism," *NTT* 56 (1955): 36–52, esp. 44.
32 So Dalman, *Einleitung und wichtige Begriffe*, 115; *Introduction and Fundamental Ideas*, 141.
33 *Einleitung und wichtige Begriffe*, 114; *Introduction and Fundamental Ideas*, 140.
34 Wilhelm Brandt, *Die jüdischen Baptismen* (BZAW 18; Giessen: Alfred Töpelmann, 1910), 113.
35 Hippolytus, *Haer.* 9.13.2.
36 In Eusebius, *Hist. eccl.* 4.22.7.
37 Kurt Rudolph, *Die Mandäer* (FRLANT 74–75; 2 vols.; Göttingen: Vandenhoeck & Ruprecht, 1960–1961), 2:380.

can now also add Samaritan Aramaic.[38] Furthermore, new texts have fairly recently emerged from the Cairo Geniza that provide an actual Jewish Aramaic designation for John the Baptist. One would think that this unprecedented evidence for the Jewish Aramaic name for John would have garnered some attention in the incessant flow of monographs on John the Baptist, but one searches in vain. In short, Taylor-Schechter Misc. 35.87 and 35.88 have preserved Aramaic fragments of the *Toledhoth Yeshu* and contain several consistent references to *yohanan masbeana* ("John the Baptizer").[39] Evidence is thus triangulating in from several directions that this root *sba* may well be the original Aramaic behind baptism in the earliest Jerusalem community as well as with John the Baptist. If this is the case, the earliest Aramaic-speaking community in Jerusalem had a distinctive designation for its baptism that aligned it with the Jewish baptizing groups and clearly set it apart from other groups.

Evidence of the self-consciousness of the early Jerusalem community is found both in general ideas, such as the notion that there was a limited period after Jesus's death for the Lord to appear,[40] as well as in adoption of specific and distinctive terminology for this group. Paul's repeated comments on the "collection for the saints" make it apparent that the Jerusalem community called themselves "the holy/saints" in a very special sense. It is often forgotten that this usage is essentially foreign to standard Greek idiom;[41] thus, the early usage in the Jerusalem congregation likely derives from Jewish Aramaic *qadishaya*. 2 Cor 8:14 ("their abundance") and Rom 15:27 (Gentile believers are *obliged* to them because the Gentiles have become partakers of *their* spiritual matters) disclose that this group considered itself spiritually better endowed; Paul shares their special name with Gentile believers, but his repeated and unqualified

---

38 Abraham Tal, *A Dictionary of Samaritan Aramaic* (HO 1.50.2; Leiden: Brill, 2000), 720–721.
39 Published by Louis Ginzberg, "Ma'aseh Yeshu," in *Ginze Schechter* (3 vols.; New York: Hermon, 1928–1929), 1:324–338, esp. 329–338, with corrections and additions in William Horbury, "The Trial of Jesus in Jewish Tradition," in *The Trial of Jesus* (ed. Ernst Bammel; SBT 2nd ser. 13; London: SCM, 1970), 103–121, esp. 117–121; and William Horbury, "A Critical Examination of the Toledoth Jeshu" (Ph.D. diss., University of Cambridge, 1970), 90–91. The references to John the Baptist are found in Taylor-Schechter Misc. 35.87, folio 1 recto, lines 16 and 23, and Taylor-Schechter Misc. 35.88, folio 1 recto, line 2.
40 So the implication of 1 Cor 15:8, explicitly defined in Acts 1:3 as "forty days." Gnostics and Ophites thought the period was "eighteen months" according to Irenaeus, *Haer.* 1.3.2 and 1.30.14; the Mart. Isa. 9:16 has 545 days, while the *Ap. Jas.* (NHC I 2.19–20) mentions 550 days.
41 See, e.g., Robert Hodgson, Jr., "Holiness (NT)," *ABD* 3:249–254, esp. 249. Details on Greek usage are found in Eduard Williger, *Hagios: Untersuchungen zur Terminologie des Heiligen in den hellenisch-hellenistischen Religionen* (RVV 19.1; Giessen: Töpelmann, 1922).

references to the collection or ministry "for the saints"[42] reveal his awareness, and even adoption, of the exclusive claim. It is hardly an accident that the term "the holy," in turn, discloses a special relationship with the arrival/day of the Lord and judgment.[43] Other terms indicate that the group conceived of itself as a building, under construction doubtless by God and bearing the name not of the temple (*haikla*), but rather "church," though it is difficult to determine what word was used for this church.[44] Cephas[45] correlates with the term "pillars" (*'amudaya*),[46] which in turn was likely related to the designation "the Just" and was also likely synonymous with the "respected,"[47] while "the Twelve" likely related to the mission in and around Palestine by the "apostles" (*shelihaya*)— apparently something of a new word—whom Paul expects to find in Jerusalem (Gal 1:19) and who have a right to live off the church (1 Cor 9:4–6, 14). Internal financial issues of this community are also at stake in the employment of the word "poor" (*ebyonaya*).[48]

These are the pieces of the puzzle that remain to be explored in detail; nevertheless, a general picture of a distinctive and self-conscious community clearly emerges.

---

42 1 Cor 16:1; 2 Cor 8:4; 2 Cor 9:1; Rom 15:25; cf. 2 Cor 9:12 ("needs of the saints"); Rom 15:31.

43 E.g. 1 Thess 3:13; 1 Cor 6:2; see further passages and the discussion in, e.g., Hodgson, *ABD* 3:251–252.

44 Possibilities include *kenishta*, *qehala*, *'edta*, and *sibura* (cf. Joachim Jeremias, *Golgotha* [Angelos.B 1; Leipzig: Eduard Pfeiffer, 1926], 69).

45 Peter Lampe's arguments ("Das Spiel mit dem Petrusnamen—Matt. xvi. 18," *NTS* 25 [1978–1979]: 227–245, esp. 233) that the Aramaic word means just "stone" have been refuted by the evidence from Qumran; see Joseph A. Fitzmyer, *To Advance the Gospel: New Testament Studies* (New York: Crossroad, 1981), 115.

46 Cf. Philipp Vielhauer, *Oikodome: Aufsätze zum Neuen Testament Band 2* (TB 65; ed. Günter Klein; Munich: Chr. Kaiser, 1979), 6–8, on building terminology.

47 Str-B 3:537: Abraham was designated "the pillar of the world" and was seen as one of the main "righteous" (Str-B 3:186).

48 Gal 2:10; Rom 15:26.

Did Jesus, in the Memory of His Earliest Followers, Ever Nurse the Sick?

Steven Thompson

An increasing stream of recent Gospel scholarship designates Jesus a healer.[1] "Jesus should be put in the general category of being a healer, even though an equivalent noun is not actually used of him in the Gospels."[2] A widespread and almost unchallenged assumption in this scholarship is that accounts of Jesus's healings were intended by Gospel writers and editors to be read and understood as miraculous. In the words of Maurice Casey, "The study of Jesus's healing ministry has traditionally been dominated by the Christian agenda of miracle."[3] But was this what they intended? This pair of assumptions, that Jesus was presented primarily as a healer and that his healings were to be understood as miraculous, dominates current scholarship, to the neglect of other aspects of Jesus's engagement with the sick. In his recent summary of this approach, Justin Meggitt declared, "Although subsequent generations of Christians would become almost fixated by Jesus's reputation as a miracle worker ... there are good reasons to look closely at the earliest records of this activity."[4] This chapter takes up Meggitt's call for that closer look. It poses and answers the question, "did Jesus, in the memory of his earliest followers, sometimes administer basic nursing care to the sick, rather than always healing them?"

While Synoptic healing pericopes remain under intense scholarly scrutiny, the thesis of this chapter, that Jesus sometimes provided basic nursing care for the sick, is not addressed. This chapter's focus is thus very specific. It does *not* inquire whether the sick whom Jesus encountered were healed, either "miraculously" or "naturally." Its goal is to answer the question, "did Jesus, in the

---

1 James D.G. Dunn, *Jesus Remembered* (Christianity in the Making 1; Grand Rapids: Eerdmans, 2003), 677; Justin Meggitt, "The Historical Jesus and Healing: Jesus' Miracles in Psychosocial Context," in *Spiritual Healing: Scientific and Religious Perspectives* (ed. Fraser Watts; Cambridge: Cambridge University Press, 2011), 17.
2 Maurice Casey, *Jesus of Nazareth: An Independent Historian's Account of His Life and Teaching* (London: T&T Clark, 2010), 245.
3 Casey, *Jesus of Nazareth*, 237. Casey does not address the possibility that nursing care is behind any Gospel healing account.
4 Meggitt, "Historical Jesus and Healing," 17.

memory of his earliest followers, ever provide basic nursing care for the sick?" After reporting the results of a fresh examination of selected Synoptic Gospel passages against their most relevant Jewish and Hellenistic backgrounds, the chapter will then conclude there is some limited Gospel evidence that, in the memory of his early followers, Jesus on occasion provided basic nursing care for the sick.

1 Methods

Four methods have been interwoven in the research behind this chapter. The first draws on and applies insights from the anthropology of healthcare in traditional societies. The second uncovers attitudes towards and practices for dealing with the sick in Palestinian Jewish society, including expectations of the fate of the sick in Jewish eschatology. The third approaches the Jesus of the Gospels through Luke Timothy Johnson's "experience-interpretation model." It avoids the complexities of the repeated quests for the historical Jesus, and settles for a more modest task—recovering the Jesus who survived in the memories of his earliest followers. The fourth method is a fresh semantic examination of key healthcare vocabulary. These methods will now be summarized.

1.1 Anthropology of Healthcare in Traditional Societies

Key insights of healthcare anthropologist Arthur Kleinman have proven crucial for the research behind this chapter. Kleinman organized healthcare activity, as practiced in traditional societies, into three categories: popular, folk, and professional. He defined the "popular" category as the "lay, non-professional, non-specialist, popular culture arena in which illness is first defined and health activities are initiated."[5] While numerous studies of Jesus's healing incorporate Kleinman's categories, most of them bypass his first, "popular," category and attempt to locate Jesus in the second, "folk," category.[6] This chapter reads

---

5   Arthur Kleinman, *Patients and Healers in the Context of Culture* (Berkeley: University of California Press, 1980), 50. His method has been applied to Gospel healing accounts by Elaine Wainwright, *Women Healing/Healing Women: The Genderization of Healing in Early Chrsistianity* (Oakville, CT: Equinox, 2006), 34–35. His approach is also cited by Hector Avalos, *Health Care and the Rise of Christianity* (Peabody, MA: Hendrickson, 1999), 19–23. However, Avalos largely ignores Kleinman's "popular" category of healthcare.
6   Kleinman's postion, including his "popular" category, informs the approach to the Gospels by

Gospel healing accounts within the framework provided by Kleinman's "popular," category instead of his "folk" category. This has proven crucial for the findings.

Another of Kleinman's insights informing this research is what he considered the mistake of studying healers and the sick in isolation from one another. To do so distorts perceptions of both and can conceal important aspects of healer-patient transactions. He advocated "the crucial health care *transactions* as the central subject for clinically oriented anthropological research" (italics original).[7] He also cautioned against assuming that the healer-patient relationship constituted a dyad. Extensive experience convinced him of the presence and influence of extended family and community.[8]

Finally, this chapter incorporates Kleinman's insights into what he termed a culture's healthcare system. Working within a culture's healthcare system, healer, patient, and family benefit, because the system first "provides psychosocial and cultural treatment (and efficacy) for the illness by naming and ordering the experience of illness, providing meaning for that experience," then by "treating the personal, family, and social problems that constitute the illness."[9]

1.2 Healthcare in Jewish Belief and Practice

This chapter draws on beliefs and practices surrounding treatment of the sick current in Second Temple Judaism, making use of them in order to better construct a plausible social setting for Jesus. Doing so enhances the probability that his ministry included nursing care of the sick. Expressions in the Hebrew prophets that led to an expectation that the benefits to accompany the coming, messianic "Son of David" included treating and healing the sick have also been examined. While these passages focused mainly on healing, some include what can be considered metaphors implying the application of basic treatment of the sick.

The well-documented Jewish obligation to visit the sick (*bikkur cholim*), as described in rabbinic texts, provides arguably the strongest indirect support that Jesus, in line with the requirements and expectations of Jewish society, sometimes visited the sick and provided basic nursing care.

John Pilch, *Healing in the New Testament* (Minneapolis: Fortress, 2000), 61–70. Pilch does not raise the possibility that Jesus nursed the sick, however.

7 Kleinman, *Patients and Healers*, 205.
8 Kleinman, *Patients and Healers*, 205.
9 Kleinman, *Patients and Healers*, 360.

Finally, Jewish treatment communities, established by Essenes and *Therapeutae*, testify to Jewish society's recognition of the need to provide nursing care. The existence of such communities strengthens the case for nursing treatment as one facet of the ministry of Jesus.

1.3   Seeing Jesus through the Eyes of His Earliest Followers

There has been a move by Luke Timothy Johnson to replace quests for the historical Jesus with a quest for the Jesus that emerged from accounts drawn from memories of his earliest followers. Johnson has put forward four dimensions of the New Testament that should be considered in uncovering the "real" Jesus. The first he called anthropological: "the texts result from really human persons interpreting their experience, and seeking to understand their experience with available cultural symbols." The second is historical: "the historical dimension demands coming to grips with the cultural 'otherness' of the writings." The third is literary: "texts in their entirety," rather than fragmented, should be the basis for finding the "real Jesus." The fourth is religious: "The New Testament was written by Christian believers for other Christian believers, or to convince those who were interested in Christian belief."[10] Johnson's approach has been employed in this research.

1.4   Semantics of Relevant Healthcare Expressions in the Classical Languages

Before leaving the methods section, it is important to note the semantic conundrum attached to key Hebrew, Aramaic, and Greek vocabulary. "If disease, illness, and sickness are relative concepts, health is all the more so," declared medical historians Darrel Amundsen and Gary Ferngren.[11] This applies especially to the English word "healing." Its large semantic range has been pointed out by J. Keir Howard, who cited John Wilkinson's account of the orthodox medical fraternity's reluctance to use the word "healing" because of its "weasel" nature, and its (mis)use in alternate medicine.[12] This caution from Wilkinson and Howard, both of whom are physicians and well-versed in New Testament

---

10   Luke Timothy Johnson, *The Real Jesus* (New York: HarperCollins, 1996), 171–174.

11   Darrell W. Amundsen and Gary B. Ferngren, "The Perception of Disease and Disease Causality in the New Testament," in *Aufstieg und Niedergang der römischen Welt* (ed. Wolfgang Haase; Berlin: de Gruyter, 1996): 2935.

12   J. Keir Howard, *Disease and Healing in the New Testament: An Analysis and Interpretation* (Lanham, MD: University Press of America, 2001), 3. Howard cites John Wilkinson, "Healing in Semantics, Creation and Redemption," *Scottish Bulletin of Evangelical Theology* 4 (1986): 17–37.

studies, should alert readers to the need to push beyond the overused "healing" to translate key Greek terms θεραπεύω and ἰάομαι, without careful attention to their semantic range within Hellenistic Greek, as well as close attention to their context in the New Testament. The most recent of Wilkinson's published studies on the NT vocabulary of healing appeared in his 1998 monograph.[13]

The initial stimulus for the research behind this chapter came from the extensive and detailed research into the language of healing in the Greek world and in the NT by Louise Wells. Her monograph constitutes the benchmark contribution to this topic.[14] NT scholars have failed to take full advantage of her work, and it deserves wider attention.[15] Amundsen and Ferngren have provided a much briefer contextualization of key NT healthcare vocabulary.[16]

2 Where were the Sick in the Greco-Roman World?

In the world of the New Testament, prior to the ready availability of clinics and hospitals, the sick were more likely to be publicly visible. For those who had homes, treatment typically began there: "sick people who had homes were usually nursed there."[17] This also would have been the practice in ancient Israel, and in Palestine during the Second Temple era.[18] In homes they would have typically been treated first by family using traditional remedies. Physicians made house calls, as did herbalists, exorcists, astrologers and other healthcarers. Some healers operated small inpatient clinics, ἰατρεῖα[19] (Latin

---

13 John Wilkinson, *The Bible and Healing: A Medical and Theological Commentary* (Edinburgh: Handsel Press, 1998), See chapter 7, "The Words for Healing."
14 Louise Wells, *The Greek Language of Healing from Homer to New Testament Times* (Berlin: Walter de Gruyter, 1998).
15 The monograph has been subjected to an unduly critical review by David Aune in *Review of Biblical Literature* 07/05/2000 (https://www.bookreviews.org/pdf/2539_1767.pdf) which magnified its weaknesses and diminished its contributions.
16 Amundsen and Ferngren, "Disease Causality in the New Testament," 2941–2943.
17 See Gillian Clark, "Roman Women," in *Women in Late Antiquity* (ed. Peter Walcott; Greece & Rome Studies; Oxford: Oxford University Press, 1996), 63.
18 Avalos, *Health Care and Christianity*, 251–253. For recent discussion of the house as locus for healing, see Walter Wilson, "The Uninvited Healer: Houses, Healing and Prophets in Matthew 8.1–22," *JSNT* 36 (2013): 65–68.
19 The term ἰατρεῖον is found in Plato (*Rep.* 3.405a). The much later νοσοκομεῖον, "infirmary" first appears in fourth-century church fathers Athanasius and Basil of Caesarea.

tabernæ).[20] Infirmaries existed for Roman soldiers and on large estates for estate workers and slaves.

For those who could travel, there were temples dedicated to gods of healing. Chief among these was the Asclepieion, a temple dedicated to Asclepius (Latin *Æsculapius*), the chief Greek hero/god of healing.[21] Visitors to one of these Asclepieia were typically admitted overnight to give the god opportunity to communicate in a dream what was needed for healing. Treatment was sometimes included. Some Asclepieia offered patients longer stays. After being healed, patients were expected to pay by means of a sacrifice.[22]

Those lacking resources for physicians, clinics, or visits to temples, and who lacked family and home, had recourse to the streets and squares of cities and towns across the Greco-Roman world. Anyone strolling those streets and squares would likely be confronted by a range of the sick in a variety of states and conditions, many isolated and alone, or dependent for support on fellow street dwellers. The Gospels contain several references to the sick in these public places. Their presence could evoke sympathy, as in the Roman Christian noblewoman Fabiola. She established a hospital in Rome c. 390 C.E., "gathering the poor sick from public squares and personally nursing many of them."[23] Finally, banishment was a response to some sick people. The Island of Aesculapius in the river Tiber near Rome, the site of an *asclepieion*, had become a dumping ground for sick and worn out slaves until the Emperor Claudius halted the practice.[24]

According to the Qumran Temple Scroll's message expressing hopes for a renewal and extension of the purity legislation of Deuteronomy, a leper colony was to be established east of Jerusalem, plus two additional communities in the same region, to isolate those suffering various bodily discharges.[25] This

---

20   Cicero, writing c. 50 B.C.E., used *taberna* to refer to a medical clinic (*Cluentius* 178). The "house of the surgeon" in Pompei, which yielded a cache of surgical instruments, was probably an upmarket *taberna*.
21   The best-known were located in Epidaurus, Cos, Athens, Pergamum and Smyrna. For an older but still-useful survey, see Martin P. Nilsson, *Geschichte der griechischen Religion*. Vol. 2: *Die hellenistische und römische Zeit* (3rd ed.; Handbuch der Altertums Wissenschaft; Munich: Beck, 1974), 108–113.
22   For an extensive survey of the leading *Asklepeia* and their relevance to the New Testament, see Wells, *Greek Language of Healing*, 13–101.
23   Jerome, *Ep. 77*. Cited by Gary B. Ferngren, *Medicine and Healthcare in Early Christianity* (Baltimore: Johns Hopkins University Press, 2009), 129.
24   Suetonius, *Claud*. 25.2.
25   11QTempleScroll 46:17–18.

expressed intention to isolate at least certain sick in order to protect Jerusalem from impurities is significant because the home of Simon the Leper was in Bethany, east of Jerusalem (Mark 14:3, Matt 26:6).

3 Nursing the Sick in the Hebrew Bible and in Post-Biblical Jewish Sources

The New Testament's understanding of, and approach to, sickness and treatment had its grounding in the monotheism of the Hebrew Bible.[26] YHWH could bring sickness, and remove it, from his people.[27] Brief Hebrew Bible references to this dimension of YHWH's relationship to his covenant people typically employ the imagery of his "hands-on" involvement in causing and removing sickness: "I shatter (מחץ) and I heal/treat (רפא); no one can pull you away from my hand" (Deut. 32:39). Eliphaz the Temanite, echoing this passage, declared of YHWH "He causes pain (כאב), but he bandages (חבש); he shatters (מחץ), but his hands also heal (רפא)" (Job 5:18). The second strophe of Psalm 146:8 includes medical treatment among the benefits of YHWH's touch, without actually specifying hands: "Yahweh, [the One] giving sight to the blind, Yahweh, [the One] straightening up (זקף) the bowed down (כפף)." The Qumran *Messianic Apocalypse* (4Q521) applies this Psalm passage to YHWH's future intervention on behalf of his people. Fragment 2 cites Ps 146:8, then adds "And YHWH will perform glorious acts such as have never existed, just as he sa[id,] [for] he will heal/treat (רפא) the badly wounded (חללים) and will make the dead live, he will proclaim good news to the poor ..." (lines 9–12).[28] Finally, according to Psalm 147:3 YHWH "treats (רפא) those whose hearts were shattered, and bandages (חבץ) what pains them."

When Israelites cared for their sick, they were following the example of YHWH, their physician: "I am YHWH the One healing (רפא) you" (Exod 15:26).[29]

---

26 See Peder Borgen, "Miracles of Healing in the New Testament," *ST* 35 (1981): 96.

27 An extended summary of this view is available in Morton Kelsey, *Healing and Christianity: A Classic Study* (Minneapolis: Augsburg, 1995), 27–32.

28 My translation; text from Florentino Martínez and Eibert Tigchelaar, *The Dead Sea Scrolls Study Edition*. Vol. 2: *4Q274–11Q31* (Leiden: Brill, 1998): 1044–1045. Meggitt, "The Historical Jesus and Healing," 40, suggested "Jesus held up his healings as evidence of his status as the one expected (in language amost identical to 4Q521) ..." See also Casey, *Jesus of Nazareth*, 238.

29 This has been developed by Audrey Dawson, *Healing, Weakness and Power: Perspectives on Healing in the Writings of Mark, Luke and Paul* (Milton Keynes, England: Paternoster, 2008), 30–32; 229.

This has implications for reconstructing the theological and eschatological expectations of Jewish people of that era. It should have, for example, cushioned the community from an uncritical expectation that, in the age to come, Messiah would resort too easily or excessively to magic and miracle in bringing about the restoration promised by the prophets.[30]

3.1   Son of David

Treatment, at least metaphorically, was one of the blessings to be brought by a coming royal descendant of David. This was most explicit in Ezekiel's extended prophetic indictment against the shepherds of Israel: "The weak (nifal ptc of חלה) you have not returned to strength (piel of חזק), the sick (qal ptc of חלה) you have not healed/treated (piel of רפא), the mangled (שבר) you have not bandaged (חשב) ..." Ezek 34:4. Yahweh's solution is to, himself, take the place of Israel's failed shepherds: "the mangled (שבר) I will bandage (חשב)" (v. 16).[31] Further on, the prophecy specified that the specific divine agent, the one who would carry out Yahweh's shepherding mission, will be "my servant David" (v. 23). Here of course "David" would have been understood by Ezekiel's readers to refer to a descendant, or "son" of David. The importance of this prophetic promise of a future Son of David shepherd/healer for Israel has been the subject of considerable scholarly attention.[32] In Mark and Matthew the title is used of Jesus in passages where people approach him for treatment of sickness. Ezekiel 34 was of great importance for the Evangelists according to Wayne Baxter. It was "the only text that most unambiguously presents the coming Davidic Shepherd as a healer and thus, best serves as Matthew's warrant for connecting Jesus's healing activity to the christological title Son of David."[33] Baxter fails, however, to see and apply the "treatment" motif in Ezekiel 34.

The "son of David" most associated with healing in Jewish expectations was Solomon. Considerable attention has been given by both ancient and recent writers to the wide-ranging and sometimes fanciful exorcism and

---

30   This position has been elaborated especially by Howard, *Disease and Healing in New Testament*, 32–38.

31   For a more extensive presentation of the christological relevance of Ezk 34, see Wayne Baxter, "Healing and the 'Son of David': Matthew's Warrant," *NovT* 48 (2006): 41–46. He successfully resists applying "Solomon as exorcist" to Jesus.

32   Earlier work includes Dennis Duling, "Solomon, Exorcism, and the Son of David," *HTR* 68 (1975): 235–252; Duling, "The Therapeutic Son of David: An Element in Matthew's Christological Apologetic," *NTS* 24 (1977): 392–410; Armin Baum, "Die Heilungswunder Jesu als Symbolhandlungen—Ein Versuch," *EuroJTh* 13 (2004): 5–14; Baxter, "Son of David," 36–50.

33   Baxter, "Son of David," 50.

healing powers attributed to Solomon, most fully elaborated in the Testament of Solomon.[34] "By the 1st century C.E., King Solomon—the only individual reigning monarch to be called 'Son of David' in the Hebrew Bible—had acquired the reputation in Jewish circles as a great exorcist and healer."[35] But from the first, traditions also attributed to Solomon discernment and insight into the properties of plants. These begin with a reference to his outstanding botanical knowledge, first named in 1 Kgs 4:33 (LXX): "He spoke concerning woody plants, from the cedar of Lebanon to the hyssop which grows out of walls." This was later expanded to include wisdom about "varieties of plants, and the powers (δυνάμεις, implying medicinal efficacies) of roots."[36] Josephus expanded the scope of Solomon's botanical wisdom: "he spoke a parable (παραβολὴν εἶπεν, here in the sense "he spelled out the comparison") concerning every kind of tree from the hyssop to the cedar."[37]

"Son of David" was applied to Jesus most deliberately in Matthew's Gospel. This has been the subject of considerable analysis during the past 40 years.[38] The relevance of these studies for our topic is limited because they focus nearly exclusively on Solomon's reputed ability to exorcise demons. There is no reference in Solomonic texts to conventional nursing care for the sick.

3.2 Jewish Healing Communities of the Second Temple Era

Several Jewish communities/movements included treatment of illness as part of their mission. This section traces accounts of their approach.

3.2.1 Therapeutae

Among Egyptian Jewish Groups the *Therapeutae* were known for their focus on both healing and worship of God. This dual focus was acknowledged in their name, θεραπεύται. Because of its ambivalent meaning, Philo could use it to

---

34 For detailed introduction and analysis, see Dennis Duling. "Testament of Solomon: A New Translation and Introduction," *OTP* 1:935–959.
35 John Meier, *A Marginal Jew: Rethinking the Historical Jesus*. Vol. 2: *Mentor, Message, and Miracles* (New York: Doubleday, 1994), 689.
36 Wis 7:20.
37 *Ant.* 8.2.5 (44). Note Aristotle's identical use of *parabolē* referring to "comparison" in *Pol.* 1264b5.
38 In addition to Duling's articles and that of Baxter, cited above, see Kim Paffenroth, "Jesus as Anointed and Healing Son of David in the Gospel of Matthew," *Bib* 80 (1999): 547–554; Richard Van Egmond, "The Messianic 'Son of David' in Matthew," *JGRChJ* 3 (2006): 41–71; Lidja Novakovic, *Messiah, the Healer of the Sick* (WUNT 2.170; Tübingen: Mohr Siebeck, 2003), especially 185–190. None mentions Jesus treating the sick, however.

describe both of their vocations—"healers" and "worshippers." As he declared, "The vocation of these philosophers is at once made clear from their title of *therapeutae* and *therapeutrides*, a name derived from θεραπεύω, either in the sense of 'cure' because they profess an art of healing better than that current in the cities which cures only the bodies, while theirs treats also souls ..."[39] ἡ δὲ προαίρεσις τῶν φιλοσόφων εὐθὺς ἐμφαίνεται διὰ τῆς προσρήσεως· θεραπευταὶ γὰρ καὶ θεραπευτρίδες ἐτύμως καλοῦνται, ἤτοι παρόσον ἰατρικὴν ἐπαγγέλλονται κρείσσονα τῆς κατὰ πόλεις—ἡ μὲν γὰρ σώματα θεραπεύει μόνον, ἐκείνη δὲ καὶ ψυχάς ... Philo draws attention to their "contemplation of nature and the contents of the natural world."[40]

3.2.2 Essenes

The name "Essene" could be derived from the Aramaic plural term for healers/physicians, אסיין.[41] This fits with their description by Josephus:

> They display an extraordinary interest in the writings of the ancients, singling out *in particular those which make for the welfare of soul and body* (μάλιστα τὰ πρὸς ὠφέλειαν ψυχῆς καὶ σώματος ἐκλέγοντες); with the help of these, and with a view to the *treatment of diseases* (θεραπείαν παθῶν), they make investigations into medicinal roots and the properties of stones.[42]

According to Philo, among the Essenes, "if anyone is sick (ἀσθενήσειεν) he is nursed (νοσηλεύεται) at the common expense and tended (θεραπευόμενος) with care (ἐπιμελείαις) and thoughtfulness (φροντίσιν) by all."[43]

These reports of treatment of the sick by *Therapeutae* and Essenes support the construct that Second Temple Jewish society included centers where health practitioners integrated spiritual insight and *materia medica* with attentive nursing care. In the following section evidence from rabbinic sources will be summarised which sustains this construct and extends it into mainstream Jewish society.

---

39 *Contempl.* 2.1 (471) (Colson, LCL).
40 Philo, *Contempl.* 11.83 (485) (trans. adapted from Colson, LCL). See also Colson's note "a" on pp. 168–169. My literal translation does more justice to the text. Colson assumed that the *Therapeutae* would "deal only with the theological side of physic" so he paraphrased "the contemplation of nature *and what it has to teach*."
41 Argued by Geza Vermes, *Post-biblical Jewish Studies* (Leiden: Brill, 1975), 19–29.
42 *J.W.* 2.8.7 (136) (Thackery, LCL) (italics supplied).
43 καὶ μὴν εἴ τις αὐτῶν ἀσθενήσειεν, ἐκ τῶν κοινῶν νοσηλεύεται θεραπευόμενος ταῖς ἁπάντων ἐπιμελείαις καὶ φροντίσιν. Philo, *Hypoth.* 11.13 (Colson, LCL).

3.3   Visiting the Sick according to Rabbinic Sources

The main component of Jewish custom and belief to support the argument that Jesus, in the memory of his followers, sometimes nursed the sick, is the venerable Jewish custom of visiting the sick. Historian of Jewish medicine Fred Rosner declared, in describing Jewish medical practice of the Talmudic era, that these visits to the sick included more than polite bedside conversation. Three essential duties were imposed on the visitor: (1) to encourage by word, (2) to cook and clean, (3) to pray. "These three activities are all essential components of what is know as *bikkur cholim*, or visiting the sick, and are applicable to this very day."[44] The Hebrew noun בִּיקוּר expresses "visiting with the intent to help"; "inspecting"; "attending."[45] "It is the holy duty incumbent upon everyone to visit the sick."[46] "[T]he duty of visiting the sick knows no limits (of time or rank)."[47]

In carrying out *bikkur cholim*, the Jewish people believed they were only following God's example. According to Genesis Rabbah: "R. Simla said: We find that the Holy One, blessed be He, recites the benedictions over bridegrooms, adorns brides, visits the sick and buries the dead … Whence do we know that He visits the sick? As it is written, 'And the Lord appeared to him by the terebinths of Mamre.'"[48] Note how the opening of Gen 18 is linked to the end of ch. 17. As 99 year-old Abraham recovered from circumcision (Gen 17:24–27), "Yahweh appeared (niphal of ראה) unto him" (Gen 18:1).[49] The rabbis then declared that Yahweh's followers should follow his example of visiting the sick, supporting it in midrashic fashion by another link to Torah, this time to Deut 13:5: "You shall walk after the Lord your God," and Exod 18:20: "You will show them the way they should walk." The occurrence of "walk" (הלך) in both passages affirmed visiting the sick to be *halakah*-mandated conduct.[50] The example of the prophet Isaiah, who visited king Hezekiah during his illness (Isa 38:1) was also cited.

---

44   Fred Rosner, "Jewish Medicine in the Talmudic Period," *ANRW* II 37.3 (1996): 2890.
45   In Mishnaic Hebrew *bikkur cholim* became the standard term to express "visit (the sick)" according to Marcus Jastrow, *Dictionary of the Targumim*, s.v. בִּיקוּר (p. 165).
46   Rosner, "Jewish Medicine," 2890.
47   Jastrow, *Dictionary of the Targumim*, s.v. בִּיקוּר (p. 165), referring to b. Ned. 39b and b. Metzi'a 30b.
48   *Genesis Rabbah*, Parashah Eight, Midrash Thirteen in Wilfred Shuchat, *The Creation according to the Midrash Rabbah* (Jerusalem, NY: Devora, 2002), 332–333.
49   Rosner cites b. Sotah 14a in addition to Gen. Rab. 8.13 in support.
50   According to Rosner, "Jewish Medicine," 2890, citing *b. Qamma* 100a and *b. Metzi'a* 30bz.

The visitor came expecting to serve by cleaning, washing, cooking, and feeding, as need dictated. It is especially significant to note the role of rabbi Akiba (c. 40–137 C.E.) as both promoter and practitioner of *bikkur cholim*. As the leading Palestinian rabbinic authority of his era, his example and influence were unmatched. "Rabbi Akiba propounded: He who does not visit the sick is like a shedder of blood."[51] This stark view was echoed and explained by later rabbinic voices:

> R. Dimi (c. 320 C.E.) said: "He who visits the sick causes him to live, while he who does not causes him to die." How does he cause [this]? Shall we say that he who visits the sick prays that he may live, whilst he who does not prays that he should die, "that he should die!" can you really think so? But [say thus:] He who does not visit the sick prays neither that he may live nor die.[52]

Furthermore, the reviving and even healing potential of *bikkur cholim* emerges in an anecdote about Akiba:

> R. Helbo once fell ill. Thereupon Rabbi Khana went and proclaimed: "Rabbi Helbo is sick." But none visited him. He rebuked them [sc. the scholars], saying, "Did it not once happen that one of R. Akiba's disciples fell sick, and the Sages did not visit him?" So R. Akiba himself entered [his house] to visit him, and because they swept and sprinkled the ground before him, he recovered. "My master," said he, "you have revived me!"[53]

Note the "healing" impact of this visit, expressed by the sick person—could it be classed a "miraculous" healing?

A person's higher social standing did not free them from visiting the sick. Nor was there a set number of visits which, when achieved, freed the visitor from making further visits.

> It was taught: There is no measure for visiting the sick. What is meant by, "there is no measure for visiting the sick?" ... Abaye explained it: Even a great person must visit a humble one. Raba said: [One must visit] even a hundred times a day. R. Abba son of R. Hanina said: He who visits an

---

51   b. Ned. 40a, cited in Rosner, "Jewish Medicine," 2891.
52   b. Ned. 40a, translation from RabbinicTraditions.com.
53   b. Ned. 40a, cited in Rosner, "Jewish Medicine," 2891.

invalid takes away a sixtieth of his pain. Said they to him: If so, let sixty people visit him and restore him to health? He replied: The sixtieth is as the tenth spoken of in the school of Rabbi, and [providing further that] he [the visitor] is of his affinity.[54]

Even multiple visits could not be expected, on their own, to remove all pain, however, so the really pain-relieving visits must be made by members of the patient's extended family.

Finally, there was even rabbinic support for visiting sick gentiles: "Our Rabbis have taught: 'We support the poor of the heathen along with the poor of Israel, and visit the sick of the heathen along with the sick of Israel, and bury the poor of the heathen along with the dead of Israel, in the interests of peace.'"[55]

3.4 Summary

As Israel's "physician" YHWH, in a few Hebrew Bible passages, assumed a metaphorical "hands-on" role in his treatment of their diseases (Deut 32:39; Job 5:18; Ps 146:8). They in turn were to have a hands-on role caring for their sick. Hebrew Bible and later Jewish depictions of the coming age included treatment as a feature of the work of the Son of David. In response to this eschatological expectation, Jewish communities such as the *Therapeutae* and Essenes practiced medical care and maintained treatment centers. In post-biblical Judaism, visiting the sick was considered a duty commanded in Torah from which no one was excluded because of social status. Such visits were to include practical, hands-on nursing care.

When placed against this Hebrew and Jewish background, Jesus would have appeared antisocial and indifferent to Torah and *halakah* had he *not* visited the sick and provided the expected nursing care. In the following section, Gospel accounts of Jesus's interaction with the sick will be examined for supporting evidence.

4 Gospel Reports of Jesus's Ministry to the Sick

This section reports findings from following Meggitt's suggestion that "there are good reasons to look closely at the earliest records of [Jesus's healing and exorcism] activity" for incidental evidence that Jesus practiced *bikkur*

---

54 b. Ned. 39b, translation from RabbinicTraditions.com.
55 b. Git. 61a, translation from RabbinicTraditions.com.

cholim.⁵⁶ The suggestion that Jesus sometimes visited the sick and provided basic nursing care has not been seriously addressed anywhere in the literature surveyed in preparation of this chapter.⁵⁷

4.1   Mark 6:5—Treating a Few Sick?

The possibility that Jesus sometimes treated the sick in a conventional manner appropriate to their culture, even if not always healing them, struck this writer while reading the Gospel report that Jesus was unable, because of the disbelief of his fellow townspeople, to do supernatural healings in Nazareth. He had to content himself with healing a few people (Mark 6:1–5). The contradiction between "unable to do any powerful acts" and "healing a few sick persons" in verse 5 disappears if the verse is read within a different cultural and semantic context. The following literal translation will be justified in the explanatory notes which follow: "and [Jesus] was unable to do a single powerful work, but upon a few sick, placing his hands, he treated [them]."

καὶ οὐκ ἐδύνατο ἐκεῖ ποιῆσαι οὐδεμίαν δύναμιν,
εἰ μὴ ὀλίγοις ἀρρώστοις ἐπιθεὶς τὰς χεῖρας ἐθεράπευσεν·

4.1.1   Notes

*οὐδεμία here functions as an adjective qualifying δύναμιν. It is translated "*no work of power, miracle, wonder*" in BDAG s.v. οὐδεμία 1, where the double negative οὐκ ... οὐδεμίαν is also noted. This double negative results in "reinforcing negation with another negator ... 'any at all'" according to Muraoka (citing Tob 2:13 S).⁵⁸

*εἰ μή after a negative introducing a concessive clause is usually translated "except." This translation and understanding of Mark 6:5, that Jesus actually performed a few healings, despite the declaration he could do *no* powerful works *at all*, is nearly universal. However, εἰ μή can also introduce an adversative clause, assuming the role usually taken by ἀλλά which would be correctly translated adversatively with "but ..."⁵⁹ Close scrutiny of all 37 Gospel occurrences

---

56 Meggitt, "Historical Jesus and Healing," 17.
57 Duling has come closest to doing so by emphasizing the wide, generalized picture of Jesus's healing that emerges from Matthew's Gospel. See his "Therapeutic Son of David," 393–398.
58 T. Muraoka (ed.), *A Greek–English Lexicon of the Septuagint* (Leuven: Peeters, 2009), s.v. οὐδείς, οὐδεμία II.b (512 f.).
59 This is acknowledged in BDF § 448(8), citing likely Aramaic influence for Synoptic Gospel occurrences. The current German edition, Friedrich Wilhelm Blass, Albert Debrunner,

of εἰ μή suggests it is best translated concessively ("except ...") in 28 passages (13 in Mark, 14 in Matthew, 10 in Luke), while in seven passages it should be translated adversatively ("but ..."): Mark 6:5, 9:9, Matt 5:13, 24:36, Luke 4:26, 27, 17:18, and probably 18:19. Semantic evidence thus clearly allows translating εἰ μή with "but" in Mark 6:5.

*ἐπιθεὶς τὰς χεῖρας. This expression is extremely rare in classical Greek.[60] The few occurrences express emotional attachment in face of loss: the dying Eteocles "heard his mother and, stretching out a sweaty hand toward her ..." (κἀπιθεὶς ὑγρὰν χέρα).[61] It also describes a hand gesture in speech: "... toward the burnt offerings he stretched out the right hand ..." (τοῖς ἐμπύροις ἐπέθηκε τὴν δεξιὰν χεῖρα).[62] The only non-biblical occurrence in the context of sickness is in a description in the Hippocratic corpus of applying manual pressure for pain relief:

> But the physician, or some person who is strong, and not uninstructed, should *apply the palm of one hand to the hump*, and then, *having laid the other hand upon the former*, he should make pressure, attending whether this force should be applied directly downward, or toward the head, or toward the hips. Τὸν δὲ ἰητρὸν χρὴ ἢ ἄλλον, ὅστις ἰσχυρὸς καὶ μὴ ἀμαθής, ἐπιθέντα τὸ θέναρ τῆς χειρὸς ἐπὶ τὸ ὕβωμα, καὶ τὴν (40) ἑτέρην χεῖρα προσεπιθέντα ἐπὶ τὴν ἑτέρην, καταναγκάζειν, προσ- ξυνιέντα, ἤν τε ἐς ἰθὺ ἐς τὸ κάτω πεφύκῃ καταναγκάζεσθαι, ἤν τε πρὸς τῆς κεφαλῆς, ἤν τε πρὸς τῶν ἰσχίων.[63]

In Jewish Greek sources the expression frequently describes priests placing hands on sacrificial victims. It also describes the ritual for transferring leadership and spiritual authority from Moses to Joshua (Num 27:18, 23; Deut 34:9). Other uses include the gesture of putting one's hand upon one's head or mouth to signal shame (2 Sam 13:19, Mic 7:6), or to signal respect and subordination to another, especially in conversation (Judg 18:19; Job 31:27; Wis 8:12). Thieves put

---

and Friedrich Rehkopf, *Grammatik des neutestamentlichen Griechisch* (18th ed.; Göttingen: Vandenhoeck & Ruprecht, 2001) §448.9, shortens the discussion and reference list, but preserves the suggestion of Aramaic influence. Note that in BDAG s.v. εἰ (p. 278), εἰ μή is also translated adversatively, "but."

60 The following data has been accessed using the *Thesaurus Linguae Graecae* (TLG) searchable database of Greek literature, based at the University of California (Irvine campus): www.tlg.uci.edu.
61 Euripides, *Phoen.* 1439.
62 Aristides (2nd-century B.C.E. historian), frg. 2.10–11.
63 *Artic.* 47.39–40.

out hands [to steal?] according to Jer 30:2. A single occurrence expresses treatment of a leper: "he shall call out in the name of God and shall place his hand on the place and brush away the leprosy" ἐπικαλέσεται ἐν ὀνόματι θεοῦ αὐτοῦ καὶ ἐπιθήσει τὴν χεῖρα αὐτοῦ ἐπὶ τὸν τόπον καὶ ἀποσυνάξει τὸ λεπρόν (2 Kgs 5:11).

A sketch of the Aramaic expressions for the laying-on of hands will begin with סמך, which occurs in 1Q20 (*Gen. Apoc.*) 20:29: "he prayed and *laid his hands* upon his head and the plague departed from him and the evil [spirit] was gone and he lived."[64] This passage is unique among Jewish healing accounts. No other makes reference to laying-on of the healer's hands using the Aramaic סמך. It is also used in rabbinic sources for the laying-on of hands in ordination.[65] It occurs in Tg. Neophiti Num 27:23 "he laid his hands on him ..."; Lev 1:4 "put his hand on the head of the burnt offering ..."; Num 27:18 "Lay your hand on [Joshua] ..."

Another Aramaic term, יהב, expresses the use of hands specifically in treatment: "he put (יהב) his hand on the tooth and treated (אסי) it."[66] The verb also occurs in the expression "place your hand on your eye."[67] Thus in Aramaic as in Greek, the vocabulary used to describe the extension of the hand in medical treatment does not of itself denote or connote healing. It simply expresses the first approach, an extension of a hand of the healthcare person for the purpose of diagnosis or treatment. Only if the context of the expression calls for it does ἐπιθεὶς τὰς χεῖρας connote healing, whether miraculous or otherwise.

*θεραπεύω has been regularly translated "heal" in English Bibles at least since the Authorised King James Version of 1611. This plus the assumption that Jesus always healed miraculously has helped to "immunize" translators and expositors against past attempts to nuance the semantic range of θεραπεύω, ἰάομαι, and related NT verbs, and make room for the translation "treatment." W.M. Ramsay over a century ago argued that according to Acts 28:8–10, when Publius was prostrated by sickness, Paul healed him (ἰάομαι) by prayer and

---

64 Cited in David Flusser, "Healing through the Laying-on of Hands in a Dead Sea Scroll," *IEJ* 7 (1957): 107–108. But Hebrew סמך is not used in the Hebrew Bible for healing, according to David Daube, *The New Testament and Rabbinic Judaism* (London: Athlone Press, 1956), 228.

65 Flusser, "Laying-on of Hands," 108.

66 Gen. Rab. 306.7 (pagination of Theodor and Albeck), and Koh. Rab. 4b(19) as cited in Michael Sokoloff, *Dictionary of Jewish Palestinian Aramaic* (3rd ed.; Baltimore: Johns Hopkins University Press, 2002), s.v. אסי (67).

67 y. Ḥag. 77d(57), as cited in Sokoloff, *Dictionary of Palestinian Aramaic* s.v. יהב [p. 236].

laying-on of hands. But when other islanders arrived hoping for the same, they were, in Ramsay's words, "cured [more correctly, 'received medical treatment']" which Luke expressed with θεραπεύω.[68] He further stated that "Now in the strict sense ἐθεραπεύοντο as a medical term, means 'received medical treatment' ..."[69]

In her recent and extensive study of selected Greek healing terms, Louise Wells concluded that ἰάομαι in the LXX conformed largely to its use in the wider Greek world, including the *Asklepieia*: "It is the God-word in the Septuagint, describing divine healing and clothing God's healing promises."[70] In Mark and Matthew, when occurring in passive voice, it tends "to describe the intervention of God."[71] However, when those Gospels use θεραπεύω, she concludes

> It is significant that the synoptists, particularly Mark and Matthew, describe Jesus' activities and behaviour with the verb θεραπεύω. In Asklepiadic literature as well as the Septuagint, this verb group more frequently describes human treatment or service, whereas ἰάομαι describes the action of both Asklepios and the Septuagint god [sic].[72]

She further argued that some occurrences of θεραπεύω *cannot* mean "cured" because they describe what has happened as *treatment*, ahead of any cure, as in the report of Marcus Julius Apellas, treated at the Aeginan *Asklepieion*. According to the inscription, the priest told Apellas, "you have been treated" (τεθεράπευσαι). The context makes clear that the healing continued well after the priest's declaration.[73]

4.1.2 Implications for Mark 6:5

The implications which flow from recognizing there are two contrasting assertions joined back-to-back in Mark 6:5 seem to have been almost universally overlooked. Interpreters assume the passage refers only to "miraculous" healings.[74] The nuances of the Markan passage suggested here are probably rendered even more invisible to most readers also because of the influence exerted

---

68 William Ramsay, *Luke the Physician and other Stories in the History of Religion* (London: Hodder & Stoughton, 1908; repr., Grand Rapids: Baker, 1956), 16.
69 Ramsay, *Luke the Physician*, 17.
70 Wells, *Greek Language of Healing*, 119.
71 Wells, *Greek Language of Healing*, 159.
72 Wells, *Greek Language of Healing*, 227.
73 Wells, *Greek Language of Healing*, 38–39, 276–278. She cites *Inscriptiones Graecae* IV2 1, no. 126, line 20 (dated c. 160 C.E.).
74 This is typified by Dunn, *Jesus Remembered*, 692.

by the Matthean parallel, which omits any reference to treatment: "and he did not do there many powerful works, because of their unbelief" (13:58). The Lukan parallel (4:16–30) does not refer to healing or treating but focuses on Jesus's sermon.

Is there further Gospel evidence, beyond Mark 6:5, to support the hypothesis that down-to-earth, normal, non-miraculous treatment of the sick was part of the ministry of Jesus?

4.2 Mark 1:31—A Helping Hand?

According to Mark 1:31, Jesus visited Peter's mother-in-law who was in bed with a fever. "He raised her up grasping [her] hand. Then the fever left her" ἤγειρεν αὐτὴν κρατήσας τῆς χειρός· καὶ ἀφῆκεν αὐτὴν ὁ πυρετός. According to Julius Preuss, in a section of his work dealing with uses of hands and fingers in ancient Jewish literature, "A [Jewish] physician who visits his patient 'takes the latter's palm, obviously to palpate the radial pulse.'"[75] A non-physician visitor extends a hand to the patient to help raise him:

> R. Johanan once fell ill and R. Hanina went in to visit him. He said to him: Are your sufferings welcome to you? He replied: Neither they nor their reward. He said to him: Give me your hand. He gave him his hand and he raised him. Why could not R. Johanan raise himself? They replied: The prisoner cannot free himself from jail.[76]

Note this use of the hand clearly referred to helping raise R. Johanan, either to a sitting position in his sickbed, or to raise him to his feet. The gesture itself expresses care and support, but not healing.

4.3 Mark 3:1–6: Sabbath "Work" or Miraculous Healing?

The healing account of Mark 3:1–6 is set during the Sabbath in a Galilean synagogue, attended by Jesus, and by a man with a paralyzed hand/arm: "[Jesus] says to the man, stretch out the arm. And he stretched [it] out and his arm returned [to its earlier position]." λέγει τῷ ἀνθρώπῳ· ἔκτεινον τὴν χεῖρα. καὶ ἐξέτεινεν καὶ ἀπεκατεστάθη ἡ χεὶρ αὐτοῦ (Mark 3:5).[77] In his reconstructed Aramaic original of this pericope in its Palestinian setting, Casey wrote "We must infer

---

75 Julius Preuss, *Biblical and Talmudic Medicine* (trans. F. Rosner; North Vale, NJ: Aronson, 1993), 51. He cites Midr. Ps 73:1.
76 b. Ber. 5b, as cited in Preuss, *Biblical and Talmudic Medicine*, 51.
77 For the reconstructed Aramaic "returned to him," see Casey, *Jesus of Nazareth*, 263.

that this is not a miracle story ... we have a healing story which is not a miracle ..."[78] Since there is no known rabbinic legislation prohibiting the performance of miracles on the Sabbath, one must acknowledge Casey's point: the issue behind the verbal exchange was treatment or therapeutic intervention, not miraculous healing. Jesus's treatment resulted in restored function—"his arm returned [to its original position]."[79] It was treatment on the Sabbath—prohibited "work"—that stirred his opponents into immediate action, according to all Synoptic accounts. Matthew's account makes good sense when read against the assumption that Sabbath treatment was the issue: "They (Pharisees) asked him 'Is it lawful to treat/provide therapy (θεραπεῦσαι) on the Sabbath?'" (Matt 12:10). Luke's account also focused on whether Jesus would treat on the Sabbath (εἰ ἐν τῷ σαββάτῳ θεραπεύει, Luke 6:7).

5 Jesus as "Therapeutic Son of David" according to Matthew

The expression "Therapeutic Son of David" was coined by Duling to highlight his thesis that "Matthew's view of Jesus' healing is more broadly based than Mark's."[80] Matthew preferred the verb θεραπεύω, sometimes using it to replace the healing and exorcism vocabulary found in Mark's parallel passages. While Duling stopped short of re-defining θεραπεύω to include "treating the sick," he drew attention to Matthew's focus on "treating" as a core component of Jesus's ministry. Note how this is stated in the two following Matthean summaries of Jesus's ministry.

5.1 *Matthew 4:23*

"And he travelled around the whole of Galilee, teaching in the synagogues, and proclaiming the good news of the kingdom, and treating every sickness and every malady among the people." This passage names the three basic components of Jesus's mission approach—"*teaching, proclaiming,* and *treating/healing* every disease and sickness among the people.*"

   Καὶ περιῆγεν ⸀ἐν ὅλῃ τῇ Γαλιλαίᾳ⸃
   διδάσκων ἐν ταῖς συναγωγαῖς αὐτῶν καὶ
   κηρύσσων τὸ εὐαγγέλιον τῆς βασιλείας καὶ

---

78 Maurice Casey, *Aramaic Sources of Mark's Gospel* (Cambridge: Cambridge University Press, 1998), 176.
79 Casey, *Aramaic Sources of Mark*, 175.
80 Duling, "Therapeutic Son of David," 393.

> θεραπεύων πᾶσαν νόσον καὶ
> πᾶσαν μαλακίαν
> ἐν τῷ λαῷ.

Matthew saw this balance of components as the core of Jesus's mission.[81]

5.2 Matthew 9:35

In Matt's second summary of Jesus's mission, "treating" again parallels teaching and proclaiming:

> Καὶ περιῆγεν ὁ Ἰησοῦς τὰς πόλεις πάσας καὶ τὰς κώμας
> διδάσκων ἐν ταῖς συναγωγαῖς αὐτῶν καὶ
> κηρύσσων τὸ εὐαγγέλιον τῆς βασιλείας καὶ
> θεραπεύων πᾶσαν νόσον καὶ
> πᾶσαν μαλακίαν.

Duling not only observed the more widespread, broad healing activity of Jesus in Matthew, he also noted Matthew's toning-down of miraculous elements of Mark's accounts.[82] However, he stopped short of considering that Matthew's θεραπεύω could include treating as well as healing.

6 Nursing the Sick in Gospel Parables

Several parables in the Synoptic Gospels which refer explicitly or implicitly to nursing the sick are relevant for this study. They take for granted a form of "hands-on" social engagement already well established in Jewish society. Nursing the sick could fit smoothly into their scenarios.

6.1 Sheep versus Goats (Matt 25:36–44)

The parable of the sheep and the goats (Matt 25:36–44) provides a "back to the future" glimpse of the type of Christian engagement which counts most for or against Jesus's followers in the final judgment. The specific forms of engagement are repeated in a finely-structured account no less than four times, making clear their importance. Note that sheep were rewarded for providing food

---

81 The healing component of Jesus's three-fold ministry continued after the teaching and preaching cease according to Joseph Comber, "The Verb *Therapeuo* in Matthew's Gospel," *JBL* 97 (1978): 432.

82 Duling, "Therapeutic Son of David," 397.

and drink for the hungry, welcoming strangers, clothing the naked and visiting the sick. Key terms for treating the sick include ἐπισκοπέω "I was sick and you *cared for* me" (vv. 36, 43), ἔρχομαι "I was sick and you *came to* me" (v. 39), and διακονέω "I was sick and you did not *assist* me" (v. 44). The help expected for the sick here is practical nursing care of the sort called by *bikkur cholim*.

6.2   Good Samaritan (Luke 10:33–38)

When the Good Samaritan saw the victim, he σπλαγχνίζομαι "had compassion," προσέρχομαι "approached him," καταδέω "bandaged his wounds," ἐπιχέω "poured on oil and wine," ἐπιβαβίζω "put him on his donkey," ἄγω "led him to the inn," and ἐπιμέλομαι "attentively cared for him." This seven-step rescue process included on-the-spot first aid, transportation, and nursing at the inn—a prime demonstration of *bikkur cholim*.[83]

6.3   Treating the Sick in the Commissioning of the Twelve (Mark 3:13; 6:7; Matt 10:1; Luke 9:1)

If treating the sick was part of Jesus's ministry, one would expect it to emerge as part of the commissioning of the twelve. In Mark's first and second commission accounts Jesus gave the twelve ἐξουσία over τὰ δαιμόνια (3:15) and unclean spirits (6:7). In Matthew's and Luke's parallels, following Q, the twelve are called not only to perform exorcisms, but also to attend to what might be termed the outer physical manifestations of inner spiritual possession of persons. Matthew 10:1: "[Jesus] gave [disciples] authority over unclean spirits to exorcise them, and to *treat* every physical malady and bodily weakness," ἔδωκεν αὐτοῖς ἐξουσίαν πνευμάτων ἀκαθάρτων ὥστε ἐκβάλλειν αὐτὰ καὶ θεραπεύειν πᾶσαν νόσον καὶ πᾶσαν μαλακίαν.[84] Note the Lukan parallel ἐξουσίαν ἐπὶ πάντα τὰ δαιμόνια καὶ νόσους θεραπεύειν "authority over all things *daimonic* and all physical maladies *to treat*" (10:9).

Giovanni Bazzana argued that "In sum, it is clear that Q missionaries were entrusted with a medical activity ..." He further asserted "The Q commission (Matt 10, Luke 10) shows some features that equate the Jesus missionaries to Greco-Roman medical practitioners."[85] While overstating his case by equating

---

83 "Jesus's parable of the Good Samaritan furnished the pattern for the Christians' care of the sick ..." Ferngren, *Healthcare in Early Christianity*, 144–145.

84 The translations "physical malady" and "bodily weakness" are from BDAG, s.v. νόσος (p. 679) and μαλακία (p. 613).

85 Giovanni Bazzana, "Early Christian Missionaries as Physicians: Healing and its Cultural Value in the Greco-Roman Context," *NovT* 51 (2009): 235, 250. His case on p. 236 for the

the twelve with physicians, he was correct in his attempt to restore focus on a treatment component in the accounts of the commission of the twelve.

6.4 Treating the Sick in the Post-resurrection Gospel Commission

Jesus's post-resurrection gospel commission in Mark's longer ending, while probably not Markan, is clearly early Christian. The σημεῖα ("signs") to accompany new believers in Mark 16:18 include apparently supernatural ones: exorcising demons, speaking new languages, safely handling serpents and poison. The first and last σημεῖα, exorcisms and laying hands on the sick, appear earlier in Mark. The others appear here for the first time. But σημεῖον can also designate an ordinary, non-supernatural "sign or distinguishing mark whereby someth. is known, *sign, token, indication*" as in Mark 13:4.[86] The wording of this final "sign" to accompany believers is familiar Markan language, echoing Mark 6:5: "upon the sick they will place hands, and they will recover." Note the similarities between Mark 16:18 (however, note the textual problem) and 6:5:

ἀρρώστους   χεῖρας ἐπιθήσουσιν   καὶ καλῶς ἕξουσιν   (16:18)
ἀρρώστοις   ἐπιθεὶς τὰς χεῖρας   ἐθεράπευσεν   (6:5)

While Mark's post-resurrection gospel commission account is nearly always read as supernatural, nothing prevents this clause being yet another Markan reference to the basic nursing care sometimes practiced by Jesus and continued by his discples.

7 The Sick and Their Treatment in New Testament Epistles

The New Testament epistles record no instance of miraculous healing, and only a single case of instruction to practice healing by laying-on of hands, anointing and prayer. Paul's epistles testify to the presence of sick persons in the believing communities, and even among his own ministry team, including himself. "Many" believers in Corinth were weak and sickly because of their abuse of the Eucharist. Some had died in consequence (1 Cor 11:30). Paul's assistant Epaphroditus was "deathly sick" καὶ γὰρ ἠσθένησεν παραπλήσιον θανάτῳ (Phil 2:27). Paul was physically sick (ἀσθένεια τῆς σαρκὸς, Gal 4:13) when he first

---

twelve being paid for treatment seems countered by Jesus's declaration "freely you have received; freely give!" (Matt 10:8).

86 Quotation from BDAG s.v. σημεῖον (p. 920).

evangelized the Galatians. His own "thorn in the flesh" was not removed, and the reason given him was because "[God's] power in sickness/weakness (ἀσθενείᾳ) is perfected." Paul responded "I will gladly boast in my "sicknesses/weaknesses" (ταῖς ἀσθενείαις μου) that the power of Christ may pitch its tent over me!" (2 Cor 12:9).

7.1 Caring in the Epistles

Paul urged believers to "help the sick" (ἀντέχεσθε τῶν ἀσθενῶν, 1 Thess 5:14). He clearly assumed that care for the sick should be practiced by believers, praising the Galatians for their hospitality to him (very likely including nursing care) during that first visit, treating him "like an angel, as [they would have welcomed] Christ Jesus himself" (ὡς ἄγγελον θεοῦ ἐδέξασθέ με, ὡς Χριστὸν Ἰησοῦν, Gal 4:14).

Timothy was advised to drink a little wine because of his stomach and his recurrent sickness (τὸν στόμαχον καὶ τὰς πυκνάς σου ἀσθενείας, 1 Tim 5:23), and apostolic assistant Trophimus was left behind (presumably in someone's care) because he was sick (ἀσθενοῦντα, 2 Tim 4:20). James anticipated sickness among believers whom he addressed: "Is anyone of you sick?" (ἀσθενεῖ τις ἐν ὑμῖν, Jas 5:14). Only here is there any anticipation of miraculous healing.

7.2 Is Care of the Sick among Paul's "Spiritual Gifts"?

Paul, in his three listings of the spiritual gifts (χαρίσματα), clearly separated "gifts of healings" (χαρίσματα ἰαμάτων) from "workings of power" (ἐνεργήματα δυνάμεων). In his first list, 1 Cor 12:9–10, χαρίσματα ἰαμάτων is fourth, while ἐνεργήματα δυνάμεων is fifth. In his second list (v. 28) the two are reversed: δυνάμεις is fourth and χαρίσματα ἰαμάτων fifth. The two remain separate in his third list (vv. 29–30): μὴ πάντες δυνάμεις; μὴ πάντες χαρίσματα ἔχουσιν ἰαμάτων.

The noun ἴαμα, occurring only in 1 Corinthians 12 in the NT, can be translated "remedy" in most of its ten LXX occurrences, some of which could also be translated "restoration of health" or "recovery."[87] For example, Jer 40:6 (LXX) where ἴαμα is paralleled with συνούλωσις, "healing of a wound." In Jer 37:17 (LXX) it is paralleled with ἰατρέω. These passages illustrate its usage for medical treatment. In the extensive works of the 2nd-century C.E. medical author Galen, ἴαμα occurs over 220 times, illustrating its primary semantic setting. The word itself has no supernatural or miraculous connotation.

---

87 Muroaka (ed.), *Greek-English Lexicon of the Septuagint*, s.v. ἴαμα (p. 336), which is defined as (a) "restoration of health"; (b) "treatment aimed at restoration of health."

1 Peter draws on the Pauline χαρίσματα in an admonition to exercise these gifts, which include looking after fellow believers: "let each, as he has received a spiritual gift, look after (διακονοῦντες) the others, as responsible stewards of the varied grace of God ... look after [one another] (διακονεῖ) from a position of the strength which God furnishes" (1 Pet 4:10–11 ἕκαστος καθὼς ἔλαβεν χάρισμα εἰς ἑαυτοὺς αὐτὸ διακονοῦντες ὡς καλοὶ οἰκονόμοι ποικίλης χάριτος θεοῦ ... τις διακονεῖ, ὡς ἐξ ἰσχύος ἧς χορηγεῖ ὁ θεός). Here as in 1 Corinthians 12, the connotation is care rather than miracle.

7.3 *Summary of New Testament Evidence*

The Synoptic Gospels record numerous healings performed by Jesus which were to be understood as immediate and miraculous. They also record Jesus commissioning his disciples to continue healing as part of the Gospel commission. The continuation of these dramatic healings, especially by Peter and Paul, is recorded in Acts. But evidence in the Synoptic Gospels also indicates that Jesus's followers were convinced of the continued importance of care for one another, including the sick.[88] They also provide glimpses of Jesus treating the sick, sometimes using touch and *materia medica*.

On at least one occasion (Mark 6:5) Jesus, in the memory of his followers, simply nursed the sick. He expected his followers to do likewise, according to their recall of several of his parables. The Gospel Commission also reminded them to include nursing the sick.

The epistles in their turn provide evidence that Jesus's earliest followers in fact included nursing their sick among their activities. Dispersed through the epistles, especially in passages of admonition, are references to the sick, and to the need to care for them.

8 Early Christian Care for the Sick

The final support for the hypothesis that Jesus in the memory of his earliest followers sometimes nursed the sick is drawn from deep and widespread commitment of many early Christians to follow his example by caring for the sick. This well-documented commitment is probably the single most influential factor leading to the establishment of hospitals. According to historian of ancient healthcare Gary Ferngren,

---

88   This is the position of Dawson, *Healing in Mark, Luke, Paul*, 323. "Mark and Luke emphasise Jesus's teaching that believers must care for one another (e.g. Mark 12:31; Luke 6:31)."

The concept of the church's care of 'the poor' was basic to the founding of he earliest hospitals. The hospital was, in origin and conception, a distinctively Christian institution, rooted in Christian concepts of charity and philanthropy. There were no pre-Christian institutions in the ancient world that served the purpose that Christian hospitals were created to serve, that is, offering charitable aid, particularly health care, to those in need.[89]

8.1   Early Christians Explain Their Care for the Sick

When Eusebius of Caesarea composed his *Ecclesiastical History* shortly after 311 C.E., he sincerely believed that both *Theraputae* and Essenes, as described by Philo, were communities of early Jewish converts to Christianity, arguing that they arose in response to John Mark's preaching mission to Alexandria: "The number of men and women who were there converted at the first attempt was so great, and their asceticism was so extraordinarily philosophic, that Philo thought it right to describe their conduct and assemblies and meals and all the rest of their manner of life."[90] Eusebius further believed that Philo, impressed by these early Jesus followers, journeyed to Rome to consult with the apostle Peter during the reign of the emperor Claudius.[91] In obvious dependence on Philo, Eusebius went on to cite the ambivalent meaning of *Therapeutae*: "It was given either because, like a physician, they relieve from the passions of evil the souls of those who come to them and so cure and heal them, or because of their pure and sincere service and worship of the Divine."[92] Eusebius stated his belief that the community's title, *Therapeutae*, whether their own or whether assigned them by Philo, served prior to the time the word "Christian" became available to them.[93] He repeated his conviction that, in describing the *Therapeutae*, Philo was actually describing the earliest Alexandrian followers of Jesus.[94]

8.2   Church Historians on Early Christian Nursing Care for the Sick

The most influential early twentieth-century historian of the early church, Adolf von Harnack, argued that care for the sick was the core function of early Christianity. He went so far as to label early Christianity "a religion of healing"

---

89   Ferngren, *Healthcare in Early Christianity*, 124.
90   *Eccl. hist.* 2.16.2 (Lake, LCL).
91   *Eccl. hist.* 2.16.2.
92   *Eccl. hist.* 2.17.3 (Lake, LCL).
93   *Eccl. hist.* 2.17.4. Cf. Acts 11:26.
94   *Eccl. hist.* 2.17.24 (Lake, LCL).

(*Religion der Heilung*) in his 1892 monograph, *Medicinisches aus der ältesten Kirchengeschichte*.[95] He argued that from the beginning, treating the sick was a key part of the Christian's mandate, citing 1 Thess 5:14 "help the sick!"[96] He provided a valuable survey of early Christian sources on the matter of caring for the sick.[97] In it he employed the noun *Krankenpflege*, "nursing" nearly a dozen times as he summarized his findings and developed his thesis that nursing of the sick, medicine, and Christianity were closely related from earliest times.[98]

Ferngren, writing more than a century later, critiqued and modified Harnack's view that early Christianity was a religion of healing: "The emphasis on *caring* more than *curing* constituted the chief ministry of the early Christian community to the sick …"[99] But he did not challenge Harnack's focus on the important place of nursing care in the early churches: "Wherever a church was founded (and the church was an urban institution), it became a focal point for the care of the sick."[100] Rodney Stark, approaching early Christianity from a sociological perspective, argued that this core, widespread commitment to providing simple nursing care for the sick was a major factor in the rapid spread of Christianity across the Roman empire.[101]

Over against Harnack's and Ferngren's position is that of Hector Avalos, whose goal was to "focus on how people in the first and second centuries might have viewed the advantages of the messages of healing reflected in early Christian literature …"[102] After comparing his view of early Christian healthcare with

---

95   Adolf von Harnack, *Medicinisches aus der ältesten Kirchengeschichte* (Leipzig: Hinrichs, 1892), 96. Repeated in his *Die Mission und Ausbreitung des Christentums in den ersten drei Jahrhunderten* (Leipzig: Hinrichs, 1924), 129, 136. Note that the title of the chapter, *Das Evangelium vom Heiland und von der Heilung*, has been misleadingly translated "The Gospel of the Savior and of Salvation" in *The Mission and Expansion of Christianity in the First Three Centuries* (trans. James Moffatt; London: Williams & Norgate, 1908; repr., New York: Harper, 1956), 101. While *Heiland* is correctly translated "Savior," *Heilung* should have been translated "healing."
96   "… nehmt euch der Kranken an." Harnack, *Mission und Ausbreitung des Christentums*, 147.
97   Harnack, *Medicinisches aus der ältesten Kirchengeschichte*, 15–66.
98   Harnack, *Medicinisches aus der ältesten Kirchengeschichte*, v–vi, 62–64, 107–111.
99   Ferngren, *Healthcare in Early Christianity*, 145. This aspect of early Christian care for the sick has not been acknowledged by Avalos.
100 Ferngren, *Healthcare in Early Christianity*, 145.
101 Rodney Stark, *The Rise of Christianity* (Princeton, NJ: Princeton University Press, 1996). This is his thesis in ch. 4, "Epidemics, Networks, and Conversion" (73–94) and ch. 7, "Urban Chaos and Crisis: The Case of Antioch" (147–162).
102 Avalos, *Health Care and Christianity*, 2.

the alternatives, Avalos pointed out the advantages of what he considered to be uniquely Christian: simple therapeutic rituals (mainly laying-on of hands), centrality of faith and prayer, free (no fees charged), available at all times and seasons (no Sabbath restrictions, or long waits to see doctors during certain seasons), highly portable (no sacred locations requiring patient travel).[103] While Avalos cited the work of Harnack and Ferngren, he did not address the issue of nursing for the sick, but limited himself to an understanding of early Christian healing as described in most of the Gospel accounts.[104]

In an extensive monograph examining mainly the language of medicine and healing employed by early church fathers, Michael Dörnemann stated that according to Ignatius, local bishops were responsible for overseeing the funding and administration of healthcare for members and others taken into church care.[105] He also noted that the majority of the patristic authors he researched expressed skepticism about miraculous healings.[106]

Audrey Dawson concluded her monograph on healing in Mark, Luke, and Paul with a brief sketch of her view of the place of healing in the post-New Testament church. She seemed to follow Avalos in downplaying evidence that the earliest Christians cared for the sick to any extent: "it seems that ordinary human care for the poor and ill became eventually an important part of the church's work."[107] Dawson stated that the high view of care for the sick in the teaching (but not the action) of Jesus did not immediately take root in the early church. It was only in the second century that "[o]rganized systems of healthcare developed ..."[108] Evidence cited by Harnack and Ferngren makes clear to the contrary that there was widespread acceptance among early Christians that basic nursing-type care for the sick was part of practical Christian faith. While a variety of treatments could be employed, Christians cared for the sick because

---

103 Avalos, *Health Care and Christianity*, 119.
104 The following histories of early Christian healing contain no reference to basic nursing care: Evelyn Frost, *Christian Healing: A Consideration of the Place of Spiritual Healing in the Church of To-day in the Light of the Doctrine and Practice of the Ante-Nicene Church* (London: Mowbray, 1949); R.J.S. Barrett-Lennard, *Christian Healing After the New Testament: Some Approaches to Illness in the Second, Third and Fourth Centuries* (Lanham, MD: University Press of America, 1994); Avalos, *Health Care and Christianity*; Kelsey, *Healing and Christianity*.
105 Michael Dörnemann, *Krankheit und Heilung in der Theologie der frühen Kirchenväter* (Tübingen: Mohr Siebeck, 2003), 333.
106 Dörnemann, *Krankheit und Heilung*, 348.
107 Dawson, *Healing in Mark, Luke, Paul*, 236.
108 Dawson, *Healing in Mark, Luke, Paul*, 236.

of the teaching and example of Jesus himself. Prayer, anointing and laying-on of hands were also available for the sick, and no doubt many of them benefitted from these and other forms of healthcare.

9 Conclusion

This chapter has argued that in developing what may be called the Christian "theology of therapy" as well as a theology of health, early Christians were prompted largely by their collective recall that Jesus not only healed the sick, but also on occasion provided basic nursing care. Bible translators, expositors, historians, and churchmen have generally failed to note this little-documented feature of Jesus's ministry, due in part to their preoccupation with the miraculous and supernatural nature of most Gospel healing accounts.

When Jesus nursed the sick, he was fulfilling one of the expectations that his Jewish peers believed to be a requirement of *halakah*, and that would be revived in the eschaton. His caring visits to the sick also demonstrated Jesus's compliance with the expectations of Jewish society. A number of his disciples and apostolic followers continued his practice because they understood that in doing so, they complied with his example, and his commission. Early Christian healthcare from its beginning was thus characterised by caring as well as curing, laying the foundation for today's widespread Christian involvement in care for the sick.

The Kingdom of God is among You: Prospects for a Q Community

Sarah E. Rollens

1 Introduction

As one of the earliest witnesses to the Jesus movement, the Sayings Source Q—one of the sources that Matthew and Luke used to compose their Gospels[1]—tempts scholars to use it to reconstruct the "first Christian community." This temptation is even greater given the many ostensible references to a group mentality in Q and the ubiquitous symbol of the kingdom of God within the text, which is often understood as a unified program for the community. There are, however, a number of problems with this enterprise, including the undertheorized notion of "community" with which scholars often work and the nebulous nature of the concept of "kingdom" in Q. In addition, recent opinions about the authors of Q as scribal figures[2] should cause us to call into

---

1 For an excellent overview of issues related to hypothesizing and reconstructing Q, see John S. Kloppenborg, *Excavating Q: The History and Setting of the Sayings Gospel* (Minneapolis: Fortress, 2000), 55–111. Since this essay examines how scholars have used Q for discerning social history of its community, issues of theorizing and reconstructing the text will not preoccupy us here. When references to the text of Q are included, this essay relies on the International Q Project's reconstruction (*The Critical Edition of Q: Synopsis including the Gospels of Matthew and Luke, Mark and Thomas with English, German, and French translations of Q and Thomas* [ed. James M. Robinson, Paul Hoffmann and John S. Kloppenborg; Hermeneia Supplement Series; Minneapolis: Fortress, 2007]).

2 John S. Kloppenborg, "Literary Convention, Self-evidence and the Social History of the Q People," in *Early Christianity, Q and Jesus* (ed. John S. Kloppenborg and Leif E. Vaage; Semeia 55; Atlanta: Scholars Press, 1991), 77–102; William E. Arnal, *Jesus and the Village Scribes: Galilean Conflicts and the Setting of Q* (Minneapolis: Fortress, 2001); Sarah E. Rollens, *Framing Social Criticism in the Jesus Movement: The Ideological Project in the Sayings Gospel Q* (WUNT 2.374; Tübingen: Mohr Siebeck, 2014); Giovanni Bazzana, "Basileia and Debt Relief: The Debts' Forgiveness of the Lord's Prayer in Light of Documentary Papyri," *CBQ* 73 (2011): 511–525 and his recent monograph *Kingdom and Bureaucracy: The Political Theology of Village Scribes in the Sayings Gospel Q* (Leuven: Peeters, 2014); to a more limited extent: Alan Kirk, *The Composition of the Sayings Source: Genre, Synchrony, and Wisdom Redaction in Q* (NovTSup 91; Leiden: Brill, 1998); and Alan Kirk, "Administrative Writing, Oral Tradition, and Q," paper presented at the annual meeting of the Society of Biblical Literature, Q Session (San Antonio, TX, 2004);

question older presumptions about the "Q community." This essay sorts through these issues to see if "community" remains a useful concept when applied to Q.

Although this essay concerns Q, many of the theoretical issues raised are applicable to *any* Greco-Roman text behind which we might purport to identify a community. Q is an especially valuable test case for two reasons, however. For one, Q is often treated as a repository of the historical Jesus's most "authentic" teachings, which makes it all the more prized in the eyes of those interested in understanding the reception and transmission of Jesus sayings in a communal context.[3] For another, according to some, Q may stand as a link between the earliest oral traditions and the Synoptic Gospels.[4] Here again, were we able to identity a "community," it would provide a crucial insight into the hazy early years of the first Jesus movement. In theory, there is thus much to be gained in this pursuit, but I will argue that the foundations upon which this enterprise rests are rather shaky. It will be clear, moreover, that biblical studies is in dire need of new ways to understand the connection between authors and communities in the ancient world.

2   Data Pointing to a Q Community

The early interest in the Q community was predominantly theological. As John S. Kloppenborg noted more than two decades ago, this interest was based largely on "[t]he categories of form criticism, [which] were invoked to produce a description of the 'community', mapping the contents of the document onto various ecclesial functions: catechesis, exhortation, mission, polity and discipline, instruction on the last things and so forth."[5] Even though this

---

Ronan Rooney and Douglas E. Oakman, "The Social Origins of Q: Two Theses in a Field of Conflicting Hypotheses," *Biblical Theology Bulletin* 38 (2008): 114–121.

3   To substantiate this point, one only need consider how central a role Q has played in the research by participants of the Jesus Seminar. See, for example, John Dominic Crossan, *The Historical Jesus: The Life of a Mediterranean Jewish Peasant* (New York: HarperCollins, 1991) or James M. Robinson, *The Gospel of Jesus: In Search of the Original Good News* (San Francisco: HarperSanFrancisco, 2005).

4   James D.G. Dunn, "Q1 as Oral Tradition," in *The Written Gospel* (ed. Markus Bockmuehl and Donald A. Hagner; Cambridge: Cambridge University Press, 2005), 45–69. Somewhat differently, James M. Robinson, "The Q Trajectory: Between John and Matthew via Jesus," in *The Future of Early Christianity: Essays in Honor of Helmut Koester* (ed. Birger Pearson; Minneapolis: Fortress, 1991), 173–194.

5   John S. Kloppenborg, "City and Wasteland: Narrative World and the Beginning of the Sayings

overtly theological agenda has waned, it has long been common to speak of a "community" behind Q.[6]

Even when scholars do not speak in terms of a single "community," it is often presupposed behind language of preaching, mission activity, or oral tradition, as well as in references to a group of "disciples" as the audience of Q. For instance, Harry T. Fleddermann, in his recent translation and extensive commentary on Q, views Q as largely addressed to a coherent collection of Jesus's disciples.[7] Perhaps the best example of this tendency to see Q as the expression of a discrete group carrying out preaching and mission activity was Gerd Theißen's influential sociological study of earliest Palestinian Christianity.[8] As is well known, Theißen attempted to correlate Q and other early texts' rhetorics of marginality with the voluntary homelessness of the missionaries in the early Jesus communities. James D.G. Dunn, on the other hand, is much more subtle in envisioning a community, since it follows from his understanding of how oral tradition functions. Oral tradition, he stresses, "is essentially *communal* in nature,"[9] so if Q is treated as an oral tradition, someone working from this position can automatically start searching for a community that generated it.[10] Likewise, for those beginning with the assumption that Q's "instructions" speak

---

Gospel (Q)," in *How Gospels Begin* (ed. Dennis E. Smith; Semeia 52; Atlanta: Scholars Press, 1990), 145–160 (152).

6 E.g., Paul Meyer, "The Community of Q" (PhD thesis; University of Iowa, 1967); John S. Kloppenborg, *The Formation of Q: Trajectories in Ancient Wisdom Collections* (SAC; Philadelphia: Fortress, 1987); Helmut Koester, *Ancient Christian Gospels: Their History and Development* (2nd ed.; London: T&T Clark, 1992), 164; Leif E. Vaage, *Galilean Upstarts: Jesus' First Followers according to Q* (Valley Forge, PA: Trinity Press International, 1994), 164; Kyu Sam Han, *Q and the Temple: The Q Community's Attitude Toward the Temple* (ThD Thesis, Knox College, Toronto School of Theology, 1998); Richard A. Horsley with Jonathan A. Draper, *Whoever Hears You Hears Me: Prophets, Performance and Tradition in Q* (Harrisburg, PA: Trinity Press International, 1999); Arnal, *Jesus and the Village Scribes*, 163; Robinson, *The Gospel of Jesus*; Harry T. Fleddermann, *Q: A Reconstruction and Commentary* (Biblical Tools and Studies 1; Leuven: Peeters, 2005).

7 Fleddermann, *Q: A Reconstruction and Commentary*, passim.

8 Gerd Theissen, *Sociology of Early Palestinian Christianity* (trans. John Bowden; Philadelphia: Fortress, 1978).

9 James D.G. Dunn, "Altering the Default Setting: Re-envisaging the Early Transmission of the Jesus Tradition," *NTS* 49 (2003): 139–175 (150), emphasis original.

10 Note Kloppenborg's rather extensive critique of Dunn's reasoning that Q began as an oral tradition as opposed to a written document ("Variation in the Reproduction of the Double Tradition and an Oral Q?" *Ephemerides Theologicae Lovanienses* 83 [2007]: 53–80). He observes that when compared to other ancient documents that we know relied on written sources, Q's reproduction of its sources is actually rather "wooden."

to actual preachers or missionaries traveling around ancient Palestine, it is a simple move then to construct a community or network of communities in which they operated.

Despite this, few have made sustained arguments for the community's existence—it is just assumed to be the best descriptor for the people responsible for the document. I myself have fallen prey to the temptation to use this word, for lack of a better way of conceptualizing this group of people. The point is, thus, not to dismiss any of these studies altogether or to accuse anyone of egregious missteps, but rather to highlight how persistent this assumption is, so that we can assess the evidence on which it is based and evaluate its utility for the study of Christian origins. Toward that end, let us first outline the kinds of data in Q that have suggested to many scholars that the text speaks *for* and *to* a community—perhaps *the* earliest Galilean "Christian"[11] group.

First and foremost, Q has a distinct set of ideas about Jesus, a supposed "unique" theology. Often, for instance, it is pointed out that Q evinces little of the widespread understanding of Jesus's death by crucifixion. Rather, Q emphasizes that Jesus was rejected and killed by those to whom he was sent—just like a long series of prophets who had been sent to Israel in the past and who were subsequently rejected.[12] This theology is most evident in Q's polemic against Jerusalem (Q 11:49–51; 13:34–35), but what is usually taken to be "unique" about this theology is what it lacks: a clear statement of the salvific nature of Jesus's death and resurrection.[13] Since this theology is so different than that which

---

11   I am deliberately problematizing the self-evidently "Christian" nature of this document. I agree with those who have argued that Q lacks an explicit Christian identity and engages in rather largely intra-Jewish debates and identity construction (see William E. Arnal, "The Q Document," in *Jewish Christianity Reconsidered: Rethinking Ancient Groups and Texts* [ed. Matthew Jackson-McCabe; Minneapolis: Fortress, 2007], 119–154; Sarah E. Rollens, "The Identity of Q in the First Century: Reproducing a Theological Narrative," in *Failure and Nerve in the Study of Religion* [ed. William E. Arnal et al; London: Equinox, 2012], 177–191).

12   Arland D. Jacobson ("The Literary Unity of Q," *JBL* 101 [1987]: 365–389) has convincingly explained how Deuteronomistic theology unifies many diverse passages in Q. Q's unity has also been demonstrated by a number of other studies, which conclude that Q has a coherent narrative, spatial organization, theology, and style (e.g., Kloppenborg "City and Wasteland"; Fleddermann, *Q: A Reconstruction and Commentary*; Michael Labahn, *Der Gekommene als Wiederkommender: Die Logienquelle als erzählte Geschichte* [Arbeiten zur Bibel und ihrer Geschichte 32; Leipzig: Evangelische Verlagsanstalt, 2010]).

13   This is not to say that Jesus's death is insignificant for Q. Daniel A. Smith (*The Post-mortem Vindication of Jesus in the Sayings Gospel Q* [LNTS 338; London: T&T Clark, 2007]), for instance, argues that Q is well aware of Jesus's death, but it understands it in terms of

eventually surfaces in the Synoptic Gospels and that which Paul discusses, it is supposed that Q represents a particular "variety" of Christianity, and thus a distinct Christian group.[14] That is, a specific community was associated with *this* set of beliefs, that understood Jesus's death as a prophetic death, as opposed to other groups, that fixated on cross and resurrection theology. This suggestion is used, along with texts such as the Gospel of Thomas,[15] to support the notion of Christianity's original diversity.

Second, Q itself gives us the rhetoric of a group mentality in two major ways. For one, much of Q's material is formulated as instructions, many addressed to a plural audience. Of course, a plural audience should not automatically imply a community, but it indicates that the text presents itself as being received by a group of like-minded people. To offer one telling example, the speech in Q 12:21–33 on being free from anxieties about food and clothing is formulated in the second person plural and asks the putative audience to do several interrelated things: consider ravens, observe lilies, not worry, and seek the kingdom (κατανοήσατε, καταμάθετε, μὴ μεριμνήσητε, and ζητεῖτε). Other instructional speeches in Q, as well as its many rhetorical questions, bank on interaction with the assumed readers/listeners. Thus, grammatically speaking, our first hunch is to suppose a bounded group as the audience for this kind of instructional language.[16] In addition to plural addressees, the text is also marked by a thorough-going rhetoric of "us vs. them," which of course invites us

---

ascension instead of resurrection. Q, after all, does have conceptual language for resurrection (Q 11:31–32), but does not apply this to Jesus's death.

14   Note especially how Q and saying collections as a genre inform the model once proposed by Helmut Koester and James M. Robinson (*Trajectories through Early Christianity* [Philadelphia: Fortress, 1971]), which sought to synthesize the great variety of early Christian texts into "trajectories" that developed over time. Q, embodying a genre that was distinct from supposedly later narrative forms, stood at the beginning of these trajectories.

15   In William Arnal's recent essay ("Blessed are the Solitary: Textual Practices and the Mirage of a Thomas 'Community,'" in *The One Who Sows Bountifully: Essays in Honor of Stanley K. Stowers* [ed. Caroline Johnson Hodge et al; Brown Judaic Studies; Providence, RI: Society of Biblical Literature, 2013], 271–281), he calls into question that Thomas represents an identifiable community (so also Philip Sellew, "Thomas Christianity: Scholars in Quest of a Community," in *The Apocryphal Acts of Thomas* [ed. Jan N. Bremmer; Leuven: Peeters, 2001], 11–35). The tide is slowly shifting in biblical studies, such that the "diversity" thesis of early Christianity is now best described as a diversity of *ideas*, not necessarily of discrete *communities*.

16   One only need consider other classic instances of wisdom literature to realize that instructional language need not bear any relationship to an actual community. For instance,

to imagine a community as the "us." For instance, Q 12:8–12 depicts people "on trial," so to speak, for their allegiances who must collectively defend themselves in the face of opposition and hostility. The beatitudes (e.g., 6:22–23) also envision some sort of perceived persecution; even the so-called mission discourse in Q 10 anticipates harsh rejection by opponents. In fact, practically everywhere we look in Q, there is an "us vs. them" mentality. Q even expects a kind of eschatological banquet wherein a select group of people will be vindicated at the demise of others (13:29, 28). Thus, the very eschatological expectations in the text also reinforce a group mentality. I have argued elsewhere that this *deliberately* imbues Q with a sense of marginality,[17] but even more, I would now suggest that Q's consistent sense of victimhood and persecution has encouraged our liberal-minded proclivities to imagine a disadvantaged group lying just behind Q, using Jesus's teachings as a rallying point for their perceived injustices. This interest becomes clear in such recent studies as Richard A. Horsley's *Covenant Economics*,[18] wherein Horsley mainly focuses on ancient ethical attitudes in Jewish and Christian texts but ultimately extends his discussion to comment on modern economic abuse and exploitation of disadvantaged groups.

Third and related, Q contains many ethical exhortations and recommendations for interactions with assailants and other enemies, which has suggested that Q was responding to a set of social experiences that a group might have endured collectively. This is reflected, for example, in many of Horsley's reconstructions of earliest Christianity, based heavily on Q material,[19] for he is often found arguing that the Q performers were faced with the threat of economic exploitation and social disintegration and were actively trying to renew ancient Israelite village ethics based on the moral precepts of the Mosaic covenant. Much of the Sermon material in Q 6, one observes, concerns how to treat enemies, how to enact fair social exchange, and how to deal with exploitation, and many other passages are focused on encouraging *specific* activities in the face of opposition (Q 12:6–7; 12:8–9, 11–12). In other words, it is not just that Q's grammar anticipates a like-minded audience, but also that its advice does as well.

---

while it is easy to imagine different social settings in which Proverbs may have been used, few would try to reconstruct the "Proverbs community."

17 Rollens, *Framing Social Criticism in the Jesus Movement*, 185–189.
18 Richard A. Horsley, *Covenant Economics: A Biblical Vision of Justice for All* (Louisville: Westerminter John Knox Press, 2009).
19 Horsley with Draper, *Whoever Hears You Hears Me*; Richard A. Horsley, *Jesus and the Spiral of Violence: Popular Jewish Resistance in Roman Palestine* (San Francisco: Harper & Row, 1987), 167–284.

Fourth and still related, many have argued that the ethical teachings in Q are more than just a list of idealizations—they are programmatic. This program, many suggest, is realized in the expectations or the expression of the kingdom of God. As I have shown elsewhere, the kingdom of God is treated as a touchstone when scholars reconstruct the Q community, and so it is often used as a window into the Q group's beliefs and activities.[20] We are tempted all the more to do this when Q's Jesus says things such as, "The kingdom of God is not coming visibly ... The kingdom of God is among you" (Q 17:20–21) or when he explains how the kingdom "reaches" people (10:9) when Q's envoys enter their homes.[21] This all feeds into the assumption that knowing about the kingdom of God in Q—that is, identifying the semantic content of the metaphor—immediately tells us about the community of people behind the text. Moreover, the treatment of the kingdom as a kind of program of ethical ideals that can be *lived* invites us to envision a group *striving* to achieve this expression.

We are hardly done though. There are even more ways that scholars have put Q to work as a document representing an intentional community. Some have seen Q as endorsing or reflecting a mission to the Gentiles,[22] which must

---

20 As in Burton L. Mack, *The Lost Gospel: The Book of Q and Christian Origins* (San Francisco, Calif.: HarperCollins, 1993); Horsley with Draper, *Whoever Hears You Hears Me*; Crossan, *The Historical Jesus*; Fleddermann, *Q*; James M. Robinson, *Jesus: According to the Earliest Witness* (Minneapolis: Fortress, 2007).

21 Although Luke is the only author to preserve a version of this saying, the International Q Project includes this passage in its reconstruction in *The Critical Edition of Q* (Robinson, Hoffmann, and Kloppenborg, eds., *The Critical Edition of Q*; cf. John S. Kloppenborg, *Q, the Earliest Gospel: An Introduction to the Original Sayings and Stories of Jesus* [Louisville, KY: Westminster/John Knox], 50–51). Generally speaking, when *Sondergut* material is included in the reconstruction of Q, it must be conceptually similar to other material already known to be in Q; it must come within or very near a Q context in either Matthew or Luke; and it must contain ideas which would be difficult to imagine Luke or Matthew fabricating. If a passage has a parallel in Thomas, then that also makes it a good candidate, for it may indicate that it was part of an earlier collection to which Q and Thomas has access. This passage satisfies a number of these criteria: it fits with Q's other notions of the immediacy of the kingdom and God's providence; it has a parallel in Gos. Thom. 3; and it seems difficult to imagine that Luke would invent this sort of passage which is at odds with his other statements about the future kingdom (Luke, as is well known, is famous for his delayed eschatology, since he has to reconcile his beliefs with his present reality in which Christianity is still actively spreading).

22 Koester, *Ancient Christian Gospels*, 159; Helmut Koester, "The Sayings of Q and Their Image of Jesus," in *Sayings of Jesus: Canonical and Non-Canonical: Essaying in Honor of Tjitze Baarda* (ed. William L. Petersen et al.; NovTSup 89; Leiden: Brill, 1997), 137–154 (154); Fleddermann, *Q*.

surely be the product of a self-conscious Christian community. Some have argued that particular features of Q are overtly concerned with identity formation, analyzed with such concepts as Deuteronomistic theology[23] or Northern Israelite identity,[24] and have thus concluded that the text's identity markers are *so* strong than it cannot be *other* than the expression of a particular community. Finally, we may also consider the sparse evidence for the community "rituals" that Q might endorse. Q talks about baptism (ch. 3), has a vague reference to taking up the cross (14:27), and may even promote some kind of missionizing activity as well (ch. 10). I will not dwell on these latter points too much, because the references to baptism and imitation of Jesus in Q are hardly programmatic: they do not appear to be either initiation rites or even actions by which community members can expect to identify one another.[25] And as I now turn to in the assessment, the supposed recommended behavior for the "Q group" needs some serious rethinking, too, because there are certainly other social forms that make sense behind the text.

3 Assessment

If we step back and assess these data that are usually used to construct a Q community, it is rather weak. A heavy dose of in-group language and some ethical exhortations do not a community make. It is our unfounded assumption that we must assume a coherent community when this sort of language is present. Stanley Stowers noted in his recent discussion of "communities" in earliest Christianity that we too often assume that there must be a "tight fit between a writer and a highly coherent social group with commonality in belief and practice."[26] In fact, as critical historians, our first impulse when we see this language should be to assume that the coherent community is *not* there and that the language is in fact trying to *create* it. Indeed, this is how

---

23 Jacobson, "The Literary Unity of Q."
24 Richard A. Horsley, "The Historical Context of Q," in *Whoever Hears You Hears Me: Prophets, Performance and Tradition in Q* (ed. Richard A. Horsley with Jonathan A. Draper; Harrisburg, PA: Trinity Press International, 1999), 46–60.
25 Q certainly expects to receive rejection, akin to Jesus's rejection, so his life becomes a template for its experience. There is a difference, though, between *using* Jesus's life as a template for understanding present experiences and *prescribing* present actions on the basis of his deeds.
26 Stanley Stowers, "The Concept of 'Community' and the History of Early Christianity," *Method & Theory in the Study of Religion* 23 (2011): 238–256 (248).

Stowers proposes we should treat Paul's letters—not as a *reflection* of a community that is already in place, but as the very attempt to construct a not-in-place community out of a collection of individuals with diverse interests and commitments.[27] In addition, the presence of plural addressees in Q, unfortunately, indicates very little on its own, otherwise we would have to posit a community for every instructional wisdom text from the ancient world, a venture that would approach absurdity. More to the point, we ought to distinguish between a text's goals of reaching—even better, *constructing*—a like-minded audience and the reality of that group ever existing. We should not expect everyone who read or heard a text to be ideologically aligned with its interests. In fact, for every collection of ideas in a text that might have been the basis for community formation, it is equally plausible that there was an actual audience of the text that *rejected* those ideas as sufficient for its identity. In other words, there need be no direct relationship between a text's projection of community identity and an actual community; to conclude this would be to accept the text's own self-promotion, but it would fail to adopt the critical eye of the historian.

That Q seems to have a programmatic concept in the kingdom of God is not especially compelling either for imagining a community. Above all, the kingdom's referent is rather unclear when one begins to examine the different uses to which it is put in Q. Scholars have proposed that it refers to everything from an ethic based on "the renewal of Israel in its basic social form, the village community"[28] to "something like the 'lordship of God' over historical affairs"[29] to "the present state of the disciples as a way of being with God in the world."[30] The Q document itself is not even clear on whether the kingdom is a present or future phenomenon. So on one hand, the concept is so nebulous that we can hardly correlate it with a calculated social program. On the other hand, it might be *deliberately* nebulous so as to function in a variety of ways, giving the document potential to resonate with a multiplicity of audiences. In fact, we know that it eventually *did* resonate with a wider audience, since Matthew and Luke—both probably rather removed from the ordinary affairs of rural villages (the socio-historical context that is usually proposed

---

[27] Stowers, "The Concept of 'Community' and the History of Early Christianity," 242–244.

[28] Richard A. Horsley, "The Kingdom of God as the Renewal of Israel," in *Whoever Hears You Hears Me: Prophets, Performance and Tradition in Q* (ed. Richard A. Horsley with Jonathan A. Draper; Harrisburg, PA: Trinity Press International, 1999), 260–276 (270).

[29] Douglas E. Oakman, *Jesus and the Peasants* (Matrix; Eugene, OR: Cascade Books, 2008), 215.

[30] Fleddermann, *Q: A Reconstruction and Commentary*, 144–145.

behind Q)—saw something special in it. In other words, it is entirely understandable that the kingdom is not a symbol with one consistent referent. The concept itself is the authoritative and rhetorically unifying device for a range of socio-political commentary: it is able to encompass ideas about the providence of God, notions about the future and the judgment entailed therein, and socio-ethical commentary, among other things—all because of the uses to which the symbol is put.[31] Considered from this perspective, we should thus not expect it to be any sort of a reflection of a particular community.

In terms of Q's endorsement of community ritual, there is really nothing to support a collection of individuals engaged in any routine activity prescribed by the document. Q talks about baptism, as noted, but many Jewish and Christian texts do this—we hardly need to correlate a text with a community when we observe this. That critique is actually beside the point, though: the notion that Q must be used in a ritualistic sense reveals a *modern* understanding of religion which imagines a community with regular beliefs and practices stemming from some authoritative, textual source. Recall Martin Luther's rationale for what rituals should be practiced by churches: he only endorsed those that were recorded in what he assumed to be accurate textual reports of Jesus's life, i.e., what he considered authoritative, literary sources. Even many modern Catholics base their official dogma and ritual activity on authorized statements from Church leaders. Since we are so used to observing these sorts of authoritative templates for belief and action in contemporary religious forms, it is easy to expect Q to act as a similar template in antiquity.

Furthermore, although the notion that a community behind Q was engaged in a Gentile mission is still debated,[32] it seems clear to many that the positive examples of Gentiles in Q are there for *argumentative* purposes. They function as shaming devices for the real people that Q's authors hoped to be in their audience[33] and do not point to the self-conscious mission of a bounded community.

---

[31] An analogous (albeit contemporary) example is the concept of "democracy" in the Western world. In its most basic form, democracy implies equal political participation. But, depending on who is deploying the term, it can be made to encompass all manner of things, such as ideas about racial or gender equality, notions of free enterprise and individual civic responsibility, and even presumptions about the evolution of political processes in contemporary society (i.e., democracy represents the most sophisticated form of political representation among modern societies).

[32] See recently, Fleddermann, *Q*.

[33] Paul Meyer, "The Gentile Mission in Q," *JBL* 89 (1970): 405–417; Jonathan L. Reed, "The Social Map of Q," in *Conflict and Invention: Literary, Rhetorical, and Social Studies on the*

Stowers has pointed out that the very fact of identifying a text's distinct "theology" has often been enough for many scholars to hypothesize a community. In his words:

> [T]he author's theology might be seen as the thought that was created or developed in a particular community, the theology that defined or differentiated the community from other communities ... [t]he writer might be seen as composing a story about Jesus that in almost every detail addressed the issues and needs of a particular community.[34]

As I began this essay by pointing out, that Q has a distinct theology of Jesus is a crucial point for understanding early Christian and Jewish diversity and has been critical for recent attempts to redescribe Christian origins, but this alone hardly implies that a special group of "Christians" must have all assented to all of Q's propositions about Jesus. Interestingly, Q's theology has also been used to *challenge* the suggestion of a distinct Galilean community behind the document, although still preserving theoretically problematic notions of "community"; Birger Pearson focuses on Q's theology in his recent attempt to dismiss a distinct "Q community."[35] He begins with the assumption that theological diversity implies a proliferation of communities—which as I have noted, is not an automatic consequence of the diversity thesis (see n. 15)—, but then fails to accept that Q could be a distinct witness to this diversity. Instead, he falls back on associating Q's theology with a "known" community (the "community" supposedly evidenced in Acts) and interprets Q's theology in light of Acts' ideas. This is a clever move if one is trying to control the diversity of Christian origins and protect Acts as its main representative, but it is not one required by the evidence. Thus, we can see that conclusions regarding whether Q's theology was unique or not are often tied to pre-existing assumptions about the earliest "Christian communities" in ancient Palestine.

These attempts to find the Q community end up engaging in precisely the enterprise that Stowers and others have called into question. This enterprise relies on an idealized concept of community, which is indebted firstly to Eusebius's and the author of Acts' heavy hands in imagining the origins of the Christian tradition,[36] and secondly to modern notions of the interiority of religion,

---

Sayings Gospel Q (ed. John S. Kloppenborg; Valley Forge, PA: Trinity Press International, 1995), 17–32, here 22; Kloppenborg, *Excavating Q*, 192–193.

34 Stowers, "The Concept of 'Community' and the History of Early Christianity," 240–241.
35 Birger Pearson, "A Q Community in Galilee?" *NTS* 50 (2004): 476–494.
36 Stowers, "The Concept of 'Community' and the History of Early Christianity," 252.

especially that it is merely a set of ideas that exists "out there" to be expressed through individual believers. When it comes to Q, much of this, unfortunately, comes down to wishful thinking. It is wishful thinking in a small sense, that each text has a community writing it or using it. This kind of wishful thinking is precisely the "undertheorized" way that community has been set to work thus far, operating in the absence of argumentation and evidence.[37] But it is also wishful thinking in a larger and more troubling sense, that the earliest discernible form of Christianity *must* have had a coherent community behind it,[38] molding its beliefs and actions and expressing its identity—and in many cases, this picture results because few have endeavored to think more creatively about the evidence and the possibilities. It is worth pointing out, as well, that this is a very Weberian notion of how a tradition develops: a founder's words and deeds are institutionalized into the beliefs and practices within the community of a founder's immediate followers.[39] This mode of historical development is not *a priori* impossible, but we should be cognizant of the wider purpose that it serves when it comes to something like Q: if one accepts Weber's model of institutional development (a.k.a. routinization of charisma), one has done two interrelated things: (1) accepted uncritically the insider's version of Christianity's rise, in this case the version promoted by the Synoptic Gospels, Acts, and Eusebius, among others; and (2) retained, in a rather unjustifiable way, an unbroken link from Jesus to later Christianity. This model, of course, ignores a huge amount of diversity and disagreement among our sources (in particular, what exactly *were* the original words and deeds of Jesus if they were going to be institutionalized in an early community? And if authors fabricate some of them, how does that affect this development?), and it also amounts to a form of essentialization: there must be some *essential* set of ideas that is retained within different forms of Christianity and transmitted down through the ages. This essentializing model is premised on the confidence that the historical Jesus lies at the beginning of the chain of institutionalization and that some facet of him has been preserved and transmitted by his followers, so if we just work backwards rigorously, we will arrive at his original "charisma."

Yet because of the theological potential of this model (i.e., Jesus is somewhere at the beginning of it), many were only too happy to rely on it find answers to their own theological questions. So, in a sense, I would argue that many early notions of the Q community simply lacked the desire to understand

---

37 Stowers, "The Concept of 'Community' and the History of Early Christianity," 245.
38 Typified in Pearson's "A Q community in Galilee?"
39 Max Weber, *Theory of Social and Economic Organization* (trans. A.R. Anderson and Talcott Parsons; New York: Citadel Press, 1947 [1922]).

it in any way other than as a larger extension of Jesus's original circle of disciples.[40] Why challenge the model of Jesus's teachings and deeds sedimenting into the Q community when it accomplishes so much theological work? For, a proponent of this view might hold, if we can't find a community behind Q—the earliest Christian document that we can discern—how are we going to imagine the uninterrupted spread of the Jesus tradition from Galilee to elsewhere in the Roman Empire?

This is precisely the point: this trajectory has guided our work thus far, and even once it is problematized, we have no other good model for thinking about how and why a person or collection of persons would preserve a text such as Q, except to appeal to the romanticized notion of community and to presume that everyone in the "community" ordered their lives around this programmatic text. So: what happens when we try out a new model?

4 Reimagining a Q Community

In addition to the theoretical caveats about the mishandling of the term community, another important reason to assess the utility of "community" has to do with recent opinions of the Q people and their activity. A number of scholars have recently made persuasive arguments that Q's authors ought to be identified as mid- or low-level administrative figures, likely some sort of scribes.[41] This is evident not only in the literary form of Q but also in its content. But this invites us to speculate about what the social formation was that sustained a project like Q? Must we fall back on the notion of community to imagine its production? If we seriously entertain this alternate social configuration for Q's authors, what are the ramifications for imagining a Q community? As I would like to suggest, they are rather serious.

Although many agree with the identification of Q's authors as scribes, some still appeal to peasant communities as the best analogues for the Q people and

---

40 As in Pearson, "A Q community in Galilee?"; Dunn, "Q1 as Oral Tradition." This assumption invites a new set of questions, of course, regarding how we should sociologically understand Jesus's disciples. Were they students following a teacher? Were they outcasts opting for an alternative mode of social exchange? Were they devotees to a popular healer? These queries are not necessarily related to Q and thus exceed the bounds of this essay.

41 For an overview of this discussion, see Rollens, *Framing Social Criticism in the Jesus Movement*, 135–141. Giovanni Bazzana's monograph (*Kingdom and Bureaucracy*) comparing features in Q to the structure and language found in documentary papyri make this almost incontestable, in my opinion.

contend that Q is a direct reflection of a peasant community.[42] However, these studies may be focusing on the wrong sort of social actors; rather, it is the people who *direct* and *shape* social movements, not the mass of followers, who are the best points of comparison for Q's authors. In a recent monograph, I examine other examples of "middling figures" who engage in social activism and use them to better understand the Q scribes.[43] Even when viewed cross-culturally, these figures often have a great deal in common, including a sense of socio-economic marginality (whether perceived or real), a drive toward intellectual creativity, and the skills to help a group construct a coherent identity. These features make a great deal of sense of what we see in Q, including its rather sophisticated literary form, its rhetoric of marginality, its attempt to orient a diverse audience toward the Jesus movement, and its preoccupation with aligning Jesus and his followers with Israelite prophets from the past. Q is not the spontaneous expression of a cohesive peasant group whose identity is already in place due to occupying a similar socio-economic position over against elite figures. Rather, Q is addressing a range of people and is synthesizing their interests in order to bring into being (ideally) a kind of constituency. It is trying to reorient these all within the confines of its ideology, to make many people *potentially* part of its group, but there is no "community" yet in reality.

Moreover, this does not seem to be a natural kind of identity formation—the rhetoric of Q is evidence for the *effort* it took to fashion a new identity around Jesus, to construct myths, to establish allegiances, and to counter alternative interpretations. This realization changes how we understand central features of Q. For instance, if Q is considered thus, the so-called Mission Instructions in Q 10 may be better understood as a reflection of scribal competition over who is authorized to interpret and preserve the shared cultural tradition, rather than as evidence for discrete activities of the community. That is, instead of reflecting a situation in which entire towns have rejected the "missionaries" of the "Q community," the harsh rhetoric against the Galilean towns might indicate that some scribes within a local village network (those clustered around the Northern rim of the lake) had challenged the authority of the scribes responsible for Q. The references to the disbelieving Galilean towns could thus be understood as a kind of exaggerated rhetorical metonymy. I am not hinging my entire interpretation of Q's authors on this example, but rather, using it to show that if we

---

42 Especially Horsley, *Jesus and the Spiral of Violence*; Horsley with Draper, *Whoever Hears You Hears Me*; Oakman, *Jesus and the Peasants*; Horsley, *Covenant Economics*.

43 Rollens, *Framing Social Criticism in the Jesus Movement*.

jettison "community" in favor of a different configuration of people behind Q, other interpretations of this passage are just as compelling as "mission activity" in Lower Galilee.

To explore Q's authors along these lines forces us to admit that we can only really speculate about a loose affiliation of authors who might be arguing "with" the Q document. The community behind Q is only evident if we let Q's authors convince us that it is there, especially if we misinterpret broad socio-political appeals as a reference to a "religious" community just because they are in a text that has been conventionally treated as "religious." So wishful thinking once again enters the picture: this time it is the authors of Q who are wishing a unified "Jesus" constituency into being instead of we who are wishing a primitive Christian community into being. To accept Q's authors at their word would accomplish many things, but in Bruce Lincoln's words, it would not be scholarship.[44]

Comparing the Q scribes to other analogous figures who shape and direct social movements has thus suggested that the notion of "community" in this very early period of Christian origins is in dire need of redescription. Not only is a coherent community not evident in Q, but the very activity that produced its "group mentality" needs rethinking. The identity in Q was sustained by frequent attention to the text (i.e., revision and redaction), probably some intentional interaction with other villages in ways that capitalized on scribal networks that were already in place, and a significant amount of intellectual maintenance and surveillance for the whole endeavor. Moreover, these scribal networks were in place for a particular reason, namely, that they were directly related to the administrative activities of the authors. We must admit, as well, that there is nothing particularly special about the ethical ideals that Q promotes and appends to the figure of Jesus—indeed many scholars have shown how they have counterparts in contemporary Jewish writing and even some philosophical discourse[45]—so generating a "community" around these ideas should not be assumed to automatically follow. If this document *became* programmatic at some point for a particular collection of people, it would take intellectual work to tell people why *this particular configuration* of ideas

---

44 Bruce Lincoln, "Theses on Method," *Method & Theory in the Study of Religion* 8 (1996): 225–227.

45 E.g., Kloppenborg, *The Formation of Q*; Downing, *Christ and the Cynics: Jesus and Other Radical Preachers in First-century Tradition* (JSOTSup 4; Sheffield: JSOT Press, 1988); Migaku Sato, *Q und Prophetie: Studien zur Gattungs- und Traditionsgeschichte der Quelle Q* (WUNT 2.29; Tübingen: J.C.B. Mohr, 1988); Vaage, *Galilean Upstarts*; Kirk, *The Composition of the Sayings Source*.

mattered to them. This, I would claim, it what the primary goal of Q is: the framing of an ideology to promote an identity associated with Jesus, maintained by the authority of the text's authors. So what we have in Q is a window into the meticulous creation of an ideology, but it is challenging to move from those ideals to a "community" that embodied all of its facets. Not only does the evidence not permit this leap, but the whole enterprise is founded on a modern notion of religion: that it is an interior set of beliefs that must correlate to believers' own attitudes and practices.[46] It sounds plausible enough (although many would certainly contest this rather Protestant way of conceptualizing religion[47]), but as critics have shown, what it means to be "religious" in non-modern contexts can be far more complicated or even different altogether.[48] To promote ideals in a written text is notably not the same as having them sustained in a self-conscious community.

To focus on Q's authors as constructing and maintaining an ideology through the text shifts us to a new kind of social configuration behind Q. As Stowers has pointed out, to treat every text as a reflection of a community makes early Christian literature "unique" in the sense that everywhere else in the ancient Mediterranean world "a writing is studied as the product of an individual writer working in a particular social and historical context, not as the product of a community."[49] The Q scribes, especially when viewed alongside other middling figures who participate in and direct social movements, are precisely these "networks of literate or specialized cultural producers"[50] on which Stowers suggests we should focus, instead of the ill-defined category of community. Attention to these figures brings into focus the way that authors configure or reconfigure a shared cultural tradition, such as the sayings attributed to Jesus or elements of Israel's epic history, in order to make them meaningful to a variety of people, a skill that cannot be accomplished by just anyone.

---

46 This view, which privileges an individual's belief as the central feature of religion, is indebted to thinkers such as Friedrich Schleiermacher, Rudolph Otto, and Martin Luther, among others.

47 Jonathan Z. Smith, *Drudgery Divine: On the Comparison of Early Christianities and the Religions of Late Antiquity* (Chicago: University of Chicago Press, 1990).

48 This critique was very clearly expressed by Talal Asad, *Genealogies of Religion: Discipline and Reasons of Power in Christianity and Islam* (Baltimore: Johns Hopkins University Press, 1993), esp. 27–79. More recently: Daniel Dubuisson, *The Western Construction of Religion: Myths, Knowledge, and Ideology* (trans. William Sayers; Baltimore: Johns Hopkins University Press, 2003); Brent Nongbri, *Before Religion: A History of a Modern Concept* (New Haven: Yale University Press, 2013).

49 Stowers, "The Concept of 'Community' and the History of Early Christianity," 247.

50 Stowers, "The Concept of 'Community' and the History of Early Christianity," 250.

In short, nothing in Q indicates a "community" akin to that which Eusebius and the author of Acts imagined, wherein the ideas of Jesus and his mission generated a spontaneous "Christian" community of believers which based their ideas and actions on his original words and deeds.[51] "Community" in Q is only present insofar as there is an idealized identity that is promoted when someone sets their stylus to a papyrus, when it comes to expression in a text, when it constructs an implied audience, and when this audience is set in relation to other expressions of identity. Thus, community is not "natural"; the rhetoric of community results from creative and innovative ideological work that has to synthesize a broad range of interests into a new configuration, even if this synthesis takes place only at the rhetorical level. When it comes to ancient documents, moreover, we are in no position to assess the extent to which this document correlated to the beliefs and practices of individual people—that question itself is steeped in modern conceptions of religion.

5   Conclusion

Previous attempts to unearth a Q community have failed for two main reasons. First, the actual evidence in the document is too scant to construct a group who used this text as a template on which it crafted its identity. Simply having a distinct set of beliefs about Jesus and proposing a series of ethical ideals is hardly enough to suppose a fixed group constructing its identity on the basis of this document. Yet, because Q has been treated as an indispensable moment in the development of Christianity—often as *the* link between the historical Jesus and the Synoptic Gospels—many have supposed that a passionately dedicated "Christian" community *must* have been responsible for its composition and survival, and so they have worked hard to extract its programmatic beliefs, informed largely by modern notions of what religion essentially is or must be. Second, the theoretical grounds on which this interest has been based are highly problematic. It is wishful thinking on our part to assume a community behind each and every text,[52] and even wishful thinking on our authors' part to presume that a "unified" community would be generated by a few words on a page. On the other hand, if we take seriously recent proposals for Q's authors,

---

51   Stowers, "The Concept of 'Community' and the History of Early Christianity," 252.
52   Dunn makes this similar critique, but his protest seems to be guided by the desire not to fracture the one "Christian" community in antiquity. My argument here is that assuming *any* "community" behind a text is problematic, theological proclivities aside, and to insist that the community would be self-consciously "Christian" is even more questionable.

we perceive a new configuration of the people behind Q, perhaps not the "community" some may have been looking for, but instead, a network of interested intellectuals constructing and engaging with the text. In any case, the desire to redescribe the "Q community" is a much-needed move both forward and away from a relatively uncritical enterprise that saw intentional "Christian" communities lurking in the background of all Jesus-centered texts.

An Imminent Parousia and Christian Mission: Did the New Testament Writers Really Expect Jesus's Imminent Return?

Mark Keown

It is commonly held in NT scholarship that there was expectation of an imminent parousia within the first generation of the church.[1] For example, I.H. Marshall, writing in 1970, states, "[o]n this point there is there is *complete agreement* among scholars."[2] It is commonly viewed that this hope was dashed and that later writings such as Luke-Acts, the inauthentic Paulines, and some of the General Epistles reflect the church dealing with the so-called "delay of the *Parousia*." The expectation of an imminent Parousia is especially held for Mark's[3] Gospel (especially Mark 9:1; 13:30)[4] and the undisputed Pauline Epistles (e.g. Rom 13:12; 1 Cor 7:26; Phil 4:5).

This essay will explore this claim from the perspective of Mark and Paul. I will argue that, while it is likely that there were Christians who considered that the Parousia was imminent (e.g. 2 Thess 2:1–2;[5] 2 Pet 3:4),[6] it is unlikely the authors of Mark and the Pauline corpus held to a view of an imminent Parousia. I am not the first to argue this. Many have argued against an imminent Parousia in Mark and Paul on a text by text basis.[7] Rather, I will argue that this is unlikely on three other connected grounds.

---

1 K.H. Jobes, *1 Peter* (BECNT; Grand Rapids: Baker Academic, 2005), 52. See also A.L. Moore, *The Parousia in the New Testament* (Leiden: Brill, 1966), 92–107.
2 I.H. Marshall, *Luke: Historian and Theologian* (London: Paternoster, 1970), 129 (emphasis mine).
3 I will use "Mark" as author of the second Gospel Mark whether penned by John Mark or another. Authorship is not critical to this discussion.
4 Moore, *Parousia*, 98 also notes Matt 10:23. See also John 21:22–23; 2 Pet 3:4. See also C.L. Holman, "The Idea of an Imminent Parousia in the Synoptic Gospels," in *Studia Biblica et Theologica* 3 (1973): 20–27.
5 C.A. Wanamaker, *The Epistles to the Thessalonians: A Commentary on the Greek Text* (NIGTC; Grand Rapids: Eerdmans, 1990), 131.
6 The opponent's mockery may suggest the Petrine community were expecting an imminent Parousia; cf. R.B. Bauckham, *2 Peter, Jude* (WBC 50; Dallas: Word, 1998), 289.
7 E.g. on Mark 9:1 and 13:30, see James R. Edwards, *Mark* (PNTC; Grand Rapids: Eerdmans; Leicester: Apollos, 2002), 259–261, 405. On Rom 13:12, see L. Morris, *The Epistle to the Romans* (PNTC; Grand Rapids: Eerdmans; Leicester: IVP, 1988), 471. On 1 Cor 7:26, see A.C. Thiselton,

First, it is clear that Mark and Paul (along with Luke and Matthew)[8] believed that the gospel must be proclaimed to *all the nations of the world* before the Parousia. Second, in light of our knowledge of the speed and extent of the initial mission, the first Christians' understanding of the known world makes it unlikely that they expected the mission's completion within a generation. Third, I will explore first-century understandings of the known world suggesting it encompassed large parts of Europe, southern Russia, central to eastern Asia, and northern Africa and, as such, great swathes of the mission were incomplete by the time of the writing of the NT. Assuming that the thinking of these writers was coherent, the idea that they held to an imminent Parousia becomes tenuous.

1 The Cosmic Mission Statements in Mark and Paul and Their Implications for an Imminent Parousia

In this section, I will explore indications that Mark and Paul believed that the gospel needed to be preached to people in every part of the known world. This implies that it is unlikely that they considered that Jesus would soon return but anticipated an interim period of substantial if unknown length before his return. During this time, they expected that the gospel would penetrate the inhabited world as they knew it.

1.1 *Mark*

In the past it has often been assumed that Mark reflects the hope of an imminent Parousia.[9] More recent interpreters of Mark, however, have argued against

---

The First Epistle to the Corinthians: A Commentary on the Greek Text (NIGTC; Grand Rapids: Eerdmans, 2000), 573. On Phil 4:5, see M.J. Keown, *Philippians* 2 vols.; (EEC; Bellingham, WA: Lexham Press, 2017), 2:336–340.

8 See also Matt 24:9, 14; 25:32; 26:13; 28:18–20; Luke 12:30; 21:24; 24:46–47; 17:30; John 1:7, 29; 3:16–17; 4:42; 5:23; 6:33; 8:12, 26; 11:19; 12:32; 13:35; 14:31; 17:21, 23; Acts 1:8; 28:30–31; 13:47; Heb 2:15; 8:11; 2 Pet 3:9; 1 John 4:14; 5:19; Jude 15; Rev 5:9; 7:9; 12:5; 14:8; 15:4; 18:3, 23; 21:24, 26; 22:2, 22, cf. Acts 14:16. The case made in this essay applies to these writings equally.

9 E.g. T.W. Manson, *The Teaching of Jesus: Studies in Its Form and Content* (Cambridge: Cambridge University Press, 1963), 277–284; I.H. Marshall, *The Gospel of Luke: A Commentary on the Greek Text* (NIGTC; Exeter: Paternoster, 1978), 757; J.D. Crossan, "Living Earth and Living Christ Thoughts on Carol P. Christ's 'Finitude, Death, and Reverence for Life,'" *Semeia* 40 (1987): 115; C.E.B. Cranfield, *The Gospel According to St Mark: An Introduction and Commentary* (Cambridge: Cambridge University Press, 1959), 417; C.A. Evans, *Mark 8:27–16:20* (WBC 34B; Dallas: Word, 2001), 361–362.

this on various fronts, however. These include those like N.T. Wright who argue that Mark's Jesus had no expectation of a Parousia at all.[10] Some argue that reading an imminent Parousia into texts such as Mark 9:1 and 13:30 is inappropriate on exegetical grounds.[11] I will not replay these debates but will focus on the tension that exists between any notion of an imminent Parousia and the Markan expectation of a mission of cosmic scope before the Parousia.

The clearest statement of a cosmic commission in Mark is found in the longer endings of the Gospel. However, these are almost certainly later additions to the Gospel's original text. The traditional long ending of Mark does, however, confirm that some Christians from the second century on held an expectation of a cosmic mission (Mark 16:15).[12] Even without these endings there are three verses in close proximity that indicate that Mark understood that the Christian message would need to go to the entire inhabited world (Mark 13:10, 27; 14:9). I will briefly look at each in turn.

1.1.1 Mark 13:10

Mark 13:10 is the clearest Markan statement of a cosmic gospel mission: "And the gospel must first be proclaimed to *all nations* (εἰς πάντα τὰ ἔθνη)."[13] It is common to read this as: an interpolation, a prophecy after the fact, a saying of Jesus from another setting,[14] a Markan editorial insertion,[15] or a gloss from the early church.[16] However, the verse is found in all extant versions of Mark

---

10 N.T. Wright, *Jesus and the Victory of God* (Christian Origins and the Question of God; London: SPCK, 1996), 339–368.
11 See e.g. Edwards, *Mark*, 259–261, 395, 404; Holman, "The Idea," 20–28.
12 On longer endings, see B.M. Metzger, *A Textual Commentary on the Greek New Testament* (2nd ed.; London; New York: United Bible Societies, 1994), 102–107.
13 Evans, *Mark 8:27–16:20*, 303 notes D rearranges the text, πρῶτον δεῖ κηρυχθῆναι τὸ εὐαγγέλιον ἐν πᾶσι τοῖς ἔθνεσιν, shifting the emphasis but leaving the meaning the same.
14 J.A. Brooks, *Mark* (NAC 23; Nashville: Broadman & Holman, 1991), 210; W.L. Lane, *The Gospel of Mark* (NICNT; Grand Rapids: Eerdmans, 1974), 460–461.
15 Very widely held, see e.g. Evans, *Mark 8:27–16:20*, 310; J. Marcus, *Mark 8–16* (AB 27; New Haven: Yale University Press, 2005), 884–885; V. Taylor, *The Gospel According to St Mark* (2nd ed.; London: Macmillan; New York: St Martin's, 1966), 507; R. Pesch, *Das Markusevangelium* (HTKNT 2/1–2; Freiburg: Herder, 1977), 2.285; W. Marxsen, *Der Evangelist Markus: Studien zur Redaktionsgeschichte des Evangeliums* (FRLANT 67; Göttingen: Vandenhoeck & Ruprecht, 1956; 2nd ed., 1959), 119–120; P. Stuhlmacher, *Das paulinische Evangelium—1: Vorgeschichte* (FRLANT 95: Göttingen: Vandenhoeck & Ruprecht, 1968), 284 n. 2; R.A. Culpepper, *Mark* (SHBC; Marcon: Smyth & Helweys, 2007), 456.
16 See e.g. Cranfield, *Mark*, 399–400; G.R. Beasley-Murray, *Jesus and the Last Days: The Interpretation of the Olivet Discourse* (Peabody, MA: Hendrickson, 1993), 402–403; E. Branden-

and, aside from *a priori* rejection of missional statements in Mark as interpolations or redactions, there is no reason to question its authenticity. Further, this verse cannot be "after the fact" because the gospel had most definitely not been preached in every known nation at the time of Mark's writing in the 60s or early 70s (see below). Additionally, as a version of this verse is found in Matt 24:14, there is little reason to dispute that it is an original saying of Jesus (cf. Luke 21:24). This conclusion is supported with Mark 13:27 and 14:9, both of which similarly speak of the cosmic scope of the mission (see below).[17] Finally, while it can never be proven that Jesus said this, the writer of Mark includes it here indicating that this is *the author's perspective* at the time of writing.

The relationship of this verse to the previous is disputed.[18] Some see it as continuous with the previous: "for they will deliver you over to councils, and you will beaten in synagogues, and you will stand before governors and kings for my sake, to bear witness before them and to all the nations."[19] The second part of v. 10 would thus imply that "it is necessary first for the gospel to be proclaimed."[20] Taken in this manner, "all nations" in Mark 13:10 is limited to those in which the disciples will face the Jewish and Gentile officials mentioned in v. 9.[21] However, few accept this reading, rightly preferring to attach καὶ εἰς πάντα τὰ ἔθνη to what follows.[22] Even so, v. 10 does in a sense continue the thread of v. 9 which foretells believers standing and testifying to Christ before a range of governing authorities. It clarifies that they will do this as they engage in evangelizing *all* the nations of the world.

"The gospel" (εὐαγγέλιον) is the announcement of the "good news" of Jesus Christ and God's Kingdom.[23] In Mark's Gospel it is the story of Jesus Christ from the John's ministry to Jesus's resurrection (Mark 1:1; 16:8). It is the message of

---

burger, *Markus 13 und die Apokalyptik* (FRLANT 134; Göttingen: Vandenhoeck & Ruprecht, 1984), 30–32.

17 Brooks, *Mark*, 210 correctly: "[t]here simply is no valid reason he could not have made the statement."
18 Cranfield, *Mark*, 398 notes some MSS insert δὲ after πρῶτον, but rejects this.
19 See e.g. Marcus, *Mark 8–16*, 885 who sees 13:9–13 and 13:9b–10 as a chiasmic unit.
20 See e.g. G.D. Kilpatrick, "The Gentile Mission in Mark and Mark xiii.9–11," in *Studies in the Gospels: Festschrift for R.H. Lightfoot* (ed. D.E. Nineham; Oxford: Blackwell, 1955), 145–158. The effect is the same. If "all nations" is attached to the former, Mark 13:9–10 speaks of believers testifying before governing authorities throughout the world.
21 A.Y. Collins, *Mark* (Hermeneia; Minneapolis: Fortress, 2007), 606.
22 See R.H. Gundry, *Mark: A Commentary on His Apology for the Cross* (Grand Rapids: Eerdmans, 1993), 768; Evans, *Mark 8:27–16:20*, 310.
23 On the Jewish and Greco-Roman background of εὐαγγέλιον as a proclamation of the good news of God's victory to Israel in exile and of imperial good news, see especially

the Kingdom received with repentance and faith (Mark 1:14–15), for which the disciples must "lose" their lives to experience salvation and reward (Mark 8:35; 10:29). This message must be proclaimed to all nations (14:9, cf. 16:15). "Must" (δεῖ) indicates that the command a divine imperative as in other instances in Mark's account of Jesus (Mark 8:31; 9:11; 13:7, 14, cf. 9:11; 14:31).

"First" (πρῶτος) can indicate either priority or sequence. If priority (cf. Mark 6:21; 9:35, 44; 10:31; 12:28, 29), it means that the preaching of the gospel to all nations is the *first priority* for the disciples and readers of Mark.[24] Alternatively, πρῶτος can speak sequentially of the gospel being preached to all nations before other events come to pass (Mark 3:27; 4:28; 7:27; 9:11, 12; 12:20; 14:12, cf. Mark 16:9). In favor of *priority* is the absence of any "then" statement. However, Matthew's reading of this verse is sequential, adding "and *then* the end will come." Matthew draws out what is implicit in Mark 13:6–13: "the end is *not yet*" (v. 7); "the *beginning* of birth pains" (v. 8); "the gospel must *first* be preached to all nations" (v. 10); and "you will hated by all for my name's sake but the one who endures *to the end* will be saved" (v. 13).[25] As such, it is best read sequentially—before the end will come, first the gospel must be proclaimed through the nations of the world.

"All nations" is πάντα τὰ ἔθνη. In early Greek thought ἔθνος had a range of meanings and developed to mean a "nation, people" (e.g. Herodotus, *Hist.* 1.101; 9.106). In Rome it was used of the provinces (e.g. Appian, *Bell. civ.* 1.2.1). It could also be used of a class of people, caste, or tribe (Plato, 776d), priestly orders (*OGIS* 90.17), trade associations, or class, rank or status (Plato, *Rep.* 420b). In later Greek it was used of "foreign, barbarous nations" as opposed to the Greeks (e.g. Aristotle, *Pol.* 1324ᵇ10).[26] "Thus ἔθνος received a slightly unfavorable connotation and moved in the direction of βάρβαροι" (Barbarians).[27] The LXX usually translates *'am* with λαός and *gôy* with ἔθνος. Λαός normally stands for the elect people whereas ἔθνη for the "Gentiles" indicating that ἔθνος was determined by Israel's self-understanding as God's chosen people as opposed to the nations or Gentiles.

Mark uses ἔθνος six times in a Jewish manner of Gentiles as opposed to Jews (Mark 10:33, 42; 11:7), and once generally of nations at war (Mark 13:8). Here

---

G. Friedrich, "εὐαγγελίζομαι, εὐαγγέλιον, προευαγγελίζομαι, εὐαγγελιστής," in *TDNT*, 2:707–737.

24 R.G. Bratcher and E.A. Nida, *A Handbook on the Gospel of Mark* (UBSHS; New York: UBS, 1993), 402.
25 Similarly Evans, *Mark 8:27–16:20*, 310.
26 LSJ, 480.
27 N. Walter, "ἔθνος," in *EDNT*, 1:382.

it either means, "all the Gentile nations," or "all the world's nations including Israel." Likely it is the latter; Mark indicating the nations including Israel (the subject of Jesus's preaching in Mark) will receive the gospel.[28]

The adjective πᾶς indicates "*all*" nations. Some take πάντα τὰ ἔθνη as hyperbole, referring to the "somewhat limited geographical perspective: the Roman Empire and the peoples just beyond its borders."[29] France takes an even narrower perspective, reading Mark 13 as limited to the fall of Jerusalem.[30] However, to limit it thus is unlikely and unnecessary. As we will argue below, however we interpret the preaching of the gospel to all nations, the idea that the gospel was preached in every known nation of the ancient world by the writing of Mark by 70 C.E. is simply not plausible.

Rather, it should be defined by the Jewish and prevailing Roman understanding of the known world which is far greater than the Roman Empire, encompassing large portions of Europe, Africa, across to China and India, and extensive parts of Russia (below).[31] It thus really means, "all the nations that there are." As such, Mark in 13:10 is stating that the gospel of the Kingdom *must* be preached to all the nations that there are.[32]

In that the Fall of Jerusalem came in 70 C.E., at best the gospel had penetrated only as far west from Israel as Greece, Asia Minor, Rome, and perhaps Spain (Acts 13–28; Rom 1:15; 2 Tim 1:17, cf. Rom 15:24, 28).[33] South, it had reached into some areas of North Africa (Acts 2:10; 8:26–39).[34] It had possibly reached into Arabia by Pentecost pilgrims and Paul (see further below, Acts 2:11; Gal 1:17;

---

28 See K.L. Schmidt, "ἔθνος," in *TDNT*, 3:369.

29 Evans, *Mark 8:27–16:20*, 310.

30 R.T. France, *The Gospel of Mark* (NIGTC; Grand Rapids: Eerdmans, 2002), 498–505. See also Wright, *Jesus and the Victory*, 339–366 who ignores Mark 13:10 in his analysis. For critique, see D.A. Carson, "Matthew," in *The Expositor's Bible Commentary Vol. 8* (ed. F.E. Gaebelein and J.D. Douglas; Grand Rapids: Zondervan, 1984), 492–494; Gundry, *Mark*, 768.

31 E.J. Schnabel, *Early Christian Mission* (2 vols; Downers Grove, IL: IVP, 2004), 1:345 sees a broader scope stating, "is not … limited to the Roman Empire but extends from Scythia to Ethiopia, from Spain to possibly India." This is promising but is still inadequate (below).

32 Schnabel, *Mission*, 1.345. Cranfield, *Mark*, 399, notes this "does not mean that the world will necessarily get steadily more Christian or that the end will not come till all men are converted."

33 On Paul in Spain, see O.F.A. Meinardus, "Paul's Missionary Journey to Spain: Tradition and Folklore," *BA* (1978): 61–63. With Schnabel, *Mission*, 1:1271–283, I am unconvinced that Paul ever reached Spain; rather, he likely went east to Philippi and other churches in Greece and Asia (see Keown, *Philippians*, forthcoming).

34 R.H. Smith, "Ethiopia (Place)," in *ABD*, 2:665: "Ethiopia included modern Sudan and Ethiopia (Abyssinia)."

4:25) and perhaps further by other unspecified preachers. The gospel was certainly not fully established in or beyond the Roman regions, and large parts of what we call Asia, Europe, and Africa were barely, if at all, touched.

It is unclear whether Mark's Jesus envisages the gospel being preached to every individual of every nation, preached once in some part of the nation, preached so that the governing authorities have taken note of it,[35] preached so that some had responded and representatives had travelled to Jerusalem,[36] or preached to the point that there are established Christian churches who are engaged in mission across it. The latter would seem most likely as the vision of the missionaries of the NT was not merely individual salvation, but the establishment of churches. Jesus's own ministry in Israel described in Mark 1–12 helps us understand that the gospel is preached to a nation. He has preached in Aramaic[37] through all the towns and villages of Israel (Mark 1:38–39; 6:6, 56; 8:27). The community he established then preached the gospel through Jerusalem, Judea, and Samaria subsequent to his resurrection embedding the gospel in the first nation (cf. Acts 1:1–8:4). Now it must go to all nations in the same way. So, at the least, it means that the gospel is embedded in communities of Christ's followers and these Christians are spreading the gospel in its region.

Marcus claims that Mark, "as a member of the Pauline Mission ... probably thinks that this eschatological prerequisite of world wide evangelization is nearly completed (cf. Rom 15:23–24; Col 1:23) and therefore the end is imminent."[38] However, neither of the verses referenced indicate Paul or Mark considered that the evangelization of the world was near completion. Romans 15:23–24 speaks of Paul's *desire* to go to Spain and says nothing about the completion of worldwide evangelization. We don't know if he even got there. Further, Rom 15:20–21 implies the *converse* of Marcus's claim with Paul wanting to go where Christ has *not* been proclaimed at all. I will discuss Col 1:23 below. Suffice to say here that this verse is not an expression of the completion of world evangelization (further below).

For Mark then, the gospel *must* first be preached to all the nations of God's world. This recalls v. 7, "but the end is *not yet*" and anticipates v. 13, "the one who endures to *the end* ..." Matthew 24:14 more explicitly adapts and connects

---

35   R.L. Cooper, *Mark* (HNTC 2; Nashville, TN: Broadman & Holman, 2000), 218.
36   R.D. Aus, "Paul's Travel Plans to Spain and the 'Full Number of the Gentiles' of Rom. XI 25," *NovT* 21 (1979): 232–262. See for critique Schnabel, *Mission*, 2:1295–1297.
37   *The Eerdmans Bible Dictionary* (ed. Allen C. Myers; Grand Rapids: Eerdmans, 1987), 72.
38   J. Marcus, *Mark 1–18* (AB 27; New York: Doubleday, 2000), 73–75. Similarly, M.E. Boring, *Mark* (Louisville: Westminster John Knox, 2006), 384: Mark 13:10 is "a declaration about the church's world wide proclamation of the gospel *in his own time.*"

Mark 13:10 to the end of the age rendering it, "And this gospel of the kingdom will be proclaimed throughout *the whole world* as a testimony to *all nations*, and *then the end* will come." Thus, before the end, for Mark and Matthew, the gospel *must* be proclaimed to every nation of the world.[39] Schnabel rightly cautions against drawing the end too tightly together with the completion of the mission, noting that Jesus does not in Mark explicitly state that the end comes *as soon as* all nations receive the gospel.[40] Accepting the caution, the two seem to be linked in the minds of Mark and especially Matthew.

1.1.2 Mark 13:27

Mark's vision of cosmic mission is seen again in Mark 13:27 where Mark's Jesus envisages a day when he will send his angels to gather God's elect, "from the four winds, from the ends of the earth to the ends of the heaven." This picks up the LXX of Zech 2:6 (2:10 MT) in particular (cf. Deut 30:4; 13:8) and applies it to Christian believers. The "angels" here can be taken supernaturally of heavenly angels gathering in the elect (cf. Mark 1:13; 8:38; 12:25; 13:32), or as gospel messengers (cf. Mark 1:2) going in every direction preaching and so gathering God's people.[41] The parallel to Mark 8:38 where the Son of Man "comes in the glory of his Father with the holy angels" and "angels in heaven" in v. 32 strongly suggest the former is to be preferred.[42]

"The four winds" are the four points of the compass:[43] north, south, east, and west.[44] The previous clause indicates that the ends of the earth cannot be limited to any single place (e.g. Spain), but the zenith of the world in *every* direction.[45] To "the ends of the heaven" emphasizes the totality of this

---

39 In Luke "the times of the Gentiles are fulfilled" in Luke 21:24 speaks of a similar notion; the Lukan Commission (Luke 24:47) refers to *proclamation* of "repentance and forgiveness of sins" to "*all nations*, beginning from Jerusalem." Similarly, Acts 1:8 speaks of witness "to the ends of the earth."

40 Schnabel, *Mission*, 1.346.

41 R.T. France, *Jesus and the Old Testament* (London: Tyndale, 1971), 238.

42 France, *Mark*, 536 notes he changed his mind on this on the basis of Mark 8:37.

43 E.g. William Hendriksen, *Exposition of the Gospel According to Mark* (NTC 10; Grand Rapids: Baker, 1953), 537; John R. Donahue and Daniel J. Harrington, *The Gospel of Mark* (SP 2; Collegeville, MN: Liturgical, 2002), 375.

44 The four points of the compass. On God gathering his people from a four-"cornered" earth, see: Ezek 7:2; 38:15; Isa 11:12; 24:16; Job 37:3; 38:13; Matt 24:31; Rev 7:1 (H. Sasse, "γῆ," in *TDNT*, 1:679).

45 For "ends of the earth," see Deut 13:7; 28:49, 64; 33:17; 1Sam 2:10; Job 28:24; Pss 2:8; 22:27; 46:9; 48:10; 59:13; 61:2; 65:5, 8; 67:7; 72:8; 98:3; 135:7; Prov 17:24; 30:4; Isa 5:26; 24:16; 40:28;

gathering from every part of God's world where people are found.[46] The three clauses form an emphatic construct highlighting the entire inhabited world at the point of Christ's return.[47] With Mark 13:10 in mind, this verse speaks of the return of Christ when God gathers those who have responded by repentance and faith to the gospel (1:15) from the world's many nations.[48] Mark 13:37 thus reinforces that the gospel will be preached across all the nations of the world before the end of the age.

It is noticeable that there is no time frame set in place and believers are told that the specific time is unknown even by Jesus and the angels (Mark 13:32). Clearly, specific speculation is unfruitful, as history painfully shows. However, it will be preceded by a time of suffering (θλῖψις) followed by (μετά) a series of cosmic signs including a darkened sun and moon, falling stars, and a shaking of the heavenly powers. "That tribulation" refers to the events in Mark 13:5–23 or 13:14–23.[49] It was common to use θλῖψις in Jewish prophetic and apocalyptic material of great suffering.[50] The astral signs are drawn from particularly from Isaiah 13:10 and 34:4. Both Isaianic references refer to forthcoming judgment on the nations; first, Babylon (Isa 13:10); and second, *all the nations* (Isa 34:4). While some limit this to the fall of Jerusalem,[51] more likely it is apocalyptic language to describe the theophany which culminates history. As Edwards puts it, "[o]bviously, this is not a description of the fall of Jerusalem or any other historical cataclysm, but a metahistorical event that includes history but subsumes and supersedes history."[52] With that said, this language should not be

---

41:5, 9; 42:10; 43:6; 45:22; 48:20; 49:6; 52:10; 62:11; Jer 10:13; 16:19; 25:31, 33; 51:16; Dan 4:22; Mic 5:4; Zech 9:10; Matt 12:42; Luke 11:31; Acts 1:8; 13:47. Associated with the hope around the Messiah (e.g. Ps 2:8; Mic 5:4) and Servant (e.g. Isa 42:10; 49:6). Often it has the sense of the very extent of the nations of the earth.

46 Deut 4:32; 30:4; Ps 19:6; Isa 13:5.
47 Evans, *Mark 8:27–16:20*, 330; France, *Mark*, 536: "This is the fulfilment of the vision of v. 10, that the εὐαγγέλιον will be proclaimed to all nations," cf. H. Traub, "οὐρανός," in *TDNT*, 5:516–517.
48 Edwards, *Mark*, 48.
49 E.g. Evans, *Mark 8:27–16:20*, 327.
50 E.g. Isa 8:22; Jer 6:24; Zeph 1:15; Mic 2:12; Hos 7:12; Obad 12, 14; Nah 1:7; Hab 3:16; Dan 12:1; 1 Macc 9:27; 4 Ezra 5:1–2; 1 En. 18:2; 2 Bar. 25.
51 France, *Jesus and the Old Testament*, 231–233; T.R. Hatina, "The Focus of Mark 13:24–27: The Parousia, or the Destruction of the Temple?" *BBR* 6 (1996): 43–66; B.M.F. van Iersel, "The Sun, Moon, and Stars of Mark 13, 24–25 in a Greco-Roman Reading," *Bib* 77 (1996): 84–92.
52 Edwards, *Mark*, 402.

read over-literally, as this kind of language is found across OT prophetic and Jewish apocalyptic material and speaks figuratively of great disaster.[53]

However we take it, "then" (τότε) the Son of Man will come in the clouds with great power and glory. While some see this as Jesus's enthronement rather than return, most likely it draws on Dan 7:13–14 and speaks of Jesus's return.[54] Clearly, Mark 13:37 confirms what is found in Mark 13:10; namely, the cosmic scope of God's mission in the interim between Jesus's ascension and return.

1.1.3 Mark 14:9

The cosmic scope of the mission is again found in Mark 14:9 where Mark's Jesus speaking of the woman who anointed him: "And truly, I say to you, wherever the gospel is proclaimed *in the whole world*, what she has done will be told in memory of her." Some suggest here a later gloss.[55] However, as with Mark 13:10 this lacks textual evidence. Likely, it is an original saying of Jesus,[56] and certainly a saying of Mark's Jesus. Here the scope is "in the whole world" (εἰς ὅλον τὸν κόσμον).[57] As with Mark 13:10 and 13:27 this should not be

---

[53] On darkened astral bodies, see Isa 13:10, 13; Ezek 32:7–8; Joel 2:10, 31; 3:15; Amos 8:9; Eccl 12:2; 2 Esd 5:5; 7:39; Dan 8:10; LAE 46.1; T. Mos. 10:4–5; Sib. Or. 3:796–803; T. Levi 4:1, cf. Isa 24:23. On heaven and earth shaken, see: Judg 5:5; Amos 9:5; Mic 1:4; Hab 3:6; Nah 1:5; Pss 18:7; 114:7; Job 9:6; T. Mos. 10:1; 1 En 57:2; 4 Ezra 5:1–2; As. Mos. 10:5; 1 En. 80:2; Sib. Or. 3:796–797; 2 Bar. 25. For a full discussion of the signs attending the coming of the Messiah, see Str-B 4/2.977-1, 015.

[54] Evans, *Mark 8:27–16:20*, 329.

[55] E.g. R. Bultmann, *The History of the Synoptic Tradition* (trans. J. Marsh; rev. ed.; Oxford: Blackwell; New York: Harper & Row, 1963), 36–37; Z. Kato, *Die Völkermission im Markusevangelium* (EHS 23.252; Frankfurt am Main: Lang, 1986), 155–159; J. Gnilka, *Das Evangelium nach Markus* (2 vols.; EKKNT 2.1–2; Zürich: Benzinger; Neukirchen-Vluyn: Neukirchener Verlag, 1978), 2:225; S.E. Johnson, *A Commentary on the Gospel According to St. Mark* (BNTC; London: A. & C. Black, 1972), 224; E. Schweizer, *The Good News according to Mark* (Richmond, VA: John Knox, 1970), 290; M.D. Hooker, *The Gospel According to Saint Mark* (BNTC; London: A. & C. Black, 1991), 330.

[56] Evans, *Mark*, 2:362; J.V. Bartlet, *St Mark* (NCB; New York: Oxford University Press, 1922), 375; A.E.J. Rawlinson, *St Mark* (6th ed.; London: Methuen, 1947), 198; A.W.F. Blunt, *The Gospel According to Saint Mark* (CB; Oxford: Clarendon, 1939), 247; Lane, *Mark*, 494–495; Taylor, *Mark*, 534; Cranfield, *Mark*, 417–418; R.P. Martin, *Mark: Evangelist and Theologian* (Exeter: Paternoster; Grand Rapids: Zondervan, 1972), 202.

[57] J. Jeremias, "Markus 14,9," ZNW 44 (1952–1953): 103–107 suggests angels proclaiming judgement, not the church. Pesch, *Mark*, 2:335–336 suggests angels remembering the woman before God. For critique, see Schnabel, *Mission*, 1:347. On ὅλον τὸν κόσμον, see Wis 11:22; 17:19; 18:24; 2 Macc 3:12; 8:19; Matt 16:26; 26:13; Mark 8:36; Luke 9:25; Rom 3:19; Col 1:6; 1 John 2:2; 5:19 in which Nero is the "Lord of the whole world" (*Ditt. Syll.*³ 814.31; cf. *Ditt. Or.* 458.40).

reduced.[58] As Schnabel says, "Jesus speaks again of an international worldwide proclamation of the good news at the beginning of the passion story."[59]

In Mark then, we have three verses which clearly indicate the cosmic scope of the gospel mission Jesus's disciples are to engage in. The three descriptions in these verses—"all nations," "the four winds," "from the ends of the earth to the ends of heaven," and "the whole world"—are parallel and speak of the same reality—the gospel will be preached in every part of God's world where people are found. At the least, this will include all areas known to the first-century followers of Jesus (see further below). If people existed in lands beyond the knowledge of the first Christians, it would also include these.

1.2 Paul

Paul has nothing quite equivalent to the Commissions of the Synoptic Gospels. However, there are clear indications that he understood the scope of the mission was to the whole inhabited earth.

In Rom 1:5 Paul speaks of preachers ("we")[60] having received "grace and apostleship to bring the obedience of faith for the sake of his name amongst *all the Gentiles*" (ἐν πᾶσιν τοῖς ἔθνεσιν).[61] Taken straightforwardly, Paul's vision is that believers from *every nation* will respond to the gospel with the obedience that springs from faith.[62] Dunn writes that this clause "reminds us that Paul seriously contemplated this outreach being achieved within his own lifetime."[63] This is patently flawed. First, Paul also states in Rom 15:19a that he had completed the ministry of the gospel *only* along the north-east Mediterranean from Jerusalem to Illyricum in western Greece.[64] Yet, Paul

---

58 R.E. Brown, *The Gospel According to John I–XII: A New Translation with Introduction and Commentary* (AB 29; New York: Doubleday), 453, sees here and at John 12:2 a possible allusion to Midr. Rab. on Sir 7:1 comparing the spread of a good name "from one end of the world to another" to the spread of the fragrance of perfume from bedroom to dining room.

59 Schnabel, *Mission*, 1:347.

60 Morris, *Romans*, 48: an epistolary plural. More likely, as J.D.G. Dunn, *Romans 1–8* (WBC 38A; Dallas: Word, 1998), 16, says, the apostles. Likely it also includes the others in the Pauline team and any others who proclaim the true gospel.

61 Dunn, *Romans 1–8*, 18, considers this should be rendered Gentiles rather than nations. The difference is minimal.

62 Morris, *Romans*, 51 notes "[i]t may perhaps indicate the largeness of his vision." On the "obedience that springs from faith," see BDAG, 1028; J. Cottrell, *Romans: Volume 1* (CPNIVC; Joplin, MO: College Press, 1996), 5.

63 Dunn, *Romans 1–8*, 18.

64 Schnabel, *Mission*, 2:1295.

considered himself obligated to *all Gentiles*, Barbarians included, and no doubt was fully aware that there were enormous swathes of known inhabited land in the world (see Rom 1:15, below). In these regions Paul (or other preachers) would need to learn new languages and cultures, cross land and sea into dangerous territory, and find fresh points of connection. Part of this area was Spain, which has not heard the gospel, and Paul hoped to reach there (Rom 15:20–21, 24, 28). Paul at this stage was likely in his fifties and had weathered a huge amount of suffering (esp. 2 Cor 11:26–31) making it unlikely he had too many years of active ministry left.[65] As such, there is nothing to indicate Paul expected to complete the mission to the Gentiles in this verse or any other.[66]

In Rom 1:8, Paul speaks of the faith of the Roman church being "proclaimed in *all the world*" (ἐν ὅλῳ τῷ κόσμῳ). This is taken by most commentators tightly with the passive voice verb (καταγγέλλεται), the faith of the Romans reported by *other* Christians.[67] However, the agency is not clear and may indicate, at least *in part*, Roman self-involvement in evangelization (cf. Phil 1:14–18a).[68] Whether or not this is the case, most agree that Paul is speaking hyperbolically and so this does not indicate that Paul considered the gospel mission had been completed.[69]

Paul also speaks of the cosmic scope of his mission when he expresses his desire to come to Rome to gather a harvest among the Romans "as among *the rest of the Gentiles*" (ἐν τοῖς λοιποῖς ἔθνεσιν) (Rom 1:13). "The rest of the Gentiles" is shorthand for "the Gentiles I have already preached among" and is defined

---

65 By this point Paul had walked 8–10,000 miles; so E.J. Schnabel, *Paul the Missionary: Realities, Strategies and Methods* (Downers Grove, IL: IVP Academic, 2008), 121. Any further travel by was challenging for an aging man.

66 Rom 16:26 also speaks of the gospel "having been made known (γνωρισθέντος) to all nations." However, this may be a later insertion (see Metzger, *Textual Commentary*, 470–471). There are also many other indications in Romans that the gospel mission is incomplete (e.g. Rom 1:5–15; 15:19–28). If authentic, this is speaking of the present revelation of the gospel which continues, not its completion. It forms an inclusio with 1:5.

67 E.g. Morris, *Romans*, 56; Robert H. Mounce, *Romans* (NAC 27; Nashville: Broadman & Holman, 1995), 65.

68 See M.J. Keown, *Congregational Evangelism in Philippians* (Milton Keynes, UK: Paternoster, 2008), 74–75 n. 23.

69 E.g. Mounce, *Romans*, 56; Dunn, *Romans 1–8*, 28; B. Witherington III and D. Hyatt, *Paul's Letter to the Romans: A Socio-Rhetorical Commentary* (Grand Rapids: Eerdmans, 2004), 42; T.R. Schreiner, *Romans* (BECNT 6; Grand Rapids: Baker Books, 1998), 49; D.J. Moo, *The Epistle to the Romans* (NICNT; Grand Rapids: Eerdmans, 1996), 57.

by Romans 15:19a;[70] those in the short arc from Jerusalem to Illyricum in western Greece.[71] This is a small part of the ancient world. He still wants to go to Spain and is indebted to all.[72] This is clear in the next verse where he refers to his obligation to preach to "Greeks and Barbarians" (Ἕλλησίν τε καὶ βαρβάροις) (Rom 1:14). This combination of terms effectively means "all the Gentiles."[73] "Greeks" here means those who have embraced the Hellenistic mindset and life including the Romans whose love and adoption of Greek culture was strong. "Barbarians" does not here carry its common Roman negative connotations,[74] but indicates the many Gentile peoples beyond the Roman Empire. In that Paul has hardly ventured at all among the Barbarians and had many left to evangelize in the Empire to the west of Italy to Spain and beyond, the mission likely has many years left beyond his own life to be anywhere near complete.

Rom 11:25 speaks of τὸ πλήρωμα τῶν ἐθνῶν, "the *fullness of the Gentiles*" coming into God's people before the consummation. While some interpret the clause in ingenious ways,[75] it likely refers to God's understanding of the full number of Gentiles believing,[76] i.e. the completion of the Gentile mission. While this lacks an explicit link to the consummation as in Matt 24:14, it is suggestive that Paul held this link. Aus and Riesner limit this to Paul completing

---

70 Dunn, *Romans 1–8*, 32, correctly: "particularly the congregations established by him in Asia, Macedonia, and Greece."

71 Morris, *Romans*, 62, correctly: "we need not take it to mean that he had worked among all the other Gentiles without exception."

72 Cottrell, *Romans*, 1:13, incorrectly states: "[b]y the time Paul wrote Romans he had preached the gospel to a large portion of the Gentile world." As we will note below, he had only preached in a small portion of the Gentile world.

73 Dunn, *Romans 1–8*, 33: "a standard phrase to include all races and classes within the Gentile world." See also C.E.B. Cranfield, *Romans* (2 vols.; ICC; Edinburgh: T&T Clark, 1975, 1979), 1:83: "the sum of Gentile mankind;" Schnabel, *Mission*, 2:970: "to proclaim the gospel to all people without any distinction." Morris, *Romans*, 63 suggests this may include Jews. However, this is unlikely as it would mean Jews are either Greeks or Barbarians which is unlikely (similarly, Schreiner, *Romans*, 55).

74 See further H. Windisch, "βάρβαρος," in *TDNT*, 1:546–549.

75 Morris, *Romans*, 420: it can also mean "the fullness of the blessing of the Gentiles" (e.g. J. Cottrell, *Romans: Volume 2* [CPNIVC; Joplin, MO: College Press, 1996], 11:25), the "full contribution of the Gentiles," or "the Gentiles as a whole." J.D.G. Dunn, *Romans 9–16* (WBC 38B; Dallas: Word, 1998), 680 sees πλήρωμα as equivalent (not exactly) to those of Israel in 11:12, cf. the 144,000 of Revelation.

76 Mounce, *Romans*, 224; Schreiner, *Romans*, 621; Moo, *Romans*, 719; R.C.H. Lenski, *The Interpretation of St. Paul's Epistle to the Romans* (Minneapolis: Augsburg, 1936), 727; William Hendriksen, *Exposition of Paul's Epistle to the Romans* (NTC 12–13; Grand Rapids: Baker, 1953), 224.

the arc from Jerusalem to Spain associating Spain with Tarshish in Isa 66:19.[77] However, this is limiting Paul's vision of "every nation" to northern rim of the Mediterranean, which is unjustified.

In Gal 2:7–9, a mission to all humanity is reflected in the assigning of the mission to the circumcised to Peter and the uncircumcised to Paul. Paul's theology of Abraham draws on Genesis and the promise that all the nations will be blessed through Abraham's seed (Gal 3:8; Gen 12:3; 18:18; 22:18; 26:4). For Paul, this seed is Jesus (Gal 3:16) and so implies that the gospel of Jesus will in some way penetrate all the nations of the earth, i.e., "in Christ Jesus the blessing of Abraham might come to *the nations*" (Gal 3:14, cf. Rom 4:13, 17–18).[78]

Colossians 1:23 states the gospel "has been preached (τοῦ κηρυχθέντος) in all creation under heaven (ἐν πάσῃ κτίσει τῇ ὑπὸ τὸν οὐρανόν)." While this could be read to indicate the completion of the gospel mission; it clearly does not;[79] in Colossians the mission is continuing and incomplete. To begin with, the use of the aorist does not necessarily imply something past and complete. As Porter states, *"the temporal reference of a participle is established relative to its use in context."*[80] There are clear indicators in the context of Colossians that Paul is not here necessarily speaking hyperbolically or referring to something complete. In Col 1:5–6 Paul writes that the gospel is bearing fruit and growing (imperfective aspect: καρποφορούμενον καὶ αὐξανόμενον) in the whole world (ἐν παντὶ τῷ κόσμῳ). This clearly implies an incomplete and continuing mission. In addition, Paul indicates that is own mission of proclamation and suffering is present and ongoing (Col 1:24¬25, 29; 2:1; 4:2, 4). His mission goal that all people come to full Christian maturity is clearly ongoing (Col 1:28). Further, his prayer request in 4:2–4 for fresh doors for the gospel and clarity of proclamation indicates ongoing mission. Paul also refers to the Colossians' ongoing mission in

---

77 Aus, "Paul's Travel Plans," 232–262, argues Paul believed his mission was complete when he brought Spaniards to Jerusalem fulfilling Isaiah's prophecy that "all flesh" worshiping God (Isa 66:23). See also R. Riesner, *Paul's Early Period: Chronology, Mission Strategy, Theology* (Grand Rapids: Eerdmans, 1998), 245–253. See for critique Schnabel, *Mission*, 2:1295–297.

78 Paul's reconciliation theology is also cosmic (Rom 11:15; 2 Cor 5:19; Eph 1:10). Similarly, cosmic submission in Phil 2:10–11 recalls Isa 45:22–23 and speaks of God's message penetrating all humanity. See also Rom 10:18; 16:26; 1 Tim 2:6; 3:16.

79 See for differing perspectives P.T. O'Brien, *Colossians, Philemon* (WBC 44; Dallas: Word, 1998), 71; F.F. Bruce, *The Epistles to the Colossians, to Philemon, and to the Ephesians* (NICNT; Grand Rapids: Eerdmans, 1984), 79; J.D.G. Dunn, *The Epistles to the Colossians and to Philemon: A Commentary on the Greek Text* (NIGTC: Grand Rapids: Eerdmans; Carlisle: Paternoster, 1996), 112.

80 Stanley E. Porter, *Idioms of the Greek New Testament* (2nd ed.; Sheffield: JSOT Press, 1994), 188 (italics his).

urging them to act and speak wisely, graciously, winsomely, and responsively to outsiders.[81] Finally, there are indications of ongoing ministry from a range of co-workers (Col 1:7–8, 4:7–17).

The factors noted above indicate that Paul (or the non-Pauline writer of Colossians) considered that the mission should reach through the whole world and that it was incomplete and ongoing. If this is Paul, he is likely in Rome in the early 60s[82] and near the end of his life, yet the mission is far from fulfilled. If it is a post-Pauline author, it is even later. It is clear that Paul's vision for the gospel included its preaching in the whole world, and this was ongoing, growing, and far from complete.

Some limit the scope of Paul's viewpoint to Spain,[83] the region of Japheth (Gen 10:2–5),[84] and others to the Roman Empire only. However, as shown above, Paul's perspective includes Barbarians (Rom 1:15), Scythians (Col 3:11), and generally "the Gentiles," i.e. the entire human race (above). This wider concern is indicated in his early mission to Arabia (above).[85] Paul's vision was for the ultimate evangelization of all Gentile nations. It is "hardly plausible Paul alone regarded the fulfillment of the missionary commission of the risen Lord to go from Jerusalem to the ends of the earth as his personal task."[86]

---

81   On this verse, see my essay in the next volume in this series, "Paul's Vision of Evangelization and the Church: Taking the Debate Forward," in *Christian Origins and the Formation of the Early Church*, ed. Stanley E. Porter and Andrew W. Pitts, TENTS; ECHC 5 (Leiden: Brill, forthcoming).

82   Bruce, *Colossians*, 193–196; O'Brien, *Colossians*, xlix–liv. Otherwise Ephesus in 52–55 C.E. or 54–57 C.E.

83   Aus, "Paul's Travel Plans," 232–262; Riesner, *Paul's Early Period*, 245–253. Dunn, *Romans 9–16*, 864 argues Paul did the northern half of a circle with others the southern (Egypt, Alexandria, North Africa). This lacks evidence.

84   J.M. Scott, "Luke's Geographical Horizon," in *The Book of Acts in its Greco-Roman Setting* (ed. D.W.J. Gill and C. Gempf; The Book of Acts in its First-Century Setting 2; Exeter: Paternoster, 1994), 522–544; J.M. Scott, *Paul and the Nations: The Old Testament and Early Jewish Background of Paul's Mission to the Nations with Special Reference to the Destination of Galatians* (WUNT 84; Tübingen: Mohr-Siebeck, 1995), 135–180. See Schnabel, *Mission*, 2:1298–1299 for critique.

85   Schnabel, *Mission*, 2:1296 rightly notes Paul never hints at plans for mission work in the well-known regions of Moesia, Scythia, Gaul, or Germania (or North Africa, or east of Arabia for that matter).

86   Schnabel, *Mission*, 2:1296.

2 The Speed and Extent of the Initial Phase of Mission

I will now consider the manner of the initial spread of the gospel noting that the speed and spread of the gospel makes it unlikely that Mark, Paul, and other thinking first generation Christians thought the evangelization of the nations would be a quick process. This makes the expectation of an imminent Parousia unlikely. Our knowledge of the spread of Christianity in the first phase is drawn from Acts and the Epistles along with snippets from tradition.

2.1 Acts

Acts gives some detail on the potential spread of the gospel from Pentecost (Acts 2:8–11), the evangelization of Israel (Acts 1–11), Syria (Acts 9:29; 11:19–26), Cyprus (Acts 13), Asia (Acts 13–14, 19), Greece (Acts 16–17, 20), and Rome (Acts 28). Much of this was led by Paul with others (Acts 9, 13–28). The list of Pentecost pilgrims suggests the gospel may have been shared by converts to the region of modern Iran or that of the Parthians (Parthians, Medes, Elamites, Mesopotamia), Syria (Judea),[87] Asia Minor or Turkey (Cappadocia, Pontus, Asia, Phrygia, Pamphylia), North Africa (Egypt, Cyrenian Libya), and Rome. Bock rightly notes that "the locales [mentioned at Pentecost] likely indicate the scope of the Jewish Diaspora settlement."[88]

Unlike Acts 8:4, there is no indication given that these pilgrims went out with an evangelistic mindset. Further, if they did so, this occurred *before* the conversion of Cornelius, the Antiochian mission and the Jerusalem Council (Acts 10–11; 15). It is likely, then, any mission was Jewish in flavor and focused on Diaspora Jews. If any new Gentiles were converted, they were likely initiated into the church not only by faith and baptism but with the taking on of key Jewish cultural boundary markers, especially circumcision. In that Luke implies that the intentional Gentile mission began with the Cornelius's family (Acts 10–11) and then in Antioch by those scattered in the Sauline persecution (Acts 8:4; 11:19–21), it is questionable that there was any initial intentional evangelistic mission beyond God-fearers and proselytes to evangelize Greeks. Notably, Paul visits Asia Minor and engages in mission suggesting that he does not consider the region evangelized despite Luke's account of Pentecost (Acts 19). It is unlikely, then, that we should consider that regions reached by Pentecost pilgrims were believed by Paul to be fully evangelized.

---

87 M. Hengel, "Paul in Arabia," *BBR* 12 (2002): 47–66 considers "Judea" here is likely "larger Syria," including the whole region.

88 D.L. Bock, *Acts* (BECNT; Grand Rapids: Baker Academic, 2007), 103.

2.2 Paul and Other New Testament Writings

Looking beyond Acts, Paul's letters indicate ministry in Arabia (likely Nabataea, Gal 1:17),[89] Syria, and Galatia (Gal 1:21, cf. Acts 9:30; 11:25–26). Romans 15:19a speaks of the completion of Paul's work along the northwestern rim of the Mediterranean from Jerusalem to western Greece. From this, we can surmise that Paul had completed to his own satisfaction the planting of churches in the main centers across this region. He thus felt free to move further west. If we date the beginning of Paul's ministry in this region from 31/32 C.E.[90] and Romans in 57 C.E.,[91] it has taken Paul twenty-five or so years to complete this work to his satisfaction. It is unclear whether Paul considers *the whole work of the gospel* complete or whether he envisaged a period of ongoing evangelization from others and his churches.[92] It is likely that Paul did not mean that *all gospel ministry* in the region was complete; rather, *his* gospel ministry was complete with the gospel founded (1 Cor 3:10–11; Eph 2:20). This meant that gatherings of believers were established and from these bases the gospel could spread (cf. 1 Thess 1:8;[93] Acts 13:48; 19:10).[94]

Paul expresses his intention to move west to Spain in Rom 15:24, 28. It is unclear whether he intended to travel by foot or ship. If by foot, he would likely have traveled north through Italy from Rome, through southern Gaul, and onto the Iberian Peninsula. If by ship, he may have intended to visit the islands of Sardinia or Corsica as he did Cyprus on his first missionary journey (Acts 13). Whichever of these he had in mind, he clearly considers Spain unevangelized in 57 C.E. He still has to travel to Jerusalem with the Collection (Rom 15:24–32) meaning it will be sometime before he returns via Rome, if at all. As noted above, it is uncertain whether Paul he ever made it to Spain.

---

[89] See F.F. Bruce, *Paul: Apostle of the Free Spirit* (Milton Keynes, UK: Paternoster, 1977), 81–82; Schnabel, *Mission*, 2:1032–1045.

[90] Schnabel, *Mission*, 1031.

[91] E.g. Moo, *Romans*, 3.

[92] See W.P. Bowers, "Fulfilling the Gospel: The Scope of the Pauline Mission," *JETS* 30 (1987): 185–198 who limits this to the establishment of churches in main centers. However, it likely also refers to these churches continuing the gospel mission in their region (so Dunn, *Romans 9–16*, 864; P.T. O'Brien, *Consumed by Passion: Paul and the Dynamic of the Gospel* [Homebush West, NSW: Lancer/Anzea, 1993], 36–43).

[93] J.P. Ware, "The Thessalonians as a Missionary Congregation: 1 Thessalonians 1,5–8," *ZNW* 83 (1992): 126–131; Keown, *Evangelism*, 250–261.

[94] Further, see M.J. Keown, "Congregational Evangelism in Paul: The Paul of Acts," *Colloquium* 42.2 (2010): 231–251.

1 Peter gives evidence of Christian gatherings in the "Roman provinces comprising all of Asia Minor north of the Taurus mountain range."[95] If we accept Petrine authorship, these are established by the mid-60s C.E. If the letter is not from Peter, these Christian gatherings are established by the 70s to 80s. Titus confirms that there was a Cretan Christian community by the writing of that letter which is either in the mid-60s if it is Paul's letter, or in the 70s to 80s if not. Colossians, Ephesians, 2 Timothy, and Revelation 2–3 indicate that there are Christian communities in many of the cities of western Asia by the mid-late first century. However, it is doubtful that the existence of these churches indicates the completion of the mission in these regions; rather, the gospel is planted and the work of completing the work was underway.

2.3 Tradition

Beyond this biblical data, there is some tenuous evidence from later tradition. Schnabel lists traditions concerning the apostles engaging in intentional international mission.[96] Some earlier documents speak of a cosmic mission. 1 Clem. 42:1–4 (ca. 90–100 C.E.) states the apostles "went forth proclaiming the good news ... preached throughout the countryside and in the cities ..." Preaching of Peter 3a (100–120 C.E.) (Agraphon 10, in Clement of Alexandria, *Strom.* 6.5.43) records that Jewish believers will "after twelve years go out into the world." Again in Pre. Pet. 3b (Agraphon 9; in Clement of Alexandria, *Strom.* 6.648) it is recorded that the faithful apostles were sent "into the world to preach the gospel to people throughout the world ..." Finally, in the Epistle to the Apostles 30 (100–150 C.E.?), Jesus says to the apostles: "Go you and preach to the twelve tribes and preach also to the gentiles and to the whole land of Israel from sunrise to sunset and from South to North, and many will believe in the Son of God." These give evidence of an intentional cosmic mission, but says nothing of the extent or completion of the task.

Later tradition is more specific, speaking of Jesus or the Twelve dividing the world into twelve regions and each disciple engaging in mission to a specific area. For example, Acts of Pet. 5 (ca. 180–190 C.E.) suggests Peter was instructed to travel to Rome. Apollonius (ca. 200 C.E.) in Eusebius (*Hist. eccl.* 5.18.14) mentions that Jesus instructed the Twelve to remain in Jerusalem for twelve years. Acts of Thomas 1:1 (ca. 200–240 C.E.) states that the apostles "portioned out the regions of the world in order that each one of us might go into the region that fell to him by lot, and to the nation to which the Lord sent him."

---

95   J.R. Michaels, *1 Peter* (WBC 49; Dallas: Word, 1998), 9.
96   Schnabel, *Mission*, 1:527–533.

Origen (185–254 C.E.) according to Eusebius (*Hist. eccl.* 3.1.1.) noted in his Genesis Commentary (Vol. 3) that the "holy Apostles and disciples of our Savior were scattered throughout the whole world" by lot, associating Thomas with Parthia, Andrew with Scythia, John with Asia, and Peter to the dispersion of Asia and then Rome. In the Acts of Pet. 12 Apos. 1:9–20; 5:11–14 (second/third century; NHC 6.1) the apostles agreed to fulfill the ministry to which Jesus appointed them, taking ships, and notes that "it is necessary for us to spread the word of God in every city harmoniously." The Letter of Peter to Philip 134:18–26; 140:7–15, 23–27 (second/third century; NHC 7.2) notes that "the apostles parted from each other into four winds in order to preach. And they went by a power of Jesus, in peace." Didascalia Apostolorum 23 (ca. 250 C.E.) states that they "divided the world into twelve parts, and were gone out to the gentiles into all the world to preach the word." Acts of Philip (fourth century) notes that Jesus "divided the apostles according to city and country, so that each one would depart to the place that had been allotted to him." Thus Peter went to Rome, Thomas to Parthia and India, Matthew to innermost Parthia, Bartholomew to Lycaonia, Simon Cananaeus to Spain, Andrew to Achaia, John to Asia, Philip to the Greeks. As above, all speak of a cosmic mission, but do not speak of its completion. Further, these do not constitute the full range of the known world without reference to Gaul, Britain, Germany, or east to China. They do not suggest that the mission was completed by the apostles.

The *Fragments of Polycarp* a. 5–12 (third century) note that unspecified people, likely the apostles, "went out in the whole inhabited world so that each one of them might complete his course within the regions which were assigned to them, while they completed the preaching about the kingdom of heaven throughout the whole of his creation, according to the testimony of the apostles." This can be interpreted as the completion of the commission; however, more likely it refers to each completing their personal mission rather than the absolute completion of the preaching of the gospel to every nation. At best, they had established the church, but this does not indicate the completion of the mission. The Syriac Acts of John (ca. 500 C.E.) records that the apostles each "travelled to the country and the region for which he had received responsibility through the grace." This again speaks of a cosmic mission but not its completion.

Schnabel questions whether this evidence suggests that there was a mission planning conference in Jerusalem twelve years after Christ's departure (41/42 C.E.) with the apostles leaving Jerusalem at the time of Agrippa's persecution and engaging in international mission.[97] However, these traditions are

---

97 Schnabel, *Mission*, 1:530–533 on the basis of the Indian nature of the *Acts Thom.* and Rom

late and lack coherency.⁹⁸ Further, even if the apostles did engage in international evangelization such as Thomas in India,⁹⁹ their effectiveness is unclear and there is absolutely no indication that they completed the evangelization of the known (or unknown) world.

We can conclude then that there is good evidence that the early Christians understood that the gospel would go to all nations and that the apostles were prominent in this mission. However, there is little evidence that it was believed that this mission was complete in the NT or the early church.

3 The First-Century Understanding of the Extent of the Nations

The discussion to this point begs the question: "what did first-century people understand as the extent of the nations?" Of course, no analysis can decisively prove that the NT writers Mark and Paul held the same perspective as that which we discern. However, it seems reasonable to assume their worldview would coincide with that of the people of their world.¹⁰⁰

Acts and the letters give information that there was early Christian contact with people from beyond Italy, Asia Minor, and Greece including Ethiopia (Acts 2:10; 8:27, cf. 13:1), Arabia (Acts 2:11; Gal 1:17), Scythia (Col 3:11), and more generally, Barbarians (Rom 1:14, cf. Diogn. 5:1–5). Beyond this we need to consult non-biblical sources to define further the extent of the known world.

Schnabel does a thorough analysis of the geographical self-understanding in the first century.¹⁰¹ He notes that the record of Greek sea voyages (*periploi*) of the fifth century B.C.E. already indicate knowledge of Sierra Leone in West Africa, Britain, the Arabian Peninsula to Pakistan (Indus River), India, the Caspian Sea, Iceland, the Baltic Sea, the northern Indian Ocean (Erythraean Sea), the Black Sea, and the Mediterranean ("Inner Sea").¹⁰² The *Peutinger*

15:20; 1 Cor 9:5; 15:5, 7; Gal 6:13. However, this only confirms apostolic missionary activity and not gospel penetration which is unknown.
98   See Schnabel, *Mission*, 1:530 for a summary of the objections to the historical credibility of these traditions.
99   See Schnabel, *Mission*, 1:880–895 argues that the tradition stands up to scrutiny. I consider this possible, but tenuous.
100 Schnabel, *Mission*, 1:469–478. Further, Paul was well educated and well-travelled as was Mark (Phlm 24, cf. Acts 12:25; 15:37, 39; Col 4:10; 2 Tim 4:11).
101 Schnabel, *Mission*, 1:444–499.
102 Schnabel, *Mission*, 1:444–446.

Table, likely based on first-century sources, is a map from Britain to China.[103] Maps indicate a similar extent of knowledge.[104] Geographical works like Strabo (64 B.C.E.–21 C.E.) and earlier works indicate awareness of Europe to Britain, northern Asia to India, Asia (Turkey), the Persian Gulf, Assyria, Syria, Arabia, Egypt, Libya, and Mauretania. Pliny the Elder (23/24–79 C.E.) describes an area including large parts of Europe including Spain, Gaul, and Germany; the Russian Steppe area (e.g. Scythians with uncountable numbers of tribes); north Africa; and west including India, China (*Seres*), and the Malay Peninsula.[105] Josephus mentions Germany (e.g. *J.W.* 1.672), Gaul (e.g. *J.W.* 1.5, 397), Spain (e.g. *J.W.* 2.374), Libya (e.g. *J.W.* 1.99), Persia (*J.W.* 1.143), and Scythians (*J.W.* 7.90). The "ends of the earth" for Josephus in the north included the Germans and Scythians, in the west Gades in Spain (*J.W.* 2.363), in the south Ethiopia (e.g. *J.W.* 2.382), and in the east India (*J.W.* 2.385) and China (*Ant.* 1.147).[106]

Coming to the disciples, Schnabel suggests that the "nations" would at a minimum include all the peoples of the world and the "ends of the earth" would include to Ethiopia in the south, India in the east, Scythia in the north, and Spain in the west.[107] However, from the above analysis it is also likely that they knew of the "silk people" (*Seres*) of China in the east with contact known from the second century B.C.E. and a marked increase in imports in the first century B.C.E.[108] Further, they were no doubt aware of all or most of western and central Europe including at least Gaul,[109] Germany,[110] and Britain.[111] Contact with Europeans, Scythians, Africans, and Indians would no doubt have given them awareness of the great swathes of Barbarian humanity in every direction.

---

103 Schnabel, *Mission*, 1:447.
104 Schnabel, *Mission*, 1:448–452.
105 Schnabel, *Mission*, 1:452–463.
106 Schnabel, *Mission*, 1:468–469.
107 Schnabel, *Mission*, 1:470.
108 Schnabel, *Mission*, 1:495–497.
109 Rome's contact with Gaul can be dated from the third century B.C.E.; see "Gaul," in *Encyclopedia Britannica* (http://library.laidlaw.ac.nz:2114/EBchecked/topic/227066/Gaul).
110 Rome's contact with Germanic tribes can be dated from the first century B.C.E., see "Germany" in *Encyclopedia Britannica* (http://library.laidlaw.ac.nz:2114/EBchecked/topic/231186/Germany/58083/Coexistence-with-Rome-to-ad-350).
111 Roman contact with Britain can be dated from the mid-first century B.C.E. with its conquest in the mid-first century C.E. See "United Kingdom," in Encyclopedia Britannica (http://library.laidlaw.ac.nz:2114/EBchecked/topic/615557/United-Kingdom/44735/Roman-Britain).

4   Conclusion

I conclude then that it is unlikely that Mark or Paul (or the other NT authors) considered that the Parousia was imminent. They did recognize that Jesus would ultimately return. They understood that there was a period of mission between Jesus's ascension/Pentecost which involved the evangelization of every nation in the world. By the time of the NT documents, because of the speed of evangelization to this point, they were aware that this would not be a fast process but would involve a substantial (undefined) period of preaching, the establishment of churches, and the evangelization of whole nations. How long they envisaged this taking is unclear, but likely they imagined a time of many decades and perhaps centuries rather than an imminent consummation of history. Those passages that supposedly point to an imminent Parousia then should be not be read in this way. Rather, they use the language of imminence to convey the urgency of responding to the gospel wholeheartedly. Whether the writers of the NT imagined the evangelization of the world taking 2000 years is to me unlikely, but who knows?

Christian Origins and Imperial-Critical Studies of the New Testament Gospels*

Warren Carter

A review of New Testament studies over the last century clearly indicates that the discipline has always been in a state of flux with new methods posing new questions about these ancient texts and, depending on the method, about the communities, ancient and modern, who engage/d them. In this ever-changing landscape, imperial-critical approaches are a recent development. This article—by a participant in this emerging field of study—is both explanatory and evaluative. It suggests some factors that account for the rise of imperial-critical work on the canonical Gospels over the previous two or so decades, delineates the leading methods that eclectic imperial-critical Gospel work has employed, and engages some of the issues concerning this approach that require further attention. Basic to the analysis is the claim that any version of the origins of the early Jesus movement must account for its negotiations of the Roman imperial world.

Imperial-critical work on New Testament texts emerged in the 1990s. Though some contemporary Hebrew Bible work has increasingly foregrounded engagement with empires,[1] imperial-critical studies have largely examined New Testament texts. It would of course be misleading to suggest that there has been no previous attention to interactions between the early Jesus movement and its writings with the Roman empire. One such example was Adolf Deissmann's ground-breaking work, *Light from the Ancient East*.[2] Yet it is true that

---

* An earlier version of this paper was presented at the Society of Biblical Literature annual meeting, November 2014. I thank Eric Thurman and Jeremy Punt for helpful and insightful responses. Bibliographic entries are representative not exhaustive.
1 See, for example, the essays by Norman Gottwald, Walter Brueggemann, and Jon Berquist, in *In the Shadow of Empire: Reclaiming the Bible as a History of Faithful Resistance* (ed. Richard Horsley; Louisville: Westminster John Knox, 2008); David M. Carr and Colleen M. Conway, *An Introduction to the Bible: Sacred Texts and Imperial Contexts* (Malden, MA: Wiley, 2010); Anathea Portier-Young, *Apocalypse Against Empire: Theologies of Resistance in Early Judaism* (Grand Rapids: Eerdmans, 2011); Leo Perdue and Warren Carter, *Israel and Empire: A Postcolonial History of Israel and Early Judaism* (ed. Coleman Baker; London: Continuum, 2012), 1–128.
2 Adolf Deissmann, *Light from the Ancient East. The New Testament Illustrated by Recently Dis-*

generally twentieth-century New Testament scholarship has not paid adequate attention to interactions between the early Jesus movement and the imperial world.

Since the 1990s, imperial-critical studies have been redressing this neglect of the canonical Gospels' negotiation of Roman imperial power through journal articles,[3] edited collections of studies,[4] monographs,[5] and the programs of various sections of the annual meeting of the Society of Biblical Literature. Beginning in the 1990s, the Paul and Politics section promoted work in the Pauline tradition and thereby provided impetus for wider exploration across the canon.[6] Since 2004, another section, the Jesus Traditions, Gospels and Negotiating the Roman Imperial World section, has promoted work in the Gospels.[7]

---

covered Texts of the Graeco-Roman World (London and New York: Hodder and Stoughton, 1910).

3 For example, *Union Seminary Quarterly Review* 59 (2005): 1–186.

4 *The Gospel of Matthew In Its Roman Imperial Context* (eds. John Riches and David Sim; JSNTSup 276; London: T&T Clark, 2005); *Luke-Acts and Empire: Essays in Honor of Robert L. Brawley* (ed. David Rhoads, David Esterline, and Jae Won Lee; Eugene, OR: Wipf and Stock, 2011); B. Salier, "Jesus, the Emperor, and the Gospel According to John," in *Challenging Perspectives on the Gospel of John* (ed. John Lierman; WUNT 2.219; Tübingen: Mohr Siebeck, 2006), 284–301.

5 For example, Ched Myers, *Binding the Strong Man: A Political Reading of Mark's Story of Jesus* (Maryknoll, NY: Orbis, 1988); Marianne Bonz, *The Past as Legacy: Luke-Acts and Ancient Epic* (Minneapolis: Fortress, 2000); Warren Carter, *Matthew and Empire: Initial Explorations* (Harrisburg, PA: Trinity Press International, 2001); Adam Winn, *The Purpose of Mark's Gospel: An Early Christian Response to Roman Imperial Propaganda* (WUNT 2.245; Tübingen: Mohr Siebeck, 2008); Warren Carter, *John and Empire: Initial Explorations* (New York: T&T Clark, 2008); Tom Thatcher, *Greater than Caesar: Christology and Empire in the Fourth Gospel* (Minneapolis: Fortress, 2009).

6 The section has published three volumes of paper presentations. See *Paul and Empire: Religion and Power in Roman Imperial Society* (ed. Richard Horsley; Harrisburg, PA: Trinity Press International, 1997); *Paul and Politics: Ekklesia, Israel, Imperium, Interpretation* (ed. Richard Horsley; Harrisburg, PA: Trinity Press International, 2000); *Paul and the Roman Imperial Order* (ed. Richard Horsley; Harrisburg, PA: Trinity Press International, 2003). Subsequently the section undertook a multi-year dialogue with several classical scholars including Karl Galinsky; see *Rome and Religion: A Cross-Disciplinary Dialogue on the Imperial Cult* (ed. Jeffrey Brodd and Jonathan Reed; Atlanta: Society of Biblical Literature, 2011).

7 Since 2004, emphases in the section's programing have directed attention to methods of imperial-critical work, interaction between John's Gospel (the so-called spiritual Gospel) and Rome's world, presentations of slavery in the Gospels, healings and exorcisms, covenant traditions and imperial negotiation, the Gospel of Thomas and empire, interactions between

1 Focus and Emergence of Imperial-Critical Work on the Gospels

Imperial-critical work on the Gospels explores the diverse ways in which the Gospels negotiate the Roman imperial world. It understands and engages the NT Gospels as products of the Roman empire, namely the extensive area, people, and resources over which the central city of Rome exercised its power and extended its control. Michael Mann identifies four "networks of power" that exercised Roman hegemony and that inhabitants of the empire had to negotiate: ideological claims, military strength, economic resources, and socio-political administration.[8] Imperial-critical approaches identify these structures of imperial power and recognize that the Gospels emerge from, are enmeshed in, and engage this world of empire in which power was located in the hands of a small, wealthy, high-status elite. Imperial-critical work thus investigates, makes visible, and evaluates the represented interactions between this pervasive context of empire and the New Testament Gospels.

These interactions are multivalent. The often simultaneous strategies span, for example, validation, accommodation, cooption, ambivalence, self-protective protest, challenge, imitation, reinscribing, competition, attack, the formation of alternative communities, contestive practices, exposure of imperial strategies, imaginative narratives and fantasies of destruction, etc., and combinations thereof. The term *negotiation* signifies the existence of such multiple and often simultaneous strategies for making one's way in or engaging a world of imperial power, its structures and personnel. Imperial-critical work assumes that the context of the Roman empire is of key importance for interpreting the Gospels and their narratives, the climax of which is Jesus's resurrection after death on a Roman cross at the hands of a Roman governor and his elite allies.

The approach does not direct attention only to obvious manifestations of Roman presence in the texts (e.g. Pilate, the centurion at the cross). Rather it is concerned more holistically with uncovering and scrutinizing the pervasive, often unspoken and implicit, experiences, institutions, and impact of imperial ways of structuring reality that the texts assume, from which they emerge, and which they engage in various ways.

In addition to this examination of the Gospels, imperial-critical work evaluates, critiques, and exposes the neglect of imperial dynamics in existing schol-

---

Jesus traditions and imperial realities encountered in the Galilee, parables as imperial negotiation, teaching Jesus traditions/Gospels as acts of imperial negotiation, and the Gospels and material culture.

8 Michael Mann, *The Sources of Social Power* (New York: Cambridge University Press, 1986), 22–28.

arship. In doing so, its readings frequently contest the non-political, spiritualized, religious reading strategies that much Gospel interpretation has employed. Moreover, with a focus on matters of power and societal visions and structures, imperial-critical approaches are well placed to consider the implications of imperial-critical readings for contemporary ecclesial and neo-imperial contexts. I will develop these dimensions further below.

A number of factors account for the emergence of imperial-critical Gospel studies, partly as a reaction against the limited purview of existing historically-dominated methods, and partly as an embracing of new questions and approaches.

One factor reacts against the imperializing impact on the scholarly guild of depoliticized and spiritualized interpretations or readings of NT texts. Such readings have, more often than not, focused on ideas and concepts ("doctrine"), avoiding socio-political factors, bodies, relationships, and societal interactions. Even though much New Testament scholarship has, since the enlightenment, concentrated on the historical circumstances of the New Testament texts and communities, ironically the extent of the history deemed relevant for actual investigation has frequently been very circumscribed. Scholars have often, for example, concentrated selectively on particular questions of provenance (who wrote what to whom, when, where, why and how), directing attention to the circumstances of the recipients' lives as small ecclesial groups, frequently involving disputes over religious practices, personnel and doctrines, and especially concentrating on interactions with synagogues. Each of these circumstances poses its own particular challenges, and investigations over several centuries have provided valuable insight and understanding. But frequently absent from these reconstructions has been investigation of the texts and their recipients as part of and in relation to the larger overarching context, structures, practices, personnel, and commitments of the Roman imperial world. This neglect of the interaction between the Roman-imperial world and the New Testament texts and communities is striking especially since the latter are generally focused on one crucified by the Romans and "everybody knows" that the early Christian movement emerged in a Roman-controlled world.

A second and related factor accounting for the emergence of imperial-critical Gospel studies involves the hegemonic understanding of religion as a private matter of individual choice that has often operated in NT scholarship. Not surprisingly, the religious commitments of western interpreters who straddle ecclesial and scholarly worlds have valued individual religious matters and personal piety and have employed this framework to shape investigations of the Gospels. In the Roman world, however, religion was as much, if not more so, communal and civic as it was private and individual. In weighing the relationship between "individual experience" and "collective activity," whether in the context of households, villages, tribes, voluntary associations, towns, cities and the empire, James Rives comments, "What is clear enough is that the social dimension of religion in the Roman world was extremely important in its own right … in defining group identity and … in articulating social hierarchies."[9] One consequence of Rives' insight is that to engage the NT canonical Gospels as "religious" documents must lead into, not away from, the socio-political dimensions of the empire.

A third factor impacting the emergence of imperial-critical gospel studies involves an overemphasis on and isolation of ethnicity. Much scholarship has given almost exclusive attention to matters of ethnicity, foregrounding the interaction between Jews and Gentiles in the early Jesus movement and notably the justifications for Gentile inclusion and mission. There is no doubt that matters of ethnicity were important for the early Jesus movement but attention to it as the leading or dominant dynamic has often meant neglect of discourses involving power, gender, and societal status, and their attendant intersectionalities. This focus on ethnicity has failed to recognize the importance of intersectionalities in that Roman imperial practices frequently connected ethnicity with claims about social status and gender. Claims of Roman superiority aligned with claims of the superiority of elites and the inferiority of non-elites, and the superiority of males over females. Rome's male-dominated power groups commonly employed a ruling strategy of forming alliances with local provincial elites, the predominantly male "power" groups of provinces and/or their leading cities, thereby forming a multi-ethnic, largely male, ruling elite concerned with protecting its common interests. Social status and the common interest of the powerful elite in maintaining the status quo provide more often a unifying focus, much more than ethnicity.

Fourth, this restricted focus on ethnicity has often been fed by extensive training for New Testament scholars in the diversity and vibrancy of first-century Jewish life and traditions. While the discovery of the Dead Sea Scrolls in the mid-twentieth century and subsequent renewed attention to other collections of Jewish literatures have helpfully revised negative stereotypes of first-century Judaism,[10] this attention has often not recognized that Jewish identity and practices appear in a complex world that involves larger political forces such as Roman imperial power. Imperial-critical studies trouble this exclusive

---

9   James Rives, *Religion in the Roman Empire* (Oxford: Blackwell, 2007), 105–157, esp. 106.
10 See, for example, the helpful discussion of George W.E. Nickelsburg, *Ancient Judaism and Christian Origins: Diversity, Continuity, and Transformation* (Minneapolis: Fortress, 2003).

Jewish focus not by an antithesis between "things Jewish" and "things Roman" but by recognizing that Jewish communities, like Jesus communities, also interacted with a complex world of Roman power.

Fifth, when attention has been paid to the Roman empire by New Testament scholars, this attention has often misrepresented its structures and reach. Foremost is an unfortunate linguistic choice, deeply ingrained in the discourse of New Testament scholarship, that depicts the empire as a "New Testament background." Such nomenclature significantly diminishes the imperial foreground of socio-political, economic, cultural, and religious structures which the Jesus movement engaged. The language of "background" for the empire falsely relegates the dominant imperial power, Rome, to the wings or backdrop—continuing the stage image—and positions a very small marginal and powerless group on center stage. Such a drastic historical misrepresentation distances Jesus-believers from the empire, thereby rendering invisible the numerous ways in which Jesus-followers negotiated that imperial world. Another historical misrepresentation, common in popular sentiments, has foregrounded persecution as the dominant dynamic facing early Jesus-followers—despite the lack of evidence for first-century Jesus-followers being subjected to daily, empire-wide, life-and-death persecution. More adequate formulations are needed.

Sixth, postcolonial perspectives have foregrounded previously silenced, neglected, and marginal voices and groups. They have focused attention on the means, impacts, and legacies of imperial power over colonized peoples, on ways colonized folks talk and/or write back, and on the hybridity, ambivalence, and mimicry that marks the third space of such interaction.[11] And they have provided theory, concepts, and language in theorizing and for talking about these dynamics of power. Numerous studies of the experiences of colonized peoples, pioneered for instance in the ground-breaking work of Frantz Fanon and Edward Said,[12] have provided New Testament scholars with a body of theoretical and lived knowledge that provides insights and language for investigating the NT writings and communities that also originate among colonized peoples. Increasing numbers of scholars from former colonies of European powers with first-hand experience of colonial power have also enriched understandings within the discipline. These studies have shown that relationships involving imperial power are much more complex than a restricted focus on persecution, a simplistic "fight or flight" alternative, or an opposition-accommodation dualism employed by some early imperial-critical studies.

---

11 For example, Homi Bhabha, *The Location of Culture* (London: Routledge, 1994).
12 Frantz Fanon, *The Wretched of the Earth* (New York: Grove, 1963); Edward Said, *Culture and Imperialism* (New York: Random House, 1993).

And seventh, as often happens in New Testament studies, impetus for exploring new questions within the discipline has come from contemporary situations outside of it. These situations include international discourse over the roles of superpowers such as the United States in the global village,[13] as well as studies of empires and their legacies in disciplines such as literary and international relations studies, historical studies, and especially various and multidisciplinary forms of postcolonial studies.

How, then does imperial-critical work undertake the task of exploring how the canonical Gospels negotiate the Roman imperial world?

2   Methods

Imperial-critical studies do not employ a monolithic method, but are eclectic, interdisciplinary, intertextual, and perspectival.

The approach finds one starting point in forms of historical-critical studies, particularly the vast and complex discipline of classical and archaeological studies that investigate the cluster of first-century structures, constructs, and conditions that comprise (something of) the Roman empire experienced by Jesus-followers.[14] Material, especially monumental and artifactual remains (numismatics, artwork, domestic furnishings etc.) along with various literary and other written works (graffiti, inscriptions, papyri), provide the bulk of the source materials.[15] Among more recent studies has been attention to matters of gender,[16] including work on gender and constructions of masculinity in the

---

13   For example, the influential study, Michael Hardt and Antonio Negri, *Empire* (Cambridge, MA: Harvard University Press, 2001).

14   For example, *Experiencing Rome: Culture, Identity, and Power in the Roman Empire* (ed. Janet Huskinson; London: Routledge/Open University, 2000); Christopher Kelly, *The Roman Empire: A Very Short Introduction* (New York: Oxford University Press, 2006); Neville Morley, *The Roman Empire: Roots of Imperialism* (London: Pluto Press, 2010).

15   On sources, see, for example, the essays in *A Companion to the Roman Empire* (ed. David Potter; Oxford: Blackwell, 2006), 23–112. On epigraphy, Ramsay MacMullen, "The Epigraphic Habit in the Roman Empire," *American Journal of Philology* 103 (1982): 233–246; Greg Woolf, "Monumental Writing and the Expansion of Roman Society in the Early Empire," *Journal of Roman Studies* 86 (1996): 22–39; on architecture and monumentality, William MacDonald, *The Architecture of the Roman Empire. II. Urban Reappraisal* (New Haven: Yale University Press, 1986); Edmund Thomas, *Monumentality and the Roman Empire: Architecture in the Antonine Age* (Oxford: Oxford University Press, 2007).

16   Maud W. Gleason, *Making Men: Sophists and Self-Presentation in Ancient Rome* (Princeton: Princeton University Press, 1995); Gleason, "Elite Male Identity in the Roman Empire," in

Gospels.[17] In addition, there is increasing attention to the circumstances and lives of non-elites.[18] And there is much debate on how the Roman economy was structured.[19]

There are, however, limits and numerous obstacles to such investigation and construction. Sources, often from winners and elites, especially male elites, do not mention the Jesus movement. They are interested in the powerful and the exercise of power in politics, wars, and the lives and roles of "great men," with establishing when, what, and how something happened. The Jesus movement, however, was not a powerful and elite movement that exercised any political or military power. It was not under the patronage of great men. It was a subculture that has to be viewed from below, not from above, located within larger imperial structures, and understood as a collective movement marked by powerlessness.

Historical inquiry known as "People's History" helpfully foregrounds such perspectives.[20] This approach values any human activity, common folks and their everyday socioeconomic conditions and structures within the larger imperial world. Crucial matters pertain to the distribution and exercise of power and resources, along with the complex negotiated interactions between

---

Life, Death, and Entertainment in the Roman Empire (ed. D.S. Potter and D.J. Mattingly; Ann Arbor: University of Michigan Press, 1999), 67–84; Craig Williams, *Roman Homosexuality* (2nd ed.; Oxford: Oxford University Press, 2010).

17   Colleen Conway, *Behold the Man: Jesus and Greco-Roman Masculinity* (Oxford: Oxford University Press, 2008); and the essays by Jerome Neyrey, Janice Capel Anderson and Stephen Moore, Tat-siong Benny Liew, Eric Thurman, and Colleen Conway in *New Testament Masculinities* (ed. Stephen Moore and Janice Capel Anderson; Semeia Studies 45; Atlanta: Society of Biblical Literature, 2003), 43–180.

18   For example, Jerry Toner, *Popular Culture in Ancient Rome* (Cambridge: Polity Press, 2009); Robert Knapp, *Invisible Romans* (Cambridge, MA: Harvard University Press, 2011); Teresa Morgan, *Popular Morality in the Early Roman Empire* (Cambridge: Cambridge University Press, 2007); and the essays in *The Oxford Handbook of Social Relations in the Roman World* (ed. Michael Peachin; Oxford: Oxford University Press, 2011).

19   Peter Temin, *The Roman Market Economy* (Princeton: Princeton University Press, 2013).

20   Eric Hobsbawm, "History from Below—Some Reflections," in *History from Below: Studies in Popular Protest and Popular Ideology in Honor of George Rudé* (ed. Frederick Krantz; Montreal: Concordia University Press, 1985), 63–73; Peter Burke, "Overture: The New History, Its Past, Its Future," in *New Perspectives in Historical Writing* (ed. Peter Burke; University Park: Pennsylvania State University Press, 1992), 1–23; Jim Sharp, "History from Below," in *New Perspectives on Historical Writing* (ed. Peter Burke; Cambridge: Polity Press, 1991), 24–41; *A People's History of Christianity: Christian Origins* (ed. Richard Horsley; Minneapolis: Fortress, 2005).

dominant and subordinated groups. Dynamics and intersectionalities of power, gender, ethnicity, and social status constitute vital dimensions.

Historical and classical studies, viewed through and in relation to People's History, provide a starting point for identifying some of the dynamics impacting the production and reception of the Gospels such as the role of military power, vast economic disparities and exploitation including taxes and tribute, slavery, extensive poverty and food insecurity, the concentration of political power in the hands of a small elite, alliances between Rome and provincial, urban elites, the significance of the imperial cult especially in the east and promoted by agonistic provincial elites, societal structures, urban and rural material realities, and the foundational claims of the ruling ideology and so forth.

Yet the limited and partial nature of the surviving data, its bias toward elites, public political events, and military actions, and the relative invisibility of non-elites and their discreet and self-protective actions means these sources cannot provide an adequate picture of the vast range of human and communal experience within the empire. Not only does the partial nature of the literary, material, or monumental/artifactual remains present one problem, so also does the challenge of relating the various existing pieces to each other. Importantly, material, monumental, or artifactual remains gain significance in the context of larger, complex, imperial structures of power relations which the archaeological record itself cannot reconstitute.

Social-science models of empires usefully provide a wholistic framework, a heuristic view or map of the imperial structure that allows dots to be joined and the significance of individual pieces of existing data to be seen in relation to the whole. Dennis Duling discusses numerous models of empires in an important article.[21] The model of Gerhard Lenski's agrarian-aristocratic empires, modified by John Kautsky's inclusion of commerce and trade, has been especially helpful for imperial-critical work.[22] Lenski focuses on the exercise of power, posing the question, "who gets what and why?" and emphasizing the significant verticality in imperial social stratification. Other models of empires, for example those offered by A.J. Motyl, Michael Doyle, and Barbara Bush have received much

---

21 Dennis Duling, "Empire: Theories, Methods, Models," in *The Gospel of Matthew in Its Roman Imperial Context* (ed. John Kenneth Riches and David C. Sim; London: T&T Clark International, 2005), 49–74.

22 Gerhard Lenski, *Power and Privilege: A Theory of Social Stratification* (Chapel Hill: University of North Carolina Press, 1984); John H. Kautsky, *The Politics of Aristocratic Empires* (Chapel Hill: University of North Carolina Press, 1982).

less attention.²³ Similarly, others have provided more economically centered approaches such as Steven Friesen's very helpful attention to socio-economic strata.²⁴

Models of the larger structure of Rome's empire, nuanced and elaborated by classical and archaeological studies, and infused by people's history approaches, allows the function and significance of specific dynamics to be seen in relation to the whole.

Necessary, however, is access to how non-elites negotiate massive differentials of power. Several approaches provide access including People's History work. The work of cultural anthropologist James Scott has been widely used in imperial-critical studies precisely because it has been so useful.²⁵ Scott recognizes that whenever power and control are asserted in societies like Rome's empire, non-elites express opposition and resistance. He rejects the claim that the absence of violence means the absence of protest and the ready compliance of non-elites as Antonio Gramsci, for example, claims.²⁶ Rather, Scott argues that nonelites find self-protective rather than open violent resistance that qualifies apparent compliance.

Disguised forms of resistance to *material* domination may involve pilfering, foot-dragging, poaching, and cheating on taxes. Disguised forms of resistance to *status* domination comprise non-expressions of honor (a sneer, no greeting), anger, subversive songs or stories, rumors, and disarming acts of seizing initiative from the powerful like carrying a soldier's pack further than the stipulated mile, or handing over one's garments to expose the harshness of the powerful one's demand (Matt 5:38–42).²⁷ Disguised forms of resistance to *ideological* domination involve the development of a dissident subculture such as

---

23   Michael W. Doyle, *Empires* (Ithaca: Cornell University Press, 1987); A.J. Motyl, *Imperial Ends: The Decay, Collapse, and Revival of Empires* (New York: Columbia University Press, 2001); Barbara Bush, *Imperialism and Postcolonialism* (Harlow: Pearson Longman, 2006).

24   Steven Friesen, "Poverty in Pauline Studies: Beyond the So-called New Consensus," *JSNT* 26 (2004): 323–361; for a somewhat revised version, Bruce Longenecker, *Remember the Poor: Paul, Poverty, and the Greco-Roman World* (Grand Rapids: Eerdmans, 2010), 36–59.

25   James Scott, *Weapons of the Weak; Everyday Forms of Peasant Resistance* (New Haven: Yale University Press, 1985); Scott, *Domination and the Arts of Resistance: Hidden Transcripts* (New Haven: Yale University Press, 1990). For discussion of Scott's work in relation to the Gospels, see *Hidden Transcripts and the Arts of Resistance* (ed. Richard Horsley; Semeia 48; Atlanta: Society of Biblical Literature, 2004).

26   Scott, *Domination*, 70–107.

27   Walter Wink, "Jesus' Third Way: Nonviolent Engagement," in his *Engaging the Powers* (Minneapolis: Fortress, 1992), 175–193.

millennial religions (the eschatological expectations in Paul and the Gospels), social banditry, or world-upside-down imagery. Scott argues that where there is autonomous space away from the always-controlling eyes of the elite, non-elites nurture alternative versions of reality or hidden transcripts. These hidden transcripts of counter-ideology contest and negate the elite's dominant public version, assert the honor and dignity of the powerless, keep alive hopes and visions of different forms of societal interaction, imagine another world, and legitimize self-protective (and occasionally publicly rupturing) forms of dissent.

In Scott's terms, the Gospel stories of Jesus crucified by Rome, raised by God, and returning in power, can be seen as alternative transcripts that expose the limits of Roman power and contest (even while they also imitate) the public transcript, or elite, "official," normalizing view of reality. Jesus articulates and enacts a transcript of the empire of God that condemns imperial domination, repairs its damage through Jesus's healings, exorcisms, and feedings, and imitatively mimics and anticipates the establishment of God's justice. Jesus exemplifies the politics of disguise and anonymity, notably through his proclamation and demonstrations of the rumor of God's imminent removal of Rome's world and establishment of God's empire. The Gospels also recognize that Jesus occasionally ruptures the political order with direct challenges to the ruling powers (the temple attack) who respond by executing him.

I have dwelt on Scott's work because it has been so useful. But it is time, I think, to explore and employ some other theorists that might pose some different questions and provide further insights.

At hand of course is the disputed and diverse multidisciplinary discipline of postcolonial studies with its focus on the exercise and effects of imperial power in relation to race, ethnicity, hybridity, marginality, gender, diaspora, etc.[28] According to R.S. Sugirtharajah, postcolonial studies unmask and resist the complex assertions and reassertions of imperial power for both colonized and colonizer, while also imagining and structuring an alternative world,[29]

---

28 For some useful introductions, Bill Ashcroft, Gareth Griffiths, and Helen Tiffin, eds., *The Post-Colonial Studies Reader* (New York: Routledge, 1995); Leela Gandhi, *Postcolonial Theory: A Critical Introduction* (Edinburgh: Edinburgh University Press, 1998); Robert Young, *Postcolonialism: An Historical Introduction* (Oxford: Blackwell, 2001); Achille Mbembe, *On the Postcolony* (Berkeley: University of California Press, 2001); Robert Young, *Postcolonialism: A Very Short Introduction* (Oxford: Oxford University Press, 2003).

29 R.S. Sugirtharajah, *Asian Biblical Hermeneutics and Postcolonialism: Contesting the Interpretations* (Maryknoll, NY: Orbis, 1998), 17.

and displaying a "proactive moral involvement" that addresses "the needs and aspirations of the exploited."[30] Edward Said has emphasized a "contrapuntal reading" of imperial sources that engages both official and resistant discourse, especially the interactions between the two.[31] To do so means a refusal to accept colonialist readings as definitive depictions of the past and present, and an embracing of hitherto silenced voices of subordinated groups with their experiences of marginalization, hybridity, and new identity. Attention to the power dynamics between ruler and ruled has shown that such relationships are very complex.

Imperial-critical work on the canonical Gospels, then, employs a range of approaches to foreground the inquiry into the diverse ways in which the Gospels negotiate Roman power. Among the cluster of methods are historical-critical studies, especially classical studies, social-science approaches, especially models of empire, people's history approaches that focus on the powerless and non-elites, studies of how the powerless negotiate power including "the arts of resistance," postcolonial and ideological studies involving matters of identity, gender, ethnicity, and social status.

3 Questions and Issues

I identify four issues that have emerged in several decades of work on Christian origins employing imperial-critical approaches to the canonical Gospels.

3.1 *Nomenclature*

The first issue concerns nomenclature. Throughout this article, I have used the language of imperial-critical studies or approaches to refer to this field of inquiry. Others have used the language of "empire studies." I prefer the former nomenclature of imperial-critical approaches. The use of the term "critical" aligns the method with other critical approaches used for the study of New Testament Gospels such as historical-critical, feminist-critical, or narrative-critical approaches. The term also foregrounds the critical, discerning, or evaluative nature of the approach. That is, the nomenclature of imperial-critical studies or approaches signifies a thoughtful or evaluative approach to these writings

---

30 R.S. Sugirtharajah, "Postcolonial Theory and Biblical Studies," in *Fair Play: Diversity and Conflicts in Early Christianity* (ed. Ismo Dunderberg, Christopher Tuckett, and Kari Syreeni; Leiden: Brill, 2001), 541–552, esp. 547, 552.

31 Said, *Culture and Imperialism*, xv.

through the lens of identifying imperial structures that a Gospel text inscribes, along with discerning the way/s in which a text advocates negotiation of those structures.

The use of the term "critical" with the sense of "discerning," and consistent with its use by other critical methods, addresses a common misunderstanding of imperial-critical approaches or empire studies. The term and the work it denotes do not signify a unilateral stance of opposition toward the Roman empire. The term and the work it denotes do not assume or create an oppositional dualism of "Rome bad, Gospels good." Such an oppositional dualism is impossible for various reasons. Historically such a verdict on the Roman empire is not sustainable nor is it accurate for the Gospels. The Gospels readily inscribe their own empire (βασιλεία) in mimicry of Rome's but also in competition with it in depicting an empire of cosmic proportions in that Jesus returns to out-muscle (judge) the imperial status quo and establish God's rule over all creation (Mark 13:24–27; Matt 24:27–31;[32] Luke 12:35–40; John 5:26–30; 12:47–48[33]). Clearly in these cosmic imperial scenarios there is both opposition to, contest with, and imitation of imperial ways. The term "imperial-critical" foregrounds the importance of interactions between imperial realities and the Gospels, and signifies multivalent presentations and forms of negotiation (not monolithic opposition).

3.2   *Imperial-Critical Approaches and Postcolonial Work*

The second issue concerns the relationship between imperial-critical work and postcolonial work, and, more accurately, the relationship between historically-oriented work that concerns the NT texts and the Roman empire and work that attends more to theorizing the ongoing contemporary experience and legacy of colonizer-colonized interactions. Elisabeth Schüssler Fiorenza has criticized imperial-critical work for not engaging these contemporary issues enough and called it to do so.[34] Others have seen a focus on the ancient world and a neglect of contemporary social-colonial structures as a point of differentiation between imperial-critical work and postcolonial studies. Stephen Moore elevates the latter while castigating empire or imperial-critical studies

---

32   Warren Carter, "Are There Imperial Texts in the Class? Intertextual Eagles and Matthean Eschatology as 'Lights Out' Time for Imperial Rome (Matthew 24:27–31)," *JBL* 122 (2003): 467–487.

33   Warren Carter, *John and Empire: Initial Explorations* (New York: T&T Clark, 2008), 336–342.

34   Elisabeth Schüssler Fiorenza, *The Power of the Word: Scripture and the Rhetoric of Empire* (Minneapolis: Fortress, 2007), 2–7.

for (supposedly) evading difficult contemporary disparities of power by its focus on the past.³⁵ Moore, however, does concede that imperial-critical work is "not without teeth" in wrestling with the question as to whether biblical texts can be said to resist empire.

Others, however, have seen a much greater alignment between the two areas of investigation. Fernando Segovia, for example, sees postcolonial studies as an umbrella entity engaging imperial power across a vast spectrum of human history involving three arenas: (1) the ancient world, (2) reception histories, and (3) the contemporary world.³⁶ By this he means postcolonial biblical criticism can have three areas of focus: (i) analysis of the imperial-colonial formations of the biblical texts, (ii) analysis of interpretations of these texts in relation to the imperial-colonial formation of "western hegemony and expansion," and (iii) analysis of interpretations in relation to imperial-colonial formations of contemporary globalization.

This threefold spectrum is vast to say the least. Attempting to embrace it all runs the risk of superficial consideration, perhaps, necessitating selective attention, with imperial-critical work more often examining the negotiation of imperial structures in the text's originating circumstances. Segovia especially notes and laments the relative absence of attention to empires such as those of Assyria, Babylonia, Persia, Macedonia, and Rome.³⁷ Such neglect significantly impacts study of the emerging Jesus movement in the imperial-colonial context of the Roman Empire, and study of the role of Christianity in various imperial formations over the last two millennia. In Segovia's formulation, imperial-critical work would be one arena of a larger postcolonial enterprise.

R.S. Sugirtharajah offers a similar three-part grid for the interests of postcolonial biblical work: (1) the "scrutiny of biblical narratives for their colonial involvement," (2) the rereading of biblical texts "from the perspective of postcolonial concerns such as liberation struggles of the past and present," and (3) drawing "attention to the inescapable effects of colonization and colonial

---

35   Stephen Moore, "Paul after Empire," in *The Colonized Apostle: Paul through Postcolonial Eyes* (ed. Christopher D. Stanley; Minneapolis: Fortress, 2011), 9–23, esp. 22.

36   Fernando Segovia, "Mapping the Postcolonial Optic in Biblical Criticism: Meaning and Scope," in *Postcolonial Biblical Criticism: Interdisciplinary Intersections* (ed. Stephen Moore and Fernando Segovia; London: T&T Clark, 2005), 23–78, esp. 64–76.

37   Fernando Segovia, "Postcolonial Criticism and the Gospel of Matthew," in *Methods in Matthew* (ed. Mark Allan Powell; Cambridge: Cambridge University Press, 2009), 194–237, esp. 215–216. See now Perdue and Carter, *Israel and Empire*.

ideals on interpretive works."[38] Again the agenda is huge, yet within this vast spectrum, both Segovia and Sugirtharajah recognize the interaction between biblical texts and imperial structures as one legitimate area of inquiry. And given a vast spectrum, some selection of focus seems appropriate.

Assuming that it is desirable for work in New Testament studies to address contemporary issues and circumstances, it should be said that a focus of imperial-critical work on the New Testament text's negotiation of the Roman empire does not necessarily mean indifference to contemporary expressions of imperial/colonizing power. Imperial-critical work opens the way to such investigations by at least three means. One means concerns attention to the Gospels' after-lives. Imperial-critical work has been oriented to interactions between the Gospels and the Roman empire. Yet the attempt to determine the Gospel texts' and movement's interactions with the Roman world enables the evaluation of the continuing influence of these texts on the interactions of subsequent readers with imperial and ruling powers. This work thus raises questions for contemporary readers about the neocolonial structures, visions, and interactions of our own world.

Second, it is undeniable that imperial-critical work has pioneered investigations of New Testament texts in relation to the structures and impacts of empires in ways that have been accessible to contemporary readers. In doing so, imperial-critical work has raised important questions about the origins and interpretations of these important texts. In addition to raising questions about reading strategies for these texts, imperial-critical work has also posed for contemporary audiences, especially those belonging to ecclesial and seminary communities, important questions about the challenges, benefits, and victims of contemporary imperial power. Questioning reading strategies and problematizing the imperial accommodation and mimicry of New Testament texts that are so important for some contemporary readers and faith communities are important and contemporary political acts. Unencumbered by some types of theoretical discussions that have often obfuscated postcolonial work—Sugirtharajah comments that "vagueness [has often been] a cardinal virtue"[39] of such work—and marked by a constant attention on biblical texts, imperial-critical approaches have gained a hearing among and created space for contemporary audiences to be aware of, engage, and evaluate not

---

38   R.S. Sugirtharajah, "Postcolonial Theory and Biblical Studies," in *Fair Play: Diversity and Conflicts in Early Christianity: Essays in Honour of Heikki Räisänen* (ed. Ismo Dunderberg, C.M. Tuckett, and Kari Syreeni; NovTSup 103; Leiden: Brill, 2002), 546–547.
39   Sugirtharajah, "Postcolonial Theory," 541.

only their sacred texts, not only their strategies of reading, not only treasured interpretations, but also contemporary neo-imperial realities. Imperial-critical approaches have fostered readings of the biblical writings in relation to the worlds from which they have emerged and in which they are engaged, focusing attention on interactions between the New Testament texts and the power dynamics and societal structures of empires, ancient and contemporary.

And third, it should also be recognized that the act of writing and publishing writings is not the only means by which those involved in imperial-critical work might engage contemporary issues of power, injustices, and societal visions, structures, and practices.

3.3 Theory and Investigating the History of Scholarship

A third issue comprises two take-aways from this consideration of the interaction of imperial-critical and postcolonial approaches. One matter concerns theory. While much postcolonial work in our discipline has been overtheorized and has often been neglectful of New Testament texts, it is fair to say that some imperial-critical work has been naïve and undertheorized. That is, much early work and even some more recent work has been far too monolithic in posing only an oppositional or antithetical relationship between the early Jesus movement and the Roman empire. Increasingly, though, through the numerous methods outlined above—including postcolonial work on ambivalence, hybridity, and mimicry—there has been a growing recognition that the relations of power between dominant and dominated are much more complex and multivalent. Imperial-critical work on the Gospels must continue to be funded by theory concerning power dynamics, empires and the experiences of the colonized.

A second take-way from this spectrum of postcolonial approaches concerns imperial-critical attention to the history of Gospel interpretation. While imperial-critical work redresses a general neglect in New Testament scholarship concerning negotiation of Roman power, it has paid little specific attention to the history and contours of this neglect across the discipline. In the history of Gospel scholarship, how have matters of imperial negotiation been avoided? In what circumstances and by what choices have spiritual and religious readings, or non-imperial readings, been preferred and thereby distanced the Gospels from imperial-political realities? Conversely, in what occasions and under what circumstances have political readings emerged? What hierarchies of knowledge have controlled interpretive options and methods within the guild? It remains for imperial-critical work to expose not only imperial dynamics in Gospel texts but also in the scholarly and interpretive guilds and the history of Gospel interpretation.

3.4 Rome and Judaism

A fourth issue concerns a supposed binary between imperial-critical work concerned with interactions between the Gospels and Rome on one hand, and scholarship concerned with interactions between the Gospels and early Judaism. One of the comments I have heard from some scholars on imperial-critical work is that they were trained in the early Jesus movement in relation to early Judaism and not classics or anything to do with the Roman empire, so they will continue to give attention to early Judaism without concern for Roman imperial power.

Such a formulation, however, is problematic. It posits two distinct cultural and political entities that are understood to have nothing to do with each other, Judaism and the Roman empire. But such a division makes no sense of the complexities of the ancient world and the emergence of the early Jesus movement. As most scholars of the early Jesus movement know, Judaism was not an entity separated and isolated from Hellenistic culture.[40] But nor were Jewish folks, whether in the land or in the diaspora, separated and isolated from the Roman world. Rome too had to deal with Jewish structures, traditions, practices etc. The Gospel writings that emerge from the early Jesus movement are shaped and contextualized by a Jewish milieu even as they also negotiate Roman power. They tell the story of one crucified by a (typical) alliance of a Roman governor and the Rome-sanctioned, provincial, Jerusalem ruling elite.[41] The question to be addressed concerns how these various cultural-political spheres interact with one another.

I have suggested in relation to Matthew's Gospel that the notion of horizontal violence developed by Frantz Fanon and Paulo Freire has much interpretive fecundity.[42] It has become something of a commonplace in Matthean studies that the Gospel emerges in relation to conflicts with a synagogue community, whether before, during, or after the Matthean community's separation.[43]

---

40   The classic discussion is, of course, Martin Hengel, *Judaism and Hellenism* (Philadelphia: Fortress, 1974).
41   The alliance is recognized by Anthony Saldarini, *Pharisees, Scribes and Sadducees in Palestinian Society: A Sociological Approach* (Grand Rapids: Eerdmans, 2001).
42   Warren Carter, "Matthew: Empire, Synagogues, and Horizontal Violence," in *Mark and Matthew 1: Comparative Readings: Understanding the Earliest Gospels in their First-Century Settings* (ed. Eve-Marie Becker and Anders Runesson; WUNT 2.271; Tübingen: Mohr Siebeck, 2011), 285–308; Fanon, *Wretched of the Earth*, 52–54; Paulo Freire, *Pedagogy of the Oppressed* (rev. 20th anniversary ed.; New York: Continuum, 1999), 44.
43   For a survey of these options, see Graham Stanton, "The Origin and Purpose of Matthew's Gospel: Matthean Scholarship from 1945–1980," *ANRW* 2.25.3: 1890–1951. For an argument

Interpreters have universally elaborated these intense conflicts as religious matters arising from the challenges of reconstruction in the post-70 CE context.

The notion of horizontal violence, though, places the conflicts in the context of the negotiation of imperial power by both synagogues and Jesus communities. Crucial to this shared task of imperial negotiation is the recognition that the destruction of Jerusalem and its temple in 70 C.E. was a fresh assertion of Roman imperial power. The notion of horizontal violence recognizes that when assertions of power are made in a society from above, from a dominant imperializing power, these assertions are typically accompanied by expressions of violence not toward the dominating power but among oppressed groups. Violence toward each other rather than against the oppressor is one means by which oppressed groups mimic their oppressor but redirect their resentment and envy in self-protectively negotiating that power.[44] I have suggested that the violence—verbal and physical—between the Jesus-group and its opponents evident in Matthew's narrative embodies such dynamics. In this model, the conflictual interactions between synagogues and Jesus-followers in Matthew's narrative are not adequately comprehended as isolated religious matters but are caught up in assertions of imperial power and the difficult task of negotiating them. Things Jewish (including Matthew's Gospel) and things Roman are not separated or isolated spheres. Their interactions need much greater recognition.

---

favoring a separation already completed, see Donald Hagner, "Matthew: Christian Judaism or Jewish Christianity?" in *The Face of New Testament Studies: A Survey of Recent Research* (ed. S. McKnight and G. Osborne; Grand Rapids: Baker Academic, 2004), 263–282. For an argument locating Matthew's group within a synagogue, see Anthony Saldarini, *Matthew's Christian-Jewish Community* (Chicago: University of Chicago Press, 1994). For evaluation, see Warren Carter, "Matthew's Gospel: Jewish Christianity, Christian Judaism, or Neither," in *Jewish Christianity Reconsidered: Rethinking Ancient Groups and Texts* (ed. Matt Jackson-McCabe; Minneapolis: Fortress, 2007), 155–179.

44 The phenomenon of horizontal violence is evident in the increasing divisions among Judeans and Jerusalemites during 69–70 C.E. as Roman pressure intensifies (Josephus, *J.W.* 4.377–397, 503–584; 5.1–38). David Abernethy notes increasing horizontal violence between Hindus and Moslems in India, and between competing groups in Kenya and Malaya under British imperialism, in Vietnam under French control, and in the former Belgium Congo. See David Abernethy, *The Dynamics of Global Dominance: European Overseas Empires, 1415–1980* (New Haven: Yale University Press, 2000), 147–161.

4 Conclusion

Imperial-critical work on the canonical Gospels, employing a cluster of diverse methods, has helped enormously to put the presence of Roman power on the agenda of much contemporary Gospel scholarship. Over recent decades, investigation into aspects of the intersections between the Gospels of the emerging Jesus movement and the imperial world has gained momentum and visibility in international and national scholarly meetings, in the scholarly guild, in publishers' catalogues, and certainly among PhD candidates questing for dissertation topics. Basic to this hermeneutical and contextual work on the canonical Gospels is the claim that any version of the origins of the early Jesus movement must engage and account for its negotiations of the Roman imperial world.

"No Stone Left upon Another": Considering Mark's Temple Motif in Narrative and History*

Adam Winn

Over the last sixty years of Gospel scholarship, interpreters have given significant attention to the role of the temple institution (by this we refer to both the temple itself and the leadership of the temple) in Mark's Gospel, though the nature of such inquiry has varied. Such inquiries fall broadly into two critical approaches to the Gospels, either redaction criticism or narrative criticism. Redaction-critical studies have been particularly interested in how the evangelist's presentation of the temple both shaped and was shaped by the situation of the Markan community.[1] These studies have involved (a) using the Markan text, in particular Mark's treatment of the Jewish temple, to reconstruct the situation of Mark's community, and (b) assessing the way in which Mark's treatment of the temple might address the reconstructed situation of Mark's community. Narrative criticism, which was in large part a response to the disproportionate historical interests of modern biblical scholarship (including that of redaction critics), sought to understand the literary scope and nature of Mark's treatment of the temple institution, as well as the way in which that treatment fit into the larger narrative of the Gospel.[2] These narrative studies sought to demonstrate that Mark's treatment of the temple was a unified literary motif, one that played a vital role in the narrative theology of Mark's Gospel. The present study seeks to bring the questions and interests of both these methods together in its analysis of the place of the temple in Mark's Gospel. As with the narrative critics, this study pays attention to the entirety

---

* The following essay is found in revised form in chap. one and six of Adam Winn, *Reading Mark's Christology under Caesar: Jews, the Messiah and Roman Imperial Ideology* (Downers Grove, IL: IVP, 2018).
1 For examples, see Willi Marxsen, *Mark the Evangelist* (trans. James Boyce et al.; Nashville: Abingdon, 1969); Werner H. Kelber, *The Kingdom in Mark: A New Time and a New Place* (Philadelphia: Fortress, 1974); S.G.F. Brandon, *The Fall of Jerusalem and the Christian Church: A Study of the Effects of the Jewish Overthrow of* A.D. *70 on Christianity* (London: SPCK, 1951), esp. 185–205; Donald Juel, *Messiah and Temple: The Trial of Jesus in the Gospel of Mark* (SBLDS 31; Missoula, MT: Scholars Press, 1977).
2 For examples, see Timothy C. Gray, *The Temple in the Gospel of Mark: A Study in Its Narrative Role* (WUNT 2.242; Tübingen: Mohr Siebeck, 2008; repr. Grand Rapids: Baker, 2010); John Paul Heil, "The Narrative Strategy and Pragmatics of the Temple Theme in Mark," *CBQ* 59 (1997): 76–100; David Seeley, "Jesus' Temple Act," *CBQ* 55 (1993): 263–283.

of Mark's Gospel and to the final product of the Gospel rather than to its literary sources or its redactional history. But as with redaction critics, this study is interested in the historical situation of Mark's community, particularly the way in which a reconstruction of that community helps us understand both Mark's narratival treatment of the temple institution and also the way this treatment of the temple might address the situation of Mark's community.[3]

At the outset, let me state my awareness of the limitations that come with asking questions about Mark's community and reading Mark's Gospel from the vantage point of a reconstructed Markan community, limitations duly noted by many narrative critics. The primary limitation is the uncertainty that accompanies any effort to reconstruct Mark's community. While evidence can be, and has been, put forth for Mark's provenance, date, and audience, such evidence has led scholars to various and even opposite conclusions, results that clearly evince the uncertain nature of such conclusions. In light of such a limitation, narrative critics have sought to read Mark's narrative with minimal attention given to the historical setting and situation of the Gospel's intended audience, with the only identity of the reader coming from what can be directly implied from the text itself. While such readings of the text have the advantage of not being contingent upon uncertain historical reconstructions, they indeed have their own problems, including the inability to resolve certain narrative tensions, and to perceive meaning in a narrative that most certainly was shaped by the specific historical situation of its author and audience. The analogy of a puzzle might be helpful here. Narrative critics are seeking to construct a puzzle without all the pieces, which inevitably creates difficulty in assembling the puzzle properly. In this study (like many redactional studies), we are attempting recreate the missing pieces (the pieces of the author and audiences setting) in order to assemble the puzzle, but the uncertainty in such recreations raises doubts as to whether the puzzle has been properly assembled.

As I undertake this study, I am keenly aware of its limitations as well as the value of studies that do not ask the questions presently being asked. I in no way

---

3 For some narrative critics that view the text as a closed world, this approach violates the very nature of narrative criticism, as it considers Mark's real/intended audience. However, in a recent essay on narrative criticism and Mark's Gospel, Mark Allan Powell has provide a broad understanding of narrative criticism, and has noted that narrative criticism can be devoted to a wide variety of goals, including that of recovering authorial intent or the way in which a text would have been understood by its intended audience (see "Narrative Criticism: The Emergence of a Prominent Reading Strategy," in *Mark as Story: Retrospect and Prospect* [ed. Kelly R. Iverson and Christopher W. Skinner; RBS 65; Atlanta: SBL, 2011], 19–44, esp. 28–32). Powell also provides several examples of narrative critical studies on Mark, as well as other Gospels, that are interested in questions regarding the real or intended audience of the Gospel (see Powell, "Narrative Criticism," 30–31).

presuppose that the questions of this study are the most important questions that can be asked of Mark's Gospel, nor do I presuppose that readings generated by the answers to such questions are superior to other readings. In fact, I acknowledge the great value in narrative-critical readings of Mark's Gospel that have no regard for Mark's intended audience, and I will rely a great deal on such readings. But I do presuppose that the questions about Mark's community and the way in which Mark's text is shaped by that community, as well as the way in which that community shapes Mark's text, are valid and important questions, questions that can lead to good and useful readings of Mark's Gospel despite the contingent and uncertain nature of the answers to such questions. With all historical reconstruction, there are varying degrees of uncertainty, but this fact should neither stop us from pursuing such reconstruction, nor eliminate its value.

This study is divided into two sections. The first section will analyze the narrative and narrative function of the temple motif in Mark 11:1–13:2. It will begin with a survey of the scope and nature of Mark's treatment of the Jewish temple institution, and will then consider how this temple motif functions within the Gospel's narrative. The second section will analyze the historical function of Mark's temple motif, beginning with a brief treatment of Mark's audience and that audience's concern for the Jewish temple. It will then consider the historical realities surrounding the aftermath of the destruction of Jerusalem and its temple throughout the Roman world, particularly the role that this destruction played in Roman imperial propaganda and the possible impact of this propaganda on the fledgling early church. Finally, the chapter will consider the ways in which Mark's temple motif could be a response to Roman propaganda and an attempt to address the crisis that such propaganda had created for the early church.

1 The Temple in Mark 11:1–13:2: Narrative Considerations

In the first ten chapters of Mark's Gospel, the temple is completely absent. In ch. 11, the temple and its leadership bursts onto the scene with tremendous narrative force, and dominate the next two chapters of the Gospel. While there is little debate as to the centrality of the temple and its leadership in Mark 11–12, there is less agreement as to centrality of the temple in subsequent chapters of the Gospel. While many interpreters see the temple dominating Mark 13, some see it playing a less significant role (or none at all!).[4] Some interpreters argue

---

4 For interpreters who see the temple playing a major role in Mark 13, see for example Gray,

that the temple plays a dominant role in Mark's passion narrative (chs. 14–15), while others might recognize it as a lesser motif among many.[5] Our focus in this essay will be Mark 11:1–13:2, in which the centrality of the temple is undisputed.

Mark 11–12 is widely recognized as a distinct literary unit in Mark's Gospel, one that is dominated by the temple and its authorities. The Triumphal Entry (11:1–11) ends with Jesus entering the temple, looking around, and departing. The following day, Jesus enters the temple again, overturns the tables of the money changers, brings a temporary halt to certain activities, and speaks words of judgment against the temple institution—actions that result in the temple authorities seeking a way to kill him (11:15–18). These actions in the temple are "sandwiched" between pericopes related to a fig tree that Jesus condemns on the day of the temple action (11:12–14) and which is found withered the following day (11:21–22). As many interpreters have recognized, these "fig tree" pericopes play a vital role in interpreting Jesus's action in the temple and thus are inseparable from Mark's treatment of the temple. Jesus then offers teachings to his disciples on faith, prayer, and forgiveness (11:23–25), teachings that on the surface seem rather incongruent with the previous material that addresses the temple, but which recent narrative studies have more closely tied to Mark's temple motif. After these teachings, Jesus and his disciples enter Jerusalem and the temple and there are confronted by the temple authorities who question the Jesus's authority (11:27–33). After demonstrating that these temple authorities stand in opposition to the work of God (11:30–33), Jesus tells the parable of the vineyard, a parable that harshly critiques the temple authorities and predicts their destruction (12:1–12). After a series of encounters with various members of the temple leadership (12:13–37), Jesus offers a scathing critique of the temple authorities, a critique that is then illustrated and substantiated by the story of a widow who gives all that she has to the temple treasury (12:38–44). Finally, in what I will argue is the last episode of this distinct literary unit, Jesus explicitly predicts the temple's destruction (13:1–2). The dominance of the temple and its authorities in these two chapters of Mark strongly suggests the presence of a distinct and intentional temple motif constructed by the

---

Temple, 94–155; R.T. France, *The Gospel of Mark* (NIGTC; Grand Rapids: Eerdmans, 2002), 494–546; J. Marcus, "The Jewish War and the Sitz im Leben of Mark," *JBL* 111 (1992): 441–462. For interpreters who see the temple playing little to no role in Mark 13, see Adam Winn, *The Purpose of Mark's Gospel* (WUNT 2.245; Tübingen: Mohr Siebeck, 2008), 70–76 and Morna D. Hooker, *The Gospel According to Saint Mark* (Peabody, MA: Hendrickson, 1991), 303–316.

5 For interpreters who emphasize the role of the temple in Mark's passion narrative, see Gray, *Temple*, 156–197 and Juel, *Messiah and Temple*.

evangelist. But what is the nature and literary function of this motif? The following analysis will yield a clear understanding of both.

1.1 The Triumphal Entry (11:1–11)

While the temple is not explicitly mentioned until the very end of the triumphal entry, it is the final destination of the entry, and is presupposed as such throughout the pericope. Jesus enters the city to great fanfare, as the crowds place both cloaks and branches before him, and clearly identify him as Israel's Messiah who has been sent by God and who will bring salvation (Ὡσαννά) through the establishment of the kingdom of David.[6] It is noteworthy that the crowds cite Ps 117:26 (LXX), εὐλογημένος ὁ ἐρχόμενος ἐν ὀνόματι κυρίου ("blessed is the one who comes in the name of the Lord"). Psalm 118 (117 LXX) is a famous Jewish pilgrimage hymn, and thus the crowd's citation of this Psalm indicates that they, along with Jesus, are making pilgrimage to the temple.[7] Yet, this pilgrimage is unlike all previous pilgrimages because the long-awaited Messiah is a participant, and the people hope that this pilgrimage to the temple, unlike all previous pilgrimages, will result in the establishment of the messianic kingdom of David. With such an understanding of the triumphal entry narrative, Mark's description of Jesus's (and presumably the crowd's) arrival at the temple is profoundly significant, and the narrative builds anticipation for the reception that Jesus will receive. However, the reader experiences an anticlimax in place of an expected climax. Jesus enters the temple with the twelve, looks around, and then leaves because of the late hour. The lack of any reception for Jesus in the temple is striking, and it stands in stark contrast to the reception Jesus receives from those making pilgrimage to the temple. Unlike the pilgrims, the temple leadership fails to recognize God's Messiah and apparently has no interest in his establishment of the kingdom of David. Through this sharp contrast between the pilgrims and the temple authorities, the Markan evangelist seems to have designed this pericope to communicate the failure of Israel's leadership, a motif that will only become more prominent as the narrative moves forward.

---

6   Francis Moloney argues that the people's acclamation and desire for the kingdom of David is misguided and stands in contrast with the Gospel's clear teaching that Jesus will bring about the Kingdom of God (*The Gospel of Mark* [Peabody, MA: Hendrickson, 2002], 219–220; see also Gray, *Temple*, 21–22, and France, *Mark*, 434). However, such a conclusion seems unnecessary as the kingdom of David could certainly be synonymous with the Kingdom of God in a Second Temple Jewish context, i.e., it is a descendant of David that will (re)establish God's Kingdom. The everlasting kingdom that God promises to David's descendants in 2 Sam 7:16 would not be understood as a kingdom other than God's own kingdom.

7   See Gray, *Temple*, 20–23.

1.2 A Fruitless Fig Tree and a Fruitless Temple (11:12–21)

There has been much debate surrounding how Jesus's action in the temple should be understood. Is Jesus simply cleansing the temple of unjust and immoral practices, or is Jesus committing an act of symbolic judgment and destruction of the temple institution? Much of this debate has focused on the historical Jesus, but our present focus is on Mark's narrative presentation of Jesus's actions. Mark presents the following actions of Jesus in temple: (1) driving out the πωλοῦντας and ἀγοράζοντας ("the sellers" and "the buyers"), (2) overturning the tables of the money changers, (3) overturning the seats of those selling doves, and (4) preventing vessels from being carried through the temple. While these actions have long been understood by Markan interpreters as Jesus "cleansing" what he perceives as a corrupt temple, there seems to be a growing trend of interpreting these actions as a symbolic judgment and destruction of the temple.[8] Here we will consider three areas of evidence in order to adjudicate between these two interpretive possibilities: (1) Jesus's actions, (2) Jesus's teaching, and (3) the intercalation of the fig and temple-action pericopes.

1.2.1 Jesus's Actions

For those who understand Jesus as cleansing a corrupt temple, it is difficult to explain some of the actions of the Markan Jesus. We are told that Jesus drives out both those who are selling and those who are buying from the temple. Those who favor a "cleansing" reading of this pericope must understand such actions in terms of Jesus driving out sellers who are cheating the buyers. But as Timothy Gray rightly notes, how would such a motive explain the Markan Jesus driving out the buyers as well as the sellers? The buyers can only be victims in this ring of corruption, so why then are they kicked out of the temple as well when they have done nothing wrong? Such an interpretation fits better with the Lukan parallel, in which the Lukan evangelist omits the reference to "buyers." But Mark's inclusion of buyers along with sellers seems to convey a cessation of all activity in the temple, an action that is more consistent with a symbolic act of destruction rather than a cleansing.

---

8 For Markan interpreters who understand Jesus's temple action as a cleansing of the temple, see Vincent Taylor, *The Gospel According to St. Mark* (London: Macmillan, 1952), 460–461; J. Marcus, *Mark 8–16: A New Translation with Introduction and Commentary* (AYB 27A; New Haven: Yale University Press, 2009), 781–795; France, *Mark*, 442–447; Craig A. Evans, *Mark 8:27–16:20* (WBC; Nashville: Thomas Nelson, 2001), 181–182. For those who understand the same action as a symbolic judgment, see Moloney, *Mark*, 222–226; Gray, *Temple*, 25–43; J.R. Daniel Kirk, "Time for Figs, Temple Destruction, and House of Prayer in Mark 11:12–25," *CBQ* 74 (2012): 509–527.

And what is to be made of Jesus's action of turning over the tables of the money changers and seats of those selling doves? As Sanders and others have pointed out, both the changing of money and the buying of animals were services essential for pilgrims to participate in the temple cult.[9] As such, these actions by Jesus halt the ability of such pilgrims to participate in the cultic activity that brought about the expiation of sins. Such actions by Jesus would thus be more consistent with a symbolic destruction of the temple institution and the cessation of its cultic activity than with merely a cleansing of a corrupt temple. Yet others have proposed that the aim of these actions was not the prevention of the cultic activity that such economic exchanges enabled, but rather the price of the gouging of poor pilgrims that both the money changers and sellers of doves were engaged in. Perhaps such a reading is supported by Jesus's citation of Jeremiah and the reference to the temple being a den of robbers. While it is possible that these actions can be fit with either reading (cleansing or destruction), perhaps determinative here is Mark's use of the word καταστρέφω which more often refers to "destroying" rather than "over-turning."[10] Such a violent description of Jesus's actions toward the money changers and the sellers of doves seems more consistent with the picture of symbolic destruction and the cessation of necessary temple business than it does with the eradication of price gouging that might have plagued economic activity in the temple.

Finally, we are told that Jesus prevents anyone from carrying any vessel (σκεῦος) through the temple. In this context, it seems most likely that σκεῦος refers to cultic vessel used in the daily operations of the temple, including a vessel that was used to transport the gifts and offerings of the temple worshippers.[11] The prevention of such actions seems odd if the focus of Jesus's actions is cleansing the temple of corruption, as the movement of cultic vessels through the temple would be completely unrelated to such corruption. But what then might the significance of this action be? Kelber keenly observes that

> [T]he obstruction of the vessel's transport effects the cessation of the temple's cultic function. In the view of Mark, therefore, Jesus not only puts an

---

9 See E.P. Sanders, *Jesus and Judaism* (Philadelphia: Fortress, 1985), 61–65 and Jacob Neusner, "Money-Changers in the Temple: The Mishnah's Explanation," *NTS* 35 (1989): 288–289.
10 See Gray, *Temple*, 27.
11 See Gray, *Temple*, 29; Moloney, *Mark*, 223; Kelber, *Kingdom*, 99–102; William R. Telford, *The Barren Temple and the Withered Fig Tree: A Redactional-Critical Analysis of the Cursing of the Fig-Tree Pericope in Mark's Gospel and Its Relation to the Cleansing of the Temple Tradition* (JSNTSup 1; Sheffield: JSOT Press, 1980), 93 n. 102.

end to the temple's business operation, but he also suspends the practice of cult and ritual. At this point, the temple no longer operates. It is shut down in all its functions.[12]

Bringing a halt to the entirety of temple operations, including the offering of sacrifices, seems much more consistent with understanding Jesus's temple action as a prophetic act that points to the *permanent* end of temple operations, namely the imminent destruction of the temple itself.

1.2.2 Jesus's Teachings

E.P. Sanders concludes that the scripture citation in Mark 11:17 should not be attributed to the historical Jesus and that it was best understood as a redactional move on the part of the evangelist to present Jesus's actions as a cleansing rather than a symbolic destruction.[13] Many Markan commentators have followed this line of thinking, and have concluded that this Scripture citation supports interpreting the actions of the Markan Jesus in terms of cleansing a corrupt temple.[14] But recent studies have argued compellingly that this citation is in fact consistent with interpreting Jesus's action in the temple as a symbolic destruction. Daniel Kirk has argued that these Old Testament texts, when understood within their original context, are quite compatible with interpreting Jesus's action as a symbolic destruction of the temple. In addressing the first part of the citation (Isa 56:7), Kirk rightly notes that Isaiah 56 is an eschatological vision of God's salvation and deliverance.[15] This vision includes God's declaration that his house, the temple, "shall be called a house of prayer for all nations" (Isa 56:7). But such a reality does not characterize the present (first) temple due to its failing leaders.[16] The prophet describes these leaders as "blind sentinels" (Isa 56:10) and "shepherds having no understanding" (Isa 56:11). Kirk argues that this passage plays a role in Israel's eschatological expectations, particular the expectation of a new and restored temple, one to which God would draw all nations—such an expectation can be seen in Tob 13:8–11; 14:5–7; 1 En. 90.28–39; and the Temple Scroll from Qumran (11QT^a [11Q19] 29:7–10).[17] As

---

12 Kelber, *Kingdom*, 101.
13 Sanders, *Jesus and Judaism*, 66.
14 See Marcus, *Mark*, 788 and Adela Yarbro Collins, *Mark: A Commentary* (Hermeneia; Minneapolis: Fortress, 2007), 526.
15 Kirk, "Time for Figs," 515.
16 See Gray, *Temple*, 33–34.
17 See Kirk, "Time for Figs," 515–516; and Gray, *Temple*, 33–34.

such, Mark's citation of Isa 56:7 is reflecting the eschatological expectations for a new temple, and thus implies the destruction of the present (second) temple that, due to its contemporary "blind guides," clearly falls short of such expectations.

Perhaps the failure of the present temple (and its leadership) to embody the eschatological temple that Isaiah prophesied would alone be enough to justify a symbolic act of destruction from Jesus. But does the citation of Jer 7:11 shift the focus of Jesus's teaching to cleansing rather than destruction? Such is the contention of Sanders, who sees the reference to the temple being a "den of robbers" as an indictment of the temple's leadership and the corrupt practices that they employ within the temple. Yet Gray argues that in both the citation of Isaiah and Jeremiah, it is the temple itself that is in focus, not the temple's leadership. In Isaiah, the focus is on the *temple's* function as a "house of prayer," and in Jeremiah, the focus is on the *temple* that has become a *den* in which robbers/bandits dwell. To be sure the context of these passages critique the temple's leadership, but the citations themselves have the temple in focus. Additionally, Kirk argues that interpreters have wrongly understood the identification of the temple as a "den of robbers/bandits."[18] Jeremiah's reference to the temple as a den of robbers is not describing corrupt behavior within the temple itself, but it is critiquing Israel's belief that the temple will protect them regardless of their wicked behavior that took place outside of the temple. Thus, the temple is presented as a place where robbers come for safe haven after they have committed their crimes, not a place where they actually commit their crimes. It is for just such an attitude that Jeremiah 7 predicts the destruction of the Jerusalem Temple. Thus, this teaching of the Markan Jesus is best understood not as an attempt to end corrupt commercial practices in the temple, but rather as an indictment of those who trust in the temple as a safe haven for the people of God, even when they are not living in accordance with such an identity.[19]

When the Scripture citations used by the Markan Jesus are understood within their proper context, they no longer support the conclusion that Jesus's temple action is one of cleansing. Instead, they seem to clearly support the notion that Jesus is condemning the present temple and its leadership. Jesus demonstrates that the present temple is not the eschatological temple promised by Isaiah, and that it is instead like the former temple that was destroyed by the Babylonians because it houses those who have misguidedly

---

18   Kirk, "Time for Figs," 518–520.
19   Kirk, "Time for Figs," 519.

believed the temple would protect them despite their evil ways. Jesus's teaching clearly implies that the present temple awaits the same fate as that of Solomon.

1.2.3   The Cursing of the Fig Tree

Perhaps the most compelling evidence for interpreting Jesus's action in the temple in terms of a symbolic judgement rather than a cleansing is the Markan intercalation of the account of the cursed/withered fig tree with the account of Jesus's temple action. The intercalation of two pericopes is widely recognized as a common redactional technique of the Markan evangelist, one that suggests to the reader that the two pericopes are mutually interpretive.[20] Thus, the cursing and subsequent withering of the fig tree is intended to provide the reader with an interpretive lens for understanding the significance of Jesus's action in the temple. The literary connection between the two is quite straightforward. Just as Jesus finds a fruitless fig tree (a common symbol in the Hebrew Bible for Israel and its temple), he also finds a fruitless temple. Jesus's cursing of the fig tree then aids the reader in interpreting Jesus's action in the temple. Just as Jesus's words declare that the fig tree will never bear fruit again, Jesus's actions in the temple declare that it too will never bear fruit. When Jesus and his disciples see the fig tree the following day, it has withered from the root. The reader is intended to see that the parallels between the fig tree and the temple continue. Just as the fig tree withered after Jesus's curse, so also will the temple experience the destruction that Jesus's action symbolized. It is important to note here that the intercalation loses its meaning if Jesus's action in the temple is understood as a cleansing rather than a symbolic judgment. In no way can the cursing/withering of the fig tree be understood in terms of "cleansing" or "purification." Thus, if one understood Jesus's temple action in terms of cleansing, such an understanding would create an unnatural divorce between the two pericopes that Mark seems to have intentionally intercalated.

In summary, we conclude that Jesus's action in the temple is best understood as a symbolic act that is prophesying the destruction of the Jerusalem Temple. The fig-tree pericope not only supports such a reading but itself functions as a symbolic presentation of both the temple's corruption and impending destruction.

1.3   *Jesus's Teaching on Faith, Prayer, and Forgiveness (11:22–25)*

The intercalated fig-tree and temple-action pericopes are immediately followed by teachings of Jesus that, at first glance, seem quite unrelated to the

---

20   For a thorough treatment of this interpretation, see Telford, *Barren Temple*.

temple or its destruction. But recent studies have demonstrated a stronger connection between these teachings and Jesus's judgment of the temple than have previously been recognized. A good starting point is Jesus's statement about "this mountain." While traditional interpretations have understood "this mountain" in a generic sense, i.e., any mountain, it has been suggested that the mountain referenced may be a specific mountain, namely Mount Zion on which the temple sat.[21] Such an identification improves the narrative flow of the passage as it creates a clear connection between the teaching on faith and Jesus's symbolic judgment of the temple. In response to the disciples' amazement at Jesus's power to destroy the fig tree, Jesus responds by saying that their own faith could do far more, including the destruction of the temple itself—the event that Jesus's actions just predicted.[22]

Jesus's teaching on prayer (11:24) also finds a connection to the temple, and its future destruction. As Jesus has just reminded the reader, the temple's eschatological purpose is to become a house of prayer. Yet here Jesus tells his disciples that their prayer will be powerful and effective if it is accompanied with faith—a teaching that implies that the eschatological house of prayer might be connected to Jesus's disciples and their community of faith rather than a physical temple.[23]

The teaching on forgiveness (11:25) finds a similar connection to the temple. One of the primary functions of the temple was to serve as the place where, through sacrifice, Israel experienced atonement and the forgiveness of sins. But if Jesus's action in the temple was a symbolic judgment, the end of the sacrificial system might be implied. Thus, in Jesus's teaching on forgiveness, we may well see the evangelist claiming that there has been a transition in the locus of atonement, from the temple to the new community of God's people. No longer is God's forgiveness tied to the temple, but it is tied to the community's willingness to forgive the sins of others.[24] Thus, the focus of Jesus's teaching on faith, prayer, and forgiveness could be directly related to his judgment of the temple, as it functions to establish the new messianic community as a replacement of the temple itself.

1.4 The Question of Jesus's Authority (11:26–33)

The following day while Jesus is entering the temple, he is confronted by the temple authorities, "the chief priests, the scribes, and the elders." The reader is

---

21 Telford, *Barren Temple*, 58–59; Gray, *Temple*, 48–53.
22 See Heil, *Narrative Strategy*, 79; Kirk, "Time for Figs," 522–523.
23 See Gray, *Temple*, 54; Kirk, "Time for Figs," 523–527; Heil, *Narrative Strategy*, 79–80.
24 See Gray, *Temple*, 54–55; Kirk, "Time for Figs," 523–527; Heil, *Narrative Strategy*, 79–80.

reminded of Jesus's passion predictions, the first of which mentions all three of these groups, while the third mentions both the chief priests and scribes. Thus, the reader knows that these groups will be responsible for Jesus's death, a death that they began plotting immediately after Jesus's action in the temple (11:18). In v. 28 they ask Jesus, "By what authority are you doing these things? Who gave you this authority to do them?"[25] Presumably, they are questioning Jesus's authority to challenge the authority of the temple, and as the stewards of the temple, their own authority as well. The reader clearly knows the answer to the question already, as the Gospels has demonstrated that Jesus wields the power of God himself (e.g., Mark 2:5; 4:39; 5:35–43; 6:48). Thus, the question functions to highlight the temple authorities' opposition to God—the stewards of God's temple and people stand in opposition to God's authority. Jesus responds to these questions with a question of his own, a question about the authority of John's baptism that demonstrates the temple leaders' ongoing opposition to God through their opposition to his messengers.

1.5 *The Parable of the Wicked Tenants (12:1–12)*

Immediately following the question regarding Jesus's authority, Jesus tells the present temple authorities a parable about a landowner who plants a vineyard and leaves it in the hands of tenant farmers. The landowner sends servants to collect his portion of the produce from the tenants, but the tenants mistreat the servants and even kill one of them. Finally, the landowner sends his son, but in hopes of receiving the son's inheritance, the tenants mistreat and kill the son. Jesus states that as a result of the tenants' actions, the landowner will destroy the tenants and give the vineyard to others. Interpreters widely agree that this Markan parable is an allegory, and there is little debate as to the meaning of its various referents. The landowner is clearly God, while the vineyard is Israel and the tower is best understood as the temple. The tenants are clearly the leadership of Israel both past and present, including the current temple authorities—a point made quite clear by the statement in v. 12 that Jesus's audience, the temple authorities, "realized that he told this parable against them." The servants are the former prophets of Israel who suffered at the hands of Israel's leadership, and the son is clearly Jesus who the readers of Mark have been told will suffer and die at the hands of the "elders, chief priests, and scribes," Jesus's very audience for this parable (Mark 8:31). Thus, the parable clearly functions as an indictment of these temple authorities and again presents them as enemies of God and his messengers. But this pericope

---

25 All scripture citations are from the NRSV translation unless otherwise noted.

also includes a prophecy of their impending destruction as God's punishment for their rejection of his son. While this prophecy focuses explicitly upon the destruction of Israel's current leadership, the temple authorities, when taken together with Jesus's action against the temple itself, the parable might also imply the destruction of the temple.

1.6 Questions for Jesus (12:13–34)

Following the parable of the wicked tenants, the conflict between Jesus and the temple authorities continues, as they present Jesus with three successive questions in an attempt to undermine his authority—all of these questions are posed to Jesus while he is in the temple precincts.

The first question, regarding the paying of taxes to Caesar, is brought to Jesus by some of the Pharisees and the Herodians, but we are told that these two groups are sent by the temple authorities themselves with the purpose of trapping Jesus. Without addressing the numerous interpretive issues related to this pericope, it is only necessary for our purposes to note that Jesus thwarts the attempt of his opponents, leaving them amazed. Jesus is then approached by the Sadducees, the religious sect to which the temple authorities belong. They present a question that seeks to illustrate the folly of belief in resurrection and ultimately undermine the authority of Jesus. But again, Jesus thwarts these opponents by demonstrating his authority as an interpreter of Torah and by implication undermining their own. Finally, Jesus is approached by one of the scribes, a group that Mark commonly identifies with the temple authorities. The scribe asks Jesus which of the commandments is the greatest, to which Jesus responds with the double love commandment (12:29–31). In a rather striking break from the pattern of the previously asked questions, the scribe agrees with Jesus and the two seem to find unity over this issue. But what is remarkable for our purposes is the statement by the scribe that such love of God and neighbor is "more important than all whole burnt offerings and sacrifices." Thus, the triadic questioning of Jesus by those representing the temple authorities culminates in a statement (from a member of that very group!) that radically marginalized the temple's primary function!

In conclusion, these three questions accomplish the following in relation to the temple institution: (1) they continue to present the temple authorities as opponents of God and his messengers; (2) they further demonstrate the superiority of Jesus's over the temple authorities; (3) they culminate in a statement that marginalizes the primary function of the temple.

1.7 The Temple and the Poor (12:35–44)

After making rather esoteric comments about the Messiah and the Son of David (vv. 35–37),[26] Jesus, still teaching in the temple, gives a scathing critique of the scribes, in which he condemns their ostentatious self-presentation, their false motives for righteous behavior, and their "devouring" of the possessions of widows. Jesus unmasks the righteous outward appearance of the scribes and reveals their true wickedness, wickedness that is evinced in their oppression of widows rather than their Torah-prescribed protection (see Exod 22:21–24; Deut 24:17, 19–22; 27:19). For such wickedness, these leaders of Israel will receive "excessive" judgment from God. Again, the temple authorities are presented as God's enemies and thus recipients of God's impending judgment.

Immediately following this condemnation of the scribes, an episode follows in which Jesus is observing people giving money to the temple treasury. After seeing the affluent give large sums of money, a widow provides an extremely small sum of money. Jesus then declares that this woman has given more than the wealthy donors, because they have given out of abundance, and she has given out of her poverty—in fact, she has given all that she had for sustaining her life. This pericope has traditionally been interpreted in terms of costly giving and the role that one's heart plays in the true evaluation of one's gift. But such interpretations have failed to give proper attention to the narrative flow of this passage, in particular the immediately preceding condemnation of the temple authorities for devouring the possessions of widows. Some interpreters have seized on the undeniable connection between these two pericopes, and have offered a radically different interpretation of the widow's gift. Instead of understanding the widow's actions as an ideal for giving that should be followed, the story of her giving should be seen as an illustration of what Jesus has just condemned the temple authorities for doing, namely devouring the possessions of widows.[27] The story illustrates the way in which Israel's leadership has perverted the will of God—instead of caring for the needs of this impoverished widow as Israel's Scriptures command, they have taken the small amount of money she has. Instead of sustaining her life as God requires, they have stolen it for the sake of the temple. Again, the wickedness of the temple

---

26 While on the surface, these comments appear to have little connection to the temple, Gray has made an interesting case for just such a connection—see Gray, *Temple*, 79–90.

27 For examples, see Addison G. Wright, "The Widow's Mite: Praise or Lament?—A Matter of Context," *CBQ* 44 (1982): 256–265; Moloney, *Mark*, 246–247; Ched Myers, *Binding the Strong Man: A Political Reading of Mark's Story of Jesus* (Maryknoll, NY: Orbis, 1992), 320–322; Evans, *Mark*, 284–285.

authorities is clearly illustrated. The appointed stewards of God's people and temple have turned against him and have become his opponents.

1.8   Predicting the Temple's Destruction (13:1–2)

Most Markan interpreters contend that Mark 11–12 form a distinct literary unit, and that a new literary unit begins with Mark 13, but here I contend that the literary unit beginning in Mark 11 finds its conclusion in Mark 13:2, with a new literary unit beginning in Mark 13:3. There are several reasons for such a conclusion. First, the literary unit begins with Jesus's entrance into Jerusalem which concludes with his arrival in the temple. It seems quite natural that this literary unit would conclude with Jesus's departure from the temple, a departure that is described in 13:1. Second, virtually all action and teaching in Mark 11–12 take place in the temple, and Jesus's prediction of the temple's destruction in Mark 13:2 takes place as Jesus is exiting the temple. It is not until Mark 13:3, when we are told that Jesus is on the Mount of Olives opposite the temple, that the narrative introduces a change of location. Such a change in location, from the temple/temple mount (Mark 11–13:2) to the Mount of Olives (Mark 13:3) suggests an intentional literary transition, from one distinct literary unit to another. It is noteworthy that Jesus never returns to the temple in Mark's Gospel, which suggests that Mark 13:1–2 is the conclusion of a temple-centric literary unit in Mark. Third, Mark 13:2 functions as an excellent summary of and conclusion to the "temple motif" that we have analyzed in Mark 11–12. The motif clearly presents the temple and its leadership as corrupt and destined for destruction. Thus, Jesus's prediction of the temple's destruction simply makes explicit what has been implicit from the point of Jesus's temple action in Mark 11—the wicked temple institution is beyond redemption, and its destruction is both certain and deserved. Fourth, the connection between Mark 13:1–2 and Mark 13:3–37 is unclear and far less certain that many Markan interpreters presume. The only possible connection between the temple and the Olivet discourse is the reference to the "desolating sacrilege" and the subsequent suffering described in vv. 14–19. But such a connection is uncertain, as the "desolating sacrilege" might not be referencing the Jerusalem temple at all.[28] And even if Mark 13:14–19 is referring to the destruction of the temple, the focus of the passage seems to be the parousia itself, for which the events of vv. 14–19 are only the immediately preceding eschatological signpost rather than the chapter's main event.[29] Mark 13:1–2 has a much clearer and certain literary connection to Mark 11–12, which

---

28   See Winn, *Purpose*, 70–76.
29   While N.T. Wright (*Jesus and the Victory of God* [Minneapolis: Fortress, 1996], 361–365) and R.T. France (*Mark*, 530–540) have argued that Mark 13:26–27 is not describing the Parousia,

focuses more upon the corruption of the temple institution than does Mark 13:3–37, which primarily focuses on the parousia and the events leading up to it. Thus, we conclude that Mark's treatment of the temple in Mark 11–12 fittingly culminates in Jesus's explicit prophecy of the temple's destruction. The current temple and its leadership have failed to fulfill their divine purpose, and have in fact become enemies of God. As a result, the temple institution will be utterly destroyed.[30]

1.9 The Temple in Mark 11:1–13:2: A Summary

We opened this section with an overview of the prominence of the temple institution in Mark 11:1–13:2 and a claim that a clear temple motif is present in these chapters. After offering an analysis of this Markan material, it should be overwhelmingly clear that the nature of this motif is thoroughly negative. Mark clearly communicates that the current temple is corrupt and that it cannot be identified with the eschatological temple that God had promised through the prophets. Even its function as a place of atonement for Israel's sins is undermined. The temple leadership has not only failed to welcome God's final messianic agent, but they have directly opposed him and even plotted to kill him. Their opposition to God is further evinced in their destruction of widows, a group regularly protected by the Torah and the prophets. As a result of its grave failings, God's eschatological agent Jesus condemns the temple, prophesying its destruction and the removal of its leadership.

1.10 The Narrative Function of Mark's "Anti-Temple" Motif

Now that we have clearly identified and properly characterized the temple motif in Mark 11:1–13:2, we now consider its purpose and function in Mark's

---

but rather the realties that accompanied the destruction of Jerusalem (note that Wright and France do not agree on all details related to the interpretation of these verses), I and others remain unconvinced of such a position (e.g., Boring, *Mark*, 373; Evans, *Mark*, 329–330; Collins, *Mark*, 614–615 et al).

30 Some will contend that I have created an unnecessary "either/or" dilemma, and that Mark 13:1–2 can serve as a "hinge" passage that both concludes Mark 11–12 and begins Mark 13:3–37—for such a position, see France, *Mark*, 464, and Eugene Boring, *Mark: A Commentary* (NTL; Louisville: WJK, 2006), 353. I am willing to concede that such a mediating position is plausible, but with this concession I would assert two important points: (1) while Mark 13:1–2 might both conclude Mark 11–12 and introduce Mark 13:3–37, its narrative emphasis resides with the former rather than the latter; and (2) I have significant reservations about the substantive connection between Mark 13:1–2 and the following eschatological discourse (see Winn, *Purpose*, 70–71).

Gospel. Recent narrative studies of Mark 11–12 have made compelling cases that the "anti-temple" motif that dominates these chapters not only communicates the corruption and subsequent destruction of the Jerusalem temple institution, but that it also makes a claim about a new "temple" that will replace the old.[31] This temple will truly be a place of prayer for all nations, and it will be the location in which God's people experience the forgiveness of their sins. Unlike the old temple, this temple is not a physical building, but it is the new eschatological community of God's people, obviously including the Markan community itself. Thus, the anti-temple motif in Mark functions to teach the readers of the Gospel their identity as the new temple of God that has replaced the old temple. The functions of the old temple find their fulfilment in this new temple.

It is not my intention to debate the merits of this position, and I am presently willing to accept such a reading without contention. Instead, my present intention is to push such a conclusion even further by asking to what end or for what purpose Mark seeks to present his readers as the new temple of God. Such a question presses beyond the narrative itself, and broaches the question of the historical function of the narrative, i.e., why did the evangelist seek to communicate to his readers that they were the new temple? What realities motivated such a message, and what goals did the evangelist seek to accomplish with such a message? It is to just such questions that we now turn our attention.

2   Mark's Anti-Temple Motif: Historical Considerations

Historical reconstruction is essential for any attempt to ascertain the way that a text was intended to function in its original context. For the purposes of this study, our reconstruction will be limited to the issue of the ethnic identity of Mark's intended audience, that audience's concern for the Jewish temple, and realties that might impact that audiences concern for the Jewish temple. We will then consider how Mark's Gospel might address the concerns of its audience.

2.1   *The Ethnic Identity of Mark's Intended Audience*

Regarding the ethnic identity of Mark's intended audience, the specific question under consideration is whether that audience was primarily Jewish or Gentile? The text itself gives us significant clues for answering this question,

---

31   See Gray, *Temple*, 90–93, 198–200; Kirk, "Time for Figs", 522–527; Heil, "Narrative Strategy," 76–100.

clues that have led most Markan interpreters to conclude that Mark's audience is primarily Gentile in its constitution. While some have put forward Mark's translation of Aramaic words as evidence for a Gentile audience, it is quite likely that Greek-speaking Jews would also be equally unfamiliar with Aramaic. More telling is Mark's explanation of Jewish practices for his readers. Perhaps the best example is found in Mark 7:3–4: "For the Pharisees, and all the Jews, do not eat unless they thoroughly wash their hands, thus observing the tradition of the elders; and they do not eat anything from the market unless they wash it; and there are also many other traditions that they observe, the washing of cups, pots, and bronze kettles." Clearly, it seems unlikely that such an explanation of Jewish practices would be necessary for an audience that was primarily Jewish. And that Mark specifically refers to "all the Jews" seems to suggest a separation between the Jews and his primary audience. Similarly, Mark has to explain for his readers that Sadducees did not believe in the resurrection (12:18), something that Jews, even Hellenistic Jews, would already know. He also explains for his reader that the "Preparation day" was the day before the Sabbath (15:42), again something that would be well known by all Jews. These examples within Mark's Gospel strongly suggest an intended audience that is primarily, if not wholly, Gentile. If the audience was primarily Jewish, an author would likely not need such clarifications, and could rely upon the majority to help explain Jewish customs to the minority. Mark's interest in a Gentile mission (11:17; 13:10; 14:9) might also suggest a Gentile audience. It is noteworthy that in the Matthean parallels to Mark 11:17 and 13:10, the Matthean evangelist, who is widely recognized as writing to a primarily Jewish audience, omits these references to a Gentile mission. In light of the above evidence, it seems highly probably that Mark is written for an audience that is primarily Gentile, and this study moves forward assuming such an audience.

If Mark's audience was primarily Gentile, the question must be asked: what interest did Gentile Christians have in the Jewish temple? That the evangelist devotes a major section of the Gospel to the Jewish temple and its future suggests that his Gentile readers must have had some interest in it. But such an interest stands in stark contrast with the evidence we see throughout the New Testament. In Paul's undisputed letters, which are without question our best window into the interests and concerns of early Gentile Christianity, we see no interest in or concern for the Jerusalem temple. In fact, the only "temple" that Paul refers to is the church itself, which he identifies as God's temple. But even in such an identification, the Jerusalem temple plays virtually no role. Paul never makes a case that the Jerusalem temple is corrupt and thus needs to be replaced by the people of God. He never even uses language of "newness" when describing the church as the God's temple, i.e., the church is the "new" temple of God. In identifying the church as God's temple, Paul never presents the church as taking on the cultic functions of the temple. It seems that the Jerusalem temple played virtually no role in Paul's missional and pastoral work among Gentile churches, even in instances where Paul identifies those churches with God's temple. And while the value of the book of Acts for reconstructing Paul's missionary work is debated, it is noteworthy that the temple plays no role in Acts' depiction of Paul's proclamation of the gospel to the Gentiles (particularly given the fact that the temple seems to play a prominent role in other parts of the book of Acts). Thus, all the existing evidence that we have portrays an early Gentile Christian church that has no interest in the Jerusalem temple.

This apparent lack of interest in the Jerusalem temple among Gentile Christians stands in stark contrast to the Gospel of Mark's, and presumably its audience's, interest in that very temple. This contrast raises the question of what could have led to the existence of such interest where none before existed. Attempts to explain the *literary* purpose of Mark's anti-temple motif, as strong as they may be, are unable to answer this question. If the motif functions to demonstrate that the church or the Markan community is the new temple that has replaced the old—a theory proposed by narrative critics and noted above—the question still remains, why would Mark's Gentile readers, who presumably have no interest in the Jerusalem temple, care? Thus, this study will offer an historical explanation for the emergence of a Gentile Christian concern for or interest in the Jerusalem temple. Such an explanation will then be used to understand the historical function and purpose of Mark's literary "anti-temple" motif.

2.2   *Catalysts for Gentile Christian Interest in the Jewish Temple*

When one asks what historical realities that post-date the undisputed Pauline letters might explain the emergence of Gentile Christian concern for the Jewish temple, two obvious and related possibilities emerge: the Jewish Revolt against Rome and the destruction of the Jewish temple itself. It is my contention that the latter option has far greater explanatory power than the former. While the Jewish Revolt could certainly peek Gentile interest in the happenings in Galilee and Judea and raise curiosity as to how this situation would be resolved, it is hard to see how the revolt alone would lead to increased interest in the temple itself. Up until the end of the revolt, the fate of the temple was quite uncertain. If Rome was victorious, there was no assurance that it would destroy the Jerusalem temple. Perhaps one could argue that Mark's anti-temple motif functioned prophetically, and that the evangelist was looking forward to the temple's destruction and explaining the reason for such a destruction to his community. But the question must be asked: for what purpose? If the Gospel's intended audience had little interest in the temple, why would Mark devote such a larger portion of his Gospel to the temple's destruction and the reasons for its destruction? Why would Mark's Gentile audience care? To what end would such a prophetic word be needed? And with the temple still standing and its future uncertain, the rhetorical power of such a prophetic message would be significantly mitigated, as Mark's readers would naturally take on a "wait and see" approach. The rhetorical value of such a move by the Markan evangelist is minimal at best.

I propose that the actual destruction of the temple is able to offer a far more plausible explanation for increased Gentile-Christian interest in the temple. To make such a case, we must consider the role that the destruction of the temple played in Roman imperial propaganda, and the impact that such propaganda would have had upon Gentile Christians.

2.3   Vespasian and the Destruction of Jerusalem and the Jewish Temple[32]

After the death of Nero, the Roman empire experienced political chaos and civil war. Nero had no successor, and as a result, Rome experienced four successive emperors in a single year. Galba, a Roman governor who had rebelled against Nero was first appointed to the Principate. After a short time, he was replaced by one of his fellow conspirators, Otho, who betrayed him. Otho was then opposed and defeated by the general Vitellius. Vitellius was then opposed and defeated by the general Vespasian, who had been serving in Galilee and Judea, putting down the Jewish Revolt per the appointment of Nero in 66 C.E. After securing the Principate through military power, Vespasian sought to legitimize and stabilize his position, lest his reign be as short-lived as his three predecessors. These efforts at legitimization involved an expansive propaganda campaign that sought to demonstrate that Vespasian held the Principate by divine right, and not simply by powerful legions. A significant piece of this propaganda was Vespasian's victory over the Jewish rebels in Jerusalem and the destruction of the Jewish temple. Vespasian seems to have presented his success over the Jews as a major victory, and one that ended a major threat to the stability of Rome's empire and brought to it peace and prosperity. To understand the importance of such claims, an understanding of the way ancients

---

32   Much of the information in this section is indebted to the excellent work of Jason A. Whitlark, found in his monograph *Resisting Empire: Rethinking the Purpose of the Letter to the Hebrews* (LNTS 484; London: T&T Clark, 2014), especially chapter eight, 160–188. My thanks to Jason not only for this work, but also for a handful of informal conversations regarding this material.

understood victory in battle and war is crucial. J. Rufus Fears refers to such understanding as the "theology of Victory."[33] When traditional ways of sanctioning political power had failed, people in the ancient Mediterranean world often recognized victory in battle as a means of legitimizing political power. Such military success functioned to legitimize the power of Alexander and his successors, as well as that of Rome's first emperor, Augustus. Victory in battle was perceived as an epiphany of the goddess Victory. The logic of the theology of victory works in the following way. The gods granted *felicitas* (good fortune or luck) to those who demonstrated *virtus* (courage, manliness, and aggression) in battle. To those whom the gods had granted excessive *virtus*, the goddess Victory would be manifest to them through military victory. Thus, victory demonstrated the gods' choice of one potential ruling power or figure over another, i.e., the victor over the vanquished. But the theology of victory went beyond simply winning in battle. Such military victory had to result in peace and prosperity for victory to legitimize the claimant's divine right to rule.[34]

Vespasian seized on this theology of victory in order to legitimize his reign, and did so by promoting his victory over the Jews in a wide variety of ways. Perhaps most noteworthy was the triumph that Vespasian and his son Titus received in celebration of their victory over the Jews. Josephus offers a vivid description of this triumph (*J.W.* 7:117–159).[35] Vespasian and Titus emerged from the temple of Isis dressed in purple imperial robes, adorned with laurel crowns, and seated on ivory thrones. The procession that commenced was a visual display of the theology of victory. Seven hundred captive Jewish soldiers marched in the procession, and scenes of the war itself were reenacted for the crowds, including, depictions of slaughtered Jewish battalions, fleeing Jewish soldiers, siege engines destroying Jewish strongholds, Roman soldiers breeching Jewish ramparts, and the conflagration of the Jewish temple. Spoils of war were prominently displayed, including sacred vessels from the Jewish temple itself, a golden table, candlesticks, lampstands and even a Torah scroll. Enormous statues of Roman gods were carried in the procession, signaling the source of Roman power and greatness, as well as the superiority of Roman gods over the God of the Jews. The prosperity that this victory had secured for Rome was evinced through the tremendous wealth that was displayed throughout

---

33 See J. Rufus Fears, "Theology of Victory at Rome: Approaches and Problems," *ANRW* 17 2:736–826.

34 The description in this paragraph of Rome's "theology of Victory" is greatly indebted to both Jason Whitlark, *Resisting Empire*, 167–168 and J. Rufus Fears, "Theology of Victory."

35 See also Winn, *Purpose*, 164–165.

the triumph: great pieces of art formed from gold, silver, and ivory, large purple tapestries, and vessels adorned in gold and precious gems, finely dressed participants, including the Jewish captives themselves, and rare species of live animals. Josephus concludes his description of the triumph by saying, "For the city of Rome kept festival that day for her victory in the campaign against her enemies, for the termination of her civil dissensions, and for her dawning hopes of felicity" (J.W. 7.157). With these words, Josephus recognizes that this military victory over the rebellious Jews and the hope and prosperity that it created legitimized the reign of Vespasian.

Vespasian also promoted this victory through coinage by reinstituting the *capta*-type that commemorated military victory. Such coins were used by Augustus, who used military victory as a means of legitimizing his power.[36] But these coins were not minted by Augustus's Julian-Claudian successors, who legitimized their power through their familial connection to Augustus. The *Judaea Capta* coin, a series of coins that commemorated Roman victory over the Jews, was minted throughout Vespasian's reign, signaling the prominent role that his victory over the Jews played in the foundation of the myth of the Flavian dynasty.[37] The coins bear a number of different images, including Jewish captives bound to a palm tree, Romans towering over but ignoring Jewish captives, and the winged goddess Victory fixing a shield to a palm tree, the Roman symbol for Judea.[38] On the latter coin, the shield bears the inscription OB CIVES SER(VATOS), "for the security of the citizens," an inscription that expresses the belief that victory over the Jews served to secure the stability of the empire.[39]

Vespasian also promoted his victory over the Jews by appropriating the temple tax, a tax paid by every Jewish male for the upkeep of the Jewish temple, to the *fiscus Judaicus*, a tax that would now be paid by all Jewish males for the rebuilding and upkeep of the temple of Jupiter. Through the payment of this tax all Jews were reminded of the power of Rome, and more particularly the superiority of Jupiter Maximus to the God of Israel.

Flavian victory over the Jews also featured prominently in Roman buildings and monuments. Shortly after his triumph celebrating victory over the Jews, Vespasian began construction on the temple of Peace, which was funded by the

---

36 For discussion on these coins, see Whitlark, *Resisting Empire*, 166–167, and Jane Cody, "Conquerors and Conquered on Flavian Coins," in *Flavian Rome: Culture, Image, Text* (ed. A. Boyle and W. Dominik; Leiden: Brill, 2003), 103–123.
37 For a list of these coins, see Whitlark, *Resisting Empire*, 166 n. 27.
38 See Whitlark, *Resisting Empire*, 166.
39 Whitlark, *Resisting Empire*, 166.

spoils of the Jewish War. At its completion in 75 C.E., it housed the vessels from the Jewish temple that had been paraded in Vespasian's triumph (see above).[40] The temple of Peace was a reminder that the Jewish Revolt was a threat to Rome's peace and prosperity, and that Vespasian had secured both through his victory over the Jews. Though completed a decade after the Jewish war, the arch of Titus clearly commemorates the Flavian victory over the Jews. Panels of the arch depict the triumph of Titus, his crowning by the goddess victory, and the spoils of war taken from the Jewish temple.[41] Another arch dedicated to Titus and located in the Circus Maximus (81 C.E.) also commemorated the defeat of the Jews. Supposedly this arch bore an inscription claiming that Titus and Vespasian were the first to ever conquer the city of Jerusalem.[42] Though false, this claim further establishes the importance attributed to this event by the Flavian family. If a decade later the Flavian defeat of the Jews still played a prominent role in the dynasty's narrative, it seems safe to conclude that this event played a prominent role in the propaganda used by Vespasian to legitimize his power.

2.4 The Implications and Challenge of Vespasian's Propaganda for Early Christians

It seems clear that Vespasian's victory over the Jews played an important role in his attempts to legitimize his reign. But how would such propaganda impact Christians living in the Roman world? To understand this impact, we must understand the implications of Vespasian's propaganda for the God of Israel. Vespasian's victory over the Jews not only communicated that he was chosen by the gods to rule over the world, but it also communicated that the gods who made such a choice, the gods of Rome, were greater than the God of the vanquished Jews. Vespasian's propaganda thus implies a challenge to both the honor and power of the God of Israel. Through the destruction of his house and the defeat of his people, the God of Israel had been shamed by the victorious Romans. Such challenges to God's honor and power are not without precedent in the history of Israel. The prophets writing in the wake of the Babylonian exile and the destruction of both Jerusalem and the first Jewish temple, refer to the mockery and derision of Yahweh that such events had generated. Ezekiel 36:20 records YHWH describing Israel's exile to the nations in the following way, "When they came to the nations, wherever they came, they profaned my holy name, in that it was said of them, 'These are the people of the LORD, and

---

40 Whitlark, *Resisting Empire*, 164.
41 Whitlark, *Resisting Empire*, 165.
42 Whitlark, *Resisting Empire*, 165.

yet they had to go out of his land.'" In Deutero-Isaiah (48:9–11), YHWH claims that he will deliver Israel from exile for the sake of his own name, and so that his own name will not be profaned—presumably, such profanation is coming from Israel's enemies because of the apparent failure of their God. In describing the nations that have defeated Israel, YHWH says, "Their rulers howl ... and continually, all day long, my name is despised" (Isa 52:5). If the former destruction of Jerusalem and its temple led to the mockery of Israel's God by pagan nations, it seems quite likely that, given the Roman theology of victory, the most recent destruction of Jerusalem and the temple would lead to the same mockery.

How might such mockery of the God of Israel impact early Christian communities? The God of Israel is clearly the God of early Christians as well, and thus Vespasian's propaganda struck at the heart of Christian religious convictions. The impact of such propaganda on Jewish Christians would likely be minimal given their deep monotheistic roots, but it would likely be much greater on Gentile Christians and recent converts from Greco-Roman paganism. Among such fledgling Christians, Vespasian's propaganda would likely lead to serious questions regarding the legitimacy of their new faith. Might their commitment to a crucified savior be misguided, particularly when the God of that savior had also been defeated by Roman power? Pressure exerted from pagan family and friends who evoked the theology of victory could be persuasive indeed to Gentile Christians. Such questions and circumstances would require a strong answer in order to keep these Christians from abandoning their new faith and returning to the familiar gospel of Roman *pax et securitas*.

A related issue is that of Christian mission among Gentiles. Such a mission was important to the author and intended audience of Mark (Mark 13:10, etc.). But clearly Vespasian's propaganda regarding the destruction of both Jerusalem and the Jewish temple would stand as a major roadblock to Christians who were trying to convince Gentiles to devote their lives to the Jewish Messiah and Son of God, Jesus and his Father, the God of Jews. Even for those interested in such a conversion from Roman paganism, a strong answer to Flavian propaganda would likely be necessary. That a century later Irenaeus was still responding to pagan claims that the destruction of the Jerusalem temple undermined both Christian claims and the power and honor of Yahweh is strong evidence for the existence of the crises I have outlined here (*Haer.* 4.4). If Christians a century later had to provide an apologetic for the destruction of the Jerusalem temple, how much more would such an apologetic be needed for Christians living in the immediate aftermath of that destruction?

2.5 Mark's "Anti-Temple" Motif and Flavian Propaganda

The above argumentation brings us back to the issue of Gentile Christian interest in the Jerusalem temple. A logical catalyst for such interest, interest that presumably did exist not among Gentile Christians of the Pauline era, is the Roman destruction of the Jerusalem temple in 70 C.E. I contend that no other historical reality provides a better explanation for the sudden emergence of Gentile Christian interest in the Jerusalem temple than that temple's destruction by the Romans.

This connection between Gentile Christian interest in the temple and the temple's destruction bring us directly to the "anti-temple" motif of Mark's Gospel, and offers us a logical explanation for why a Gentile Gospel has such a strong interest in the Jerusalem temple, devoting over two chapters to it. I propose that Mark's "anti-temple" motif functions to respond to the Flavian propaganda related to the Jerusalem temple and that the motif addresses the crises that such propaganda would create for Mark's Gentile community. In response to the Roman theology of Victory that fueled Flavian propaganda, Mark argues that the Jerusalem temple was destroyed because it and its leadership were thoroughly corrupt and had turned against the purposes of YHWH. This corruption was identified by God's appointed Messiah and was verified by the temple authorities' rejection and execution of that Messiah. Long before Rome turned its attention to a rebellious Judea, YHWH's Messiah Jesus had recognized a rebellious temple institution and had prophesied its utter destruction. Thus, through his "anti-temple" motif, Mark robs Flavian propaganda of its power, and transfers that power to YHWH and his Messiah Jesus, the true ruler of the world. Consequently, Rome and its emperor simply become pawns in the plans of the God of Israel.

Such a move by the evangelist is hardly without precedent. Similar arguments are made by the Jewish people in response to Babylon's destruction of the first temple. Throughout the exilic and post-exilic prophets, the reason for the temple's destruction was not the inferiority of Yahweh to the gods of pagan nations, but rather Yahweh's punishment of an unfaithful people. In Isa 42:24–25 the prophet writes:

> Who gave up Jacob to the spoiler, and Israel to the robbers? Was it not the LORD, against whom we have sinned, in whose ways they would not walk, and whose law they would not obey? So he poured upon him the heat of his anger and the fury of war; it set him on fire all around, but he did not understand; it burned him, but he did not take it to heart.

In Lamentations, the source of Judah's destruction is consistently identified as YHWH rather than foreign nations, and this destruction is clearly a result of Judah's wickedness: "How the Lord in his anger has humiliated daughter Zion! He has thrown down from heaven to earth the splendor of Israel; he has not remembered his footstool in the day of his anger" (2:1). The prophets also depict Babylon as a pawn of YHWH that will be used to punish Israel. Jeremiah 25:8–9 states:

> Therefore thus says the LORD of hosts: Because you have not obeyed my words, I am going to send for all the tribes of the north, says the LORD, even for King Nebuchadnezzar of Babylon, my servant, and I will bring them against this land and its inhabitants, and against all these nations around; I will utterly destroy them, and make them an object of horror and of hissing, and an everlasting disgrace.

Ezekiel 21 depicts Babylon as a sword in the hand of YHWH that will be used to punish his people. I propose that the Markan temple motif is following the precedent of Israel's prophets, and is a narratival attempt to make the same argument in response to the second temple's destruction as these prophets made in response to the first temple's destruction.

It is noteworthy that the Gospel of Mark would not be alone in making such an argument in response to Rome's destruction of the Jerusalem temple. The late first-century Jewish apocalypse 2 Baruch, though coded as a response to the Babylonian destruction of the first temple, is truly addressing the Roman destruction of the second. Here the destruction of the temple is orchestrated by God who uses foreign nations as pawns for his purposes.[43] Similarly, the *Apocalypse of Abraham* (a late first- or early second-century C.E. text), describes the Roman destruction of the Jerusalem temple (ch. 27), and it attributes this destruction to the power of YHWH, who allows the destruction of the temple because of Jewish infidelity. But perhaps most significant is Josephus's explanation for the temple's destruction.[44] Josephus attributes the destruction of Jerusalem and the temple to the will of God (*J.W.* 7.358–360) as an act of

---

43 For discussion, see Philip F. Esler, "God's Honour and Rome's Triumph: Responses to the Fall of Jerusalem in 70 C.E. in Three Jewish Apocalypses," in *Modeling Early Christianity* (ed. Philip F. Esler; London: Routledge, 1995), 255–258.

44 For the following arguments, I am greatly indebted to work of Steve Mason ("Figured Speech and Irony in T. Flavius Josephus," in *Flavius Josephus and Flavian Rome* [ed. J. Edmondson et al.; Oxford: Oxford University Press, 2005], 260–265) and Jason Whitlark (*Resisting Empire*, 175–176).

judgement against the actions of Jews (*J.W.* 1.10–12). Again, Rome is presented as an agent or tool of God that engaged in a war that it truly wanted no part of (*J.W.* 1.10). Perhaps nothing illustrates Rome as God's agent more than the following quote of the Roman general and future Flavian emperor, Titus: "God indeed … has been with the war. God it was who brought down the Jews from these strongholds; for what powers have human hands or engines against these towers" (*J.W.* 6.410–411).

If narrative critics are correct regarding the literary purpose of Mark's temple motif, namely that it identifies Mark's community as the new temple of God that replaces the old, then the motif would not only offer Mark's community a counter argument to Flavian propaganda, but it would go a step further. In addition to defending the community and the God of Israel from shame, it would also function to empower the community by giving it a new identity. The Gospel makes the claim that long before the Roman destruction of the temple, YHWH had already created and entered a new eschatological temple, namely Mark's community itself. Thus, Rome did not destroy the house of YHWH, but an empty and corrupt shell. The true home of YHWH, the true house of prayer, and the true place in which atonement for sins is found is the new people of God who follow God's Messiah, Jesus. In this context of Flavian propaganda, the words of Jesus in Mark 11:23 take on new significance, as with these words, Jesus tells the Markan community that through faith, they have more power at their disposal than that of powerful Roman legions. While Rome was able to destroy the Jerusalem temple (albeit as pawns of YHWH), Jesus tell his disciples that, through faith, they have the power to cast the entire temple mount into the sea. Thus, far from being a sign of divine favor upon Rome, the destruction of the Jerusalem temple is presented as a sign of divine favor upon the Markan community, establishing it as the true dwelling place of God and divine power.

3 Conclusion: The Markan "Anti-Temple" Motif as Both Pastoral Response and Missional Empowerment

As discussed above, Flavian propaganda would have been a significant blow to the fledgling faith of new Gentile converts to the Christian faith. It might even have posed serious difficulties for well-established Gentile Christians whose faith was waning under persecution (or its threat) and the delay of the parousia. Flavian power that had been enacted in a tangible way over the God of Israel might lead some to question whether the resurrected Jesus could truly rival such power. Thus, through an "anti-temple" motif, the Markan evangelist takes this crisis head on and offers a pastoral response to the concerns of a

Gentile Christian community. He assures them that the destruction of Jerusalem temple was not evidence of Rome's power over the God of Israel, but that it was instead the God of Israel judging a corrupt and defunct institution, one God had already replaced. Rome and its newly appointed emperor were merely pawns used to accomplish the purposes of God and his Messiah—a Messiah who decades before had predicted the destruction of Israel's temple.

In addition to causing a potential crisis for Gentile Christians, Flavian propaganda also presented a major obstacle for any Christian engaged in Christian mission. Such Christians would be hard pressed to convince pagan Gentiles that Jesus, the Son of the God of Israel, was true lord and savior of the world in the face of Rome's victory over Jerusalem and the destruction of the Jewish temple. For Gentiles steeped in the theology of victory, recent events had decidedly favored the gods of Rome and Rome's emperor. Mark's "anti-temple" motif provides Christian missionaries with a means of dealing with this obstacle and a means of answering the questions and challenges they would encounter as they sought to spread the gospel of Jesus.

The Holy Spirit as Witness of Jesus in the Canonical Gospels

Judith Stack

1 Introduction

All of the canonical Gospels portray the Holy Spirit as an agent of witness to the identity of Jesus as the Christ and Son of God—an identity that the early Christian communities confessed and from which they also drew their communal identities as believers in and disciples of Jesus. Some aspects of the work of the Spirit seem to have been perceived differently in the communities or are at least articulated differently by the authors (or final redactors[1]) of the Gospels, yet there are notable areas of overlap as well, the most consistent being the perception of the Holy Spirit as an agent of witness to Jesus and thus the focus of this exploration.

2 The Holy Spirit in Mark

Given its relatively brief length, the interest in and development of the perspective on the role of the Holy Spirit as a witness to Jesus's identity evident the Gospel of Mark is significant. The identity of Jesus to which the Spirit witnesses is at least two-fold: as the anointed messianic king ("son of God") and as the apocalyptic agent of God's will who is both motivated and empowered by the Holy Spirit.

Mark begins his Gospel with an assertion about Jesus's identity: that Jesus is the Christ, and some manuscripts add "son of God." Whether the υἱοῦ τοῦ θεοῦ[2] was original to Mark's writing, the later development of Mark's portrayal of Jesus's identity—and the relationship of the Spirit to it—substantiates the correlation of the terms that we see in the less reliable manuscripts as representative of Mark's perspective if not his original writing.

---

[1] The scope of this paper will be, as indicated above, simply to trace synchronically the theme of Spirit-as-witness in the final-form texts of Matthew, Mark, Luke, and John. In this sense it will serve only as a prolegomenon to the further work of exploring the historical interrelations of these texts and traditions.

[2] Or υἱοῦ θεοῦ.

This perspective is made evident as soon as Jesus appears in Mark. Jesus comes to be baptized by John, and just as he is coming up out of the water, the heavens are opened and the Spirit descends upon Jesus and God declares that Jesus is "my son, the beloved." The seeming simultaneity of the coming of the Spirit and the declaration of Jesus's identity as son of God ties these inextricably, a tie that will be developed as the Gospel progresses. But essential also to this tie is the apocalyptic context set by both the symbolic-allusive depiction of John the Baptist and the rending of the heavens in the Spirit's descent. John's attire and manner is reminiscent of Elijah (2 Kgs 1:8), the return of whom was an expected harbinger of the eschaton (Mal 4:5–6). Further, the heavens being rent asunder (σχιζομένους) would have been a disruption of the created order indicative of the sorts of apocalyptic cosmological disruptions attendant upon the end of the age.[3] This combination of the attestation of Jesus's identity by the voice of God and the coming of the Spirit within an apocalyptic scenario is significant for grasping Mark's point.

The first aspect to note is the now commonly recognized connection between the title "son of God" and the kings of Israel, particularly David as the paradigmatic and ideal king of Israel. Such terminology is a feature of many of the royal Psalms,[4] and those Psalms took on Messianic significance during the Second Temple Period.[5] The Spirit of the Lord coming upon a man was understood as a feature of the process of becoming anointed as king (cf. 1 Sam 10:1–6 and 16:13–14), thus the combination of the descent of the Spirit onto Jesus and declaration of his divine sonship would have had royal connotations, but put in an apocalyptic scenario, the connotations become distinctly messianic and eschatological. The presence of the Spirit and particularly its connection to eschatological expectations identifies Jesus as the messianic agent of God for the end of the age, an identity in which the Spirit will play a significant role.

This identity to which the Spirit will attest is immediately indicated as, after the baptism "the Spirit cast out (ἐκβάλλει) Jesus into the wilderness" (1:12) where

---

[3] Note esp. Joel 2:30–31 which foretells anomalous heavenly portents connected with "the day of the Lord" (a text which was apparently significant for some in the early church: see Acts 2:17–20) and which were also connected with the giving of the God's Spirit (Joel 2:26–29). Cf. 1 En. 91:16.

[4] Pss 2, 45, 72, 89, and 110.

[5] Adela Yarbro Collins and John J. Collins, *King and Messiah as Son of God: Divine Human and Angelic Figures in Biblical and Related Literature* (Grand Rapids: Eerdmans, 2008), 55–58. See also the discussion in this essay of the parallel passage in Matthew and potential parallels between Jesus's baptism and David's anointing (see below).

he is tempted by Satan.[6] The first act of the Spirit of God within Jesus is to set him conflict with apocalyptic powers of evil, a conflict which will continue in the litany of exorcisms[7] that characterize the first nine chapters of the Gospel. This is part of the Spirit's role of witnessing and attesting to Jesus in that Jesus's Spirit-instigated conflict[8] results in the subsequent demonstration of Spirit-empowered dominion over the demonic powers. Given that God must be in conflict with the powers of evil, Jesus must indeed be filled with the Spirit God to not only enter into this conflict but also prevail against such powers. Indeed the presence of the Spirit of God in Jesus is such that, not only does it witness to Jesus's identity through its empowerment of his exorcisms, it compels the spiritual entities around it (the demons) also to attest to Jesus's identity: "I know who you are, the Holy One of God,"[9] "You are the Son of God,"[10] "Jesus, Son of the Most High God."[11] So the Spirit becomes the agent of witness to Jesus's identity as the apocalyptic, royal-messianic Son of God as well as the motivating agent within Jesus.

The source of Jesus's power over demons is, of course, precisely the issue at stake in the Beelzebul controversy (3:22–30), and although Mark does not make as explicit as Matthew that the source of Jesus's power is God's Spirit (Matt 12:28; cf. 12:18), the dualistic framework of apocalyptic thought leaves God's Spirit as the only option for empowerment when diabolical power has been eliminated through Jesus's persuasive logic. Jesus's opponents' inability or unwillingness to acknowledge the attestation of Jesus's identity by the Spirit and its agency within him makes them culpable of unforgiveable blasphemy, "for they had said, 'He has an unclean Spirit'" (Mark 3:30).

---

[6] It is unclear whether Jesus's statement to the disciples in Mark 14:38 alludes to this connection between the Spirit and being in a place of temptation. Given this early incident "Watch and pray that you may not enter into temptation; the Spirit indeed is willing, but the flesh is weak" could indicate that the disciples ought to pray that God will prevent the Spirit from taking them, like Jesus, into a place of temptation, and that the Spirit is willing (or ready or even eager, cf. Rom 1:15) to do this. There is not, however, enough contextual evidence to assert this parallel with confidence.

[7] E.g. Mark 1:25.

[8] The use of ἐκβάλλω in Mark 1:12 shows that it is always the Spirit that is driving Jesus into the conflict, verbally anticipating the use of this word for Jesus's own Spirit-empowered casting out.

[9] Mark 1:24.

[10] Mark 3:11.

[11] Mark 5:7.

The Spirit's role in witnessing to Jesus is not, however, manifest only through Jesus. Or at least Jesus predicts such.[12] In the "little apocalypse" of Mark 13, Jesus tells his followers:

> But see to yourselves: they will hand you over to councils and to synagogues to be beaten, and you will stand before rulers and governors for my sake in testimony to them. And the gospel must first be proclaimed to all the Gentiles. And when they arrest you and hand you over, do not worry beforehand what you are to say, but say whatever is given you in that hour, for it is not you who are speaking, but the Holy Spirit.[13]

Jesus thus predicts that the Holy Spirit's vocation of witnessing to Jesus is not confined to working through Jesus himself, but will be continued in his followers who will, apparently also be filled with the Spirit, and this is again set within an explicitly apocalyptic context. This also sheds some light on the otherwise obscure prediction of John the Baptist that Jesus will "baptize you with the Holy Spirit" (1:8).

And while the context of disciples' Spirit-empowered witness is obviously envisioned in a post-resurrection scenario, even before Jesus's death, the disciples are depicted as participating in at least one of Jesus's Spirit-empowered activities: that of exorcising unclean Spirits. "And he called the twelve, and began to send them out two by two, and gave to them authority over unclean Spirits" (6:7). Thus even before Jesus's resurrection, the disciples participate in Jesus's apocalyptic, Spirit-empowered activity of confronting the diabolical powers.[14]

The final passage in which we see the witnessing activity of the Spirit is the crucifixion, but here we need to pay attention to some of Mark's more subtle literary craft to grasp his message. While the Spirit is not specifically referred to in Mark 15 there are elements that set up the scene as both apocalyptic and

---

12 It is perhaps worth noting that the reliability of Jesus's predictions has proleptically been affirmed through the reference in Mark 12:36 to David's Spirit-inspired prophetic abilities: "David himself, inspired by the Holy Spirit, declared, 'The Lord said to my Lord, Sit at my right hand …'" Since Mark has already established for the reader that this same Holy Spirit now empowers Jesus, his prophecies can be taken to be as reliable as David's are deemed to be, since the same Spirit inspires both.

13 All NT translations are mine based on NA27 unless otherwise noted.

14 This ability is apparently, for Mark, linked to the authority of Jesus's name, not from any close association with Jesus himself as we see demonstrated in 9:38–40 in the discussion of another successful exorcist who uses Jesus's name but is not among the disciples.

parallel to the baptism. We have a scene in which apocalyptic elements are invoked: the officially posted charge against Jesus is that he is the "king of the Jews," and messianic language figures heavily in the derision of the onlookers (15:26 and 32). He is also derided as one "who would destroy the temple and build it in three days"—such destruction being understood as a significant catastrophe and its rebuilding a miraculous sign indicative of God's reign.[15] The darkening of the sun recalls the prophecies of the coming of the Day of the Lord.[16] Finally, the onlookers misunderstand Jesus's cry of dereliction as a call to Elijah. This not only calls to mind the prophecy of Malachi 4 mentioned earlier (and thus eschatological hopes) but also the way in which Mark has portrayed John the Baptist in those terms and thus his call to repentance in light of the coming kingdom. It may also in this way allude the last passage in which the figures of John and Elijah were related, that is, Jesus's question about his perceived identity and Peter's confession of Jesus as the Messiah (Mark 8:27–30).[17] This passage is, of course, followed then by Jesus's prediction of his imminent Passion, thus further connecting the pericopes. The rebuke of Peter as "Satan" for trying to dissuade Jesus from his path to suffering and death (8:31–33) also serves to alert the reader that the upcoming Passion and crucifixion will be an event of apocalyptic conflict. This is reinforced by Jesus's struggle in Gethsemane: the temptation in the garden to reject the path to the cross here at the end of Jesus's ministry parallels the temptation in the wilderness at the beginning of his ministry.[18]

As we move then into the crucifixion, Mark has constructed the narrative to lead us to expect some level of parallelism with the baptism. And the narrative does not disappoint. As Jesus dies on the cross, Mark says he ἐξέπνευσεν. This does, of course, mean "breathed his last" but more literally "expired," that is, expelled [his] spirit/breath. Mark is depicting this as, in some sense, Jesus's unbaptism—the departure of the Spirit that descended upon Jesus and has been the motivating agent of his work as well as, correlatively, the validating mark of

---

15 Cf. 1 Sam 7:4–17. Also Jub. 1:9, and cf. Jub. 8:19. And of course this claim of destruction and rebuilding is a charge against Jesus at his trial (Mark 14:56–58).

16 Isa 13:10, 34:4, 50:2–3; Joel 2:10, 31; Amos 8:9.

17 Matthew, of course, in his version of this incident will explicitly connect the work of the Spirit to Peter's perception and confession of Jesus's identity. Perhaps Mark expects his readers to be sophisticated enough to make the connection without explicit direction.

18 The fleeing νεανίσκος at the end of the garden temptation (Mark 14:51) may even indicate a reversal of the appearance of the ministering angels in 1:13 given his seeming extraneousness and that the personage in the tomb after the resurrection—a being identified in the other Synoptic Gospels as one or more angels—is also called by Mark a νεανίσκος.

his identity now departs. This parallelism is reinforced by, at the departure of the Spirit, the rending of the temple curtain with the same terminology (ἐσχίσθη) as the rending of the heavens at its descent. This movement of the Spirit is, just as at the baptism, accompanied by a declaration of Jesus's divine sonship and thus Davidic-messianic identity—this time, however, not by the voice of God but by an unlikely witness: the nearby centurion who saw οὕτως ἐξέπνευσεν. Whether we are to take his testimony at face value or whether it is, as some have suggested, perhaps a sarcastic remark on the ignominy of the death of this "king of the Jews," the reader is expected to recognize the validity of the confession "Surely this was the/a son of God" and to connect it to the power of the Spirit to evoke even from Gentile executioners and demons the correct testimony of Jesus's identity.

3 The Spirit in Matthew

At key junctures in Matthew's narrative of the life of Jesus, the Holy Spirit is referred to as a witness to his identity and with respect to the disciples' task of both faithful following and partnership in Jesus's mission, indicating the author's and community's sense of the Spirit's role in their own continuation of the work started by Jesus and imparted by him to the disciples.

As in Mark, one of the first explicit references to the Spirit in Matthew is in connection to Jesus's interaction with John the Baptist. In Matthew, after some protest by John, Jesus is baptized by him: "And when Jesus was baptized, immediately he came up from the water, and behold, the heavens were opened, and he saw the Spirit of God coming down like a dove coming upon him, and behold, a voice from heaven saying, 'This is my Son, the beloved, with whom I am well pleased'" (Matt 3:16–17). The ambiguity of the pronouns makes it unclear if the one seeing the descent of the Spirit is Jesus or John,[19] but perhaps it is not important to Matthew's point. The emphasis is on the simultaneity of the coming of the Spirit and the affirmation by God of Jesus's sonship and God's declaration of divine approval.

The connection between the Spirit coming upon Jesus and God's approval and proclamation of Jesus as son is perhaps meant to be reminiscent of King David. As has been often pointed out, the idea of the king being the or a son of God, particularly David as the paradigmatic and ideal king of Israel, is a feature

---

19 An ambiguity that some copyists perhaps tried to resolve by the addition of "to him" after "the heavens were opened."

of many of the royal Psalms,[20] and those Psalms took on Messianic significance during the Second Temple Period.[21] Further corroborating this connection is the similarity of this scene to David's anointing by Samuel: "Then Samuel took the horn of oil and anointed him in the midst of his brothers. And the Spirit of the LORD rushed upon David from that day forward" (1 Sam 16:13). Jesus's baptism with water by the prophet John parallels the anointing of David with oil by the prophet Samuel, and in both stories the "son of God" receives the Spirit. Jesus's status as Davidic Messiah and Son of God are thus mutually reinforced both by the allusion to David and the combination the voice of God and the coming of the Spirit in the baptism.

Before Jesus arrives for baptism, however, John's proclamation refers to Jesus and the coming Spirit with a different emphasis. Matthew reports that John preached that "he who is coming after me is more powerful than I, whose sandals I am not worthy to carry. He will baptize you in the Holy Spirit and fire" (3:11). Before we even see Jesus receive the Spirit in baptism, we are told that he himself will impart the Spirit to others in his own baptizing work. The connection with fire, however, lends a note a judgment, since John continues saying, "His winnowing fork is in his hand, and he will clear his threshing floor and gather his wheat into the barn, but the chaff he will burn with unquenchable fire." When put in conversation with some of Matthew's later parables, particularly the Wheat and the Tares to which this seems to allude, there is a potential interpretation that those who are "wheat" will be baptized in and receive the Spirit and those who are chaff or tares will receive fire, but regardless, there is an underlying connection of the Spirit with judgment, and that those who, in the context of John's previous preaching, are expected to be judged unfaithful are identified with the Jewish religious leadership (3:7–10) who will be depicted as inveterately opposed to Jesus.

But the baptism narrative is not the first mention of the Spirit in Matthew. The first and very early mention of the work of the Spirit is in 1:18–20:

> Now the birth of Jesus Christ was thus: his mother Mary, having been betrothed to Joseph, before they came together was found to be with child from the Holy Spirit ... But as he pondered these things, behold an angel of the Lord appeared to him in a dream, saying, "Joseph, son of David, do not fear to take Mary as your wife, for that which is begotten in her is from the Holy Spirit."

---

20 Pss 2, 45, 72, 89, and 110.
21 Collins and Collins, *King*, 55–58.

The assertion of Spirit's role in the initial generation of Jesus demonstrates the community's sense that the attestation of Jesus by the Spirit was not a surprising development at the baptism but was its role from the start. And we again see the combination of connection to David with the assertion of Jesus's divine sonship. Further, in v. 21 we are introduced to two other aspects of Jesus's identity: that "he will save his people from their sins" and be understood as "God with us." Jesus as the embodiment of God's presence on earth has a distinctly Johannine accent and is a recurring theme of no small significance in Matthew.[22]

Perhaps this idea of attestation of identity is also behind Matthew's assertion that after his baptism Jesus was "led into the desert by the Spirit to be tested by the devil" (4:1). The attestation of Jesus's sonship without confirmation through Jesus's ability to resist temptation would be mere assertion. And it seems no small, locutionary quirk then that the first two temptations of the devil are preceded by the clause "If you are the son of God ..." The question on the table is whether Jesus *is*, as the text has been asserting, the son of God filled with and empowered by the Holy Spirit; he demonstrates that he indeed is, but not by satisfying the devil's requirements for affirmation but by resisting and in so doing, showing himself faithful. For Matthew, because the Spirit is always involved in attesting to Jesus identity, it is she who leads Jesus to the proving grounds of his identity and thus is again the agent of attestation.

Jesus's identity vis-à-vis the Spirit is, in fact, at the heart of one of the longest and most contentious disputes that Matthew relates between Jesus and his opponents. The Beelzebul controversy of ch. 12 revolves around the fundamental question of which (or what sort) of spirit is empowering Jesus and his work. It is a complex passage, but there are three main points pertinent to our exploration:

- The works that Jesus does (exorcisms) are works acknowledged as works of God's Spirit within the wider community ("by whom do your sons cast them out?" 12:27) and indeed are more: signs that "God's reign has come upon you," undoing the reign of Satan (12:25–29).
- To label these works of God's Spirit as works of the devil is to go beyond impugning Jesus ("speaking a word against the Son of Man") to impugning

---

22   Note the thorough exploration of this theme by Andries van Aarde in *God-With-Us: The Dominant Perspective in Matthew's Story, and Other Essays* (Pretoria: Periodical Section of the Nederduitsch Hervormde Kerk van Afrika, 1994) as well as David D. Kupp in *Matthew's Emmanuel: Divine Presence and God's People in the First Gospel* (SNTSMS 90; Cambridge: Cambridge University Press, 1996).

the Spirit herself as from the devil, and demonstrates a level of intransigence against the work of God that can only end in judgment (12:31–42).
- The failure of Jesus's opponents to acknowledge the work of the Spirit in Jesus (and by extension his identity), and indeed their active opposition to it, shows that they, not he, are filled with "unclean Spirits" (12:41–45).

But the question of what people are to make of Jesus's identity based on these Spirit-empowered works is not one that Matthew has introduced without preparation. While Jesus's opponents are, apparently, bent on intentional misconstrual of the Spirit's attestation through works indicative of the kingdom, John the Baptist and his disciples demonstrate greater openness to recognition as Matthew relates in the previous chapter.

> Now John, hearing in prison about the works of the Christ, sent word through his disciples and said to him, "Are you the Coming One, or shall we expect another?" And Jesus answered them, "Go and tell John what you hear and see: the blind receive their sight and the lame walk, lepers are cleansed and the deaf hear, and the dead are raised up, and the poor have good news preached to them." And blessed is the one who is not σκανδαλισθῇ by me.
> Matt 11:2–6

Matthew here indicates—and perhaps Jesus himself claimed—that Jesus's works are indicators of his identity. John's obvious willingness to accept these as Spirit-empowered works consistent with the coming Kingdom and as markers of Jesus's role in bringing that Kingdom and his identity thus contrasts with the rejection of these by the Scribes and Pharisees in ch. 12. And lest the readers be in any way confused regarding what Spirit is animating and empowering the works of Jesus and what that means, Matthew's narrator alerts the readers by means of the fulfillment quotation that falls between these two sections:

> ... In order that might be fulfilled that which was declared by the prophet Isaiah [42:1]: "Behold, my servant whom I have chosen, my beloved with whom my soul is well pleased. I will set my Spirit upon him, and he will announce judgment to the Gentiles."
> Matt 12:17–18

In the midst of stories about how Jesus's miraculous deeds relate to his identity, Matthew communicates the community's perspective that these were empowered by the Holy Spirit and were in fact demonstrations of Jesus's infilling with

God's Spirit and thus his identity as the eschatological "Coming One." The Spirit bears witness to Jesus's identity through works that are harbingers of the Kingdom and indicative of Jesus role with respect to the Kingdom.

These stories also help shed light on a previous and significant mention of the Spirit earlier in Matthew. In ch. 10, the "Missionary Discourse," Jesus commissions his disciples to do precisely the things that he has been doing in previous chapters and continues to do in chapters 11 and 12—preach, heal, raise the dead, cleanse lepers, and cast out demons (10:7–8)—things that, as we have seen, are portrayed as demonstrations of the presence of the Spirit and indications of Jesus's identity as Son of God. Jesus also predicts that his disciples will experience the same sort of rejection that Jesus experiences, and since we do not see any such rejection of the disciples within the timeframe of the narrative, it seems that these predictions point beyond that timeframe to that of Matthew's community (or perhaps their predecessors who were closer to Jesus's own time).

It is in this context of rejection and persecution that Matthew's implicit evocation of the activity of the Spirit in the mighty works of the disciples becomes an explicit assertion of the Spirit's infilling of the disciples and indeed their own identity vis-à-vis God. Jesus says:

> Beware of people, for they will deliver you over to courts and flog you in their synagogues, and you will be dragged before both governors and kings for my sake, to bear witness to them and to the Gentiles. When they hand you over, do not be anxious how you are to speak or what you are to say, for what you are to say will be given to you in that hour. For it is not you who are speaking, but the Spirit of your Father speaking through you.
> Matt 10:17–20

Here we have an important indication of the community's sense of their own identity. Their witness as well as their deeds are, like those of their Master, understood to be through the agency of the Spirit. Thus their witness, which apparently includes not only announcing the imminence of the kingdom but also acknowledging Jesus before people (v. 32), is empowered by the Spirit, or more precisely is actually accomplished by the Spirit. So Matthew claims that the Spirit's action as witness to the identity of Jesus is not restricted to its role or presence in and with Jesus but to be similarly active in and animating of the disciples' varieties of witness even after Jesus is no longer physically present. The identification of the disciples with Jesus through the work of the Spirit is so profound that Jesus here also calls the Spirit not just the Spirit of *his* Father but the Spirit of *their* Father, indicating a level of filial identification usually more associated with the Johannine tradition. The Spirit witnesses to Jesus as the Son of God, but the disciples also are to consider God their Father,[23] and as with Jesus, the activity of the Spirit is one of the ways in which this relationship is affirmed.

This connection between the Father and the identity-confirming Spirit is also notable in one of the key Matthean christological passages: Peter's confession. Here, when the question of Jesus's identity is explicitly posed ("Who do people say that I am"), Peter's ability to perceive and articulate that identity is attributed to the activity of God's Spirit:

> [Jesus] said to them, "But who do you say me to be?" Answering Simon Peter said, "You are the Christ, the Son of the living God." And answering, Jesus said to him, "Blessed are you, Simon Bar-Jonah! For flesh and blood has not revealed this to you, but my Father who is in heaven."
> Matt 16:15–16

The ability of the disciples (here represented by Peter) to genuinely confess the identity of Jesus as Son of God is attributed to the work of God just as the revelation of Jesus's sonship was portrayed earlier in the baptism as the tandem work of the voice of God and the witness of the Spirit. This is reinforced again in the next scene.[24]

Upon the Mount of Transfiguration, there is in some sense a reenactment of the baptism. Jesus's transfigured, shining appearance and descent of the cloud parallels the descent of the Spirit and the affirmation by God's voice that Jesus is the beloved son is linguistically identical, though with the addition of the admonition to "listen to him":

---

23   While God's fatherhood of not only Jesus but the disciples as well may seem like a more typically Johannine idea, this is not an isolated occurrence in Matthew. See also 5:16, 45, 48; 6:1–18 (eight times), 26, 32; ch. 11 and 23:9.

24   It should be noted, of course, that the aftermath of Peter's confession shows that the revelatory inspiration and the confession it engenders can be fleeting. As soon as Jesus begins to predict his rejection, suffering, and death, Peter seems to lose his ability to perceive the Spirit-given perspective of the Father and shows himself liable to misunderstand Jesus's messianic identity to a such a degree that he becomes no more perceptive than a mere mortal and in articulating that perspective becomes a snare to Jesus and aligned with God's and Jesus's enemy, Satan.

[Jesus] was still speaking when, behold, a bright cloud overshadowed them, and a voice from the cloud said, "This is my beloved Son, with whom I am well pleased; listen to him."
>Matt 17:5

This combination of the presence of the Spirit symbolically infilling and thereby attesting to Jesus's identity in conjunction with the verbal attestation of the voice of the Father both harkens back to the baptism and sets the stage for the final reference to the Spirit in the Great Commission. Before that, however, there are two more subtle but important instances where the Spirit and witness to Jesus's identity are linked.

In Matt 22:42, Jesus poses a question to the Pharisees regarding the identity of the Messiah: "What do you think about the Christ? Whose son is he?" In his response to their reply that the Christ is David's son, "He said to them, 'How is it then that David in the Spirit, calls him Lord?'" (22:43). Matthew here attributes to the work of the Spirit even David's (perhaps unwitting) witness to Jesus's identity as Lord,[25] thus explicitly encompassing into the circle of witnesses to Jesus those in the Hebrew Bible who were filled with the Spirit, a move made perhaps more subtly and symbolically in the Transfiguration by the presence of Moses and Elijah.

One of the most interesting connections between the activity of the Spirit and witness to Jesus's identity occurs during the crucifixion, at the moment of Jesus's death:

> And Jesus again crying out with a loud voice, released his Spirit and behold, the curtain of the temple was split in two, from top to bottom and the earth shook and the rocks were split in two … And the centurion and those with him keeping watch over Jesus, seeing the earthquake and

---

25   While Jesus's role as "Lord" has not been one of the aspects of his identity emphasized thus far in our exploration, it is not a small element in the overall characterization of Jesus since κύριος is used numerous times with reference to Jesus and not simply as a respectful form of address from others but by Jesus with reference to himself. See esp. Matt 7:21–22, 10:24–25, 21:3, and arguably multiple times in the parables of chs. 24 and 25. Whether this should be taken as an assertion of identification with Yahweh given the many times God is referred to as "the Lord" in Matthew is not guaranteed, but it is probable given the other evidence. For our purposes, however, the aspect to note is that whatever weight "Lord" ought to be given as a facet of Jesus's identity for Matthew, David's proclamation of it is seen as the work of the Spirit.

the things that happened, were extremely frightened, saying, "Truly this was the Son of God!"

Matt 27:50–51, 54

Whether the centurion and his companions realize the full import of it, their confession of Jesus's identity accords exactly with the previous confession made of Jesus when the Spirit has been depicted as moving around Jesus—that is, in his baptism and during the Transfiguration. Unexpectedly, however, this time the affirmation does not come from the voice of the Father in heaven, but from voices of those wielding earthly power and charged with overseeing Jesus's death, and that death is the moment of the Spirit's movement. The community's sense that even those opposed to Jesus must acknowledge his identity when the Spirit is sent forth seems apparent.

Finally, after Jesus's resurrection, he appears to his disciples on the mountain. Jesus's commissioning to make more baptized disciples—persons who perceive Jesus's identity and attest to it through both their words and actions, as he has been instructing them—is "in the name of the Father and of the Son and of the Holy Spirit" (Matt 28:19). The identity of the new disciples ritually enacted in baptism will be not just an identity in Jesus, but also in the Father and the Holy Spirit. This is apparently the baptism in the Holy Spirit referred to in John the Baptist's preaching, and the impartation of the Spirit in baptism is inextricably linked with the Father and Jesus the Son—though this is hardly surprising given the interconnectedness shown earlier in Matthew between the Holy Spirit, the Spirit of the Father, and Jesus. The community's sense of the inseparability of the works of these three is apparent, and it is through all three that the ongoing, Jesus-commissioned work of the community in going and making disciples is understood to take place.

Thus, Matthew's portrayal of the work of the Holy Spirit is multifaceted but consistent: the Spirit witnesses to Jesus's identity as Son of God and Messiah by infilling Jesus and activating the works that he does that are signs of the Kingdom and that themselves become witnesses to his identity. Times of the Spirit's movement are times of particularly clear articulation of Jesus's identity as Son of God. Further, the disciples (and others') ability to perceive and articulate this identity in witness is likewise enabled by the Spirit such that they are also portrayed as filled to some extent with this same Spirit and thereby come to share in Jesus's identity as children of God.

4 The Spirit in Luke

If the Markan portrayal of the Spirit's witnessing role had an apocalyptic bent and the Matthean portrayal a David-Messianic tendency, Luke's portrait draws heavily on the tradition of the Holy Spirit as the inspiring agent of the prophets.[26] The greatest concentration of Luke's references to the Spirit occur in the early chapters of his Gospel.

As in all of the Synoptic Gospels, the Holy Spirit is mentioned very early in the Gospel of Luke. In the appearance of Gabriel to Zechariah, the angel says that the child that Zechariah will father will be "filled with the Holy Spirit even from his mother's womb" (1:15). The angel then also says that the child "will go before [the Lord] in the Spirit and power of Elijah, to turn the hearts of the fathers to the children, and the disobedient to the good sense of the righteous to make ready for the Lord a people prepared" (1:17). Luke thus immediately connects the Holy Spirit with the Spirit at work in one of the paradigmatic prophets of the Jewish scriptures, Elijah.[27] This is reinforced with the other passage that focusses on Zechariah, that is the birth and naming of John and Zechariah's prophecy regarding him: "And Zechariah his father was filled with the Holy Spirit and prophesied saying … And you, child, will be called a prophet of the Most High, for you will go before the Lord to prepare his way" (1:67, 76). The Holy Spirit leads Zechariah to prophesy and part of the prophecy he declares is the future prophetic vocation of the child whom Gabriel has already declared will be filled with the Holy Spirit. The Holy Spirit for Luke is, first of all, the Spirit that enables prophecy—that is, the declaration of the truths of God that may be unclear to those without the insight given by the Spirit.

Between these two passages related through the person of Zechariah, however, we have two other references to the Spirit. When Gabriel appears to Mary, he says to her: "The Holy Spirit will come upon you …" (1:35). While this has often been taken to refer to the miraculous conception of Jesus,[28] the terminology of the Spirit coming upon (or being put upon) one has prophetic

---

26 As with Matthew, the fact that Luke seems to have drawn on Mark as a source means that Mark's emphasis and points on the role of the Spirit are not eliminated, but they are recast into a different context which at some points results in a different emphasis. We will focus on the instances where these recast points seem to give a different message than they did in Mark.

27 Elijah may even be taken as symbolic of the prophets in general, given that he appears with Moses (symbolic of the Law) in the Transfiguration.

28 It is perhaps, then, only the "the power of the Lord will overshadow you" that is in direct response to Mary's question of "how shall this be?"

implications.[29] Particularly important in this regard is Joel 2:28–29: "And it shall come to pass afterward, that I will pour out my Spirit on all flesh; your sons and your daughters shall prophesy ... Even upon the menservants and maidservants in those days, I will pour out my Spirit." Given that Mary then calls herself the "maidservant of the Lord" (Luke 1:38), she seems to have correctly grasped the angel's allusion.[30] And of course, when Mary visits Elizabeth, she declares a prophecy (or prophetic poem or song—the Magnificat) in which, without directly referring to the child she carries, she articulates Luke's vision for the mission of Jesus and his place within God's plan. The Holy Spirit has come upon her as Gabriel declared, and she is thus able to prophesy about the God's future for Israel.[31]

The second reference to the Spirit in this section serves as a confirmation of the angel's declaration that Zechariah and Elizabeth's child will indeed be filled with the Holy Spirit as a prophet: "And when Elizabeth heard the greeting of Mary, the baby leaped in her womb" (1:41). Elizabeth interprets this for us as a leap of joy by the yet-unborn prophet at hearing the voice of "the mother of my Lord" (1:44). It says also that Elizabeth herself "was filled with the Holy Spirit" and thus she also prophesies, recognizing the roles of Mary, her blessedness, and also the importance of the child that she is carrying (1:42–45).

The next references to the Spirit carry on the theme of the Spirit as the agent of prophecy and particularly prophetic testimony regarding Jesus and his identity. When Jesus is brought to the temple:

> There was a man in Jerusalem by the name of Simeon and this man was righteous and devout, looking for the consolation of Israel, and the Holy Spirit was upon him, and it had been revealed to him by the Holy Spirit that he should not see death before he had seen the Lord's Christ, and he came in the Spirit into the temple.
>
> Luke 2:25–27

---

29 See for example Num 11:25–26, 29; 1 Sam 10:6, 10; 19:23; 2 Sam 23:2; Isa 59:21; Ezek 11:5.

30 This means that it is the "power of the Most High" that is the agent of Jesus's incarnation rather than the Holy Spirit proper, a distinction that is important here exegetically, although it might be hair splitting or theologically problematic from a Trinitarian perspective.

31 It should be clear, however, that as with prophecy in the Hebrew Bible/Old Testament, prophecy here involves "forth-telling" (that is, declaring how things stand from a divine perspective) quite as much as "foretelling"—and that, in fact, the foretelling is a logical extension of the articulated divine perspective on the situation.

Upon encountering Jesus, Simeon declares that he has now seen God's salvation and that the child will be "a light for revelation for the Gentiles and for glory to [God's] people Israel" and that he "is placed for the falling and rising of many in Israel and for an opposed sign (and a sword will pierce your own soul too) in order that the thoughts of the hearts of many may be revealed" (2:32–35). The connection between Simeon being filled with the Spirit and his revelation and declaration of Jesus's identity is clear and consistent with Luke's previous depictions. The Holy Spirit enables prophetic revelation and speech, and that these are connected to the person and mission of Jesus.

As we move into the narrative of the Baptism and Temptation, the previous observations on Mark's and Matthew's versions of these stories pertain here as well to the extent that Luke's versions are basically identical, although the preceding material in Luke's narrative suggests a number of further observations on these passages. Luke's depiction early on of John's infilling with the Holy Spirit serves to establish the reliability of his prophetic witness and thus both the urgency of his call to repentance in light of the coming judgment (3:7–14) and the truth of his statements about the "one mightier" than he, particularly the implicit indication that this mightier one (i.e., Jesus) is the Messiah and, more explicitly, eschatological judge (3:15–17). John's witness then combines with the witness of the voice of God and the filling of Jesus with the Spirit to depict Jesus as a particularly prophetic Messianic Son of God.

The importance in Luke of the Spirit leading Jesus into the wilderness (4:1) in the Temptation narrative probably has the same connotations as in Matthew: the Spirit as a witnessing and attesting agent to Jesus's identity leads him to the proving grounds of that identity in order for his identity to be witnessed to through his victory over temptation and, by extension, his mastery of the diabolical powers. Luke, in fact, seems to make this result clearer by his addition at the end of the narrative of the short statement that, after the temptation, "Jesus returned in the power of the Spirit into Galilee and a report concerning him went out through all the surrounding country" (4:14). It does not say what this report was, but Jesus empowerment with the Spirit after his overcoming of temptation apparently is related to the dissemination of this report—yet another indication of the perception that the Spirit evokes witness to Jesus's identity, if even in the somewhat ambiguous form of a "report."

A uniquely Lukan episode follows in which Jesus himself testifies about himself and the presence of the Spirit in him. A number of things are notable in Jesus's reading and commentary in the Nazareth synagogue (4:16–24). The first is that Jesus's reading from Isaiah begins with the declarations that "the Spirit of the Lord is upon me" (4:18), a circumstance that has already been established in the baptism and is tied both to the prophetic office and to God's declaration of Jesus as the beloved Son. Jesus's next statement that God "has anointed me" refers to his messianic identity, and the quotation closes with an indication, again, of Jesus's prophetic function as a proclaimer of God's favor and what that entails (4:18–19). This initial witness by Jesus's to his identity is met favorably: the Spirit working through Jesus is effective in its attestation for "all spoke well of him" (4:22). Interestingly, however, Jesus's most explicit articulation of his identity—as that of a prophet—eventually causes his hearers to be "filled with rage" (4:28); this however simply serves to confirm the validity of Jesus's identity, since "no prophet is accepted in his hometown" (4:24). The initial acceptance of the witness points to the effectiveness of the testifying work of the Spirit, while the rejection serves to confirm the content of it.

Another uniquely Lukan construction is the introduction to the passage in 10:21–22. Though the rest of the content of the passage is essentially identical to Matt 11:25–27, Luke introduces his iteration of this material with: "In that same hour, he rejoiced greatly in the Holy Spirit and said ..." What follows is another important passage about Jesus's identity—"All things have been handed over to me by my father, and no one knows who the son is but the father, and who the father is but the son and the one to whom the son wills to reveal [him]." Again, a connection is made by Luke between the Holy Spirit and the declaration of some aspect of Jesus identity, in this case his unique position of knowledge and revelation vis-à-vis the Father.

Another uniquely Lukan reference to the Spirit occurs in 11:13: "If you then, being evil, know how to give good gifts to your children, how much more will the Father in heaven give the Holy Spirit to those who ask him!" While in its immediate context, the implication of this is not clear, in the next chapter, we have an exhortation by Jesus to his disciples in which the significance is clarified:

> Everyone who confesses me before humans, the Son of Man also will acknowledge before the angels of God, but the one who denies me before humans will be denied before the angels of God. And everyone who speaks a word against the Son of Man, it will be forgiven him, but the one who blasphemes the Holy Spirit will not be forgiven. And when they bring you before the synagogues and the rulers and the authorities, do not be anxious about how you should defend yourself or what you should say, for the Holy Spirit will teach you in that hour what is necessary to say.
> Luke 12:8–12

The Holy Spirt that the Father will give to those who ask will be the Spirit that enables confession of Jesus before all opponents and in settings with potentially life-threatening consequences. This is, obviously, the same Spirit who enabled prophets of the past to declare the truths revealed to them despite danger and opposition from rulers and religious leaders. And, of course, Jesus himself is portrayed in just such a way. Through his Spirit-inspired declaration of his identity, he comes into conflict with the existing powers (as prophets do) and suffers the consequences.

Thus, finally, as Jesus expires (ἐκπνέω) on the cross, he cries, "Father, into your hands I place my Spirit!" (23:46), a statement unique to Luke's Gospel. As in Mark and Matthew, we again have something like a reversal of the baptism, but here Jesus's own agency in returning the Holy Spirit to the Father is emphasized. The Holy Spirit's function as witness and attesting agent to and through Jesus has been accomplished.[32]

So, in Luke's Gospel, the Holy Spirit is depicted in a way that emphasizes the traditional prophetic function of the Spirit, but in such a way that what the Spirit reveals from God (through Jesus and through others filled with the Spirit) is Jesus's role in God's plan for Israel, a role that includes (as in the other Synoptic Gospels) being the Davidic-Messianic King/Son of God, but with an emphasis on the prophetic aspect of that identity.

5 The Spirit in John

The first explicit reference to the Spirit[33] in John's Gospel occurs in Jesus's encounter with John the Baptist. Although John does not here baptize Jesus (in contrast to the Synoptics), there are significant similarities in the encounter.

> The next day [John] saw Jesus coming toward him, and said, "Behold, the Lamb of God, who takes away the sin of the world! This is the one of whom I said, 'After me comes a man who is ahead me, because he was prior to me.' I myself did not know him, but in order that he might be revealed to Israel, I came baptizing with water." And John bore witness saying "I observed the Spirit descend from heaven like a dove, and it remained on him. I myself did not know him, but he who sent me to baptize with water

---

32 Obviously, however, Luke does not think that the Holy Spirit is done witnessing to Jesus's identity, as the Book of Acts makes clear.

33 One might argue that the later connections in John between the Spirit and the word(s) of Jesus and thus of God (since they are the same) may indicate that the Spirit is also being invoked in the use of *logos* in the Prologue, but the complexity and resultant necessary length of such an argument put that exploration beyond the scope of this brief essay.

> said to me, 'He on whom you see the Spirit descend and remain, this is the one who baptizes with the Holy Spirit.' And I have seen and have borne witness that this is the Son of God."
>
> John 1:29–34

The community's understanding of John's vocation as exclusively to prepare for and bear witness to Jesus[34] is emphasized here, but it is clear that it is only the presence of the Spirit coming and remaining upon Jesus that enables John to fulfill that vocation and bear witness to the identity of Jesus as the Son of God, Lamb of God, and baptizer in the Holy Spirit. John's testimony based on the Spirit's activity also leads Andrew to identify Jesus as the Messiah/Christ (1:40–41). Thus the Spirit is identified as the definitive witness to Jesus's identity and also becomes the catalyst for the human witness of John the Baptist and Andrew.

Interestingly, the only other explicit connection linguistically between the Spirit and witness to Jesus comes in the Farewell Discourse. Here Jesus discusses the hatred and persecution that the disciples will face and "all these things they will do to you on account of my name, because they do not know him who sent me" (15:21). However, he says to the disciples:

> But when the Advocate comes, whom I will send to you from the Father, the Spirit of truth, who proceeds from the Father, he will bear witness about me. And you also will bear witness, because you have been with me from the beginning.
>
> John 15:26–27

Here we see explicit indication that the Spirit will bear witness to Jesus.[35] The disciples, in the face of persecution and rejection, however, are promised to have a vocation like that of John the Baptist: to witness to the identity of Jesus, and this witness they will give is based on the witness of the Spirit of truth sent to them from the Father.

Since this Spirit proceeds from the Father, this passage also extends a connection back to one of the major passages regarding witness to Jesus. In 5:31–37, Jesus says:

---

34 Cf. John 1:6–8, 15, 19, and 23.
35 Note also that the Spirit will "glorify" Jesus because "he will take what is mine and declare it to you" (John 16:14). The connection between glorifying and bearing witness to Jesus bears further exploration.

> If I alone bear witness about myself, my witness is not true. There is another who bears witness about me, and I know that the witness that he witnesses about me is true. You sent to John, and he has borne witness to the truth. Not that the witness that I receive is from man, but I say these things so that you may be saved. He was a burning lamp and shining, and you were willing to rejoice for a while in his light. But the witness that I have is greater than that of John. For the works that the Father has given me to complete, the very works that I am doing, bear witness about me that the Father has sent me. And the Father who sent me has himself borne witness about me.[36]

The overlap of the ideas of witness by the Father and witness by the Spirit is hardly surprising given that the Spirit remains on Jesus, that Jesus and the Father are one (10:30 and 17:21–23), and that "God is spirit" (4:24).

It is also notable here that Jesus points in 5:36 to his works, commissioned by the Father, as witnesses to himself. This is reiterated in 10:25: "I told you, and you do not believe. The works that I do in my Father's name bear witness about me." This may refer to the "signs" that Jesus does in John, or may in fact refer to Jesus's impending death understood as his moment of glorification. Perhaps both are in view as works given to him by the Father that bear witness. So, the witness of the Father and Spirit are interconnected and, indeed, in important ways inseparable. Moreover, Jesus expects these works (and presumably their witness) to be carried on and even extended by the disciples after his departure: "Truly, truly, I say to you, whoever believes in me will also do the works that I do; and greater works than these will he do, because I am going to the Father" (14:12).

The interconnection in 15:26 between *truth* and the Spirit, however, is also significant and serves to expand the scope of our examination. The Spirit is called the Spirit of truth not only in 15:26 but in 14:17 as well where Jesus tells the disciples, "You know him, for he dwells with you and will be in you." Also germane to our examination are Jesus's words to the disciples in 16:7–15:

> If I do not go away, the Advocate will not come to you. But if I go, I will send him to you. And when he comes, he will convict the world concerning sin and righteousness and judgment ... When the Spirit of truth comes, he

---

36 Similar assertions are made in John 8:17–18: "In your Law it is written that the testimony of two people is true. I am the one who bears witness about myself, and the Father who sent me bears witness about me."

will guide you into all the truth, for he will not speak on his own authority, but whatever he hears he will speak, and he will declare to you the things that are to come. He will glorify me, for he will take what is mine and declare it to you. All that the Father has is mine; therefore I said that he will take what is mine and declare it to you.[37]

Several things are notable here: the Advocate-Spirit is the Spirit of truth and will come to the disciples to guide them into all truth and glorify Jesus, and that the authority of the Spirit's words comes from the Father. The use of παράκλητος for the Holy Spirit here suggests the judicial motif that has been underlying the use of witness language in John and thus reinforces the prominence of the question of Jesus's identity and the work of the Spirit understood in relation to it.

This "Spirit of truth" terminology is, however, made even more significant by Jesus's explicit identification of himself with truth: "I am the way, the truth, and the life" (14:6). The narrator claims that Jesus is "full of grace and truth" (1:14) and that "grace and truth came through Jesus" (1:17). If the Spirit is identified with truth and Jesus is also, it seems that Jesus is filled with the Spirit of truth which is also the Spirit from the Father. While this is perhaps a more circumambulatory way to make the point than what we saw in Matthew, the point does seem to be that the Spirit in Jesus serves to witness to his sonship because the Spirit that infills him is the Holy Spirit from the Father. Thus when it says that John the Baptist "has borne witness to the truth" (5:33), the witness is both to Jesus and to the presence of God's Spirit of truth which infills Jesus and renders him "the Truth" as well, and these dual aspects were also present narratively in John the Baptist's initial witness to Jesus in ch. 1.

Thus, the Spirit in Jesus is a witness to his identity and the Spirit is and will be given to the disciples in part to enable their witness to Jesus. The giving of the Spirit is, in fact, one of Jesus's works to which John the Baptist witnesses: "He who sent me to baptize with water said to me, 'He on whom you see the Spirit descend and remain, this is he who baptizes with the Holy Spirit'" (1:33). Later in 3:34, either John the Baptist or the narrator says, referring to Jesus, "For he whom God has sent utters the words of God, for he gives the Spirit without measure." And it says in 7:37–39:

---

37   Notes the similar idea in John 14:26: "But the Advocate, the Holy Spirit, whom the Father will send in my name, he will teach you all things and bring to your remembrance all that I have said to you."

On the last day of the feast, the great day, Jesus stood up and cried out, "If anyone thirsts, let him come to me and drink. Whoever believes in me, as the Scripture has said, 'Out of his heart will flow rivers of living water.'" Now this he said about the Spirit, whom those who believed in him were to receive, for as yet the Spirit had not been given, because Jesus was not yet glorified.

Here the Spirit is symbolically linked with water, hearkening back to the idea that Jesus will baptize in the Holy Spirit. Further, since Jesus's "glorification" is linked with his crucifixion (12:23; 13:31), it is not surprising that when Jesus dies we see a reappearance of these in combination. When Jesus dies, he bows his head and he παρέδωκεν—"gave up" or perhaps better, "handed over," "delivered," or "transferred"—his Spirit (19:30).[38] Then upon being pierced with a spear by one of the soldiers, water—symbolic of the Spirit—and blood flow out (19:34). Yet, for all the obvious symbolism here, the giving of the Spirit does not seem either to be completed here nor, on the other hand, begun. This seems to be a middle moment. In 14:17, Jesus says "... the Spirit of truth, whom the world cannot receive, because it neither sees him nor knows him; you know him, for he dwells with you, and will be in you." Here it seems that the Spirit is already given to the disciples.

Yet further complicating the picture is that the most obvious moment of bestowal of the Spirit is when Jesus appears to the disciples after his resurrection: "Jesus said to them again, 'Peace be with you. As the Father has sent me, even so I am sending you.' And when he had said this, he breathed on them and said to them, 'Receive the Holy Spirit'" (20:21–22).

Jesus's task of baptizing in the Holy Spirit seems to be one which the community was thoroughly convinced he completed, but perhaps different strands of the tradition saw the giving as happening at different points or in varying stages of intensity or completion. The key element however is that the Spirit is indeed passed on to the disciples, and that this transference is related to witness (15:26) and the sending forth of the disciples after the resurrection (20:21).

---

38   Note that this is different from Matthew's terminology. Matthew has ἀφῆκεν—released or let go the Spirit.

6 Conclusion

As should be apparent, similarities in the understanding of the work of the Spirit as an agent of witness in the Gospels are striking. All show evidence of their author's/communities' belief that the descent of the Holy Spirit was a witness to Jesus's sonship in his encounter with John the Baptist, and that John also proclaimed that Jesus would baptize in the Holy Spirit. For Matthew this occasion is fraught with Davidic-Messianic overtones, for Mark apocalyptic, and for Luke prophetic (though these overlap and are not exclusive emphases), but these notes are more muted in the Johannine tradition.[39]

All of the Gospels indicate in various ways that Jesus's works are motivated by the Holy Spirit and thus become a witness themselves to his identity, a witness which tends to polarize his adherents and opponents. All expect the Spirit to be at work in the disciples as a witnessing power active through them, particularly in times of duress, although again this is articulated differently, and all expect the disciples to continue doing the Spirit-empowered works of Jesus when he is not present.

Some of the greatest divergence in the Gospels' portrayals of the relationship of the Spirit to witness is in the depiction of Jesus's passing on of or baptizing in the Spirit. In Mark it is unclear when this happens (perhaps at the promised meeting in Galilee), for Luke the bestowal of the Spirit is depicted in Acts, and in Matthew and John this is potentially part of the final commissioning scenes of the Gospels, although in John the giving of the Spirit is either understood to be multi-phased (including earlier stages) or was understood differently in the component traditions of that Gospel since Jesus's breathing upon the disciples is not the first indication of their infilling. Further, in John there is a real bestowal of the Spirit onto the disciples as part of their sending, whereas in Matthew, it seems that it is the disciples who will impart the Holy Spirit to new disciples as part of their baptizing. It seems that if Jesus baptizes in the Holy

---

[39] This study has focused on the Spirit's role in witness to the identity of Jesus, and this role seems to sum up and indeed exhaust understanding of the work of the Spirit in the Synoptics. John, however, has other references to the Spirit that are not as easily connected with the theme of witness: in Jesus's conversation with Nicodemus, the Spirit is essential for being born into the Kingdom of God; in the conversation with the Samaritan woman, Jesus tells her that true worshippers will worship in Spirit and in truth and that this is what the Father seeks; Jesus says that the Spirit gives life and that Jesus's words are Spirit and life (6:63). All of these bear further examination, with both synchronic and diachronic approaches, regarding their relationship (or lack of it) to the Spirit-as-witness perspective.

Spirit, in Matthew it will be through the disciples. Also, the note of judgment associated with Jesus's baptizing in the Spirit that is present in Matthew and Luke is absent in John and Mark.[40]

While this essay has not advanced proposals about the historical relationships among these elements in the various Gospels, it seems apparent that the component traditions shared many of the same perspectives on the role of the Holy Spirit, whether because of shared experiences of the historical Jesus, shared sources, or similar needs and experiences within the communities that caused these ideas to be relevant and formative for the communities' identities. These same factors of historicity, sources, and community needs may be at work in the divergences as well.

---

40 A case could potentially be made that in John this association exists because Jesus's words "are Spirit" (6:63) and are certainly inspired by the Holy Spirt and given by God and that this then associates the Spirit with judgment since Jesus says, "The one who rejects me and does not receive my words has a judge; the word that I have spoken will judge him on the last day" (12:48).

New Exodus Traditions in Earliest Christianity

Nicholas Perrin

1 Introduction

Whereas Paul's broad and creative use of the Scripture has been widely recognized for some time, it has only been within the past several decades that scholars have demonstrated a collective interest in the narrative-substructure of the apostle's writings and—so it is sometimes argued—its architectonic function within his argument. One such architectonic narrative-substructure claimed to lie just beneath the surface of Paul's discourse is the Exodus story.[1] It has been argued that Paul, precisely by invoking the scriptural accounts of Israel's escape from Egypt, sought to ground his gospel within what was for first-century Judaism *the* redemptive story. Along these lines, it is further maintained that the apostle's recurring and largely implicit correlation between the Exodus and the Christ-event, far from serving a merely metaphorical or rhetorical purpose, is foundational to his understanding of both events. In this case, the redemption wrought by Christ is not merely the anti-type of the Exodus but rather its recapitulative extension.

While this particular understanding of Paul—his hermeneutic and his concept of redemptive history—has not gone unchallenged,[2] it remains to be asked whether the alleged strong linkage between *kerygma* and Exodus should be considered peculiar to Paul or characteristic of early Christian preaching

---

1 One of the early formulations of this position in the contemporary discussion was Harald Sahlin, "The New Exodus of Salvation according to St. Paul," in *The Root of the Vine: Essays in Biblical Theology* (ed. Anton Fridrichsen et al.; New York: Philosophical Library, 1953), 81–95. More recent reiterations include, representatively, Sylvia C. Keesmaat, *Paul and His Story: (Re)Interpreting the Exodus Tradition* (JSNTSup 181; Sheffield: Sheffield Academic, 1999); William N. Wilder, *Echoes of the Exodus Narrative in the Context and Background of Galatians 5:18* (Studies in Biblical Literature 23; New York: Peter Lang, 2001); B.J. Oropeza, "Echoes of Isaiah in the Rhetoric of Paul: New Exodus, Wisdom and the Humility of the Cross in Utopian-Apocalyptic Expectations," in *The Intertexture of Apocalyptic Discourse in the New Testament* (ed. Duane F. Watson; Symposium Series 14; Atlanta: Society of Biblical Literature, 2002), 87–112; Todd A. Wilson, "Wilderness Apostasy and Paul's Portrayal of the Crisis in Galatians," *NTS* 50 (2005): 550–571.

2 See most notably J.L. Martyn, *Theological Issues in the Letters of Paul* (Edinburgh: T&T Clark, 1997); Martyn, *Galatians: A New Translation with Introduction and Commentary* (AB 33a; New York: Doubleday, 1997).

in general. Scholars have not only detected Exodus motifs within a number of NT writings, but also assigned these motifs an essential theological function within their respective discourses.[3] But these same texts post-date Paul's period of activity and their appropriation of the Exodus storylines could easily be explained as the traces of Pauline influence, whether in radicalized or merely residual form.

By examining the pre-history of the accounts of the Feeding of the 5,000 and Jesus's Walking on the Water, I wish in this essay to explore whether there may be any evidence that earliest Christianity outside of Paul posited—whether explicitly or implicitly—a correlation between the Exodus and the Christ-event. Of course because it is impossible to date identifiable pre-Gospel traditions with any precision, a study of this kind cannot dogmatically stipulate whether such traditions pre-date Paul. At the same time, since the transmission of Jesus materials within the earliest Palestinian community seems to have felt no impress from the apostle's thought, any detection of Exodus themes in the former would suggest an independent interest in the same redemptive story.[4] Moreover, if pre-Gospel traditions can be shown as appropriating Exodus imagery as theologically crucial elements in their accounts of Jesus, then this in turn would suggest that Israel's story of origin played a foundational role not only for Paul, but also for the early church across the board. On the other hand, if these two texts, which are generally agreed to reflect Exodus motifs on a redactional or compositional level, betray no indication of the same tendency in prior stages of tradition, this would strengthen the impression that Paul's use of Exodus was an isolated phenomenon.

---

3 Two texts outside Paul and the Gospels seem to have drawn more than a little interest in this regard: Hebrews and Revelation. For Hebrews, see, e.g., Matthew Thiessen, "Hebrews and the End of Exodus," *NovT* 49 (2007): 353–369, and "Hebrews 12.5–13, the Wilderness Period, and Israel's Discipline," *NTS* 55 (2009): 366–379. For Revelation, see David Mathewson, "New Exodus as a Background for 'the Sea Was No More' in Revelation 21:1C," *TJ* 24 (2003): 243–258; Laslo Gallus, "The Exodus Motif in Revelation 15–16: Its Background and Nature," *AUSS* 46 (2008): 21–43; Benjamin G. Wold, "Revelation's Plague Septets: New Exodus and Exile," in *Echoes from the Cave: Qumran and the New Testament* (ed. Florentino Garcia Martinez; STDJ 85; Leiden: Brill, 2009), 279–297.
4 Much of this depends on the dating of Mark (and Q). Assuming with many scholars that the Second Gospel was composed in the closing years of the 60s, the realm of "pre-Markan tradition" would reach from this point back to the life of Jesus in the early 30s.

2   Exodus Motifs in the Markan Accounts of the Feeding of the 5,000 and Jesus Walking on Water

The miracle which has come down to us as the Feeding of the 5,000 has attracted considerable attention not only on account of its being the only miracle attested in all four canonical Gospels, but also on account of its putative antiquity among the Jesus traditions. One of the most commonly cited defenses of such antiquity is found in Paul J. Achtemeier's study, "Toward the Isolation of Pre-Markan Miracle Catenae."[5] Applying the scalpel of redaction criticism, Achtemeier argues that a sizeable portion of 4:35–8:26 can be traced back to two discrete collections, both of which follow the same patterned sequence involving (1) a sea miracle, (2) three healing miracles, and (3) a feeding miracle. On this reconstruction, the Feeding of the 5,000 had already been attached at the end of a string of miracles well before arriving at Mark's editorial doorstep. Achtemeier's analysis, which will be taken up in more detail below, corroborates the *communis opinio* in at least one important respect: if the feeding story does not stem from an actual event within the life of the historical Jesus, it originates at a very early date within the tradition.[6]

Given the primitiveness of the Feeding of the 5,000, it is all the more interesting to note its intimations of Passover imagery. This is palpable in the first instance where Mark records that Jesus has the people recline (ἀνακλῖναι) (6:39), a posture characteristic of festive meals, the Passover not least among them. The fact that the crowds are instructed to assume this physical position on Jesus's initiative indicates a degree of intentionality on his part. If the feeding does indeed have the markings of a Passover meal, the evangelist has also left indications that it is Jesus who stages the event as such. Second, the

---

5 *JBL* 89 (1970): 265–291; reprinted in Paul J. Achtemeier, *Jesus and the Miracle Tradition* (Eugene, OR: Cascade, 2008), 55–86. Subsequent citations of this article follow the pagination of the reprinted version. See also Paul J. Achtemeier, "The Origin and Function of the Pre-Markan Miracle Catenae," *JBL* 91 (1972): 198–221; reprinted in *Jesus and the Miracle Tradition*, 87–116.

6 J.P. Meier (*A Marginal Jew: Volume II: Mentor Message, and Miracles* [New York: Doubleday, 1994], 966) is representative of a sizeable swathe of historical Jesus scholarship when he writes: "I think the criteria of multiple attestation and of coherence make it more likely than not that behind our Gospel stories of Jesus feeding the multitude lies some especially memorable communal meal of bread and fish, a meal with eschatological overtones celebrated by Jesus and his disciples with a large crowd by the Sea of Galilee." For a critical engagement with Achtemeier's article, see Robert M. Fowler, *Loaves and Fishes: The Function of the Feeding Stories in the Gospel of Mark* (SBLDS 54; Chico, CA: Scholars Press, 1981), 24–31.

sequence of verbs describing Jesus's handling of the bread and fish (take, bless, break, give [v. 41]) are similar to what we find in the Lord's Supper (14:22) and likely as well to what Mark's readers would have heard in their experience of the sacramental liturgy (cf. 1 Cor 11:23–24).[7] Because the early church consistently set the Lord's Supper squarely within the context of a Passover meal (1 Cor 10:1–22), and because, too, there is little sign of Markan intrusion at 6:41 and 14:22, it is entirely plausible that the Feeding of the 5,000, in its pre-Markan form, was regarded as a kind of anticipatory Last Supper and, by extension, a kind of Passover meal. Third, the Passover-*esque* quality of the meal is further supported by the notice that the event took place when the grass was green (6:39) and late in the day (6:35).[8] The force of the latter detail, however, is offset by the fact that the late hour has its own function within the plot of the pericope: it provides the occasion for Jesus and the disciples to consider the crowd's physical needs. In any case, the crowd's reclining posture, the Eucharistic shading of Jesus's actions, and the notice of time—all these raise the possibility that the Feeding of the 5,000, even in its pre-Markan stage, was understood as a kind of Passover meal.

That the second evangelist at least utilized the first feeding along these lines may be argued on the basis of the larger narrative context, involving both the second feeding (8:1–10) and the discussion centering on the yeast of Pharisees and Herod (8:14–21). In his warning to the disciples in the latter passage, Jesus seeks to draw out—albeit in a highly oblique manner—the meaning of the feeding miracles. Here he implies that the disciples' failure to understand the significance of the feedings is connected to their succumbing to the invasive presence of "yeast," that is, toxic attitudes associated with Jesus's enemies. While interpreters of 8:17–21 have devoted considerable energy to resolving the significance of the number of leftover-laden baskets from the two feedings, as a preliminary step to explicating Jesus's admonition, more consideration needs to be given to the fact that Jesus's mention of "the yeast of Pharisees and the yeast of Herod" in metaphorical connection with the two feedings is slightly odd, even *mal à propos*, apart from the expectation that the disciples were already thinking about yeast in the first place.[9] Given Mark's well-known cor-

---

7 The objection of Fowler (*Loaves*, 134–147) against reading the two feeding miracles in light of Mark 14 would be stronger were it not for the virtually indubitable fact that Mark's hearers would have been quite familiar with the Eucharist quite apart from its rehearsal from the written Gospel.

8 Commentators generally understand the "green grass" as corroborative of springtime Passover; likewise, the meal was initiated in the late afternoon (see Jub. 49:19; Josephus, *J.W.* 6.9.3).

9 Following Schmithals and Gnilka, Robert A. Guehlich (*Mark 1–8:26* [WBC 34a; Dallas: Word],

relating of Passover with Jesus's death within the last week (Mark 11–15), which suggests a narratival sensitivity to calendrical setting, we have no better option than to offer that the evangelist thought of these two meals as the opening and closing feasts of *Massot* (Feast of Unleavened Bread), respectively.[10] Thus, far from being doublets of an isolated account of a single meal or as nothing more than the evangelist's recasting of Israel's experience of manna (Exod 16), the Feeding of the 5,000 and the Feeding of the 4,000 make far better sense as two discrete celebrations falling within the Passover week, where the former functions as the initial "holy convocation" (*miqrā-qōdeš*) inaugurating the week-long Passover festival and the latter serves as its climactic counterpart.[11]

Here it may be objected that any attempt to link the Feeding of the 4,000 (8:1–10) with the celebratory close of the Passover week flounders on the strong hints, issued by the evangelist himself, that the meal included Gentiles among its numbers.[12] This Gentile presence can certainly be surmised not only on account of Mark's staging the second feeding as part of a larger tour of Gentile territories (7:24–37), but also on account of Jesus's remark that the people have come "from afar" (*apo makrothen*), a phrase doubling as a shorthand descriptor of Gentiles (8:3).[13] Since uncircumcised Gentiles were prohibited from taking part in Passover (Exod 12:43, 48) and presumably the Feast of Unleavened Bread as well, this certainly gives some pause to the suggestion that Mark's second feeding miracle included Gentiles and functioned as the closing feast of the Passover week.

422) states that Jesus's mention of leaven has an "awkward presence in 8:14–21 [and] makes it an unlikely candidate for being the core of a Markan created narrative."

10   The relevant text from Leviticus is worth quoting: "On the first day you shall have a holy convocation; you shall not work at your occupations. For seven days you shall present the LORD's offerings by fire; on the seventh day there shall be a holy convocation: you shall not work at your occupations" (Lev 23:7–8; cf. also Exod 12:17–20; 23:15).

11   Especially following the influential study of Frans Neirynck (*Duality in Mark: Contribution to the Study of the Markan Redaction* [BETL 31; Leuven: Leuven University Press, 1973]), the vast majority of scholars have sought to explain the presence of two feedings (as opposed to one) as being the by-product of Mark's peculiar penchant for doubling. Comparison with the manna feeding of Exodus 16 is standard in the commentaries; see, e.g., Morna D. Hooker, *The Gospel according to St. Mark* (BNTC; London: A&C Black, 1991), 164–165; R.T. France, *The Gospel of Mark* (NIGTC; Grand Rapids: Eerdmans, 2002), 262; Adela Yarbro Collins, *Mark* (Hermeneia; Minneapolis: Fortress, 2007), 332.

12   So, classically, Alan Richardson, *The Miracle Stories of the Gospels* (London: SCM, 1956), 97–98; Werner Kelber, *The Kingdom in Mark: A New Place and a New Time* (Philadelphia: Fortress, 1974), 56–60.

13   See, e.g., Joel Marcus, *Mark 1–8* (AB 27; New York: Doubleday, 2000), 487.

But given Mark's deep interest in the Gentiles, more precisely, his recurring point that the Gentiles are now also to be included within the purview of God's salvific purposes,[14] it seems that the argument could just as well, if not more fittingly, be turned in the opposite direction. Because we find in Mark's Jesus one who exorcises the demons of the Roman Decapolis (5:1–20), declares his messiahship in Gentile hinterlands (8:27), calls for a house of prayer "for all nations" (11:17), and—more immediately—gives "bread" to the Syro-Phoenecian woman (7:24–30), we must suppose that the evangelist would have regarded a "Gentile Passover meal" not as an impossible contradiction, but more likely as an oxymoronic symbol, speaking powerfully to one of his thematic concerns. From another angle, it may also be argued that it is precisely the meal's status as a Passover meal that provides the best explanation of the Gentile presence, for among all the feasts it was this cultic meal which was seen, at least by some, as possessing an inherent sanctifying efficacy.[15] Finally, I believe that understanding the two feedings as the first and last meals of *Massot* makes richer sense of the narrative itself. If the Evangelist intended the two feedings to mark off the annual festival dedicated to identifying and expelling contaminating yeast, then this corresponds handsomely with the plotline of the intervening pericopae. For in these passages Jesus not only locates—as any *Massot* celebrant would—the true source of cultic impurity (7:1–22), but also identifies those who may now be considered ritually pure (7:24–30). From Mark's point of view, it seems that Jesus's redefinition of the Passover feasts goes hand-in-hand with a corresponding redefinition of cultic purity. In sum, the presence of Gentiles at the second feeding does not undermine the argument I am making, but in fact bolsters it.

Although I wish to distance myself from an interpretation which conceives the first feeding as a recasting of the manna miracle of Exodus 16 *simpliciter*, it would certainly be a mistake to ignore the overtones of a miraculous desert feeding or downplay the obvious comparisons with Moses.[16] Like Moses, Jesus

---

14 See Kelly R. Iverson, *Gentiles in the Gospel of Mark: Even the Dogs under the Table Eat the Children's Crumbs* (LNTS 339; London: T&T Clark, 2007).

15 The remarks of Philo (*Spec.* 2.145) on the Passover are apropos: "In this festival many myriads of victims from noon till eventide are offered by the whole people, old and young alike, raised for that particular day to the dignity of the priesthood … on this occasion the whole nation performs the sacred rites and acts as a priest with pure hands and complete immunity." See also Nicholas Perrin, *Jesus the Temple* (Grand Rapids: Baker Academic; London: SPCK; 2010), 175–179.

16 Jubilees (49.23) explicitly locates the first Feast of Unleavened Bread in the wilderness and by the sea, just as we have it Mark: "For this feast you observed with nervousness when you

feeds the crowds and takes on a shepherding role (6:34). Moreover, he orders the crowd in groups of "hundreds and fifties" (6:40), forging an obvious association with the Mosaic organization of Israel (Exod 18:21). But the collage of images is christological in import: it is a composite sketch, serving to show that Jesus, in feeding the 5,000, is taking on the mantle once donned by Moses. With this association firmly in place, along with the insights which 8:1–21 shed on the first feeding event, we surmise that Mark, in his recounting of the two feedings, has in mind not simply the Passover week of Jesus's day, but the very first Passover, beginning in Exodus 12.[17]

3   Jesus Walks on the Water as Exodus Motif in Mark

In this connection, it may be asked whether this line of argument is strengthened on consideration of the subsequent water-walking scene (6:45–52), tightly linked as it is with the feeding miracle through Mark's characteristic "and immediately" Καὶ εὐθὺς (v. 45). Some would undoubtedly say so, at least those who posit correspondence between Jesus Walking on Water and the crossing of the Red Sea (Exod 14).[18] Jesus's declaration to be I AM (ἐγώ εἰμι) (v. 50), the hour of the fourth watch (6:48), the blowing of the wind against the water (v. 48), his intention to "pass by" (παρελθεῖν) (v. 48)—all these among other features, so it is argued—conspire to invoke the Exodus. After all, in Israel's foundational story, it is the Lord, the I AM ἐγώ εἰμι (Exod 14:4, 18), who kept night vigil (Exod 12:42), who sent a strong (east) wind (Exod 14:21) during the morning watch (Exod 14:24), and who would eventually self-reveal through "passing by" (Exod 33:19–23; 35:6; 1Kgs 19:11).[19] Likewise, Jesus's "walking on the sea" (v. 49) has invited

---

went out from Egypt until you entered into the wilderness of Sur because you completed it on the shore of the sea" (translation from *OTP* 2:142).

17   In his own accounts of the feeding miracles, Matthew apparently builds on this understanding, for he follows Mark in recording the number of men who ate, but in both feedings adds—in imitation of the Passover account of Exodus 12—the phrase "besides women and children" (Matt 14:21; 15:38; cf. Exod 12:37).

18   Bertil Gärtner, *John 6 and the Jewish Passover* (ConNT 17; Lund: Gleerup, 1959), 30–37; John Paul Heil, *Jesus Walking on the Sea: Meaning and Gospel Functions of Matt. 14:22–33, Mark 6:45–52, and John 6:15b–21* (AnBib 87; Rome: Biblical Institute Press, 1981); William R. Stegner, "Jesus' Walking on the Water: Mark 6:45–52," in *The Gospels and the Scriptures of Israel* (ed. Craig A. Evans and William R. Stegner; JSNTSup 104; Sheffield: Sheffield Academic, 1994), 212–234.

19   Stegner ("Walking on the Water," 222) tentatively suggests the possible relevance of Job 9:11: "Lo, he passes by me, and I see him not; *he moves on (parelthē)*, but I do not perceive him."

comparison with both Moses and the God of Israel who walks on water (Ps 77:14–15, 19–20 MT; Job 9:8b). For many, the echoes of Exodus in 6:45–52 are perceptible; their frequency and volume place beyond doubt the pericope's deep dependence on the story of Israel's crossing.

Yet here we must be cautious, for not all scholars are equally impressed by a *basic* comparison between Jesus Walking on the Water and the Exodus. For many interpreters of Mark, the Gospel sea miracle offers a more generalized account of epiphany. Along these lines, the stray hints of Exodus contained in 6:45–52, however deliberately invoked, must be considered as incidental for the evangelist's purposes. After all, it is typically argued, the evangelist's interest lies not so much in establishing a typological connection with the Exodus, but in staking a christological claim through the manifestation of Jesus's powers over nature. Questions may also be raised against an Exodus matrix. For example, had Mark 6:45–52, as an isolated tradition, been designed to render Jesus's water miracle as a recapitulated Exodus, would we not come to expect more clues to this effect? Would we not also expect more sense as to how to interpret certain details (Jesus intention to pass the disciples by, the stilling of the wind) which do not apparently cohere with the Exodus story? Whatever rich and provocative allusiveness may obtain, it is arguably insufficient warrant for relating the entire plot-structure of the pericope back to the Exodus story.

Of course similar reservations may be registered in regards to the Feeding of the 5,000 as a self-contained unit. However true it may be that the episode contains several promising links with Israel's central redemptive story, the cumulative strength of such discrete links arguably falls short. In the end, the points of contact between the pericope of the first feeding miracle and the Exodus narrative remain isolated and of a superficial nature. Like the pericope of Jesus's Walking on Water, the Feeding of the 5,000 possesses on its own insufficient signs of its dependence on the Exodus story in any sort of structural way; neither can the story be convincingly shown to be radically rooted in any prior narrative grammar. Thus far one may fairly judge the Feeding of the 5,000 and Jesus Walking on Water as *isolated traditions*.

It is of course a separate question as to whether Mark has arranged and deployed these traditions with a view to rooting them in the Exodus, thereby investing them with a redemptive-historical significance that they did not independently possess. Given the assorted studies of recent decades which have set themselves to exploring Mark's interest in the Exodus-motif,[20] the answer

---

20 J.W. Bowman, *The Gospel of Mark: The New Christian Jewish Passover Haggadah* (StPB 8; Leiden: Brill, 1965); William M. Swartley, "The Structural Function of the Term 'Way'

to this question seems to me unavoidable: the evangelist not only appropriated the redemptive story *par excellence* as a basic framework for much of his Gospel, he also applied this same framework to—or even deduced it from—his reception of these two miracles. The latter claim may be demonstrated very simply on pointing out that Mark places the Feeding of the 5,000 just prior to Jesus Walking on Water. If by themselves the two events show only tangential relation to Israel's founding moment, then together the feeding miracle and the sea miracle undergo redefinition by virtue of their mimicking the Exodus narrative on a structural level: a wide-scale sacred meal (Exod 12–13) followed by divine intervention at sea (Exod 14). Together the two pericopae establish a reciprocal hermeneutical relationship; the meaning generated by both far outstrips the interpretive sum of their individual contribution. As events forged together, they hold a firm anchor within the Exodus story.

4 The Conjoining of the Feeding of the 5,000 and Jesus Walking on Water: Markan or Pre-Markan?

This insight only makes more acute the question as to whether it was Mark who first conjoined the Feeding of the 5,000 and Jesus Walking on Water, or whether this complex goes back to a pre-Markan tradition. For a number of years, their convergence in the pre-Markan tradition went unquestioned. This, however, would change on the publication of Achtemeier's essay cited above, alongside an earlier work by Thierry Snoy.[21] For Achtemeier, it was the evangelist who first collocated the Feeding of the 5,000 and Jesus Walking on Water. This follows, virtually by necessity, from the nature of his argument.

Achtemeier argues that two similarly structured but separate catenae circulated within the pre-Markan tradition. The remains of those catenae (whose oral or graphic texture remain unstipulated) come to surface in two blocks of material in the second Gospel. They are as follows:

(*Hodos*) in Mark's Gospel," in *The New Way of Jesus: Essays Presented to Howard Charles* (ed. William Klassen; Kansas: Faith and Life Press, 1980), 73–86; Marcus, *Mark, passim*; Rikki E. Watts, *Isaiah's New Exodus and Mark* (WUNT 2.88; Tübingen: Mohr-Siebeck, 1997; repr. Biblical Studies Library; Grand Rapids: Baker, 2000).

21 "La Redaction marcienne de la marche sur les eaux (Mc. VI 45–52)," *ETL* 44 (1968): 205–241; 433–481.

Catena I	Catena II
Stilling of the Storm (4:35–41)	Jesus Walks on Water (6:45–51)
Gerasene Demoniac (5:1–20)	Blind Man of Bethsaida (8:22–26)
Woman with a Hemorrhage (5:25–34)	Syrophonecian Woman (7:24b–30)
Jairus' Daughter (5:21–23, 35–43)	Deaf-Mute (7:32–37)
Feeding of the 5,000 (6:34–44, 53)	Feeding of the 4,000 (8:1–10)

The proposal certainly has its attractions. The final configuration of the catenae, which Achtemeier arrives at with only a little redactional-critical legerdemain, establishes a satisfying symmetry between the two catenae; the simplicity of this schema also grants the explanation an intrinsic probative value. On the assumption that Mark indeed made use of pre-existing traditions, one finds Achtemeier's argument to be generally persuasive.

However, in reconstructing the alleged break between the two catenae, Achtemeier's case stands on somewhat shakier ground, not only because it cuts against the grain of accepted scholarship, but also because the evidence he brings to bear at this point is not entirely compelling. According to our author, the Feeding of the 5,000 (6:30–44) fell at the tail end of a chain of miracles. As I have pointed out, this move is necessary to establish two catenae of similar shape, but he argues the point primarily on the basis of alleged geographical incongruities caused by the mention of Bethsaida at 6:45 ("Immediately he made his disciples get into the boat and go on ahead to the other side, to Bethsaida"), which in turn betrays textual dislocation at just this juncture. First, there is the apparent disconnect between Jesus's intention to go to Bethsaida and the actuality of his landing with the disciples in Genessaret (v. 53).[22] Second, Achtemeier draws attention to the phrase "to the other side to Bethsaida" (εἰς τὸ πέραν πρὸς Βηθσαϊδάν) (v. 45), which one might expect to be reserved for boat voyages to the east side of the sea.[23] Both of these problems, Achtemeier argues, following Snoy, can be explained by the evangelist splicing 6:45–52 into an original version of the feeding 6:30–44, which originally ended with the notice of the disciples landing in Gennesaret (6:53), only to fail to spot the discrepancy himself.[24] Such reworking in turn gives just cause for thinking that

---

22 "Miracle Catenae," 74.
23 Achtemeier, "Miracle Catenae," 75.
24 Achtemeier, "Miracle Catenae," 77. See Snoy, "Redaction," 205–241, 433–481.

Mark attempted to forge a transition at this juncture. Although Achtemeier also finds traces of redaction as further evidence of the evangelist's attempt to combine the two pericopae, again, the geographical difficulties maintain primary importance for his point.[25]

In my view, this particular component (namely, that Mark attached the two catenae at the break between 6:44 and 6:45) within Achtemeier's larger argument is not the strongest link in the chain. In the first place, the alleged geographical difficulties are not as jarring as they may appear. Mark only says that Jesus made his disciples go πρὸς Βηθσαϊδάν, that is, "to" or "towards" Bethsaida. That the boat lands at Genessaret rather than the intended destination of Bethsaida is certainly a source of interest and puzzlement, but given that the two towns were both situated on the north shore of the Sea of Galilee and separated only by distance of a few miles, one wonders whether the original audience would have seen the change in final destination as the navigational catastrophe it is sometimes made out to be.[26] More to the point, the switch from the expected Bethsaida to Genessaret is liable to narrative-critical explanation. It is likely in order to register the disciples' unwillingness to go forward with Gentile mission that the evangelist indicates that the episode terminates with an abortive trip to Gentile territory (Bethsaida), which results in the disciples being re-routed back into nearby Jewish territory (Genessaret).[27] Second, it is also not clear, as Achtemeier suggests, that the phrase "to the other side to Bethsaida" (εἰς τὸ πέραν πρὸς Βηθσαϊδάν) must bear reference to an eastward journey across the sea. The word πέραν simply means "on the other side" and the Gospel tradition, within Mark and without, contains several curious instances where "the other side" (πέραν) patently refers even to an area on the west side of the Jordan.[28] While of course the Snoy/Achtemeier dislocation

---

25 "Miracle Catenae," 76–77.
26 An intriguing explanation presents itself in noting that the disciples had been fighting the wind all night. Since Genessaret is just due west along the shore from Bethsaida (Julias), the disciples' arriving at the former point rather than their intended destination may be explained by the wind, which in this case must have been a strong easterly wind. Perhaps Mark inserts this detail for the sake of the particularly astute and well-versed reader: it was after all an easterly wind which blew against the Red Sea thereby allowing the children of Israel to cross (Exod 14:21). I leave this only as a suggestion.
27 So Iverson, *Gentiles*, 40; Elizabeth Struthers Malbon, "The Jesus of Mark and the Sea of Galilee," *JBL* 103 (1984): 363–377; Struthers Malbon, *Mark's Jesus: Characterization as Narrative Christology* (Waco, TX: Baylor University Press: 2009), 40–41.
28 See Mark 5:1, 21; Matt 19:1; John 1:28; 6:25. Fowler (*Loaves and Fishes*, 59) calls the equation of πέραν in Mark with the east side of the sea "a common error."

theory cannot be absolutely ruled out, geographical concerns are not compelling enough to justify the hypothesis.

More serious obstacles to our supposing that Mark conjoined the Feeding the 5,000 (Mark 6:30–44) with Jesus Walking on the Water (6:45–52) arise on consideration of John 6, where the feeding (John 6:1–15) and the sea miracle (6:16–24) are brought together side-by-side and in the same order that Mark presents them.[29] The obstacles come at two separate levels. First, if we subscribe to Bultmann's theory of a signs-source, which most would see as including both the Feeding of the 5,000 and Jesus Walking on the Water, then the argument that Mark initiated the combination becomes very difficult.[30] Second, even if we dispense the theory of a signs-source, we must then suppose that John here depended on Mark. However, notwithstanding renewed calls within recent decades for seeing the Fourth Gospel as drawing on the Synoptic tradition, several convincing studies render dependence at this particular juncture rather dubious.[31] Indeed, given that Mark's version of the feeding seems to reflect a stronger Eucharistic emphasis than John's, and given too that it is John rather than Mark who gives the historically credible rationale for Jesus's bringing the feeding to a hasty close (namely, in the crowds desire to make him king [John 6:15]), a reasonably good case can be made, on these grounds and others, for the greater antiquity of the Fourth Gospel's account.[32] The Johannine combination of the feeding and the sea-walking also seem to have roots deep in history—all quite independent of Mark.

---

29 Achtemeier ("Miracle Catenae," 75) recognizes the point in passing. Matthew preserves the same order as well: Feeding of the 5,000 (14:13–21) and Jesus Walks on Water (14:22–33).

30 On the signs-source in general, see Robert T. Fortna, *The Fourth Gospel and Its Predecessor* (Philadelphia: Fortress, 1988); Urban C. von Wahlde, *The Earliest Version of John's Gospel: Recovering the Gospel of Signs* (Wilmington, DE: Michael Glazier, 1989).

31 C.H. Dodd, *Historical Tradition in the Fourth Gospel* (Cambridge: Cambridge University Press: 1963), 196–211; Raymond Brown, *The Gospel According to John* (AB 29; Garden City, NY: Doubleday, 1986), 235–244; P.W. Barnett, "The Feeding of the Multitude in Mark 6/John 6," in *Gospel Perspectives*. Vol. 6: *The Miracles of Jesus* (ed. David Wenham and Craig Blomberg; Sheffield: JSOT Press, 1986), 273–293; John Painter, "Tradition and Interpretation in John 6," *NTS* 35 (1989): 421–450; Edwin D. Johnston, "The Johannine Version of the Feeding of the Five Thousand—An Independent Tradition?" *NTS* 8 (1961–1962): 151–154; cf. Ian D. Mackay, *John's Relationship with Mark: An Analysis of John 6 in the Light of Mark 6–8* (WUNT 2.182; Tübingen, Mohr-Siebeck, 2004), 290–300.

32 As offered long ago by Alfred Loisy ("Le Second Évangile," *Revue d'Histoire et de littérature Religieuses* 8 [1903]: 524).

This finding has implications for our assessment of Achtemeier's thesis. As convincing as Achtemeier's overall argument may appear, the possibility that Mark was the first to unite the two pericopae in view, the Feeding of the 5,000 and Jesus Walking on the Water, remains its Achilles' heel. This, I think, forces an adjustment in how we might conceive of the catenae, so as to retain the basic shape of Achtemeier's proposal but allow, along with Rudolf Pesch, that Mark not only received long catenae from his tradition and but also received much of his inspiration for his duplication *Tendenz* from this same tradition. In short, I would propose taking the two catenae, so helpfully marked out by Achtemeier, and combining them into one long catena or perhaps, better, into three constitutive modular components, sub-catenae perhaps.

The kind of repetition I am advocating in the pre-Markan tradition may be borne out by oral studies undertaken since the time of Achtemeier's explanation for the Markan doublets and since, too, the time of subsequent shifts to redactional (Neirynck) and narrative-critical (Fowler) explanations of the same. As is recurringly noted in the literature, repetition is a characteristic feature of the oral style.[33] For example, in a study of an extended interchange between Eumaios and Odysseus in *Odyssey* 14, Elizabeth Minchin observes the phenomenon of repetition in Homer's oral-based epic:

> The repetition of the speech-act, the bid, in this narrative segment is an example of Homer's occasional practice of repeating scenes, or elements of scenes, *seriatim*. We see such repetition, for example, in the *Iliad*: in Agamemnon's tour of inspection (*Iliad* 4.223–421), in the sequence of night-time summonses that the king initiates (*Iliad* 10.17–179), or in the funeral games described at *Iliad* 23.257–897. The repeated dining scenes at *Odyssey* 1.125–148 are a modest example of the same phenomenon

---

33 As Terence C. Mournet (*Oral Tradition and Literary Dependency: Variability and Stability in the Synoptic Tradition and Q* [WUNT 2.195; Tübingen: Mohr-Siebeck, 2004], 174–175) puts it: "[r]edundancy is perhaps *the most pervasive characteristic* of oral communication. In orally oriented cultures one cannot help but note that redundancy occurs in variegated forms and is utilized in the composition and transmission of all traditions. Many scholars have observed that this characteristic is one of the key manifestations of orally composed/performed traditions" (emphasis added). See also Richard A. Horsley, "Oral Performance and Mark: Some Implications of *The Oral and the Written Gospel*, Twenty-Five Years Later," in *Jesus the Voice, and the Text: Beyond the Oral and the Written Gospel* (ed. Tom Thatcher; Waco, TX: Baylor University Press, 2008), 45–71, esp. 63–68.

(Scott 1971). What is repeated in such scenes is the format of the whole, its underlying structure; what is repeated word for word are the physical action or actions that may be part of that event.[34]

From here Minchin offers her own explanation as to the rhyme and reason of such repetition:

> In the example we find at *Odyssey* 1.125–148, repetition is used to convey a contrast between the behavior of a civilized young man who knows how to behave in company and who is putting his understanding of etiquette into practice for the first time and that of the suitors, who have ceased to care about good manners (Scott 1971:548). The scene points up effectively the selfishness of the suitors and the inexperience, but good intentions, of Athena's young host. Likewise, in the three Iliadic cases noted above, sustained repetition, even as it carries the narrative forward, serves as a convenient and controlled means of characterization (again, by means of contrast).[35]

While it is not my intention to argue that the repetition of plot for the sake of contrast occurs in the pre-Markan tradition, Minchin's readiness to see this dynamic as occurring at the oral stage of production is noteworthy for the present study. It would not, at any rate, be difficult to show that Mark uses the same technique as Minchin argues obtains for the *Odyssey*. If so, then the possibility cannot be ruled out that Mark himself was prompted by a narrative technique existing in prior tradition.

Based on the results of this investigation, it would seem that stories of feeding, which are seen as recapitulations of Mosaic Passover meals, serve as the fundamental starting-point for the pre-Markan sub-collection or sub-catena. Closely tied to this, in two instances, are stories involving a sea setting (6:45–51 and 8:11–21). Perusing the Gospel further, we then find that this complex is typically followed by stories of miracles. Whereas Achtemeier wished to transpose the Blind Man of Bethsaida so as to preserve two sets of three miracles,[36] I am not convinced that the three-miracle pattern is a necessary component of this pattern. We are just as well served leaving the Blind Man where he is

---

34 "Serial Repetition in Homer and the 'Poetics of Talk': A Case Study from the *Odyssey*," *Oral Tradition* 14 (1999): 336–353 (347).
35 Michen, "Serial Repetition in Homer," 348.
36 "Miracle Catenae," 79–81.

in canonical Mark, that is, directly behind the Boat Discussion of 8:11–21. We can, however, discern a variant triadic pattern, involving feeding, the sea, and miracles. This may be set out as follows:

	Sub-catena 1	Sub-catena 2	Sub-catena 3
Meal	???	Feeding of the 5,000 (6:34–44, 53)	Feeding of the 4,000 (8:1–10)
Sea	Stilling of the Storm (4:35–41)	Jesus Walks on Water (6:45–51)	Boat Discussion (8:11–21)
Miracles	Gerasene Demoniac (5:1–20)	Syrophonecian Woman (7:24b–30)	Blind Man of Bethsaida (8:22–26)
	Woman with a Hemorrhage (5:25–34)	Deaf-Mute (7:32–37)	
	Jairus's Daughter (5:21–23, 35–43)		

One weakness of this reconstruction is that it lacks any feeding prior to the Stilling of the Storm (4:35–41). There are certainly ways to explain this omission: either Mark simply dropped it altogether or it was something closer to the form of one of our earlier food-oriented stores in Mark (2:13–17, 2:23–27) and was simply transposed. I will leave this an open question. Otherwise, the pattern is consistent. The association of meal, sea, and miracles in the pre-Markan tradition is invocative of the Exodus, more exactly, its constituent components of Passover (Exod 12–13), Sea Crossing (Exodus 14), and Miracles (Exod 15–17) (cf. Num 14:11, 22; Deut 4:34; 6:22; etc.). Thus, we find a transmuted Exodus pattern already repeating itself in the pre-Markan tradition. Only later did Mark incorporate these pre-existing catenae into his own Gospel text.

5 Conclusion

We return to our initial question, that is, whether there is evidence for the early Christian usage of Exodus traditions independent of Paul. More particularly, is there any evidence that such usage reflected an understanding in which the Exodus was structurally basic to the rehearsal of the *kerygma*?

Towards answering such questions, two lines of evidence have come together. In the first place, the collocation of the Feeding of the 5,000 and Jesus Walking on Water in both pre-Markan and pre-Johannine traditions suggests that the two events were wedded *qua* Exodus complex at a very early stage of the church's life. Exactly how early it is impossible to say. However, we are bound to infer that tradition on which Mark drew remained independent of and most likely prior to Q, which also grew up on Palestinian soil. In this case, these same traditions can be assigned to anywhere between the time of the historical Jesus and the middle of the first century. In any event, the *origins* of the pre-Markan tradition are likely to have preceded the earliest writings of Paul. If we hypothesize the existence of a signs-source (I shall prescind from the question here), the same pre-Pauline dating obtains *a fortiori*. Second, within the pre-Markan cycle we may hypothesize the existence of a three-fold pattern: Meal→Sea→Miracles, corresponding to Passover→Exodus→Signs & Wonders. The repetition of this pattern is explicable as characteristics of oral traditioning.

This would *not* indicate, as has been suggested elsewhere, that the pre-Markan and pre-Johannine traditions are merely tinged by colors from the Mosaic palette. Rather it appears that successive episodes of the Jesus-story were—early on and at a fundamental level—interpreted within the grid of the Exodus. The events of Exodus were not the *Farben* of the *kerygma*,[37] but the canvas; the chief redemptive event in Israel's history became a basic framework for understanding the Christ-event within the church's earliest history. This has broad implications for our understanding the Christology, soteriology, hermeneutics, and ecclesiology of the primitive community.

---

37 As Alfred Suhl (*Die Funktion der alttestamentlichen Zitate und Anspielungen im Markusevangelium* [Gütersloh: Gütersloher, 1965], 47) put it so long ago.

Sea Storms, Divine Rescues, and the Tribulation: The Jonah Motif in the Book of Matthew*

Susan M. Rieske

1   Introduction

Although by the end of the first century, the early Jesus movement was growing rapidly, that journey was anything but smooth sailing. With persecution as a threat from both the Roman imperial leaders and the Jewish establishment, these early Christians must have been plagued with questions as to how such circumstances could be ushering in the long-awaited eschaton. Speaking to these concerns, the Gospel writers employed various literary motifs to help the community locate itself within this eschatological context. One of these was the motif of Jonah, a figure who seems to take on particular eschatological nuances in the Gospel of Matthew.

Matthew alludes on more than one occasion to Jonah. While scholars have attempted to make sense of these allusions, more exploration needs to be done on the motif and the possibility of a unifying theological conception behind it. This study will attempt to make headway by doing just that. I will focus on three main narratives: the stilling of the storm (8:23–27), the sign of Jonah (12:38–42; 16:1–4) and the confession of Peter, the "son of Jonah" (16:13–20).[1] Admittedly, this study is an exploratory excursion; I will not be able to present a thorough exegetical analysis of each passage, neither will I attempt to solve the myriad of attendant exegetical problems. Instead, I will take a panoramic look at these passages against the background of Jewish conceptions of Jonah. In so doing, what will emerge is a theme that was also central in the reception of Jonah within Judaism: the theme of tribulation. Although for Matthew, who believed

---

* A portion of this essay was presented at the 2014 SBL annual meeting in San Diego, CA. Many thanks to those in the session who gave feedback and to Eva Dittmann, Jeremy Otten, and especially Nicholas Perrin who offered invaluable advice on earlier drafts of this essay.
1 I am treating the two sign of Jonah passages together. Other Jonah-like phrases noted in the Nestle-Aland Greek NT include "great joy" (Matt 2:10; Jonah 4:6); "sackcloth and ashes" (Matt 11:21; Jonah 3:5–6); "guilty of innocent blood" (Matt 23:35; Jonah 1:14); and "grieved unto death" (Matt 26:38; Jonah 4:9), as noted by Mark Allan Powell, "Echoes of Jonah in the New Testament," *WW* 27.2 (2007): 157–164. I address these briefly when pertinent to the main texts.

the Messiah had come and with him the last days, it is not just tribulation in the general sense of the term, but *the* tribulation—the period of intense distress and suffering that was to come in the eschaton.[2] Often referred to as the "messianic woes," this time period was marked by several features as highlighted in this definition by Mark Dubis:

> A tumultuous period of eschatological distress and tribulation that, according to early Judaism, was to precede the coming of the Messiah. Characteristic features include apostasy, war, earthquakes, drought, famine, pestilence, familial strife and betrayal, cosmic signs, increasing wickedness, and the scarcity of truth and wisdom. Otherwise known in the rabbinic literature as the 'birth pangs of the Messiah,' these woes lead inexorably to the birth of the final state of blessedness.[3]

As the tribulation coincided with the advent of the messiah, it was also tied directly to the end of exile as the climactic point of Israel's suffering.[4] This fact is important for our purposes, for as we will see, Jonah's own tribulation was also tied to Israel's suffering in exile.[5]

I will begin by exploring the Jewish reception of Jonah as a tribulation text, with a preliminary look at tribulation in the narrative itself. I will then address the three primary Matthean passages, taking soundings for echoes of tribulation. My goal will be to determine whether Matthew extends the same Jonah-tribulation connection found in Judaism through his Jonah motif—although

---

[2] Several have persuasively argued this for Matthew and the other Gospel writers. Typically, the persecution of John the Baptist is seen as inaugurating this time period. See Albert Schweitzer, *The Mystery of the Kingdom of God: The Secret of Jesus' Messiahship and Passion* (trans. Walter Lowrie; New York: Dodd, Mead, 1914), 219–273; Schweitzer, *The Quest of the Historical Jesus: First Complete Edition* (ed. John Bowden; trans. W. Montgomery et al.; rev. ed.; Minneapolis: Fortress, 2001), 330–397; Dale C. Allison, *The End of the Ages Has Come: An Early Interpretation of the Passion and Resurrection of Jesus* (Philadelphia: Fortress, 1985); C. Marvin Pate and Douglas Welker Kennard, *Deliverance Now and Not Yet: The New Testament and the Great Tribulation* (New York: Peter Lang, 2003); Brant James Pitre, *Jesus, the Tribulation, and the End of the Exile: Restoration Eschatology and the Origin of the Atonement* (WUNT 2.204; Tübingen: Mohr Siebeck, 2005).

[3] Mark Dubis, "Messianic Woes," in *Eerdmans Dictionary of the Bible* (ed. D.N. Freedman; Grand Rapids: Eerdmans, 2000), 890–891. Cited in Pitre, *Tribulation*, 5.

[4] Convincingly drawn out by Pitre, *Tribulation*, 83, 90, 115, 128–129.

[5] I will use the anarthrous "tribulation" broadly for both Israel's past tribulation and that to come in the eschaton. For the eschatological tribulation, I will use the term "the tribulation" or "messianic woes."

refracted, of course, through his own eschatological lens. This is, in fact, precisely what this study suggests. Thus, in Matthew, when Jonah surfaces, so do echoes of the tribulation.

2 Jonah and Tribulation within Judaism

It is not difficult to see how the Jonah narrative became a tribulation text for Jews suffering in exile, considering the centrality of the theme of exile in the story itself. Scholars have long noted Jonah's exilic dimensions, arguing that the prophet served symbolically for Israel. Like Israel, Jonah was called to a mission to the nations, but in disobedience he rejected this call and was disciplined by Yahweh through a time of suffering in the sea—his "exile." His prayer, recounting his near death experience in the sea storm, fills in the picture: he is outside the land, longs to see the temple, is in "prison" (cf. Isa 42:7; Ps 107:10–16; Lam 3:34) and calls to God for deliverance (Jonah 2:1–9). Yahweh answers and restores him to the land, typifying Israel's hope for their own restoration (Jonah 2:9–10).[6] The crisis of exile and its accompanying sufferings is one of the key facets of the story.

Alongside this exilic focus, "tribulation" is mentioned explicitly in Jonah's recounting of his sufferings in his prayer:

> I called to the LORD out of my *distress* (θλίψει, צרה) and he answered me; out of the belly of Sheol I cried, and you heard my voice. You cast me into the deep, into the heart of the seas, and the flood surrounded me; all your waves and your billows passed over me.[7]
>
>   Jonah 2:2–3 [2:3–4 MT/LXX].

While the term θλῖψις (and variations of the verb θλίβω) is used for various types of distress, Israel so consistently experienced θλῖψις that it became a bedrock term in their salvation history, used often for afflictions (including exile) brought upon them by Yahweh to elicit repentance (cf. Deut 4:29–30;

---

6 For exilic themes in Jonah, see Ehud Ben Zvi, *Signs of Jonah: Reading and Rereading in Ancient Yahud* (JSOTSup 367; London: Sheffield Academic, 2003), 127–128; Daniel L. Smith-Christopher, *A Biblical Theology of Exile* (Minneapolis: Fortress, 2002), 130–135; Timothy J. Stone, "Following the Church Fathers: An Intertextual Path from Psalm 107 to Isaiah, Jonah and Matthew 8:23–27," *JTI* 7 (2013): 37–55.

7 English translations of OT, NT and the Apocrypha are from the NRSV.

Judg 10:6–16).⁸ Also, as it is here in Jonah, θλῖψις is often accompanied by the action of "crying out" (צעק, זעק, קרא; βοάω, κράζω, ἀναβοάω LXX) for deliverance (Judg 10:6–16; Neh 9:27; Ps 107 [106 LXX]; 120:1 [119:1 LXX]; cf. Jonah 2:9). In addition to recurring cycles of this distress, a time of eschatological θλῖψις also awaited Israel at the culmination of their history (Dan 12:1; Zeph 1:14–18).⁹ With such deep theological significance in this term along with the way it is framed in Jonah's prayer, Israel certainly would have seen its own experience of θλῖψις in that of Jonah.

Alongside the use of θλῖψις, the sea storm imagery itself carried tribulation overtones. Sea storm narratives were widespread in antiquity with the storms customarily representing divine judgment (as also in Jonah 1:4–16).¹⁰ Thus, within Judaism, storm language became associated with God's judgment of exile, including the final tribulation of the eschaton.¹¹ This is perhaps most explicitly seen in Ps 107 (106 LXX), which focuses not only on exile but explicitly on tribulation, seen in the fourfold refrain with the tribulation/cry out dynamic: "Then they cried to the LORD in their trouble (θλίβεσθαι, צרר) and he delivered them from their distress" (vv. 6, 13, 19, 28). Most importantly, it depicts tribulation through vivid sea storm imagery, akin to Jonah's (Ps 107 [106 LXX]:23–32).¹² Such imagery, as we will see shortly, was a foundational part of tribulation symbolism in later Judaism as well.

---

8   As Heinrich Schlier, "θλίβω, θλῖψις," *TDNT*, 3:139–148, esp. 142, states, "it predominantly denotes the oppression and affliction of the people of Israel or of the righteous who represent Israel."

9   Schlier, "θλίβω," 3:139–148.

10 See Pamela Lee Thimmes, *Studies in the Biblical Sea-Storm Type-Scene: Convention and Invention* (San Francisco: Mellen Research University Press, 1992), 29–80; David J. Ladouceur, "Hellenistic Preconceptions of Shipwreck and Pollution as a Context for Acts 27–28," *HTR* 73 (1980): 435–449; Gary B. Miles and Garry W. Trompf, "Luke and Antiphon: The Theology of Acts 27–28 in the Light of Pagan Beliefs about Divine Retribution, Pollution, and Shipwreck," *HTR* 69 (1976): 259–267.

11 See Isa 28:2, 17; 29:6; 30:30; Ezek 13:10–16; Wis 16:15–16; Sir 39:28–29; 2 Esd 13:11, 37; 2 Bar. 53:7; 3 Bar. 16:3; Sib. Or. 3:689–692; 8:204–205; 1 QHᵃ 10:27–28; 11:13–18; 14:22–24. This association stemmed in part from the Noahic flood, a metonymy for God's judgment including that in the tribulation (Dan 9:26; Zeph 1:3; Jub. 23:18; Matt 24:36–39//Luke 17:26–27). See Dorothy M. Peters, *Noah Traditions in the Dead Sea Scrolls: Conversations and Controversies of Antiquity* (Leiden; Brill, 2009), 22–26. For the flood background of Jonah, see Hyun Chul Paul Kim, "Jonah Read Intertextually," *JBL* 126 (2007): 499–504, 521.

12 Thimmes, *Sea-Storm*, 127–132; Stone, "Following," 42–46.

Among the handful of times Jonah is mentioned in extra-biblical Jewish literature, three texts in particular highlight the tribulation theme.[13] One is the petition of Eleazar for God's deliverance found in 3 Maccabees:

> The three companions in Babylon who had voluntarily surrendered their lives to the flames so as not to serve vain things, you rescued unharmed, even to a hair, moistening the fiery furnace with dew and turning the flame against all their enemies. Daniel, who through envious slanders was thrown down into the ground to lions as food for wild animals, you brought up to the light unharmed. *And Jonah, wasting away in the belly of a huge, sea-born monster, you, Father, watched over and restored unharmed to all his family.* And now, you who hate insolence, all-merciful and protector of all, reveal yourself quickly to those of the nation of Israel—who are being outrageously treated by the abominable and lawless Gentiles. Even if our lives have become entangled in impieties in our exile, rescue us from the hand of the enemy …
>
> 3 Macc 6:6–10

Here Jonah is placed beside two other heroic figures who were delivered not only from life-threatening danger, but from exilic persecution; this may indicate that Jonah was also viewed as a recipient of persecutory acts (by the Gentiles or the "sea-born monster" itself; cf. Jer 51:34).[14] At the very least, here Israelites in exile appropriate the story of Jonah—and specifically its tribulation sequence—for their own exilic suffering, appealing to Yahweh for similar divine deliverance.

A second text which connects Jonah with tribulation is found in the prayers in the Mishnaic tractate Taanith, to be recited on fasting days as Israel petitions Yahweh for deliverance from exilic suffering:

---

13   For a broader discussion on Jewish reception of Jonah, see Simon Chow, *The Sign of Jonah Reconsidered: A Study of Its Meaning in the Gospel Traditions* (ConBNT 27; Stockholm: Almqvist & Wiksell International, 1995), 25–44; Gregory C. Jenks, "The Sign of the Prophet Jonah: Tracing the Tradition History of a Biblical Character in Ancient Judaism and Early Christianity," in *How Jonah Is Interpreted in Judaism, Christianity, and Islam: Essays on the Authenticity and Influence of the Biblical Prophet* (ed. Mishael Caspi and John T. Greene; Lewiston, NY: Mellen, 2011), 11–51.

14   As Chow, *Sign of Jonah*, 205, notes, early Christian art also characteristically depicted Jonah with these figures, highlighting the idea of deliverance from trouble or death. Interestingly, depictions of Jonah diminished after the time of Constantine, likely due to the abatement of Christian persecution. See Graydon F. Snyder, *Ante Pacem: Archaeological Evidence of Church Life before Constantine* (Macon, GA: Mercer University Press, 1985), 49.

He who answered Jonah in the belly of the fish may He answer you and hear the voice of your crying [this day], Blessed are Thou, O Eternal, who answerest in time of distress (צרה).[15]

m. Ta'an. 2:4

In this text, which likely should be dated early,[16] we find the term "distress" (צרה) the same term used in Jonah's prayer. The significance of this connection comes to light upon examining the other refrains. The syntax of each parallels the one above, although each one focuses on a different OT figure(s) with a corresponding characteristic of Yahweh, as seen below:

1) "Abraham on Mount Moriah ... the redeemer of Israel."
2) "our ancestors at the red sea ... Who rememberest things forgotten."
3) "Joshua at Gilgal ... Who hearest the sound of the Shofar."
4) "Samuel in Mizpah ... Who hearest that cry."
5) "Elijah on Mount Carmel ... Who hearest prayer."
6) *"Jonah in the belly of the fish ... Who answerest in time of distress."*
7) "David and Solomon, his son, in Jerusalem ... Who has compassion on the land."[17]

Viewed beside the other six, it becomes clear that the predominant theme connected to Jonah is the theme of distress (צרה)—tribulation. Furthermore, as in 3 Maccabees, Jews suffering in exile appeal to Yahweh's deliverance of Jonah in a petition for their own.

A third document pertinent to our study is *1QHodayot*, the most significant document on the eschatological tribulation from Qumran. Written in the first person, the author clearly believes he is suffering in the messianic woes.[18] While this text does not mention Jonah directly, the writer describes his persecutory sufferings with Jonah-like imagery:

---

15 From Chow, *Sign of Jonah*, 41–42. Bracketed words are supplied by Chow, noting a translational error. For primary text, see *Mishnayoth* (trans. Philip Blackman; New York: Judaica Press, 1990), 417–418.
16 Dietrich Correns, "Jona und Salomo," in *Wort in der Zeit: Neutestamentliche Studien: Festgabe für Karl Heinrich Rengstorf zum 75. Geburtstag* (Leiden: Brill, 1980), 86–94. See also Chow, *Sign of Jonah*, 41–42.
17 Blackman, *Mishnayoth*, 417–418.
18 Pitre, *Tribulation*, 91–96.

> I (have become) like a sailor in a ship in the raging seas: their waves and all their breakers roar over me, a whirlwind (without a) lull for taking breath without a track to take a straight path over the surface of the water. The deep thunders at my sigh, (my) so(ul nears) the gates of death.
> 1QHª 14:22–24

While this might merely be a general image of sailors in a sea storm, in addition to the thematic parallels to Jonah, a lexical link is found between the Qumran phrase "their waves and all their breakers roar over me" (גליהם וכול משבריהם עלי, 1QHª 14:23) and Jonah's "all your waves and your billows passed over me" (כָּל־מִשְׁבָּרֶיךָ וְגַלֶּיךָ עָלַי עָבָרוּ, Jonah 2:3 [2:4 MT]).[19] Thus, here we have a clear text on the tribulation in which the writer may be alluding to Jonah. At the very least, it is noteworthy that this writer likens his "tribulational" persecution to a threatening sea storm, a fact with potential significance for Matthew's own Jonah allusions.

Undoubtedly in the first two texts, and perhaps also in the third, the story of Jonah was appropriated by Jewish writers for their own experience of tribulation in exile. In the same vein, Jonah stood as a figure of deliverance from tribulation, and his story was appealed to by Israelites as they cried out to Yahweh for their own deliverance. While there may be more Jonah-tribulation associations to be found within this literature, these few examples offer solid evidence that tribulation was central in the conception of Jonah within Second Temple Judaism.

3   Jonah and Tribulation in Matthew

Given the Jewish reception of Jonah as a tribulation text, we now need to ask whether Matthew himself viewed it as such. Of course, if so, Matthew would

---

19 Psalm 42:7 (42:8 MT, כָּל־מִשְׁבָּרֶיךָ וְגַלֶּיךָ עָלַי עָבָרוּ MT) may also be in play. The sea storm sequence in Ps 107 is typically confirmed as the backdrop of this text and other sea storm imagery in the scroll (cf. the hushing or lull of the sea [דְּמָמָה, Ps 107:29; 1QHª 14.23]). See Svend Holm-Nielsen, *Hodayot: Psalms from Qumran*, (ATDan 2; Aarhus: Universitetsforlaget, 1960), 44 n. 21, 58 n. 28, 59 n. 30, 96 n. 45; Julie Hughes, *Scriptural Allusions and Exegesis in the Hodayot* (STDJ 59; Leiden: Brill, 2006), 198, 204. Hughes, although somewhat tentative, points to verbal parallels with Jonah (cf. 172 n. 151, 199, 201 n. 68, 205). Ps 107, however, has a long history of being connected to Jonah. For example, the Targum on the Psalms sees the sea storm portion as a prophecy of Jonah. See *The Targum of Psalms* (trans. David M. Stec; ArBib 16; Collegeville, MN: Liturgical, 2004), 198.

have re-infused Jonah with special meaning for his own community gathered around the person and work of Jesus and, thus, likely suffering persecution. We will begin our endeavor to answer this question with the first main port of entry into this motif, the stilling of the storm.

3.1   The Storm of Tribulation: Matthew 8:23–27

> And when he got into the boat, his disciples followed him. A windstorm arose on the sea, so great that the boat was being swamped by the waves; but he was asleep. And they went and woke him up, saying, "Lord, save us! We are perishing!" And he said to them, "Why are you afraid, you of little faith?" Then he got up and rebuked the winds and the sea; and there was a dead calm. They were amazed, saying, "What sort of man is this, that even the winds and the sea obey him?"
>
> Matt 8:23–27

Shared resonances between the Jonah story and the stilling of the storm narrative have been well established with scholars noting the following thematic parallels:[20]

Jonah	Thematic parallel	Matthew
1:3	Main character enters a boat	8:23
1:4	Violent sea storm arises	8:24
1:4–5	Boat and its occupants are in danger	8:24–25
1:5	Main character is sleeping	8:24
1:5	Men on the boat are frightened	8:25–26
1:6	Main character is awoken by men on the boat	8:25
1:6	Men ask main character for help	8:25
1:12, 15	Sea is calmed by intervention of main character and divine power	8:26
1:16	Men on boat express awe/reverence	8:27

---

20   Lexical parallels accompany the thematic. This chart is an adaptation from lists in Lamar Cope, *Matthew: A Scribe Trained for the Kingdom of Heaven* (CBQMS 5; Washington, DC: Catholic Biblical Association of America, 1976), 96–97 and Paul F. Feiler, "The Stilling of the Storm in Matthew: A Response to Günther Bornkamm," *JETS* 26 (1983): 404–405. See also W.D. Davies and Dale C. Allison, *A Critical and Exegetical Commentary on the Gospel according to Saint Matthew* (3 vols.; ICC; Edinburgh: T&T Clark, 1991), 2:70.

It is noteworthy that the portion of Jonah to which Matthew points is his time in the storm, *the tribulation sequence*. While Jesus represents Jonah in this scene, with the preceding passage focused on those attempting to evade Yahweh's mission (cf. 8:18–22), a Jonah parallel certainly would have reminded Matthew's readers of Jonah's attempt to evade his own mission, exhorting them against doing the same. Significantly, Jesus is the model of an *obedient* Jonah, embarking on Yahweh's mission, incidentally, to the Gentiles.[21] The disciples, of course, are to "follow" (ἀκολουθέω) this "new Jonah" in this mission, no matter what the cost (cf. 8:22–23).[22]

Part of this cost is, undoubtedly, tribulation. Considering the strong connection between tribulation and sea storm imagery we saw above (in Jonah, Ps 107, and *1QHodayot*), the messianic woes might be symbolized in the storm itself. It is perhaps not inconsequential that the earliest Christian interpreters in the throes of persecution saw this storm symbolizing such.[23] Furthermore, at least one other storm in Matthew (in the parable of the wise and foolish builder in Matt 7:24–27) has been seen by a majority of scholars as having an eschatological tenor, possibly pointing directly to the tribulation.[24] The storm in the story of Jesus's walking on the water (Matt 14:22–33) might also be viewed similarly.[25]

---

21   Crossing the sea in the Gospels is customarily connected to Gentile mission. On Jonah and the Gentile mission, see David Moffitt, "The Sign of Jonah and the Prophet Motif in the *Gospel of Matthew*: Moving Toward the Gentile Mission," in *How Jonah Is Interpreted in Judaism, Christianity, and Islam: Essays on the Authenticity and Influence of the Biblical Prophet* (ed. Mishael M. Caspi, and John T. Greene Lewiston; NY: E. Mellen, 2011), 233–245. I am not dismissing the Gentile emphasis in the Jonah motif; to the contrary, we should remember that the Gentile mission was one of the end goals of the tribulation. See C. Marvin Pate and Douglas Welker Kennard, *Deliverance Now and Not Yet: The New Testament and the Great Tribulation* (New York: Peter Lang, 2003), 204, 210, 214–215, 228–229, 405, 407, 454.

22   On the metaphorical use of ἀκολουθέω here, see Günther Bornkamm, "The Stilling of the Storm in Matthew," in *Tradition and Interpretation in Matthew* (trans. Percy Scott; Philadelphia: Westminster, 1963), 52–57; Jack Dean Kingsbury, "The Verb AKOLOUTHEIN ('To Follow') as an Index of Matthew's View of His Community," *JBL* 97 (1978): 56–73.

23   Tertullian, *De baptismo* 12; Hippolytus, *De antichristo* 59. See Davies and Allison, *Matthew*, 2:69.

24   See R.T. France, *The Gospel of Matthew* (Grand Rapids: Eerdmans, 2007), 296–297; John Nolland, *The Gospel of Matthew: A Commentary on the Greek Text* (Grand Rapids: Eerdmans, 2005), 342–344; Davies and Allison, *Matthew*, 1:719–722. On the storm as final judgment, see Ulrich Luz, *Matthew 1–7: A Commentary* (trans. Wilhelm C. Linss; Hermeneia; Minneapolis: Fortress, 2007), 385–388. Interestingly, the Matthean account of this parable highlights the storm with more intensity (cf. Luke 6:46–49).

25   Robert H. Gundry, *Matthew: A Commentary on His Handbook for a Mixed Church under*

All things considered, we could certainly do worse than to imagine that the storm in this passage echoes the tribulation.[26]

A second hint of the tribulation may be found in Matthew's unique description of the cause of the storm as an "earthquake" (σεισμός).[27] Earthquakes characteristically represented God's judgment, including the eschatological tribulation.[28] We see this even within Matthew's own narrative, as earthquakes (σεισμοί, Matt 24:7) are predicted as part of the tribulation. Thus, Matthew's seismic shock may an important cross point for Matthew's Jonah-tribulation grid.

Third, we should note the "great calm" (γαλήνη μεγάλη, Matt 8:26; cf. σεισμός μέγας, Matt 8:24) that follows the earthquake-generated storm. This mimics the pattern where the geologic violence of the tribulation is followed by peace and restoration of the created order.[29] Thus, a storm and an earthquake with a great calm following may point to the tribulation-restoration sequence.

Lastly, this narrative may serve as a foreshadowing of Jesus's death and resurrection, which has tribulation significance.[30] This might be deduced first by Jesus's sleeping/waking sequence, as sleep was a common metaphor for death with awakening symbolizing resurrection (cf. Matt 27:52).[31] Another

---

   Persecution (Grand Rapids: Eerdmans, 1994), 295–302, connects that passage to this one and highlights the storm there as persecution.

26 If Stone, "Following," 49, is right that this sea crossing is "a symbolic enactment of Israel's return from exile" then it would follow easily that the storm represents the tribulation, the pinnacle of Israel's exilic suffering.

27 So Günther Bornkamm, "σείω," *TDNT*, 7:196–200; Bornkamm, "Stilling," 56; Ulrich Luz, *Matthew 8–20: A Commentary* (trans. James E. Crouch; Hermeneia; Minneapolis: Fortress, 2001), 20; Donald Senior, *Matthew* (ANTC; Nashville: Abingdon, 1998), 101–102; Eduard Schweizer, *The Good News according to Matthew* (trans. David E. Green; Atlanta: John Knox Press, 1975), 221. Bornkamm notes the eschatological significance in the earthquakes at Jesus's death and resurrection (27:54; 28:2).

28 See Isa 29:5–6; Zech 14:4–5; 2 Esd 9:3; Sib. Or. 3:675–681, 752; 4:58–59; 2 Bar. 27:7; *T. Levi.* 4:1; As. Mos. 10:4; Apoc. Ab. 30:8; Matt 24:7//Mark 13:8//Luke 21:11; Rev 6:12; 8:5; 11:13, 19; 16:18.

29 See Zech 14:6–8; Sib. Or. 3:659–660; Jub. 23:27–31; 1 En. 91.16. R. Reed Lessing, "Amos's Earthquake in the Book of the Twelve," *CTQ* 74 (2010): 258, notes connections to the prophets in which eschatologically framed earthquakes precede re-creation (cf. Amos 9:11–15; Joel 2:18–26).

30 That this narrative foreshadows Jesus's death and resurrection goes back to Jerome, *Commentaire Sur S. Matthieu* (SC 242; Paris: Cerf, 1977), 1:163 and Thomas Aquinas, *Commentary on Matthew* (trans. John Henry Parker; Catena Aurea; London: Rivington, 1842), 1: 323. Stone, "Following," provides exegetical support for this view.

31 Stone, "Following," 52–53. See Dan 2:1–2; 2 Macc 12:45; Sir 30:17; John 11:11–14; Acts 7:60; 13:36; 1 Cor 7:39; 11:30; 15:6, 18, 20, 51; Eph 5:14; 1 Thess 4:13–17; 5:10; 2 Pet 3:4. For a multitude of Greek and Jewish references, see Craig S. Keener, *The Gospel of John: A Commentary*

connection to Jesus's death and resurrection can be found in the use of σεισ-μός (8:24), which may intentionally foreshadow the σεισμοί occurring at Jesus's death and resurrection, geologic events which only Matthew includes (27:54; 28:2).[32] If indeed this passage proleptically represents Jesus's death and resurrection—which would correlate well with Jonah who himself served symbolically for death and resurrection—the tribulation may not be far from the horizon.[33] While I will not here restate the arguments connecting Jesus's death and the tribulation, Allison's words are representative of several scholars: "the messianic woes had shown themselves above all in the passion and death of Jesus."[34] As for resurrection, in Jewish eschatology, tribulation was often depicted as its precursor.[35]

Thus, in this Jonah-framed maritime story, it is quite possible that Matthew is beginning to triangulate Jesus, Jonah and the tribulation. In this passage, Matthew presents Jesus as a Jonah figure with the disciples following him in his mission, encountering a "storm" of tribulation along the way. If we are on target, we might expect to see a trajectory of similar themes continuing through the remaining Jonah passages.

3.2   *The Sign of Tribulation: Matthew 12:38–42; 16:1–4*

> Then some of the scribes and Pharisees said to him, "Teacher, we wish to see a sign from you." But he answered them, "An evil and adulterous generation asks for a sign, but no sign will be given to it except the sign of the prophet Jonah. For just as Jonah was three days and three nights in the belly of the sea monster, so for three days and three nights the Son of Man will be in the heart of the earth. The people of Nineveh will rise

---

(Peabody, MA: Hendrickson, 2003), 2:840–841 nn. 53–58. As Luz, *Matthew 1–7*, 28, points out, the twice-repeated term ἐγείρω for Jesus's rising up (8:25–26) is a Mattheanism connected to resurrection (14:2; 8:15; 27:64; 28:6, 7).

32   Stone, "Following," 53.

33   For Jonah as a symbol of death and resurrection in Judaism, see Chow, *Sign of Jonah*, 27–44.

34   Allison, *End of the Ages*, 173, also 26–82; 115–141. As Pitre, *Tribulation*, 381–508, esp. 383, notes, Schweitzer, Jeremias, Allison, Wright, and Dunn have linked Jesus's death to the eschatological tribulation, arguing that the evangelists and Jesus himself portrayed it as such. Interestingly, the phrase noted as a possible Jonah allusion in the Nestle-Aland text, "exceedingly grieved unto death" (Matt 26:38; Jonah 4:9), occurs in the Garden of Gethsemane narrative, a passage replete with tribulation themes.

35   See Dan 12:1–2; Isa 26:17–19; 2 Esd 7:26–44; 9:1–13. Pitre, *Tribulation*, 124, 187–188.

up at the judgment with this generation and condemn it, because they repented at the proclamation of Jonah, and see, something greater than Jonah is here! The queen of the South will rise up at the judgment with this generation and condemn it, because she came from the ends of the earth to listen to the wisdom of Solomon, and see, something greater than Solomon is here!"

Matt 12:38–42

The Pharisees and Sadducees came, and to test Jesus they asked him to show them a sign from heaven. ² He answered them, "When it is evening, you say, 'It will be fair weather, for the sky is red.' And in the morning, 'It will be stormy today, for the sky is red and threatening.' You know how to interpret the appearance of the sky, but you cannot interpret the signs of the times. An evil and adulterous generation asks for a sign, but no sign will be given to it except the sign of Jonah." Then he left them and went away.

Matt 16:1–4

Notorious for being a *crux interpretum*, the sign of Jonah is plagued with complexities, several occurring in these two passages. Keeping the focus on tribulation, I will key in on: (1) the nature of the sign, (2) the generation reference, (3) the quotation of Jonah, and (4) the storm imagery.

Both pericopae begin with a request by the Jewish leaders for a "sign" (σημεῖον, 12:38; 16:1). As they just witnessed healing miracles (12:22–30), they were likely asking for something more, possibly even an eschatological sign announcing the arrival of the messianic age. Within Judaism, signs served as characteristic harbingers of the eschaton; among these, in fact, were cosmic anomalies. As the sign is called a σημεῖον ἐκ τοῦ οὐρανοῦ in 16:1, with οὐρανός in the two verses following referring to the sky in a geological sense, it is possible they were looking for such here.[36] This, of course, would also be one of the "signs of the times" (σημεῖα τῶν καιρῶν, Matt 16:3). Furthermore, in the other main Matthean context where σημεῖον appears, it clearly carries eschatological import, as the disciples ask Jesus for a σημεῖον of Jesus's coming and "the end of the age" (συντελείας τοῦ αἰῶνος, Matt 24:3; cf. 24:30). The Jewish leaders would have undoubtedly considered this sign as a sign of blessing for themselves; as such, Jesus refuses to grant it. If a sign of the messianic age is in view here, the messianic woes would certainly also be on the horizon.

---

36 Davies and Allison, *Matthew*, 2:580.

Second, the reference here to "an evil and adulterous generation" (γενεὰ πονηρὰ καὶ μοιχαλίς, 12:39; 16:4) has significance pertaining to the tribulation. This γενεά appears several times in Matthew's Gospel, seemingly referring to a similar group of people (11:16; 12:39, 41, 42, 45; 16:4; 17:17; 23:36; 24:34). It is characteristically cast in a negative light and often as persecutors of the heralds of the kingdom (cf. 23:29–36).[37] Even in this context, which is saturated with the theme of persecution,[38] the γενεά are presented as the opponents of Jesus and John (11:16–19), condemned to eschatological judgment (12:41–42), and likened to a household of demons (12:43–45), a comparison that may, in fact, point to their violence against the elect.[39] Interestingly, a strikingly similar wicked generation appears in Second Temple literature as a central feature of the eschaton. One text it appears in is the Apocalypse of Weeks. In this work, which divides history into periods of "weeks," a "perverse generation" arises in the critical seventh week (1En. 93:9).[40] At the end of that week, an elect remnant also arises (93:10), brings an end to "violence" and "deceit"— the deeds of the perverse generation—and executes judgment, which continues into the eighth week (91:11–12).[41] The ninth and tenth weeks disclose the consummation of this time with the final judgment and eschatological restoration (91:14–17). Notably, this generation is connected explicitly with the tribulation; not only do the terms "violence" and "deceit" serve as trademarks of this time period, but the order of events also fits the characteristic sequence:

---

37 See M. Meinertz, "'Dieses Geschlecht' im Neuen Testament," *BZ* 1 (1957): 283–289; Evald Lövestam, *Jesus and "This Generation": A New Testament Study* (Stockholm: Almqvist & Wiksell, 1995); Neil D. Nelson, "'This Generation' in Matt 24:34: A Literary Critical Perspective," *JETS* 38 (1995): 385. In Nelson, see esp. 373 n. 17 for scholars who recognize its pejorative nature. See also Susan M. Rieske, "What Is the Meaning of 'This Generation' in Matthew 23:36?" *BSac* 165 (2008): 209–226, although I have since modified my view to include the temporal aspect with "this generation" applied to Jesus's contemporaries.

38 See Gundry, *Matthew*, 203–204.

39 Demons were often associated with such. See Elaine Pagels, "The Social History of Satan, the 'Intimate Enemy': A Preliminary Sketch," *HTR* 84 (1991): 105–128; Pagels, "The Social History of Satan, Part II: Satan in the New Testament Gospels," *JAAR* 62 (1994): 17–58.

40 Translation from George W.E. Nickelsburg and James C. VanderKam, *1Enoch: The Hermeneia Translation* (Hermeneia; Minneapolis: Fortress, 2012). As George W.E. Nickelsburg, *1Enoch 1: A Commentary on the Book of 1Enoch* (Hermeneia; Minneapolis: Fortress, 2001), 447, notes, Deut 32 lies in the background. Incidentally this is the same source text for Matthew.

41 Nickelsburg, *1Enoch 1*, 447. Although the weeks are split in two chapters (93 and 91), scholars concur they belong together in the apocalypse. See Nickelsburg, *1Enoch 1*, 414–415.

the tribulation is followed by the emergence of the elect, which in turn is followed by judgment on evildoers.[42]

A second crucial text where an "evil generation" is mentioned is the eschatological discourse of Jubilees (Jub. 23:14). This generation parallels that of 1 Enoch in several key ways: the generation engages in violence (23:14–21), it precedes the arising of an elect remnant (23:26–31), and it arises concurrently with the eschatological tribulation, which here gets full disclosure (23:11–14; 22–25).[43]

One last text in the Sibylline Oracles is worth quoting in full, not only because an eschatological generation is mentioned in conjunction with tribulation, but a "sign" is also mentioned:

> But whenever this sign (σῆμα) appears throughout the world, children born with gray temples from birth, afflictions (θλίψεις) of men, famines, pestilence, and wars, change of times, lamentations, many tears; alas, how many people's children in the countries will feed on their parents, with piteous lamentations. They will place their flesh in cloaks and bury them in the ground, mother of peoples, defiled with blood and dust. O very wretched dread evildoers of the last generation (γενεῆς), infantile, who do not understand that when the species of females does not give birth, the harvest of articulate men has come.[44]
>
> Sib. Or. 2:154–164

Again, an evil generation (the "last" of that age) arises during a time of great tribulation.[45] Furthermore, as here in Matt 12 where the generation is given a "sign"—the sign of Jonah—this generation is also given a sign of the end. Notably, here the sign is tribulation itself.[46] As we will explore shortly, this fact may be significant for our understanding of the sign of Jonah. Nonetheless, it is clear that the idea of a wicked eschatological generation arising concur-

---

42 Pitre, *Tribulation*, 45.
43 As in 1 Enoch and Matthew, this text draws on Deut 32.
44 *OTP*, 1:317–472. Greek from *Die Oracula Sibyllina* (ed. Johannes Geffcken; GCS 8; Leipzig: Hinrichs, 1902). While the dating and the extent of Christian redaction on the oracles is debated, Collins affirms this portion as Jewish, and as such it might be dated at the turn of the era before Matthew's time. See *OTP*, 1:330–331.
45 This one too is accompanied by the rising of an elect remnant (Sib. Or. 2:168–169, 174–175).
46 Other Second Temple texts also speak of the "sign" of tribulation in the eschaton (Sib. Or. 3:796–807; 4:173; 2 Bar. 25:1–4).

rently with the tribulation was alive and well in Judaism's matrix of ideas.⁴⁷ With the similarities between these generations and Matthew's—both in their evil nature and their association with tribulation (cf. Matt 24:3–35)—it is likely that by referencing this evil generation, Matthew is announcing the arrival of the eschatological tribulation.

A third nod to the tribulation within these pericopae is found in Matthew's quotation from Jonah, which points directly to his time of tribulation: "Jonah was three days and three nights in the belly of the sea monster" (ἦν Ιωνας ἐν τῇ κοιλίᾳ τοῦ κήτους τρεῖς ἡμέρας καὶ τρεῖς νύκτας, Jonah 2:1 LXX; Matt 12:40). These words immediately precede the prayer of Jonah discussed above, which is also introduced by a repetition of the identical phrase, τῆς κοιλίας τοῦ κήτους (Jonah 2:2 LXX). Considering the way scriptural quotations customarily points to broader literary contexts, Matthew is likely pointing to this very prayer.⁴⁸ As already noted, Jonah's prayer begins with "tribulation" (θλῖψις, צרה; Jonah 2:3 MT/LXX). Considering Matthew's use of the LXX here, it is unlikely that he would *not* have noticed the term θλῖψις—the very term used consistently for the eschatological tribulation in his Gospel (24:9, 21, 29).⁴⁹ The parallel between Jesus's time after death ("in the heart of the earth") and Jonah's time of distress in the whale highlights Jesus's own time of tribulation.⁵⁰

The three day reference in this quotation may also carry tribulation significance. This time period has been long considered to be the climax of Jesus's

---

47 See also 1Q28b (1QSb) 3:7; CD 1:12–2:1; 1QpHab 2:6–7; 7:1; Tg. Isa. 57:3; m. Soṭah 9.15; b. Ketub. 112b; b. Sanh. 97a–98a.

48 C.H. Dodd, "The Old Testament in the New," in *The Right Doctrine from the Wrong Texts?: Essays on the Use of the Old Testament in the New* (ed. G.K. Beale; Grand Rapids: Baker, 1994), 176, states that NT authors "often quoted a single phrase or sentence not merely for its own sake, but as a pointer to a whole context—a practice by no means uncommon among contemporary Jewish teachers ... The reader is invited to study the context as a whole, and to reflect upon the 'plot' there unfolded."

49 Its use in the parable of the sower (13:21) may also point to the tribulation. Davies and Allison, *Matthew*, 2:401, note the same triangulation of θλῖψις, σκανδαλίζω, and persecution in the messianic woes of Matthew's eschatological discourse (24:9–10). For a convincing argument on the centrality of the tribulation in the Markan parable, see Nicholas Perrin, *Jesus the Priest* (Grand Rapids: Eerdmans, forthcoming), ch. 3. For representative uses of θλῖψις with persecution, see 1Macc 5:16; 4Macc 14:9; 18:15; Acts 11:19; 14:22; 20:23; Eph 3:13; Phil 1:17; Col 1:24; Rev 2:10; 7:14.

50 As many argue, this prayer is likely retrospective, and, thus, his time in the whale is included in his sufferings and is seen as God's final act of judgment upon Jonah. See Hans Walter Wolff, *Obadiah and Jonah: A Commentary* (trans. Margaret Kohl; Minneapolis: Augsburg, 1986), 132–133.

conflict with evil as it correlated with a presumed descent into hell.[51] This view rests partly on Jewish interpretations of Jonah's own sojourn as a war against evil.[52] Although scholars are divided on this issue, this idea should not be ruled out and would certainly fit with notions of the tribulation, where conflict with evil escalates. More significant, however, is the oft-cited Hosea passage where after a time of "tribulation" (θλῖψις, צר, Hos 5:15), Israel calls out, "Come, let us return to the LORD; for it is he who has torn, and he will heal us; he has struck down, and he will bind us up. After two days he will revive us; on the third day he will raise us up, that we may live before him" (Hos 6:1–2). This passage, which has a distinctly eschatological flavor in the rabbinic literature, certainly indicates a symbolic connection between three days and tribulation.[53] This symbolism is also noted in this popular Yalqut reflection, "God leaves the righteous no longer than three days in distress."[54] This latter idea also highlights divine vindication, which comes through Jesus's and Jonah's respective "resurrections." Interestingly, even being brought safely through a sea storm symbolized the same.[55] Such vindication likely plays a role in the meaning of the sign, as Jesus's deliverance confirms him as God's righteous prophet, guaranteeing judgment for the γενεά who persecutes him (12:41–42).[56] Ironically, while Jesus is delivered from his tribulation, his persecutors will suffer their own. Thus, just as in Sib. Or. 2:154–164 where the initial wave of tribulation serves as a sign to the wicked eschatological generation, it does here as well, only in a quite different manner.

---

51 Luz, *Matthew 8–20*, 217 and n. 41.
52 Otto Betz, "Jesu Heiliger Krieg," *NovT* 2 (1957): 116–137.
53 See Harvey K. McArthur, "On the Third Day," *NTS* 18 (1971): 81–86; Hans F. Bayer, *Jesus' Predictions of Vindication and Resurrection: The Provenance, Meaning, and Correlation of the Synoptic Predictions* (WUNT 2.20; Tübingen: J.C.B. Mohr, 1986), 143–144, 205–211; Joachim Jeremias, "Die Drei-Tage-Worte der Evangelien," in *Tradition und Glaube* (ed. Gert Jeremias, Heinz W. Kuhn, and Hartmut Stegemann; Göttingen: Vandenhoeck & Ruprecht, 1971), 221–229.
54 Noted by Luz, *Matthew 8–20*, 217. George M. Landes, "Three Days and Three Nights Motif in Jonah 2:1," *JBL* 86 (1967): 446–450 and Johannes Baptist Bauer, "Drei Tage," *Bib* 39 (1958): 354–358 conclude that the reference basically conveys a short period of time which was just long enough to be life-threatening.
55 See Charles H. Talbert and John H. Hayes, "A Theology of Sea Storms in Luke-Acts," in *Jesus and the Heritage of Israel* (ed. David P. Moessner; Harrisburg, PA: Trinity Press International, 1999), 267–283; Ladouceur, "Hellenistic Preconceptions"; Miles and Trompf, "Luke and Antiphon."
56 Similarly, see Bayer, *Jesus' Predictions*, 110–145.

Lastly, in these pericopae, sea storm imagery again emerges as Matthew's Jesus chides the Jewish leaders for their ability to forecast sea storms but their inability to understand the signs of the times (16:2–3).[57] If we are right that sea storm imagery related to Jonah symbolizes tribulation in Matthew, then this imagery confirms our Jonah-tribulation paradigm. The irony is vivid: while the Jewish leaders can forecast a storm in the natural world, they fail to recognize the coming cosmic storm of tribulation—one, in fact, brought on by their own persecution.

Thus, in these passages, Matthew seems to be in line with other Jewish writers who zeroed in on tribulation in Jonah. Even if this sign of Jonah carries the meaning in Matthew that most scholars attach to it—the death and resurrection of Jesus[58]—this certainly leaves room (three days and three nights in fact) for tribulation. However, as the following pericope makes clear, Jesus will not be the only one to suffer these messianic woes; his disciples will as well.

3.3 Tribulation for the Son of Jonah: Matthew 16:17–19

> Now when Jesus came into the district of Caesarea Philippi, he asked his disciples, "Who do people say that the Son of Man is?" And they said, "Some say John the Baptist, but others Elijah, and still others Jeremiah or one of the prophets." He said to them, "But who do you say that I am?" Simon Peter answered, "You are the Messiah, the Son of the living God." And Jesus answered him, "Blessed are you, Simon son of Jonah! For flesh and blood has not revealed this to you, but my Father in heaven. And I tell you, you are Peter, and on this rock I will build my church, and the gates of Hades will not prevail against it. I will give you the keys of the kingdom of heaven, and whatever you bind on earth will be bound in heaven, and whatever you loose on earth will be loosed in heaven." Then he sternly ordered the disciples not to tell anyone that he was the Messiah.
>
> Matt 16:13–20

---

57   Cf. Luke 12:54–56. Luz, *Matthew 8–20*, 347 notes this as a classic weather rule for mariners in antiquity but also notes that these verses might be a later addition. For discussion on this text-critical issue, see T. Hirunuma, "Matthew 16:2b–3," in *New Testament Textual Criticism: Its Significance for Exegesis: Essays in Honour of Bruce M. Metzger* (ed. Eldon Jay Epp and Gordon D. Fee; Oxford: Clarendon, 1981), 35–45.

58   See Chow, *Sign of Jonah*, 64–65, 70, 88–91; Luz, *Matthew 8–20*, 213–223; Joachim Jeremias, "Ἰωνᾶς," *TDNT*, 3:406–410; Paul Seidelin, "Das Jonaszeichen," *ST* 5 (1952): 119–131.

Many battles have been waged over this controversial passage, and it is not my intention to enter into the fray here. I will focus primarily on how Jesus's address of Peter as Σίμων Βαριωνᾶ (16:17) might fit into Matthew's Jonah-tribulation matrix, especially considering two contextual factors: the emphasis on persecution and the reference to the "gates of Hades."

As has been argued, Σίμων Βαριωνᾶ is likely the Greek version of the Aramaic יוֹנָה בַּר (Βαρ = בַּר) which translated yields "son of Jonah," a rendering with which most translations agree. Although some have argued for a different understanding,[59] considering Matthew's keen attention to Jonah, especially just a few verses prior (16:4), this phrase likely serves as an additional Jonah allusion.[60]

The phrase "son of Jonah" most probably carries the connotation of likeness, representing that which would characterize Peter's life and ministry (cf. Jesus's naming of Jesus and John as "sons of thunder," Mark 3:17). It may also depict succession or even "spiritual" sonship, which would carry the idea of following in one's footsteps.[61] While there might be subtle foreshadowing here of Peter's denial that mirrors Jonah's flight from his own mission (Matt 26:30–35, 58–75), in this context, Peter does not primarily follow the Jonah of the Hebrew scriptures, but the "new Jonah," Jesus himself, who has already been portrayed as such twice in Matthew (seen above). Thus, as the "son of Jonah," Peter's life will mirror that of Jesus—and if Jesus as Jonah signifies tribulation then Peter as the "son of Jonah" would signify the same.

The first aspect pointing to the theme of tribulation is the strong emphasis on persecution in the context.[62] This passage not only marks a turning

---

59 For example, Luz, *Matthew 8–20*, 362 n. 59, among others, attempts to reconcile this with John 1:42 and 21:15–17, arguing that ιωνᾶ is a variant form of "John" with no reference to Jonah.

60 See Gundry, *Matthew*, 332; M.D. Goulder, *Midrash and Lection in Matthew: The Speaker's Lectures in Biblical Studies, 1969–71* (London: SPCK, 1974), 387–388; Herbert M. Gale, "A Suggestion Concerning Matthew 16," *JBL* 60 (1941): 257. An allusion to Jonah here certainly meets the criteria set forth by Richard B. Hays, *Echoes of Scripture in the Letters of Paul* (New Haven: Yale University Press, 1989), 29–32.

61 "Spiritual" family connections may be indicated by the reference to the "Father" in heaven who revealed truth to him (16:17), connections which would be passed on through Jesus.

62 Robert W. Wall, "Peter, 'Son' of Jonah: The Conversion of Cornelius in the Context of Canon," *JSNT* (1987): 79–90, suggests that Luke sees Peter as being like Jonah in his ministry to the Gentiles. There is likely truth to this, considering Peter's unique role in unifying Jews and Gentiles in the community. In this context, however, suffering eclipses the Gentile mission in prominence.

point in the narrative towards Jesus's passion,[63] but within close proximity to this Jonah reference lies the idea that *the persecution of the disciples will mirror that of Jesus*. As Matthew narrates three verses following, "From that time on, Jesus began to show his disciples that he must go to Jerusalem and undergo great suffering at the hands of the elders and chief priests and scribes, and be killed, and on the third day be raised" (16:21).[64] Shortly afterwards, Matthew inserts Jesus's promise that those who follow Jesus will endure similar suffering (16:24–25). While resurrection is also reflected in these verses, persecutory suffering comes to the surface prominently with expansive descriptions (i.e. πολλὰ παθεῖν ἀπὸ τῶν πρεσβυτέρων καὶ ἀρχιερέων καὶ γραμματέων, 16:21) and the distressed response of Peter and the disciples indicating that the danger of suffering is on the forefront of their minds (cf. 16:22; 17:23). The movement from the suffering of Jesus to the suffering of disciples certainly elucidates how this "son of Jonah" will follow after the "new Jonah." Furthermore, it brings another tribulation echo to the surface.

A second support for the Jonah-tribulation connection is found in the "gates of Hades" (πύλαι ᾅδου, Matt 16:18), a standard expression denoting death and/or mortal danger. Peculiar here, however, is that these "gates" seem to be on the offensive.[65] While this phrase, of course, could simply imply death,[66] it likely carries more semantic payload. First, "Hades," is the Greek equivalent of "Sheol" (שְׁאוֹל/ᾅδου, Jonah 2:2 [2:3 MT/LXX]) with which Jonah described his own tribulation.[67] While undoubtedly death is in view, this "Sheol" reference may have carried connotations of evil for Matthew, as in Jewish apocalyptic literature Sheol/Hades was both the destiny of evildoers and the realm of evil spirits.[68] In

---

63 See France, *The Gospel of Matthew*, 612.
64 Being the first time "three days" is mentioned after Jonah's "three days," this may be a subtle reference back to that text (12:40). So also R.T. France, *Jesus and the Old Testament: His Application of Old Testament Passages to Himself and His Mission* (Downers Grove, IL: InterVarsity, 1971), 54–55.
65 As Joachim Jeremias, "πύλη," *TDNT*, 6:924–928, notes "κατισχύειν when followed by a genitive is always active ('to vanquish') in Jewish Greek." For πύλαι ᾅδου, see Isa 38:10; Wis 16:13; 3 Macc 5:51; Ps. Sol. 16:2. Cf. 1 QH^a 11:17 and Ps 107 (106 LXX):18.
66 Jack P. Lewis, "'The Gates of Hell Shall Not Prevail Against It' (Matt 16:18): A Study of the History of Interpretation," *JETS* 38 (1995): 349–367, demonstrates the dominance of this view throughout history.
67 It might also be compared to the land with "bars" (בְּרִיחַ/μοχλός, Jonah 2:6 [2:7 MT/LXX]).
68 See 1En. 56:8; 99:11; 102:11; 103:7; Jub. 7:29; 22:22; 24:31. See Otto Betz, "Felsenmann Und Felsengemeinde: Eine Paralells zu Matt 16:17–19 in den Qumranpsalmen," *ZNW* 48 (1957): 70–72; Philip Johnston, *Shades of Sheol: Death and Afterlife in the Old Testament* (Leicester, England: Apollos, 2002), 81–83.

fact, the apocalyptic dimensions of this phrase, along with the expectation of a great unleashing of evil in the last days, has led some to see this as a reference to the rulers of the evil realm rushing forth from their gates to attack the people of God (cf. 1QH^a 11:16–18, 26–28; Rev 6:8; 9:1–11; 11:7).[69]

This view, in fact, finds support from the verse following referencing the "keys of the kingdom of heaven" (τὰς κλεῖδας τῆς βασιλείας τῶν οὐρανῶν, Matt 16:19), likely alluding to the "gates" of heaven; the two sets of gates serving as antitypes, with both opening to let something out.[70] Evil rulers come forth from the gates of Hades, while angelic powers come forth from the gates of heaven.[71] Interestingly, in the same 3 Maccabees text above that references Jonah, immediately after Eleazar's prayer against the persecution, God "opened the heavenly gates," and two angels descend, opposing the forces of the enemy and binding them with shackles (3 Macc 6:18–19; cf. binding and loosing, Matt 16:19). In the same context, Jews on the brink of martyrdom speak of lying at the πύλαι ᾅδου (3 Macc 5:51). Matthew (perhaps with the Maccabean martyrs in mind) may be conflating both ideas: the πύλαι ᾅδου represent both death by martyrdom and the unleashing of the evil powers behind it. As such, vv. 18–19 taken together highlight the cosmic warfare between good and evil forces, fought on the battleground of God's people, although the evil forces certainly will not have the victory. Such a portrait fits squarely within the frame of the eschatological tribulation—evil escalates against the people of God as the kingdom of God breaks in (cf. Matt 11:12).[72]

In Matthew's purview, however, it is not Israel but the community (ἐκκλησία) of Jesus that is the target of the attack.[73] Certainly, this includes Peter,

---

69 See Joel Marcus, "The Gates of Hades and the Keys of the Kingdom (Matt 16:18–19)," *CBQ* 50 (1988): 443–455, who cites K. Weiszäcker, *Untersuchungen über die evangelische Geschichte, ihre Quellen und der Gang ihrer Entwicklung* (Freiburg: Mohr, 1864), 494 n. 2; Jeremias, "πύλη," TDNT 6:927; Davies and Allison, *Matthew*, 2:639–634.

70 Marcus, "Gates of Hades," 446–448. In 3 Bar. 11:1–2 the angel Michael holds the "keys of the Kingdom of heaven" (ὁ κλειδοῦχος τῆς βασιλείας τῶν οὐρανῶν) to open its "gate" (πύλη). Cf. also 1 En. 9:2; 2 Bar. 10:18; 4 Bar. 4:4; Matt 23:13; Rev 1:18.

71 I am adapting Marcus's view; he states "the gates of heaven open to permit the extension of God's dominion from the heavenly sphere to the earthly one," but thinks the kingdom of heaven here "should be understood not as a reference to a *place* but as a term for *God's manifestation of his kingly power*" (italics his). See Marcus, "Gates of Hades," 447. I am persuaded, however, that Matthew has the heavenly *realm* in view. Likely, this power parallels that of Eleazar, being appropriated through prayer.

72 See Marcus, "Gates of Hades," 447–448; Otto Betz, *What Do We Know about Jesus?* (trans. Margaret Kohl; Philadelphia: Westminster, 1968), 52–53.

73 Based partly on temple imagery, several scholars have connected this passage to the house on the rock in the parable of the wise and foolish builders (Matt 7:24–27). See France,

the "son of Jonah" himself. However, with the corporate focus here—and if Peter serves representatively for the disciples[74]—we might allow for a wider net implying not just one "son of Jonah" but many "sons (and daughters) of Jonah" who will follow Jesus into tribulation.[75] If so, we come full circle back to the stilling of the storm, where the disciples follow Jesus figuratively into tribulation—incidentally, the same picture of discipleship we see here (16:24–26). And just as the "new Jonah" is delivered from tribulation and vindicated through resurrection, Jesus will do the same for his disciples, bringing judgment on their persecutors and giving everyone their due reward (16:27–28). Perhaps it is of some significance, then, that both the "son of Jonah" and all those "persecuted because of righteousness" are called "blessed" (μακάριος, 5:10–11; 16:11), for those who suffer through tribulation will be the ones to inherit the kingdom of heaven (5:11). Thus, with the kingdom in view, this particular Jonah passage not only points to the messianic woes, but offers hope for those suffering Jonah-like tribulation.

4   Conclusion

Through this brief exploration, we have sought to investigate whether the eschatological tribulation may be an integral part of Matthew's Jonah motif. After recognizing the centrality of tribulation in the Jewish reception of Jonah, we examined the three primary narratives in Matthew to explore whether he continues this Jonah-tribulation paradigm in his Gospel, framed of course by his own eschatological convictions. Indeed, echoes of the tribulation seemed

---

The Gospel of Matthew, 297; Gundry, *Matthew*, 134–135; Schweizer, *The Good News according to Matthew*, 191; Michael Patrick Barber, "Jesus as the Davidic Temple Builder and Peter's Priestly Role in Matthew 16:16–19," *JBL* 132 (2013): 942. As already mentioned, that parable has eschatological nuances, with the storm itself perhaps representing the tribulation (see n. 27). If Matthew intends to evoke that parable here, another Jonah- sea storm- tribulation connection might be confirmed.

74   See, classically, Georg Strecker, *Der Weg der Gerechtigkeit: Untersuchung zur Theologie des Matthäus* (FRLANT 82; Göttingen: Vandenhoeck & Ruprecht, 1971), 205.

75   Even if one wishes to assert a more prominent foundational role for Peter, in his acting as the spokesperson for the disciples (as many have affirmed), Jesus's response might be extended to them and, subsequently, all who make the same confession. On this delicate balance in Peter's portrayal, see Jack Dean Kingsbury, "The Figure of Peter in Matthew's Gospel as a Theological Problem," *JBL* 98 (1979): 67–83; Markus Bockmuehl, *Simon Peter in Scripture and Memory: The New Testament Apostle in the Early Church* (Grand Rapids: Baker Academic, 2012), 73–77.

to emerge at several points. If these soundings are accurate, we might conclude that as Jonah was a figure of tribulation for Israel, he was equally a figure of tribulation for the new community, re-infused, of course, with messianic significance. Thus, in Matthew, Jonah serves as a symbol of tribulation for the new people of God centered on a new "Jonah" figure—Jesus himself—whose journey through tribulation guides his followers through their own journey of suffering. As I offer this proposal, however, I realize we have only scratched the surface of this important motif. In addition to a more thorough treatment of these passages, one might also examine other "Jonah-esque" phrases, explore connections to Matthew's other tribulation texts, or test these insights against broader New Testament conceptions of Jonah and/or tribulation. Many questions remain. Yet, while this study has not completely lifted the fog from this important motif—or the tribulation to which it points—perhaps it has helped pave a way through the murky waters surrounding both.

The Parables of Jesus and Socrates

Adam Z. Wright

1   Introduction[1]

In 1937, Swiss scientist Fritz Zwicky began to study the gravitational forces in a far away constellation named Coma Berenices, which can be found roughly three hundred million light years away from the earth. What he found was puzzling: the movement of the galaxy clusters within the constellation were moving at a very fast rate; much too quickly for the amount of mass that Zwicky was able to calculate visually. Perhaps what puzzled Zwicky the most was how the planets, which were circulating at such a fast rate, stayed in orbit. Under the normal laws of physics, planets have the potential to become detached from their orbit and be flung off into space if they move too quickly. As it turns out, the phenomenon that Zwicky had discovered was what scientists now call "dark matter" or "dark energy." These phenomena are called "dark" because they are completely invisible, yet they account for over 90% of all gravitational force in the entire cosmos, and they explained why Zwicky was unable to see what caused the planets to move so quickly and yet remain within orbit.

But what does a discussion about the discovery of dark matter and energy have to do with Greek philosophy and the New Testament? The answer is this: even though Greek philosophy may not always be easily detected in the New Testament, we can be sure that certain philosophical schools were integral to how the ancients understood both themselves and their respective contexts, including both Christian and Jewish contexts. By extension, this essay will argue that in order for New Testament writers to have successfully dialogued with certain groups, allusions to philosophy were unavoidable. Not only this, but already established philosophical questions may have been rather influential for helping the earliest Christians shape statements about their beliefs. This will be illustrated by how the Parable of the Sower, found in each of the Synoptic Gospels, addresses certain questions concerning belief and disbelief, knowledge and ignorance. It will be argued that the ways in which Jesus talks about belief, for example, echo the ways that Socrates talks about it in the Parable of the Cave. This does not mean that the Synoptic Gospels directly imitated

---

[1] The following information comes from Neil DeGrasse Tyson and Donald Goldsmith, *Origins: Fourteen Billion Years of Cosmic Evolution* (New York: Norton, 2014), 64–67.

Plato's *Republic*, but it means that Jesus and Socrates (the Synoptics and Plato) are in dialogue with one another because they are addressing the same topic.

With regard to philosophy, I would like to make some clarifying comments concerning what it is and how the term will be used in this essay. Philosophy is an appropriate term for describing the ways in which we discuss the answers to certain questions. But philosophy is not theology, nor is it science. According to Bertrand Russell, theology consists of speculations on matters that are unascertainable with regard to definite knowledge. Science, on the other hand, appeals to human reason rather than to authority. Said another way, "all *definite* knowledge belongs to science; all *dogma* as to what surpasses definite knowledge belongs to theology."[2] The reason, therefore, why the teachings of Jesus in the Parable of the Sower occupy the place of philosophy is because of their practical applicability. In other words, the teachings of Jesus are applicable to general human life, and are concerned with philosophical categories like ethics and metaphysics. Not only this, but the teachings of Jesus apply themselves directly to existential queries, namely how humanity understands itself in the here and now with regard to the Kingdom of God.

More specifically, thinking about the Parable of the Sower in philosophical terms is helpful. As will be seen below, the most prominent features of the parable are concerned with knowledge and ignorance. Jesus's comments on this subject are an attempt to qualify the true nature of knowledge and the avenues by which one comes to a position of knowledge. This kind of dialectic was common in the ancient world, and first century readers of the parable would have made a number of connections with other dialectics concerning the same topic. Again, this is not to say that the Synoptic tradition was directly emulating Plato, for example, but it means that, by establishing the same topic, the Synoptic tradition is in communication with other dialectics concerned with the same topic.

The question then becomes: how can we be certain that two texts are in communication with each other, and are these two texts discussing the same philosophical topic? The purpose of this essay is to argue that, in the Parable of the Sower, the Synoptic writers are in communication with Platonic notions of knowledge and ignorance. This communication is not always obvious, which means that philosophy may occupy a role similar to that of dark matter: its effects may be detected even when the cause of those effects are not readily seen.

---

2   Bertrand Russell, *History of Western Philosophy and its Connection with Political and Social Circumstances from the Earliest Times to the Present Day* (London: Allen and Unwin, 1979), 13.

2   Method

For a long time, New Testament scholars have suggested several different methods by which one can either prove or disprove communication between two texts.[3] Some of these methods draw correlations on the word-level, which means that two texts are in communication because they share one or two words in common. Others go further and draw correlations at the sentence or paragraph level, which would mean that longer strings of shared vocabulary items and grammatical syntax indicate communication. Still others have avoided these kinds of correlations and suggest allusion (conscious or unconscious) and paraphrase, which would mean that two texts can be in communication without any shared vocabulary items at the word, sentence, or paragraph levels; this kind of communication is much more difficult to prove since one needs to develop a fairly robust set of criteria in order to do so.

The method adopted in this essay states that we should first begin our examination of textual communication with the topical level of discourse, and doing so has two advantages.[4] The first is that this method can accommodate two texts that share a topic yet employ different vocabulary, syntax, and lines of reasoning. The second reason is that shared topics accommodate

---

[3] I have made note of many such studies in Adam Z. Wright, "Detecting Allusions in the Pauline Corpus: A Method," in *Paul and Gnosis* (ed. Stanley E. Porter and David I. Yoon; PAST 9; Leiden, Brill, 2015), 59–79. See also Hughson T. Ong, "Is 'Spiritual Gift(s)' a Linguistically Fallacious Term? A Lexical Study of Χάρισμα, Πνευματικός, and Πνεῦμα," *ExpTim* 125 (2014): 583–592; Hughson T. Ong, "Reconsidering the Meaning and Translation of Πνευματικός and Πνεῦμα in the Discourse Context of 1 Corinthians 12–14," in *Modeling Biblical Language: Selected Papers from the McMaster Divinity College Linguistics Circle* (ed. Stanley E. Porter, Gregory P. Fewster, and Christopher D. Land; LBS 13; Leiden: Brill, 2016), 309–338.

[4] Two presumptions should be stated at the outset of this study. The first is that ancient peoples asked a number of questions about: creation; the nature of humanity; the problem of wrong-doing and ethics; death and the afterlife. As we might expect, the ancients strove to answer these questions but did so in very different ways. This is why a topical-level examination works: because two different groups say very different things about the afterlife, for example, it does *not* mean that they are not asking the same question, namely, "is there an afterlife and how do we think about it?" The second presumption asserts that the ancients communicated with one another in both positive and negative ways. While this may appear rather puerile, many of the objections to a connection between the New Testament and Greek philosophical texts is that the New Testament writers might not have had any exposure to such texts. I find this to be an incredible assertion since, based on my reading of both the New Testament and early Church history, the earliest Christians dealt with a number of issues pertaining to Jewish/Gentile interactions.

all kinds of allusion (both conscious and unconscious)[5] and paraphrase which could either seek to sustain meaning or subvert it.[6]

The question then becomes, "how do we know exactly what the topic of a given text is?" I have argued elsewhere that a topic can be discerned based on the most prominent features of a text.[7] This can be decided by determining the ways in which an author uses verbal aspect to render frontground material. For example, an author could create the background of a discourse using the perfective aspect and make an item prominent by then employing the imperfective or stative aspects. Thus, one will read a string of aorist tense-form verbs, which make up the background, and then read a present (or perfect) tense-form verb—which verbs are more prominent.

Thus, we allow the linguistic features of a text to determine the topic. From there, we are able to take note of the similarities and differences (*emulatio* or *aemulatio*) between the text in question and another text that shares the same topic. In what follows, I will examine the Parable of the Sower using this method.

---

5 Allusion is the most difficult of all categories to detect. The reason I say this is because of the many different ways that allusion can manifest itself. Sometimes, allusion is an unconscious act thereby placing more emphasis on the reader's interpretive act rather than on the writer's creative act. Alternatively, allusion can be a part of the writer's creative act but not the reader's interpretive act. This leads one to place more emphasis on the text than on the writer's creative act or the reader's interpretive act. This has, by and large, come to be known as the "hermeneutical triangle": the consistent relationship between writer, reader, and text.

6 In the ancient world, a writer could emulate a text's meaning or subvert it, a process known as either *emulatio* or *aemulatio*, respectively. Such acts on the part of the writer were meant either to confirm or subvert a reader's expectation. In many cases, an author would signal an allusion, or a set of forth-coming allusions, by using an "Alexandrian footnote" such as "it has been said" or "you have read before that ..." Such a "footnote" orients the reader's expectations which would then be subverted if the act of *aemulatio* was employed.

7 Prominence is perhaps one of the most important components of any linguistic analysis. As Robert Longacre quips, "Discourse without prominence would be like pointing to a piece of black chalkboard and insisting that it was a picture of black camels crossing black sands at midnight." This point is well-taken. One of the major ways that Greek writers indicate prominence is through the use of verbal tense choices. This is illustrated by what Stanley Porter calls "planes of discourse": background, foreground, and frontground verb tenses. In what follows, we will be assessing which tenses are being used by various authors and using this information to determine a topic based on the prominence of the verbal tenses. See Wright, "Pauline Allusion"; R.E. Longacre, "Discourse Peak as Zone of Turbulence," in *Beyond the Sentence: Discourse and Sentential Form* (ed. J.R. Wirth; Ann Arbor, MI: Karoma, 1985), 83; Stanley E. Porter, *Idioms of the Greek New Testament* (Biblical Languages: Greek 2; 2nd ed.; Sheffield: Sheffield Academic, 1994), 302–305.

3 Famous Teachers: Jesus and Socrates[8]

Jesus and Socrates provide, for many reasons, an excellent point of comparison between the Judaeo-Christian tradition and the Greek philosophical tradition. But before I make any serious inquiries into a particular text, I would like to begin this essay with some preliminary observations about why a comparison of Socrates and Jesus is appropriate for the current study.

The first observation concerns the challenges that both Jesus and Socrates present to the historian. This is due, in large part, to the fact that neither Jesus nor Socrates themselves wrote anything down. As a result, historians must rely on the writings of their followers. The life and ministry of Jesus are recorded in the four canonical Gospels which were, presumably, each written by certain eyewitnesses to the events of Jesus's ministry.[9] The Synoptic Gospels present, overall, a similar portrait of Jesus's ministry, whereas John's Gospel departs from the others with regard to the chronology of certain events. Similar issues are presented to the Socratic historian who must rely on the works of Plato, Xenophon, and Aristophanes for an account of Socrates' life and work, all of whom present Socrates in different and, at times, contradictory ways.[10]

And so, historically speaking, we have two extraordinary teachers about whose lives—most certainly their early lives—we have very little information with the exception of a few biographical points. For example, we do know that Jesus was born in Bethlehem as a lower-class peasant and his birth was accompanied by a number of supernatural occurrences. We know nothing else about his childhood, however, except that which is described in a very short pericope that recounts the actions of Jesus at the age of twelve (Luke 2:41–52). Information about the adulthood of Jesus is restricted to certain events surrounding his ministry, but we have little biographical information except those things which can be derived from the events of the ministry itself. We also know that Jesus did not acquire employment during his adult years and, instead, devoted all of his time to his ministry thereby relying on others to fund his ministry (Luke 8:3). Though the exact date is debated, Jesus was killed in his early thirties because of the things said and done during his ministry, after which he was resurrected from the dead and appeared to his followers.

---

8   I would like to thank Luke S. Gordon for his help in developing this section.
9   For the purpose of this essay, I am taking the position that the canonical Gospels represent the earliest witness to the life and ministry of Jesus. As a result, I will not be taking into account other accounts of Jesus's life, such as pseudepigraphical writings and gospels.
10 Russell, *History*, 101.

The early life of Socrates, much like that of Jesus, is largely unknown. We do know, however, that Socrates was born in 469 BCE in Athens to a moderate social status. His father was an Athenian sculptor named Sophroniscus and his mother was named Phaenarete, though we have no other information pertaining to his birth or activities as a child. He did not acquire employment, but spent his time engaged in discussion about philosophy, a task he understood as a divine calling and to be of the utmost importance. This philosophical work roused the authorities to a point where they placed arrested Socrates, placed him on trial, and ordered his execution. He died in 399 BCE at the age of 70.[11]

The second observation that I would like to make concerns the social, economic, and religious impact Jesus and Socrates had on their respective contexts. Jesus, much like Socrates, subverted the social, economic, and religious standard of his time, and such subversion resulted in certain accusations that led to his death. Religiously speaking, Jesus, as the son of God, challenged—if not completely changed—the way people thought about Judaism in the first century; this much can be attested by the nature of Paul's letters, particularly the letter to the Galatians.[12] The main reason why Jesus was eventually killed was because he claimed to be God's son, a statement that resulted in the charge of blasphemy (Mark 14:62–64). Socrates never claimed to be divine in any way, but the main accusations against him stated that he was guilty of introducing new divinities and teaching the youth of Athens accordingly. Thus, from the perspective of both sets of accusers, Jesus and Socrates were guilty for introducing new and blasphemous ways of thinking about and understanding God.

These accusations, from the perspective of those who think of Jesus and Socrates as being innocent, are unfounded because of the reasons why Jesus and Socrates began their work. Theologically speaking, both men thought of their work as having been inspired by God.[13] In the Synoptic Gospels, Jesus's

---

11 Russell, *History*, 101.

12 The problem I am referring to here is the problem of whether Gentile believers should adopt Jewish customs such as circumcision or other aspects of the Law. Paul addresses the issue of "a different gospel" in Galatians, a problem that could point towards two separate councils that discussed this very issue (Acts 11, 15).

13 A large part of the accusation against Socrates for introducing new gods is the result of his testimony that a "daemon" guided much of what he said and did. This daemon was the divine source from which Socrates received his instruction, and it placed him into a direct relationship with the divine—something to which no one else had access. Socrates states that, "I shall not speak as my word whatever I shall say, but shall refer you to a trustworthy speaker ... the god at Delphi" (*Apol.* 20e). See W.K.C. Guthrie, *Socrates* (Cambridge: Cambridge University Press, 1971), 84.

baptism features a validation from God shortly before he begins his public ministry (Matt 3:17; Mark 1:11; Luke 3:22). Like Jesus, Socrates began his work after hearing from a divine source: the Oracle at Delphi—a mouthpiece of the "god of Delphi"[14]—who proclaimed that there is no person wiser than Socrates.[15] The main goal of Socrates's work was then to prove the god wrong, a process that led to the conclusion that the wisest people are those who think themselves unwise. The conclusion at which Socrates eventually arrives is that only God is wise and that humanity's wisdom is worth little in comparison. He thus sees his work as a means of validating God's words because, according to Socrates, "God cannot lie, for that (lying) is impossible for him."[16]

Economically speaking, we can note a number of similarities between what Jesus and Socrates thought about money and the power that comes from having a lot of money. Jesus often spoke negatively about money: "You cannot serve God and money" (Matt 6:24) or "Truly I say to you, a rich person shall never enter the kingdom of heaven" (Matt 16:26). Likewise, Socrates spoke negatively about money: "To honour wealth and at the same time adequately to possess soundness of mind among one's fellow-citizens is impossible" (*Rep.* 555c) and "for one who is exceptionally good to be also exceedingly rich is impossible" (*Laws* 743a). Jesus even spoke out against the attainment of great power: "For what does a person profit if he gains the whole world and yet loses his soul?" (Matt 16:26). Likewise, Socrates speaks out against great power: "And yet in exchange for your soul you would not be willing for the absolute power over all Greeks and barbarians to come to you" (*Alc.* 2.141c). Each of these examples illustrates the way in which Jesus and Socrates thought about the marginalized as well. For example, a number of Jesus's parables describe the ways in which certain marginalized people should be thought of as equal (Luke 10:25–37).

---

14   *Apol.* 20e.
15   Gutherie notes the apparent contradiction of Socrates's reaction: "to set out to prove the god a liar would be a strange way of obeying him." This is probably because Socrates understood the oracle to be a riddle. In the *Apology*, Socrates points out the strange nature of the oracle: "What can the god mean? What is his riddle? I know very well that I am not the least bit wise. What does he mean by saying that I am the wisest? He can't be lying: that would not be right for him" (*Apol.* 21b). Treating the oracles as riddles was common practice, so it makes sense that Socrates set out to refute the obvious meaning of the riddle, that he was unwise, only to prove that he was the wisest. Gutherie, *Socrates*, 87.
16   *Apol.* 21b. According to Russell, the *Apology* is largely religious in tone. This is largely due to the ways in which Socrates justifies his work, and seeks to invalidate the claim that he is "introducing new gods" by pointing out that his work actually began as a result of divine inspiration. See Russell, *History*, 105.

The third observation concerns the ironic nature of their work. Irony works, or appears, only when the reader understands the greatness of a character or situation when those in the narrative do not. It is clear that, in both narratives, neither Jesus nor Socrates were recognized properly or understood correctly. To explain what I mean, I will draw attention to three ironic aspects of their work: the irony of their humility; how Jesus and Socrates ironically realized truth; how the missions of both Jesus and Socrates were truly validated after their deaths.

The first ironic aspect concerns the ways that both Socrates and Jesus advocated humility despite their apparent greatness. This is certainly true of Jesus who, as the expected Messiah, promoted his death as vindication rather than kingship; presumably why Peter took such exception to such promotion (Mark 8:31–32). This message is further illustrated by the ways which Jesus presents success, namely that the greatest will become the least and the least will become the greatest (Matt 19:30; 20:26; 23:11). Socrates also admonished humility in a number of ways. In addition to proving that he was not the wisest, Socrates taught that the greatest teachers were those who served, "one who has not served could never become a praiseworthy master, and one should pride himself on having served well rather than on having ruled well" (*Laws* 762e). Such humility can also be tied into issues of social justice. It was mentioned above that Jesus sought to close the gap between the privileged and the disenfranchised, such as when he tells the rich young ruler to sell all that he owns and give it to the poor (Mark 10:21). Socrates also said a lot about issues of social justice, even going so far as to say that one should *never* perform an injustice on another (*Crito*, 49b). Jesus, in turn, taught that one should always resist the evil a person may do, going so far as to retaliate to such evil with kindness (Matt 5:38–42).[17]

The second ironic aspect concerns the fact that neither Jesus nor Socrates was truly monumental until after their deaths.[18] This may be due to the fact that death was the only means by which their respective messages could be

---

17   Further comparisons between Jesus and Socrates on the issue of retaliation can be found in W.K.C. Guthrie, *History of Greek Philosophy* (6 vols.; Cambridge: Cambridge University Press, 1971), 3:113; David Gill, "Socrates and Jesus on Non-Retaliation and Love of Enemies," *Horizons* 18 (1991): 246–262.

18   This may reflect the concept of a "death tradition" which has been mentioned in a number of places: see Herbert A. Musurillo, *The Acts of the Pagan Martyrs: Acta Alexandrinorum* (Oxford: Oxford University Press, 1954; repr. New York: Arno, 1979), 236–246; David Seeley, *The Noble Death: Graeco-Roman Martyrology and Paul's Concept of Salvation* (JSNTSup 28; Sheffield: JSOT Press, 1990) 83–141; Gregory E. Sterling, "Mors Philosophi: The Death of Jesus in Luke," *HTR* 94 (2001): 383–402.

accepted. If their messages were accepted before their deaths, then their entire message would be invalidated because the effects of it being accepted would diminish their humility. Said another way, if Jesus was made king of Israel, his entire message would then become invalid. This is precisely what makes their deaths so ironic and why no one ever truly accepts Jesus's message within the Gospel narrative.[19] What is more, those closest to Jesus eventually abandon him. One may be tempted to view this as a rather anticlimactic element within the narrative, but it is a necessary element that points towards his death and resurrection as the ultimate vindication. So much can be said for Socrates as well, who accepted death as a vindication for a life well-lived. This kind of life, for Socrates, was vindicated by a kind of resurrection. Though expressed differently, Socrates states that death is a simple transition from this world into the next.[20] The reason why this is important is because, in order for others to recognize that their respective messages were valid, their death and resurrection was necessary.

The third ironic aspect regards the ways that Jesus and Socrates attained, and taught about, moral consciousness. Jesus, much like Socrates, engaged in conversation and discussion with a large number of people and both became important public figures in their respective contexts. Their efforts, however, were largely unaccepted, at least at first. Socrates's mission was infused with the irony that, no matter how hard he tried to refute the god's oracle that he was wisest, he would only be proven wise. Kierkegaard understood this aspect of the Socratic mission to be pregnant with significance. Kierkegaard explains the irony here by suggesting that Socrates's efforts were primarily negative in nature. His continual search for his own ignorance, however, allowed him to disassociate from all conventional sources of wisdom and illustrate how, once a person rises above all preconceived conventions of thought, he or she truly begins to live. This necessitates that social conventions make for artificial realities, and it is only when a person transcends them that he becomes aware of how small he is when compared to the vastness of, in Platonic terms, the Ideal.[21] This means that, in order for Socrates to become great, he had to become least.

---

19 I have argued this point elsewhere, and it is important to note that the irony of the Gospels is illustrated by the way that those who "should" recognize Jesus as the Son of God and Messiah do not, while those who "should not" recognize Jesus, in fact, do. For the full argument, see Adam Z. Wright, "Recognizing Jesus: A Study of Recognition Scenes in the Gospel of Mark," *JGRChJ* 10 (2014): 174–193.

20 Russell, *History*, 110.

21 James Beckman, *The Religious Dimension of Socrates' Thought* (Waterloo, ON: Wilfrid Laurier University Press, 1979), 128. See also Kierkegaard, *The Concept of Irony*.

In some senses, Socrates had risen above all determinations of life and therefore constitutes a world historical turning-point: to see God truly, one must release themselves from what they see and look beyond it to what is unseen. Said another way by Beckman, "Socratic irony represented a necessary first, negative phase in an authentic human existence, and was only a preparation for the leap of faith, the ultimate, consummate, phase in an authentic human existence."[22]

Hegel provides another perspective on the irony of Socrates's mission. He thought that Socrates "attained intellectual insight into the abstract, universal principles of moral conduct through individual reflection on his own consciousness."[23] Beckman comments on this by saying, "Socrates represents the dawn of moral consciousness insofar as there emerges with him the consciousness of self as an independent critical subject over against the social organism."[24] Said another way, Hegel understands Socrates as one who steps away from the constraints of social moral consciousness and appeals to an individual standard beyond that of the *polis*. Socrates therefore represents critical moral reasoning that challenged the old, unreflective, and non-rational synthesis.[25]

The theories of both Kierkegaard and Hegel are applicable to Jesus as well, whose ministry, as mentioned above, is quite ironic. Jesus extends our understanding of morality beyond mere convention. Jesus asserts that morality is much more than simply following the rules of the Law. Countless times throughout the Gospel tradition, Jesus challenges his listeners to think of morality in terms of the most inner part of a person's psyche:

> Listen to me, everyone and understand this: Nothing outside of a person can defile them by going into them. Rather, it is what comes out of a person that defiles them ... what comes out of a person is what defiles them. For it is from within, out of a person's heart, that evil thoughts come—sexual immorality, theft, murder, adultery, greed, malice, deceit, lewdness, envy, slander, arrogance and folly.
>
> Mark 7:14–15, 20–22

By doing so, Jesus challenges a number of religious and social normalities and goes beyond them. This is important, because what Jesus is essentially doing

---

22   Beckman, *Religious Dimension*, 129.
23   Beckman, *Religious Dimension*, 129.
24   Beckman, *Religious Dimension*, 129.
25   Beckman, *Religious Dimension*, 129.

here is similar to that of Socrates: Jesus expects a person to examine themselves and understand their sin, not to be told what their sin is from an outside source. With regard to what was said concerning Kierkegaard above, Jesus should be then understood as one who transcends social, moral convention in order to understand that morality is not collective but is necessarily individualistic. This is illustrated in a number of instances throughout the Synoptic tradition, especially with regard to neglecting certain tenets of the Law in favour of healing marginalized people (Mark 5:25–34).[26] Hegel's view of Socrates is less helpful here, since we have limited access to Jesus's inner dialogue. But, Hegel might read Mark 5:25–34 and suggest Jesus goes beyond the social moral consciousness to appeal to a standard beyond it.

The ironic nature of Jesus and Socrates can be summed up, then, in the following ways. First, both Jesus and Socrates embody a level of humility that seems counterintuitive to their greatness. As mentioned, this produces a level of irony because the audience of the narrative understand and recognize their greatness while those within the narrative do not. This leads us to consider how neither Jesus nor Socrates, nor their messages, was truly recognized or accepted until after their deaths. This is an important point because death was the only means by which their messages could be truly validated. This leads to the fact that Jesus and Socrates were killed for attaining a sense of moral consciousness that threatened a social consciousness contemporary to them.

In what follows, two parables will be examined in relation to one another: Jesus's Parable of the Sower and Plato's Parable of the Cave. Each of these parables discuss the ways that people either know or do not know, recognize or do not recognize, truth. This examination will pay special attention to particular issues of linguistic prominence which will, in turn, provide some evidence for whether or not the New Testament is in communication with this aspect of Greek philosophy. To reiterate the method stated above, any similarities that may be found do not suggest that Mark, for example, was aiming to imitate Plato. Instead, communication between texts may reveal an author's attempt to emulate or subvert another text's meaning. This can only happen, however, if both texts are, in some way, addressing the same topic which is in

---

26   I have in mind here what is said concerning bleeding in Lev 15:19–30. Since this woman pushes through a crowd to reach Jesus, she would have caused a number of people that she came in contact with to be ceremonially unclean. What is more, her touching of Jesus's cloak would have caused Jesus to become unclean. Jesus finds her touch particularly prominent compared to the others who were pushing against him which is a point I will refrain from commenting on here (v. 30). The point, however, is that Jesus transcends purity regulations in favour of healing the woman.

this case is knowledge and ignorance. This process may generate two very different answers to the same question: what is the truth and how do we know it?

4 The Parable of the Cave

Plato becomes the mouth piece for Socrates with regard to this section. Much of what we can know about Platonic metaphysics, and his philosophy in general, can be derived from the Parable of the Cave. This parable draws a distinction between reality and appearance, and this distinction is undoubtedly religious at its core.[27]

A true philosopher, according to Socrates, is not someone who simply loves knowledge; vulgar curiosity does not make a philosopher.[28] A philosopher is concerned with reality, and it is when a person ascertains reality that they become truly wise. Reality is therefore separated from appearance. Said another way, the things we see around us in the world are only an appearance, or representation, of the reality that exists in a super-sensible eternal world.[29]

This led to Plato's theory of "ideas" or "forms." This theory is, according to Russell, partly logical and partly metaphysical. It is logical in the sense that it deals primarily with general words. He uses the example of a cat: there are many individual animals which we can refer to as a "cat." But we could be referring to something entirely different with each use of the word "cat" because not all cats are the same. An animal is a "cat" because it participates in some general nature that is common to all cats. We cannot dispense the use of a more general word like "cat" but we must understand that it refers to something kind of universal *catness*. This catness is not born when a cat is born nor does it disappear when a cat dies; it has no position in either time or space and is therefore eternal.

Metaphysically speaking, catness must be embodied by a certain ideal cat, which is created by God and is completely unique. Using another example, there may be many beds, but there is only one ideal or *form* of a bed, and just as a reflection of a bed in a mirror is not the real bed, so are various particular beds merely copies of the ideal bed. The philosopher, or wise person, will be concerned only with the ideal bed and not the particular beds

---

27   Russell, *History*, 135.
28   Russell, *History*, 136.
29   Russell, *History*, 136.

found in the world around us. This, of course, creates a distinction between those who pay attention to the ideals and those who pay attention to only the particulars, and Socrates explains this distinction using the Parable of the Cave.

The parable can be paraphrased in the following way.[30] Those who pay attention to the particulars are like prisoners in a cave who are able to look in only one direction because they are bound. Behind them is a fire that casts shadows on the wall in front of them, both shadows of themselves and of any other objects that lie behind them. They regard the shadows of those objects as real, and have no notion of the objects from which they originate. At some point, one person frees himself and escapes from the cave and sees, for the first time, the light from the sun. In addition, he sees real things and becomes aware that he has been deceived by the shadows in the cave. If he is a responsible philosopher, he sees it as his duty to educate those who are still prisoners in the cave; he will tell them the truth about reality and lead them towards freedom. However, he will have difficulty persuading them to leave the cave since, entering the cave again, he is unable to see the shadows as clearly as he did due to the fact that he has been outside in the sun—to those remaining in the cave he will appear stupider than before his escape.

At first glance, this parable is probably referring to the life of Socrates and the results of his efforts to enlighten those around him, an effort that resulted in his being imprisoned and sentenced to death. This parable could also be interpreted, according to Russell, to mean that a Good person must come and live amongst those who have never seen the truth. "It would seem," he says, "that God Himself, if He wishes to amend His creation, must do likewise; a Christian Platonist might so interpret in Incarnation."[31] A third option can also be

---

30 Plato's parable can be found in *Rep.* 514a–521d.
31 Russell, *History*, 144–145. Russell finds a problem with this interpretation, however, and suggests that "it remains completely impossible to explain why God was not content with the world of Ideas. The philosopher finds the cave in existence, and is actuated by benevolence in returning to it; but the Creator, if He created everything, might, one would think, have avoided the cave altogether." His point is well-taken because the Platonic view of God is one that can only conceive ideal things. However, he assumes that worlds, as he uses the word, are things which cannot change. This would mean, according to Russell, that the Ideal world always remains ideal, and the world of impressions necessarily remains a degree removed from Ideal. This departs from a Judaeo-Christian worldview which states that God originally created the world as "good," a word that could be construed as ideal. Though Christianity and Platonism do not converge in every respect here, it does suggest that Platonists and Christians are asking a similar question with regard to nature of reality and knowledge about other realities.

suggested, though not necessarily distinct from the first two. Those who are unenlightened are given a chance to become enlightened by someone who truly knows. The parable is then a commentary on the reasons why some people are enlightened while others remain unenlightened. It is also a commentary on what happens to those who attempt to elucidate the truth: they are ultimately rejected or thought of as stupid. In the case of Socrates—and by extension, Jesus—the one who delivers the truth is killed. Given this interpretation, the Cave parable has much in common with the Sower parable which will be discussed below.

5 Jesus and the Kingdom of God: Knowing and Not Knowing

The Parable of the Sower, from this point referred to as simply "Sower," is found in each of the Synoptic Gospels (Matt 13:1–23; Mark 4:1–20; Luke 8:1–15). In this parable, Jesus is interested in describing a process of attaining knowledge, a process expressed in the phrase γνῶναι τὰ μυστήρια τῆς βασιλείας τοῦ θεοῦ ("to know the mysteries of the kingdom of God"), a phrase which can be found in all of the Synoptic accounts of the parable: Matthew 13:11, Mark 4:11, and Luke 8:10. Each explanation of the Kingdom includes a quotation from Isaiah 6, which indicates that not everyone will understand Jesus's explanation because he speaks in parables. A discussion of William Wrede's "Messianic Secret" notwithstanding, one is left to speculate as to why Jesus chooses to disclose information about the Kingdom in a manner that not everyone would understand. It is certainly possible that each evangelist's inclusion of the Isaiah quotation is meant to explain *why* not everyone understood Jesus. In other words, Isaiah provides a context according to which the evangelists can explain why the crowds, when presented with certain knowledge, choose to ignore it. A similar concept can be found in the allegory of the cave described above: why, when presented with the truth, do some people continue to live in ignorance? In what follows, an analysis of the Sower will be conducted with respect to linguistic prominence. It is possible that the Parables of the Sower and Cave are in communication even though their explanations of the source of reality and truth are quite different.

Matthew's discourse begins with the boundary ἐν τῇ ἡμέρᾳ ἐκείνῃ (13:1) which establishes the context in which Jesus told the parable. The background of the discourse is established with a string of perfective verbs until 13:3, in which Jesus begins to use the imperfective (λέγων) thereby establishing the foreground. Jesus then switches back to the perfective to describe the details of the parable with the exception of an imperfect verb (ἐδίδου) in 13:8. This continues until 13:9 in which Jesus reverts to the imperfective aspect (ὁ ἔχων ὦτα ἀκουέτω). Jesus reverts back to a perfective aspect in 13:10 which could be considered a discourse boundary (προσελθόντες), at which point Jesus begins to explain what he means by the parable. He switches back and forth between perfective and imperfective aspects with the exception of a couple of stative aspects (δέδοται, δέδοται) in 13:11.

Mark's version of the Sower begins similar to Matthew's with a boundary marker (καὶ πάλιν ἤρξατο διδάσκειν παρὰ τὴν θάλασσαν) in 4:1, yet he chooses a catenative construction (ἤρξατο διδάσκειν) as opposed to Mathew's aspectually vague verb ἐκάθητο.[32] Unlike Matthew's Jesus, Mark's Jesus establishes the foreground with an imperfective verb in 4:1, and then reverts to the perfective in 4:2. Verse 3 begins with an imperfective aspect, most likely indicating prominence, followed by a string of perfective verbs that continue until 4:9 at which point Jesus reverts to the use of more imperfective aspects. Verse 11 features a stative verb (δέδοται) which echoes Matthew's method of rendering prominence. The explanation of the parable continues with Jesus switching between perfective and imperfective verbs until 4:13 at which point Jesus uses another stative verb (οἴδατε). Jesus then continues his explanation by switching between background and foreground verbs until 4:20.

Luke begins his version of the sower without a boundary marker which indicates that parable be read in light of 8:1–3. Luke establishes the background with several perfective verbs throughout vv. 4–8 intermingling imperfective verbs throughout. The explanation of the parable contains a stative verb (δέδονται) in 8:10, thereby establishing prominence, from which point Jesus continues with either perfective or imperfective verbs.

Each account of the sower contains the stative verb δέδονται (Matt 13:11; Mark 4:11; Luke 8:10) which indicates the most prominent, or salient, feature of the discourse. What is more, this verb is connected with knowledge, rendered by the verb γνῶναι, in each of the accounts. Because the meaning of the stative verb used here is cognate to "give," we may rightly conclude that the evangelists want to emphasize Jesus's ability to give knowledge or, more aptly, correct knowledge. This may allude to the Parable of the Cave in the sense that Jesus could represent the person who has left the cave and returns for the purpose of revealing the truth. This position of knowledge is contrasted with those who are ignorant by the evocation of the Isaiah quote which emphasizes a certain group's inability to correctly understand the knowledge given

---

32   Stanley E. Porter, *Linguistic Analysis of the Greek New Testament: Studies in Tools, Methods, and Practice* (Grand Rapids: Baker Academic, 2015), 271.

to them. This contrast is mostly clearly illustrated in Mark's Gospel because of his use of a stative verb (οἴδατε) in 4:13.

We can conclude that the content of the Sower parable is meant to address the giving of true knowledge by someone who truly understands. We can also conclude that there are two groups of people: those who understand and accept the knowledge that Jesus provides and those who do not. We cannot be sure, outside of the reasons given in the parable itself, why certain people must remain in ignorance. We can be sure, however, that Jesus wants to make a clear distinction between those who understand and those who do not.

At this point, the connection, or communication, between the parables is obvious: both are concerned with knowledge and ignorance of truth. The Parable of the Cave details a person's vision of truth by conveying it in terms of understanding the reality of things—when a person leave the cave, they see things for how they really are. Jesus is described in a similar way as the person who teaches about the truth (the Kingdom). The Sower also describes the kind of person who hears the word and produces a large crop; a phrase which is meant to be understood metaphorically as someone who understands the truth and lives successfully because of it. These kinds of people are juxtaposed with others who, for some reason, are unable to understand the truth and, therefore, live unsuccessfully.

6 Conclusions

The Parables of the Cave and Sower are in communication with one another with regard to their topic: knowing and not knowing. If we accept that both parables are addressing the same topic, we can more readily accept differences in their presentation without disregarding the communication that exists between them. The Parable of the Cave asserts Socrates as the knowledgeable person who returns to the metaphorical cave to enlighten those who still live inside. Likewise, the Parable of the Sower asserts that Jesus teaches about the kingdom of God as one who is most knowledgeable of it. Both parables describe the ignorance of those who do not accept the message of truth from the one who speaks it, and both describe the negativity aimed towards those teachers of truth.

Though there are a number of similarities between the parables which may suggest *emulatio*, a number of differences suggest that the Parable of the Sower addresses the question of knowledge and ignorance in different ways and with different language. It is unlikely that the Parable of the Sower seeks to subvert the meaning of the Parable of the Cave through the process of *aemulatio* since both parables achieve, more or less, the same message concerning knowledge and ignorance. It is most plausible, then, to suggest that both parables are concerned with addressing the reasons why certain people reject such extraordinary teachers.

PART 4

The Jewish Mission and Its Literature

∴

Why Have We Stopped Reading the Catholic Epistles Together? Tracing the Early Reception of a Collection

Darian Lockett

In the historical development of the New Testament canon, the four Gospels and the Pauline letters were received and recognized as distinct collections early in the process. Jens Schröter notes the "two most important collections, which stand at the beginning of the emergence of the New Testament" are "the four Gospels and the Letters of Paul" while "Acts and the Catholic Letters, which are closely connected with Acts in terms of the history of the canon," came shortly after.[1] In this regard, Adolf Harnack's view of the crucial role of Acts in the development of the New Testament canon is still relevant. Harnack argued,

> Acts is in a certain way the key to understanding the idea of the New Testament of the Church, and has given it the organic structure in which it stands before us. By taking its place at the head of the "Apostolus" the Acts first made possible the division of the Canon into two parts and justified the combination of the Pauline Epistles with the Gospels. It is also possible to speak of a threefold division, in which the Acts (together with the Catholic Epistles and Revelation) formed the central portion.[2]

Schröter then summarizes Harnack's position: "Acts is therefore the writing that combines the various parts of the New Testament canon—Gospels, Letters of Paul, Catholic Letters—with one another and brings to expression the intention that becomes recognizable behind that compilation."[3] In the end, Harnack understood the historical meaning of Acts (its content) as quite different from its canonical function within the New Testament. In many of the early codices it is the combination of Acts and the Catholic Epistles—the *Praxapostolos*—which forms a canonical link between the four-fold Gospels on one side and the

---

[1] Jens Schröter, *From Jesus to the New Testament: Early Christian Theology and the Origin of the New Testament Canon* (Baylor–Mohr Siebeck Studies in Early Christianity 1; Waco, TX: Baylor University Press, 2013), 273.

[2] Adolf Harnack, *The Origin of the New Testament: And the Most Important Consequences of the New Creation* (trans. J.R. Wilkinson; London: Williams and Norgate, 1925; repr. Eugene, OR: Wipf and Stock, 2004), 67.

[3] Schröter, *From Jesus to the New Testament*, 274.

Pauline Letter collection (including Hebrews) on the other. Understanding the development of the New Testament canon and its reception from this perspective draws attention to several issues that are not usually in view when considering the reception history of James, Peter, John, and Jude. Whereas the journey of each of these texts into the New Testament are commonly viewed as unrelated stories, knowing the Catholic Epistles functioned as a collection within the eventual New Testament canon suggests one should consider them together. This picture of canonical development suggests that by the end of the canonical process the Catholic Epistle collection functioned in tandem with the Book of Acts, and thus it is as the *Praxapostolos* that the Catholic Epistles find their role within the New Testament canon as a discrete collection. But this already assumes a particular understanding of "Catholic" in the label "Catholic Epistles."

Should the seven letters of James, 1–2 Peter, 1–3 John, and Jude be called "General Letters" or "Catholic Epistles"? There is some ambiguity as to whether these two terms are merely interchangeable or if there is a principled difference in their denotation. For many in New Testament scholarship the labels are interchangeable. "General" or "Catholic" refers to a genre designation, namely, circular letters addressed to a "general" audience. This perspective asserts that among the letters contained in the New Testament there are a hand full addressed to a general readership unlike the Pauline letters which are typically directed to specific addressees.

However, especially in light of modern historical-critical treatment of the Catholic Epistles, if the primary designation is one of genre—the general nature of the addressees—it is difficult to define the limits of the collection. On one hand, Hebrews and Revelation could be considered "general" letters because of the broader nature of their audiences. While on the other hand, there is doubt whether 2 or 3 John, with such a specific address, could qualify as "general" letters.[4] If grouped by genre the collection would include Hebrews and Revelation and exclude 2 and 3 John and likely Jude as well.

There is historical precedent for understanding the term "catholic" as descriptive of a letter written to a general audience. By the end of the second century the term "catholic" was used to describe the general address of individual letters. For example, Apollonius, recorded in Eusebius, notes that the Montanist Themiso "dared, in imitation of the apostle [John] to compose an

---

[4] Similarly there is doubt whether Jude is a general letter. Richard Bauckham argues that "we should not see it as a 'catholic letter' addressed to all Christians, but as a work written with a specific, localized audience in mind" (*Jude, 2 Peter* [WBC 50; Waco, TX: Word, 1983], 3); see also, Stephan J. Joubert, "Persuasion in the Letter of Jude," *JSNT* 58 (1995): 75–87.

epistle general [καθολικήν τινα σθνταξάμενος ἐπιστολήν]" (*Hist. eccl.* 5.15.5). Eusebius also reports that Dionysius of Alexandria was "most useful to all in the general epistles which he drew up for the churches [ὑπετυποῦτο καθολικαῖς πρὸς τὰς ἐκκλησίας ἐπιστολαῖς]" (*Hist. eccl.* 4.23.1). Clement of Alexandria described the letter written after the Jerusalem Council in Acts 15:23–29 as a "catholic epistle of all the apostles [τὴν ἐπιστολὴν τὴν καθολικὴν τῶν ἀποστόλων ἁπάντων]" (*Strom.* 4.15.97, line 3). Later in the sixth century, this description was applied to the seven canonical letters of James through Jude because of their general address. Leontius of Byzantium notes, "They are called catholic because they were written not to one single people like Paul's [letters], but in general to all [ἀλλὰ καθόλου πρὸς πάντα]" (*De Sectis, act* 2.4).[5] In addition, Origen describes especially 1John and perhaps 1Peter as individual "catholic" letters, however, it is not completely clear if this is because of their general address (1John in *Comm. Jo.* 1.22.137; 2.23.149; and 1Peter in *Comm. Jo.* 6.35.175; cf. Eusebius, *Hist. eccl.* 6.25.5). What is clear is that understanding the term "catholic" as reference to letters with general audiences was current from the second century onward, and perhaps even earlier.

However, the term "catholic" not only described the scope of a letter's audience but also was used to refer to a discrete collection of letters within the New Testament canon. This latter understanding, though once common before the advent of historical-criticism, is now quite rare. The concern of this paper is the early reception history of the Catholic Epistles—the discrete collection of James, 1–2 Peter, 1–3 John, and Jude as received in the early church. Though one must keep in mind that the Catholic Epistles functioned along with Acts in the New Testament canon, this paper attempts to identify when the term "Catholic Epistles" functioned as a label for this discrete canonical collection of letters. Eusebius, along with the general consensus coming after him, constitutes a kind of *terminus post quem* for such use. Establishing such use by the time of Eusebius, the paper then works back in time considering any evidence that suggests how early a Catholic Letter collection—in whole or in part—might have taken shape. This earliest reception history will comprise early citation and use of these letters as well as manuscript evidence indicating their collection together. Finally, this chapter will consider the hermeneutical implications for reading these letters together and briefly suggests why modern readers and commentators no longer read Catholic Epistles together as a significant collection.

---

5   I am indebted to Karl-Wilhelm Niebuhr ("Die Apostel und ihre Briefe: Zum hermeneutischen und ökumenischen Potental des Corpus Apostolicum im Neuen Testament," in *Paulus und Petrus: Geschichte—Theologie—Rezeption* [ed. H. Omerzu and E.D. Schmidt; Leipzig: Evangelische Verlagsanstalt, 2016], 273–292) for this reference.

1 Reception of the Catholic Epistles in the Early Church[6]

1.1 *Catholic Epistles as a "Terminus Technicus": Eusebius and Following*

In Eusebius we find what some consider the first reference to the "Catholic Epistles" considered a technical designation for a discrete collection.[7] Following an elaborate record of the martyrdom of James, the Lord's brother, Eusebius notes:

> Such is the story of James, whose is said to be the first of the Epistles called Catholic [ἡ πρώτη τῶν ὀνομαζομένων καθολικῶν ἐπιστολῶν]. It is to be observed that its authenticity is denied [ἰστέον δὲ ὡς νοθεύεται μέν], since few of the ancients quote it, as is also the case with the Epistle called Jude's, which is itself one of the seven called Catholic [τῶν ἑπτὰ λεγομένων καθολικῶν]; nevertheless we know that these letters have been used publicly with the rest [μετὰ τῶν λοιπῶν] in most churches.
>
> *Hist. eccl.* 2.23.24–25

Both James and Jude are considered as members of a larger collection of letters called "Catholic," and further, Eusebius indicates that James stood at the front of the collection. James's authenticity was disputed due to lack of attestation by the "ancients," however both James and Jude were nevertheless "used publicly with the rest in most churches." Though critical of James due to lack of use by the ancients, Joseph Mayor's caution against any hasty conclusion that Eusebius was therefore suspicious of James is worth repeating. "His own practice," Mayor noted of Eusebius, "betrays no suspicion of its genuineness, as he not only recognizes it as an authority ... but in one passage quotes James iv.11 as

---

6 To my knowledge there are only four scholars who have discussed the early reception history of the Catholic Epistles as a discrete collection at any significant length: David Nienhuis, *Not by Paul Alone: The Formation of the Catholic Epistles Collection and the Christian Canon* (Waco, TX: Baylor University Press, 2007), 29–97; David R. Nienhuis and Robert W. Wall, *Reading the Epistles of James, Peter, John and Jude as Scripture: The Shaping and Shape of a Canonical Collection* (Grand Rapids: Eerdmans, 2013), 17–39; Jacques Schlosser, "Le Corpus Épîtres des Catholiques," in *The Catholic Epistles and the Tradition* (ed. Jacques Schlosser; BETL 176; Leuven: Leuven University Press, 2004), 3–41; and finally, Karl-Wilhelm Niebuhr, "Die Apostel und ihre Briefe."

7 Painter notes: "In saying 'first of the Epistles named Catholic,' Eusebius provides the first known reference to the Catholic Epistles ...,' yet he denies this is a specific reference to a collection per se (John Painter and David A. deSilva, *James and Jude* [Grand Rapids: Baker Academic, 2012], 10).

Scripture (*Comm.* [*Ps.*] P. 648 Montf.), in another quotes James v.13 as spoken by the holy Apostle (ib. p. 247)."[8]

That James and Jude were used in "most churches" indicates, to some degree, Eusebius's reception of tradition about these letters. It was the practice of a wide scope of churches to use these letters, and their use throughout the church was along "with the rest" or "with the remaining [letters]." It seems likely that Eusebius means that James and Jude are used publicly "with the remaining [letters]," that is, the rest of the received, apostolic letters. Thus the passage suggests that Eusebius not only received a tradition of using these letters, "as in most churches," but that tradition also included referring to these letters with the label "Catholic Epistles."

The fact that Eusebius only mentions James and Jude is significant. John Painter notes that, "James and Jude, the brothers of Jesus, form an inclusion around the [Catholic Epistle] collection," that is, the two brothers of Jesus "form ... the bookends of this collection."[9] And thus,

> That would explain why Eusebuis, when he names James as the first of the seven C.E., also names Jude, and no other from the collection. To name the first and the last was to identify this *collection*. This might have been necessary, given that references to a catholic epistle was used in a nonspecific way in earlier sources.[10]

If Painter is correct, then it is possible that the tradition of a Catholic Epistle collection starting with James, including 1–2 Peter, 1–3 John, and finally concluding with Jude, was already a received collection that was recognized by Eusebius's audience with the mere reference to the first and last letters of the collection. Whether one accepts the plausibility of this observation or not, it is clear that Eusebius is aware of a collection of letters comprised of James, Jude, and five other unnamed letters which he expects his readers to recognize by the label of "Catholic Epistles."

In another key passage, Eusebius names each of our seven letters yet does not use the label "Catholic Epistles." Eusebius writes:

> At this point it seems reasonable to summarize the writings of the New Testament which have been quoted [τὰς δηλωθείσας]. In the first place

---

8   Joseph Mayor, *The Epistle of St. James* (London: Macmillan, 1897), xlix.
9   John Painter, "The Johannine Epistles as Catholic Epistles," in *The Catholic Epistles and Apostolic Tradition* (ed. Karl-Wilhelm Niebuhr and Robert W. Wall; Waco, TX: Baylor University Press, 2009), 248–249.
10 Painter, "The Johannine Epistles as Catholic Epistles," 458 n. 11 (*emphasis* added).

should be put the holy tetrad of the Gospels. To them follows the writing of the Acts of the Apostles. After this should be reckoned the Epistles of Paul. Following them the Epistle of John called the first, and in the same way should be recognized the Epistle of Peter. In addition to these should be put, if it seem desirable, the Revelation of John, the arguments concerning which we will expound at the proper time. These belong to the Recognized Books [ὁμολογουμένοις]. Of the Disputed Books [ἀντιλεγομένων] which are nevertheless known to most are the Epistle called James, that of Jude, the second Epistle of Peter, and the so-called second and third Epistles of John which may be the work of the evangelist or of some other with the same name.

Hist. eccl. 3.25.1–5

Though much of the scholarly focus on this passage has revolved around the criteria for Eusebius's categorization of canonical texts, there are more interesting indications relevant to the Catholic Epistle collection. Eusebius explicitly speaks of canonical sub-collections, namely, the Gospels and Pauline Epistles. He refers to these collections as complete units, not needing to enumerate the contents of either collection. It is likely that this is because these groupings of texts had become standard in the tradition. In other words, Eusebius has received the tradition of a four-fold Gospel collection comprised of Matthew, Mark, Luke, and John along with a fourteen-letter collection attributed to Paul which included Hebrews,[11] and, though he does not mention it here, Eusebius is aware of a second collection of letters called the Catholic Epistles—as clearly evidenced in *Hist. eccl.* 2.23.24–25. It is therefore plausible, when reading both passages together (viz., 2.23 and 3.25), that they form a trajectory that indicates Eusebius received or understood the Catholic Epistles as a discrete collection.

Contrary to much of the (Eastern) manuscript evidence surveyed below, Eusebius lists the Pauline letter collection immediately after Acts registering no knowledge of the *Praxapostolos*. After noting 1 John and 1 Peter immediately after the Pauline Letters, Eusebius lists the five remaining Catholic Epistles and labels them as "disputed" (*antilegomena*). Whereas Eusebius refers to Gospels and Paul's Letters as canonical units, he lists the remaining New Testament texts with their reception as individual books in mind. Leaving aside Acts, which he lists along with Gospels and Pauline Letters, it seems Eusebius is

---

[11] Eusebius speaks of the "fourteen letters of Paul are obvious and plain, yet it is not right to ignore that some dispute the Epistle to the Hebrews ..." (*Hist. eccl.* 3.3.5).

focused on the remaining texts expressing a concern over their authority and reception through citation in the early church. Though in the end one would not want to disassociate canonization and authority, this passage might indicate that whereas the Catholic Epistles were recognized as a discrete collection their degree of authority, as witnessed by early citation, was still under consideration.[12] As least this hesitancy would suggest that these letters went through a longer process as they were received into the New Testament canon.

If Eusebius was writing sometime before 300 C.E. and his work reflects previous tradition regarding the reception of these letters, then we can consider the Catholic Epistles a relatively fixed canonical sub-collection at least by the close of the third century.[13] From Eusebius onward, the Catholic Epistles are limited to seven in number, with the names of the authors always being James, Peter, John, and Jude and this collection of letters was often attached to Acts. About fifty years after Eusebius, Cyril of Jerusalem records a canon list that, in part, states: "Receive also the Acts of the Twelve Apostles; and in addition to these the seven Catholic Epistles of James, Peter, John, and Jude [δέχεσθε ... πρὸς τούτοις δὲ καὶ τὰς ἑπτά, Ἰακώβου, καὶ Πέτρου, καὶ Ἰωάννου, καὶ Ἰούδα καθολικὰς ἐπιστολάς]; then as a seal upon them all, and the last work of disciples [ἐπισφράγισμα δὲ τῶν πάντων, καὶ μαθητῶν τὸ τελεθταῖον], the fourteen Epistles of Paul" (*Catech.* 4.36).[14] In canon 60 of the Synod of Laodicea, the seven Catholic Epistles are counted by name after the four Gospels and Acts and before the Pauline letters. Athanasius's Easter Letter lists the "Acts of the Apostles and seven letters, called Catholic, by the apostles [καὶ ἐπιστολαὶ καθολικαὶ καλούμεναι τῶν ἀποστόλων ἑπτά], namely one by James, two by Peter, then three by John, and after these, one by Jude. After these [πρὸς τούτοις] there are fourteen letters by Paul" (*Ep. Fest.* 39.5). And roughly thirteen years after Athanasius, Amphilochius

---

12   In a brief, yet illuminating, discussion regarding the function of the label "Catholic Epistles," Brevard Childs argued that the term "catholic" never referred to a letter which was (more) "canonical" than others. He notes, "the term remains a useful one to designate a collection of New Testament writings which is distinct from the Gospels and the Pauline corpus" (*The New Testament as Canon: An Introduction* [Minneapolis: Fortress, 1984], 495). Childs, and perhaps Eusebius too in this passage, does not use the label directly to claim a kind of superior canonical authority over other canonical letters, such as Paul's—the label was not canonically significant in this way. However, contrary to Wall and Nienhuis (*Reading the Epistles*, 5), this does not mean that Childs denied that the term "Catholic Epistles" referred to a discrete, canonical collection of letters within the New Testament (see Darian Lockett, "Are the Catholic Epistles a Canonically Significant Collection? A Status Quaestionis," *CurBR* 14.1 [2015]: 62–80).

13   Nienhuis, *Not by Paul*, 69.

14   As cited in Nienhuis, *Not by Paul*, 77.

(ca. 380 C.E.) notes a degree of variation. He says, "Of the Catholic Epistles [καθαλικῶν ἐπιστολῶν] some say we must receive seven [ἑπτά φασιν], but others say only three should be received—that of James, one, and one of Peter, and those of John, one. And some receive three [of John], and besides these two of Peter and that of Jude a seventh [ἑβδόμην]" (*Iambi ad Seleucum*).[15] Though Amphilochius registers some variation in number, he is clearly working within a tradition that received the seven Catholic Epistles. With Jerome, this terminology was also introduced in the Latin West (*Vir. ill.* 1–2).

Thus with Eusebius, and strengthened by the following tradition, the seven canonical letters of James, 1–2 Peter, 1–3 John, and Jude were received for the most part as a fixed collection in largely the same order and often associated with Acts. According to the material considered so far, the collection of seven Catholic Epistles was evidently known and largely fixed by the end of the third century. Is there any indication that this collection, or a portion thereof, existed earlier?

1.2 Indications of a Catholic Epistle Collection before Eusebius

The history of the development before this point is more difficult to determine. There are a few slight but suggestive indications that the Catholic Epistle collection was known before the time of Eusebius.

1.2.1 Origen (184/5–253/4 C.E.)

Like Eusebius, Origen was aware of canonical sub-collections as he specifically refers to the four-fold Gospel. In a fragment preserved by Eusebius, Origen notes, "in the first of his [*Commentaries*] *on the Gospel of Matthew*, defending the canon of the church he gives his testimony that he knows only four Gospels ... which alone are unquestionable in the Church of God under heaven ..." (*Hist. eccl.* 6.25.5). Beyond the four Gospels, Origen frequently cites 1 Peter and 1 John calling both texts "catholic epistles" (*Comm. Jn.* 6.175.9 and *Comm. Jn.* 1.138, 2.149 respectively). Though this is a frequent description used by Origen, it is unclear exactly what he means by the title. In the passage from Eusebius, Origen goes on to quote from 1 Pet 5:13 to which he offers the preface: "Peter acknowledged ... in the catholic epistle [ἐν τῇ καθολικῇ ἐπιστολῇ], speaking in these terms ..." (*Hist. eccl.* 6.25.5). It is difficult to know whether Origen refers to 1 Peter as part of a Catholic Epistle collection, or if, as was a current usage, he merely was referring to 1 Peter's general audience.

---

15   See also Bruce M. Metzger, *The Canon of the New Testament: Its Origin, Development, and Significance* (Oxford: Clarendon, 1997), 314.

Furthermore, Origen says: "Peter ... has left one acknowledged [ὁμολογουμένη] epistle, and, it may be, a second also; for it is doubted [ἀμφιβάλλεται]" (*Hist. eccl.* 6.25.8). The passage continues with a reference to the letters of John: "He has left also an epistle of a very few lines, and, it may be, a second and a third; for not all say that these are genuine" (*Hist. eccl.* 6.25.9). Furthermore, in several places Origen refers to James (*Comm. Jo.* 19:6; *Comm. Rom.* 4:1, 8, 9:24; *Hom. Exod.* 3:3, 8:4; *Hom. Lev.* 2:4; *Hom. Job* 7:1; *Sel. Ps.* 31:5; *Fr. Jo.* 126).[16] Though Origen does not refer to Jude, 2 Peter, 2–3 John, or James as catholic epistles, he does use the label with reference to 1 Peter and 1 John. This may indicate that Origen understood the label as reference to letters addressed to general audiences, but it is hard to know this with confidence. At least Origen knows of all of the seven letters and uses the label catholic epistle for two of them. From this limited evidence, Nienhuis concludes that, "despite having all the ingredients in his possession, Origen shows no awareness of a discrete canonical collection called the C.E."[17] It is not clear that the silence on Origen's part constitutes such a definitive conclusion; however, admittedly one would expect him to describe all seven letters as "Catholic" if Origen himself viewed them as a discrete canonical collection (but even this concession does not rule out the possibility that these seven letters were received as a discrete collection either by Origen or in other areas of the church).

1.2.2   Clement of Alexandria (150–215 C.E.)

There is a suggestive passage from Clement preserved in Eusebius that possibly indicates he was aware the term "Catholic Epistles" referred to a discrete collection. According to Eusebius, Clement had written in his *Hypotyposeis* "concise explanations of all the Canonical Scriptures [ἐνδιαθήκοι γραφαί], not passing over even the disputed writings [τὰς ἀντιλεγομένας], I mean the Epistle of Jude and the remaining Catholic Epistles ... [καὶ τὰς λοιπὰς καθολικὰς ἐπιστολάς]" (*Hist. eccl.* 6.14.1). Though the Letter of Jude is mentioned, it is unclear

---

16   See Mayor, *Epistle of James*, cxlvii and Nienhuis, *Not by Paul*, 55–60. Nienhuis rightly points out that Origen registered a hesitant acceptance of James (the letter is found ἐν τῇ φερομένῃ Ιακώβου ἐπιστολῇ; *Comm. Jn.* 19.23.152); however, this is far from a position of doubt on Origen's part. Nienhuis seems to move beyond the evidence when he concludes, "in Origen's day the letter was still in its early use and was not fully authoritative even to those in Origen's audience ... Indeed, his appeal to the letter is that of a document recently arrived" (56).

17   Nienhuis, *Not by Paul*, 63.

which of the Catholic Epistles he means here. This might demonstrate that, whereas Clement could use τὴν ἐπιστολὴν τὴν καθολικὴν to describe a letter of general address (see above), in this passage Clement possibly refers to something more. Though he does not enumerate the contents of the collection it is possible that he is referring to "the remaining Catholic Epistles" as a discrete collection. Of course this is not a list of texts included in the Catholic Epistles, and one should be cautious in drawing conclusions about the exact contents of Clement's "remaining Catholic Epistles."

Three later witnesses shed slightly more light on Clement's work. Fragments of Clement's *Hypotyposeis* are preserved in Latin by the sixth-century author, Cassiodorus. In *Adumbrationes in Epistolas Catholicas*, Cassiodorus preserved Clement's commentaries on 1 Peter, 1–2 John, and Jude. In a second text, *Institutiones Divinarum et Saecularium Litterarum*, Cassiodorus remarks, "The presbyter Clement of Alexandria ... has made some comments on the Canonical Epistles [*epistolis ... canonicis*], that is to say the first epistle of St. Peter, the first and second epistles of St. John, and the epistle of James [*et Iacobi* (erroneously for *Iudae?*)]."[18] Because his previous work preserves the actual commentaries on 1 Peter, 1–2 John, and Jude, many scholars believe Cassiodorus erroneously mentions "the epistle of James" where he likely means "the epistle of Jude." Nienhuis points out the third witness to Clement's *Hypotyposeis*. Admittedly quite late, the ninth-century Byzantine Patriarch Photius commented on the *Hypotyposeis* in his work called *Bibliotheca* claiming that Clement's work "is supposedly an interpretation of Genesis, Exodus, the Psalms, St. Paul's epistles, the Catholic Epistles, and Ecclesiastes."[19] Though Nienhuis expresses little trust in the document as a source for the precise contents of the *Hypotyposeis*, it is suggestive that in this later witness the title Catholic Epistles refers to a discrete collection of texts as it stands in the list beside "St. Paul's epistles." It is plausible that Clement was aware of a collection of Catholic Epistles on which he had commented.

1.2.3 Tertullian (160–225 C.E.)

Though Tertullian knew and used 1 Peter (directly quoting the letter once, *Scorp.* 12.2) and 1 John (citing it several times), and is the first Western witness to affirm the letter of Jude (*Cult. Fem.* 1.3.1–3), he never refers to these texts with

---

18 *De institutione divinarum litterarum* 1.8.4 (R.A.B. Mynors, *Cassiodori Senatoris Institutiones* [Oxford: Clarendon, 1937], 29); as cited in Nienhuis, *Not by Paul*, 49.

19 *Bibliotheca Photii Patriarchae* cod. 109, as cited in Nienhuis, *Not by Paul*, 49.

the title Catholic Epistles. He refers to James of Jerusalem and is careful to demonstrate the consistency between Paul and the Pillar apostles, yet he never refers directly to the letters of James, 2 Peter, or 2–3 John.

1.2.4 The Muratorian Fragment

The Catholic Epistles are also mentioned in the Canon Muratori: "the epistle of Jude and two of the above-mentioned John are counted/used [*habentur*] in the catholic [*in catholica*] church/epistles" (69). This reference is questionable in several respects, however. Not only is the date of the fragment uncertain, but so too is the meaning of *in catholica*, which may refer either to the "catholic church" (as most suppose) or, perhaps, to a collection of the Catholic Epistles.[20] Geoffrey Hahneman notes,

> Elsewhere in the Fragment the Church is always called *ecclesia catholica* (ll. 56, 61, 66, 73, 78), and a mere *catholica* would be uniquely interpreted here as 'Catholic Church'. According to Katz, however, *catholica* frequently stood for *epistola catholica*, and 1 John was sometimes considered to be the catholic epistle *par excellence* ... Katz's suggested Greek [original] would be translated something like: "Certainly the epistle of Jude and two [epistles] of the aforementioned John are held in addition to the catholic [epistle]."[21]

If, as seems likely, *in catholica* refers to "the catholic epistle" what is the significance? On one hand, along with Origen this vague reference in the Muratorian canon could merely refer to 1 John as a letter with a general address; however, if, like Origen, 1 John is *the* "catholic epistle" then the author would be connecting Jude and two other letters of John (2 and 3 John?) to 1 John. Though very slight, this possibility could suggest a partial collection of the Catholic Epistles.

At any rate, the selection of only Jude and two of the Johannine letters is unique. This is idiosyncratic in terms of both contents and order. Hahneman again notes,

> The absence of 1 Peter (and James) is extraordinary, and most probably implies omissions in the Fragment. The letters found in the Fragment, namely 2 (and 3?) John and Jude, are elsewhere found only in larger col-

---

20 Niebuhr, "Die Apostel und ihre Briefe."
21 Geoffrey Mark Hahneman, *The Muratorian Fragment and the Development of the Canon* (Oxford: Oxford University Press, 1992), 16.

lections of the catholic epistles ... Jude, which is listed before the letters of John in the Fragment, was usually listed last among the catholic epistles both in the East, where the order James, Peter, John, Jude was standard, and in the West, where the order varied.[22]

This again is suggestive of a partial collection.

1.2.5 Irenaeus (130–200 C.E.)

As one of the earliest witnesses to express recognition of canonical sub-collections, namely, the four-fold Gospel canon (*Haer.* 3.11.8) and a thirteen-letter Pauline corpus, Irenaeus does not mention a Catholic Epistle collection. He does clearly refer to 1 Peter (*Haer.* 4.9.2) and 1 John by name and there is some evidence that he quoted from 2 John 7–8; however, he merely cites this content along with several passages from 1 John as coming form the epistle of John (*Haer.* 3.16.5–8). Also, Irenaeus mentions the pillars of Peter, James, and John (*Haer.* 3) in the context of arguing for the harmony of apostolic doctrine—he does not demonstrate knowledge of the letters of James, 2 Peter, 3 John, or Jude.

2 An Early Reception History: Reception in the Manuscript Evidence

The presence or absence of canon lists or early citation is by no means the only criterion for determining how far the canon process might have developed at any given period. The manuscript tradition must be taken together with the above evidence for a composite picture of the early reception of the Catholic Epistles as a collection. The manuscript evidence strongly suggests a four-fold Gospel collection originating in the early second century. Stanley Porter notes that, "There appears to be a strong line of continuity from the second century to the fourth, with our four canonical Gospels emerging as a whole together out of the second century."[23] And with respect to the Pauline corpus, Porter notes,

---

22 Hahneman, *The Muratorian Fragment*, 181.
23 Stanley E. Porter, *How We Got the New Testament: Text, Transmission, Translation* (Grand Rapids: Baker Academic, 2013), 106. See also Francis Watson, *Gospel Writing: A Canonical Perspective* (Grand Rapids: Eerdmans, 2013). It is significant that these manuscripts regularly connect the four canonical Gospels with no instances where an apocryphal Gospel is included. J.K. Elliott comments, "There are no manuscripts that contain say Matthew, Luke, and Peter, or John, Mark, and Thomas. Only the Gospels of Matthew, Mark, Luke, and John were considered as scriptural and then as canonical" ("Manuscripts, the Codex, and the Canon," *JSNT* 63 [1996]: 107).

there is strong evidence that a collection of at least thirteen Pauline epistles was circulating by 200 C.E. at the latest.[24]

Though this broad picture of the manuscript evidence is clear, the corresponding evidence for the early history of the Catholic Epistles is extremely fragmentary. Though we cannot obtain a clear view regarding the contents and the order of the Catholic Epistles in these early collections, we can add to the image already created by the evidence above. A suggestive observation is that, to our knowledge, the Catholic and Pauline Epistles were never included in the same manuscript during their transmission. That is, before the major codices which include the entire New Testament with Catholic and Pauline Epistles as discrete collections, individual letters from either collection did not, as a rule, circulate together. One special case is P[72] (third or fourth century), which contains Jude and 1–2 Peter along with several other ancient Christian texts.

2.1 Papyrus and Parchment Fragments

Contained in the Bodmer papyri (P.Bodmer VII–VIII), P[72] comprises several early Christian works including 3 Corinthians then Jude and finally 1–2 Peter.[25] It is an odd collection of texts, which many scholars have suggested was for private devotional use, with three of the Catholic Epistles in an unusual order. Both the pagination and scribal hand suggest that Jude and 1–2 Peter were from a previous manuscript, either together from another collection or as individual documents.[26] Tommy Wasserman has attempted to reconstruct what he calls the "Bodmer codex" where he argues that 1–2 Peter and Jude were actually written by the same hand,[27] even though they follow different originals (1 Peter is closest to Codex Vaticanus where 2 Peter and Jude contain

---

24 Porter, following some of the evidence offered by David Trobisch, suggests that Paul's letter collection could originate from the mid-second century (if not earlier) (*How We Got the New Testament*, 110).

25 The text contains, in order: the *Nativity of Mary*, 3 Corinthians, *Odes of Solomon* 11, Jude, Melito's *Homily on the Passion*, a fragment of a liturgical hymn, the *Apology of Phileas*, Ps 33:2–34:16 [LXX], and 1–2 Peter.

26 Eldon Jay Epp, "Issues in the Interrelation of New Testament Textual Criticism and Canon," in *The Canon Debate* (ed. Lee Martin McDonald and James A. Sanders; Peabody, MA: Hendrickson, 2002), 485–515, esp. 491–493.

27 David Trobisch agrees (*The First Edition of the New Testament* [Oxford: Oxford University Press, 2000], 30), and further notes: "The selection and sequence of P[72] may best be explained as an irregular and singular exemplar, one that left no traces in the later manuscript tradition" (34).

Western readings).[28] Wasserman argues for a process of collection that brought the various manuscripts together into the codex now represented by P^{72} and was bound together in the early fourth century. Porter notes that, "If this is true, it indicates that by as early as the third century, 1 Peter, 2 Peter, and Jude were considered a subcorpus and copied together, even if they were bound with other manuscripts for particular theological purposes."[29]

There are three witnesses to James, all from the third century: P^{20} (James 2:19–3:2, 4–9), P^{23} (1:10–12, 15–16), and P^{100} (3:13–4:4; 4:9–5:1). Porter notes that P^{100} contains pagination on both sides of the same leaf. "The page numbers … indicate," he argues, "that page 1 was the beginning of the Epistle of James. Since Hebrews probably was included with the Pauline Epistles, it is possible either that both P^{23} and P^{100} were manuscripts of just the Epistle of James or that they were the first book in a collection of the Catholic (or General) Epistles."[30] Of course we cannot know this for sure because the page numbers alone could otherwise indicate that there were a number of other texts in the codex. However, Porter concludes that, if the former is "the case, there is evidence of the Catholic Epistles being gathered together possibly by the second century and almost assuredly by the third."[31]

Larry Hurtado notes that the fragmentary parchment codex 0232 (P.Ant. 1.12), containing a small portion of 2 John 1–9 on the front and back of a single page, "may have originally contained a collection of writings ascribed to the apostle John, a 'Johannine Corpus.'"[32] The fragment contains page numbers originating from a different scribal hand, which indicate that the codex was of a significant enough size to contain several texts. Colin Roberts originally calculated that the preceding 163 pages would have constituted so much space that, rather than the Catholic Epistles, the codex more likely contained the Gospel of John, Revelation, and 1 John. From this Charles E. Hill concludes "Thus this does create a prima-facie likelihood that 0232 was indeed once part of an edition of the Johannine corpus."[33] However, Michael J. Kruger has argued that there is not enough space for all the Johannine texts. Kruger discovered that Roberts's

---

28 Tommy Wasserman, *The Epistle of Jude: Its Text and Transmission* (ConBNT 43; Stockholm: Almqvist & Wiksell, 2006), 31, 42–50.
29 Porter, *How We Got the New Testament*, 123.
30 Porter, *How We Got the New Testament*, 123.
31 Porter, *How We Got the New Testament*, 124.
32 Larry W. Hurtado, *The Earliest Christian Artifacts: Manuscripts and Christian Origins* (Grand Rapids: Eerdmans, 2006), 39. This is the thesis of Charles E. Hill, *The Johannine Corpus in the Early Church* (Oxford: Oxford University Press, 2004).
33 Hill, *The Johannine Corpus in the Early Church*, 455–456.

calculation of four hundred words per page was incorrect and grossly overestimated the size of the original codex. Rather than four hundred *words*, it is actually four hundred *letters* per page, which, in turn, indicates a much shorter codex. Based on this revised calculation, Kruger argues "this manuscript likely contained the book of Hebrews and a full collection of the Catholic Epistles."[34] Though, as Kruger notes, one cannot be completely confident that the original codex contained some or all of the Catholic Epistles, for the purposes of the present paper, such an insight is an important argument against the early circulation of a Johannine corpus. Porter's research affirms this conclusion: "There is little transmissional or manuscript evidence to indicate a usual gathering of the Johannine writings as a subcorpus—even in the major codexes, which did not keep John's Gospel, the three Johannine Epistles, and the book of Revelation together."[35] Rather, the evidence here indicates that the letters of John either circulated individually or as a group of Catholic Epistles, not in a collection of Johannine texts.

2.2 Major Codices

The major majuscule codices of the fourth and fifth century regularly combine Acts and the Catholic Epistles into the *Praxapostolos*[36] and place it either before (Vaticanus and Alexandrinus) or after (Sinaiticus) the Pauline corpus.[37]

---

34 Michael J. Kruger, "The Date and Content of P. Antinoopolis 12 (0232)," *NTS* 25 (2012): 254–271. Though C.H. Roberts argued 0232 constitutes our earliest copy of 2 John (third century) and also is evidence of an early Johannine corpus, Kruger contests both these assertions. Based on the size and material of the manuscript and the scribal hand Kruger argues for a fourth or early fifth century date for 0232 (270).

35 Porter, *How We Got the New Testament*, 121.

36 David Trobisch makes an interesting observation from the manuscript evidence regarding the *Praxapostolos*. Noting that NA27 describes the contents of most manuscripts using only four letters (*e* = Gospels, *a* = Praxapostolos, *p* = the Letters of Paul, *r* = Revelation of John), Trobisch notes that, "The editors refer to Acts and the General Letters using a single notation (*a*). If a significant number of manuscripts containing the Book of Acts without the General Letters or the General Letters without the Book of Acts existed, this notation would not suffice" (*The First Edition of the New Testament*, 26).

37 Sinaiticus: four Gospels, fourteen Pauline letters (with Hebrews between 2 Thessalonians and 1 Timothy), Acts with the Catholic Epistles (in the order of James, Peter, John and Jude—interestingly there is a roughly two column space between Acts and James), Revelation then followed by *Barnabas* and part of *Hermas*. Vaticanus (following what is the typical Eastern order): four Gospels, Acts with the Catholic Epistles (James, Peter, John, and Jude), the Pauline letters (with Hebrews after 2 Thessalonians), yet the manuscript ends with Hebrews 9:13 (thus we do not know which texts were included at the end of the

The order of the Catholic Epistles in all three follows the canonical order (James, Peter, John, and Jude), a rather fixed tradition in the East since Athanasius.[38] In the Western tradition, the four Gospels and Acts are immediately followed by the Pauline corpus so that Acts and the Catholic Epistles are separated. This order is evidenced by, among others, the Vulgate and as well as by the majority of Byzantine manuscripts, and was preserved up to the Council of Trent. In addition to this, sometimes in the Western tradition, 1–2 Peter precedes James (Augustine, Rufinus, but not in the Vulgate). Strikingly, the bilingual Greek-Latin codex Bezae Claromontanus preserves a table of contents in Latin between the text of Philemon and Hebrews. In the table of contents, Philemon is followed by the seven Catholic Epistles in the order: 1–2 Peter, James, 1–3 John, and Jude. Suggestively, this order corresponds to the *varia lectio* of Gal 2:9 in the Greek part of the codex where Peter is mentioned first (which indicates once again that ordering of the Catholic Epistles was strongly influenced by the list of apostles in Galatians).[39]

Finally, one can also refer to so-called "additions" in biblical manuscripts (difficult to date when they were added) appearing both in *super-* or *subscriptiones* or lists of contents. These too serve as evidence for the reception of the Catholic Epistles. For example, in Alexandrinus the Gospels are followed by Acts along with the Catholic Epistles. At the end of Jude there is an addition in a different hand: πράξεις τῶν ἁγίων ἀποστόλων καὶ καθολικαί ("acts of the holy apostles and catholic [epistles]").[40] Not only do we see the "Catholic Epistles" so labeled as a collection, but also this passage testifies to an understanding of Acts and the Catholic Epistles as a unified collection in the New Testament. Alexandrinus also contains a table of contents added in the seventh or eighth century which, after the four Gospels and before the fourteen

---

codex). Alexandrinus: four Gospels, Acts with the Catholic Epistles (James, Peter, John, and Jude), fourteen letters of Paul (with Hebrews between 2 Thess and 1 Tim), Revelation along with *1–2 Clement* and the *Psalms of Solomon* (which is not part of the text, but in the table of contents).

38 D.C. Parker (*New Testament Manuscripts and Their Texts* [Cambridge: Cambridge University Press, 2008], 286) notes that this is the order most common in the manuscripts; see also Nienhuis, *No by Paul*, 71–73, 91–97, and Kruger, "Date and Content of P. Antinoopolis," 266.

39 Based upon this observation, Niebuhr concludes: "Dies belegt, wie bewusst den christlichen Abschreibern die Reihenfolge der einzelnen biblischen Schriften und die mit ihr gegenbenen intertextuellen Beziehungen waren" ("Die Apostel un ihre Briefe"). And thus is evidence of a growing, if not received, notion of a canonically significant collection and arrangement of texts.

40 Trobisch, *The First Edition of the New Testament*, 52.

letters of Paul and the Apocalypse of John, has the term καθολικαί ζ' ("catholic [epistles] 7"). *Inscriptiones* or *subscriptiones* accompanying the Catholic Epistles often include ἐπιστολή then the named author or some add καθολική as well. These titles are quite uniform in identifying the author of the text (not the recipients as in the Pauline corpus).

3   Conclusion

In recent research, some scholars argue that the origin of the collection of Catholic Epistles dates back to a canonical collection from as early as the second century,[41] while others argue that such a canonical collection did not exist earlier than the testimonies from the second half of the fourth century, with variations existing according to different regions of early Christianity. The sparse evidence for some of the epistles before Origen, in particular for James, adds to the difficulties in constructing the history of the Catholic Epistles collection. In the Syriac tradition, the Catholic Epistles are testified only from the fourth century onwards, and initially only included James, 1 Peter, and 1 John. On the other hand, testimony in the early fathers for the rather marginal letters of Jude (in Clement, Tertullian, Origen) or 2–3 John (in Clement, Irenaeus, Origen) is much better than for James.[42]

Harry Gamble rightly observes the need to consider the development of the New Testament canon as "a collection of collections."[43] Reception history and the manuscript evidence indicates that the four Gospels and the Letters of Paul were incorporated into the New Testament canon early in the process. The Catholic Epistles finally entered the New Testament canon as a collection as well; however, much of the evidence above suggests that individual letters from this collection circulated individually for a time. Jens Schröter notes that "The compilation of Acts + Catholic Letters is finally to be explained by the fact that in both cases it is a matter of writings that first enter into the history of the collection of binding corpora subsequent to the Gospels and Letters of

---

41   C.-B. Amphoux and J.-B. Bouhot, eds., *La Lecture liturgique des Épîtres catholiques dans l'Église ancienne* (Lausanne: Zèbre, 1996), and Trobisch, *The First Edition of the New Testament*.

42   Neibuhr, "Die Apostel un ihre Briefe."

43   Harry Y. Gamble, "The New Testament Canon: Recent Research and the Status Quaestionis," in *The Canon Debate* (ed. Lee Martin McDonald and James A. Sanders; Peabody, MA: Hendrickson, 2002), 275.

Paul, whereas they circulated for quite a long time as individual writings."[44] Even though these letters did have a past where they circulated individually, they finally entered the canon as a collection toward the end of the canonical process, as early as the second half of the second century. Furthermore, this discrete letter collection was joined to Acts during the formation of the canon to form the *Apostolos*, or what Schröter calls "the apostle portion" of the New Testament.[45] Therefore, a final account of the canonical development of the Catholic Epistles must observe a period of individual circulation culminating in a collection of all seven letters together in a discrete corpus suggested by the growing (if inconsistent) use of the label "Catholic Epistles" to refer to this discrete collection and then the association of the Catholic Epistles as a collection with the Acts of the Apostles.

The issue at hand is whether these seven letters should be read in isolation from each other, taking their individual historical situations as the single, determinative context for their interpretation, or whether their collection as Catholic Epistles into a discrete canonical sub-unit and the connection of the Catholic Epistles with Acts as the *Praxapostolos* within the larger New Testament canon should constitute a further context within which they are interpreted. This question raises the issue of whether subsequent judgments regarding the Christian canon *clarify* or *obscure* the meaning of the Catholic Epistles. Famously, Harnack argued that "Canonization works like whitewash; it hides the original colors and obliterates all the contours," hiding "the true origin and significance of the works."[46] The historical-critical approach to biblical studies rejects later judgments regarding the collecting and ordering of the canon as anachronistic to their right interpretation, and thus emphasizing the text's situation in *history* over against its situation in the *canon*.

---

44 Schröter, *From Jesus to the New Testament*, 290.
45 Schröter notes that the reception of the Catholic Epistles along with Acts "represented the apostle part of the canon, [Mit diesen zusammen stellate sie den Apostelteil des Kanons dar] whereas the letter collection of Paul had always stood for itself and had no need of legitimation from Acts. By contrast, the Catholic Letters, from which for a long time only 1 Peter and 1 John enjoyed uncontested acceptance, could be shown to belong to the canon through a book in which there was talk of James, Peter, and John [viz, Acts]. This corresponds to the intention, which was discernible since Irenaeus, of expanding the witness of Paul through that of the original apostles, a function that was now also taken over by the Catholic Letters. In the course of this, it was probably not least the fact that they were seven in number that played a role in the arrangement together that ultimately took place of the Catholic Letters in their own corpus of writings in the canon" (*From Jesus to the New Testament*, 290–291).
46 Harnack, *The Origin of the New Testament*, 140–141.

However, Schröter is correct to argue that "historical-critical interpretation of the New Testament texts and a theology of the New Testament do *not* exclude each other—and neither should they be dissolved into each other—but stand in a tension-filled dynamic in relation to each other ..."[47] Rather than pitting historical-critical description against reception-historical significance, it is actually the fundamental role of canon that allows for taking up both together. Again, Schröter notes,

> the emergence of the New Testament canon is—in contrast to what Wrede [and Harnack] thought—not an arbitrary establishment of ancient church bishops and theologians that through historical criticism has become antiquated in the meantime and therefore unimportant. Rather, the formation of the New Testament belongs to those developments of the early church in which fundamental characteristics of Christian faith manifest themselves.[48]

Presumably then, the reason modern scholarship has had such a reaction against reading the Catholic Epistles as a discrete collection is because of the anachronistic criterion of canon. Yet, if Schröter is correct, historical-critical and reception-historical interpretation of the Catholic Epistles need not exclude one another. This survey of the early reception history suggests that the collection and arrangement of the Catholic Epistles took place during the canonical development of the New Testament and constitutes an important hermeneutical context for interpreting these letters. Thus, reading the Catholic Epistles as a discrete canonical collection is not merely theologically permissible, but also, as this description of their reception history suggests, enjoys (a degree of) early historical support.

---

47   Schröter, *From Jesus to the New Testament*, 330 (*emphasis* original).
48   Schröter, *From Jesus to the New Testament*, 337–338.

A Jewish Denial: 1 John and the Johannine Mission

Matthew Jensen

The proclamation that "Jesus is the Christ" lies at the core of the spread of Christianity and the mission of the early church. The Synoptic Gospels relate this identification at their turning points (Mark 8:29; Matt 16:16; Luke 9:20) and its demonstration is John's stated purpose (20:31). It is so central to the mission of the early church that Acts employs it as a summary of the apostles' teaching: the twelve (5:42), the newly converted Saul (9:22) who continued to use it throughout his ministry as Paul (17:3; 18:5), and even Apollos (18:28).[1]

However, even though this same summary statement also occurs in 1 John, on one occasion it is in a very different context. It does not summarise what the author of 1 John taught but rather it describes what the antichrists were denying (2:22).

This essay examines 1 John in order to understand what it reveals about the Johannine mission. An initial section sets the context of the Johannine mission by exploring what is said about John's mission in Irenaeus, Revelation, Acts, and Paul. Then the essay examines 1 John in detail in order to ascertain who the audience of the mission were and what message they heard. Finally, some conclusions about where 1 John fits in the Johannine mission timeline or trajectory are suggested.

1 The Johannine Mission outside of 1 John

The New Testament documents describe how the apostles followed a missionary agenda outlined by the risen Jesus (Matt 28:18–20; Luke 24:45–49; Acts 1:8) and consequently how the earliest church spread from Jerusalem to the known world. There is debate about the number of apostolic missionary movements and for the purpose of this essay on the Johannine mission, two positions are noteworthy. On the one hand, Barnett argues that there were three apostolic

---

[1] This essay assumes the general reliability of Acts as a historical source. For the reasons for this assumption and discussion of the limits of the historical reliability of Acts, see C.J. Hemer, *The Book of Acts in the Setting of Hellenistic History* (WUNT 49; Tubingen: Mohr Siebeck, 1989), 3–19; C.K. Barrett, "The Historicity of Acts," *JTS* 50.2 (1999): 515–534; D. Marguerat, *The First Christian Historian: Writing the "Acts of the Apostles"* (SNTSMS 121; Cambridge: Cambridge University Press, 2002); E.J. Schnabel, *Acts* (ZECNT; Grand Rapids: Zondervan, 2012), 38–41.

missions—Peter and John to the disapora Jews, James to the Jerusalem community, Paul to the Gentiles. Barnett cites as evidence the grouping together of Peter and John in Acts 3–4, 8, the common teaching that is unique to 1 Peter and John's Gospel,[2] and the long term friendship of Peter and John.[3] On the other hand, Ellis argues that there were four missionary movements—each of Peter, John and James to the circumcision, and Paul to the nations.[4] Ellis prefers to establish his case on the evidence of Galatians 1–2 where Peter is described without reference to John (1:18), indicating that they were seen to be separate individuals, and is later listed in the group of the three pillar apostles (2:9). This evidence plus the existence of a distinct group of literature commonly recognised as belonging to the Johannine community or school (John, 1–3 John, Revelation) makes Ellis's proposal more likely: there was an independent mission associated with the apostle John.[5]

There is little evidence describing the Johannine missionary movement and as a result the picture developed is only able to be in broad detail. The four main sources of information outside of 1 John are Irenaeus, Revelation, Acts, and Paul.[6] This first section reviews these sources in order to establish a context for understanding the Johannine mission within which 1 John originated.

---

2 "Feed my sheep" (1 Pet 5:2; John 21:15–17); "born again" (1 Pet 1:3, 22; John 3:3, 5); "you will follow later" (1 Pet 3:18–22; John 13:36; 21:19, 22). See Paul Barnett, *Jesus and the Rise of Early Christianity* (Downers Grove, IL: InterVarsity Press, 1999), 325.

3 Barnett, *Jesus and the Rise*, 300.

4 E. Earle Ellis, *The Making of the New Testament Documents* (BibInt 39; Leiden: Brill, 1999), 33–47.

5 The issue of the relationship between the apostle John and the Elder John will not be addressed in this essay as the mission movement itself is the issue. The movement started with the apostle and may or may not have continued with the elder. For a recent review of the issue of the Johannine Community, see Wally V. Cirafesi, "The Johannine Community Hypothesis (1968–Present): Past and Present Approaches and a New Way Forward," *CurBR* 12 (2014): 173–193.

6 John's Gospel is not included in this list because of the inherent difficulties associated with mirror-reading a narrative text. For an understanding of John's Gospel which accords somewhat with the position of the present paper, see J. Louis Martyn, "A Gentile Mission That Replaced and Earlier Jewish Mission?" in *Exploring the Gospel of John: In Honor of D. Moody Smith* (ed. R. Alan Culpepper and C. Clifton Black; Louisville: Westminster John Knox, 1996), 124–144. For the view that the Gospels were not written for a specific community but rather a broad audience, see R. Bauckham, "For Whom were the Gospels Written?" in *The Gospels for All Christians: Rethinking the Gospel Audiences* (ed. R. Bauckham; Grand Rapids: Eerdmans, 1998), 9–48.

1.1 The Johannine Mission according to Irenaeus

Irenaeus has a few scattered references to John that reveal something about his final mission base and his message towards the end of his life.

John is presented as residing in Ephesus from where he wrote the Gospel (*Haer.* 3.1.1), fled the bathhouse because Cerinthus was inside (*Haer.* 3.3.4), and remained until the reign of Trajan in 98 C.E. (*Haer.* 2.22.5; 3.3.4). Little can be ascertained about when John moved to Ephesus but his movement to a Gentile city (with a large Jewish community) may indicate his mission audience as both Jews and Gentiles or Jews of the diaspora. Little is said about the content of John's teaching other than it was consistent with the other apostles (*Haer.* 2.22.5), is contained in John's writings, is about the plan of salvation, declares that there is one God who created heaven and earth and spoke by the law and the prophets, and that there is one Christ, the Son of God (*Haer.* 3.1.1–2; 3.11.1–2).

In sum, Irenaeus places John in Ephesus until the reign of Trajan (98 C.E.) and presents John as teaching doctrine that is consistent with the other apostles.

1.2 The Johannine Mission according to Revelation

The material in the book of Revelation is consistent with Irenaeus. Although the genre of the book of Revelation poses some difficulties for historical investigation, it is possible to ascertain some information from the epistlatory frame about the Johannine mission.

John wrote to the seven churches in Asia (1:4) from the island of Patmos (1:9). That is, John's base of operations, apparently due to exile (1:9), is in Asia and the letter he records to the seven churches commences first of all to the Ephesian church (2:1), which is where Irenaeus claims John resided until 98 C.E. Since these churches are in Asia, John's audience may have included Gentiles.[7] Yet the nature of the letter to the seven churches with its continual appeal to Old Testament themes, language, and characters assumes a familiarity with the Old Testament that warns against too readily ruling out any Jewish contingent in the audience. The missionary message contained in Revelation also bears similarities with the descriptions of John's message in Irenaeus but has some differences. There is one plan of salvation but it is Jesus's death and resurrection that achieves this salvation (1:5–6). Further, revelation contains some ethical

---

[7] The imperatival refrain at the end of each of the letters to anyone who has an ear to hear what the Spirit says to the churches (2:7, 11, 17, 29; 3:6, 13, 22) indicates that the audience is wider than just the seven churches named.

teaching in the closing (22:11, 15) and the teaching about the return of Christ to judge is more prominent (1:7; 22:12, 20) than the brief description of Irenaeus.

So from Revelation it appears that the Johannine mission was to Asia and as such may have had both Jews and Gentiles as its audience. The teaching discussed how Jesus's death and resurrection achieved the plan of salvation with the return of Christ to judge having a more prominent place than described in Irenaeus.

1.3 The Johannine Mission according to Acts

Even though John is not a main character in Acts, he is the second apostle listed (1:13) and often accompanies Peter in the opening chapters that deal with the Jewish mission in and around Palestine. From these references it is possible to glean a number of different pieces of information about his mission. The inadvertant mentioning of John in Acts makes this material historically reliable.

First, the descriptions of John occur in the context of the earliest churches' mission to Jews and Samaritans. John accompanies Peter to the temple to pray (3:1), is imprisoned by the priests and Sadducees (4:1), and appears before the Sanhedrin (4:5–7). Later, the Jerusalem apostles send John and Peter to Samaria to confirm the Samaritan acceptance of the Word of God (8:14). Further, John is described as preaching the gospel in Samaritan villages on his return trip to Jerusalem (8:25). The only other reference to John is to identify which James was killed by Herod in Jerusalem (12:1).[8]

Second, John's mission is located in Jerusalem and its surrounds. John is described as going to the temple to pray (3:1) and appearing before the Sanhedrin (4:5–7). Unlike the general church population in Jerusalem, John did not leave Jerusalem at the outbreak of persecution following Stephen's death (8:1). He went to Samaria (8:14) but returned to Jerusalem (8:25). There is no further reference to John in Acts so it is impossible to date John's movement from Jerusalem to Asia in general and Ephesus in particular.[9]

Third, John's missionary message is the same as the other apostles, in particular, Peter. Even though Peter is recorded as speaking in the incidents when Peter and John are together (3:12; 4:8), the narrator describes them both speaking (4:1) and teaching (4:2) the crowd. Further, even though the speech is put

---

8 There is another John referred to in Acts but, in order to avoid this second John being confused with John the apostle, he is idenfied as John Mark (12:12, 25; 13:5, 13; 15:37).

9 Ellis, *Making of the New Testament*, 234 argues from the use of Gospel traditions that the Johannine mission was probably based in southern Palestine until 60 C.E. because Luke uses common traditions with John when he was writing his Gospel during Paul's Caesarean imprisonment in 58–60 C.E.

into Peter's mouth, the speeches are riddled with the first person plural. It is both Peter and John who are the object of the crowd's inspection (ἡμῖν—3:12) and who witnessed the resurrection (ἡμεῖς μάρτυρές ἐσμεν—3:15). The Sanhedrin warns both of them not to speak or teach (4:17–18) and both Peter and John answer that they will not stop speaking (4:19–20). That is, Acts records Peter's speeches as representing the views of both Peter and John.

So, from Acts it can be concluded that John's mission was to Jews and Samaritans in and around Jerusalem with a message in common with the other apostles, in particular as a witness to the resurrection.

1.4 The Johannine Mission according to Paul

Paul only discusses John on one occasion, in his autobiographical material in Galatians 1–2. Again, the incidental reference to John means that the information is probably historical reliable.[10] Paul reveals three things about John and his mission.

First, Paul discloses that John's mission was to the Jews (or, more literally, to the "circumcision"). In Gal 2:1–10, Paul recounts his meeting with James, Cephas, and John, the "pillar" apostles (2:9), in order to discuss his gospel. The result of this meeting was recognition (ἰδόντες—2:7) about the intended mission audience of Paul, James, Cephas, and John. Paul was entrusted with the gospel to the uncircumcision (ἀκροβυστία) just as (καθὼς) Peter had been to the circumcision (περιτομή). Paul restates the position in 2:8–9 with respect not just to Peter but to James and John as well. Paul would go to the nations (τὰ ἔθνη—2:8, 9), while the other three apostles would go to the circumcised (περιτομή—2:8, 9). There is no geographical refinement, only the socio-religious description.

Second, though Paul does not always mention John in Jerusalem, he does speak of him being there as late as the middle of the century. Paul's first visit to Jerusalem resulted in his meeting with Cephas and James (1:18–19). There is no mention of John, and Paul is at pains to record every apostle who he met on that visit (1:19). Yet when describing his second visit to Jerusalem fourteen years later ("Επειτα διὰ δεκατεσσάρων ἐτῶν πάλιν ἀνέβην εἰς Ἱεροσόλυμα—2:1), Paul met John along with James and Cephas (2:9). The dating of Paul's second visit to Jerusalem according to Galatians is difficult. The sequence "Επειτα μετὰ ἔτη τρία ἀνῆλθον εἰς Ἱεροσόλυμα (1:18) ... "Επειτα διὰ δεκατεσσάρων ἐτῶν πάλιν ἀνέβην εἰς

---

10 Barnett, *Jesus and the Rise*, 300 states that this "passage, more than any other in the New Testament, explains the subsequent *actual* history of the apostolic age" (*emphasis* original).

Ἱεροσόλυμα (2:1) could be read either consecutively (17 years) or concurrently (14 years).[11] If the most conservative historical approach is followed then John was conducting a mission to the circumcision for at least 14 years prior to the Jerusalem meeting with the intention of continuing with this mission audience after meeting Paul. Since Paul's Damascus Road meeting of Jesus seems to be 34 C.E., then John was at mission among the Jews until at least 48 C.E.

Finally, the content of John's mission message appears to be the same as that of Paul and the other apostles. John was not involved in compelling Titus to be circumcised (2:3). Further, Paul's gospel message was not seen to be at odds with the other apostles but rather Paul argues it was the same with the difference being the mission audience (2:2, 7).[12] Additionally, Paul's ethical concern for the Jerusalem church matched their desires (2:10). That is, the message of John's mission with regards to salvation, law keeping, and ethical concern for the poor, seem in keeping with Paul.

So from Paul it seems that John's mission was to the socio-religious group known as the circumcision, was located in a geographical area within a short distance of Jerusalem, continued until at least 48 C.E., and contained the same gospel message as Paul.

1.5 Summary

Irenaeus indicated that John had Ephesus as his mission base until 98 C.E. and continued to teach the same message as the other apostles. This is consistent with Revelation where John was writing from Patmos to the seven Asian churches presumably made up of both Jews and Gentiles. The message was consistent with Irenaeus's record but added more explicit teaching about the return of Christ as judge. Though this was the endpoint of the Johannine mission, both Acts and Paul attest to the origin of the Johannine mission being

---

11   Those who read it consecutively include Frank J. Matera, *Galatians* (Collegeville, MN: Liturgical, 1992), 71; J.D.G. Dunn, *A Commentary on The Epistle to the Galatians* (London: A. & C. Black, 1993), 71; C.K. Barrett, *A Critical and Exegetical Commentary on the Acts of the Apostles* (2 vols.; ICC; Edinburgh: T&T Clark, 1998), 2:711. Those who understand it as concurrent include D. Wenham, "Acts and the Pauline Corpus, II. The Evidence of the Parallels," in *The Book of Acts in Its First Century Setting*. Vol. 1: *Ancient Literary Setting* (ed. B.W. Winter and A.D. Clarke; Grand Rapids: Eerdmans, 1993), 226–243; R. Bauckham, "James and the Jerusalem Church," in *The Book of Acts in Its First Century Setting*. Vol. 4: *Palestinian Setting* (ed. R. Bauckham; Grand Rapids: Eerdmans, 1995), 469–470; Douglas J. Moo, *Galatians* (Grand Rapids: Baker, 2013), 8–18.

12   Contra F.C. Baur, *Paul the Apostle of Jesus Christ: His Life and Works, His Epistles and Teaching* (repr., Peabody, MA: Hendrickson, 2003).

to Jews in and around Jerusalem. The mission remained in this location until at least Paul's second Jerusalem visit (48 C.E.) and had a message that was in accord with the other apostles—with Peter in the witness to the resurrection of Jesus and with Paul in respect to justification by faith, the place of the law and concern for the poor.

2 The Johannine Mission in 1 John

With this context established, the second part of this essay examines 1 John in order to ascertain what it reveals about the Johannine mission. It will focus on the issues of the identity of the opponents, the audience, and the message, because there is so little evidence about the location or the date, and because any decision about the location and the date is predicated on the placement of 1 John in the trajectory of the Johannine mission just outlined. So, for instance, if the opponents are identified as Docetic, then it is argued that 1 John was written late to affirm the incarnation to a Gentile audience who would have felt the pull of the Greek philosophy which undergirds Docetism.

2.1 *The Opponents and Audience*

The first explicit description of the opponents is in 1 John 2:18–23.[13] These antichrists have left the community (2:18–19) and deny the identification of Jesus with the title Christ (2:22). That they were once part of the community indicates that recognising them will help in answering the questions about the audience of the letter and the mission as a whole. Their denial is usually associated with Cerinthian teaching, Docetism, or some form of Gnosticism. However, this is unlikely.[14] There is better evidence to suggest that the opponents were Jews who denied the apostolic message that identified Jesus as the Christ.[15]

First, the syntax of the denial appears to indicate that the opponents were Jewish. Ascertaining the subject of an εἰμί clause is difficult but Goetchius,

---

13   J.M. Lieu, "'Authority to Become Children of God': A Study of 1 John," *NovT* 23 (1981): 211.

14   For an extended critical discussion of the opponents, see Daniel R. Streett, *They Went Out from Us: The Identity of the Opponents in First John* (BZNW 117; Berlin: de Gruyter, 2011), 5–111.

15   T. Griffith, *Keep Yourselves from Idols: A New Look at 1 John* (JSNTSup 233; London: Sheffield Academic, 2002); M.D. Jensen, *Affirming the Resurrection of the Incarnate Christ: A Reading of 1 John* (SNTSMS 153; Cambridge: Cambridge University Press, 2012), 107–135; B. Olsson, *A Commentary on the Letters of John: An Intra-Jewish Approach* (Eugene, OR: Pickwick, 2013).

Carson, and Porter seem correct when they argue that the subject is the arthrous noun.[16] Wallace is unconvincing in his critique of this position and in his suggestion that word order indicates the subject.[17] This is because Wallace relies on the premise that 1John was written to Gentiles on the basis of 5:21.[18] The appeal to 5:21 is not syntactical but rather historical and, as such, it begs the question because the historical situation can only be ascertained through a close examination of the syntax and the meaning that it conveys. Further, Griffith and Olsson have all demonstrated the plausibility of 1John being written to a Jewish audience without recourse to the syntax of 2:22.[19] Wallace's suggestion of using word order to ascertain the subject has one key text that indicates its unviability: John 5:15 contains the answer of the man whom Jesus healed: Ἰησοῦς ἐστιν ὁ ποιήσας αὐτὸν ὑγιή.[20] Under Wallace's word order rule, Ἰησοῦς is the subject of the clause.[21] However, from context the question that the healed paralytic is answering is not "who is Jesus" but who "made you well" (ὁ ποιήσας με ὑγιή—5:11). This requires ὁ ποιήσας αὐτὸν ὑγιή to be the subject and Ἰησοῦς the complement. The repeated vocabulary emphasizes the point and the word order directly contradicts Wallace's suggested new rule. This clause demonstrates the inconsistency of Wallace's word order suggestion.

So the syntax of 2:22 indicates that the subject of the clause Ἰησοῦς οὐκ ἔστιν ὁ Χριστός is ὁ Χριστός. That is, the denial of the antichrists is that the "Christ is Jesus." This clause should therefore be understood as addressing the question "Who is the Christ/Son of God?" a question that Carson argues reflects a Jewish concern.[22]

Second, those who denied the identification of Jesus as the Christ were understood to also deny the Father and the Son (2:22). Given the christological

---

16 E.V.N. Goetchius, "Review of *Towards a Descriptive Analysis of ΕΙΝΑΙ as a Linking Verb in New Testament Greek*," *JBL* 95 (1976): 147–149; D.A. Carson, "The Purpose of the Fourth Gospel: John 20:31 Reconsidered," *JBL* 106 (1987): 639–651; S.E. Porter, *Idioms of the Greek New Testament* (2nd ed.; Sheffield, JSOT Press, 1994), 109.
17 Daniel B. Wallace, *Greek Grammar Beyond the Basics: An Exegetical Syntax of the New Testament* (Grand Rapids: Eerdmans, 1996), 43–47.
18 Wallace, *Greek Grammar*, 46.
19 Griffith, *Keep Yourselves from Idols*, 171–179; Olsson, *The Letters of John*. See also Jensen, *Affirming the Resurrection*, 107–135 and Streett, *The Went Out from Us*, 157–166.
20 D.A. Carson, "Syntactical and Text-Critical Observations on John 20:30–31: One More Round on the Purpose of the Fourth Gospel," *JBL* 124 (2005): 711.
21 Wallace, *Greek Grammar*, 44.
22 Carson, "The Purpose of the Fourth Gospel," 643–646. Goethius, "Review," 148 notes the same syntactical construction is used in Acts in the context of the gospel being preached to Jews (5:42; 9:22; 17:3; 18:5, 28).

context, it is best to understand this Father/Son language against the backdrop of Ps 2:7, where God declares the Messiah to be his Son. When the apostate Jews who have left the community deny the identification of Jesus as the Christ, they are denying God the Father and his appointed Messiah. They cannot claim to have the Father (a Jewish claim, see Rom 2:17) because they deny his Son, and if they want to have the Father still, they need to confess his Son (John 2:23).

Third, the first person plural pronouns in 2:19 are usually understood to refer to "Christians." This assumes a clear distinction between "Christians" and "Jews"—a distinction that is not reported as occurring in the mind of the earliest church.[23] The "Christian" message started inside Judaism and was completely Jewish. The apostles were not starting a new religion (Christianity) but proclaiming the fulfilment of Judaism. It is anachronistic to read a clear distinction back into this verse. With this assumption removed, the first person plural in 2:19 can be understood to refer to Judaism. The author and his community thought that they were the one true version of Judaism and those who denied that "the Christ was Jesus" had left this true version to follow some other (in their view aberrant) form of Judaism. They never really belonged to Judaism because if they did they would have recognised the identity of Jesus as the Christ and seen in him the fulfilment of their Old Testament expectation.

Even with these reasons for identifying the opponents (and the audience) as Jewish, there are four common objections that need to be answered.

First, Brown argues that 1 John is not in the style expected for arguing with Jews since there is a lack of Old Testament quotations cited to support 1 John's argumentation.[24] The perceived absence of Old Testament quotations in 1 John is an argument from silence and, therefore, does not demonstrate Brown's critique. Further, the critique does not take into account the many Old Testament intertextual links or the extent of Jewish thought evident in 1 John. The discussion between Carson and Lieu demonstrates the growing acceptance that 1 John is dependent on the Old Testament.[25] Since 1 John displays Old

---

23   The distinction also does not appear explicitly in the Roman historians until Pliny (*Ep.* 10.96–97). Prior to Pliny, Nero's blaming of the fire of Rome on Christians (Tacitus, *Ann.* 15.44.2–5) may indicate that by 64 C.E. there was a difference between Christians and Jews but the disctinction was not evident in 49 C.E. when Claudius expelled the Jews from Rome over a dispute about Chrestus, i.e. Christ (Suetonius, *Claud.* 25.4).

24   R.E. Brown, *The Epistles of John* (AB 30; Garden City, NY: Doubleday, 1982), 52; J.A. du Rand, *Johannine Perspectives* (Johannesburg: Orion, 1991), 168.

25   D.A. Carson, "John and the Johannine Epistles," in *It is Written: Scripture citing Scripture* (ed. D.A. Carson and H.G.M. Williamson; Cambridge: Cambridge University Press, 1988), 256; J.M. Lieu, "What was from the Beginning: Scripture and Tradition in the Johannine

Testament influence and Jewishness in its exegetical methods, this objection to identifying the opponents as Jewish does not hold.

Second, Lieu argues that this "intriguing" identification, although "making sense of the scriptural echoes and parallels with other texts usually deemed 'Jewish,'" fails to explain why the author often describes "Jesus as the Son of the Father" and regularly places the term "Christ" in the context of discussion of Jesus's sonship.[26] This objection is not understood as a weakness when the Old Testament is appreciated as the matrix of reflection the author of 1John follows. The Father and Son language should be read in the context of Ps 2:7 where the Father God declares the Messiah to be his Son. This interpretation concords with Hengel's and Kruse's observation that, in 1John, the titles "Christ" and "Son of God" are both messianic and almost interchangeable.[27] That the discussion of 'the Christ' occurs in the context of Jesus being the Son of the Father (2:22–23) seems to support the identification of the opponents as Jewish rather than weaken it.

Third, 2:19 seems to indicate that the false teachers were once part of the group with John, not just non-Christian Jews.[28] This objection falls foul of the assumption that there are two different religions—Judaism and Christianity. If, as has been argued above, there were not two religions but one (Judaism), then it makes perfect sense for John to be referring to those who left as once part of the group.

Fourth, Jews would never claim to be sinless (1:8, 10) and would need no command to avoid idolatry (5:21). This fails to understand the problems of Israel depicted in the Old and New Testaments. Jeremiah 2:35 quotes the words of faithless Israelites who claim they have not sinned (LXX οὐχ ἥμαρτον), the same words used in 1John 1:10. Further, the Old Testament consistently warns against

---

Epistles," NTS 39 (1993): 459; D.A. Carson, "'You Have No Need that Anyone Should Teach You' (1John 2,27): An Old Testament Allusion that Determines the Interpretation," in *The New Testament in Its First Century Setting: Essays on Context and Background in Honour of B.W. Winter on His 65th Birthday* (ed. P.J. Williams, A.D. Clarke, P.M. Head, and D. Instone-Brewer; Grand Rapids: Eerdmans, 2004), 274.

26 J.M. Lieu, *I, II & IIIJohn: A Commentary* (Louisville: Westminster, 2008), 105–106. See also M. Morgen, *Les épîtres de Jean* (Paris: Cerf, 2005), 106–107 who argues that the concept of "Son" is the larger christological concept in 1John and determines the meaning of "Christ."

27 M. Hengel, *The Johannine Question* (London: SCM, 1989), 59; R. Schnackenburg, *The Johannine Epistles* (New York: Crossroad, 1992), 146; C.G. Kruse, *The Letters of John* (Grand Rapids: Eerdmans, 2000), 174.

28 I.H. Marshall, *The Epistles of St. John* (NICNT; Grand Rapids: Eerdmans, 1978), 17; Brown, *Epistles*, 52; Schnackenburg, *Epistles*, 18; Lieu, *I, II, IIIJohn*, 105.

idolatry (Exod 20:4; Lev 19:4; Deut 5:8) and condemns Israel when it commits idolatry (Isa 1:29; Ezek 6:4–13; 8:10; Hos 8:4–6). Additionally, the New Testament reports the claims of the 'rich young ruler' to have kept the law (Matt 19:20; Mark 10:20; Luke 18:21), and Paul describes his pre-conversion understanding of himself as being righteous and blameless (Phil 3:6). So neither of these objections weakens the identification of the opponents as faithless Jews who have left the true Israel. Rather they seem to support the contention because they demonstrate that these were issues faced by first-century Jews.

So, it seems best to identify the opponents as Jews who were rejecting the identification of Jesus with the promised Christ. As they were part of the community from which they departed, it appears that the audience was also Jewish. There is no indication whether this group is located in Palestine or is part of the diaspora. However, the lack of formal epistolary form could indicate that 1 John is a circular letter to which shorter letters (like 2–3 John) were appended for specific situations and thus the question of the geographical situation of the audience is moot.

2.2 *The Message of 1 John*

This essay will examine the message of 1 John on two levels. First, given this volume's interest in transmission of traditions, 1 John makes explicit references to a message that the audience had heard prior to the letter (2:7–8, 18, 24; 3:11; 4:3). Second, 1 John itself contains a message that is consistent with the teaching of the other Christian missions noted above.

2.2.1 The Traditional Message: 'What You Heard'

There are five places in 1 John where the author refers to a message that the audience has heard before. The content of this teaching can be grouped together into three topics: the commandment to love (2:7–8; 3:11), the coming of the antichrist (2:18; 4:3), and the resurrection of Jesus (2:24). Given that the audience was Jewish, some of these traditions may not refer to the missionary movement's preaching but to teaching associated with the Old Testament. A decision between these possibilities will be made in each case.

The first tradition that the audience has heard before the receipt of this letter is the old commandment (2:7). The audience has had this old commandment from the beginning but it is also a new commandment because in the new age marked by the passing of darkness and the dawning of light (2:8), the audience is now able to keep the commandment. In the context, this commandment is brotherly love (2:9–11). The commandment is drawn from Lev 19:18 which a Jewish audience would have heard repeatedly from the Old Testament but it is also new because Jesus not only obeyed the commandment (ἐν αὐτῷ "in him," 2:8) but also restated it in his teaching (John 13:34). This commandment is again referred to in 3:11 with the Old Testament example of Cain used to illustrate its content. So the first tradition that 1 John refers to is the commandment to love one's brothers—a tradition found in the Old Testament but realised in the Gospel traditions associated with Jesus, not just in the Johannine mission (John 13:34) but also in those associated with James (Matt 22:39–40), Peter (Mark 12:31–33), and Paul (Luke 19:27).

The second tradition that 1 John refers to is the teaching of a coming antichrist (2:18; 4:3). This antichrist will deny that the Christ is Jesus (2:22) and be unable to confess that Jesus is the Christ who came in flesh (4:2). The tradition is not located directly in the Old Testament since it is a refusal to identify Jesus with the office of the Christ. However, the opposition of people to God's chosen king is an Old Testament theme (Ps 2:1–3). Further, it also occurs in the Gospel tradition as recorded in the synoptics (Matt 24:24; Mark 13:22). 1 John may be the first occurrence of the word "antichrist" (ἀντίχριστος) and thus this may be one of distincitive teachings of the Johannine mission, but the concept has its roots in the Old Testament.

Finally, there is a reference to the message that the audience heard from the beginning. They are commanded to remain in this message with the promise that if they do, then they will remain in the Son and the Father (2:24). The message itself is not elaborated on further but in the context it has to do with the identification of Jesus with the Christ (2:22). In particular, the repeated vocabulary of 2:24 from the opening verses (1:1–3) seems to indicate that the message is the eyewitness testimony of the authors.[29] Since this message is "from the beginning," it likely indicates that the opening prologue contains a description of the authors mission message. The message is one of life (τοῦ λόγου τῆς ζωῆς) matching with the promise of eternal life referred to in 2:25. This life is not the incarnation as so commonly assumed but the testimony to the resurrection of the incarnate Christ.[30] The preaching of 1:1–3 contains material also recorded in the Gospel traditions associated with both John (20:19–29) and Luke (24:36–43).[31]

Thus, a close examination of 1 John reveals references to traditional material in its message. It draws on the Old Testament teaching about brotherly love and opposition to God's anointed but in both cases the tradition is understood in light of Jesus. The tradition also contained teaching about Jesus's physical

---

29 ἀπ' ἀρχῆς (1:1; 2:24 twice); ἀκούω (1:1, 3; 2:24 twice).
30 Jensen, *Affirming the Resurrection*, 62–72.
31 Note in particular the use of the verb ψηλαφάω (1 John 1:1; Luke 24:39).

resurrection ensuring eternal life. These traditions were evident in the messages of the other missionary movements.

2.2.2 1 John and the Other Apostolic Mission Messages

Paul, Luke, and Revelation describe the mission message of John. This section reviews what they depict and outlines areas in 1 John where this occurs.

First, Paul is at pains to state that his gospel is in agreement with the pillar apostles, in our case John (Gal 2:2, 7). In Galatians, Paul's gospel contains at least two key themes—justification by faith (2:16) and Jesus's death for sin (1:4; 2:20). Although 1 John does not contain teaching explicitly on justification, it does indicate that belief is the means by which someone is born of God (5:1) and overcomes the world (5:5). Further, Jesus's death in 1 John is the means of propitiation (2:2; 4:10) as his blood cleanses the audience from all sin (1:7). This teaching about Jesus's death for sin is not just consistent with Paul's gospel but is also in line with the recorded teaching of the Johannine mission in Acts 3:15, 18; 4:10; and Rev 1:5. Additionally, even though Paul does not explicitly mention the resurrection in his gospel summaries in Galatians (though see 1 Cor 15:3–11), both Acts and Revelation indicate that John taught about Jesus's resurrection. In Acts 3:15, Peter uses the first person plural pronoun to describe both him and John as witnesses to the resurrection (see also 4:10) and Revelation discusses Jesus's resurrection in 1:5. As previously discussed, 1 John affirms the resurrection of Jesus as part of its traditional material. It even does this in the same eyewitness language used in Acts.[32] Thus, 1 John contains the same gospel message described in Paul, Acts, and Revelation with regards to faith, the death of Jesus for sin, and the physical resurrection.

Second, Paul records that the pillar apostles did not compel Titus to be circumcised (Gal 2:3). This acceptance of the Gentiles into the plan of God without law obedience is not reflected in 1 John. In fact, there is no mention of circumcision or any of the normal Jew/Gentile issues that occur in the rest of the New Testament (e.g. food sacrificed to idols). Even though this is an argument from silence, its very omission may indicate that the audience was Jewish and had no issues about relating to Gentiles, a point which would fit with John's mission to the Jews and place 1 John early in the history of the Johannine mission. The only possible reference to Gentiles in the book could be in 1 John 2:2 where it states that Jesus died for not just the sins of the audience but those of the whole world. This nod in the direction of the Gentiles may mean that 1 John was written after Paul met with the pillar apostles in Jerusalem (48 C.E.).

---

[32] Jensen, *Affirming the Resurrection*, 71.

Third, Gal 2:10 records the directive of the pillar apostles for Paul to remember the poor. This same ethical concern is evident in 1 John's teaching about brotherly love (2:9–11) and is worked out specifically in the discussion of 3:16–18 that addresses supporting those brothers in need.

Finally, it was noted that Revelation emphasized Jesus's return to judge (1:7; 22:12, 20) in its mission's teaching. A similar teaching also occurs in 1 John 2:28–29 where Jesus is depicted as returning to the shame of some, and 4:17 where the day of judgment is discussed in the context of the confession that the Son of God is Jesus (4:15).

2.3 *Summary*

1 John appears to be written to a Jewish audience in the context of the denial of some Jews that the Christ is Jesus (2:22). The author explicitly uses some traditional teachings common to the other apostolic missions (the love commandment, the coming of antichrists, the physical resurrection). Additionally, the teaching attributed to the Johannine mission by Paul, Acts, and Revelation is generally evident in 1 John. The notable exception to this is any reference to circumcision or any other specifically Jewish practise that divided Jews from Gentiles.

3 Conclusion: The Place of 1 John in the Johannine Mission

The Johannine mission started in Jerusalem with a Jewish target audience. The apostle John seems to have worked in and around Jerusalem in southern Palestine until at least his meeting with Paul in 48 C.E. At some point after that, the mission moved base to Asia Minor (probably Ephesus) before John was exiled on the island of Patmos. This geographical movement seems to have broadened the target audience to include Gentiles, though not removing its original focus on Jews (in this case diaspora Judaism).

Since 1 John is written to Jews in the context of some faithless Jews denying that the Christ is Jesus, it would appear that 1 John was more likely written before the mission center moved to Asia and before the widening of the missionary audience. It was probably not written before the meeting with Paul in Jerusalem given its reference to Jesus's death being for both Jews and Gentiles (2:2).

Love One Another and Love the World: The Love Command and Jewish Ethics in the Johannine Community

Beth M. Stovell

The development of the "love command" in Jesus's teaching and its implementation in the early Christian community as a social boundary marker has been the topic of much discussion. Many locate this development within the Johannine corpus, particularly in the Johannine epistles, and argue that the "love command" functions in an exclusive fashion, reinforcing group identity. Yet one may ask whether these formulations have adequately considered the social context of the perpetuation of the "love command" in the Johannine community, particularly in relation to the ethics of the Jewish mission. Using conceptual mapping theories developed by Giles Fauconnier and Mark Turner and emotion theories developed by Zoltán Kövecses among others, this paper examines the conceptions of love, the law, and boundary line formation in Jewish literature of the Second Temple period to understand the social phenomenon occurring in the early Johannine community depicted in the "love command" in Johannine literature. Besides providing a new methodology to approach the love command in Johannine literature, this paper will argue that love in the Johannine epistles demonstrates a conception of love consistent with the ethics present in Hellenistic Judaism including the following conceptions: love is the fulfillment of the law, love is seen through compassion to others, love is shown in deeds and we do deeds because of love, love is a gift from God, love is serving in good-will without self-interest, love creates harmony and makes us children of God, and love is modeled by Jesus, who is a great leader of the faith.

This chapter will argue that applying emotion theory to the Johannine letters view of love demonstrates continuity with Jewish conceptions of emotions associated with love in the Second Temple period. While the Elder expresses these views of love within the context of the community, it is likely that love in relation to the law extended love outside the community via the Jewish notion of good works, modeled by Jesus in his ministry. The idea of love as a new "command" and the need to obey this command suggests coherence between notions of law and of love implicit in the Johannine community. Detailing major conceptions of love in the Second Temple period provides the grounding for the roots in the Hellenistic Judaism present in Johannine literature more broadly.

1 The "Love Command" in Johannine Scholarship

Before exploring the new theories suggested for analysis of the Johannine vision of love and law, we will first identify major trajectories in past scholarship around the "love command" specifically in assumptions about John's community related to the love command. Approaches to the love command in Johannine literature have often been deeply impacted by the approaches taken in the reconstruction of the Johannine community more generally as well what approaches to Johannine scholarship as a whole particular scholars have taken. In her overview of trends in Johannine literature more broadly, Gail O'Day identifies several trajectories within Johannine scholarship in the late twentieth century and focuses on the following categories: historical criticism, social world criticism, literary criticism and ideological criticism.[1] More recently, scholars like Tan Yak-hwee have described these trajectories in more detail and suggested new ways of formulating the Johannine community based on an awareness of postcolonial criticism.[2] One can line up each of these approaches alongside studies of the "love command" in Johannine literature.

1.1 *Historical Criticism and the Love Command*

Within the historical approach, we find studies of the love command as part of the debates around the formation of the Johannine community in the writings of Käsemann, Richter, Brown, and Martyn. Typically these studies focus more on the love command as a means to understand the history *behind* the Johannine community rather than as a topic to be engaged in itself. Scholars in following this perspective have often focused on the exclusive nature of love in Johannine literature. For example, Käsemann especially stressed the limitations of love in Johannine literature, pointing to passages like John 3:16 as later redactions.[3] Brown argued that the exclusive love that found in the Johannine literature points to the sectarian quality of the Johannine community, seeing a parallel with "narrower inner-communitarian concept of 'love' found in the Qumran community."[4]

---

[1] Gail R. O'Day, "Johannine Literature," in *The New Testament Today* (ed. Mark Allan Powell; Louisville, KY: Westminster/John Knox, 1999), 70–85.

[2] Yak-Hwee Tan, *Re-Presenting the Johannine Community: A Postcolonial Perspective* (Studies in Biblical Literature; New York: Peter Lang, 2008).

[3] Ernst Käsemann, *The Testament of Jesus: A Study of the Gospel of John in the Light of Chapter 17* (Philadelphia: Fortress, 1978), 59–61.

[4] Raymond E. Brown, *Epistles of John* (AB 30; Garden City, NY: Doubleday, 1982), 271–272.

Unfortunately, at times scholars have assumed that the conception of love itself in an almost propositional sense is already understood and is a means to a deeper history, rather than asking the question of how notions of love as an emotion were conceived in the Second Temple writings. Further, several scholars have leveled arguments against the selectivity of some of these form critical approaches. For example, Reinhartz's critique of Martyn's description of the Johannine communities' development falls into the camp of historical criticism; however, Reinhartz's reappraisal of the relationship between the Johannine community and its Jewish neighbors provides a new way of dealing with the Johannine community that opens the door for new appraisals of the love command.[5] Further, some scholars discussing Johannine ethics have questioned whether notion of sectarianism is the best way to approach the question of Johannine ethics.[6]

1.2 *Literary Criticism and the Love Command*

Literary criticism has been another approach to Johannine studies developing out of Alan Culpepper's work into a wide array of various forms of literary criticisms.[7] Often these literary approaches come as a response to the historical approach. For example, Francis Moloney develops his literary approach to love in John's Gospel in part as a response to previous historical approaches to love in the Johannine corpus. We see this in Moloney's introduction as he laments the more sectarian perspectives on the Johannine corpus and community that believe the call to love another has narrowed love in John's writings until it has "lost its breadth and limitlessness"[8] or become morally bankrupt (citing Jack T. Sanders).[9] In response, Moloney suggests a more robust view of Johannine

---

5 Adele Reinhartz, "The Johannine Community and Its Jewish Neighbors: A Reappraisal," in *What is John?* Vol. 2: *Literary and Social Readings of the Fourth Gospel* (ed. Fernando F. Segovia; Atlanta: Scholars Press, 1998), 111–138.

6 Johannes Nissen, "Community and Ethics in the Gospel of John," in *New Readings in John* (ed. Johannes Nissen and Sigfred Pedersen; Sheffield: Sheffield Academic, 1999), 194–212.

7 For further discussion of these trajectories in literary criticism and their developments since Culpepper, see Tom Thatcher and Stephen D. Moore, eds., *Anatomies of Narrative Criticism: The Past, Present, and Futures of the Fourth Gospel as Literature* (Society of Biblical Literature Resources for Biblical Study; Atlanta: Society of Biblical Literature, 2008).

8 Moloney quotes Herbert Preisker, *Das Ethos des Urchristentums* (Darmstadt: Wissenschaftlichte Buchgesellschaft, 1968), 205. See Francis J. Moloney, *Love in the Gospel of John: An Exegetical, Theological, and Literary Study* (Grand Rapids: Baker, 2013), 7.

9 See Moloney, *Love in the Gospel of John*, 7. Moloney cites Jack T. Sanders, *Ethics in the New Testament: Change and Development* (London: SCM, 1985), 91–100.

conceptions of love, but primarily focuses on this broader vision in the Gospel of John rather than its impact on the Johannine epistles.

Sjef van Tilborg provides one of the major monographs on love in the Johannine corpus within the arena of literary criticism, focusing specifically on love in the Fourth Gospel. Van Tilborg uses a narrative-critical approach. Ultimately, many scholars have found untenable van Tilborg's account of "imaginary homosexual behavior" that despite its name is nonetheless not actually homosexual, but in van Tilborg's explanation a form of pederastia, where love for the *pais* becomes initiation for entry into God's love. Notably some have critiqued the model of relationships between men and women that van Tilborg assumes.[10]

The difficulties with these literary approaches to the "love command" in Johannine literature is that they often limit their scope to focusing primarily on how love is depicted within the narrative construction of the biblical text and do not spend as much time exploring how love as an emotion would have been understood in that ancient context and thus impacting the way love is conceived within the narrative. These approaches can at times also devalue the place of culture alongside history as means of more deeply understanding the conception of love.

1.3 Sociocultural Criticism and the Love Command

Among the early scholars to use sociocultural criticism regarding the construction of the Johannine community and its developing symbolism, Wayne Meeks in his 1972 article "The Man from Heaven in Johannine Sectarianism" views Johannine symbolism as sectarian and ultimately anti-Jewish. According to Meeks, the Jews are the ones who are "from below" ignorant of Jesus's identity, unlike Jesus himself as seen in Jesus's encounter with Nicodemus in John 3. As Meeks explains, the motif of ascent and descent serves a purpose in creating an exclusivist vision for the Johannine community "demolishing the logic of the world, particularly the world of Judaism, and progressively emphasizing the sectarian consciousness."[11]

---

10 Sjef Van Tilborg, *Imaginative Love in John* (BibInt; Leiden: Brill, 1993), 248. Among those who have questioned the validity of van Tilborg's finding, see Ismo Dunderberg, "The Beloved Disciple in John: Ideal Figure in an Early Christian Controversy," in *Fair Play: Diversity and Conflicts in Early Christianity* (ed. Ismo Dunderberg, Christopher Tuckett, and Kari Syreeni; NovTSup 103; Leiden, Brill, 2002), 243–272, 262 n. 72. Tan critiques this model that Tilborg claims is democratic, yet Tan notes that Tilborg's model is patriarchal and hierarchical in its very nature, thus eschewing equal role of women in this "democracy." See Tan, *Re-Presenting the Johannine Community*, 23–24.

11 Wayne A. Meeks, "The Man from Heaven in Johannine Sectarian," *JBL* 19 (1972): 71.

While Meeks's approach does not focus specifically on the conception of love in the Johannine literature, his sociocultural assumptions regarding the Johannine community in their exclusivist and sectarian directions provides the foundation for other sociocultural approaches that do address the concept of love. For example, Malina and Rohrbaugh provide a sociocultural approach to the love command in Johannine literature. Malina and Rohrbaugh argue that the language of love/hate is part of the "anti-language" strategies employed by the "anti-society" community.[12] Malina and Rohrbaugh argue that this anti-language serves two purposes: to maintain social cohesion and inner group identity and to "resocialize" group members with a different ideology from the surrounding social world as a way of creating "emotional anchorage."[13]

The value of sociocultural criticism is its ability to examine the concept of love as more than simply a literary convention and to think carefully about the impact of sociocultural patterns on the biblical text. However, the downside of these approaches is that they apply analysis of modern sociocultural phenomena to ancient contexts to understand the conceptions of love in those ancient contexts, which can at times lead to assumptions around similar conceptions of love to our modern conceptions. This study will suggest an alternative way to approach the Johannine community's conception of love.

1.4 Ideological Criticism and the Love Command

Gail O'Day uses a feminist approach to discuss the Johannine community and uses the love command as part of her ideological critique. In her article on John for the *Women s Bible Commentary*, O'Day argues that the love command functions in a positive manner joining together men and women. She describes the key role of loving one another as a means of transforming the community. While this love command is sectarian in O'Day's view, it is nonetheless a source of liberation.[14] Similarly, Tan uses a postcolonial

---

12   Love/hate are one of these "anti-language" pairings along with above/below, life/death, and light/darkness. For discussion of the "love/hate" pairing, see Bruce J. Malina and Richard L. Rohrbaugh, *Social-Science Commentary on the Gospel of John* (Minneapolis: Augsburg Fortress, 1998), 86–88. Similarly, Joan Campbell builds on and refines Malina's notion of the Johannine community as an anti-society and Michael Halliday's notion of anti-language to describe kinship relations in the Johannine community. See Joan Campbell, *Kinship Relations in the Gospel of John* (CBQMS; Washington, DC: Catholic Biblical Association of America, 2007). For her discussion of anti-language and anti-society, see pp. 163–180.

13   Malina and Rohrbauch, *Social-Science Commentary of the Gospel of John*, 7.

14   Gail R. O'Day, "John," in *Women s Bible Commentary: Expanded Edition with Apocrypha* (ed. Carol A. Newsom and Sharon H. Ringe; Louisville: Westminster John Knox, 1998), 390–393.

approach to demonstrate how the love command in John's Gospel becomes a means to bring the marginalized disciples back to the center, who is Jesus. The love command, according to Tan, includes both obedience and dependence as demonstrated in passages like John 15.[15] Tan argues that the love command becomes a notion of self-identity for the early Christian community because it is embodied in the love of Jesus to others. As Tan explains, "therefore, the community is thrust an identity, one patterned after Jesus, and, in so doing, they claim their marginality and validate the claim from the 'center,' namely Jesus."[16] Using post-colonial concepts, Tan explains how this reciprocal love is "vital and empowering in light of the foreboding reality of the hatred of the 'world' (15:18–27)." Tan argues that through this love, the community finds strength to resist the 'world' and comes to learn "about themselves, their relationships to each other and their place in the world." Tan further argues that this reciprocal love "organizes social existence and social reproduction" of the Johannine community.[17]

In contrast, other feminist scholars and other forms of ideological critics have seen the love command as primarily upholding the patriarchal status quo and not encouraging equal treatment to women and/or marginalizing other people groups.[18] Some have responded with feminist readings of Johannine literature as a means to correct these problems. For example, Adele Fehribach, in *The Women in the Life of the Bridegroom*, argues that Mary, the mother of Jesus, could be seen as a "woman who works within the cultural constrains of her time to accomplish the 'love command'" through her praxis-oriented approach to the situation at Cana in John 3.

In *Love Commands in the New Testament*, Pheme Perkins focuses on the love commands as a means to examine New Testament ethics. Her chapter "God as Love: The Johannine Tradition" provides both negative and possible positive readings of the "love command" in Johannine literature. While Perkins notes the seemingly exclusive nature of the love command in Johannine literature and the internal focus of the Johannine community, Perkins also

---

15 Tan, *Re-Presenting the Johannine Community*, 123–132.
16 Here Tan cites Gayatri Chakravorty Spivak, *Outside in the Teaching Machine* (New York: Routledge, 1993), 55. See Tan, *Re-Presenting the Johannine Community*, 181.
17 Tan here quotes Bill Ashcroft, Gareth Griffiths, and Helen Tiffin, *Post-Colonial Studies: The Key Concepts* (London: Routledge, 2000), 71. Tan, *Re-Presenting the Johannine Community*, 181.
18 Tan provides a helpful overview of these positions in Tan, *Re-Presenting the Johannine Community*, 31–40.

suggests several ways in which the love commands in the Johannine literature can be located within their cultural context pointing to a broader scope to the love command. First, Perkins associates the love command as Jesus's testament in ways that overlap with the testaments in Hellenistic Jewish wisdom traditions.[19] (This insight will be explored in more depth in our discussion of the conceptualization of love in Hellenistic Judaism below.) As Perkins notes, "there are suggestions of a somewhat more universal scope to the love of the Johannine community"; towards this end she points to two characteristics that suggest this scope: (1) "formulation of the double command in 1Jn 4:21" which suggests that "neighbor" could "anyone with whom one has dealings"[20] and (2) the evangelistic vision of God as love "directed toward the salvation of the whole world (Jn 3:16; 1Jn 4:9f., 14)."[21] This suggests that while ideological criticism and criticism that focuses on ethics provide interpretations of the Johannine love command is sometimes contradictory perspectives, some of these approaches provide the same for some universal application to the love command alongside the traditional view of the love command as purely internally focused.

1.5 Law and Love and Linguistic Approaches to Love

Besides these various forms of criticism that impact past scholarship on the love command in Johannine literature, the distinction between love and law in the Johannine epistles can often be impacted by a scholar's preconceived notions of the distinction between law and gospel. While in his commentary on 1–3 John, David Rensberger acknowledges that action necessarily comes out of love, Rensberger makes a strong distinction between love and law. Rensburger makes the point abundantly clear as he states, "This is the good news, the gospel message, according to the Johannine letters: God is love, God sent Jesus into the world out of love, and we now have an opportunity to love. For the elder, love is not law, but gospel."[22]

Similarly, Rensberger describes the exclusivism of the command to love in his article on Johannine ethics in such a way that it leads other scholars like Philip Tite to speak of "the eliticism of the Fourth Gospel's love theology" citing

---

19 Pheme Perkins, *Love Commands in the New Testament* (New York: Paulist, 1982), 104–105.
20 Here Perkins cites Rudolf Schnackenburg, *Das Johannesbriefe* (Freiburg: Herder, 1970), 121–122. See Perkins, *Love Commands in the New Testament*, 120.
21 Perkins, *Love Commands in the New Testament*, 120.
22 David Rensberger, *The Epistles of John* (Westminster Bible Companion; Louisville: Westminster John Knox, 2001), 5.

Rensberger's article as his source.²³ However, it is certainly worth noting that Rensberger's approach does not cast the Johannine community as the "elite," but as the oppressed.²⁴

Yet Rensberger's approach appears to miss the intricate overlap between love of one's neighbor as a key outworking of the law itself and appears to assume that law and gospel must be opposing ideas rather than that some aspect of the law could be seen as essential to the gospel message itself. This is unfortunate because it causes one to question whether the "love command" is indeed a "command" at all, in the sense this word is used elsewhere in Scripture in relation to the Law.

Besides separating love and law from one another, another recurring problem is that love is most commonly approached at the word level for analysis. Due to the extensive works of Spicq and Nygren discussing love from a linguistic perspective at the word level,²⁵ much of Johannine study has long depended on these studies of love as foundational for their understandings of love in Johannine literature. These approaches received substantial criticism from James Barr among others. James Barr's essay on the words for love in biblical Greek provides helpful clarity on the use of the term love in the LXX while also unraveling previous arguments that assumed both that the LXX and the New Testament usage of the Greek word ἀγάπη is largely unique. Instead Barr argues that the gap between ἀγάπη and φίλος is not as broad as thought and that what we find in the LXX is the following: "Basically, however, we are saying that within the LXX the choice of was a feature of continuity with contemporary usage, and not least of contemporary religious usage; the effort to portray it as a supreme example of discontinuity was completely wrong."²⁶

While noting the criticisms of Barr and others, recent studies on love have still often assumed this stance less critically than is warranted. Varghese in his

---

23   Tite cites David Rensberger, "Love for One Another and Love for Enemies in the Gospel of John," in *Love of Enemy and Nonretaliation in the New Testament* (Louisville, KY: Westminster John Knox, 1992). See Philip L. Tite, *Conceiving Peace and Violence: A New Testament Legacy* (Lanham, MD: University Press of America, 2004), 92 n. 64.

24   David Rensberger, "Oppression and Identity in the Gospel of John," in *Recovery of Black Presence* (Nashville: Abingdon, 1995), 77–94; David Rensberger, *Johannine Faith and Liberating Community* (Philadelphia: Westminster, 1988), 117–124.

25   See Anders Nygren, *Agape and Eros* (trans. Philip S. Watson; Philadelphia: Fortress, 1953); Ceslaus Spicq, *Agape in the New Testament* (trans. Marie Aquinas McNamara and Mary Honoria Richter; 3 vols.; St. Louis: Herder, 1963–1966).

26   See James Barr, "The Word Love in Biblical Greek," in *The Glory of Christ in the New Testament: Studies in Christology in Memory of George Bradford Caird* (ed. L.D. Hurst and N.T. Wright; Oxford: Clarendon, 1987), 3–18.

Imagery of Love in the Gospel of John attempts to correct this by looking at love at the level of imagery, but does not use theories of emotion or metaphor as effectively as might have been beneficial to overturn the typical approach, and includes a section that depends on the *TDNT* and *TDOT* definitions that suffer from many of the same errors critiqued by Barr. Rather than using recent theories of imagery, metaphor, or emotion studies, Varghese instead maintains a tradition approach incorporating linguistic, syntactical, semantic, narrative analysis alongside historical-critical analysis. Varghese focuses on three images used in relation to love: bridegroom-bride, friendship, covenant.[27] Yet these three images are not all the images used in relation to love in the Johannine literature, nor are they the ones more readily apparent in the Johannine epistles (the focus of this paper). In contrast to many of these studies, this study will provide an important distinction between studying the word "love" or ἀγαπάω and studying the conception of love in the Second Temple period by clarifying the levels of emotion moving above the word level to the level of metaphor and discourse. It will also incorporate recent emotion theories as a means of providing additional insight into the study of the Johannine depiction of love.

1.6 Conclusions

Approaches to the "love command" in the Johannine corpus and community have tended to develop out of the approaches that biblical criticism scholars are appropriating to address the question. At times, scholars how are focused on historical critical analysis have studied love in the Johannine corpus through complex analysis of the Johannine communities' historical development. In these historical studies, there has often been a reciprocal relationship between, on the hand, the perceived attitudes of the community related to love within the community versus to those outside the community and, on the other hand, how the community included or rejected neighboring parties whether Jews, Jewish Christians, or other religious groups derived from Judaism or Christianity (e.g., Johannine sectarianism, Johannine docetism, Johannine gnosticism, etc.). The problem with these studies is that they can at times become circular: our analysis tells us that the Johannine community had a particular vision of love that we deduce impacts their community development, but by the same evidence we deduce that the community development tells us what the vision of love for the community was.[28] Such circularity suggests the need for a new approach to the question of the "love command."

---

27   John Varghese, *Imagery of Love in the Gospel of John* (AnBib; Rome: Gregorian and Biblical Press, 2009).

28   An example of this is the following logic: We know the Johannine community is sectar-

Further these approaches leave several remaining questions: What has been the impact on Johannine scholarship of refinements in understanding Hellenistic Judaism? How was the emotion of love conceived? How did love relate to conceptions of the law and the double command in the Synoptics? If the Johannine corpus represents a form of Jewish Christianity, how do recent studies of Jewish ethics and Jewish Christianity impact Johannine study? These questions will be examined as part of the exploration of a new method to the love command.

2 A New Approach to the "Love Command" in Johannine Literature

In view of the past history of approaches to the "love command" in Johannine scholarship, this chapter suggests a new approach that utilizes recent studies of emotion and its impact on social identity and relates this to recent work on Jewish ethics within Jewish Christianity. First, we identify some of the recent developments in studies of emotions and social identity that provide the foundations for this new approach to the "love command." Next, we examine the major steps involved in analyzing the conceptions of love and law in relation to the ethics of the Jewish mission.

2.1 *Developments in Emotion Studies and Social Identity*

Recently discussions in the field of cognitive linguistics have begun providing illuminating insights into the study of biblical texts.[29] This approach has impacted the study of metaphor in biblical study, but as some scholars like Janet Soskice have pointed out, the study of Scripture offers numerous spaces for analysis of imagery because theology itself is described through the use of abstract language. Abstract language by its very nature is necessarily described in terms of metaphorical language. Love is one of the abstract terms used

---

ian, thus their vision of love represents these sectarian conceptions of love and we know that the Johannine community is sectarian based on our analysis of their conceptions of love.

[29] Examples include Anne Moore, *Moving beyond Symbol and Myth: Understanding the Kingship of God of the Hebrew Bible through Metaphor* (Studies in Biblical Literature; New York: Peter Lang, 2009), 216–258; Bonnie Howe, *Because You Bear This Name: Conceptual Metaphor and the Moral Meaning of 1 Peter* (BibInt; Leiden: Brill, 2006); P. van Hecke, "Conceptual Blending: A Recent Approach to Metaphor Illustrated with the Pastoral Metaphor in Hos 4:16," in *Metaphor in the Hebrew Bible* (ed. P. van Hecke; BETL; Leuven: University Press/Peeters, 2005), 215–231.

throughout Scripture to explore the relationship within the Godhead, the relationship within the Christian community, and the relationship between the Christian community and the world around it. Thus, applying cognitive modes of analysis are helpful to understand not only how love is *explained* within biblical literature, but also how love was *conceptualized* by those writing biblical literature and in the cultures that surrounded them.

Recent studies on emotion have explored how emotions are conceived, how cross-cultural experiences impact conceptions of emotion, and how the conceptualization of emotions is related to social identity. Zoltán Kövecses has spent his academic career exploring the conceptualization of emotions. His research has impacted disciplines across the humanities including (but not limited to) anthropology, economics, archaeology, history, and religion. Most pertinent for our study is Kövecses's study of the metaphors of emotion. In *Metaphor and Emotion*, Kövecses ranks basic emotion terms ranked in relation to one another (vertical hierarchy of concepts: emotion, anger, annoyance; similarly one might rank emotion, love, expressions related to love). Kövecses has explored how love is conceptualized in the English language through love metaphors.[30]

The strength of Kövecses's work is that it provides a foundation for comparison across cultures for how emotion metaphors are conceived. However, a limitation of Kövecses's early research is that it tends to locate emotion metaphors generally (and thereby love metaphors specifically) using only a target and source model. This tends to limit discussions of love metaphors to single types of metaphors (e.g., love is a journey, love is a physical force, etc.) rather than to show how conceptions of love work alongside other conceptual metaphors. Thus, to more fully understand the conceptualizations of metaphors of emotion and in our case the conception of love, it is helpful to team the early work of Kövecses with the research of Giles Faucconier and Mark Turner who have argued that conceptual metaphors are often blended to create new

---

30   This is particularly developed in Kövecses, *Metaphor and Emotion: Language, Culture, and Body in Human Feeling* (Studies in Emotion and Social Interaction; Paris: Editions de la Maison des sciences de l'homme, 2000), 26–29. Kövecses also discusses love metaphors in his earlier works. See Zoltán Kövecses, *The Language of Love: The Semantics of Passion in Conversational English* (Lewisburg, PA: Bucknell University Press, 1988); Zoltán Kövecses, "A Linguist's Quest for Love," *Journal of Social and Personal Relationships* 8 (1991): 77–97, which develop a study of love metaphors specifically, and Zoltán Kövecses, *Emotion Concepts* (New York: Springer-Verlag, 1990); Kövecses, *Metaphors of Anger, Pride, and Love: A Lexical Approach to the Structure of Concepts* (Pragmatics & Beyond; Philadelphia: Benjamins, 1986).

conceptual frameworks.[31] This process of analyzing the blends of different conceptual metaphors is described as "conceptual mapping."[32]

2.2 Social Identity and Emotions

While there has been some work in New Testament study on the relationship between social identity and emotions and an even smaller amount of focused work on social identity in relation to love in the Johannine corpus specifically,[33] much of this analysis has not had the advantage of recent developments in identifying intergroup emotions and on studying the sociology of emotions. Recent studies have distinguished between individual emotion studies and intergroup emotions. In the modern Western context of many interpreters, there is a tendency to think in terms of individual emotions (based on impact of Enlightenment individualism). However, within ancient contexts, it is often more accurate to discuss how we understand communal intergroup emotions. We see the necessity of this because of the consistent use of plural forms related

---

31 Kövecses identifies the value of this work in his second edition of his introduction to metaphor. See Zoltan Kövecses, *Metaphor: A Practical Introduction* (2nd ed.; New York: Oxford University Press, 2010). See also *VLLXX: Papers Presented to László Varga on his 70th Birthday* (ed. Péter Szigetvári; Eötvös Loránd University, Budapest, 2013) html: http://seas3.elte.hu/VLlxx/.

32 See Kövecses's discussion of these developments: http://seas3.elte.hu/VLlxx/kovecses.html.

33 Raimo Hakola has examined social identity in the New Testament broadly and specifically in the Johannine community in Raimo Hakola, "The Counsel of Caiaphas and the Social Identity of the Johannine Community (John 11:47–53)," in *Lux Humana, Lux Aeterna* (Göttingen: Finnish Exegetical Society; Vandenhoeck & Ruprecht, 2005), 140–163; Hakola, *Identity Matters: John, the Jews and Jewishness* (NovTSup 118; Leiden: Brill, 2005); Hakola, "Social Identities and Group Phenomena in Second Temple Judaism," in *Explaining Christian Origins and Early Judaism: Contributions from Cognitive and Social Science* (ed. Petri Luomanen, Ilkka Pyysiäinen, and Risto Uro; BibInt; Leiden: Brill, 2007), 259–276; Hakola, "The Johannine Community as Jewish Christians? Some Problems in Current Scholarly Consensus," in *Jewish Christianity Reconsidered* (ed. Matt A. Jackson-McCabe; Minneapolis: Fortress, 2007), 181–201; Hakola, "The Burden of Ambiguity: Nicodemus and the Social Identity of the Johannine Christians," *NTS* 55 (2009): 438–455; Hakola, "The Reception and Development of the Johannine Tradition in 1, 2 and 3 John," in *Legacy of John: Second-Century Reception of the Fourth Gospel* (NovTSup 132; Leiden: Brill, 2010), 17–47. The *T & T Clark Handbook to Social Identity in the New Testament* provides a helpful overview of some of the ways social identity has been explored in New Testament studies including an article by Rikard Roitto on love and social identity in 1 John. See *T & T Clark Handbook to Social Identity in the New Testament* (ed. J. Brian Tucker and Coleman A. Baker; New York: T&T Clark, 2014).

to love and other emotions. Thus it is helpful to learn from recent analysis of the sociological aspects of emotions and valuable to think about intergroup dynamics related to love in recent work on intergroup emotions.[34]

Among the key elements recently developed in studies of emotions in psychology and within cognitive linguistics is the relationship between emotions and ethics. While it is not possible to rehearse here the entire history of philosophy related to emotion and ethics (which is extensive),[35] it is helpful to state a few misconceptions that have developed out of certain philosophical understandings of emotions in relation to ethics. This helps to demonstrate how emotions have been misunderstood as purely subjective and separate from reason, and how ethics have long been seen as necessarily determined based on reason with a strong distrust of emotions in relation to ethics. However, recent studies on emotion have emphasized that the divide between emotion and reason is actually an arbitrary one that is not backed up philosophically or scientifically and that the notion of ethics as ever purely a matter of reason devoid of emotion is faulty logic and thereby impossible.

2.3   *Studying Emotions in Scripture*

Several recent studies have examined the role of emotions in Scripture with an awareness of recent advancements in our understanding of emotion in the spheres of psychology and cognition.[36] Within biblical studies, some studies have developed out of Kövecses's work. For example, a recent article explores anger in the Old Testament and its implications for research on emotions in Scripture.[37] Among these works, some of the prominent studies exploring emotion in the New Testament are by Matthew Elliott. In his monograph, *Faithful Feelings: Rethinking Emotion in the New Testament*, Elliott delves into the complexities of recent studies of emotion to show their value both in the New Testament and in subsequent interpretations of the New Testament. Specifically,

---

34   See Eliot R. Smith and Diane M. Mackie, "Intergroup Emotions," in *Handbook of Emotions*, (ed. Michael Lewis, Jeannette M. Haviland-Jones, and Lisa Feldman Barrett; New York: Guilford Press, 2010), 428–439.

35   See Robert C. Solomon, "The Philosophy of Emotions," in *Handbook of Emotions*, 3–16.

36   See Matthew A. Elliott, *Faithful Feelings: Rethinking Emotion in the New Testament* (Grand Rapids: Kregel, 2006).

37   See E.J. van Wohlde, "Sentiments as Culturally Constructed Emotions: Anger and Love in the Hebrew Bible," *BibInt* 16 (2008): 1–24; Zacharias Kotzé, "A Cognitive Linguistic Approach to the Emotion of Anger in the Old Testament," *HTS* 60 (2004): 843–862; Paul A. Kruger, "A Cognitive Interpretation of the Emotion of Anger in the Hebrew Bible," *JNSL* 26 (2000): 181–193.

Elliott's work on love as an emotion and the value of carefully considering how we explain the nature of this emotion provides a jumping off point for revisiting how notion of love have been explained previously related to the Johannine corpus.[38]

Unlike previous discussions of emotions and particularly love that separate emotions from reason, Elliott provides a different way of understanding 1John that will prove helpful to this study. Elliott's approach sees love in 1John as packaging the conception of love with knowledge and action. As Elliott explains,

> I will argue that the facts point to the total interconnectedness and interdependence of emotion and reason (Elliott, 2005). This interconnectedness is clearly seen in how the New Testament handles emotion. For example, in 1John, knowledge, love, and action are packaged together. True knowledge results in genuine love and right action flows out of genuine love. John does not see love as knowledge or as action; rather, the three—love, knowledge, action—are linked together in a unified and interdependent whole (Brown, 1982; Carson, 2000; Marshall, 1978). Interpreters have often mistakenly belittled or excluded emotional love from the triad, based on their world view when the biblical text points to emotion as absolutely essential.[39]

Extending Elliott's initial remarks on 1John to a more extensive study of the concepts associated with emotion in Second Temple Judaism and early Christianity allows for greater exploration of how love was conceptualized within Johannine literature and the ability to examine how this may have impacted social dynamics in the Johannine community. This will entail an exploration of how law and love are related within Second Temple Judaism and early Christianity. As noted above, emotions and ethics are related concepts and thus this examination of love naturally leads to a discussion of how these conceptions of love and law impacted the ethics of the Jewish mission and Johannine literature.

2.4   Ethics of the Jewish Mission in Relation to Law and Love

The tendency described above within Johannine scholarship to separate love from law (and emotion from reason as noted in discussions of past scholarship

---

38   See Matthew A. Elliott, "The Emotional Core of Love: The Centrality of Emotion in Christian Psychology and Ethics," *Journal of Psychology and Christianity* 31 (2012): 105–117.

39   See Elliott, "The Emotional Core of Love," 109.

on emotion) has caused some scholars to miss the intricacies of conceptual relations between love and law as related to the ethics of the Jewish mission and as related to the Johannine corpus. Yet recent studies have explored the relationship between the Johannine corpus and the Jewish mission highlighting how Johannine literature reflects tendencies of Hellenistic Judaism grouping it with other biblical texts of Hellenistic Judaism such as James and Hebrews.[40] For example, Perkins discusses how Johannine literature appears to echo much of Hellenistic Jewish wisdom writings in describing love as Jesus's testament similar to Testament of Joseph, etc.[41] The subsequent section will explore conceptions of love and law in relation to the ethics of the Jewish mission by exploring conceptions of love, the law, and boundary line formation in Jewish literature of the Second Temple period. This will provide grounding for discussing the conceptualization of love and Law in Johannine literature, depicted in the "love command" and related passages.

3 Conceptions of Love and Law in Second Temple Judaism

In order to analyze the conception of love in Second Temple Judaism, initial work needs to be done to discuss the universality of emotion in comparison to cultural specificity, then the group specificity, then individual specificity of a conception of emotion.[42] Kövecses provides a helpful clarification that he is focused on descriptions of love rather than expressions of love.[43] Some researchers have suggested based on cross-cultural research that love is among five general and possibly universal emotions present in 11 languages

---

40   Cynthia Long Westfall, "The Hebrew Mission: Voices from the Margins?" in *Christian Mission: Old Testament Foundations and New Testament Developments* (ed. Stanley E. Porter and Cynthia Long Westfall, MNTS; Eugene, OR: Pickwick, 2011), 187–207.
41   Perkins, *Love Commands in the New Testament*, 104–105.
42   There have been a variety of studies on cross cultural emotion metaphors. For a survey and for an analysis of Chinese and English emotion metaphors, see Chapter 3 "Emotion Metaphors," in *The Contemporary Theory of Metaphor: A Perspective from Chinese* (ed. Ning Yu; Human Cognitive Processing Series; Philadelphia: Benjamins, 1998), 49–82. See also Kövecses's discussion of universality in the conceptualization of emotions in Chapter 8 of Kövecses, *Metaphor and Emotion*, 139–163 and cultural variation in the conceptualization of emotions in Chapter 9 of Kövecses, *Metaphor and Emotion*, 164–181. Kövecses discusses these ideas in greater detail in Kövecses, *Metaphor in Culture: Universality and Variation* (Cambridge: Cambridge University Press, 2005).
43   Kövecses, *Metaphor and Emotion*, 2–3. Examples of expressions of emotions in English could be "yuk!" for disgust or "wow" for feeling enthusiastic or impressed.

along with happiness, sadness, anger, and fear.[44] However, this cross-cultural research has demonstrated that while these emotions may be universal the *conception* of these emotions and the *descriptions* of these emotions vary from culture to culture. Within Second Temple Hellenistic Judaism, the conception of love includes the following concepts: (1) Love encourages mercy in God and is shown through mercy to others; (2) Love is enacted through deeds and these deeds garner love from God; (3) Love is the fulfillment of the law; (4) Love is a crown upon the head; (5) The sign of love is selflessness; (6) Love is a gift from God and the power of piety comes from love; (7) Love makes us children of God (family metaphors); (8) Love is directed by the divine word/the Law of Moses and leads to the right path.

Examining a variety of literature from within Second Temple Judaism, we find a variety of examples in which love and law appear to be conceptually related with one another. For example, we find love for one's neighbor or brothers associated with fulfillment of the law.[45] The diversity of dating of these texts provides evidence on both sides of the Johannine corpus's creation of a similar perspective on love and law, in which Christian additions to Jewish texts appear to generally be in continuity with Jewish texts prior to the Jewish-Christian split. Notably several of these conceptions of love include the notion of law as related to love.

3.1 Love is Also Seen through Compassion or Mercy to Others (*Love and Deeds, Actions*)

These appear to echo Deuteronomic laws related to loving God and showing mercy to others. The Psalms of Solomon are usually dated to the first century B.C.E.[46] There is much on the Psalms of Solomon that discuss God's love for us and our response of love toward him in relation to our response to God's law.

---

44 Nico H. Frijda, Suprapti Markam, Kaori Sato, and Reinout Wiers, "Emotions and Emotion Words," in *Everyday Conceptions of Emotion: An Introduction to the Psychology, Anthropology and Linguistics of Emotion* (ed. James A. Russell et al.; Nato Asi Series; Series D: Behavioural and Social Sciences 81; Dordrecht, The Netherlands: Kluwer, 1994), 121–143.

45 Adele Yarbro Collins highlights the relationship between these passages and the double love command in Mark's Gospel. See Adele Yarbro Collins, "The Reception of the Torah in Mark: The Question of the Greatest Commandment," in *Pentateuchal Traditions in the Late Second Temple Period: Proceedings of the International Workshop in Tokyo, August 28–31, 2007* (ed. Akio Moriya and Gōhei Hata; JSJSup 158; Leiden: Brill, 2012), 227–242.

46 Kenneth Atkinson, *I Cried to the Lord: A Study of the Psalms of Solomon's Historical Background and Social Setting* (Leiden: Brill, 2004).

Pss. Sol. 4:25: "Let your mercy, O Lord, be upon all them that love you."

Pss. Sol. 6:6: "And every request of the soul that hopes for him the Lord accomplishes. Blessed is the Lord, who shows mercy to those who love him in sincerity."

Pss. Sol. 9:8: "And, now, you are our God, and we the people whom you have loved: Behold and show pity, O God of Israel, for we are yours. And remove not your mercy from us, otherwise they assail us."

Pss. Sol. 10:3: "For he makes straight the ways of the righteous, and does not pervert (them) by his chastening. And the mercy of the Lord (is) upon them that love Him in truth."

Pss. Sol. 18:3: "Your judgments (are executed) upon the whole earth in mercy; and your love (is) toward the seed of Abraham, the children of Israel."

Similar to these sentiments relating law to the treatment of neighbor in terms of mercy that extends toward the people of Israel, but also out toward the world, we find the Testament of Issachar: but love the Lord and your neighbor, show mercy to the poor and weak (T. Iss. 5:2).

3.2   *Love is Shown in Deeds and We Do Deeds because of Love*

Other writings within Hellenistic Judaism reflect the concept that love is demonstrated by the deeds that we do and/or that we do particular deeds out of love for God or one another. The Sibyline oracles speak of men who care for "deeds of love" (Sib. Or. 1:296). The Testament of Naphtali discusses the need to be wise in God as means of understanding his commandments, leading to an understanding of the deeds that must be accomplished "so that the Lord will love you" (T. Naph. 8:10) Similarly, the Testament of Gad speaks of the need to love one another "in deed, and in word, and in the intention of the soul" (T. Gad 6:1). The Apocalypse of Abraham 17:7 links righteous deeds to hospitality and "the greatness of your love towards God."

These blendings of conceptions of love and law are also found in a variety of apocalypses and within the Sibylline Oracles.[47] We find blends of love and

---

47   There is great disparity in dating these materials, but the hope is that this provides a general milieu for the conception of law and love in the time-period surround the

law similar to those found in other forms of Second Temple literature within various apocalypses as well. Apocalypse of Abraham 1:5 also reinterprets the blessing to Abraham in light of these three elements of Abraham's righteous actions, his hospitality to others, and his love: "for I have blessed him as the stars of heaven, and as the sand by the sea-shore, and he is in abundance of long life and many possessions, and is becoming exceeding rich. Beyond all men, moreover, he is righteous in every goodness, hospitable and loving to the end of his life."

In the Apoc. Sedr. 1:14, the author states, "O (how) extraordinary and paradoxical is the wonder that he who has love fulfills the law; for love is the fulfillment of the law" (Greek: ὦ τοῦ θαύματος ἐξαισίου καὶ παραδόξου, ὅτι ὁ ἔχων τὴν ἀγάπην ὅλον τὸν νόμον πληροῖ· πλήρωμα γὰρ νόμου ἡ ἀγάπη).[48]

Apocalypse of Sedrach 1:12–16 provides a commentary on John's Gospel:

> For John the theologian says: "This commandment we have from God, in order that the one who loves God should also love his brother." 13 And again the Lord says: "On these two (commandments) depend the whole law and the prophets." 14 O (how) extraordinary and paradoxical is the wonder that he who has love fulfills the law; for love is the fulfillment of the law. 15 O the power of love so immense; O the power of love without measure; 16 Nothing is more honorable than love, nor is there anything greater, either in heaven or on the earth. 17 Love is itself the principal virtue, beyond all the virtues. Love is the goal of the world. 18 It was honed in the heart of Abel; it worked with the patriarchs, it protected Moses; it made David the dwelling place of the Holy Spirit; it strengthened Joseph.

What the Apocalypse of Sedrach demonstrates is that even later traditions of Christians appear to have closely associated fulfilling the law with loving God and one another, but also see this love as extending to the whole earth. This love is described as being "so immense" as to be "without measure" and the "goal of the world."

3.3 *Love is Fulfillment of the Law*

There is a notion within Second Temple Judaism that love is the fulfillment of the law and that keeping the law is within the same conceptual frame as love.

Johannine corpus. For example, the Apocalypse of Sedrach is generally dated to between 150 to 500 C.E. However, this passage concerning love may be part of the later redactions attributed to Christian sermons on love added at a later point. See *OTP*, 1:605–607.

48 Translation by Craig Evans, *The Pseudepigrapha* (English), Oaktree Software, 2009.

This fulfillment of the law is described in terms of a love of God, a love of neighbor, and a love that extends in compassion to rest of the world. The Testaments of the Patriarchs demonstrate this:

> Therefore, *my children, love the Lord God of heaven, and keep His commandments,* following the example of the good and holy man Joseph ... *Fear the Lord and love your neighbor* ... See, children, the end of the good man; Be followers of his *compassion,* with a good mind, that you also may wear crowns of glory. For the good man has not a dark eye; for *he shows mercy to all men,* even though they be sinners.
> T. Benj. 3:1–3; 4:1–3

> So *keep the law of God, my children,* and try to live simply and in innocence; and do not be over-inquisitive about the Lord's commands, nor about the affairs of your neighbour. But *love the Lord and your neighbour,* and *show compassion* for the poor and the weak.
> T. Iss. 5:1–2

This theme is also found within the Jewish apocalyptic literature as Apocalpyse of Sedrach states succinctly: "O (how) extraordinary and paradoxical is the wonder that he who has love fulfills the law; for love is the fulfillment of the law" (Apoc. Sed. 1:14).

3.4 *Love is a Crown upon the Head*

Another conception of love in Hellenistic Judaism is as a crown upon one's head. This suggests a link between conceptions of royalty and conceptions of love. Testament of Benjamin explicitly associates these crowns with glory and with love God and one's neighbor, besides using the language of familial metaphors.

> Therefore, *my children, love the Lord God of heaven, and keep His commandments,* following the example of the good and holy man Joseph ... *Fear the Lord and love your neighbor* ... See, children, the end of the good man; Be followers of his *compassion,* with a good mind, that you also may *wear crowns of glory.* For the good man has not a dark eye; for *he shows mercy to all men,* even though they be sinners.
> T. Benj. 3:1–3; 4:1–3

Apocalypse of Abraham also uses this crown language. In this case, it is the greatness of one's love for God that becomes a crown.

Death says: "No, my lord Abraham, for your righteous deeds, and the boundless sea of your hospitality, and *the greatness of your love towards God has become a crown upon my head*, and in beauty and great peace and gentleness I approach the righteous".

Apoc. Ab. 17:7

3.5 *Love is Selfless, a Gift from God, and Serves out of Goodwill*

The Letter of Aristeas highlights two further aspects of the conception of love. Love is selfless and serves out of goodwill and love is a gift from God and the power of piety comes from love. The Letter of Aristeas states: "(The king) gave his confirmation to the answer, and asked the next man: 'To whom ought men to entrust themselves?' 'To those,' he said, 'who *serve you from goodwill and not from fear or self-interest*, thinking only of their own gain. For the one is *the sign of love*, the other the mark of ill-will and expediency'" (italics added, Let. Aris. 270).

The Letter of Aristeas has a debatable dating, but it certainly predates the Johannine corpus. Most scholars date this text to the middle of the second century B.C.E.[49] In v. 229 of the Letter of Aristeas, the interaction between the king and the man are notable in relation to love and the law. When the king asks "What is it that resembles beauty in value?" The response is to describe piety as the pre-eminent form of beauty. Notably the power of piety is said to lie in love (ἀγάπη). Love is in turn described as a "gift of God." This discussion immediately follows a discussion on the attitude of friends toward friends in v. 228. When the topic of failing arises, the response is that a person cannot fail because the seeds of gratitude are already in him, but if he does fail, he needs to stop whatever he is doing that caused the failure, but "he must form friendships and act justly. For it is the gift of God to be able to do good actions and not the contrary." Here love is linked to friendship and acting justly because these are described as "the gift of God" just as love is earlier described in this way. In fact, in this pass it seems that love and "do[ing] good actions and not the contrary" are placed in equivalent places. Verse 270 also affirms that a sign of love then is serving out of goodwill rather than fear, self-interest, or thinking of one's own gain. Love is also described as a gift from God and the power of piety comes from love. Piety is described as a chief virtue that is empowered by love. Love is God's gift. Example: "The king spoke kindly to him and then asked the

---

49 John R. Bartlett, *Jews in the Hellenistic World: Josephus, Aristeas, the Sibylline Oracles, Eupolemus* (Cambridge: Cambridge University Press, 1985) 16–17.

next: 'What is it that resembles beauty in value?' And he said: *'Piety*, for it is the pre-eminent form of beauty, and *its power lies in love*, which is *the gift of God*'" (italics added, Let. Aris. 229).

3.6 Love is Harmony and Sacrifice. Love Makes Us Children of God (*Themes of Familial Love*)

Another metaphor associated with love within Hellenistic Judaism is the notion of love as associated with familial metaphors. In several places, love is described in terms of being "children" or being born of God. Towards this end, first we can note the frequency with which love and child are associated in pseudepigraphal writings.

In the Maccabees, love is linked to familial relationships and also love is primarily described in terms of harmony and sacrifice as well as dedication to the law.

Examples include:

Brotherly love: 4 Macc 13:23: *"Brotherly love* being thus sympathetically constituted, the seven brethren had a *more sympathetic mutual harmony.*" 4 Macc 13:27: "And yet, although *nature and intercourse and virtuous morals increased their brotherly love* those who were left endured to behold their brethren, who were ill-used for their religion, tortured even to death."

Motherly love: 4 Macc 14:13: "And consider how comprehensive is the *love of offspring*, which draws every one to sympathy of affection, 14 *where irrational animals possess a similar sympathy and love for their offspring with men.*"

Throughout Second Temple Judaism, "my child" and "my children" are common phrases used when exhorting love of God, love of one another, love of one's neighbor, etc. This associates love with the familial metaphor. Many have noted how these familial metaphors play an important role in the writings of the New Testament generally. However, they are particularly key to the imagery found in the Fourth Gospel and in the Johannine epistles as many scholars have noted.[50]

3.7 Love is Directed by the Divine Word/the Law of Moses and Lead to the Right Path

In Pseudo-Orpheus (Orphica) and Aristobulus we find conceptions of love as eternal and the dependence on the divine word to direct the thoughts of one's heart as linked to remaining in eternal love. Artisobulus clarifies that Pseudo-

---

[50] See my section on familial metaphors in Beth M. Stovell, *Mapping Metaphorical Discourse in the Fourth Gospel: John's Eternal King* (LBS 6; Leiden: Brill, 2012), 217–221.

Orpheus's "Sacred Word" should be most correctly read as speaking directly of the Law of Moses. Pseudo-Orpheus (Orphica) and Aristobulus demonstrate a connection between conceptions of love as eternal and the dependence on the divine word to direct the thoughts of one's heart, leading to the right path. Aristobulus clarifies that this vision of Pseudo-Orpheus should be most correctly read as speaking directly of the law of Moses.

Dating Orphica is notoriously tricky. However, Charlesworth argues that Orphica are Jewish poems that during the second or first century B.C.E. were falsely attributed to Orpheus. These poems bear resemblances to the Jewish pseudepigraphal testaments.[51] Three times the same phrase is repeated (or a close variant): "For I am confessing things that are true. Do not allow the former closely-held appearances to deprive you of eternal love, but look to the divine word, insist upon it, directing the deep thoughts of [your] heart. Stay upon the good Path, looking only to the immortal master of the world" (Orph. 1:4–8; 2:1–5; 3:3–7). This passage suggests that the conception here of the divine word is as the source for direction that leads to eternal love. What is key to maintaining this eternal love is staying on the right path. The "divine word" becomes a means to direct one's heart via one's deepest thoughts.

Aristobulus quotes this passage from Pseudo-Orpheus in his writings. Encouraging his hearers as "my child" to listen to this instruction, Aristobulus's overarching message places emphasis on Moses as the "lawgiver" (Aristob. 2:4) The relationship between Hellenism and Judaism is also spelled out in Aristobulus, as Aristobulus is described as a philosopher standing in the tradition of Hellenistic Judaism as Aristob. 3:1 states: "Aristobulus the peripatetic [philosopher], who lived before us and was of the Hebrews, agreed that the Greeks have proceeded from the philosophy of the Hebrews." Aristobulus points to the one who translated the books of the Law as a φιλοτιμίαν (lover of honor). Aristobulus provides a helpful clarification regarding what he means when he is quoting Pseudo-Orpheus. Where Pseudo-Orpheus refers to the "divine word" as the locus of direction, Aristobulus explains that what he means by the conception of the divine word: "One must take the divine 'voice', not as a spoken word, but as the construction of deeds, just as Moses has spoken to us throughout the Law of the entire creation of the world as [being] the words of God. For he constantly [consistently?] says at each point, 'And God spoke, and it happened'" (Aristob. 4:1).

---

51   James H. Charlesworth, *The Pseudepigrapha and Modern Research* (Missoula, MT: Scholars Press, 1976), 167–168.

The "Sacred Word" in Aristobulus's description is thus creative word that is specifically linked to the Law. This law is explicitly linked to eternal love and to right action. The goal of the law is also explicitly stated thus: "The entire construction of our Law is arranged with a view toward piety, justice, self-control, and all other good things which are in keeping with the truth" (Aristob. 4.6). One might argue that here we find the notion that eternal love and the law would be linked by self-control, justice, and piety, which lead to the truth. The notion of profession of truth, which leads to holding onto eternal love is found in the key quote from Pseudo-Orpheus that we are discussing here and seems to be consistent in its appropriation on Aristobulus.

3.8 Love is Modeled by the Great Leaders of the Faith from Previous Generations

In the case of T. Iss. 5:2 we find the love metaphor and law metaphor ("law" and "commands") associated with familial metaphors ("my children"). Here love is also associated with showing compassion. "So keep the law of God, my children, and try to live simply and in innocence; and do not be over-inquisitive about the Lord's commands, nor about the affairs of your neighbour. But love the Lord and your neighbour, and show compassion for the poor and the weak" (T. Iss. 5:1–2).[52]

This association between love of God, the law, compassion, alongside familial metaphors are also found in other parts of the Testaments of the Twelve Patriarchs, particularly in presenting Joseph's exemplary role. In the Testament of Benjamin, Joseph becomes the prime example that God's children should follow because he loved the Lord, loved his neighbor, and lived with compassion:

> Therefore, my children, love the Lord God of heaven, and keep His commmandments, following the example of the good and holy man Joseph. 2 Incline your thoughts to what is good, as you know it to be with me, because he who has the right mind sees everything properly. 3 Fear the Lord and love your neighbor … See, children, the end of the good man; Be followers of his compassion, with a good mind, that you also may wear crowns of glory. For the good man has not a dark eye; for he shows mercy to all men, even though they be sinners. And though they devise with evil

---

52 Translation by Marinus de Jonge in *The Apocryphal Old Testament* (ed. H.F.D. Sparks; Oxford: Clarendon, 1984), 554.

intent concerning him, by doing good he overcomes evil, being shielded by God: and he loves the righteous as his own soul.[53]

> T. Benj. 3:1–3, 4:1–3

Thus, love in the Testament of Benjamin is conceived as including mercy and compassion even to sinners alongside love of God and love of neighbor. These descriptions of Joseph's actions appear to also be identified as "keep[ing] [the Lord God's] commandments."

In Testament of Joseph, love is linked to honor God and one's brothers, even when they do evil. As Testament of Joseph states,

> My brothers knew how my father loved me, and yet I did not exalt myself in my mind: although I was a child, I had the fear of God in my heart; for I knew that all things would pass away. And I did nor raise myself (against them) with evil intent, but I honored my brothers; and out of respect for them, even when I was being sold, I refrained from telling the Ishmaelites that I was a son of Jacob, a great man and a mighty. Do you also, my children, have the fear of God in all your works before your eyes, and honor your brothers. For every one who does the law of the Lord will be loved by Him.[54]
>
> T. Jos. 10:5–6, 11:1–2

Walter Harrelson argues that the Testament of Joseph offers a picture of patient and long suffering love that would have been particularly pertinent to Diaspora Jews dealing with relationships with foreigners. As Harrelson explains,

> this picture of love to be the most remarkable teaching in the entire Testament of the Twelve Patriarchs. It goes beyond the love of others that is commended in the other testaments. It is interiorized, made constituent of the very life of Joseph that he prefers others to himself, puts himself at the disposal of others, and never forgets that the witness of God's people Israel in the world, especially in the world of foreigners, requires patient, long-suffering love.[55]

---

53   Translation by Craig Evans, *The Pseudepigrapha* (English), Oaktree Software, 2009.
54   Translation by Craig Evans, *The Pseudepigrapha* (English), Oaktree Software, 2009.
55   Walter J. Harrelson, "Patient Love in the Testament of Joseph," *PRSt* 4 (1977): 10.

Harrelson argues that this type of love spills over into a love for others as a natural consequence:

> Joseph is addressing all of his children and relatives; his words apply to all of the people of God. His concern is not with himself. He is not saying that love of others inevitably brings the favor of God and therefore prosperity. He is not teaching the Stoic view that the self is enhanced through the love of others. He insists that such a readiness to suffer harm for the sake of love of others, and especially God's people, is a style of living that "spills over" into one's conduct with all persons, Jew and pagan alike. Thus, love of others characterizes the faithful member of the community of God's people, in whatever circumstances that member may find himself.[56]

The images of love in the Testament of the Twelve Patriarchs points its hearers to these patriarchs as examples of the love that they must show to others. This love extends not only to the Jewish community, but to all persons.

3.9 *Impact on Social Boundaries and Jewish Ethics*

The interaction between the conceptions of love and law in Hellenistic Judaism has an impact on social maintenance, social boundaries, and Jewish ethics. Work on the role of group emotions has shown that often models of ideal emotional responses become regulatory for the groups emotions.[57] In the Testament of the Twelve Patriarchs it appears that such role models are raised in the form of Abraham and Joseph. In this way the individual emotional responses of Abraham and Joseph function as exemplary for the expectations of the group emotions. We can see this in the use of plural imperatives for instruction on how to love based on the models of Abraham and Joseph. While one might expect to find these models of faith living out an exclusivist vision of love that focuses only on love for the people within the Jewish community, instead we find that love is encouraged to spill out to the nations. This suggests that while social boundaries still existed that differentiated those within the community and those outside the community, yet love still extended to those outside the community based on an adherence to the law. Here the particular models provided by Abraham and Joseph are key. In both cases, love is associated with aspects of adherence to the law. Effectively, the idea is that for one to keep the

---

56 Harrelson, "Patient Love," 11.
57 See the discussion of role models and intergroup emotion in Smith and Mackie, "Intergroup Emotions," 428–439.

law, one must live like Abraham and Joseph, living like Abraham and Joseph includes the group to extend love to those outside of the group. This may help us with distinctions between social boundaries and group emotions in the Johannine epistles.

4 Love and Law in Early Christianity and the Johannine Corpus

This section begins with an analysis of law and love conceptions in Jewish Christianity by examining these conceptions in the Epistle of James as exemplary. It will then establish the relationship between Jewish Christianity and the Johannine letters. This section will then examine the depictions of love and law in John's Gospel and the Johannine letters.

Our study of the conceptions of law and love in Second Temple Judaism have shown that extensive links join the way that love is conceived in terms of love of God, love of neighbor, and love of the world with fulfillment of the law. This idea of love as fulfillment of the law and its associations with compassion and with familial metaphors also find themselves throughout texts representing Jewish Christianity.[58] This section of the chapter will focus on representations of Jewish Christianity found within the New Testament itself. Specifically, we will examine how the royal law of love in the epistle of James may provide an example of Jewish Christianity that helps to demonstrate the presence of the trends in Hellenistic Judaism articulated above.

In Jas 2:5–10 we find articulated what the author of James calls the "royal law" of love:

> Listen, my dear brothers and sisters: Has not God chosen those who are poor in the eyes of the world to be rich in faith and to inherit the kingdom he promised those who love him? 6 But you have dishonored the poor. Is it not the rich who are exploiting you? Are they not the ones who are dragging you into court? 7 Are they not the ones who are blaspheming the noble name of him to whom you belong? 8 *If you really keep the royal law found in Scripture, "Love your neighbor as yourself," you are doing right.*

---

58   Notably the distinction between texts of Second Temple Judaism and Jewish Christianity is a tricky distinction to make, particularly with the long history of redaction between Jewish texts and Christian texts from the late second century into the fifth century C.E. This is part of the reason that I have focused exclusively on the New Testament literature representing Jewish Christianity in this section rather than trying to delineate what represents Judaism or Christianity in the previous section.

> 9 But if you show favoritism, *you sin and are convicted by the law as lawbreakers.* 10 For *whoever keeps the whole law and yet stumbles at just one point is guilty of breaking all of it.*

Notably Jas 2:8–10 defines the royal law in terms of a love for neighbor and emphasizes the link between this love and the law by stating that those who do not adhere to this sin and are lawbreakers. Yet this love of neighbor in James is not simply an insider specific form of love, but is explicitly described as those outside the community being shown either favoritism or derision. This tells us that the "love of neighbor" concept in James is not limited to those within the Jewish community, but extends to the treatment of those who enter the community from the outside. It is in the very actions related to their entry into the community where love is particularly needed. Thus, to suggest that here the love of neighbor is only an internal and exclusive concept is to miss the very aspect of this social space as a threshold space between insider and outsider. In this threshold space, love is not only valued and essential, but any act against this form of love is seen as law-breaking.[59]

Many have associated this royal law of love with other traditions of Jewish Christianity such as the Matthean and Didache traditions.[60] "Love of neighbor" in Matthew and James traditions appear to be joined with conceptions of love that emphasize love as compassion and love as fulfillment of the law. These ideas of love include an outward focus as well as an inward focus on the community that shows continuity with the Jewish ethics we have delineated above related to love and Law.

How does locating John's Epistles (and the Johannine community) in Jewish ethics change our perspective on the love command if read in light of a social location for the Johannine literature within Jewish Christianity? How might the Epistle of James alongside other Jewish Second Temple literature help us

---

59 Notably, there seems to be an extension of the law and "neighbor" in relation to the poor starting as early as Lev 19 that Jas 2 appears to be referencing.

60 Matthias Konradt, "The Love Command in Matthew, James, and the Didache: Their Place in Early Christian Literature," in *Matthew, James, and Didache: Three Related Documents in Their Jewish and Christian Settings* (ed. Hubertus Waltherus, Maria van de Sandt and Jürgen Zangenberg; Atlanta: Society of Biblical Literature, 2008), 271–288; Joel Weaver, "Heart of the Law: Love Your Neighbor (Jas 2:8–13)," *RevExp* 108 (2011): 445–451; *Matthew and the Didache: Two Documents from the same Jewish-Christian Milieu?* (ed. Hubertus Waltherus, Maria van de Sandt and Jürgen Zangenberg; Minneapolis: Fortress, 2005); Matt A. Jackson-McCabe, *Logos and Law in the Letter of James: The Law of Nature, the Law of Moses, and the Law of Freedom* (NovTSup 100; Leiden: Brill, 2001).

to fill this out more fully? First, the Epistle of James represents a Jewish Christian document likely pre-dating John's Epistles. Second, one can make a pretty convincing case that the Epistle of James represents Jewish Christianity similar to that found in John's Epistles and that we can demonstrate a particular milieu or a matrix of ideas around love, law, and boundaries in Jewish ethics. Other scholars have noted links between the Johannine epistles and the Epistle of James.[61]

4.1 Continuity and Discontinuity with Second Temple Judaism and Jewish Christianity

While not all concepts in Second Temple Judaism are in continuity with Jewish Christianity, the similarities between the perspectives on love and law portrayed in the Second Temple Judaism that we have analyzed above and the Jewish Christianity demonstrated in the Epistle of James show striking continuity. At the very least one could argue that the Epistle of James demonstrates that compassion for those in need and love for the neighbor are seen as related concepts. Further, there is a conception of God's royal law as equal to the notion of loving one's neighbor. As noted above, this neighbor cannot be understood only as an insider in an exclusivist way because the context of James 2 informs us that these potential "neighbors" in question are those entering the community for the first time and either being treated well or mistreated. Thus, it is precisely in the liminal space between insider and outsider where love as law is being emphasized. The severity of this love for those from the outside coming in is such that to not love in this fashion is described as sin and breaking of the law. This suggests that the delineation between insider and outsider in terms of love and law are more complicated in Jewish Christianity (and thereby in the Johannine epistles) than many have previously suggested.

4.2 Love and Law in Johannine Epistles

As noted in the review of literature section above, one of the assumptions of past scholarship in relation to the love commands in John's Gospel and John's epistles has been the sectarian nature of the Johannine community and teamed with this at times has been the concept of the Johannine community or the author of Johannine literature as anti-Semitic or anti-Jewish. Yet recent studies have questioned whether the Johannine community was actually sectarian and to what degree the Johannine corpus represents documents that are anti-

---

61 John Painter, "The Generosity of God in the World: Preaching from John, 1 John and James," *St Mark's Review* 219 (2012): 35–51.

Jewish. Related to this is the question of the cultural provenance of the Johannine corpus. Some scholars have made recent compelling arguments that the combination of Hellenistic and Jewish imagery in the Fourth Gospel suggests that the closest milieu is likely Hellenistic Judaism.[62]

Recently, Cynthia Long Westfall has taken this hypothesis further by examining how the Jewish mission functioned in relation to Jewish Christianity including Johannine literature. Westfall argues that there is much to justify an approach that sees John's writings in line with the larger foundations of the Jewish mission and Hellenistic brands of Jewish Christianity.[63] Reading the Johannine epistles in light of these Jewish ethics and in light of a Hellenistic brand of Jewish Christianity, one finds links not only between the Johannine epistles and Hellenistic Judaism of the Second Temple period, but also between other forms of Jewish Christianity like the Epistle of James. Such a perspective teamed with recent approaches to emotion and conceptual metaphor studies provides us with potential for new insight into the question of the love command in the Johannine epistles. This section will argue that the depictions of love and law found in 1 John echo both Jewish Christianity and Second Temple Hellenistic Judaism in notable ways. From this, I will argue that the notion of insider/outsider and exclusivism that have been assumed as part of Johannine ethics need to be rethought. Put another way, I hope to prove what Pheme Perkins found to be not provable, but potentially true: that Johannine ethics included a more expanding love for others than simply an insiders' love.

4.3 *Role of Exemplars of the Faith (e.g. Abraham, Joseph, Jesus)*

Previously we discussed the distinction between individual and intergroup emotions and applied some of these concepts to Second Temple Judaism particularly in the role of the Testaments of the Twelve Patriarchs. 1 John echoes this notion of exemplars of faith as models for group emotion. Rather than having Abraham or Joseph as models for a love that is given to insiders, but extends to outsiders as well, Jesus is lifted up as such a role model (1 John 3:16; 4:9–11). The group is encouraged to mirror the individual emotions of Jesus (who showed his love through sacrifice) in their interpersonal interactions. Notably, throughout 1 John, Jesus's love demonstrated through his sacrifice is characterized as salvific not just for insiders, but also for outsiders to the Jewish Christian community of 1 John (1 John 2:1–2). While some scholars have noted the poten-

---

62 See Stephen S. Smalley, *John the Evangelist and Interpreter* (New Testament Profiles; Downers Grove, IL: InterVarsity, 1998).

63 Westfall, "The Hebrew Mission: Voices from the Margins?," 187–207.

tial of this missional element of 1 John and other parts of Johannine literature, few have then asked how this reinterprets love and law conceptually as an intergroup emotion. It is not only the case that Jesus died for the world and saved the world, but Jesus also modeled through this love—the love that the Johannine community should show to others. The explicit group emotion intended in response to viewing this model of faith is to love like Jesus loved. The emotion of love is conceptualized in terms of the deeds done in response to others.

4.4 Individual vs. Intergroup Emotions and the Law

Noting this distinction between Jesus's individual emotion and the actions attached to this emotion as exemplar for intergroup emotion also creates a helpful parallel to the notion of law in 1 John. The law was not given primarily to individuals but to a community. While individuals are responsible to maintain the law within their own lives and bodies, nonetheless the concept of fulfillment of the law in terms of love is consistently interpersonal including externalized action as demonstrative of an internal love. The notion of law maintenance does not end because of the existence of Jesus's love in 1 John. In contrast, the notion of adherence to both the commandment to love one another and the notion of adherence to "the commandments" function as reminders to the people that maintenance of the law continually requires them to demonstrate their intergroup expression of love through the action of love within the community as well as outside the community. This is highlighted in places like 1 John 2:2–7. Jesus's propitiation is described as not only for us but the whole world. This precipitates a talk on the law and love in 1 John 2:3–6. First John 2:3 points to the necessity of obedience of God's commandments. 1 John 2:3–4 emphasizes that any claim to knowledge of God comes through this obedience. While 1 John 2:5 switches from discussion of God's commandments to God's word, there certainly appears to be a desire of setting these two notions in parallel with one another.

1 John 2:5–6 notes that obedience to God's word and following God's commandments are the way God's love is completed in us. This love explicitly looks like walking as he walked. As we have noted elsewhere, the conception of "walking" in relation to the Law demonstrates the working out of the Law. 1 John 2:6 clarifies that it is only in this walking just as he walks, that we know that we abide in him. Many have noted that ubiquitous nature of this notion of abiding throughout Jewish literature and within John's Gospel.[64] 1 John 2:7 explores

---

64   Joseph C. Dillow, "Abiding Is Remaining in Fellowship: Another Look at John 15:1–6," *BSac* 147 (1990): 44–53.

whether this "new" command is really "new" or in continuity with the "old." The answer is both/and. This suggests that the break off from Judaism is anything but complete and certainly this imagery is not anti-Jewish as some have argued.

While this passage moves into a discussion of how believers should love other believers, this notion of loving other believers does not negate the notion that there is continuity between the old commandment and the new one. As we have seen in discussion of Hellenistic Judaism and Jewish Christianity, it is not necessarily the case that because there are encouragements to love insiders to the community that a love for outsiders is thereby excluded. Instead, the continuity between the old commandment and the new one placed alongside the salvific love of Jesus and the call to model our lives on him all suggest that this love is both for the insider and reaching out to the outsider.

Below, I will briefly highlight some of the key ways that the conception of love and law found in Hellenistic Judaism and in Jewish Christianity as charted above appear to be echoed at least in part in 1 John.[65]

4.5 Love Encourages Mercy in God and is Shown through Mercy to Others

Sources in Second Temple Judaism describe love as compassion for those in need. 1 John 3:17 describes how love of neighbor involves not refusing the help the needy. This passage further explains that sharing goods function as a sign of love, not sharing goods function as a sign of not loving. While this compassion is demonstrated within the brotherhood of believers, this notion of love nonetheless resonates with larger conceptions of love and law that we have explored above. This notion of love for the other is displayed from the start in 1 John 2 in God's gift of salvation to all people, his ultimate act of mercy. 1 John prescribes a love that mirrors God's mercy through mercy to others.

4.6 Love is Enacted through Deeds and Love is a Gift from God

In Second Temple Judaism, love is described as a selfless gift that comes from God. 1 John echoes this notion of love as God's gift to us. 1 John 4:7–16 describes how God's love is given from God and that God's character is attested as love itself. This love is manifested through a gift from God in the sending of his Son (1 John 4:9–10). The Spirit is also given as part of this action of abiding love.

---

65   I will not be suggesting that all aspects of these conceptions of love and law are equally manifest in 1 John nor am I asserting that each reference to "love" would include all of these conceptions. Barr's critique of illegitimate totality transfer still holds true in this analysis. What I am suggesting is that some of these notions of love appear to be similar to what is found in 1 John.

The love of God is not only demonstrated in sending his Son, but also in the actions of Christ on our behalf. As Christ laid down his life, we lay down our lives for others (1John 3:16) showing the selflessness of love. Love is explicitly described as serving not only in words, but in deeds (1John 3:18), which echoes the notion of serving out of goodwill rather than compulsion.

4.7 Love is Fulfillment of the Law. This "New" Commandment is also Not a "New" Commandment (See Discussion of 1John 2 above)

Sources in Second Temple Judaism depict love as fulfillment of the law. Similarly, 1John 5 describes how love for God is achieved by loving the Son and keeping his commandments (1John 5:1–3). In contrast, those who do not love violate the law. The one who does not love is a liar (1John 4:20) and a murderer (1John 3:15). Love is so much the essence of fulfilling the law that without love, we sin and become lawless (1John 3:4–10).

4.8 Love Makes Us Children of God

Many scholars have noted the familial metaphors throughout Johannine literature.[66] Love is closely conceptually linked to familial metaphors in 1John. God's great love makes us called his children (1John 3:1). Love makes us born of God (1John 3:9). The language of "children" and birthing language are consistent with larger metaphorical frameworks related to childbirth and family in the Johannine corpus. Linking depictions of love to these conceptual frameworks provides a locus for love while also demonstrating the power of love to create familial links. Love creates a social identity that is intimately linked to God by the metaphor of family.

4.9 Love Modeled by Jesus, Who is a Great Leader of the Faith (Similar to Abraham, Joseph, etc.)

As noted above, Jesus is described as the model for the way emotions of love are to be expressed within the intergroup setting. The actions of Jesus provide an implicit basis for the Jewish mission that is in continuity with the Jewish ethics of love God and love your neighbor where one's neighbor can at times be understood as insider to the group and can also be understood as in a liminal space where entering the group becomes a real possibility. Thus, Jesus as role model presses into the notion of strictly divided internal and external social

---

66 For survey of these discussions on John's Gospel, see Stovell, *Mapping Metaphorical Discourse in the Fourth Gospel*, 290. For discussion of familial metaphors in the Johannine epistles, see Dirk G. Van der Merwe, "Family Metaphorics: A Rhetorical Tool in the Epistle of 1John," *Acta patristica et byzantina* 20 (2009): 89–108.

space by creating a salvific link between the two spaces. The notion that we are to walk as Jesus walked suggests that the lives of believers are also supposed to walk in ways that create this liminal space and that this kind of "walking" will make obey God's commandment and make God's love complete.

5 Conclusions

Examining conceptions of love in relation provides a new basis for examining the Johannine community. Assumptions of only internalized love in the Johannine corpus tends to overlook the overall framework of conceptions of love in Hellenistic Judaism. This study demonstrates that love and law including actions of love leading to compassion for others in the world were more common conceptions of love explicit in Second Temple Judaism and implicit in Johannine literature.

This study provides only the initial steps towards a variety of other potential future studies. Deeper understanding of distinctions between individual and intergroup emotions may prove helpful to differentiate expectations for the individual compared to responses of the group. Further exploration would also benefit studying how Jesus's love command functions as a testament and relates to the role of exemplars of the faith (e.g., Abraham, Joseph, Jesus).

Further examinations of social identity related to Jewish ethics based on these formulations could also help to demonstrate new ways of understanding the formation of social identity in the Johannine corpus.

The New Perspective (on Paul) on Peter: Cornelius's Conversion, the Antioch Incident, and Peter's Stance towards Gentiles in the Light of the Philosophy of Historiography

Christoph Heilig

1 Introduction

The development of an inner-Jewish community who believed in Jesus of Nazareth as the Messiah into the global movement of "Christianity" poses difficult historical questions at many points. Among them, the original acceptance of the first Gentiles *as Gentiles* into this group is one of the most pressing issues. Within the Protestant tradition, this historical question has, for the most part, been deeply interwoven with the theological debate about justification—and, thus, with the person of Paul.

This relatedness of historical and theological matters suggests that a shift in the perspective on Paul's thought might also entail a reconsideration of his role in the historical process that led to Christian congregations with Gentile members, especially vis-à-vis other prominent figures within the early Christian movement.

Accordingly, this essay will discuss the question of how recent trends in Pauline studies—the emergence of the so-called "New Perspective on Paul" (in the following: NPP)—have influenced the perception of the two foundational figures of Paul and Peter in relation to the historical question of how it came to be that Gentiles became an important part of the early Christian movement.

2 Peter and Paul in New Testament Scholarship

2.1 F.C. Baur

Even before the NPP the Lutheran faith-works-dichotomy had been challenged as the guiding paradigm within the protestant tradition of Pauline research. For F.C. Baur, Paul's great achievement was to be understood as offering a new point of departure for Christianity,[1] by overcoming Jewish particularism and

---

[1] Cf. F.C. Baur, *Kirchengeschichte der ersten Jahrhunderte* (vol. 1 of *Geschichte der christlichen*

transforming Christianity into an "allgemeine[s] Heilsprincip für alle Völker."[2] Thus, in his conversion he broke through the barriers of Judaism and dissolved Jewish particularism within the universal idea of Christianity.[3]

It is in this context that the inclusion of Gentiles into the Christian movement is to be understood, i.e., as the result of a religious transformation of the nationalist idea of Judaism *through Paul*.[4] In the wake of Baur, the "Antioch incident," which is recounted in Gal 2:11–21, became the prime textual proof for Paul's isolated stance within the early Christian movement in that regard— and thus also a hermeneutical key for understanding the development of early Christianity in general.[5] It offered a fixed point from which one could interpret the events leading to this clash as well as the trajectories going out from it. Here, the Jewish mission of the church of Jerusalem and Paul's law-free gospel to the Gentiles collided. In this light, the factions in Corinth (cf. e.g. 1 Cor 1:12) and elsewhere could only be understood as the lasting break between both strands in early Christianity. In this paradigm, it is only natural to read the rest of the Pauline correspondence as evidence for the *Völkerapostel* becoming increasingly isolated, being rejected in his collection for the church of Jerusalem and dying alone in the end in Rome. Also, looking in the other direction on the timeline, this incident was the defining evidence for demonstrating that the innovative Paul met a Jewish Christianity that had no interest in the inclusion of Gentile Christians.

2.2 The New Perspective on Paul

How did the NPP change this approach to Paul, Peter, and the historical problem of Gentiles as being part of the early Christian movement? First, one should

---

Kirche; 3rd ed.; Tübingen: Fues, 1863), 44: "In Paulus hat die nach dem Hingang Jesu beginnende Entwicklungsgeschichte des Christenthums einen neuen Anfangspunkt."

2 Baur, *Kirchengeschichte*, 45.

3 Baur, *Kirchengeschichte*, 45: "[I]n diesem Umschwung seines Bewusstseins [durchbrach er] auch die Schranken des Judenthums […] und [hob] den jüdischen Particularismus in der universellen Idee des Christenthums [auf]."

4 Of course, Baur also famously emphasized the conflict between the Hellenists and Hebraists in Jerusalem. But the group around Stephen is in the end only regarded as a "Vorläufer" of Paul (Baur, *Kirchengeschichte*, 42). Thus, it is only in him that the group receives "seinen eigentlichen Herold und seine principielle Begründung" (Baur, *Kirchengeschichte*, 43).

5 Cf. already F.C. Baur, "Die Christuspartei in der korinthischen Gemeinde, der Gegensatz des petrinischen und paulinischen Christenthums in der alten Kirche, der Apostel Petrus in Rom," *Tübinger Zeitschrift für Theologie* 4 (1831): 61–206, esp. 114–115. A translation of this essay (by Martin Bauspieß, Christoph Heilig, David Lincicum, Lucas Ogden, Wayne Coppins) for the SBL Press series History of Biblical Studies is currently in preparation.

note that speaking of "the" NPP is problematic in itself, because there are competing opinions on who represents this exegetical paradigm—and, thus, what even constitutes it. A root cause of this problem is that in the German-speaking sphere the close relation between Durham and Tübingen secured James D.G. Dunn a critical reception among Martin Hengel and his students, while the same was not true for N.T. Wright. As Simon Gathercole has recently pointed out, the German reactions to the NPP are marked by a clear over-representation of Dunn's particular approach.[6] This has even led to the absurd situation that an award-winning dissertation on the explicit topic of the NPP (it claims to be "a critical introduction" to the NPP in the subtitle) managed to cite Wright only in two footnotes—as an *opponent* of that exegetical tradition.[7] Similarly, it is noteworthy that an essay that was meant to critique the NPP was recently adduced by Wright as "simply set[ting] the stage for the real questions to begin."[8] The problem is aggravated by different parties trying to secure the prerogative of being the one who offers the definitive interpretation of the history of research. Thus, Wright in a recent book on the history of Pauline interpretations seeks to establish his emphasis on narrative dynamics as an integral part of the NPP—an aspect that he thinks has not been sufficiently acknowledged by his sparring partner Dunn.[9] Dunn, on the other hand, only recently published an assessment of Wright's big book on Paul, implying that Wright makes such little use of the "actual" ideas of the NPP that he should not even be regarded a proponent of that movement.[10]

Against this background, it seems advisable not to analyze the NPP as a monolithic unity but to pay special attention to how different scholars within the NPP argue within their individual approaches. In what follows, I will scrutinize in particular the contributions by Wright and Dunn. This is not to say,

---

6   Simon Gathercole, "Deutsche Erwiderungen auf die 'New Perspective': Eine anglophone Sicht," in *Die Theologie des Paulus in der Diskussion: Reflexionen im Anschluss an Michael Wolters Grundriss* (ed. Jörg Frey and Benjamin Schliesser; Biblisch-Theologische Studien 140; Neukirchen-Vluyn: Neukirchener Verlag, 2013), 115–153.
7   Ivana Bendik, *Paulus in neuer Sicht? Eine kritische Einführung in die "New Perspective on Paul"* (Judentum und Christentum 18; Stuttgart: Kohlhammer, 2010), 150 and 167.
8   N.T. Wright, *Paul and the Faithfulness of God* (London: SPCK, 2013), 1409 with regard to Jörg Frey, "The Jewishness of Paul," in *Paul: Life, Setting, Work, Letters* (ed. Oda Wischmeyer; trans. Helen S. Heron and Dieter T. Roth; Edinburgh: T&T Clark: 2012), 57–95.
9   N.T. Wright, *Paul and His Recent Interpreters* (London: SPCK, 2015), 96–102.
10 James D.G. Dunn, "An Insider's Perspective on Wright's Version of the New Perspective on Paul," in *God and the Faithfulness of Paul: A Critical Examination of the Pauline Theology of N.T. Wright* (ed. Christoph Heilig, J. Thomas Hewitt, and Michael F. Bird; WUNT 2.413; Tubingen: Mohr Siebeck, 2016), 347–358.

of course, that they are the only ones who could meaningfully be ascribed to this paradigm.[11] Still, the choice is not arbitrary. Both authors are united in that their suggestions are motivated in part by dissatisfaction with current Pauline scholarship, sharing the concern of Krister Stendahl—undoubtedly a "grandfather" of the NPP—in assuming that the whole Lutheran paradigm of a perspective oriented towards the individual "introspective conscience" was inadequate for understanding Paul's letters. Also, they each[12] offered an early and fundamental reaction to E.P. Sanders's work *Paul and Palestinian Judaism*,[13] accepting his conclusion that the Judaism of Paul's day was not a religion of work-righteousness but a religion of grace,[14] but rejecting Sanders argument that Paul's only problem with this religious pattern of "covenantal nomism" (i.e., election into the covenant by grace, "works" as an expression of the covenantal status) was that it was "not Christianity."[15] Dunn thinks that Paul's main problem with covenantal nomism was that it placed too much emphasis on "works of the Law" as "boundary markers," i.e. as demarcating the Jewish people from the rest of the world, thus burying the global scope of the Abrahamic promise[16] under a rather nationalist agenda: "[W]hat Paul denies is that God's justification depends on 'covenantal nomism,' that God's grace extends only to those who wear the badge of the covenant."[17] For Wright, this notion of the Abrahamic covenant is even more important: it bridges the

---

11 For example, the original edition of Francis Watson, *Paul, Judaism and the Gentiles: A Sociological Approach* (SNTSMS 56; Cambridge University Press, 1986) offers a reaction to E.P. Sanders that stands in greater continuity with Sanders, the "grandfather" of the NPP— and with its "great-grandfather," F.C. Baur.

12 N.T. Wright, "The Paul of History and the Apostle of Faith," *TynBul* 29 (1978): 61–88; republished as the first chapter in N.T. Wright, *Pauline Perspectives: Essays on Paul, 1978–2013* (London: SPCK, 2013). James D.G. Dunn, "The New Perspective on Paul," *BJRL* 65 (1983) 95–122; republished as the second chapter in James D.G. Dunn, *The New Perspective on Paul: Collected Essays* (WUNT 185; Tübingen: Mohr Siebeck, 2005). All page references are to the versions in the collected volumes.

13 E.P. Sanders, *Paul and Palestinian Judaism: A Comparison of Patterns of Religion* (London: SCM, 1977).

14 By contrast, the recent work of John M.G. Barclay, *Paul and the Gift* (Grand Rapids: Eerdmans, 2015), has challenged Sanders: "Sanders is right that grace is everywhere; but this does not mean that grace is everywhere the same" (p. 319). In other words: There might still be real *disagreement* between Paul and his fellow Jews regarding the concept of "grace" because not everybody adhered to the same "perfection" of that concept.

15 Sanders, *Paul*, 552.

16 Cf. Dunn, "New Perspective," 104 who sounds quite Wrightian in that passage.

17 Dunn, "New Perspective," 101.

gulf between Stendahl's emphasis on justification as a doctrine of missionary practice and Ernst Käsemann's insistence on the theological significance of justification[18] in that it is part of God's larger story with sinful humanity. Israel—and, thus, covenantal nomism—plays a role in this cosmic drama. The problem with Israel is that she did not become the light of the world—but rather part of the problem herself. It is thus through the Messiah as the representative of God's people that the worldwide family of Abraham can finally be established through faith. The category of the covenant thus remains important for Paul indeed—though it is reworked around the Messiah.

While Wright and Dunn have the same starting points and share some fronts, their interpretation of Pauline texts still differs significantly. For example, they both agree that Paul's surprising statement that those under the law are *under the curse of the law* has nothing to do with individuals not being able to attain perfect obedience through their "works" and thus falling short of righteousness. But while Dunn argues that the curse Paul has in mind is due to the fact that Judaism has used the Law in a nationalist fashion to prevent its own basic goal, the blessing for the Gentiles,[19] Wright thinks that what is presupposed is indeed the inability to fulfil the law—though not on the level of the individual, but on the level of Israel as a nation.[20]

In what follows, we will thus have to pay close attention to both how Wright's and Dunn's shared assumptions influence their interpretation of Paul and Peter regarding the "Gentile problem" and how they differ in their assessment due to specifics of their individual interpretive frameworks. We will make that comparison on the basis of Wright's and Dunn's treatment of the Antioch incident, i.e. Gal 2:11–21. Not only do we have here Paul's justification language that

---

18   See Ernst Käsemann, "Rechtfertigung und Heilsgeschichte im Römerbrief," in *Paulinische Perspektiven* (3rd ed.; Tubingen: Mohr Siebeck, 1993), 108–139. It is one of the ironic consequences of the asymmetric reception of Wright and Dunn in German-speaking scholarship that Friedrich Wilhelm Horn, "Juden und Heiden: Aspekte der Verhältnisbestimmung in den paulinischen Briefen: Ein Gespräch mit Krister Stendahl," in *Lutherische und Neue Paulusperspektive: Beiträge zu einem Schlüsselproblem der gegenwärtigen exegetischen Diskussion* (ed. Michael Bachmann; WUNT 182; Tubingen: Mohr Siebeck, 2005), 17–39, writes a piece on the Stendahl-Käsemann dispute without noting that his criticism against the "NPP" is actually an *essential* aspect of Wright's original formulation of his "new perspective" on Paul.

19   James D.G. Dunn, *A Commentary on the Epistle to the Galatians* (BNTC; London: Continuum, 1993), 170–174.

20   See his argument in N.T. Wright, "Curse and Covenant: Galatians 3.10–14," in *The Climax of the Covenant: Christ and the Law in Pauline Theology* (London: T&T Clark, 1991), 137–156.

prompted Dunn to formulate his version of the NPP, but we can also pursue here how earlier argumentative lines of scholarship are continued or dropped.

One might, on the one hand, intuitively expect that the role of Peter would receive renewed interest in the framework of the NPP compared to the old, Lutheran paradigm. For if the speech in Gal 2:14–21 does not represent a uniquely Pauline/Lutheran position on how one "gets saved by faith alone without good works" and the basic question is, instead, about who is a member of God's people, then this assumption might open up the possibility that the theological views expressed there are in larger continuity with Petrine thought than has often been assumed.

On the other hand, one should also not underestimate the degree to which the NPP is still part of a decisively Protestant-oriented, i.e. Paul-centered, tradition. And while a large part of the NPP does represent a stream of British scholarship that remains skeptical towards Baur's ideological agenda,[21] these scholars sometimes seem to underestimate their indebtedness to Baur's pioneering work.[22] Therefore, it will be of great interest to see whether Baur's general paradigm on the development of early Christianity still comes through in Wright's and Dunn's treatment of the Antioch incident.

3 Philosophy of Historiography

3.1 *Describing and Evaluating Arguments*

In his magisterial work on Peter, Markus Bockmuehl also discusses how the apostle fares in recent treatment of his more popular colleague Paul. Regarding the two proponents of the NPP discussed here—Wright and Dunn—he concludes that their assessment of Peter does not differ very much from the picture that emerges in the work of interpreters of the "old" perspective.[23] Our

---

21 Cf., e.g., Stephen Neill and Tom Wright, *The Interpretation of the New Testament, 1861–1986* (2nd ed.; Oxford: Oxford University Press, 1988).

22 For example, Wright, "Paul of History," 18 writes that "Baur saw the critique of the law as being against Jewish particularism, though he saw it as Jewish-*Christian* particularism only." This, however, clearly disregards Baur's view on the development of religious thought in general. He would have been very satisfied with statements such as this one (Wright, "Paul of History," 10): "The significant point about faith is simply that, unlike the Torah, it is available world-wide." Of course, unlike Wright, he would not have anchored this point within Jewish salvation-history itself.

23 Markus Bockmuehl, *The Remembered Peter: In Ancient Perception and Modern Debate* (WUNT 262; Tübingen: Mohr Siebeck, 2010), 48–60. One might add that the publication

analysis of the Antioch incident will aim at bringing a bit more nuance to this conclusion, by differentiating how the two sketches of the figure of Peter differ on the basis of the differing approaches within the NPP, i.e. how the different *versions* of the NPP are associated with different implications for how we should understand Peter in relation to the role of Gentiles in the early Church.

At the same time, Bockmuehl's preliminary assessment points toward an important aspect that needs to be kept in mind when approaching the issue that is in question here: The NPP is on its most fundamental level a new perspective *on Paul*. We thus need to be prepared to recognize that Wright and Dunn have not explicated everything that could be said on the basis of (their versions of) the NPP with regard to *Peter*. In fact, we should probably be prepared to encounter some inconsistencies in this respect. For no "new" approach is entirely innovative. Every attempt to make sense of a certain part of the evidence by suggesting a new explanation already presupposes a prior understanding of other evidence, which is taken as point of departure for both formulating the new hypothesis and integrating the evidence in question into that framework. Thus, a purely descriptive account of how Wright and Dunn write about Peter cannot, in the end, be wholly satisfying. We also need to pay close attention to how these authors construe their arguments and where their positions might be due to older assumptions of research that do not actually fit in well into their new paradigm. In other words, the NPP might have to say more on Peter than Wright and Dunn actually state explicitly and it is part of evaluating the NPP's *potential* to identify such points in the argument.

3.2   *Bayesian Historiography*

We thus need to take a short look at how historical arguments actually function. In raising the question of Peter's and Paul's respective roles in the integration of Gentiles into Christian communities, we enter the realm of *historiography*, the field that is "composed of representations of past events."[24] Accordingly, when inquiring about the basic rules that govern arguments in this sphere, we are making use of categories of the *philosophy of historiography*, the branch of

---

of Wright, *Paul* has not changed this significantly. Here, the Antioch incident is important inasmuch as Paul offers his views on "justification" in terms of covenantal membership in his rebuke to Peter, but Paul's relation to Peter in general is not of interest. Cf. Wright, *Paul*, 854, n. 22 and 1496–1498.

24   Aviezer Tucker, *Our Knowledge of the Past: A Philosophy of Historiography* (Cambridge: Cambridge University Press, 2004), 1.

epistemology that tries to describe the correct relations between history and evidence[25] and the appropriate procedure for using the latter in order to reconstruct the former.

As historians we are confronted with data that we try to explain as results of past processes. Our basic task, hence, is to relate evidence we observe (in the form of texts, archaeological remains, oral traditions, etc.) to historical events. Of course, regularly there is a variety of possible causal chains that could lead to the evidence accessible to us and it is our task to choose the best hypothesis. There are three basic methodological guidelines that have to be kept in mind in our quest for the *most plausible hypothesis* with regard to explaining present evidence by postulating past events.

1. We must consider whether a postulated hypothesis would make the observed evidence likely, if it were true. In other words, if we presuppose the postulated causal chain, would we be confident to bet that the observed evidence would come out as a result? We can call this aspect the *explanatory potential* of a hypothesis.
2. We also must consider whether the postulated hypothesis—regardless of whether it could explain the evidence well or not—is plausible in itself, i.e., with regard to the basic parameters it presupposes. In other words, is there background knowledge—independent of our evidence in question—that speaks in favor or against the postulated hypothesis? Thus, this aspect can be designated the *background plausibility* of the hypothesis.
3. Last, but not least, we must make sure that we do not look at a specific hypothesis in isolation but that we evaluate it comparatively to other potential explanations for the evidence. This *comparative assessment* must take into account both aspects, explanatory potential and background plausibility, in equal shares and for all competing hypotheses in the same way.

The importance of these factors can be deduced from basic axioms of probability theory and they are summarized in the so-called "Bayes's theorem." The mathematical background of these considerations does not have to occupy us here,[26] but it is important to note that this is not an arbitrary selection

---

25 Tucker, *Knowledge*, 2.
26 For discussion of this point, see the summary and the literature cited in Christoph Heilig, "Methodological Considerations for the Search of Counter-Imperial 'Echoes' in Paul," in *Reactions to Empire: Sacred Texts in Their Socio-Political Contexts* (ed. John A. Dunne and Dan Batovici; WUNT 2.372; Tubingen: Mohr Siebeck, 2014), 73–93 and chapter 2 in

of aspects. This is not to say that sometimes it might not be preferable for historical inquiries to focus on explanatory potential or background plausibility alone;[27] however, it does imply that in such cases it is not possible to speak in a meaningful way of the overall "probability" of a hypothesis and the way evidence confirms it or not. All good historiography respects these considerations—whether consciously or not—and where inferences are structured in another way, they are incomplete.[28]

If we want to evaluate hypotheses along these lines, we first have to know which data is to be regarded as our background knowledge and which constitutes the new evidence that is to be interpreted. In the end, it is only the decision of the historian that demarcates between the new evidence that must be integrated into the hypotheses in question and those elements that are accepted as the background for this interpretation, since our background knowledge is itself of course largely the result of prior inferential processes. Sometimes, one might recognize the relatedness of certain data but find it very difficult to decide which part of it should constitute the basis for further

---

Christoph Heilig, *Hidden Criticism? The Methodology and Plausibility of the Search for a Counter-Imperial Subtext in Paul* (WUNT 2.392; Tübingen: Mohr Siebeck, 2014).

27 E.g., in order to come up with potential hypothesis in the first place (explanatory potential; this is often called "abduction" in the literature) or to set some basic parameters within new hypotheses could then be found (background plausibility). Also, it is of course possible to decide that one decides between different hypotheses on the basis of explanatory virtues and not on the basis of the notion of a subjective probability. However, what is important is to keep in mind that as soon as one speaks about evidence "confirming" a hypothesis—in the sense that taking the new evidence into account raises the subjective assessment of how "probable" (i.e., how likely to be true) the hypothesis is—this process needs to follow the structure of Bayes's theorem. On the whole issue of the relationship between "abduction"/"inference to the best explanation" and Bayesian confirmation theory, see Theresa Heilig and Christoph Heilig, "Historical Methodology," in Heilig et al., eds., *God and the Faithfulness of Paul*, 115–150.

28 This happens more often in exegetical literature than one might perhaps think. As demonstrated in Christoph Heilig, *Paul's Triumph: Reassessing 2 Corinthians 2:14 in Its Literary and Historical Context* (BTS 27; Leuven: Peeters, 2017) by means of different proposals for the meaning of θριαμβεύειν in 2 Cor 2:14, the vast majority of proposals only manages to make a convincing impression by selectively focusing on only one of the mentioned important aspects. For example, it is argued that from the context of the letter we would expect a "victorious" notion or that Paul would have been more familiar with pagan epiphany processions rather than Roman victory parades (background plausibility). However, scholars supporting such views do usually not take into account how this thought might have been expressed (explanatory potential).

conclusions.[29] Historians will naturally differ in their ranking of certainty they attribute to specific hypotheses. This is not in itself a problem for historiographical discourse, as long as the interdependence of hypotheses within this net of plausibilities is recognized and made explicit so that other scholars, who do not agree with certain presuppositions, can still engage that work.[30] One could, for example, argue that since Paul should be interpreted in the framework of the NPP, Colossians can no longer be regarded as non-Pauline in content and that it should, hence, be regarded as authentic.[31] On the other hand, one might argue that the framework of the NPP should not be assumed as background knowledge, but that the inauthentic nature of Colossians rather constitutes the point of departure. One can then argue on the basis of this pre-selection of the Pauline material that Paul's theology—as apparent from Romans, for example—should be understood in the classical categories of the Reformation.[32]

The roots of the NPP in the work of Stendahl and Sanders can be interpreted as being primarily related to the aspect of the *background plausibility*: the increased knowledge about ancient Judaism made earlier assumptions concerning our background knowledge for interpreting Paul untenable. The different proposals by Wright and Dunn can then be understood as abductive

---

[29] To give an example that is related to our subject: Should we use the assumption that the letter to the Galatians was addressed to the south of Asia Minor in order to argue for the possibility of an early date of the letter involving perhaps even an argument against aligning Gal 2:11–21 with Acts 15? Or should we, conversely, argue that since both passages describe the same event the letter has to be dated late and could well be addressed to northern cities? A fair overview over positions that takes into account German as well as English literature, and that points out uncertainties in all options, is offered by Jörg Frey, "Galatians," in Wischmeyer, ed., *Paul: Life, Setting, Work, Letters*, 207–215.

[30] For this reason, I spend much space in this essay on describing how I intend to proceed. Often, difficult historiographical disputes are more in need of ordering argumentative structures instead of trying to create "new" evidence.

[31] See Wright, *Paul*, 56–61.

[32] What is *not* a feasible procedure is to argue that Colossians is inauthentic because of its NPP-content *and* to argue at the same time that Paul should not be interpreted within the framework of the NPP because his authentic letters do not display such thinking. One would rather have to offer some *independent* reason for assuming the inauthenticity of Colossians (such as its style). Otherwise, the reasoning would be *circular*. In order to avoid circularity, it is hence mandatory that each element that is adduced as background knowledge is itself the result of a correct inference, which does not make use of information that can only be derived from inferences later in the chain of argumentation.

attempts to reconstruct Paul's thinking on this basis so that the actual Pauline wording—on the Law, on justification, etc.—could be *better explained*.

In what follows we cannot in detail determine whether the explanations for specific Pauline formulations are indeed "better"[33] than the Lutheran alternatives. What we will focus on is instead the question of how statements on Peter actually follow from the conclusions achieved within the framework of the NPP and where assumptions concerning Peter might actually influence the NPP-reading of Paul.

4   Peter's Stance towards Gentile Christians

4.1   *Introduction*

Most discussion of the Antioch incident treat at length whether the preceding meeting in Jerusalem (Gal 2:1–10) is identical with the Apostolic "Council" in Acts 15 or not (but rather with the famine visit in Acts 11:29–30). After all, it would make a difference indeed in evaluating Peter's actions at Antioch if they were preceded by a formal agreement (that might even be accessible in Acts 15:23–29 if this is not a later compromise). While I do think that a decision on this issue is possible in light of the evidence, I do not think that it is wise using it as point of departure for our analysis. The parallels are close indeed but there are too many possible scenarios in which two meetings (Gal 2:1–10 and Acts 15) could be imagined side by side.[34] Whether this is plausible or not depends almost entirely on the concrete nature of the conflict that was associated with Gentile Christians. Hence, it seems better to tackle this issue of number and relation of conferences *after* having established the probable conflict at Antioch and not to use it as background knowledge for this investigation.[35]

In fact, it is surprising that Acts 15 has received so much attention as foil for understanding Gal 2:11–21, whereas Acts 11 has been largely ignored. To be sure,

---

33   "Better" means in this context: Whether a comparison of background plausibilities and explanatory potentials indeed supports the claim that the meaning of the text suggested within the NPP has a higher subjective probability.

34   Cf. e.g. Richard Bauckham, "James, Peter, and the Gentiles," in *The Missions of James, Peter, and Paul: Tensions in Early Christianity* (ed. Bruce Chilton and Craig Evans; NovTSup 115; Leiden: Brill, 2005), 135–139.

35   Bauckham's instinct seems highly recommendable from the perspective of the philosophy of historiography.

Luke's narration is not without rhetorical intentions.[36] The episode with Cornelius is used for preparing for the more widespread inclusion of Gentiles into early Christianity (Acts 11:19–26)[37] in general and Paul and Barnabas's mission (beginning in Acts 13) in particular.[38] However, what is important for our discussion is the fact that Dunn and Wright seem to be in basic agreement with each other concerning the basic historicity of this account. Hence, this narrative of the fundamental transformation of Peter's stance towards Gentiles offers a perfect point of departure for approaching the relationship between Peter and Paul in Galatians. In addition, we can follow the argument of the NPP as represented by these two authors particularly well if we make this episode the start of our investigation since with Martin Hengel we have a proponent of the Old Perspective on Paul who shares their views concerning the fundamental historical validity of this tradition.[39]

4.2 Acts and Peter's Stance towards Gentile Christians

If one reads Dunn's account of the interaction between Peter and Paul in Jerusalem and Antioch (see below), a notable feature is that his reading does *not* make much recourse to the Cornelius episode. Similarly, the episode plays no role at all in Wright's *The New Testament and the People of God*[40] nor in his assessment in *Paul and the Faithfulness of God*.[41] While Wright does not seem to

---

36 Cf. James D.G. Dunn, *Beginning from Jerusalem* (Christianity in the Making 2; Grand Rapids: Eerdmans, 2009), 387.
37 On the significance of the mission of those "Hellinists," cf. Dunn, *Jerusalem*, 299–300.
38 We cannot discuss here the mission of Philip in Acts 8:3–40, which includes the first recounted conversion of a Gentile (Acts 8:26–39). Cf. Dunn, *Jerusalem*, 290, who says that "Luke, faithful to his sources, gives the credit where credit is due, even if it somewhat cuts across his own intended programme."
39 See e.g. the discussion of Dunn, *Jerusalem*, 384–387 and Martin Hengel, *Der unterschätzte Petrus: Zwei Studien* (Tübingen: Mohr Siebeck, 2006), 86 and Hengel, *Studien zum Urchristentum* (vol. 6 of *Kleine Schriften*; WUNT 234; Tübingen: Mohr Siebeck, 2008), 72. Note that the assumption of a severe ideological clash at Antioch seems more coherent if the historicity of the Cornelius episode is rejected or if another sequence is assumed. Cf. on such arguments Lutz Döring, "Schwerpunkte und Tendenzen der neueren Petrus-Forschung," BTZ 19 (2002): 215–216. See Philip F. Esler, *Community and Gospel in Luke-Acts: The Social and Political Motivations of Lucan Theology* (SNTSMS 57; Cambridge: Cambridge University Press), 95.
40 N.T. Wright, *The New Testament and the People of God* (London: SPCK, 1992).
41 Cornelius's name is never mentioned in Wright, *Paul*.

offer an explanation for this, Dunn[42] explicitly informs us why this is the case for his argument: he thinks that Cornelius belonged to a class of "exceptional cases" and was not a "point of principle."[43]

Interestingly, Dunn's own exegesis of the Cornelius episode does not point in this direction. Rather, reading what Dunn has to say on Acts 10–11, one might actually expect him to approach the figure of Peter in Galatians as someone who actually *shares* Paul's concerns. By contrast, Dunn calls the agreement of Gal 2:6–9 an "astonishing ... decision."[44] I would like to raise the question of whether it is possible that Dunn uses as background knowledge of his assessment of the Peter-Paul interaction in Galatians presuppositions of earlier Protestant scholarship, particularly from the Baur-strand, while neglecting his own conclusions on Acts 10–11 as a proper background for interpreting these Pauline texts.

For in Dunn's own assessment, Peter's decision to baptize Cornelius seems to be important not only on a literary but also on a historical level. It might have been "exceptional" in the sense that here God was seen to have intervened himself in the development of the messianic community. However, within the book of Acts it seems to be quite obvious that the event cannot be understood as "exceptional" in the sense that it did not go hand in hand with a re-evaluation of Gentiles in general. Rather, God's exceptional treatment had to create a rule for mission.[45] After all, what we find in Acts 10–11 is not simply the conversion of a particularly devout and God-fearing man (Acts 10:2: εὐσεβὴς καὶ φοβούμενος τὸν θεόν). Instead, Cornelius is the test case for every Gentile who repents of his Gentile lifestyle (Acts 11:18: τὴν μετάνοιαν εἰς ζωήν; cf. 1 Thess 1:9–10) and acts righteously (Acts 10:35 ἐν παντὶ ἔθνει ὁ φοβούμενος αὐτὸν καὶ ἐργαζόμενος δικαιοσύνην). The relevance this insight would have had on Peter's worldview, and in particular on his formerly held assumptions concerning Gentiles, cannot be overestimated. Granting baptism to these Gentile individuals could hardly have been separated from a deep transformation of Peter's Jewish perspective on Gentiles in general. This is very plausibly reflected in Luke's account of the revelation Peter receives. Without the perception of divine command, Peter would not have baptized (or even have gone to) these Gentile individuals.

---

42 I will mostly cite Dunn's commentary on Galatians. But cf. also his "Incident at Antioch," *JSNT* 18 (1983): 3–57, which provides some additional details.
43 Dunn, *Galatians*, 104.
44 Dunn, *Galatians*, 104.
45 Cf. Jack J. Gibson, *Peter between Jerusalem and Antioch* (WUNT 2.345; Tübingen: Mohr Siebeck, 2013), 134.

Richard Bauckham has convincingly shown, building on the work of Klawans,[46] that Peter's behavior can be best explained against the background of Jewish views on impurity and holiness.[47] Second Temple Jews did not regard Gentiles as *ritually* impure, since ritual pureness was an issue for those within the covenant only,[48] but as *morally* impure, since Gentile lifestyle was connected with immoral behavior, above all idolatry, from a Jewish perspective. While contact with the ritually impure was defiling but not morally illegitimate, contact with the morally impure sphere was problematic due to the dangers of being led astray. The other important dichotomy is the one between the profane/common and the sacred/holy.[49] While Gentiles can in principle repent and lose their moral impurity, they cannot become holy, because they are inherently profane *as* Gentiles. As Bauckham summarizes,[50] "Only a Jew (circumcised if male), obedient to the Torah, could really be trusted to be morally pure, and only a Jew could be holy (not profane)." Read in light of this background, the paradigmatic significance of the Cornelius episode becomes apparent. In what follows I will give a short overview of the reading that results from this perspective.[51] At the same time I will try to point out where Dunn's exegesis seems actually to overlap quite significantly with such a reading that presupposes a *fundamental change in Peter's perception of Gentiles*.

After a short characterization of the centurion (Acts 10:1–2), the narrative begins with a vision (Acts 10:3–6) in which an angel summons him to send for Peter. While Cornelius sends for Peter (Acts 10:7–8), Peter himself receives a revelation from God (Acts 10:9–16). Peter is shocked by the call to eat "common and impure" food, which is completely against his practice (οὐδέποτε ἔφαγον πᾶν κοινὸν καὶ ἀκάθαρτον; Acts 10:14). God's response is that he himself has cleansed it (ὁ θεὸς ἐκαθάρισεν) and that it cannot therefore be "common" (10:15). The profaneness and (ritual) impurity of the animals functions as an analogy to the (moral) impurity of Gentiles.[52] Of course, Peter does not make the connection at this point in the story. But after meeting the delegates from Cornelius (Acts 10:17–23a), Peter goes from Caesarea to Joppa (Acts 10:23b–24a) on the basis

---

46 Jonathan Klawans, "Notions of Gentile Impurity in Ancient Judaism," *AJSR* 20 (1995): 285–312.
47 The following summary builds on Bauckham, *James*.
48 It is of some interest that Peter is said to have stayed at a tanner before the Cornelius episode (βυρσεύς; Acts 9:43). Cf. Dunn, *Jerusalem*, 383.
49 Bauckham, *James*, 99–100.
50 Bauckham, *James*, 102.
51 For more details see Bauckham, *James*.
52 Bauckham, *James*, 104.

of the advice of the Spirit (Acts 10:19b–20). Luke probably uses the ambiguous summons μηδὲν διακρινόμενος (cf. Acts 11:12!) intentionally: Peter is encouraged not to doubt the appropriateness of the invitation but on a fundamental level it is of course completely about "not making a distinction."[53]

Peter meets Cornelius (Acts 10:24b–26) and his relatives and friends (Acts 10:27; cf. 10:24b). Peter explains (Acts 10:28–29) that his visit is against his former Jewish instincts but that God had shown him that this behavior was inappropriate. It is important to note that Peter's former reservations towards Gentiles are described with a very strong word (ἀθέμιτος) and that the issue in question is very generally the association with Gentiles (κολλᾶσθαι ἢ προσέρχεσθαι). (In other words, there is no evidence that Peter is concerned here with the danger of ritual impurity on the basis of unclean food in a shared meal.)[54] Such a deep bias could only be overcome by Peter because God "showed" him (ἔδειξεν) that it is wrong to call any human being "common" or "impure" (μηδένα κοινὸν ἢ ἀκάθαρτον λέγειν ἄνθρωπον; Acts 10:28). *Dunn's own summary* seems to take into account these fundamental (not "exceptional") consequences: "As the law of clean and unclean served to embody and defend Israel's separateness, so its abolition meant that the time of Israel's holding itself separate from the nations was over."[55]

Peter's inquiry into the purpose of his visit (Acts 10:29b) is answered by Cornelius with a recounting of his vision (Acts 10:29–33). Peter obviously regards this narration as a confirmation (Acts 10:34–35) of his divine experience and the deduction that the ἔθνος is no longer the defining factor for God's dealing with humans (Acts 10:34–35). Luke masterfully depicts the strangeness of the situation for Peter by letting him not deduce any further thoughts from this but by letting him recount God's commission of the Messiah Jesus to *Israel* (Acts 10:36–43).[56] The end of his speech juxtaposes the sending of the apostles to the λαός with an eschatological message (Acts 10:42) and the proclamation of the prophets that "*every one* who believes in him [πάντα τὸν πιστεύοντα εἰς αὐτόν] receives forgiveness of sins through his name" (Acts 10:43 RSV; italics my own). Obviously, the listeners have this faith since, to the surprise of the Jewish believers who are present, they become filled by the Spirit just as the Jewish believers

---

53 I think Bauckham, *James*, 105 presses this point too far. He is right that the vision itself does not speak about Gentiles. However, Luke seems to envision a gradual realization and acceptance of God's strange new ways (cf. Acts 10:34) by not pointing to a concrete point in time for a full understanding.

54 Correctly Bauckham, *James*, 107–112.

55 Dunn, *Jerusalem*, 395.

56 On the resulting tensions, cf. Dunn, *Jerusalem*, 394–396.

at Pentecost were (Acts 10:44–46a; cf. explicitly in Acts 11:17). Luke explicitly interprets this as a salvation-historical event by broadening the focus from the specific instance to the gift for the "nations" (ἐπὶ τὰ ἔθνη ἡ δωρεὰ τοῦ ἁγίου πνεύματος ἐκκέχυται; Acts 10:45; cf. Acts 11:1). Seeing this act of God, Peter confirms it by baptizing the Gentile believers (Acts 10:47–48a) and staying with them for some time (Acts 10:48b).

News of this revolutionary event spreads (Acts 11:1) and when Peter comes to Jerusalem his actions are regarded as highly controversial (Acts 11:2). "Those of the circumcision" (οἱ ἐκ περιτομῆς) probably are not a specific party of the church of Jerusalem but just like in Acts 10:45 (οἱ ἐκ περιτομῆς πιστοί) Luke uses this phrase to do justice to the fact that the followers of the Messiah Jesus now were made up of Jews and non-Jews.[57] Accordingly, the accusation that Peter went into the house of Gentiles (εἰσέρχομαι), uncircumcised people, and ate (συνεσθίω) with them (Acts 11:3) was apparently a widespread concern in the congregation. Peter reacts by narrating the events (Acts 11:4), namely the vision he had received (Acts 11:5–10), the encounter with the messengers (Acts 11:11), the commission by the Spirit (Acts 11:12a; cf. Acts 10:19–20 where this confirmation by the Spirit precedes the encounter with the messengers), the journey to Caesarea (Acts 11:12b; the τινες τῶν ἀδελφῶν τῶν ἀπὸ Ἰόππης συνῆλθον αὐτῷ from Acts 10:23 are now specified as "these six brothers" [οἱ ἓξ ἀδελφοὶ οὗτοι], probably because they function as witnesses), Cornelius's own vision (Acts 11:13–14), and the "falling" of the Spirit just as at Pentecost when Peter began to speak (Acts 11:15). Peter then gives an additional insight into his motivation for baptizing Cornelius's and his associates: the baptism with the Spirit was a promise by the Lord (Acts 11:16), accordingly what happened to Cornelius and the other Gentiles was divine intervention and his decision to baptize them with water only followed this prior decision by God as an act of obedience (Acts 11:17; cf. Acts 10:47). This explanation is regarded as sufficient by the congregation in Jerusalem and it praises God for having given to Gentiles also the repentance that leads to life (τοῖς ἔθνεσιν ὁ θεὸς τὴν μετάνοιαν εἰς ζωὴν ἔδωκεν; Acts 11:18).

It is of interest that the concern that is raised is Peter's close association with Gentiles (Acts 11:3), not the fact that the gospel is applied to them in some way (Acts 11:1). However, Peter's response does not focus on justifying his "lax" standards with regard to purity issues but on demonstrating the *full membership* of the Gentile converts in the messianic community as demonstrated by the gift of the Spirit. In a strict sense, this does not explain why Peter went into the house of uncircumcised men (εἰσῆλθες πρὸς ἄνδρας ἀκροβυστίαν ἔχοντας;

---

57   So also Bauckham, *James*, 116–117.

Acts 11:3)[58] but why he accepted them as members of the messianic community *as Gentiles* (without receiving circumcision). But apparently the deduction is accepted that this change of status of Gentiles as *potential* members of the refined people of God also requires a change in approaching them. At this point Bauckham's plausible reconstruction lacks precision. He argues that "[t]he 'Gentile Pentecost' at the house of Cornelius means that both the distinction between pure Israel and impure Gentiles and the distinction between the holy people of Israel, separated for God, and the profane peoples, separated from God, have been abolished."[59] However, primarily, the elimination of this distinction is rather implied by God's *sending* of Peter to Gentiles (not just since the giving of the Spirit).[60] In some instances, Bauckham does not seem to be clear enough on this issue, for example, when he writes:[61] "That Gentiles could no longer be regarded as profane was also required by God's gift of the Holy Spirit ..." This unnecessarily seems to confuse status of Gentiles (including Cornelius before he met Peter) in general (over against Jews in general) with the status of followers of the Messiah Jesus from both realms. In fact, what Bauckham merges are actually two related but distinct issues. First, there is the equal status of believing Jews and believing Gentiles *as Gentiles*.[62] This status of membership is what is confirmed by the Spirit. Second, since only faith was necessary to reach this status, this implies that both, circumcised and uncircumcised, should be treated in the same manner, both being in need of faith and repentance. Hence, the rejection of the Messiah by Israel *also* implies a state of moral fault (cf. e.g. Acts 2:40) that requires Jews to repent and enter the messianic community (Acts 2:38) from Jews.

To sum up, we find in Acts 10–11 the recognition by Peter that it is wrong to assume moral impurity and profaneness for Gentiles *per se*. Rather, they can become members of the messianic community by repentance and faith, without becoming Jews. As Peter says later (Acts 15:8), God knows the repentant heart and purifies it through faith without making a distinction between Jews and Gentiles (οὐθὲν διέκρινεν μεταξὺ ἡμῶν τε καὶ αὐτῶν; Acts 15:9); both are saved in the same way (Acts 15:11). This implies that even before conversion it would be unfair to treat uncircumcised people as more morally impure and profane than unbelieving Jews. The way Peter counters the objections regarding his association with Gentiles, who became Gentile believers, strongly indicates

---

58 It is not plausible to limit the reference of the verb to a stay *after* the conversion.
59 Bauckham, *James*, 115.
60 Correctly noted by Dunn, *Jerusalem*, 388–389.
61 Bauckham, *James*, 114.
62 Cf. Dunn, *Jerusalem*, 398.

that the equal status confirmed by the Spirit has implications in two directions: (a) It exempts the new members of the messianic community of any moral suspicion that would have justified doubts about having, e.g., a common meal; (b) at the same time it makes clear that these Gentiles are set apart for being told "the word" so that they are on the same level as Jews who have not yet responded positively to the Christian proclamation. As Dunn points out, "Peter was now free to deal with Cornelius as he would have dealt with any fellow Jew."[63]

It seems that this state of affairs, this fundamental change with respect to the attitude towards Gentiles, needs to form our background knowledge for later developments as recounted in Galatians. In any case, there is no good reason for supposing that Luke's depiction of the acceptance of Peter's action (Acts 11:18) at that point in time is exaggerated, just because he recounts dissent on this issue later (Acts 15:1 and 5). Alternatively, one might argue that the Jerusalem church did indeed accept Peter's argument—but that Peter had not made it such a fundamental issue himself. However, if the event was as important for Peter as it is for Luke's narrative, we can assume that his account of what happened included a reference to the relevance that he attributed to this episode. It thus seems doubtful that—so Dunn elaborates—Peter's actions were accepted "as an exception" by some of the congregation.[64] It could only be accepted in principle or rejected at this point. (This does not, of course, exclude the plausible development that the issue became controversial again later, probably after the inclusion of new Jewish believers.)[65] Accordingly, the attempt by Dunn to interpret Peter's leaving Jerusalem (Acts 12:17) as indication of more openness towards the Gentile mission than James[66] is purely speculative. Such reconstructions should not be used as background knowledge for understanding later events, such as the Antioch incident. One wonders whether Dunn is here reading his understanding of the Antioch incident *back* into Peter's experience in Jerusalem. While such a move is of course possible in principle (see above on the differentiation between evidence that is to be evaluated and background knowledge), the problem seems to be here that he thereby creates tension with his own understanding of Peter's opinion of what happened in Cornelius house.

---

63   Dunn, *Jerusalem*, 396.
64   Dunn, *Jerusalem*, 401–402.
65   Bauckham, *James*, 117–118.
66   Hinted at by Dunn, *Jerusalem*, 411.

4.3 The Evidence from the Literary Context in Galatians

When Paul came to Jerusalem to visit Peter (Gal 1:18), it is well possible that both men[67] had already had their experience with Gentile converts. Of course, we cannot know this with certainty because of the difficulty in dating Cornelius's conversion.[68] However, we can at least note that the way Paul recounts his commission as Apostle to the Gentiles (Gal 1:15–17a) with the ἵνα-clause in v. 16 suggests that Gal 1:17b actually refers to missionary activity that includes non-Jews.[69] If we then take into account Peter's skepticism towards Gentiles *before* his vision and the confirmation by the Spirit, the assumption that this encounter pre-dates the first meeting with Paul seems a justifiable inference. Alternative reconstructions seem less plausible. After all, the meeting seems to have been quite uncontroversial and characterized by mutual respect.[70] The position that Peter became familiar with Paul's specific proclamation *before* the conversion of Cornelius and accepted it,[71] yes, even was influenced in his view on Gentiles by Paul,[72] only works if one presupposes that Luke's depiction of Peter's stance toward Gentiles is incorrect (which Dunn does not seem to believe).[73] Alternatively, one could take the fact of a harmonious meeting as the point of departure and argue in the other direction—namely that Paul began his "law-free" mission among Gentiles only later. But that does not seem to fit well with the way Paul structures vv. 15–17.[74] Although nothing of our larger

---

67 Cf. Bauckham, *James*, 134 on Peter's conversion of Cornelius. Cf. Dunn, *Jerusalem*, 385: "some time before 41."

68 Cf. e.g. Martin Hengel and Anna Maria Schwemer, *Paulus zwischen Damaskus und Antiochien: Die unbekannten Jahre des Apostels* (WUNT 108; Tübingen: Mohr Siebeck, 1998), 240 for a dating after Paul's first visit. This dating explains the questions of Bauckham, *James*, 134 with regard to Hengel's consistency.

69 Cf. Eckhard Schnabel, *Urchristliche Mission* (Wuppertal: Brockhaus, 2002), 990–1003 and Hengel and Schwemer, *Paulus*, 153–162 (as well as 174–213). Other reconstructions have to presuppose a later refinement of Paul's gospel or are faced with an inexplicable "gap" in Paul's missionary activity.

70 Of course, Frey, "Paulus," 207 rightly points out that for Paul the confirmation of his commissioning as apostle to the Gentiles does not seem to have been a priority of this visit. But at the same time it does not seem plausible that Paul's actual missionary praxis would not have been known to Peter (cf. Frey, "Paulus," 223; cf. also Gal 1:23).

71 Hengel and Schwemer, *Paulus*, 218–219; cf. also p. 232.

72 Hengel and Schwemer, *Paulus*, 233–235.

73 This seems to be the presupposition of Frey, "Paulus," 223, who also assumes an "erst nach und nach erfolgte Öffnung" for Gentiles.

74 Cf. Jörg Frey, "Paulus und die Apostel," in *Biographie und Persönlichkeit des Apostels* (ed. Eve-Marie Becker and Peter Pilhofer; WUNT 187; Tübingen: Mohr Siebeck, 2005), 202 and

question depends on this reconstruction and although it should be admitted that this is one of the less certain inferences, it seems, hence, appropriate to assume that when Peter and Paul met, both had already come to the conclusion that Gentiles could become part of the messianic community without being circumcised first. If this is correct, it seems beyond imagination that they would have only discussed matters of Peter's knowledge of the earthly Jesus[75] and not also the faith of Gentile believers.[76] Accordingly, there is no need for arguing that Peter's "Pauline" stance at the Jerusalem Council (Acts 15) and in the Petrine tradition might be due to the influence of Paul on Peter during this visit.[77] Exchange on this matter would have taken place within the framework of independently established but coherent boundaries.

In any case—even if Paul had begun his Gentile mission only later—when Paul went up to Jerusalem again (Gal 2:1), this time it is uncontroversial that already some years earlier Peter would already have had to have reached the important conclusion that Jews as well as Gentiles can be "acceptable" to God—and that those who are "accepted" are so in an equal way.[78] It is thus surprising that Dunn does not list Peter's distinct recognition of the end of the common Jewish perspective on Gentiles as a feature of the apostle's theology.[79] This would seem to follow naturally from Dunn's own description of the Cornelius episode, even if we allow for the possibility that there was a difference between Peter's opinion and the way his position was received in Jerusalem (see above). In any case, as long as indications to the contrary are missing, we should not assume that Peter changed his mind between meeting Cornelius and meeting Paul. Nothing in Paul's account of the meeting would suggest anything like that. Paul's main assertion is that when he presented his gospel to the inner circle of the Jerusalem church (Gal 2:2) "nothing was added" to him by those in charge (Gal 2:6). To the contrary (Gal 2:7: ἀλλὰ τοὐναντίον), they recognized that Paul's missionary success among Gentiles (Gal 2:7–9) was equally a gift by God as was the mission of Peter that apparently was known to be

---

206 for the differentiation between the formative commission at Damascus and gradual formulation of this position. However, it seems problematic to attribute the same formative influence to those mentioned in Gal 2:12 and the opponents in Galatia and Corinth (Frey, "Paulus," 212; cf. Markus Bockmuehl, *Jewish Law in Gentile Churches: Halakhah and the Beginning of Christian Public Ethics* [Edinburgh: T&T Clark, 2000], 71–72 on this).

75   Dunn, *Jerusalem*, 369.
76   Vehemently and correctly Bauckham, *James*, 138.
77   Hengel and Schwemer, *Paulus*, 234–235.
78   Dunn, *Jerusalem*, 397–398.
79   Dunn, *Jerusalem*, 414–415.

effective among Jews at that time.[80] There are no fractions visible between Paul on the one side and Peter, James, and John—and Barnabas for that matter— on the other side. Sure, Paul takes care not to attribute too much authority to οἱ δοκοῦντες (Gal 2:2, 6, 9) in the course of describing the dependency of his mission on their acceptance (Gal 2:2!). But to say that the clarification ὁποῖοί ποτε ἦσαν οὐδέν μοι διαφέρει· πρόσωπον [ὁ] θεὸς ἀνθρώπου οὐ λαμβάνει (Gal 2:6) "indicates that he himself has moved on from an earlier esteem for the pillar apostles' authority (as pillars) to a more jaundiced or querulous evaluation of that authority"[81] reads far too much into the text.[82] It might well be that the events at Antioch had made Paul cautious towards appealing too strongly to the authority of others which would make him vulnerable.[83] But there is no indication that he thought it to be a settled matter that at the time of writing that authority had taken a stance against him. Similarly, Dunn's reading of the Antioch incident seems to make him overly sensitive for possible critique directed against Barnabas in this passage.[84] In any case, even if later fraction occurred (which would have to be determined independently in any case), we should at least note that Paul depicts the meeting with the "pillars" to have been very harmonious. Dunn's reading of ἀλλ' οὐδὲ ... ἠναγκάσθη περιτμηθῆναι (Gal 2:3) as indicating that "the Jerusalem apostle had tried to persuade Paul to accede to the demand, but did not insist"[85] is an illegitimate deduction from the negation[86]—and the incomplete but emphatic διὰ δὲ τοὺς παρεισάκτους

---

80 We do not have to consider here the question of what the "division" of spheres implied exactly. Paul does not care to give more details and the most basic point is God's commissioning and not a regulation of missionary target groups. For a good discussion of the options see Schnabel, *Mission*, 951–958.

81 Dunn, *Jerusalem*, 453.

82 On the participle, see now Peter Malik, "Some Notes on the Semantics of οἱ δοκοῦντες in Galatians 2," *ExpTim* 128 (2017): 168–176.

83 Dunn, *Galatians*, 103.

84 Cf. Dunn, *Galatians*, 89 on Gal 2:1 and the order of persons, pp. 92 and 94 on the singular in Gal 2:2 and Gal 2:3 with Dunn, *Galatians*, 101 on the return of the plural in 2:5. How can Paul see himself to have been "wholly at one" with Barnabas against the false brothers while with regard to the Jerusalem agreement he no longer wants to include him in his narration of the events? (Also note the shift to the singular again in Gal 2:6–8 and the return of the plural in Gal 2:9–10, which also does not fit easily into Dunn's paradigm.)

85 Dunn, *Galatians*, 96.

86 This argument is not stronger than the assumption that Titus was *not forced* to get circumcised but got circumcised nevertheless. Gordon D. Fee, *Galatians* (Pentecostal Commentary; Blandford Forum, UK: Deo, 2007), 61 rightly calls such an unwarranted deduction "an idiosyncratic moment of interpretation."

ψευδαδέλφους (Gal 2:4) rather suggests a stark contrast between the action of the "false brothers" and the activity of the "pillars" that is described right after that (Ἀπὸ δὲ τῶν δοκούντων ...; Gal 2:6).[87] Therefore, one can conclude that in light of the Cornelius episode such a pressure from the pillars seems unlikely anyway and that the Pauline text of the second Jerusalem visit seems to be very coherent with that state of affairs. In any case, the assumption of such an attempt of the pillars to have Titus circumcised would at least presuppose a real *change* of opinion. If Gentiles were not to be regarded as impure and profane any longer and if they could become equal members of the messianic covenant and part of the covenant by faith, there is no reason for supporting the demand of the circumcision of Titus. Hence, what is actually astonishing is that Dunn calls the final decision "astonishing."[88] For it seems very much in line with the prior conviction of Peter (and probably also of his peers). Wright's assessment thus seems more in line with Dunn's own characterization of the Cornelius episode: "Paul is simply embarrassed and angry that the issue has been raised at all."[89]

Again, Dunn offers a pointer to how he thinks it might have been possible that a rather strong clash of opinions could happen at Antioch even though he seems to assume a quite radical change of Peter's perception of Gentiles through his experience with Cornelius. He thinks that there might have been "seeds of potential misunderstanding"[90] in the Jerusalem agreement, in the sense that one party might have regarded the care for the poor as in some sense degrading the status of Gentile converts. It is true indeed that the caring for the poor (Gal 2:10) might have been intended to demonstrate to conservative fractions in Jerusalem that the covenantal status of Gentile Christians was legitimate.[91] But this was certainly not regarded as a "compromise" by Paul,[92] who seems to have been quite enthusiastic about this obligation of his churches towards the "mother church" in Jerusalem.[93] No doubt, caring for the poor was important to Jewish identity, but it was certainly not a means of ethnic demar-

---

[87] Dunn, *Galatians*, 97.
[88] Dunn, *Galatians*, 104.
[89] N.T. Wright, *Galatians and Thessalonians* (New Testament for Everyone; Louisville: Westminster John Knox, 2002), 16.
[90] Dunn, *Galatians*, 114.
[91] Dunn, *Galatians*, 113.
[92] Dunn, *Galatians*, 113; Fee, *Galatians*, 70.
[93] If the meeting is identical with the "famine visit" of Acts 11:27–30, this might even be understood as an exhortation to continue something Paul already had done before. Cf. Douglas J. Moo, *Galatians* (BECNT; Grand Rapids: Baker, 2013), 138.

cation. Hence, from a NPP viewpoint it does not seem to fall within the same category as circumcision, which was designed to keep Jews and Gentiles apart. The same could be said about the "apostolic decree"—if one is willing to presuppose that Galatians 2 refers to the same event as Acts 15 and that the decree is an authentic reflection of the official agreement reached there.[94] There might have been misunderstandings later (on which see below), but if we take into account the Cornelius episode as our background knowledge, there is no reason to suppose that confirming that Gentile Christians could become equal members of the messianic community did not have clear implications for the mode of Gentile mission (and the need of circumcision).

But how then are we supposed to understand the next narrated encounter of Peter and Paul, the events recounted in Gal 2:11–14a and interpreted in Paul's speech in Gal 2:14b–21? We must acknowledge that the evidence for any reconstruction of what happened at Antioch at that point in time is very thin. In what follows, I want to present a reconstruction that aims at making as few additional assumptions as possible:

1. The conflict ultimately emerged on the basis of an action by James. Paul's wording in Gal 2:12 is best understood as implying that the "certain people" were indeed commissioned by James and that their arrival caused Peter's action (ὅτε δὲ ἦλθον is not just coincidental temporal information).
2. There is no reason to suppose that James's concern was opposed to a circumcision-free *mission of the Gentiles*.[95] Apparently, what he was concerned with was the *behavior of the Jewish Christians* (cf. Gal 2:13: οἱ λοιποὶ Ἰουδαῖοι).[96]
3. Although much of the discussion has centered on food laws in particular, it seems more plausible that the issue was association of Jewish Christians with Gentiles in general (Gal 2:12: ὑπέστελλεν καὶ ἀφώριζεν ἑαυτόν).[97]
4. There is good historical evidence for assuming that external pressure on the church in Jerusalem raised James's concern of close association

---

94 Bauckham, *James*, 127 and Bockmuehl, *Law*, 168. Against Hengel, *Petrus*, 100–102 and 120–121. I tend towards rejecting the former but accepting the latter conclusion. But nothing in this essay depends on these decisions. Rather, these are issues that should be dealt with on the basis of the discussion of more foundational questions such as the one discussed here.

95 This also implies that it is questionable to assume a break that involves a distinctive "Missionspraxis" (Frey, "Paulus," 220) at Antioch.

96 Bockmuehl, *Law*, 72.

97 Correctly Bockmuehl, *Law*, 72–73.

between Gentile Christians and Jewish Christians in Antioch.[98] If James regarded Antioch as belonging to the holy land, this would be even more plausible.[99] It seems possible that τοὺς ἐκ περιτομῆς refers to a group of persons that goes beyond those messengers from James, even if they (and James) are included.[100] And it might well be that the motivation of this group was heterogeneous (ranging from Jewish zeal for Torah to Jewish-Christian fear).

5. It is plausible in light of Peter's character that he disassociated himself from the Gentile part of the congregation out of fear (Gal 2:12: φοβούμενος).[101] This fits well with the fact that Paul describes this action, as well as Barnabas's later participation due to "group pressure," as "hypocrisy" (συνυπεκρίθησαν ... τῇ ὑποκρίσει; Gal 2:13). Dunn is right that these expressions have the same reference as οὐκ ὀρθοποδοῦσιν πρὸς τὴν ἀλήθειαν τοῦ εὐαγγελίου (Gal 2:14), but this does not change the semantics of the former.[102] Peter did not demonstrate himself to be a hypocrite because he betrayed the earlier agreement on the gospel, but because he did not act on the basis of real conviction. The accusation is quite similar to the one in Gal 6:12–13.[103] Peter, of course, might have designated his behavior very differently, as "respect" or something similar.[104]

6. *James's own* motives and aims remain largely inaccessible. We do not even know whether he—or even those who came from Jerusalem—*asked* Peter to behave in the way he did[105] or whether this was only Peter's own decision, perhaps being based on some information they brought about the critical situation in Jerusalem. The strongest evidence we have is the fact that Paul did not argue with those from Jerusalem and did not point to the agreement with James.[106] It appears as if the real problem was

---

98 Cf. e.g. Bockmuehl, *Law*, 73–75.
99 See the careful discussion by Bockmuehl, *Law*, 61–70.
100 See Moo, *Galatians*, 148 on the lexical fallacy that the phrase has to refer to Jewish *Christians* in light of its other usage in the NT.
101 See now the important study Gibson, *Peter*, which addresses background plausibility in a way that is very significant from the perspective of the philosophy of historiography.
102 Against Dunn, *Galatians*, 125.
103 Cf. on this Justin K. Hardin, *Galatians and the Imperial Cult* (WUNT 2.237; Tübingen: Mohr Siebeck, 2008), 100.
104 Cf. Hengel, *Petrus*, 98.
105 Contra Martinus C. de Boer, *Galatians: A Commentary* (NTL; Louisville: Westminster John Knox, 2011), 130.
106 This is rightly observed by Fee, *Galatians*, 71, although I do not agree with his conclusions.

what *Peter* did with the information he had received. It should be noted that nothing speaks against the possibility that James himself feared the "circumcision party," rather than being their main representative.[107] Nevertheless, it should be admitted that it does seem possible that James had raised "issues of purity"[108] for Jewish believers, as long as one does not claim that he did so with the intention of denying Gentile believers full membership in the messianic community.[109]

Let us sum up these considerations with a focus on Peter's behavior. On the one hand, there is no indication that *Peter had ever changed his view on a Gentile mission since his encounter with Cornelius.* There is in particular no reason to assume that a real change of mind occurred after the meeting in Jerusalem.

This of course was the route famously taken by Baur, who assumes that the earlier recognition of Paul's mission by the "pillars" of the church of Jerusalem lacked an "inner Haltepunkt in ihrem religiösen Bewusstsein."[110] This necessitates a reading of Gal 2:1–10 as a partial success on Paul's part, which is due, however, more to Paul's stubbornness than to real understanding on the part of the "pillars"![111] Such an interpretation seems only possible to maintain if one is not willing to accept anything of the considerations so far as background knowledge. And yet it seems to have influenced the position of Wright: on the one hand, he presupposes a real identity change for Peter since Cornelius's conversion,[112] and on the other hand, he assumes (not without a note of surprise; italics are mine): "[δικαιοσύνη] means 'membership in God's true family.' Peter *had supposed, for a moment at least, that this 'righteousness' was to be defined by Torah.*"[113] Also, the assumption that Paul narrates this event to counter "a version of the story in which Peter had the strongest arguments"—apparently Wright means arguments for why one had to become "a full Jew"—presupposes that Peter had *actually given* such an explicit explanation for his behavior.[114] By contrast, when Wright concentrates on Peter's "play-acting," he emphasizes the *tactical* nature of the change of praxis to a much higher degree.[115] This notion

---

107   Moo, *Galatians*, 148.
108   So Bockmuehl, *Law*, 80.
109   Bockmuehl, *Law*, 81.
110   Baur, *Kirchengeschichte*, 51.
111   Baur, *Kirchengeschichte*, 51.
112   N.T. Wright, *Justification: God's Plan and Paul's Vision* (London: SPCK, 2009), 95.
113   Wright, *Justification*, 100.
114   Wright, *Galatians*, 22.
115   Wright, *Galatians*, 22–23.

of surprise over the fact that "for whatever reasons, both Peter and Barnabas [were] *persuaded*"[116] (italics mine) can also be found in the account of Fee (another exegete who can be assigned to the NPP),[117] who similarly mentions the conversion of Cornelius in the immediate literary context. This justified confusion is probably an indication of incoherent assumptions.

On the other hand, Wright seems correct when he notes that "the question of eating with Gentiles was not an issue which the meeting left undecided."[118] In other words, it is not a good alternative to suppose that Peter *remained faithful* to the Jerusalem agreement but that eating with Gentiles *had simply not been addressed*. As Bauckham rightly stresses, the question of entrance into the covenant for Gentiles and the way they are approached by Jewish believers are two sides of the same coin.[119] If Gentiles could become part of the messianic community *as* Gentiles, this necessarily implied that association with them no longer was a matter of moral impurity or profaneness. Peter had learned this lesson long ago and it would be pure speculation to suggest that he again lost it later. It thus seems surprising that Dunn at one point uses the Cornelius episode in order to explicate *Paul's* thoughts but that he presupposes on the same page that Peter himself apparently did not hold that same—his own—conviction as strongly.[120]

All this is of course not to say that after the Cornelius episode and the two meetings between Peter and Paul in Jerusalem there was no room left for disagreement. At least in Acts 10:28 Peter's conviction is expressed from the perspective of a Jewish Christian, i.e., the focus is on what he was *allowed* to do (cf. ἀθέμιτος). This entailed of course a certain obligation, namely not to regard Gentile believers as profane and morally impure. But it did not, at least not necessarily, imply that one could not disassociate oneself from them for *other* reasons. The practice of keeping a distance towards Gentiles, which would be more comfortable for non-believing fellow Jews, does not contradict in itself the conviction that Gentiles are equal members of Abraham's family. In other words, Dunn is certainly right in pointing out that Peter might have "had very good reasons for his actions."[121] The conflict with Paul arose exactly because they *shared* theological views but did not agree on the question of whether

---

116   Fee, *Galatians*, 72.
117   Cf. also Fee, *Galatians*, 71 and 76 on Jerusalem (and Peter in particular) "breaking" the agreement.
118   Bauckham, *James*, 122. Contra e.g. Hengel, *Petrus*, 92–93.
119   Bauckham, *James*, 123. Contrast with Frey, "Paulus," 225.
120   James D.G. Dunn, "The New Perspective on Paul: Whence, What, Whither?" in Dunn, *The New Perspective on Paul: Collected Essays*, 28.
121   Dunn, *Galatians*, 125.

disassociating oneself from Gentile brothers and sister was incompatible with these ideas. For Peter that might simply have been a "tactically wise accommodation."[122] In what follows, I will thus assume that the incident at Antioch makes best sense before the background of (a) shared theological convictions and (b) disagreements on the compatibility of certain behavior.[123]

Before we turn to Paul's speech, I would like to point out that my reconstruction does *not* imply absolute *harmony* just because it assumes a common theological basis. Paul does not address Peter in the manner of Gal 1:8–9 because he does not assume differing opinions with regard to the gospel. Nevertheless, as κατὰ πρόσωπον αὐτῷ ἀντέστην (Gal 2:11) and τῷ Κηφᾷ ἔμπροσθεν πάντων (Gal 2:14) demonstrate, Paul's reaction to Peter's behavior was very harsh. And since Peter probably had good reasons for his drawing back and since initially he would not have, in all likelihood, regarded his behavior as contradicting their common views on Gentile mission, it is possible that Peter did not react with remorse so that the conflict would have been resolved immediately. It is exactly the fact that there is strong disagreement on behavior *despite* a common theological basis that makes Peter's reaction difficult to predict.[124] While Hengel's conclusion that both apostles "sich ... gegenseitig tief verletzt [hatten] und dadurch zu Kontrahenten [wurden]" is equally speculative,[125] the possibility cannot be excluded that, at the time of writing of the letter, there was still uncertainty with regard to how Paul's and Peter's common convictions were lived out appropriately in light of other constraints.[126] Be this as it may, with regard to even later developments, there is good evidence that the conflict did not result in a lasting break between Peter and Paul (and Jewish and Gentile missions in general as expression of the one gospel).[127] Here, the failure of

---

122 Moo, *Galatians*, 143.
123 This is also assumed by Frey, "Paulus," 225–226, who nevertheless thinks that the break at Antioch was deeper, because he attributes lasting importance to the emphasis on Torah at Jerusalem. But is it plausible to assume that these views on *Jewish halakhah* had such a deep impact on *Gentile mission*?
124 Against Thomas R. Schreiner, *Galatians* (ZECNT; Grand Rapids: Zondervan, 2010), 145: "In other words, there is every reason to believe that Peter responded positively to Paul's reprimand since Peter acted out of fear, and not based on his conviction." Acting out of fear is not equivalent to acting in a state of shock and without contemplation.
125 Hengel, *Petrus*, 85. The considerations by Hengel, *Petrus*, 158–162 can be used with equal right to argue for a much earlier reconciliation.
126 Cf. e.g. Christfried Böttrich, "Der Apostelkonvent und der Antiochenische Konflikt," in *Paulus Handbuch* (ed. Friedrich W. Horn; Tübingen: Mohr Siebeck, 2013), 108–109.
127 Cf. e.g. Christfried Böttrich, "Petrus und Paulus in Antiochien (Gal 2,11–21)," *BTZ* 19 (2002): 237–239.

Baur's paradigm to do justice to the *comparative* nature of historiographical assessments (see on our third principle of Bayesian historiography above) can be seen very clearly.[128] Still, one should acknowledge that we cannot know with certainty who was the "winner" of the argument, if it was at that time even possible to recognize one of them as such.

5 Paul's Speech within the Framework of the New Perspective

We are now in the position to move on to Paul's speech in Gal 2:14–21.[129] Regardless of how one wants to describe the precise nature of Paul's rebuke towards Peter, it should be noted that this speech, and Gal 2:11–21 in general, is in any case *not* what one would expect on the basis of the assumption of Baur's hypothesis. In other words: the explanatory potential of Baur's original paradigm is very low. For as is now widely accepted, Paul's speech presupposes that he and Peter agree fundamentally on a theological level.[130] Peter was "condemned" (2:11) in the sense that his actions after certain people from James came were not in line with his earlier praxis and conviction (2:12). Hence, when Paul addresses Peter he assumes that they share a theological knowledge (2:16),

---

128 To say that "[i]n den sämmtlichen Briefen des Apostel ... uns auch nicht die geringste Andeutung darüber [begegnet], dass in der Folge die beiden Apostel einander wieder näher gekommen sind" (Baur, *Kirchengeschichte*, 53) and to argue that the break with the church of Jerusalem remains a constant factor behind Paul's later letters is very problematic. It should be noted that such "evidence" that is sometimes adduced for lasting fractions between a "Jewish" and a "Gentile" wing in early Christianity does not confirm the Baur-hypothesis over against possible alternative reconstructions. Sure, one can *integrate*, for example, the issues at Corinth into such a framework. But it is an entirely different thing to say that it, hence, *confirms* this hypothesis. Not only is it, of course, possible to understand the same evidence in other frameworks, which do not presuppose a lasting break between Peter and Paul, but also what we actually find in the later NT tradition and beyond is precisely not what one would *expect* on the basis of such a schism (see Bockmuehl, *Peter*, 67–68).

129 It is not relevant for our purposes how much this speech resembled Paul's actual words spoken to Peter. In any case, it is what Paul regarded to be an appropriate response to Peter's behavior after some reflection. Also, it is not very important whether part of the section does not belong to the speech but is rather intended as a later commentary on Paul's response. No doubt, Paul's thoughts are meandering, but no doubt they are also a unity as they stand.

130 This is even acknowledged by Hengel, *Petrus*, 135 with regard to the first person plural in Gal 2:16.

a view on the gospel (2:14), that makes such behavior unacceptable. It is not the case that "sich der Heidenapostel in seinen Grundsätzen so tief verletzte [fühlte]," but rather that he apparently assumed—even at the time of writing his letter—that these *Grundsätze* were a common foundation of his and his colleague's mission. No doubt, Peter's behavior seemed to be terrible to Paul for its *implications* but if he had thought that Peter was explicitly arguing against the gospel, Paul's response should have looked much different (cf. 1:8–9).[131] But what would explain the text as it is? In what follows, we will analyze how Wright's and Dunn's respective versions of the NPP try to make sense of the text and how their new, "abductive" proposals are to be evaluated against the background plausibility of their suggestions.

Paul formulates two premises in Gal 2:14b: Peter is described as being a Jew (σὺ Ἰουδαῖος ὑπάρχων) and as nevertheless "living in Gentile and not in Jewish manner" (ἐθνικῶς καὶ οὐχὶ Ἰουδαϊκῶς ζῇς). It is on this basis that Paul asks: "How can you then force the Gentiles to live like Jews?" (πῶς τὰ ἔθνη ἀναγκάζεις ἰουδαΐζειν). As we have seen above, this compulsion[132] was most certainly not intended. If Peter had taken active steps to promote a Jewish lifestyle, Paul would probably have pointed this out. The pressure is rather indirect: if Gentiles recognize that they are not treated as full members of the messianic community, they have to deduce that they can only be accepted by becoming Jews (ἰουδαΐζειν thus probably includes reference to circumcision here, although this is of course not part of the semantic content itself).[133]

Read against the Cornelius episode as the background knowledge for this passage, it is reasonable to see the reference to Peter's non-Jewish way of life as a *positive* statement by Paul that aims at their shared experience. Wright seems correct in noting that besides "eating with Gentile Christians" this statement refers more generally to Peter "making no difference between himself and them," just as he had learned *"in the house of Cornelius."*[134] Dunn, in contrast, argues that the second premise echoes "the accusation made by those from James" and reflects typical intra-Jewish polemic.[135] It is only in the

---

131   Correctly noted by Schreiner, *Galatians*, 148.
132   The parallel with ἀναγκάζω in Gal 2:3 has often been noted, but it has not been recognized sufficiently that this presupposes that Peter is imagined as having *rejected* this compulsion back then. Hence, this reference can be used as additional argument for our interpretation of the second Jerusalem meeting. Cf. also Gal 6:12 for the situation in Galatia.
133   Correctly Moo, *Galatians*, 151. The focus of Hengel, *Petrus*, 96 on the "Gewissen" of the Gentiles seems to be a Lutheran interpretation that cannot be deduced from the text alone.
134   Wright, *Justification*, 95. Italics are mine.
135   Dunn, *Galatians*, 128. Cf. also his recent comment in reply to Wright in Dunn, "Insider's Perspective," 350.

inconsistency that is deduced from these premises that Dunn recognizes "Paul's own [language]."[136] It is possible indeed that Paul picks up a charge that was brought up against Peter. However, for the sake of the argument it seems necessary that Peter himself *accepted* this premise (although not, of course, the negative evaluation of this behavior). Thus, if we have an echo of conservative polemic against Peter's openness towards Gentiles (cf. Acts 11:3!), it would be plausible to assume that Paul uses this language intentionally to remind Peter of the arguments he had to face himself—and in which he had of course defended the acceptance of Gentiles *as* Gentiles. (This is confirmed by Paul's usage of the designation "sinners" in Gal 2:15 and Gal 2:17, on which see below.) Hence, the polemical statement that Peter had been living in a Gentile manner referred to the fact that he no longer distinguished between Jew and Gentile. This observation, so Wright, "was not a criticism," but, for Paul, "part of 'the truth of the gospel.'"[137]

The first person plural in Gal 2:15 indicates that we should read this verse as continuation of Paul's confrontation of Peter. How Gal 2:15–16 relates semantically to the question in Gal 2:14b is difficult to determine since no connector is used. It no longer focuses on Peter's behavior but on its consequences with regard to membership in the messianic community, the implication that Gentiles must become Jews. Syntactically,[138] it is best to regard Gal 2:15 as a nominal clause: "We [are] Jews by nature and not 'Gentile sinners.'" If this is the case, the participle in Gal 2:16 should probably be connected with the verb ἐπιστεύσαμεν: "¹⁵We are Jews ... ¹⁶ But since we know that ... [causal clause], even we have put our faith in Jesus Christ [main clause]." If one regards the δέ to be a later insertion in order to clarify the adversative function of Gal 2:16 over against Gal 2:15,[139] this reading is still possible but it might become preferable to regard Gal 2:15 as the subject that is then picked up again in the main clause in Gal 2:16:[15] "We—Jews by nature and not Gentile sinners¹⁶—even we have put our faith in the Messiah Jesus [main clause], because we know that ... [causal clause]."[140] In any case, the καὶ ἡμεῖς in Gal 2:16 seems to pick up the "Jews by nature" from Gal 2:15: "Even we—the 'Jews by birth'—have put our faith in the Messiah Jesus."

By contrast, Dunn's rendering of these verses in his commentary is quite different. He translates: "¹⁵We are Jews by nature and not 'Gentile sinners,' ¹⁶knowing that no human being is justified by works of the law but only through

---

136   Dunn, *Galatians*, 129.
137   Wright, *Paul*, 1435.
138   On the options, see Moo, *Galatians*, 173.
139   E.g. Dunn, *Galatians*, 131.
140   Cf. e.g. Boer, *Galatians*, 141.

faith in Jesus Christ, and we have believed in Christ Jesus, in order that we might be justified by faith in Christ and not by works of the law, because ..."[141] While he is in agreement with many other scholars in taking v. 15 as a nominal clause, it is suspicious that he treats the participle εἰδότες in v. 16a apparently as pointing back adverbially to that sentence. This results in the καί in v. 16b suddenly introducing the main clause. In Dunn's original, pioneering work on this passage the relation between v. 15 and εἰδότες in v. 16 is depicted as even closer. There, Dunn translates: "[15]We who are Jews by nature and not Gentile sinners, [16]know that a man is not justified by works of law except through faith in Christ Jesus."[142] Thus, the participle is translated here like an indicative verb and is totally disconnected from the main clause with ἐπιστεύσαμεν in v. 16b. On the level of content, this syntactical solution has the effect that the "being Jewish" from v. 15 is connected closely with the "insight" of v. 16a, with the result of it becoming "an accepted view of Jewish Christians."[143] It follows necessarily that any novel argumentative move has to be located in what follows after that. However, it seems very problematic to connect the participle in an adverbial way with the verbless clause in v. 15.[144]

On the basis of these syntactical observations, we can now turn to the content of Gal 2:15. Wright is correct in speaking of "a standard Jewish attitude" with regard to Paul's talk about "sinners."[145] Dunn similarly thinks that Paul is "putting himself in the shoes of a typical Jew who looked out at the rest of the world as outside the realm of God's covenant righteousness and sinful."[146] However, it seems less obvious when Dunn claims that this "is the language of conciliation" and that he was "reaching out to Peter."[147] The demarcation between ethnic Jews (φύσει Ἰουδαῖοι) and Gentiles *as sinners* (i.e., as morally impure) had been left behind by Peter since the conversion of Cornelius and Peter would, hence, not have found his own position reflected in such a designation. Also, if this expression corresponded to the attack by the people of James (an assumption which seems itself problematic due to the extreme harshness of such an attack)[148] *as well as* to Peter's position, this would imply

---

141   See e.g. Dunn, *Galatians*, 131.
142   Dunn, "New Perspective," 96.
143   Cf. Dunn, "New Perspective," 96.
144   Against e.g. Richard N. Longenecker, *Galatians* (WBC 41; Dallas: Word, 1990), 83.
145   Wright, *Justification*, 95.
146   Dunn, *Galatians*, 133.
147   Dunn, *Galatians*, 133.
148   An assumption that is of course in line with the idea that Peter's relationship to Jerusalem had become problematic because of *Peter's own* "laxness" with regard to the law (Hengel,

that Peter adopted the perspective of "those of the circumcision" as his own, although Paul says he acted out of fear. Furthermore, this reading does not seem to be able to account for the usage in Gal 2:17, where it is most plausible to assume that Paul speaks explicitly of Peter and himself as belonging in this category. Hence, Gal 2:15–16 should not be regarded as an argument that tries to convince Peter of a theological truth. Paul rather points out that his and Peter's shared conviction excludes the possibility that Gentiles would have to become Jews in order to being acceptable for God. The direction is rather turned on its head: they have become just like Gentiles, like "sinners," in order to be included in the covenant people.[149] In a certain way, this is parallel to the premise that Peter "lives in Gentile manner" (Gal 2:14b): since he has recognized that access to the messianic community is the same for Jews and Gentiles (Gal 2:15–16), he accepts Gentiles as acceptable and Gentile Christians as accepted by God and behaves accordingly (Gal 2:14b).

If our syntactical analysis of Gal 2:15–16 is correct, it follows naturally that on a semantic level a concessive function for Gal 2:15 should be assumed.[150] In other words, *although* Peter and Paul were everything a fellow Jew could have demanded (compare Gal 2:15 with Phil 3:4–6), they did not make this their basis for their "righteous" status (cf. Gal 2:16 and Phil 3:7; see also Acts 15:11). In Wright's words this means that Gal 2:15–16 offers a radical redefinition of the Jewish doctrine of election around the Messiah Jesus.[151] On this basis, many scholars believe that it is best to assume that ἐὰν μὴ διὰ πίστεως Ἰησοῦ Χριστοῦ in 2:16 is not exceptive but adversative.[152] To be sure, it should be admitted that Dunn's reading as "but only"[153] has a good explanatory potential. Nevertheless, from our discussion it has emerged that the background plausibility that Paul must convince Peter that "works of the law" (as boundary markers of the messianic community) are incompatible with faith as access to the messianic community[154] is low. Thus, it is not necessary to see in Gal 2:16 a shift from "works of the law *in combination* with faith" to "faith alone." The more common use of ἐὰν μή should not determine the rhetorical function of Gal 2:15–16 but

---

Studien, 75). However, there is not much evidence that can be adduced for shifting the main conflict in early Christianity from Peter-Paul to Peter-James. This view presupposes a problem of authority for Peter in Jerusalem that is difficult to maintain.

149 Cf. Moo, *Galatians*, 157.
150 Moo, *Galatians*, 156.
151 Cf. now Wright, *Paul*, 852–860.
152 Moo, *Galatians*, 162–163.
153 Dunn, *Galatians*, 133.
154 Dunn, *Galatians*, 138.

vice versa, having established the latter independently, i.e. on the basis of the literary and historical context.[155] We cannot go into any details of the meaning of the phrase "works of the law"[156] nor is this necessary for our purpose: whatever the exact meaning of the phrase "works of the law" is and independent of the question of whether Paul had a broader concept of works and merit, it seems very reasonable that in our context it *refers* to those deeds commanded by Torah that "divide Jew from Gentile."[157]

The last paragraph implies that the shared knowledge (εἰδότες) of Peter and Paul includes not only the *necessity* of faith in the Messiah (εἰς Χριστὸν Ἰησοῦν ἐπιστεύσαμεν)[158] *but also its sufficiency* (ὅτι ἐξ ἔργων νόμου οὐ δικαιωθήσεται πᾶσα σάρξ).[159] The issue for which faith is both a necessary (as demonstrated by Jewish Christians)[160] and sufficient (as being important for Gentile Christians) condition is the membership in God's people as expressed by the metaphor[161] of "justification," i.e., the act of being declared to be in the right by the judge.[162] The fact that Paul uses the metaphor in order to summarize common ground between him and Peter on the access of Gentiles to the covenant people does not necessitate the assumption that he did not "invent" it (Jas 2:14–26 probably is a reaction to a version of Paul's teaching). Even

---

155 In any case, see now Debbie Hunn, "Ἐὰν μή in Galatians 2:16: A Look at Greek Literature," *NovT* 49 (2007): 281–290.

156 Cf. e.g. Frey, "Jewishness," 92–94 for a recent summary of opinions.

157 Wright, *Justification*, 96. Fee, *Galatians*, 84 correctly notes with regard to the meaning "doing good works in order to gain salvation" that "One can say definitively that such is not its meaning here." Even Hengel, *Petrus*, 96 who uses the classical terminology of "heilsnotwendig[e]" works agrees on the concrete reference of the phrase. Cf. also Frey, "Jewishness," 80 on Paul and circumcision (and boundary markers in general). Frey later in this chapter criticizes aspects of the NPP, which should however—from my perspective—rather be seen as reductionist variants of the NPP (cf. Hengel, *Petrus*, 86–94, where Frey can refer to Wright as well as Dunn as sharing his views).

158 I will not discuss the genitive Χριστοῦ. This is another issue where Wright and Dunn differ (cf. Wright, *Justification*, 97). Regardless of whether the faithfulness of the Messiah played a role in bringing about the state of "righteousness," the main clause focuses on the act of faith of Jewish Christians.

159 Contra Dunn, *Galatians*, 140: "Paul was trying to move Peter away from the ambiguity of the opening statement." Dunn himself refers to Acts 11:17 as indicating "that Paul's appeal included reference to Peter's earlier experience with Cornelius."

160 Cf. Wright, *Justification*, 97–98. Wright's argument does not seem very far removed from those who oppose the NPP with regard to this point.

161 The comments by Fee, *Galatians*, 81–82 on different metaphors for expressing aspects of God's salvific work are helpful.

162 Dunn, *Galatians*, 134.

within a NPP reading that focuses on the dimension of "national righteousness," the metaphor will probably never be devoid of moral connotations insofar as the Jewish designation of Gentiles as "sinners" does not simply express Jewish national pride but (more specifically) the moral impurity of Gentiles.[163] The change from ζῶν (Ps 142:2 LXX)[164] to σάρξ (which was anyway by far the more usual combination in the LXX) might reflect this awareness that the nullification of ethnic boundary markers implied the gracious acceptance of those who were formerly outside the covenant. In light of Phil 3:3, it seems equally possible, however, that the focus is exactly on the "fleshly" mark of circumcision. In any case, the emphasis is on the insufficiency of the ἔργα νόμου. If one agrees that they refer to those marks which were meant to keep *Jews* apart from sinful Gentiles, then σάρξ, even if used intentionally with the negative connotation of "the nature of human beings as frail and weak,"[165] specifically sheds bad light on Jewish exceptionalism. And indeed, in the context Paul's focus is not to make statements regarding humanity in general but to degrade Jewish claims that would justify Peter's behavior but deny the gospel.

Accordingly, Gal 2:17a should be read as rephrasing Peter's and Paul's recognition: "We are found to be 'sinners' ourselves (εὑρέθημεν καὶ αὐτοὶ ἁμαρτωλοί) in seeking to be justified in the Messiah (ζητοῦντες δικαιωθῆναι ἐν Χριστῷ)." Dunn sees here again inner-Jewish polemic at work just as in Gal 2:15: "The surprising discovery for Paul (and Peter) was evidently that their eating with Gentiles caused them to be regarded as 'sinners,' even by their fellow believers ... the James faction still insisted on regarding Gentiles as 'sinners,' and those Jews who disregarded or treated lightly the traditional boundary lines by eating with them as equally 'sinners.'"[166] The passive of εὑρίσκω here seems indeed to signal astonishment—as any "Jew by birth" would be astonished to recognize that he was on the same level as those people he regarded as "sinners." However, it does not seem to leave open the possibility that what is "found" does not correspond to reality. The δέ rather signals a further development of the argument: if it is true that ἐξ ἔργων νόμου οὐ δικαιωθήσεται πᾶσα σάρξ (Gal 2:16), this *effectively means* that εὑρέθημεν καὶ αὐτοὶ ἁμαρτωλοί (Gal 2:17a). Wright thus seems to be on the right track when he paraphrases Gal 2:16–17a: "Yes, we are seeking to find our identity as God's people 'in the Messiah,' ... and yes, that means that in terms of the Torah as we know it we find ourselves standing alongside

---

163   Cf. above on Bauckham, *James*.
164   The use of Scripture does not imply that the "we" of Gal 2:15–16 refers to Jews in general and that Paul's ideas about "justification" were commonly held by his contemporaries.
165   Moo, *Galatians*, 159.
166   Dunn, *Galatians*, 141.

'Gentile sinners,' as in v. 15. Technically, we are 'sinners' like them."[167] Alternatively, if one regards Gal 2:17c as reacting against the whole of Gal 2:17ab, it would be possible to see the contrast not between "being 'sinner'" and "being a transgressor" and the fact that only the latter makes the Messiah a "servant of sin," but between *not* being "sinner" versus "being a transgressor." In other words, Paul might be saying: "To put our faith in the Messiah does not make us 'sinners' (= those outset the covenant) with the effect that the Messiah would become a servant of sin, but rather putting our trust in the 'works of the law' would make us transgressors and the Messiah a servant of Sin."[168] However, in light of Rom 3:3, the μὴ γένοιτο (Gal 2:17c) should probably not be understood as referring to the protasis as well (cf. also Rom 3:5–6) but only to the apodosis: Does this—the fact that Jews are also like "sinners," i.e., become members of the messianic community only by faith—mean that the Messiah is a servant of sin (ἆρα Χριστὸς ἁμαρτίας διάκονος;)?[169] Dunn himself writes: "But the implication of such an attitude was intolerable."[170] However, Dunn deduces that since the consequence is intolerable, this most also apply to the premise. Hence, Gal 2:17 is judged to be a *"reductio ad absurdum* of Peter's theology."[171] Our own exegesis in contrast allows for Gal 2:17 to be a reflection of *Peter's and Paul's common perception* that as Jews they had the same entry conditions as Gentiles. What Paul vehemently denies—probably explicitly reacting to those who would have liked seeing Jewish Christians disassociate from Gentiles[172]— is that this inevitable fact (εὑρέθημεν ...) might degrade the Messiah.

---

167 Wright, *Justification*, 98.
168 The suggestion of Bauckham, *James*, 133 goes in this direction: Paul wants to stress that if they (Peter and Paul) do not become "sinners" by placing their hope in the Messiah, then Gentiles should not be regarded as such, is interesting indeed. However, one would have to assume (a) that Gal 2:17a is denied by Gal 2:17c too and (b) that the focus on the status of Jewish Christians is only there to make deductions for Gentile Christians. But this is not confirmed by what follows in Paul's argument. Wright, *Galatians*, 27 seems to presuppose a similar logic: "This doesn't mean ... that by losing Jewish identity we are 'sinners,' as the Jews had regarded the Gentiles. On the contrary, if like Peter you reconstruct the wall between Jews and Gentiles, all you achieve is to prove that you yourself are a lawbreaker."
169 Cf. Moo, *Galatians*, 167.
170 Dunn, *Galatians*, 141.
171 Dunn, *Galatians*, 142. Similarly (although without assuming Paul picking up language from opponents), Fee, *Galatians*, 88–89: If eating with Gentiles is sin, and we have done this "because of our new relationship with God through Christ," this means that Christ is promoting sin. And that is impossible.
172 Cf. Wright, *Justification*, 98.

The rationale (cf. γάρ) for the "rejection of the logic of verse 17"[173] is offered in Gal 2:18: if "I" rebuild what I had previously destroyed, I demonstrate myself to be a transgressor (παραβάτην). The thing that is (in close analogy to Eph 2:14–15) torn down and rebuilt probably is the "those parts of the law that in various ways segregated Jews from Gentiles."[174] Paul argues here that re-erecting the division between Jews and Gentiles, re-affirming the moral impurity and profaneness of Gentiles, making a difference in treating Jewish and Gentile Christians, necessarily implies that earlier association with Gentile Christians would have to be re-evaluated as ἀθέμιτος (Acts 10:28).

How does this counter the logic of Gal 2:17? Apparently, Paul presupposes that he can assume that Peter would agree that the removal of the division between Jews and Gentiles was the will of God. This is where Gal 2:19–20 fits in: the earlier decision to accept Gentiles as Gentiles is not the result of some laxness on the side of Paul in order to please people (cf. Gal 1:10 and Gal 5:11). Rather, his life, including his outreach to Gentiles, is determined by a transformative act of God and rooted in the death of the Messiah.[175] Accordingly, accepting Gentiles as Gentiles into the messianic community must have been right and could not have been an act of "transgression" (cf. Gal 2:7–9!). And since this would constitute an inacceptable verdict, one cannot act in way that would imply it, namely by re-erecting the division. It is exactly in this case, if one decides to do re-erect that division nevertheless, that one would actually have to conclude that the Messiah had become ἁμαρτίας διάκονος after all. Dunn is certainly right that for Paul the idea that "his whole life as a Christian, in its outreach to Gentiles, was one long act of transgression, which put him beyond the pale of God's acceptance, was an impossible contradiction of what the gospel meant."[176] However, Gal 2:18 only becomes a good response to Gal 2:17 if Paul can assume that *Peter* would still have agreed on the validity of the Gentile mission. And at least on the basis of Luke's account of the Cornelius episode and everything Paul has told us so far about Peter, he had every reason to make that assumption. For against this background knowledge, one could easily argue that Peter himself could have recounted a story very similar to Gal

---

173   Moo, *Galatians*, 166.
174   Moo, *Galatians*, 167.
175   Correctly noted by Dunn, *Galatians*, 144: "Paul was anxious to make clear that his about-face regarding the law was no mere idiosyncratic decision on his part; on the contrary it was the inevitable working out of Christ's death; it was part and parcel of Jesus's own death."
176   Dunn, *Galatians*, 143. The use of the "I" to focus on *Peter* (Hengel, *Petrus*, 96–97) seems less plausible.

2:19–20! Therefore, on the one hand, the shift to the first person singular might indeed signal a focus on Paul's own person and his mission,[177] which he recognized to appear in dubious light due to Peter's behavior. However, at the same time, this does not mean that Paul has given up the hope that Peter would agree with him.[178] It is exactly the shift to the singular that calls on Peter's personal respect for Paul's calling and it should not be overlooked that Paul still assumed that he could presuppose that Peter would agree on the status of his missionary work, seeing in it the reflection of his own mission and effort.

When Paul sums up his speech by saying that he does not "nullify the grace of God" (Οὐκ ἀθετῶ τὴν χάριν τοῦ θεοῦ; Gal 2:21a), this means that he can and will not re-erect the dividing wall between Gentiles and Jews. Insisting on the Jewish law as providing the basis for being declared righteous, of being accepted as a member of the messianic community (Gal 2:21b: εἰ γὰρ διὰ νόμου δικαιοσύνη),[179] would mean that the Messiah died in vain (Gal 2:21c: ἄρα Χριστὸς δωρεὰν ἀπέθανεν), because for Paul the Messiah's death inaugurated a new period (cf. Gal 3:13–14; see already Gal 1:4!).[180] Dunn thinks that Paul inserts Gal 2:21 because he notices that "the format of an extended reminiscence of his reply to Peter at Antioch was becoming too strained, and that he must begin to address the challenge of the Galatian situation more directly."[181] Although I completely agree that the christological focus aims at providing a point of departure for turning emphatically to the Galatian situation (cf. Gal 3:1 Ὦ ἀνόητοι Γαλάται …), I think that a train of thought is recognizable throughout that leads directly to this point: Paul has dug deeper and deeper in the foundations of his conviction of God's acceptance of Gentiles into his people. This had the effect of exposing the grave results of apparently pragmatic actions of Peter on a very fundamental level while at the same time offering a very basic framework for addressing the Galatian situation.

---

177   Contra Wright, *Justification*, 99 and Wright, *Paul*, 1425 who regards the use of "I" (here and in Rom 7) as "a way of saying 'this is what happens to Jews,' without saying it as though that were something which Paul could look at from the outside." I think this misses part of the dynamics between Peter and Paul which is still at work here in Gal 2:18.
178   Cf. Dunn, *Galatians*, 144, who seems to imply this.
179   Rightly Dunn, *Galatians*, 148.
180   Cf. Dunn, *Galatians*, 149.
181   Dunn, *Galatians*, 149.

6 Synthesis: The New Perspective on (Paul on) Peter

As I have noted above, we can be quite confident that the dispute did not have lasting effects on early Christian mission, but we cannot know whether Peter re-continued associating with Gentile Christians after having been confronted by Paul. The simple fact that Paul does not recount this is no disproof—having set the stage for his argument in Galatians 3, there would not have been much sense in going back to the concrete issue with Peter.[182] Nevertheless, it might also be that Peter did not think that disassociating himself from Gentile Christians really implied "nullifying God's grace" (Gal 2:21a). One could imagine that he would have found a compromise quite appealing: after all, he could have suggested that he would keep himself at a distance from his Gentile brothers and sisters for tactical reasons while making clear to them that this did *not* imply that "righteousness is through the law" (Gal 2:21b), with the result that there would not have been pressure or need for "judaizing" (Gal 2:15). Be this as it may: although we do not know whether Peter agreed that his behavior had to have the implications Paul argued they had, Gal 2:14–21 "at least" gives us insights into the theological basis that Paul assumed to share with Peter and that served him as point of departure for pointing out these consequences.

We can thus conclude that reading Paul's speech in Gal 2:14–21 through the lens of the NPP offers a perspective on *Peter* that coheres very well with Luke's narration of the Cornelius episode in Acts 10–11.[183] In fact, the NPP seems to offer much more potential for recognizing parallels between Paul's speech and Luke's account of Peter's position than either Wright or Dunn seem to be willing to acknowledge. It is here that the Baur κληρονομία in the NPP seems to shine through: In the end, Paul remains the real hero, while Peter's own position cannot be comprehended without a good amount of surprise (Wright) or without alleging quite significant inconsistencies (Dunn). But would it be so bad if in the end the "NPP" were a "new perspective on Peter"?[184]

---

182 Against Hengel, *Petrus*, 103.

183 The resulting reconstruction has the advantage that one does not have to presuppose an almost inexplicable gap between Peter's convictions before and after the Antioch incident (cf. e.g. conclusions 5 and 6 with conclusions 7 and 8 in Hengel, *Petrus*, 163–164).

184 In a recent collection on Wright's Pauline interpretation, this "privileging" of Paul has been criticized by some contributors. See e.g. Heilig and Heilig, "Historical Methodology," 144–145 and James H. Charlesworth, "Wright's Paradigm of Early Jewish Thought: Avoidance of Anachronisms," in Heilig et al., eds., *God and the Faithfulness of Paul*, 229–230.

Tradition as Interpretation: Linguistic Structure and the Citation of Scripture in 1 Peter 2:1–10

Andrew W. Pitts

1 Peter 2:1–10 has attracted increasing interest from scholars in the last fifty years. John Elliott devoted an entire monograph to 2:4–10[1] and at least six others deal with it extensively in the context of broader discussions.[2] Several significant articles have also recently emerged.[3] Few treatments, however, have convincingly attempted to situate the passage within the overall strategy of the discourse. This occasions the need for the present study. As with other uses of the Old Testament in 1 Peter, 2:1–10 employs Scripture in the service of developing/supporting communal motifs and/or exhortations issued in connection with them. I will argue that Scripture is not interpreted by Peter primarily in a pesher-like fashion or in accordance with the practices of Jewish midrash, but in light of early Christian traditional material.

---

1 J.H. Elliott, *The Elect and the Holy: An Exegetical Examination of 1 Peter 2:4–10 and the Phrase βασίλειον ἱεράτευμα* (NovTSup 12; Leiden: Brill, 1966).

2 B. Lindars, *New Testament Apologetic: The Doctrinal Significance of Old Testament Quotations* (London: SCM, 1961); B. Gärtner, *The Temple and the Community in Qumran and in the New Testament* (SNTSMS 1; Cambridge: Cambridge University Press, 1965); W.L. Schutter, *Hermeneutic and Composition* (WUNT 2.30; Tübingen: Mohr Siebeck, 1989), 85–100, 123–138; Andrew M. Mbuvi, *Temple, Exile and Identity in 1 Peter* (LNTS 345; New York: T&T Clark, 2007); Abson Prédestin Joseph, *A Narratological Reading of 1 Peter* (LNTS 440; London: T&T Clark, 2012), esp. 88–93; David G. Horrell, *Becoming Christian: Essays on 1 Peter and the Making of Christian Identity* (LNTS 394; London: Bloomsbury, 2013), esp. 133–163.

3 E.g. F.W. Danker, "1 Peter 1:24–2:17: A Consolatory Pericope," *ZNW* 58 (1967): 93–102; K.R. Snodgrass, "1 Peter II.1–10: Its Formation and Literary Affinities," *NTS* 24 (1977): 97–106; V.R. Steuernagel, "An Exiled Community as a Missionary Community: A Study Based on 1 Peter 2:9, 10," *ERT* 10 (1981): 8–18; S. Minear, "The House of Living Stones: A Study in 1 Peter 2:4–12," *Ecumenical Review* 34 (1982): 238–248; E. Schweizer, "The Priesthood of all Believers: 1 Peter 2:1–10," in *Theology, Worship and Ministry in the Early Church: Essays in Honour of Ralph Martin* (ed. M.J. Wilkins and T. Paige; JSNTSup 87; Sheffield: JSOT Press, 1992), 285–293; R.T. France, "First Century Bible Study: Old Testament Motifs in 1 Peter 2:4–10," *Journal of the European Pentecostal Theological Association* 18 (1998): 26–48; cf. also E.W. Glenny, "The Israelite Imagery of 1 Peter 2," in *Dispensationalism, Israel and the Church* (ed. C.A. Blasing and D.L. Bock; Grand Rapids: Zondervan, 1992), 156–187.

1   **Literary Form and Linguistic Structure**

The passage has been viewed against a variety of literary backgrounds including Jewish midrash,[4] *testimonia*,[5] and early Christian hymnology.[6] Contrary to Schutter and Elliott's insistence, Wright has convincingly demonstrated that midrash is always for the sake of the biblical text cited and is not intended to contribute to a new composition,[7] as is reflected in the use of Scripture in 1 Peter.[8] Similarly, Harris's *testimonia* theory[9] has been called into serious question by scholars such as Dodd who insists that the portrayal is somewhat anachronistic since it is hard to conceive of these types of collections as early as New Testament times.[10] Neither does the passage have the fundamental characteristics of an ancient hymn, as Elliott has convincingly shown.[11] Best probably comes the closest when he argues that 2:4–10 most likely draws from early Christian traditional material, but he fails to successfully integrate the passage within the larger strategy of the discourse or to show how it is illumined by the Petrine hermeneutic set out in 1:10–12.[12] In this connection, my analysis

---

4   Schutter's central thesis is that 1 Pet 1:13–2:10 is an instance of homiletic midrash. Schutter, *Hermeneutic and Composition*, 85–100, 130–138; Elliott, *Elect*, 36–38; P.J. Achtemeier, *1 Peter* (Hermeneia; Philadelphia: Fortress, 1996), 150–151. Achtemeier is representative of a fairly common perspective on this passage when he suggests, "The similarity between this passage in 1 Peter and materials from Qumran, a similarity greater in the case of this letter than of any other NT writing, has been used as a basis for seeing in the Qumran material a possible source for these verses. There are, for example, references to a new temple (e.g., 1QS 8.4–6, using Isa 28:16); to nonmaterial sacrifice (e.g., 1QS 8.4–6; 9.3–5; 4QFlor 1.6–7); to members of the community as stones (4QpIsad, frag. i; cf. 1QH 6.25–27), perhaps even to the priesthood of the community as directly related to the new temple (e.g., CD 3.19–4.3). Additionally, the use of the OT citations in this passage in 1 Peter also bears strong resemblance to the kind of midrashic exegesis evident at Qumran, including at times pesher-like interpretation, although such exegetical procedures are by no means limited in the NT to 1 Peter."
5   For a survey of the literature on this view, see Elliott, *Elect*, 130–133.
6   E.G. Selwyn, *The First Epistle of St. Peter* (London: Macmillan, 1946), 268–281; H. Windisch, *Die Katholischen Briefe* (3rd ed.; ed. H. Preisker; HNT; Tübingen: Mohr Siebeck, 1951), 161.
7   A.G. Wright, "Literary Genre Midrash," *CBQ* 28 (1966): 105–138, 414–457.
8   Best shows how several individual texts do not align with a proper understanding of midrash. E. Best, "1 Peter II 4–10: A Reconsideration," *NovT* (1969): 270–293.
9   J.R. Harris, *Testimonies* (I–II; Cambridge: Cambridge University Press, 1916).
10   C.H. Dodd, *According to the Scriptures* (London: Nisbet, 1962), 24–27; but cf. 4QTestimonia/4Q Florilegium.
11   Elliott, *Elect*, 133–138.
12   Best, "1 Peter II 4–10," 270–293. Best does remark in a general manner that quotations of

also differs from Best due to the linguistic methodology that drives it, including especially the broader discourse concerns that Best apparently minimizes. In agreement with Best, however, I will argue in the next section of this chapter that the hermeneutic employed in 2:1–10 draws heavily from traditional material in its interpretation of Old Testament passages.

Typically, 2:1–10 is not treated as a unit. Most studies posit a break between 2:1–3 and 2:4–10.[13] Understanding 2:1–10 as a single unit, however, seems far more stable linguistically.[14] The clause structure for the passage begins in 2:1 with an independent clause forming a hypotactic structure with all of the subsequent clauses up to 2:7 where the finite verb breaks the pattern. The conditional clause in 2:3 (εἰ ἐγεύσασθε ὅτι χρηστὸς ὁ κύριος) is connected to the exhortations in 2:1–2. The circumstantial participial clause in 2:4 (see below) then expands upon the finite verb it modifies (ἐγεύσασθε) as do the subsequent embedded and dependent clauses that run up through 2:6. The author is expounding upon the manner in which the audience is expected to taste of the goodness of God. It is through their new communal identity. In 2:7–8, the chain of dependence is broken through the introduction of a finite verb in order to summarize and draw an antithesis with the audience's former identity in typical Petrine style. The positive side of the antithesis is then restated emphatically in 2:9–10 as the author draws together a plethora of Old Testament people-of-God motifs and applies them directly to his audience.

In 2:1 there is a shift away from the kinship terminology that was prominent in 1:14–25 and words for status,[15] membership among groups and classes of people,[16] and, to some extent, words from the semantic domain for people[17]

Old Testament passages in 1 Peter typically either support or advance an argument (293). And this is good as far as it goes. The theory still fails to show how quotations function within the argument and their role in the development of the argument.

13 Elliott, *Elect*, 146–147; I. Howard Marshall, *1 Peter* (IVP New Testament Commentary Series; Downers Grove, IL: InterVarsity, 1991), 65; L. Goppelt, *A Commentary on I Peter* (ed. R. Hahn; trans. and augmented by J.E. Alsup; Grand Rapids: Eerdmans, 1993), 134; Achtemeier, *1 Peter*, 149–150; J.H. Elliott, *1 Peter: A New Translation with Introduction and Commentary* (AB 37B; New York: Doubleday, 2000), 404–405; K. Jobes, *1 Peter* (BECNT; Grand Rapids: Baker Academic, 2005), 144.

14 So Snodgrass, "1 Peter II.1–10," 97–106; P.H. Davids, *The First Epistle of Peter* (NICNT; Grand Rapids: Eerdmans, 1990), 79.

15 L&N, Domain 87.

16 L&N, Domain 11.

17 L&N, Domain 9.

(4× in 2:1–10) occur most frequently.[18] The use of βρέφη[19] with ἀρτιγέννητα ensures that familial relations are no longer in view, helping to establish a new semantic environment for the coding of the new motif. The semantic similarity between βρέφη and τέκνα (1:14), however, provides cohesion through the transition from 1:25 into 2:1–3, creating texture and linkage between the paragraphs.[20] The structure of the passage is distinct when compared with the rest of 1 Peter. Instead of having exhortations followed by brief support through traditional material and theological exposition, this passage begins with a cluster of commands and then engages in an extended exposition of the communal status of the audience in support. The uninterrupted character of the explanation is suggestive of its conceptual centrality to the discourse. Scriptural quotations are used excessively in developing the motif.

Many take προσερχόμενοι in 1 Pet 2:4 as an imperatival participle,[21] but this function of the participle is limited to independent contexts and so is unjustified here.[22] The participle should be understood instead as a circumstantial participle of manner related to the finite verb in 2:3,[23] explaining the manner in which the audience has tasted of the goodness of the Lord. Typical of the style of 1 Peter, the author expounds the identity of the audience through communal applications of Scripture to the recipients, forming one of the largest collections of Old Testament passages in the New Testament. What distinguishes this passage from the ones that precede it and those that follow is the extended nature of the exposition. It develops the identity of the audience more thoroughly and more consecutively than any other passage in the letter, establishing a close connection between the community's identity and the author's

---

18 The two domains are often indistinguishable. J.T. Reed, *A Discourse Analysis of Philippians: Method and Rhetoric in the Debate over Literary Integrity* (JSNTSup 136; Sheffield: Sheffield Academic, 1997), 300.
19 L&N, Domain 9.
20 Cf. Elliott, *1 Peter*, 399.
21 Jobes, *1 Peter*, 145; D. Senior, *1 and 2 Peter* (NT Message 20; Wilmington, DE: Michael Glazier, 1980), 30; Senior, "1 Peter," 53; Minear, "House," 240; W. Grundmann, "die ΝΗΠΙΟΙ in die urchristlichen paränese," *NTS* 5 (1959): 188–205; Goppelt, *A Commentary on I Peter*, 137.
22 Cf. S.E. Porter, *Idioms of the Greek New Testament* (2nd ed.; BLG; Sheffield: Sheffield Academic, 1994), 185–186. The classic examples of this usage of the participle occur in Rom 12:9–19. Unlike the instance in 1 Pet 2:4, these participial forms seem to be unrelated to a main finite verb.
23 Cf. Elliott, *Elect*, 16; J.R. Michaels, *1 Peter* (Waco, TX: Word, 1988), 97; Achtemeier, *1 Peter*, 153; Elliott, *1 Peter*, 409; Senior, *1 and 2 Peter*, 100; W. Grudem, *1 Peter: An Introduction and Commentary* (Downers Grove, IL: IVP, 2009), 80; cf. also D. Daube, "Participle and Imperative in I Peter," appended note in Selwyn, *First Epistle*, 467–488.

rhetorical strategy for employing Scripture. Unlike many passages in 1 Peter, the exhortation is given first and then followed by an extensive application of Old Testament passages in support of the construction of the community's identity. This breaks the previous pattern of offering a brief statement of identity first, followed by an exhortation and expansion / support from traditional material, usually the Old Testament. This passage begins with an exhortation, expands it through the use of the ἵνα-clause, and then grounds it in a detailed exposition of the community's identity reflected in a mosaic of scriptural passages—especially from Isaiah and Psalm 117—concluding with the prominent statement from Hos 2:23: "You were once not a people, but now you are a people of God's own possession; once you had not received mercy, but now you have received mercy" (1 Pet 2:10). All of these passages reinforce the socio-political identity of the audience and help ground the commands associated with individual motifs.

2 Integration of Traditional Material

Scholars have often recognized the numerous affinities of 1 Peter with other New Testament material.[24] Prior to the emergence of form and tradition criticism in the 1920s, these similarities were taken to be marks of literary dependence.[25] Selwyn's essay represents the first form-critical classification of traditional material in 1 Peter.[26] He successfully argued against previous literary dependence approaches and demonstrated that New Testament literature drew upon a common body of early Christian tradition. Selwyn suggests four distinct sources for this tradition: (1) liturgical hymns, (2) 'persecution fragment,' (3) catechetical schemas, and (4) sayings of Jesus (*Verba Christi*).[27]

---

24 Extensive comparative lists noting similarities between 1 Peter and other New Testament literature have been compiled by several scholars.

25 E.g. H.J. Holtzmann, *Lehrbuch der historisch-kritischen Einleitung in das Neue Testament* (Freiburg im Breisgau: Mohr, 1885), 313–315; O.D. Foster, *The Literary Relations of "The First Epistle of Peter" with Bearing on the Date and Place of Authorship* (Transactions of the Connecticut Academy of Arts and Sciences 17; New Haven: Yale University Press, 1913), 363–538; see also F.W. Beare, *The First Epistle of Peter: Greek Text with Introduction and Notes* (3rd ed.; Oxford: Blackwell, 1970), 219.

26 E.G. Selwyn, "On the Inter-relation of I Peter and other N.T. Epistles," in Selwyn, *First Epistle*, 365–466.

27 Selwyn, *First Peter*, 17–24; Selwyn, "On the Inter-relation of I Peter and other N.T. Epistles," 365–466.

Traditional material emerges in 1 Peter broadly through the use of biblicisms (language reminiscent of Israelite tradition and Scripture) as well as through christological, kerygmatic, paraenetic, and liturgical formulae (including baptismal, catechetical, hymnic, cultic, and doxological formulae). That these formulae find their parallels in other New Testament literature reflects a common deposit of Christian tradition rather than direct literary dependence. 1 Peter 2:1–10 is extremely rich in its integration of this tradition as an interpretive framework for understanding Old Testament people-of-God motifs. In light of the hermeneutic set out in 1:10–12, the author integrates relevant aspects of early proclaimed (ἀνηγγέλη) (i.e. oral) Christian tradition into his exposition, forming the central basis for his interpretation of Israelite tradition (i.e. Scripture).

Several layers of traditional material can be identified in 1 Pet 2:1–10:[28]

2.1 Primitive Christological and Kerygmatic Tradition

1. λίθος-imagery. The development of the Jewish interpretive tradition of stone imagery in Isa 28:16 indicates a messianic application that was flexible in its details indicating a common oral tradition.[29] Christ as stone (λίθος) is not a uniquely Petrine conception. This notion formed a significant part of early Christian tradition.[30] Stone imagery is frequently applied to Jesus as Messiah within the literature of early Christianity, typically—as is the case here—involving reference to Isa 8:14, 28:16 and/or Ps 118 (117):22: Mark 12:10; Matt 21:42; Luke 20:17; Acts 4:11; Rom 9:32; Eph 2:20 (see also Barn. 6:2–4; 16:6–10; Ign. *Eph.* 9:1; Herm. *Vis.* 3; Gos. Thom. 65–66). These all reference Christ as the corner stone and/or stone of stumbling. Synoptic parallels employ Ps 118 (117):22 at the end of each rendition of the parable of the wicked man.[31] As with the Jewish Judean evidence, New Testament messianic applications of λίθος imagery

---

28 For lists of traditional material in 1 Peter 2:4–10, see C.A. Bigg, *A Critical and Exegetical Commentary on the Epistles of St. Peter and St. Jude* (2nd ed.; ICC; Edinburgh: T&T Clark, 1926), 15–24; Selwyn, "The Inter-relation of 1 Peter," 365–466; A.E. Barnet, *Paul Becomes a Literary Influence* (Chicago: University of Chicago Press, 1941), 61–59; Elliott, *1 Peter*, 20–40; Best, "1 Peter II 4–10," 279–281.

29 The Jonathan Targum of Isa 28:16 understands this passage to be messianic. De Waard argues that 1QS 8:8 is dependent upon this Targum. J. de Waard, *A Comparative Study of Old Testament Text in the Dead Sea Scrolls and in the New Testament* (Leiden: Brill, 1965), 54. This would pre-date the christological messianic application of this passage within Jewish circles. Cf. Elliott, *Elect*, 27; Jobes, *1 Peter*, 147–148.

30 Elliott, *Elect*, 28; Best, "1 Peter II 4–10," 279; for an analysis of λίθος in early Jewish and Christian literature and in 1 Peter, see Elliott, *Elect*, 26–36.

31 Elliott, *Elect*, 29–30.

are flexible and seem to rely upon an oral tradition. The development of the New Testament tradition can probably be traced back to the *Verba Christi*.³² This imagery is significant to the development of christological themes in 1 Pet 2:4–8 and as Elliott notes, "it is obvious that the group of OT pss. in 1 P 2:6–8 reflect dependence upon a common Christian tradition."³³ 1 Peter's application of the motif to Christ, however, is distinct in that the author portrays Christ as the stone *simpliciter*.³⁴ The imagery is also applied to Christians both here in 1 Peter and in primitive Christian tradition.³⁵ We already see this element of the tradition emerging in communal form among the sectarians at Qumran and this communal reading of Isaiah 28 is even said to constitute a requirement for entrance into the community (1QS 5:5; 8:17; 8:5–10; 1QH^a 6:25; 7:17; 4QIsa.d; 4QpPs 37 2:16).³⁶ This stream of tradition seems to have impacted or, at least, been reiterated in early Christianity as well (1 Cor 3:9; Eph 2:19–20).

2. Christological formulae. There is as of now no consensus regarding whether christological formulae had already been standardized into hymnic and/or creedal material at the time 1 Peter was written.³⁷ The major christological formula in the present context is "rejected by men on the one hand, but [was] chosen and is precious in the sight of God on the other" (note the μὲν ... δὲ construction) in 2:4, a brief formalized parallelism.³⁸ Both elements of the formula (rejection and election) weigh in significantly within the development of primitive tradition. In addition to the references to stone imagery in the *Verba Christi* mentioned above, rejection and suffering is also predicted in the *Verba Christi* (Mark 8:31; Luke 9:22; 17:25; cf. also Acts 7:35–37). Thus, it seems to be no coincidence that, as with the couplet in the *Verba Christi* tradition, suffering also emerges as a major token across Peter's discourse. The understanding of Christ as the elect or chosen one of God is taken over from applications of Isa 42:1 in the *Verba Christi* (Matt 12:18; Luke 9:35).³⁹ The distinction in the

---

32   Selwyn, *First Peter*, 32; Elliott, *Elect*, 32.
33   Elliott, *Elect*, 33.
34   Best, "1 Peter II 1–4," 279.
35   Best, "1 Peter II 1–4," 279.
36   Elliott, *Elect*, 26–27. Elliott notes (26), "The significant element in all these passages is that the image of stone and/or building is applied to the community as the eschatological congregation of the Last Day."
37   Elliott, *1 Peter*, 30.
38   Cf. Elliott, *1 Peter*, 30.
39   In John 1:34 P$^{66, 75}$ A B C L Θ Y 0233^{vid} f $^{1, 13}$ 33 1241 aur c f l g bo have ο υιος του θεου. ℵ* and P⁵ (ουτος εστιν ο εκλεκτος του θεου) add εκλεκτος. Even if the textual reading is not as

ascriptions of this prophecy within these two passages is noteworthy. In the Matthean tradition, Jesus applies the prophecy to himself whereas in Luke's Gospel, God alludes to the prophecy in a voice from heaven. In Luke 23:35, we discover attestation to the widespread nature of this tradition by the audience's mockery at Christ through using this title conditionally: "He saved others, let him save himself if he is the Messiah of God, the Elect One." These statements represent a common oral tradition that was pervasive enough to extend beyond community insiders and apparently was closely associated with the messianic identity of Jesus. The use of ἔντιμον with ἐκλεκτὸν may be a Petrine adaptation of the tradition or it may reflect an alternate version to what is reflected in the Gospels.

3. διὰ Ἰησοῦ Χριστοῦ. The use of διὰ Ἰησοῦ Χριστοῦ is probably an element of later Christian traditions, only represented in John's Gospel (1:17) and once in Acts (10:36), but is not infrequent within the epistolary tradition: Rom 1:8; 5:21; 7:25; 16:27; Gal 1:1; Eph 1:5; Phil 1:11; Titus 3:6; Heb 13:21; 1Pet 2:5; 4:11; Jude 25 (see also *1Clem.* 1:1; 50:7; 58:2; 59:3; Ign. *Ep.* 4:2; Ign. *Magn.* 5:2; 8:2; Pol. *Phil.* 1:3; Did. 9:4). In 1Pet 2:5 it is used to indicate the means through which the audience received communal benefits (cf. 1:11).

4. Christ as stumbling block. The portrayal of Christ as σκάνδαλον was a common element of early Christian tradition, especially for Paul: Rom 9:33; 1Cor 1:23; Gal 5:11. This conception of Christ also comes out in 1Pet 2:8 as he explains the reaction of unbelievers to the testimony of Christ in the Old Testament.

2.2 *Paraenetic Features*

1. οὖν as a transition into exhortive material.[40] Early Christian paraenetic tradition is marked by the use of the inferential conjunction οὖν as a means of relating the exhortation to previous discourse; in the *Verba Christi*: Matt 5:19, 23, 48; 6:2, 8, 9, 6:31, 34; 7:12; 9:38; 10:6, 26, 31; 13:18; 18:4; 22:9, 21; 23:3; 25:13; 28:19; Mark 10:9; 13:35; Luke 3:8 (John the Baptist);[41] 8:18; 10:2; 11:35; 14:33; 21:17;[42] in

---

likely here, the reading suggests early application of the term that reflects its messianic significance within early Christianity.

40 Cf. W. Nauk, "Das oun-paräneticum," *ZNW* 49 (1958): 134–135. Note also that throughout this paper I employ a very standard traditio-critical model of substantiating evidence for streams of tradition through listing verse references within the text.

41 It is interesting that Luke 3:18 connects the content of John's message both to an oral tradition and to paraenesis: Πολλὰ μὲν οὖν καὶ ἕτερα παρακαλῶν εὐηγγελίζετο τὸν λαόν.

42 John's use of οὖν is somewhat unique and has more of a narratival function, but there

the Apostolic Tradition: (Petrine Speeches): Acts 2:36; 3:19; (Philip's Speech): Acts 8:22; (Pauline Speeches): Acts 13:40; (Pauline Epistolary Tradition): Rom 12:1; 13:10, 12; 14:13, 16, 19; 16:19; 1 Cor 4:8, 16; 10:31; 2 Cor 8:24; Gal 5:1; 6:10; Eph 4:1, 17; 5:1, 7, 15; 6:14; Phil 2:1–2; Col 2:6, 16; 3:1–4, 5, 12; 1 Thess 4:1; 5:6; 2 Thess 2:15; 1 Tim 2:1, 8; 3:2; 5:14; 2 Tim 1:8; 2:1, 21. The function of οὖν in 2:1 serves this purpose and reflects dependence on a reservoir of traditional hortatory material (see also 1 Pet 4:1, 7; 5:1, 6).

2. The ethical function of ἀποτίθημι. In non-paraenetic literature ἀποτίθημι usually has a literal (non-ethical) connotation of being put into (prison; the tabernacle) (Matt 14:3; *1 Clem.* 43:2), taking off (one's clothes) (Acts 7:58; 2 Macc 8:35), storing (food, stones, bones) (1 Macc 1:35; 4:46; *Mart. Pol.* 13:2; 18:2). In New Testament and Greco-Roman paraenetic material, however, it takes on a more ethical function: casting off the works of darkness (Rom 13:12), putting off the old self (reflecting catechetical baptismal tradition) (Eph 4:22),[43] laying aside falsehood (Eph 4:25), setting aside sin (Heb 12:2), and introducing vice lists (Col 3:8; Jas 1:21). The function of ἀποτίθημι to introduce vices is especially relevant for 1 Pet 2:1.[44]

Colossians 3:8	James 1:21	1 Peter 2:1
νυνὶ δὲ *ἀπόθεσθε* καὶ ὑμεῖς τὰ πάντα, ὀργήν, θυμόν, κακίαν, βλασφημίαν, αἰσχρολογίαν ἐκ τοῦ στόματος ὑμῶν·	διὸ *ἀποθέμενοι* πᾶσαν ῥυπαρίαν καὶ περισσείαν κακίας ἐν πραΰτητι, δέξασθε τὸν ἔμφυτον λόγον τὸν δυνάμενον σῶσαι τὰς ψυχὰς ὑμῶν.	*Ἀποθέμενοι* οὖν πᾶσαν κακίαν καὶ πάντα δόλον καὶ ὑποκρίσεις καὶ φθόνους καὶ πάσας καταλαλιάς,

---

is also markedly less paraenetic material in John. On the use of οὖν in John, see R. Buth, "Οὖν, Δέ, Καί, and Asyndeton in John's Gospel," in *Linguistics and New Testament Interpretation: Essays on Discourse Analysis* (ed. David Alan Black et al.; Nashville: Broadman and Holman, 1992), 146–150; V. Poythress, "Testing for Johannine Authorship by Examining the Use of Conjunctions," *WTJ* 46 (1984): 351–370.

43 Cf. G. Schneider, "ἀποτίθημι," *EDNT*, 1:146.
44 Similarly, 1 Clem. 13:1: Ταπεινοφρονήσωμεν οὖν ἀδελφοί ἀποθέμενοι πᾶσαν ἀλαζονείαν καὶ τύφος καὶ ἀφροσύνην καὶ ὀργάς καὶ ποιήσωμεν τὸ γεγραμμένον λέγει γὰρ τὸ πνεῦμα τὸ ἅγιον.

In addition to what is represented above (the consistent use of ἀποτίθημι, πᾶς and κακία), each of the vice lists deploys a conjunction in order to introduce the list and enlist words from the semantic field for speech. The similarities are not exact enough to indicate literary dependence, but the affinities are certainly suggestive of a common deposit of early Christian tradition that the authors molded and incorporated for their own purposes.

3. Vice list. The catalogue of virtues and/or vices reflects a common feature of early Christian paraenesis: Matt 5:3–11, 15:19; Mark 7:21–22; Rom 1:18–32; 13:13; Gal 5:19–23; 1 Cor 5:10–11; 6:9–10; 2 Cor 6:6–7; 12:20; Eph 4:31; 5:3–7; 6:14–17; Phil 4:8; Col 3:5–9; 3:12–14; 1 Tim 1:9–10; 3:2–3; 6:4–5, 11; 2 Tim 3:2–5; Titus 1:7–8; 3:1–3; Jas 3:17; 1 Pet 4:3–4; 2 Pet 1:5–8, Jude 8, 16; Rev 9:20–21; 21:8; 22:15 (see also Wis 8:7; 1QS 4:2–14; Barn. 19–20; Did. 5:1; 1 Clem. 35:5; Pol. *Phil.* 2:2; 4:3).[45] The list of vices in 1 Pet 2:1 is typical, being complemented by a positive injunction in 2:2. This type of list is, of course, not unique to 1 Pet 2:1—similar vice lists occur in 1:22, 4:3, and 4:15. As noted above, the use of ἀποτίθημι is common in such lists.

4. Antithetical structure. Antithesis is another feature that was abundant in a whole range of paraenetic traditions including philosophical and epistolary paraenesis as well as Jewish and early Christian paraenesis.[46] Virtue-vice lists often typically take this structure, but several other forms of paraenesis take antithetical structure as well (usually the use of an imperative[s] in the first clause or set of clauses and a negative particle[s] [often with a conjunction relating the clause, typically in an adversative relation] in the second clause or set of clauses is characteristic of this form): Matt 5:17–18, 21–48; 6:19–20; 15:19; 7:1; 10:28; 10:34; 23:3; Luke 6:29, 30, 37; 10:3–4, 7; 12:28–29; John 2:16; Rom 12:9–21; 1 Cor 14:34, 39; Gal 5:1, 16; Eph 5:15; Col 3:2, 19, 22–23; 1 Thess 2:9; Titus 3:14; Jas

---

45 N.J. McEleney, "The Vice List of the Pastoral Epistles," *CBQ* 36 (1974): 203. Dryden sees the virtue-vice lists in 1 Peter as a reflection of Greco-Roman philosophy. J.D.W. Dryden, *Theology and Ethics in 1 Peter: Paraenetic Strategies for Christian Character Formation* (WUNT 2.209; Tübingen: Mohr Siebeck, 2006), 38. However, as Easton demonstrates, although virtue-vice lists were scarce in the Old Testament, in Hellenistic Jewish literature they are "fairly abundant." B.S. Easton, "New Testament Ethical Lists," *JBL* (1934): 1–12 (1).

46 For distinctions between epistolary and philosophical paraenesis, see A.W. Pitts, "Hellenistic Moral Philosophy and the Greek Epistolary Tradition: Implications for Pauline Paraenesis," in *Paul and the Ancient Letter Form* (ed. S.E. Porter and S.A. Adams; PAST 6; Leiden: Brill, 2010), 269–306. See P.Oxy. 42.3069.11–13 for an example of antithesis in epistolary paraenesis; further references to variations of antithesis in early paraenesis may be found in A.J. Malherbe, "Hellenistic Moralists and the New Testament," in *ANRW* II.26.1 (1992): 290.

1:22; 1 John 2:28 (see also 1 Clem. 21:1; 22:3; 30:6; Barn. 2:8; Ign. *Magn.* 10:2; Ign. *Tral.* 7:1; Did. 1:4, 5; 15:3). 1 Peter 2:1–2 utilizes this structure, beginning with a string of negative commands (ἀποθέμενοι), followed by a positive command directed at spiritual growth.

2.3 Liturgical Forms and Tradition

1. Catechetical baptismal schemas. The use of ἀποτίθημι indicates a baptismal context.[47] Early Christians often invoke this type of clothing imagery in association with baptismal practices, involving the putting off of clothing for the baptism itself and re-clothing after one had been immersed.[48] ἀπόθεσις is tied directly to baptism in 3:21 so that this connection is clearly made by the author as well. The term, therefore, seems to evoke two frames of reference, one of paraenesis and one of early baptismal liturgies. Schneider rightly captures this dual emphasis when he observes that ἀποτίθημι is common metaphorical language for "standard catechetical terms of [baptismal] paraenesis."[49] In 1 Peter, it takes this function, having both a liturgical and a paraenetic connotation. The metaphor of new-born children is explained by Beare in this light as a statement that remains "appropriate to the condition of converts who have just been received into the Church by baptism," citing Augustine who uses this passage as a reference to those who are "fresh in the infancy of spiritual regeneration."[50] And Selwyn and Beare note milk (2:2) and honey were often given to the newly baptized.[51] Nursing and milk (2:2) imagery were also common metaphors in early Christianity.[52]

---

47 Schneider, "ἀποτίθημι," 1:146; Selwyn, *First Peter*, 393–400; J.N.D. Kelly, *The Epistles of Peter and of Jude* (BNTC; repr., London: Continuum, 1969), 144; Elliott, *1 Peter*, 395; Achtemeier, *1 Peter*, 144.

48 For an analysis of the use of clothing imagery in the baptismal practices of the early church, see J.H. Kim, *The Significance of Clothing Imagery in the Pauline Corpus* (JSNTSup 268; London: T&T Clark, 2004), 96–101. Kim cites points to several examples of Jewish proselyte baptism (see b. Yebam. 46a, 47ab). He also observes that in Gos. Thom. 37 one is baptized naked and clothed afterwards. Similarly in Hippolytus, *Apos. Trad.* 21.3 baptism involves the candidates removing their clothing signifying the renunciation of evil spirits (21.9–10). Likewise, the Gospel of Philip ties clothing imagery to baptismal practices as does Jerome's *Ep. Fab.* 19. Kelly (*First Peter*, 83–84) adds Cyril of Jerusalem, *Myst. Cat.* 2.2; *Procat.* 4 to this list. Cf. also C.F.D. Moule, *Worship in the New Testament* (London: Lutterworth, 1961), 52–53.

49 Schneider, "ἀποτίθημι," 1:146.

50 Beare, *1 Peter*, 114.

51 Selwyn, *1 Peter*, 154–155; Beare, *1 Peter*, 117; cf. also Elliott, *1 Peter*, 399.

52 For references, see Elliott, *1 Peter*, 399; Selwyn, *1 Peter*, 154–155; Goppelt, *First Peter*, 128–130.

2. *Cultic ascriptions.* Selwyn's analysis of liturgical tradition as finding its source entirely in early baptismal practices is certainly too strong.[53] There are, however, clear liturgical motifs that can be traced back to common primitive tradition among the first Christians. The central noun in the cultic portion of the passage (2:5 and 2:9 where the priesthood is reinvoked) is ἱεράτευμα. It occurs here as part of a prepositional group with εἰς, indicating the goal of the verbal action (οἰκοδομεῖσθε [οἶκος πνευματικὸς]). The infinitive (ἀνενέγκαι [πνευματικὰς θυσίας]) points to the purpose or function of the priesthood, to offer spiritual sacrifices. Thus, the tradition of priesthood in early Christianity forms the central frame of reference for understanding the cultic motifs within this passage. Even in the most primitive forms of the priesthood tradition in the New Testament, we find a communal emphasis not present in the understanding of priesthood among the sectarians at Qumran or even within the Hebrew Bible. The Qumran priests remained distinct from common community insiders and were essential to the government and function of the community.[54] Similarly, in the Old Testament the emphasis of priesthood remains an individual notion, not something that the people of God participate in as a corporate entity.[55] Incorporation of the early streams of the Christian tradition of priesthood are seen only in 1 Peter and in Revelation. In Rev 1:6 and 5:10, language very similar to 1 Pet 2:9 is employed, both instances collocating with βασίλειος. The reference in Rev 20:6 is eschatological. All three, however—as with the references in 1 Peter—are communal, again suggesting a common reservoir of tradition. Early Christian traditional material seems to reflect an understanding of the priesthood that was not reserved for a particular order but that came as a benefit and privilege granted to all community insiders on the basis of the suffering and exaltation of Christ (διὰ Ἰησοῦ Χριστοῦ; cf. 1:11). But while primitive priesthood traditions are not as widely represented in the New Testament, the notion of spiritual sacrifices is represented more broadly (see Rom 12:1; Phil 4:8; Heb 13:5).

2.4 *Communal Tradition and the* Ecclesia Dei

Communal tradition refers to the body of oral tradition that began to emerge around the corporate identity of believers. It reflects how early Christians perceived themselves and wanted to be perceived. The most important theme that emerges in relation to this stream of tradition is the "people of God" motif.

---

53 Selwyn, *1 Peter*, 268–281.
54 E. Best, "Spiritual Sacrifices: General Priesthood in the New Testament," *Int* 14 (1960): 273–299 (273).
55 See Best, "Spiritual Sacrifices," 276–278.

Early Christianity clearly perceived itself to be the new people of God: Rom 9–11; Gal 3:26–29; 6:16; Eph 2:11–3:10. The primitive understanding of the people of God developed into an eschatological notion later embodied in the *ecclesia dei*.[56] The spectrum of this source of traditional material, therefore, is quite broad and intersects with other dimensions of the common deposit of tradition, especially those layers tied in with the original identity of the people of God (e.g. some liturgical formulas and cultic ascriptions). The author of 1 Peter clearly draws upon and substantially develops this tradition through several motifs, relating directly to the community's identity. This is seen in the application of several passages to the audience that originally referred to Israel as the people of God. Paul seems to have drawn from the same tradition in his discourse about the relationship of Gentile believers to Israel (cf. Rom 9:6 and 1 Pet 2:9—see below). The predestination of the community of believers and the damnation of unbelievers was also clearly a prevalent aspect of early Christian tradition: John 15:16; Rom 8:29–30, 33; chs. 9 and 11; 1 Cor 1:23–24; Eph 1:3–14; Col 3:12; 1 Thess 1:4; 3:3; 5:9; 2 Tim 2:10; Titus 1:1; 1 Pet 1:1–2; Rev 17:14. 1 Peter integrates this aspect of tradition into his exposition heavily in 2:4–10.

3   The Form, Function, and Interpretation of Old Testament Material

3.1   *Psalm 33:8 LXX in 1 Peter 2:3*

The first direct quotation in this passage is from Ps 33:8 LXX (34:9 MT) in 1 Pet 2:3, although it is not introduced formally.

Psalm 34:9 (MT)	Psalm 33:8 (LXX)	1 Peter 2:3 (Psalm 33:8)
וְרָאוּ טַעֲמוּ יְהוָה כִּי־טוֹב	γεύσασθε καὶ ἴδετε ὅτι χρηστὸς ὁ κύριος	εἰ ἐγεύσασθε ὅτι χρηστὸς ὁ κύριος.

Clearly, there are some changes. The mood forms for γεύομαι are different. The conditional particle is used to introduce the quotation in 1 Peter and ἴδετε is absent. The morphological change from the aorist imperative to the aorist indicative (טַעֲמוּ is also imperative) is suggestive of the fulfillment hermeneutic employed. The morphology is also constrained by the choice of the conditional

---

56   The eschatological people of God: so Elliott, *Elect*, 39.

particle as an introduction for the quotation since the particle is not used with the imperative to form a condition so that the change can hardly be said to have been informed by pesher methods. The conditional is used with the indicative to assume the truth of the reality for the sake of argument.[57] The quotation is not introduced with a citation formula—though εἰ has this function here in a very mild sense—which may be an indication that the text was drawn from memory which would account for the omission of ἴδετε.[58]

The author immediately moves from the citation to its interpretation through the λίθος-complex that runs from 2:4 through 2:8 so that traditional material serves as the most immediate base for the interpretation of the Old Testament tradition. An interpretive frame loaded with streams of primitive tradition is employed to frame the quotation in 2:4–5 before actually citing the Old Testament in 2:6–8. Below I seek to draw several parallel uses of this tradition within the New Testament that are distinct enough to rule out direct literary dependence but are similar enough to suggest reliance upon a common tradition. The relation of 2:4–6 as a direct qualification and expansion of 2:3 illustrates the author's reliance upon this tradition in the interpretive procedures and reflections upon Psalm 33 LXX. A wide range of traditional material is employed for these purposes, especially cultic ascriptions, communal tradition, and christological and kerygmatic formulae, using λίθος-imagery most directly.

The quotation functions here in a very similar way to the one employed in 1 Pet 1:24–25. As Jobes remarks,

> [T]he sentence begun in verse 2 is completed in verse 3 with another perceptual metaphor of taste in the direct allusion to LXX Ps 33. Thus, LXX Ps 33 contributes to the interpretive context within which Peter's command to crave milk should be understood, just as his use of LXX Isa 40:6–8 supports his command in 1:22, also in the imperative mood, to love one another earnestly.[59]

---

57 See S.E. Porter, *Verbal Aspect in the Greek of the New Testament with Reference to Tense and Mood* (SBG 1; New York: Peter Lang, 1989), 294–304.

58 Cf. T. McLay, *The Use of the Septuagint in New Testament Research* (Grand Rapids: Eerdmans, 2003), 26–30, esp. 26; P⁷² reads: ει εγευσαθε επειστευσατε οτι inserting επειστευσατε in place of the missing word.

59 K.H. Jobes, "'Got Milk?' A Petrine Metaphor in 1 Peter 2:1–3 Re-visited," *Leaven: A Journal of Christian Ministry* 20 (2012): 121–126; cf. also Schutter, *Hermeneutic and Composition*, 57–58; Achtemeier, *1 Peter*, 143; Elliott, *1 Peter*, 399.

But the passage has even more in common with 1:24–25 than Jobes recognizes. In concert with the context that precedes and especially with what follows, the author uses this text to help ground the exhortation in the communal identity of the audience. In previous passages, the author develops the point that the audience has been graciously included within the family of God. Similarly, in 2:2–3 the new entrance into the community (cf. ὡς ἀρτιγέννητα βρέφη [2:2]) serves as the perfect exhibition of God's kindness toward the predominantly Gentile audience.[60] Further, the clause in 2:3 is connected directly in hypotactic relation to the following clauses all the way down through 2:6, indicating that these verses function as an expansion of 2:3 that is in dependent relation to the exhortation in 2:1. In other words, the scriptural development in 2:3–6 (as well as 2:7–10—see above) supports and expands upon the communal motif in 2:3 that grounds the exhortation issued in 2:1–2, giving further development and context to the expression of communal identity throughout the letter (see the analysis of linguistic structure above).[61]

3.2 The λίθος-Complex: Isaiah 8:14, 28:16 and Psalm 117:22 LXX in 1 Peter 2:4–8

The second set of quotations is formally introduced in 2:6 and runs through 2:8. The stretch of text marked by 2:4–5 is, therefore, best understood as an interpretive frame for the quotation, typical of Petrine style (see 1:15–16; 1:22–25; 3:8–12). The supportive nature of the citation is indicated by the subordinating conjunction within the quotation formula: διότι περιέχει ἐν γραφῇ. The first quotation is a composite text from Isa 8:14 and 28:16.

Isaiah 28:16 (MT)	Isaiah 28:16 (LXX)	1 Peter 2:6
הִנְנִי	Ἰδοὺ ἐγὼ	ἰδοὺ
יִסַּד בְּצִיּוֹן	ἐμβαλῶ εἰς τὰ θεμέλια Σιων	τίθημι ἐν Σιὼν
אָבֶן	λίθον	λίθον

---

60 See J.H. Elliott, *Home for the Homeless: A Sociological Exegesis of 1 Peter, Its Situation and Strategy* (London: SCM, 1982).

61 As Elliott, *1 Peter*, 409, observes regarding 2:4, "This phrase extends the thought of 2:2–3 regarding continued fidelity to the Lord and introduces a unit (vv 4–10) that compares believers with their elect Lord and contrasts these elect believers and their honor with rejecting nonbelievers and their shame." Jobes, *1 Peter*, 145, also notices the intimate tie between these two sections. Both are wrong, however, to assume that 2:4–10 marks a new unit.

(cont.)

Isaiah 28:16 (MT)	Isaiah 28:16 (LXX)	1 Peter 2:6
אֶבֶן	[---]	[---]
בֹּחַן פִּנַּת	πολυτελῆ ἐκλεκτὸν ἀκρογωνιαῖον	ἀκρογωνιαῖον ἐκλεκτὸν
יִקְרַת	ἔντιμον εἰς τὰ θεμέλια αὐτῆς	ἔντιμον
מוּסָד מוּסָּד		[---]
הַמַּאֲמִין לֹא	καὶ ὁ πιστεύων ἐπ' αὐτῷ οὐ μὴ	καὶ ὁ πιστεύων ἐπ' αὐτῷ
יָחִישׁ	καταισχυνθῇ	οὐ μὴ καταισχυνθῇ

While an alternative text-type is not to be entirely ruled out, the LXX follows the MT quite closely so that the reading in 1 Peter should probably be viewed as a deviation from a major textual tradition instead of drawing from a divergent *Vorlage*.

The next citation is from Ps 117:22 in 2:7 with ὑμῖν οὖν ἡ τιμὴ τοῖς πιστεύουσιν, ἀπιστοῦσιν δὲ (esp. οὖν ... δὲ) serving to continue the citation formula while readjusting the interpretive frame for direct communal application (so ὑμῖν).

Psalm 118:22 (MT)	Psalm 117:22 (LXX)	1 Peter 2:7 (LXX Ps 117:22)
אֶבֶן מָאֲסוּ	λίθον, ὃν ἀπεδοκίμασαν οἱ	λίθον ὃν ἀπεδοκίμασαν οἱ
הַבּוֹנִים הָיְתָה	οἰκοδομοῦντες, οὗτος ἐγενήθη	οἰκοδομοῦντες, οὗτος ἐγενήθη
לְרֹאשׁ פִּנָּה	εἰς κεφαλὴν γωνίας	εἰς κεφαλὴν γωνίας

Unlike the citation in 2:6, this quotation from Psalm 117 follows the LXX without deviation.

The third quotation develops the λίθος-complex and shifts back to Isaiah (8:14), using καὶ as a formal continuation of cited material.

Isaiah 8:14 (MT)	Isaiah 8:14 (LXX)	1 Peter 2:8
וּלְאֶבֶן נֶגֶף וּלְצוּר מִכְשׁוֹל	λίθου προσκόμματι συναντήσεσθε αὐτῷ οὐδὲ ὡς πέτρας πτώματι	καὶ λίθος προσκόμματος καὶ πέτρα σκανδάλου

Best argues that 1 Peter has changed the case forms (the genitive and dative to nominatives) from the LXX.⁶² However, it seems more likely that a different *Vorlage* is in place here that aligns closer to the Hebrew accusative object of the preposition (וּלְאֶבֶן).⁶³ There is also more direct correspondence between the 1 Peter text and the MT: וּלְאֶבֶן נֶגֶף aligns with καὶ λίθος προσκόμματος and וּלְצוּר מִכְשׁוֹל aligns neatly with καὶ πέτρα σκανδάλου so that each element is accounted for.

The final potential quotation in 2:10 is really closer to an allusion (since no citation formula is found and major differences obtain) or may not be a reference to the Old Testament at all. If the author does refer to the Old Testament, he has radically altered the language, probably in order to serve a communal application. In 2:10 (οἵ ποτε οὐ λαὸς νῦν δὲ λαὸς θεοῦ) the author speaks with language strongly reminiscent of Hos 2:25 (LXX: Οὐ λαῷ μου λαός μου εἶ σύ).⁶⁴ The most significant alteration of the language here is the temporal reference frame. In Hosea, the waw-consecutive (וְאָמַרְתִּי) (translated by the Greek future ἐρῶ) carries temporal reference of the Hebrew discourse (although the verb itself is aspectually based);⁶⁵ in this case we probably have a consequent prophetic perfect emphasizing the present certainty of a distant action. The future sequence for the waw-consecutive here is begun in 2:23 with the qal imperfect אֶעֱנֶה and is then carried by the chain of perfects, as is typically the case with future frames of reference in Hebrew.⁶⁶ If our author reads the prophetic perfect here in light of his communal fulfillment hermeneutic, then temporal reference in the language would need to be altered in order for the passage to serve his purposes. In Greek, temporality is realized through temporal deictic features (i.e. temporal markers) and this is precisely what is used to switch the temporal frame from future to present time within the quotation. The audience was once (ποτε) not a people, but now (νῦν) they are the people of God. This applies to the statements regarding the application of God's mercy as well, alluding to the language of Hos 2:3 (MT).

Several elements in the text reflect a strong reliance upon traditional material as the primary interpretive base for the interpretation of Old Testament

---

62 Best, "1 Pet II 1–4," 276.
63 So Schutter, *Hermeneutic and Composition*, 131.
64 Achtemeier, *1 Peter*, 167; Elliott, *1 Peter*, 441.
65 Since Driver's influential work, the majority of Hebraists have understood Hebrew as an aspectually based language. S.R. Driver, *A Treatise on Hebrew Tenses and Some Other Syntactical Questions* (Oxford: Clarendon, 1881).
66 F.W. Gesenius, *Gesenius' Hebrew Grammar* (ed. and expanded by E. Kautzsch; 2nd ed. rev. and trans. by A.E. Cowley; Oxford: Oxford University Press, 1946), 132.

citations. First, the interpretive frames (2:4–5 and 2:7–8) for the quotations evidence a strong integration of primitive Christian traditional material. The quotation frame in 2:4–5 employs λίθος-imagery (λίθον ζῶντα [2:4]; λίθοι ζῶντες [2:5]), a christological formula (ὑπὸ ἀνθρώπων μὲν ἀποδεδοκιμασμένον παρὰ δὲ θεῷ ἐκλεκτὸν ἔντιμον [2:4]), themes of election (ἐκλεκτὸν ἔντιμον [2:4]),[67] and a wide range of cultic ascriptions and communal tradition (οἶκος πνευματικὸς εἰς ἱεράτευμα ἅγιον ἀνενέγκαι πνευματικὰς [2:5]). The interpretive frame employed by the author in 2:4–5 has two asymmetrical dimensions: (1) a christological dimension (2:4) and (2) a communal dimension (2:5). The second dimension is based on the first. Through coming to Christ as the living stone, the community also finds an identity as living stones (καὶ αὐτοὶ ὡς λίθοι ζῶντες). The quotation is then given in direct support for these statements drawn from early Christian tradition. Each of the first two quotations emphasizes one of the dimensions. The citation in 2:6 from Isaiah 28 gives scriptural support to the christological tradition and supplies a missing premise to the argument stated in 2:5, connecting believers as living stones to Christ as the living stone (giving support to the second dimension as well). The quotation in 2:7 is introduced through an explicit shift of the reference frame to believers, drawing a more direct correlation between the subsequent quotation and the second dimension of the interpretive frame in 2:5 while providing further support and interpretation for understanding the connection established between Christ and believers on the basis of Isa 28:16. The point is drawn out through initiating a stark antithesis, contrasting two communities—believers and unbelievers—as is typical throughout the letter. The negative side of the antithesis is built up from 2:7 all the way through 2:8. The third quotation from Isa 8:14 continues this emphasis and draws further from themes of primitive Christian tradition involving Christ as stumbling block and the notion of predestination in the interpretive comment directly following the quote. These citations construct a negative antithesis that builds up to the emphatic intersection of the diverse streams of tradition that have been the focus of the discourse in the positive affirmation of the community's identity and status as the people of God in 2:9–10. The antithetical connection between 2:9–10 and its context is signaled by δὲ joined with ὑμεῖς in order to shift the application to the community. In addition to providing a positive antithesis, these verses gather together in summary fashion

---

67 While the synoptic parallels seem to draw their references to Christ as the elect one from Isa 42:1 while the citation here clearly seems to go back to Isa 28:16: λίθον πολυτελῆ ἐκλεκτὸν using ἔντιμον for ἐκλεκτὸν, and pre-invoking the passage itself within the interpretive frame.

the threads of tradition that have run through these passages. The text functions rhetorically as a restatement of the interpretive frame used to introduce the series of Old Testament quotations in 2:4–5, bringing together christological and communal themes into one holistic statement about the audience's identity. They are "a chosen race, a royal priesthood, a holy nation, a people possessed by God." They were "once not a people, but now are the people of God"; they "had not received mercy" but now "have received mercy" (2:9, 10).

Another testimony to the use of primitive tradition as the interpretive framework for understanding the Petrine use of the Old Testament is found in the employment of stock passages and interpretations from the reservoir of early Christian tradition. One of the hallmark features of this passage is that it employs Old Testament passages and interpretations that had currency among other early Christian sources. The messianic application of stone imagery in Isaiah and Psalm 117 LXX was a significant aspect of early Christian interpretation and tradition: Mark 12:10; Matt 21:42; Luke 20:17; Acts 4:11; Rom 9:32; Eph 2:20 (see also Barn. 6:2–4; 16:6–10; Ign. *Eph.* 9:1; Herm. *Vis.* 3; Gos. Thom. 65–66).[68] Paul's application is especially noteworthy. It is similar in that Christ is seen as the stumbling block for unbelieving Israel, but it lacks the direct application to the community that 1 Peter brings in especially in 2:9–10. This seems to be indicative of a common tradition that had oral circulation among early Christians. Both authors drew from this deposit of primitive material and molded it to fit their own interpretive purposes.

A final consideration concerns the rhetorical function of Old Testament quotations in this passage. One of the hermeneutical parameters set out by the author in 1:10–12 was the theoretical justification for communal applications of the Old Testament (i.e. prophecy) to the discourse audience. Therefore, as with other implementations of Scripture in 1 Peter, Old Testament citations serve either to support and/or to develop a communal motif or an exhortation associated with a communal motif. No other passage in 1 Peter bears as rich a testimony to this principle as 1 Pet 2:1–10. In the discussion of the linguistic structure of the passage it was shown that the Old Testament citations running from 2:3–10 are in the service of grounding the exhortation regarding spiritual growth in 2:1–2. Unlike other communal motifs in 1 Peter, which amount to short stereotyped phrases, usually followed by an exhortation, 1 Pet 2:1–10 begins with an exhortation and grounds it through an extensive exposition of the identity of the community.

---

68   This list of references is copied from the above analysis for the convenience of the reader.

4 Conclusions

In addition to providing a linguistic analysis of the structure of 1 Pet 2:1–10, this essay has sought to establish two central points. First, it was shown that primitive traditional material provides a more convincing interpretive base for understanding 1 Peter's use of the Old Testament than midrash, pesher, or testimonia theories. Old Testament citations are consistently framed and explained by reference to early Christian tradition. This seems to be indicative of a close interpretive connection between the two in the mind of the author and seems to coincide nicely with the hermeneutical agenda set out by the author in 1 Pet 1:10–12. Second, it was argued that Scripture is employed strategically throughout 1 Peter and particularly in 1 Pet 2:1–10 in order to develop a communal motif or to support an exhortation(s) made in association with a communal motif.

1 Peter and the Theological Logic of Christian Familial Imagery

Matthew R. Malcolm

One of the intriguing features of earliest Christian mission, as reflected in its traditions and teaching material, is its remarkably heightened utilisation of family imagery. This is evident across the breadth of New Testament literature, and appears to have been a fairly immediate feature of the Jesus movement. My intention in this essay is to suggest that an analysis of this feature in 1 Peter enables a glimpse into the theological logic that might have accompanied and consolidated the widespread adoption of such imagery in earliest Christianity. Namely, it is applied to those whose identity is informed by the gospel of the son of God.

It should immediately be conceded that the "son of God" is not mentioned in 1 Peter.[1] However, the fact that God is identified twice within the first three verses as "father" may alert us to the possibility that a conceptualisation of Jesus or believers as son or children is not far beneath the surface.[2]

I want, then, to make an argument in three steps, first, briefly establishing that familial imagery is in fact crucial in the letter; second, considering that this is indeed representative of a broader heightening of such terminology in

---

1 This is noted as a surprising omission by Kraftchick: "Many christological images that are frequently found in other New Testament documents do not appear in 1 Peter. For example, 1 Peter never refers to the 'son of God,' although this title is implied when God is called Jesus's Father (1:3)." Steven J. Kraftchick, "Reborn to a Living Hope: A Christology of 1 Peter," in *Reading 1–2 Peter and Jude: A Resource for Students* (ed. Eric F. Mason and Troy W. Martin; Atlanta: SBL, 2014), 83–98 (88).

2 This raises the question of what it means for something to be "beneath the surface" of the words that we have in front of us. Human cognitive processes group things into categories and networks; and an author can express an element of such a category or network, which *assumes* the whole without *articulating* the whole. I refer to a cognitive network as a "conceptualisation" or a "schema." This is a normal and constant feature of human communication. In speaking of a "bride," for example, a "wedding schema" is beneath the surface for speakers and hearers who share sufficient cultural overlap, even if a wedding is never mentioned. The terminology I am using here draws on the insights of cognitive linguistics. See, for example, Farzad Sharifian, *Cultural Conceptualisations and Language* (Cognitive Linguistic Studies in Cultural Contexts 1; Amsterdam: Benjamins, 2011), 3.

early Christianity; and third, proposing that this heightening can be partially illuminated by the theological importance of an early "gospel schema" of the Son of God.

1 Familial Imagery in 1 Peter

The opening verses of 1 Peter identify the recipients as *rebirthed children of the Father of Jesus Christ*. This image takes up a significant amount of space in the letter—more than is often recognised—running from 1:3 to 2:3.[3] Furthermore, it is more than just a recurring motif in that section, but is a consistent multi-dimensional image around which most of the section is structured:

Feature	1:14–16	1:17–21	1:22–25	2:1–3
A: Appeal to Regenerate Status within God's Family				
Allusion to regenerate family status	ὡς τέκνα ὑπακοῆς	εἰ πατέρα ἐπικαλεῖσθε	φιλαδελφίαν ἀνυπόκριτον	ὡς ἀρτιγέννητα βρέφη
Pre-imperatival wrong conduct	μὴ συσχηματιζόμενοι			Ἀποθέμενοι
B: Imperative to Action Consistent with This Familial Metaphor				
Aorist imperative	ἅγιοι … γενήθητε	ἐν φόβῳ … ἀναστράφητε	ἀλλήλους ἀγαπήσατε	γάλα ἐπιποθήσατε
C: Further Basis of Appeal				
Divine action		ἐλυτρώθητε	ἀναγεγεννημένοι	
Negative		οὐ φθαρτοῖς	οὐκ … φθαρτῆς	
Scripture	ἅγιοι ἔσεσθε		ῥῆμα κυρίου μένει	χρηστὸς ὁ κύριος
Extended "you" conclusion		ὥστε τὴν πίστιν ὑμῶν	εὐαγγελισθὲν εἰς ὑμᾶς	

---

3 Larry R. Helyer rightly notes, "Paternal imagery shapes Peter's Paraenesis in 1 Peter 1:3–2:3," in Helyer, *The Life and Witness of Peter* (Nottingham: Apollos, 2012), 117.

Following the establishment of the childhood metaphor in 1:3–12, the general imperative to a renewed mindset in 1:13 issues in four specific family-imaged imperatives in 1:14–2:3. Each of these involves: (a) an appeal to regenerate status within God's family (as obedient children, father-callers, brother-lovers, newborn infants), (b) an aorist imperative to action consistent with this familial metaphor, and (c) a further basis of appeal.

It is clearly important to this "witness" (5:1) that those who are the recipients of the news of evangelists (1:12) conceive of themselves as communal children and heirs. Elliott rightly comments: "the metaphor of God as father is ... consonant with the recurrent theme of rebirth (1:3, 23; 2:2) that implies God as progenitor and the believing community as God's family or household (2:5; 4:17) and 'brotherhood' (2:17; 5:9 ...)."[4] Elliott himself has contributed significantly to discussion of the imagery of the "household" in 1 Peter, demonstrating that this domicilic setting, which is present in the New Testament more broadly as "the starting point and focal point of the 'Jesus movement' ... and the subsequent believer/Christian movement," functions as a key image of belonging to God.[5] I have no doubt that the household as the setting and social structure for the meetings and transmission of early Christianity made it a useful image of "the Christian vision of communal salvation,"[6] and Elliott's analysis offers a useful social-scientific perspective on how this came about, in contrast to the religious imagery of "Judaism and Rome."[7] My own interest here is to consider a key theological factor that allowed the imagery of familial relationship to take hold across this young sect.

2 Familial Imagery as Heightened in Early Christianity

The proposal of this essay is that the motif of communal childhood is not in itself an image of major significance in the Hebrew Scriptures or Jewish self-identification, but becomes more prominent in the light of a gospel, or *kerygma*, of God's son.

Let us consider, then, the presence of the motif in the Hebrew Scriptures and early Judaism. There are indeed a few points—especially in the context of

---

4 John H. Elliott, *1 Peter: A New Translation with Introduction and Commentary* (AB 37B; New York: Doubleday, 2000), 331.
5 See particularly chapter 4 of John H. Elliott, *A Home for the Homeless: A Social-Scientific Criticism of 1 Peter, its Situation and Strategy* (repr., Eugene, OR: Wipf and Stock, 1990).
6 Elliott, *Home*, 199.
7 Elliott, *Home*, 199.

the sojourn to inheritance—at which the Hebrew Scriptures picture the people as children of their father God (an image reinforced by the terminology of "inheritance" to describe the Promised Land): "Do you thus repay the LORD, O foolish and senseless people? Is not he your father, who created you, who made you and established you?" (Deut 32:6 NRSV).[8] Indeed, the communal childhood imagery in the first two imperatival sections of the table above (1:14–16 and 1:17–21) seems to be consciously related to the period of wilderness wandering, by the citation of Leviticus in relation to obedient children in the first section (1:16), and the mention of the "sojourn" (παροικία) of father-callers in 1:17 (cf. Lev 25:23; Deut 23:7; 26:5).[9]

However, while the language of "house" is certainly utilised to describe Israel and Judah,[10] and the language of sonship is applied to the Davidic anointed (Ps 2; 2 Sam 7), it should be conceded that the language of *familial relationship with God as father* is infrequent in the Hebrew Scriptures as a whole (and can hardly be called common even in the wilderness or kingship narratives).[11] Indeed, most of the familial language of the Hebrew Scriptures and related literature must be heard as quite literally depicting Israel as a broad family of descendants of Abraham.

What of Jewish use of such imagery around the first century? It is notable that we find early Jewish application of such imagery to proselytes. Philo

---

8   See also Deut 8:5; 14:1; Mal 2:10; cf. Jub. 1:23–25. Also relevant are the references to Israel as God's firstborn son in the exodus event: Exod 4:22–23; Hos 11:1. Robert H. Stein considers that the portrayal of God as father "is surprisingly rare in the Old Testament. There God is specifically called the Father of the nation of Israel ... or the Father of certain individuals ... only fifteen times ... This metaphor for God may have been avoided in the Old Testament due to its frequent use in the ancient Near East where it was used in various fertility religions and carried heavy sexual overtones. The avoidance of this description for God can still be found in the intertestamental literature. There its use is also rare." Robert H. Stein, "Fatherhood of God," in *Evangelical Dictionary of Biblical Theology* (ed. Walter A. Elwell; Grand Rapids: Baker, 1996), 247–248 (247).

9   For a substantial argument concerning links between 1 Peter and the exodus-wilderness experience, see Allan Chapple, "The Appropriation of Scripture in 1 Peter," in *All That the Prophets Have Declared: The Appropriation of Scripture in the Emergence of Christianity* (ed. Matthew R. Malcolm; Milton Keynes, UK: Paternoster, 2015), 155–171, 264–280.

10 As Elliott points out: *Home*, 183.

11 Schlosser furthermore points out that the image of "rebirth" is marginal in the Old Testament: it is "une catégorie tout à fait marginale dans le discours vétérotestamentaire sur Dieu (Dt 32,18; Ps 2,7; Pr 8,25): la renaissance ou, plutôt, la régénération." Jacques Schlosser, *La Premiere Epitre de Pierre* (Commentaire Biblique: Nouveau Testament 21; Paris: Cerf, 2011), 62.

describes penitent proselytes as those who have come to the "father of all," and who should thus be regarded as both friends and relatives (φιλτάτους καὶ συγγενεστάτους).¹² Aseneth is depicted in Joseph and Aseneth as becoming, in conversion to Judaism, a renewed (ἀνακαίνισον αὐτήν, 8:11) offspring of a child-loving father (πατὴρ φιλότεκνος, 12:8).¹³ This imagery is also utilised of proselytes in Rabbinic texts.¹⁴ It seems that the motif of the fatherhood of God lends itself to a depiction of Jews and Gentiles as coming into commonality; and the motif of new birth lends itself to a depiction of new religious identity.

However, it should be noted that the imagery of new birth in Christianity, and specifically in 1 Peter, is not strictly picturing conversion of non-Jewish proselytes, but is used more broadly to express a theological conviction regarding the identity of God's people, including the undoubtedly Jewish persona of Peter himself: "he has rebirthed *us* into a living hope" (1:3). Furthermore, the motif of the fatherhood of God is not adopted because he is the common "father of all," but rather he is specifically, and primarily, the "father of ... Jesus Christ" (1:3). While there is some connection between parallel uses of terminology relating to fatherhood and rebirth here then, it is not strong.

Further, the book of 1 Peter is not idiosyncratic in its use of these motifs of fatherhood and rebirth, in comparison with other documents of the New Testament.

In relation to fatherhood, Stein notes that despite apparent avoidance in the Old Testament and intertestamental literature, the "teaching of the Fatherhood of God takes a decided turn with Jesus, for 'Father' was his favourite term for addressing God."¹⁵ As well as this use by Jesus, Paul articulates clearly the conception that the filial relationship that believers enjoy with God is derived from God's identification as the Father of Jesus Christ, appropriated by the Spirit: "When we cry, 'Abba! Father!' it is that very Spirit bearing witness with our spirit that we are children of God, and if children, then heirs, heirs of God and joint heirs with Christ—if, in fact, we suffer with him so that we may also be glorified with him" (Rom 8:15–17 NRSV).

In relation to "rebirth," John's Gospel has Nicodemus as the "teacher of Israel" in representing those who must receive new birth in order to enter the

---

12   Philo, *Virt.* 179.
13   Joseph and Aseneth interestingly presents Joseph as "son of God" in some special sense (18:11), and calls upon the God of his "father Israel," who intriguingly "called [Israel?] from darkness into light" (8:10: καλέσας ἀπὸ τοῦ σκότους εἰς τὸ φῶς).
14   See b. Yeb. 22a, 48b, 62a, in all of which a proselyte is depicted as being like a newly born child.
15   Stein, "Fatherhood," 247.

kingdom of God (3:3; cf. 1:12–13).¹⁶ In Titus 3:5, God is said to have saved "us" by the "washing of rebirth," a first person plural that clearly includes the Jewish persona of Paul. A partial parallel to this comes in Gal 3:26, before Paul declares that "there is no longer Jew or Greek," where he says that "in Christ Jesus you are all children of God through faith" (NRSV). While speaking in their own voices, these different New Testament passages have a consonance with 1 Peter's striking assumption that not only proselytes but also Jews must undergo rebirth by the Father—an assumption absent in Jewish literature prior to the New Testament.

But even if backgrounds in the religious documents of Hebrew Scripture and Judaism are modest, might the New Testament documents' use of fictive kinship terms reflect the broader Hellenised environment in which these documents arose? Eleanor Dickey's analysis of Roman-era Greek letters is important:

> the difference between [earlier] classical and [Roman era] epistolary usage is particularly striking in the case of the masculine ἀδελφέ, which from its first appearance in the papyri seems to be used to colleagues and business partners more often than to relatives, and which even at that early stage does not appear to carry connotations of special affection when used outside the family.¹⁷

Dickey points out that, as well as this adoption of a convention of vocative address, Greek letters of the Roman era can exhibit the broader Greek tendency to "extend" kinship terms to those who are viewed with affection or ingratiation:

> In other types of Greek [that is, beyond epistolary Greek], extended kinship terms are clearly used as politeness features, indicating respect and/or affection for the person awarded metaphorical kinship status.¹⁸
>
> [In the epistles under examination,] terms for parents, children, and siblings can all be used to non-relatives.¹⁹

---

16   A partial parallel is found in Matt 18:3/Luke 18:17, in which it is said that the kingdom of God can only be entered by those who receive "like a little child."
17   Eleanor Dickey, "The Greek Address System of the Roman Period and Its Relationship to Latin," *CQ* 54 (2004): 494–527 (514).
18   Eleanor Dickey, "Literal and Extended Use of Kinship Terms in Documentary Papyri," *Mnemosyne* 57 (2004): 131–176 (138).
19   Dickey, "Literal and Extended," 153–154.

These useful observations should be considered, and may illuminate a number of New Testament passages. However, what we see in early Christianity is frequently slightly different to an "extended" use of kinship terminology. We can see in early Christianity a conscious—even provocative—reframing of kinship categories: "A crowd was sitting around him; and they said to him, 'Your mother and your brothers and sisters are outside, asking for you.' And he replied, 'Who are my mother and my brothers?' And looking at those who sat around him, he said, 'Here are my mother and my brothers! Whoever does the will of God is my brother and sister and mother'" (Mark 3:32–35 NRSV). Here we see that the ingratiating terminology does not express an *extension* beyond (perceived) literal kinship ties, but a potential *repudiation* of literal kinship ties in favour of the group. Presumably this phenomenon might be found in various settings. But Joseph H. Hellerman considers that in the context of first-century Mediterranean cultures it is "a distinctly Christian conception" to envisage "a surrogate family whose membership transcended traditional boundaries of ethnicity, generation (patriline), and geography (fatherland)":[20] "In both arenas—terminology and behaviour—the churches departed significantly from contemporary social alternatives in its [sic] familial emphasis."[21] It is indeed striking that despite relatively modest backgrounds in the relevant literary and social contexts, familial language is used pervasively across the breadth of early Christian literature, from very early on.

As noted above, the ministry of Jesus as depicted in the Gospels involves an unprecedented use of familial imagery: "… the community Jesus envisions (one that, indeed, he assumes is already gathering around him) constitutes a surrogate kinship group, for which membership depends upon obedience to God, not upon one's patriline."[22] Of course, the Gospels, which bear witness to this ministry, are not the earliest documents of the New Testament. However, the passage from Mark cited above, in which Jesus reframes his followers as his kin, represents relatively early Jesus tradition.[23]

---

20   Joseph H. Hellerman, *The Ancient Church as Family* (Minneapolis: Fortress, 2001), 59.
21   Hellerman, *Ancient Church*, 22.
22   Hellerman, *Ancient Church*, 66. Helyer comments, "Though the fatherhood of God is mentioned in the OT, Jesus takes it to an unprecedented level." Helyer, *Life and Witness*, 118.
23   Dale C. Allison (*Resurrecting Jesus: The Earliest Christian Tradition and its Interpreters* [New York: T&T Clark, 2005]), while deferring the question of "what Jesus himself really said or did" (151), considers this passage to be an example of "early traditions about Jesus" (150) that present him in a "provocative" (167) light, expressing an implicit "tension between Jesus and Torah" (166) that is one strand of early Jesus tradition to be grappled with. On the use of this imagery broadly in Jesus's ministry, Moxnes comments: "Jesus

The letters of Paul are certainly early among the New Testament documents, and here again we see familial imagery similar to that found in 1 Peter. N.T. Wright in fact sees Paul's theology as *epitomised* with the use of such imagery in Philemon: "… because of the Messiah, and particularly because of his death and resurrection and the 'faith/faithfulness' which that both enacted and evokes, people of all sorts (Jew and Greek, slave and free, male and female) are brought into a single family. Messiah-family."[24]

Furthermore, besides the Gospels, Pauline literature, and Petrine literature, the familial imagery of the fatherhood of God and communal childhood of believers is found in Hebrews,[25] James,[26] the letters of John,[27] Jude,[28] and Revelation;[29] that is, every segment of the New Testament canon. This heightened use of familial imagery is therefore a phenomenon of early Christianity worthy of investigation from multiple angles.

The Old Testament references, the proselyte terminology, the contemporary Greek conventions of address, the ministry of the historical Jesus and the social setting of early Christianity surely provide a number of reasons for the proliferation of such terminology in the New Testament documents. But it seems to

---

speaks to his followers of kingdom as a household, with God as father and the addressees as his children … For those who had left households, Jesus' sayings about the kingdom imagined it as a new home place … With a subversive form of rhetoric, Jesus turned the life of the wandering disciples into households of God … For hearers who had been uprooted from their place of identity, the sayings about the kingdom also served to reinstate them in a location that could give them a new identity. And kingdom as household provided a familiar place for identity." H. Moxnes, *Putting Jesus in His Place: A Radical Vision of Household and Kingdom* (Louisville, KY: WJK, 2003), 123–124.

24 N.T. Wright, *Paul and the Faithfulness of God* (London, SPCK, 2013), 17; cf. Hellerman, *Ancient Church*, 126.

25 For example, 2:11–12: "For the one who sanctifies and those who are sanctified all have one Father. For this reason Jesus is not ashamed to call them brothers and sisters, saying, 'I will proclaim your name to my brothers and sisters'" (NRSV).

26 For example, 2:15: "If a brother or sister is naked and lacks daily food …" and 3:9: "With it we bless the Lord and Father" (NRSV).

27 For example, 1 John 3:1: "See what love the Father has given us, that we should be called children of God" (NRSV).

28 Jude 1: "To those who are called, who are beloved in God the Father" (NRSV).

29 For example, Rev 3:5, in which Jesus promises, "I will confess your name before my Father and before his angels"; and 12:17, in which the "son" is shown to have siblings: "Then the dragon was angry with the woman, and went off to make war on the rest of her children, those who keep the commandments of God and hold the testimony of Jesus" (NRSV).

me that our examination of the use of this motif in 1 Peter enables a deeper glimpse into the theological logic that might have accompanied and consolidated the widespread adoption of such imagery in earliest Christianity: *it is applied to those whose identity is informed by the gospel of the son of God.*

3   The Gospel of the Son of God

I suggest that for much literature associated with the name of Peter, the "gospel" might be summarised with the fourfold schema of:

> *suffering/death of the son of God → resurrected life → attestation → eschatological vindication.*

It can hardly be doubted that christological sonship,[30] death, resurrection, and eschatology feature in early Christian *kerygmata*. That "attestation" is an appropriate element of a Petrine gospel schema, however, is perhaps worth dwelling on briefly.[31] This theme can be seen by looking across the early literature with which Peter is associated (although there is no need to insist that this element is confined to Peter or limited to the interest of a Petrine circle).

Martin Hengel points out the significance of Peter's own attestation of the resurrection in Luke's depictions of his message and identity: "Luke appropriately allows Peter and John to confess before the leading authorities of the people: 'It is impossible that we could keep silent *about that which we have seen and heard*,' and Peter can give support to his story about Jesus in the

---

30   Of course, this theme itself could be unpacked by exploring the ministry of Jesus in Galilee and Judea, as occurs in the Gospels, as well as the speech attributed to Peter in Acts 10. In other works, such as the First Epistle of Peter and the apocryphal Gospel of Peter, this ministry is assumed in the identification of Jesus as "Christ" or "King of Israel," but has no prominence.

31   This element does not appear, for example, in Achtemeier's otherwise useful summary of the importance of Christ's career in 1 Peter: "The theological logic of 1 Peter is grounded in the events of the passion of Jesus Christ: his suffering (2:21) and death, (1:19) and his subsequent resurrection (1:21) and glorification (3:21). The logic thus grounded structures both the new reality and consequently the new behavior of those who follow Christ. The letter is therefore predicated on Christology. The emphasis on the suffering of Jesus as a prelude to his exaltation forms the core of that Christology, and it is expressed in terms derived from the course of his career: suffering, death, resurrection, ascension, and exaltation, a career to which he was destined from the very beginning." Paul J. Achtemeier, *1 Peter* (Hermeneia; Minneapolis: Fortress, 1996), 37.

presence of Cornelius with the postscript: '*We are witnesses* of all that he did in the land of Judea and in Jerusalem.'"[32] Peter is universally presented as a foundational apostolic witness, whose very proclamation is an essential outcome of the prior events of suffering, death, and resurrected life.[33] He is a key witness in the accounts of the evangelists, and is listed by name in Paul's famous received tradition of the *euangelion* itself (1 Cor 15:3–5). He is celebrated in the later *Acts of Peter* as one whose life climaxes with evangelistic proclamation.[34]

The resurrection event, it seems, necessarily issues forth in Petrine attestation. But it is worth noting that across the literature that draws on Peter's persona—biblical and extra-biblical—the impetus for this attestation does not begin with the witness; it is driven from above, and from within the empty tomb itself. In Mark's Gospel, the young man at the empty tomb announces, "He has been raised! ... Go, tell!" In the Gospel of Peter, the risen Jesus himself emerges from the tomb, affirming that he has proclaimed to the dead. In the Second Epistle of Peter, God himself voices the proclamation that is later echoed in human testimony (2 Pet 1:16–21). Peter is broadly conceived, in early and late documents, as one for whom human attestation is a responsive and essential gospel outcome of the Christ event. It is thus appropriately part of a gospel schema associated with his name.

To articulate this gospel schema with some of the terminology of 1 Peter, in particular, we could say that Jesus undergoes *suffering*, is *made alive by his father*, is made known in evangelistic *announcement*, and will be revealed in *glory*:

suffering → made alive by father → announcement → glory

---

[32] Martin Hengel, *Saint Peter: The Underestimated Apostle* (trans. Thomas H. Trapp; Grand Rapids: Eerdmans, 2010 [German 2006]), 80; emphases original.

[33] Gerald O'Collins argues that Acts is in sync with the New Testament more broadly in presenting Peter as "the leading, public witness to the resurrection of Jesus from the dead." He is, first and foremost, the "Easter proclaimer." Gerald O'Collins, "Peter as Witness to Easter," *TS* 73 (2012): 263–285 (280, 281). F. Lapham points to the crucial significance of the voice of God regarding his Son on the "holy mountain" and on this basis remarks that "to Peter is accorded the special privilege of being the prime witness of the glory of the divine Christ." F. Lapham, *Peter: The Myth, the Man and the Writings: A Study of Early Petrine Text and Tradition* (London: T&T Clark, 2003), 239.

[34] Markus Bockmuehl comments, "The *Acts of Peter* ... bring together Peter's evangelistic and apologetic preaching with the theme of repentance and conversion in his own life." Markus Bockmuehl, *The Remembered Peter in Ancient Reception and Modern Debate* (WUNT 262; Tübingen: Mohr Siebeck, 2010), 201.

Jesus is the one who suffers, rises, is announced, and is glorified. In fact, it seems to me that, regardless of questions of authorship,[35] we can profitably examine the whole letter of 1 Peter with this fourfold "Petrine" gospel schema in mind. We see the elements of this schema variously distributed in depictions of Jesus Christ and his witnesses.

3.1 *Gospel Schema Seen in Jesus Christ and His Witnesses*

		Suffering	Made alive	Announced	Glory
1:1–2	Jesus	Sprinkled blood			
1:3–9	Jesus	Death	Resurrection		Revelation
1:10–12	Christ	Sufferings			Glory
1:10–12	Evangelist			Announcement	
1:13	Christ				Revelation
1:17–21	Christ	Blood/death	Resurrection	Revelation	Glory
1:22–25	Evangelist			Announcement	
2:4–8	Jesus	Rejected			
2:18–25	Christ	Suffering, cross	Justice (?)		
3:18–22	Christ	Suffering, death	Made alive	Proclamation	Authority
4:1–6	Gospel			Proclamation	
4:12–19	Christ	Sufferings			Glory
5:1–5	Peter			Witness suffering	Sharer in glory

Jesus is depicted as the one who suffered and died; rose to new life; is attested in proclamation by himself, by evangelists, and by Peter; and will be revealed in future glorious authority.

It is further worthy of note that this same schema can usefully describe the ways in which 1 Peter characterises the identity of the letter's recipients, as Christian believers.

---

35 I believe a good case can be made for Petrine authorship, although the contribution of this essay does not depend on that assumption.

3.2   *Gospel Schema Applied to Identity of Believers*

		Suffering	Made alive	Announced	Glory
1:3–9	Believers		*Birth* ...		Salvation/ inheritance
1:14–16	Believers	(former ignorance)	... children	Conduct	
1:17–21	Believers	(former futility)	... children	Conduct	
1:22–25	Believers		... children	Conduct	
2:1–3	Believers		... children	Conduct	Salvation
2:4–8	Believers		Living stones	Priests, sacrifice	
2:9–10	Believers	Not his people	His people	Priests, proclaim	
3:18–22	Believers		Saved		

The recipients are those who have themselves entered into new life, and attest the Christ event, as they look ahead to salvation at the time of Christ's revelation. The chief "new life" metaphor is, of course, that of "new birth"—which is linked at the outset to Christ's new-life resurrection (1:3).[36] What is surprising is that, although the theme of attestatory *proclamation* is not absent (2:9; 3:15), it is overtaken in significance by the theme of attestatory *conduct*. This is striking for its presence in passages where the gospel schema is applied in close parallel to Christ and to believers. For example, in 3:18–22, Christ is presented as the one who suffers in the flesh, is made alive in the spirit, and makes *proclamation* to spirits, before entering into heavenly authority. Immediately subsequently, believers are presented as those who suffer in the flesh, live by the will of God, and *conduct themselves* rightly in the face of the Gentiles, who will one day face heavenly authority. This very *conduct* is presented as somehow analogous to *proclamation* to the dead (4:6). It is for this reason that I call it "attestatory conduct."

If we are to turn our focus to the nature of this attestatory conduct, it is interesting that once again, the author seems to conceptualise it using the Petrine gospel schema we have already seen.

---

36   A second "new life" metaphor is the striking image of *living* stones.

3.3 Gospel Schema Applied to Conduct of Believers

		Suffering	Made alive	Announced	Glory
2:11–12	Believers			Conduct …	
2:13–17	Believers	… accept authority			
2:18–25	Believers	… accept, suffer	Live for righteousness		God's approval
3:1–7	Believers	… accept			
3:8–12	Believers	… bless			Inherit blessing
3:13–17	Believers	… conduct, defend			
4:1–6	Believers	Suffer			
4:7–11	Believers	Discipline, service			End of all things
4:12–19	Believers	Suffering			
5:1–5	Elders				Crown of glory
5:6–11	All	Humble, suffer			Restoration

The attestatory conduct of believers is shown to be (especially) like the suffering of Christ, and like the new life of Christ, concluding with participation in the glory of Christ.

What I am seeking to point out is that the writer seems to draw flexibly on a basic Petrine gospel schema in conceptualising Jesus, Christian identity, and Christian conduct: in the believer's identity and conduct, Christ is depicted as *suffering, made alive, announced*, and destined for *glory*.

But how does this fit with the idea (encapsulated well by Achtemeier and others) that the chief imagery for the identity and conduct of believers in 1 Peter is that of *Israel*?[37] The answer, of course, is that the Petrine gospel schema itself draws upon and renegotiates the heritage of Israel, in the light of the Christ event.

3.4 The Gospel and the Renegotiation of Israel's Heritage

The persona of the writer is foregrounded as that of a witness of the gospel of Jesus Christ, being self-consciously "a witness of the sufferings of Christ, as well as one who shares in the glory to be revealed" (5:1). In view of the sufferings and

---

[37] "Israel has become the controlling metaphor for the new people of God, and as such its rhetoric has passed without remainder into that of the Christian community." Achtemeier, *1 Peter*, 72.

future glories of the Christ, then, the writer draws upon, and renegotiates, patterns from Israel's heritage. This gospel-oriented renegotiation of the heritage of Israel is multi-faceted, and need not be neat. There are numerous images from Israel's heritage that the author draws upon, and there are multiple and flexible points of connection with his gospel schema. Among those parts of the Old Testament said to be primary backgrounds for 1 Peter, cases have been made for Psalm 34, Zechariah 9–14, Malachi, Isaiah, and the exodus-wilderness period.[38]

Without denying the significance of the other biblical backgrounds, I particularly affirm that a key pattern from Israel's heritage that fits the writer's conception of the gospel events is the movement from life-giving redemption in the wilderness, through to the final inheritance of salvation in the Promised Land:[39]

Gospel schema:	Suffering	Made Alive	Announced	Glory
Israel's heritage:	Egypt/exodus	Covenant Inauguration	Priestly proclamation	Inheritance

It is worth noting that this "wilderness" set of imagery is persistent in the letter as a means of expressing the identity and conduct of gospel figures. To revisit the data from the tables above, we see that Jesus is presented as the one who "suffered" and had his blood "sprinkled," was raised by his "Father,"

---

[38] Chapple, "Appropriation of Scripture in 1 Peter," draws special attention to the work of Bornemann, Schutter and Woan (Ps 34); Liebengood (Zech 9–14); Danker (Malachi); and Pearson, Dubis, and Mbuvi (Isaiah). Chapple himself pursues the primacy of the exodus-wilderness period.

[39] It cannot be doubted that the movement from Egypt to inheritance was a culturally ingrained schema for those who identified with Israel. It surfaces across the New Testament. In Pisidian Antioch, Luke has Paul begin his speech with God's creation of the people in Egypt and—after a period in the wilderness—their entry into Canaan "as an inheritance" (Acts 13:16–19). In 1 Corinthians, Paul depicts the exodus as the beginning of covenant life, following which came a time of "testing" in the wilderness (1 Cor 10:1–13). The letter to the Hebrews famously draws application from the period of wilderness wandering on the way to the "rest" of inheritance. In doing so it draws upon the pre-existing schematisation of this motif in Ps 95, acknowledging that this conceptualisation was already a feature of Jewish cultural memory. A similar acknowledgement is implicit in Matthew's use of Hosea's "Out of Egypt I called my son" (Matt 2:15).

is the "rejected but chosen" "living stone," "proclaims" the gospel acts of God, and secures a future "inheritance." The recipients are identified as those who have been granted "new birth" life, are now priestly "living stones" who undergo "testing" but proclaim "the mighty acts of God" through impeccable conduct during their "sojourn," and look forward to their "inheritance." All of these "gospel" themes find significant background in Israel's movement from life-giving redemption in the wilderness to final inheritance in the Promised Land.[40]

Gospel schema:	Suffering	Made Alive	Announced	Glory
Israel's heritage:	Egypt/exodus	Covenant Inauguration	Priestly proclamation	Inheritance
Presentation of Jesus:	Death/blood sprinkled; rejected; suffering	Resurrection by Father; chosen; living stone	Proclamation to the dead	Authority
Presentation of recipients:	"Former" life; present suffering	Birth as children; living stones; living for righteousness; testing	Priestly proclamation; sojourning conduct	Inheritance; restoration

It is important to note that these images have been *renegotiated* in the light of the gospel events. For example, the theme of priestly proclamation to the nations is not of major importance in the Hebrew Scriptures themselves; but in the light of the Christ event—in which attesting proclamation is crucial—the author seizes upon an opening in the priestly covenant identity of Israel and gives it new prominence. It is the gospel schema, then, that has primary governance, directing the use and renegotiation of Old Testament texts and imagery.

And it is this same "gospel renegotiating" instinct, I suggest, that contributes to the prominence of familial imagery in 1 Peter, despite relatively modest backgrounds in the Old Testament and early Judaism.

---

40   See Chapple, "Appropriation of Scripture in 1 Peter," for detailed consideration.

It is, in literature associated with Peter, the *Son of the Father* who suffers, is made alive, is announced, and is glorified: "This is my son, the beloved."[41] In the context of a work in which the identity of Jesus is a template for the identity of believers, I suggest it is this conviction about the sonship of Jesus that consolidates the use of childhood imagery for those who belong to him: *they* receive new birth from *his* father (1 Pet 1:3). On this basis the author seizes upon and amplifies suggestive Old Testament imagery related to sojourning childhood obedience, father-invocation, and infancy. Now that identity for the people of God is refracted through the gospel of Jesus Christ, it seems appropriate to the author to revisit the Scriptures and give new significance to heretofore unemphasised imagery.

While similar theological logic, in other circumstances, might consolidate the use of "adoption" imagery (Rom 8:23), in 1 Peter the Petrine gospel undergirds the imagery of "rebirth." This is not to say that the theological logic necessarily prompted the terminology; it might have confirmed terminology that had arisen through other resources—perhaps the ministry of Jesus or proselyte terminology. But it is possible that the early Christian practice of reading Psalm 2 christologically,[42] in which Jesus is said to have been "begotten" (γεγέννηκα) at his baptism, transfiguration, or resurrection, might have led to the theological reasoning that those who have come to the risen Christ have been "re-begotten" (ἀναγεννήσας). The influence of Psalm 2 would certainly fit with the Petrine interest in the declaration of sonship on the ὄρος τὸ ἅγιον (Ps 2:6 LXX; cf. 2 Pet 1:18: τῷ ἁγίῳ ὄρει).

In other words, it is possible that the theological logic of salvation through identification with the divinely begotten Son exerts a greater influence on the adoption of familial imagery in 1 Peter and early Christianity than mere "consolidation." But this is, of course, impossible to quantify. Nevertheless, the role of "theological logic" in the development of early Christianity should not be neglected. The study conducted in this essay demonstrates that the

---

41   In particular, the divine voice on the mount of transfiguration holds a place of some importance in the literature traditionally associated with Peter: Mark 9:7, "This is my son, the beloved; listen to him!"; 2 Pet 1:17–18, "For he received honour and glory from God the Father when that voice was conveyed to him by the Majestic Glory, saying, 'This is my Son, my Beloved, with whom I am well pleased.' We ourselves heard this voice come from heaven, while we were with him on the holy mountain" (NRSV; see also Acts Pet. 20).

42   This can be seen, e.g., in the Gospels' baptism and transfiguration passages; Acts 4:23–31; 13:33; Heb 1:5; 5:5. For an analysis of the christological influence of this psalm, see Aquila Lee, *From Messiah to Pre-Existent Son: Jesus' Self-Consciousness and Early Christian Exegesis of Messianic Psalms* (WUNT 2.192; Tübingen: Mohr Siebeck, 2005).

illumination of early Christian mission provided by social and literary contexts can be usefully supplemented by serious attention to the impacts of theological conviction upon imagery, language, and communication.

4 Conclusion

In considering the use of family imagery in early Christian mission, I have made a case that 1 Peter provides a window into the theological logic that consolidated the widespread adoption of such motifs. This case has come in three steps.

First, I showed that familial imagery is crucial to the letter of 1 Peter, being established in the opening verses with the fatherhood of God and the rebirth of believers. This imagery is especially utilised from 1:3 to 2:3, where believers are depicted, in a tight literary structure, as obedient children, father-callers, brother-lovers, and newborn infants. Second, I suggested that this sort of use of familial language in early Christianity occurs across the breadth of its documents in such a way that is not exhaustively explained by literary or social contexts. In particular, we see in early Christianity the prioritising of a narrow conception of the fatherhood of God (primarily "father of Jesus Christ" rather than "father of all"), the surprising application of "rebirth" imagery to not only proselytes but also Jews, and the provocative reassignment of kinship terms across otherwise firm borders. Third, I proposed that the gospel of the Son of God supplies renegotiated imagery for earliest Christianity. Specifically, I suggested that a Petrine gospel schema renegotiates the imagery of Israel's heritage in configuring both the identity of Jesus and the identity of believers in 1 Peter. One key pattern from Israel's heritage that fits the writer's conception of the gospel events is the movement from life-giving redemption in the wilderness through to the final inheritance of salvation in the Promised Land. However, this imagery is refracted and renegotiated through the gospel of the son of God who *suffers*, is *made alive*, is *announced*, and holds an inheritance of *glory*.

Thus, the imagery of the recipients as father-invoking, sibling-loving, milk-nourished children of God's household, while partially explained by a number of potential backgrounds, receives logical consolidation in the light of the governing conceptualisation of this Petrine gospel of God's son: *believers are to conceive of their own identity as arising from that of Jesus Christ, who was "made alive" by the Father.*

The extent to which this theological logic is reflective of prior Christian activity and literature is an intriguing question. The letter of 1 Peter is, of course, difficult to date precisely. It has been noted that the data relating to heightened use of familial imagery in early Christianity does appear to include the earliest documents of the New Testament (Paul) as well as early Jesus tradition (Mark), so the literary phenomenon in question is certainly early. The various factors noted above (ministry of the historical Jesus, social setting of early Christianity, Hebrew Scripture, proselyte terminology, etc.) no doubt contributed to the emergence of this phenomenon to different degrees across this time period. But the fact that the conceptualisation of Jesus as "Son" of the "Father" is also present in documents across this period makes it reasonable to speculate that this "theological logic" may have been a significant factor from soon after it was believed that living hope had been awakened "through the resurrection of Jesus Christ from the dead" (1 Pet 1:3).

Modern Authors Index

Abernethy, D. 281
Achtemeier, P.J. 337, 343–348, 498–500, 507, 510, 513, 525, 529
Adams, S.A. 506
Alexander, L.C.A. 153
Alexander, P.S. 34, 136
Allison, Jr., D.C. 101, 352, 358–359, 361–362, 365, 370, 523
Amphoux, C.-B. 409
Amundsen, D.W. 199, 200
Anderson, J.C. 271
Anderson, P.N. 36–37, 42–43, 46, 164
Anderson, R.N. 89
Arnal, W.E. 224, 226–228
Asad, T. 239
Ashcroft, B. 274, 431
Ashton, J. 171
Atkins, J.W.H. 34
Atkinson, K. 441
Aune, D.E. 130, 136, 200
Aus, R.D. 248, 255–256
Avalos, H. 197, 200, 221–222

Bachmann, M. 463
Bailey, J.A. 36
Bailey, K. 33
Baird, J.A. 91, 94
Baker, C.A. 264, 437
Baldensperger, W. 11, 12
Balla, P. 77
Bammel, E. 11, 194
Barber, M.P. 371
Barclay, J.M.G. 462
Barnet, A.E. 502
Barnett, P.W. 346, 412–413, 416
Barr, J. 433–434, 456
Barrett, C.K. 168, 412, 417
Barrett, L.F. 438
Barrett-Lennard, R.J.S. 222
Bartlet, J.V. 251
Bartlett, J.R. 445
Batovici, D. 466
Bauckham, R.B. 97–98, 132, 156, 242, 394, 413, 417, 469, 472–478, 481, 484, 492–493
Bauer, J.B. 366
Baum, A. 109, 111–114, 130–132, 203

Baumgarten, A.I. 187
Baur, F.C. 417, 459–460, 462, 464, 483, 486, 496
Baxter, W. 203–204
Bayer, H.F. 366
Bazzana, G. 216, 224, 236
Beale, G.K. 365
Beare, F.W. 501, 507
Beasley-Murray, G.R. 244
Becker, E.-M. 110, 280, 477
Becker, J. 11, 56
Beckman, J. 381–382
Bendik, I. 461
Berger, K. 91, 99, 102
Berquist, J. 264
Best, E. 7, 498–499, 502–503, 508, 513
Betz, H.D. 58, 64–65, 68–69, 90
Betz, O. 366, 369
Bhabha, H. 269
Biber, D. 92
Bigg, C.A. 502
Bird, M.F. 461
Black, C.C. 82, 413
Black, D.A. 96, 505
Blackman, P. 356
Blasing, C.A. 497
Blass, F.W. 209
Blomberg, C.L. 94–95, 346
Blunt, A.W.F. 251
Bock, D.L. 41, 96, 99, 257, 497
Bockmuehl, M. 225, 371, 464–465, 478, 481–483, 526
Bonke, M. 80
Bonz, M. 265
Borgen, P. 202
Boring, M.E. 248, 298
Bornkamm, G. 359–360
Böttrich, C. 485
Bouhot, J.-B. 409
Bovon, F. 41–42, 46
Bowden, J. 352
Bowers, W.P. 258
Bowersock, G.W. 73
Bowman, J.W. 342
Boyle, A. 304
Brandenburger, E. 244–245

Brandon, S.G.F. 283
Brandt, A.J.H.W. 192–193
Bratcher, R.G. 246
Bremmer, J.N. 228
Brodd, J. 265
Brooks, J.A. 244–245
Brown, J.K. 92
Brown, R.E. 11–12, 24–26, 31, 56, 100, 172, 175–176, 252, 346, 420–421, 427
Bruce, F.F. 255–256, 258
Brueggemann, W. 264
Bultmann, R. 28, 56, 68–69, 91–92, 96–100, 251, 346
Burer, M.H. 99
Burke, P. 271
Burkert, W. 30
Burkitt, F.C. 34
Burridge, R.A. 47, 136
Bush, B. 272–273
Buth, R. 505
Buttrick, D.G. 127
Byrskog, S. 100

Cadbury, H.J. 97
Campbell, J. 430
Cantarella, E. 110
Carr, D.M. 264
Carson, D.A. 95–96, 162, 168, 247, 419–421
Carter, W. 5, 264–265, 276–277, 280–281
Cartledge, P. 65
Casaseca, F. 81
Casey, M. 196, 202, 213–214
Caspi, M. 355, 359
Catchpole, D.R. 101–102, 190
Chapple, A. 520, 530–531
Charlesworth, J.H. 156, 170, 178–182, 447, 496
Childs, B.S. 399
Chilton, B.D. 11, 99, 178, 469
Chow, S. 355–356, 361, 367
Cirafesi, W.V. 413
Clark, G. 200
Clarke, A.D. 417, 421
Classen, C.J. 90
Clauss, M. 29–30
Cody, J. 304
Collins, A.Y. 12, 49, 50, 53–56, 245, 290, 298, 312, 317, 339, 441
Collins, J.J. 312, 317
Collins, R.F. 99, 168

Colson, F.H. 36
Comber, J. 215
Conway, C.M. 264, 271
Conzelmann, H. 99
Cook, J.G. 82
Cooper, R.L. 248
Cope, L. 358
Correns, D. 356
Cottrell, J. 252, 254
Cranfield, C.E.B. 243–245, 247, 251, 254
Crawford, S.W. 46
Cribbs, F.L. 37, 44
Crook, Z. 39–40
Cross, A.R. 69
Crossan, J.D. 4, 172–177, 179–184, 225, 230, 243
Cullmann, O. 27
Culpepper, R.A. 244, 413

Dahl, N.A. 193
Dalman, G. 188
Danker, F.W. 497
Daube, D. 211, 500
Dauer, A. 36
Davids, P.H. 499
Davies, M. 36, 91
Davies, W.D. 91, 101, 358–359, 362, 365, 370
Dawson, A. 202, 219, 222
de Boer, M.C. 482, 488
de Jong, I.J.F. 152
de Jonge, M. 448
Debrunner, A. 209
Deissmann, A. 264
DelHousaye, J. 2, 32
Delling, G. 190
Derrenbacker, Jr., R.A. 127
deSilva, D.A. 396
deWaard, J. 502
Dewey, J. 95
Dibelius, M. 11, 59, 91
Dickey, E. 522
Dietzfelbinger, C. 162
Dillow, J.C. 455
Dockery, D.S. 95–96
Dodd, C.H. 22, 56, 346, 365, 498
Dominik, W. 304
Donahue, J.R. 249
Döring, L. 470
Dörnemann, M. 222

Douglas, J.D.   247
Doyle, M.   272–273
Draper, J.A.   226, 229–232, 237
Driver, S.R.   513
Dryden, J.D.W.   506
Dschulnigg, P.   165
du Rand, J.A.   420
Dubis, M.   352
Dubuisson, D.   239
Duff, T.E.   39
Duling, D.   99, 100, 203–204, 209, 214–215, 272
Dunderberg, I.   275, 278, 429
Dungan, D.   127
Dunn, J.D.G.   32–33, 38, 96, 196, 212, 225–226, 236, 240, 252–256, 258, 361, 417, 461–465, 468, 470–473, 475–480, 482, 484, 487–496
Dunne, J.A.   466
Dupont, J.   62
Durst, M.   157

Easton, B.S.   193, 506
Edmondson, J.   308
Edwards, J.R.   242, 244, 250
Ehrman, B.D.   3, 48, 108–119, 129, 133
Eidinow, E.   134
Elliott, J.H.   497–500, 502–503, 507, 509–511, 513, 519–520
Elliott, J.K.   48, 404
Elliott, M.A.   438–439
Ellis, E.E.   98–99, 139, 413, 415
Elwell, W.A.   520
Endo, M.   41
Engberg-Pedersen, T.   58
Epp, E.J.   99, 367, 405
Erbse, H.   39
Ernst, J.   11, 160–161
Esler, P.F.   308, 470
Esterline, D.   265
Evans, C.A.   11, 100–101, 178–182, 243–247, 250, 252, 288, 296, 298, 341, 443, 449, 469

Fanning, B.M.   99
Fanon, F.   269, 280
Fantham, E.   125
Farmer, K.A.   73
Farmer, W.R.   33, 93, 108

Farrer, A.   35, 38
Fears, J.R.   303
Fee, G.D.   367, 479, 482, 484, 491, 493
Fehribach, A.   431
Feiler, P.F.   358
Ferguson, E.   50
Ferngren, G.B.   199–201, 216, 219–222
Fewster, G.P.   375
Fitzmyer, J.A.   190–191, 195
Fleddermann, H.T.   226–227, 230, 232–233
Flusser, D.   211
Forgas, J.P.   84
Förster, H.   3, 149, 152, 155–156, 164, 168–169
Fortna, R.T.   346
Foster, O.D.   501
Foster, P.   173
Fowden, G.   78
Fowler, R.M.   337–338, 345, 347
France, R.T.   247, 249–250, 286–288, 297–298, 339, 359, 369–370, 497
Fredriksen, P.   187
Freedman, D.N.   352
Freire, P.   280
Frey, J.   110, 461, 468, 477–478, 481, 484–485, 491
Fridrichsen, A.   335
Friedrich, G.   246
Friesen, S.   273
Frijda, N.H.   441
Frost, E.   222
Funk, R.   108

Gaebelein, F.E.   247
Gahan, J.J.   34
Gale, H.M.   368
Gallus, L.   336
Gamble, H.Y.   409
Gandhi, L.   274
Gärtner, B.   341, 497
Gathercole, S.   461
Geffcken, J.   364
Gempf, C.   256
Gerhardsson, B.   33
Gesenius, F.W.   513
Geyser, A.S.   11
Gibson, J.J.   471–482
Gieseler, J.C.L.   32
Gill, D.W.J.   256, 380
Ginzberg, L.   194

Gleason, M.W. 270
Glenny, E.W. 497
Glonner, G. 157
Gnilka, J. 251
Goetchius, E.V.N. 419
Goguel, M. 11
Goldsmith, D. 373
Goodacre, M. 35
Goppelt, L. 499–500, 507
Gottwald, N. 264
Goulder, M.D. 36, 38, 368
Graf, F. 53
Graham, M.P. 72
Grant, R.M. 30
Gray, T.C. 283, 285–291, 293, 296, 299
Green, J.B. 92, 94, 99
Greene, J.T. 355, 359
Gregory, A. 35–37
Griesbach, J.J. 33
Griffith, T. 418–419
Griffiths, G. 274, 431
Grudem, W. 500
Grundmann, W. 500
Guehlich, R.A. 338
Gundry, R.H. 99, 245, 359, 363, 368, 371
Guthrie, W.K.C. 378–380
Güttgemanns, E. 91, 102

Haase, W. 199
Haenchen, E. 162
Hagner, D.A. 33, 225, 281
Hahn, F. 86, 190
Hahn, R. 499
Hahneman, G.M. 403–404
Hakola, R. 437
Haldiman, K. 149
Han, K.S. 226
Hardin, J.K. 482
Hardt, M. 270
Harnack, A. 6, 393–394, 410
Harrelson, W.J. 449–450
Harrington, D.J. 249
Harris, J.R. 498
Harris, W.V. 73
Harrison, J.R. 130
Hartman, L. 192
Hata, G. 441
Hatina, T.R. 250
Haviland-Jones, J.M. 438

Hawthorne, G.F. 94
Hayes, J.H. 366
Hays, R.B. 368
Head, P.M. 33, 421
Heil, J.P. 283, 293, 299, 341
Heilig, C. 7, 459, 461, 466–467, 496
Heilig, T. 467, 496
Hellerman, J.H. 523–524
Hellholm, C. 50
Hellholm, D. 50, 53
Helyer, L.R. 518, 523
Hemer, C.J. 412
Henderson, S.W. 77
Hendriksen, W. 161, 249, 254
Hengel, M. 35, 153, 157, 257, 280, 421, 461, 470, 477–478, 481–482, 484–487, 489, 491, 494, 496, 525–526
Herder, J.G. 32
Herzer, J. 110
Hewitt, J.T. 461
Hezser, C. 2, 71–73, 77, 79, 84
Hickling, C.J. 98
Hill, C.E. 406
Hirunuma, T. 367
Hobsbawm, E. 271
Hodge, C.J. 228
Hodgson, Jr., R. 194–195
Hoffmann, P. 51, 224, 230
Hollenbach, P.W. 11
Holman, C.L. 242, 244
Holmén, T. 86
Holmes, M.W. 35, 48
Holm-Nielsen, S. 357
Holtzmann, H.J. 35, 501
Hooker, M.D. 98, 251, 286, 339
Hoover, R.W. 108
Horbury, W. 194
Horn, F.W. 463, 485
Hornblower, S. 127, 134
Horrell, D.G. 497
Horsley, R.A. 59–62, 226, 229–232, 237, 264–265, 271, 273, 347
Howard, G. 36
Howard, J.K. 199, 203
Howe, B. 435
Hughes, J. 357
Hunn, D. 491
Hurd, J. 59
Hurst, L.D. 433

Hurtado, L.W. 406
Huskinson, J. 270
Hyatt, D. 253

Instone-Brewer, D. 143, 421
Iverson, K.R. 284, 340, 345

Jackson-McCabe, M.A. 227, 281, 437, 452
Jacobson, A.D. 52, 227, 231
Janssen, M. 110
Jastrow, M. 206
Jeffers, J.S. 83
Jenks, G.C. 355
Jensen, M.D. 7, 412, 418–419, 423–424
Jeremias, G. 366
Jeremias, J. 56, 193, 195, 251, 361, 366–367, 369–370
Jervell, J. 55, 63
Jewett, R. 90
Jobes, K.H. 242, 499–500, 502, 510–511
Johnson, L.T. 99, 199
Johnson, S.E. 251
Johnston, E.D. 346
Johnston, P. 369
Jones, F.S. 4, 187
Joseph, A.P. 497
Joubert, S.J. 394
Juel, D. 283, 286
Just, F.S. 154, 164

Karris, R.J. 32
Käsemann, E. 59, 68–69, 427, 463
Kaster, R.A. 127
Kato, Z. 251
Kautsky, J.H. 272
Kautzsch, E. 513
Kaylor, R.D. 77
Keck, A. 81
Keener, C.S. 13, 28, 134, 143, 360
Keesmaat, S.C. 335
Kelber, W.H. 95, 100, 102, 283, 289–290, 339
Kelly, C. 270
Kelly, J.N.D. 507
Kelsey, M. 202, 222
Kennard, D.W. 352, 359
Keown, M. 5, 242–243, 253, 258
Keylock, L. 94–97
Kierkegaard, S. 381–383
Kilpatrick, G.D. 245

Kim, H.C.P. 354
Kim, J.H. 507
Kingsbury, J.D. 359, 371
Kirk, A. 224, 238
Kirk, J.R.D. 288, 290–291, 293, 299
Klassen, W. 343
Klawans, J. 472
Kleinman, A. 197–198
Kloppenborg, J.S. 51, 224–227, 230, 234, 238
Knapp, R. 271
Koester, H. 172–173, 181, 226, 228, 230
Konradt, M. 452
Köstenberger, A.J. 149, 161, 168
Kotzé, Z. 438
Kövecses, Z. 436–438, 440
Kraeling, C.H. 11
Kraftchick, S.J. 517
Kramer, W. 190
Krantz, F. 271
Krapp, P. 81
Kraus, T.J. 172–174
Kruger, M.J. 406–408
Kruger, P.A. 438
Kruse, C.G. 421
Kuhlmann, H. 86
Kuhn, H.W. 86, 366
Kupp, D.D. 318
Kytzler, B. 34

Labahn, A. 53
Labahn, M. 50, 54, 57, 149, 227
Ladouceur, D.J. 354, 366
Lampe, P. 195
Land, C.D. 375
Landes, G.M. 366
Lane, W.L. 244, 251
Lange, A. 34
Lapham, F. 526
LeDonne, A. 149
Lee, A. 532
Lee, J.W. 265
Lee, M.V. 89
Lee, S.-I. 188
Legras, B. 109, 115, 124
Lenski, G. 272
Lenski, R.C.H. 254
Leroy, H. 27
Lessing, R.R. 360
Lewis, J.P. 369

Lewis, M.   438
Lewis, N.   188
Lichtenberger, H.   11
Licona, M.   3, 134
Lierman, J.   36, 265
Lieu, J.M.   418, 420–421
Liew, T.B.   271
Lightfoot, R.H.   24
Lincoln, A.T.   39, 152, 154, 161, 163
Lincoln, B.   238
Lindars, B.   163, 497
Lindemann, A.   99
Lockett, D.   6, 393, 399
Lohfink, G.   192
Lohmeyer, E.   11, 59
Loisy, A.   59, 346
Long, F.J.   89
Longacre, R.E.   376
Longenecker, B.   273
Longenecker, R.N.   489
Lord, A.B.   95
Lövestam, E.   363
Lührmann, D.   173
Luomanen, P.   437
Lupieri, E.   11
Luz, U.   359–361, 366–368

MacDonald, D.R.   64
MacDonald, W.   270
Mack, B.L.   230
Mackay, I.D.   346
Mackie, D.M.   438, 450
MacMullen, R.   270
MacRae, G.W.   37, 99
Malbon, E.S.   345
Malcolm, M.R.   7–8, 517, 520
Malherbe, A.J.   506
Malik, P.   479
Malina, B.J.   430
Mann, M.   266
Manson, T.W.   243
Marcus, J.   244–245, 248, 286, 288, 290, 339, 343, 370
Marguerat, D.   412
Markam, S.   441
Marshall, I.H.   94, 109–110, 242–243, 421, 499
Martin, R.P.   35, 93, 251
Martin, T.W.   517
Martínez, F.G.   202, 336

Martyn, J.L.   335, 413, 427–428
Marxsen, W.   244, 283
Mason, E.F.   517
Mason, S.   34, 308
Matera, F.J.   417
Mathews, K.A.   95
Mathewson, D.   336
Matson, M.   2, 37–38
Mattern, S.P.   82
Mattingly, D.J.   271
Mayor, J.   397, 401
Mbembe, A.   274
Mbuvi, A.M.   497
McArthur, H.K.   366
McCarthy, C.   42, 48
McDonald, L.M.   405, 409
McEleney, N.J.   506
McHugh, J.   39
McKenzie, S.L.   72
McKnight, E.V.   99
McKnight, S.   94–95, 281
McLay, T.   510
McNicol, A.J.   127
Meade, D.   112
Meeks, W.A.   429–430
Meggitt, J.   196, 202, 208–209
Meier, J.P.   11, 204, 337
Meinardus, O.F.A.   247
Meinertz, M.   363
Merx, A.   193
Merz, A.   75, 99
Metzger, B.M.   244, 253, 400
Meyer, E.   130
Meyer, P.   226, 233
Michaels, J.R.   39, 259, 500
Milchner, H.J.   86
Miles, G.B.   354, 366
Millar, F.   188
Miller, M.   122
Miller, S.   83
Miller, Su.   164
Minchin, E.   347–348
Minear, S.   497, 500
Moessner, D.P.   366
Moffitt, D.   359
Mohri, E.   165
Moloney, F.J.   168, 287–289, 296, 428
Moo, D.J.   95–96, 253–254, 258, 417, 480, 482–483, 485, 487–488, 490, 492–494

MODERN AUTHORS INDEX

Moore, A.   435
Moore, A.L.   242
Moore, S.D.   271, 276–277, 428
Morgan, T.   271
Morgen, M.   421
Moriya, A.   441
Morley, N.   270
Morris, L.   95, 161, 168, 242, 252–254
Motyl, A.J.   272–273
Moule, C.F.D.   507
Mounce, R.H.   253–254
Mournet, T.C.   347
Mowinkel, S.   72
Moxnes, H.   523–524
Muraoka, T.   209
Murphy-O'Connor, J.   11, 57
Musurillo, H.A.   380
Myers, A.C.   248
Myers, C.   265, 296
Mynors, R.A.B.   402

Nanos, M.D.   90
Nauk, W.   504
Negri, A.   270
Neill, S.   99, 464
Neirynck, F.   339, 347
Nelson, N.D.   363
Neusner, J.   136, 289
Newsom, C.A.   430
Neyrey, J.   271
Nickelsburg, G.W.E.   268, 363
Nicklas, T.   172–174
Nida, E.A.   246
Niebuhr, K.-W.   394, 396–397, 403, 408–409
Nienhuis, D.R.   396, 399, 401–402, 408
Nilsson, M.P.   201
Nineham, D.E.   36, 245
Nissen, J.   428
Nock, A.D.   53
Nolland, J.   359
Nongbri, B.   239
Nordeval, Ø.   50
Novakovic, L.   204
Nygren, A.   433

O'Brien, B.   115, 130
O'Brien, P.T.   255–256, 258
O'Collins, G.   526
O'Day, G.R.   427, 430

Oakman, D.E.   225, 232, 237
Olsson, B.   418–419
Omerzu, H.   395
Ong, H.T.   375
Opelt, I.   127
Oropeza, B.J.   335
Osborne, G.   281
Osty, E.   37

Paffenroth, K.   204
Pagels, E.   363
Paige, T.   497
Painchaud, L.   150
Painter, J.   346, 396–397, 453
Palmer, H.   91
Papathomas, A.   191
Parker, D.C.   408
Parker, P.   36
Pate, C.M.   121, 352, 359
Patterson, S.J.   2, 49
Peabody, D.B.   127
Peachin, M.   271
Pearson, B.   60, 62, 225, 234–236
Pearson, B.W.R.   69
Pedersen, S.   428
Pelling, C.   135–136
Penner, T.C.   99
Perdue, L.   264, 277
Perkins, P.   431–432, 440
Perrin, N.   5, 92, 335, 340, 365
Perrin, No.   99–100
Pesch, R.   244, 251, 347
Peters, D.M.   354
Petersen, S.   165
Petersen, W.L.   48, 230
Pilch, J.   198
Pilhofer, P.   477
Pillinger, R.J.   34
Pitre, B.J.   352, 356, 361, 364
Pitts, A.W.   1, 3–4, 89, 130, 149, 172, 256, 497, 506
Poirier, P.-H.   150
Pokorný, P.   56–57
Porter, S.E.   1, 3–4, 7, 69, 86, 89, 91–92, 101, 104, 130, 149, 172, 174, 179, 255–256, 375–376, 387, 404–407, 419, 440, 500, 506, 510
Porter, W.J.   174
Portier-Young, A.   264

Potter, D.S. 270–271
Powell, E. 126
Powell, M.A. 129, 277, 284, 351, 427
Poythress, V. 505
Preisigke, F.G. 155
Preisker, H. 59, 428, 498
Preuschen, E. 59
Preuss, J. 213
Pyysiäinen, I. 437

Räisänen, H. 82
Ramsay, W.M. 211–212
Rau, G. 85
Rawlinson, A.E.J. 251
Redlich, E.B. 91
Reed, J.L. 233, 265
Reed, J.T. 89, 500
Rehkopf, F. 210
Reicke, B. 32
Reif, A. 34
Reinhartz, A. 428
Rensberger, D. 432–433
Reumann, J. 11, 24
Rhoads, D. 81, 265
Richards, E.R. 3, 108–109, 115, 121, 130, 132
Richardson, A. 339
Riches, J.K. 265, 272
Rieske, S.M. 6, 351, 363
Riesner, R. 77, 255–256
Ringe, S.H. 430
Rishell, C.W. 12
Rist, J.M. 32
Rives, J. 268
Roberts, C.H. 406–407
Robinson, J.M. 51, 63, 224–226, 228, 230
Robinson, J.A.T. 25, 38
Rohrbaugh, R.L. 430
Rollens, S.E. 4, 224, 227, 229, 236–237
Rooney, R. 225
Ropes, J.H. 35
Rosner, F. 206–207
Rothschild, C.K. 1–2, 11, 15, 25, 51–52, 110
Rubenstein, J.L. 76, 79, 85
Rudolph, K. 193
Ruffini, G. 73
Runesson, A. 280
Russell, B. 374, 377–379, 381, 384–385
Russell, D.A. 134–135
Russell, J.A. 441

Sahlin, H. 193, 335
Said, E. 269, 275
Saldarini, A. 280–281
Salier, B. 265
Sanders, E.P. 3, 36, 90–107, 176–177, 289–291, 462, 468
Sanders, J.A. 405, 409
Sanders, J.T. 428
Sandmel, S. 89
Sato, K. 441
Sato, M. 238
Schäfer, P. 76, 80
Schaller, M. 84
Schantz, R. 81
Schenke, G. 150
Schenke, L. 162
Schlarb, E. 173
Schlier, H. 354
Schliesser, B. 461
Schlosser, J. 396, 520
Schmeller, T. 86
Schmid, U.B. 48
Schmidt, E.D. 395
Schmidt, K.L. 45, 247
Schmithals, W. 91, 102
Schnabel, E.J. 76, 247–249, 251–256, 258–262, 412, 477, 479
Schnackenburg, R. 68, 169, 421, 432
Schneider, G. 505, 507
Schnelle, U. 169
Schniewind, J. 36
Schreiner, T.R. 253–254, 485, 487
Schröter, J. 6, 56, 393–394, 409–411
Schulz, S. 162, 164, 189, 191
Schüssler Fiorenza, E. 66, 276
Schutter, W.L. 497–498, 510, 513
Schütz, J. 11
Schweitzer, A. 352, 361, 371
Schweizer, E. 251, 360, 497
Schwemer, A.M. 477–478
Scobie, C.H.H. 11
Scott, J. 273–274
Scott, J.M. 256
Scott, S.P. 158
Seeley, D. 283, 380
Segovia, F. 277–278, 428
Seidelin, P. 367
Sellew, P. 228
Sellin, G. 59

Selwyn, E.G.   498, 500–503, 507–508
Senior, D.   360, 500
Shanks, M.A.   35
Sharifian, F.   517
Sharp, J.   271
Shellard, B.   38, 43–44
Shuchat, W.   206
Siegal, E.A.B.-A.   187
Silk, M.S.   127
Sim, D.C.   265, 272
Skeat, T.C.   47–48
Skinner, C.W.   284
Sloan, R.B.   95
Smalley, S.S.   454
Smith, D.A.   190, 227
Smith, D.E.   226
Smith, D.M.   56
Smith, E.R.   438, 450
Smith, J.Z.   63, 239
Smith, R.H.   247
Smith-Christopher, D.L.   353
Snodgrass, K.R.   497, 499
Snoy, T.   343–345
Snyder, G.F.   355
Snyder, H.G.   82
Sokoloff, M.   211
Solomon, R.C.   438
Sparks, H.F.D.   448
Spawforth, A.   127, 134
Spicq, C.   433
Spivak, G.C.   431
Stack-Nelson, J.   5, 311
Stamps, D.   89
Stanley, C.D.   277
Stanton, G.N.   98, 280
Stark, R.   221
Stegemann, H.   366
Stegner, W.R.   341
Stein, R.H.   95, 520–521
Steiner, R.   187
Steinmann, J.   11
Stendahl, K.   462–463, 468
Sterling, G.E.   380
Steuernagel, V.R.   497
Stewart, Z.   53
Stone, T.J.   353, 360–361
Stovell, B.M.   7, 426, 446, 457
Stowasser, M.   162
Stowers, S.   231–232, 234–235, 239–240

Strauss, M.   108, 130
Strecker, G.   38, 371
Streeter, B.H.   35
Streeter, W.   48
Streett, D.R.   418–419
Stuhlmacher, P.   99, 244
Sugirtharajah, R.S.   274–275, 277–278
Suhl, A.   350
Swartley, W.M.   342
Sweeney, M.A.   72
Synek, E.M.   165
Syreeni, K.   81, 275, 278, 429
Szigetvári, P.   437

Tal, A.   194
Talbert, C.H.   86, 136, 366
Talmon, S.   95
Tan, Y.-H.   427, 429–431
Tannehill, R.C.   43
Taschl-Erber, A.   165
Tatum, W.B.   11
Taylor, J.   11, 25, 31, 53, 59, 193
Taylor, V.   91, 244, 251, 288
Telford, W.R.   289, 292–293
Temin, P.   271
Thackeray, H.St.J.   35
Thatcher, T.   56, 149–150, 154, 164, 171, 265, 347, 428
Theissen, G.   71, 75, 77–78, 85–86, 91, 99, 102–107, 226
Theobald, M.   168
Thiessen, M.   336
Thimmes, P.L.   354
Thiselton, A.C.   242
Thomas, E.   270
Thompson, S.   4, 196
Thornton, C.-J.   153
Thür, G.   110
Thurman, E.   271
Thyen, H.   150, 161
Tiffin, H.   274, 431
Tigchelaar, E.   202
Tite, P.   432–433
Tiwald, M.   86
Tombs, D.   101
Toner, J.   271
Travis, S.H.   93–94
Trilling, W.   11
Trinacty, C.   119–120, 122, 124–125

Trobisch, D.   32, 405, 407–409
Trollope, W.   48
Trompf, G.W.   354, 366
Tucker, A.   465–466
Tucker, J.B.   437
Tuckett, C.M.   93, 136, 190, 275, 278, 429
Tyson, N.D.   373

Uro, R.   437

Vaage, L.E.   224, 226, 238
van Aarde, A.   318
van Belle, G.   149, 151
van Hecke, P.   435
van Iersel, B.M.F.   250
van Minnen, P.   173
van Oort, J.   154
van Ruiten, J.T.A.G.   34
van Tilborg, S.   429
van Wohlde, E.J.   438
Van de Sandt, M.   452
Van der Merwe, D.G.   457
Van der Stockt, L.   39
Van Egmond, R.   204
VanderKam, J.C.   363
Varghese, J.   433–434
Vegge, T.   50
Verheyden, J.   150
Vermes, G.   22, 46, 205
Vidas, M.   85
Vielhauer, P.   189, 195
von Gemünden, P.   77
von Harnack, A.   220–222
von Rad, G.   190
von Wahlde, U.C.   346

Wagner, G.   69
Wagner, J.   86
Wainwright, E.   197
Walcott, P.   200
Wall, R.W.   368, 396–397, 399
Wallace, D.B.   419
Wallace-Hadrill, A.   82
Walter, N.   246
Walters, P.   43
Waltherus, H.   452
Walz, C.   151
Wanamaker, C.A.   242
Wansbrough, H.   95

Ware, J.P.   258
Wasserman, T.   405–406
Watson, D.F.   335
Watson, F.   404, 462
Watts, E.J.   73
Watts, F.   196
Watts, R.E.   343
Wead, D.W.   27
Weaver, J.   452
Webb, R.L.   11, 53
Weber, M.   235
Wedderburn, A.J.M.   130–131
Weder, H.   149
Weeden, T.J.   82
Weisse, C.H.   35
Weiszäcker, K.   370
Wells, L.   200–201, 212
Wendland, P.   45
Wendt, H.W.   59
Wenham, D.   94, 346, 417
Westcott, B.F.   32
Westermann, W.L.   83
Westfall, C.L.   440, 454
Whitlark, J.A.   302–305, 308
Wickert, U.   154
Wiers, R.   441
Wilckens, U.   162
Wilder, W.N.   335
Wilkins, M.J.   73–74, 497
Wilkinson, J.   199–200
Williams, C.   271
Williams, K.D.   84
Williams, P.J.   421
Williamson, H.G.M.   420
Williger, E.   194
Wilson, T.A.   335
Wilson, W.   200
Windisch, H.   254, 498
Wink, W.   11, 273
Winn, A.   5, 265, 283, 286, 297–298, 303
Winter, B.W.   417
Wirth, J.R.   376
Wischmeyer, O.   461
Witherington III, B.   129, 253
Wold, B.G.   336
Wolfe, K.   43
Wolff, H.W.   365
Wolter, M.   131
Woolf, G.   270

Wright, A.G. 296, 498
Wright, A.Z. 6, 373, 375–376, 381
Wright, N.T. 97, 99, 104, 244, 247, 297–298, 361, 433, 461–465, 468, 470, 480, 483–484, 487–493, 495–496, 524
Wyrwa, D. 154

Yardeni, A. 189
Yoon, D.I. 375
Young, R. 274
Yu, N. 440

Zangenberg, J. 452
Zevini, G. 162

Index of Ancient Sources

Old Testament

Genesis

1–2	62
1:26	55
2:7	62
10:2–5	256
12:3	255
17	206
17:24–27	206
18	206
18:1	206
18:18	255
22:1–18	31
22:18	255
26:4	255

Exodus

1:2	53
4:22–23	520
6:45–52	342
12–13	343, 349
12	142, 341
12:17–20	339
12:37	341
12:42	341
12:43	339
12:48	339
14	341, 343, 349
14:4	341
14:18	341
14:21	345
14:24	341
15–17	349
15:26	202
16	339–340
18:20	206
18:21	341
20:4	422
22:21–24	296
23:15	339
23:20	21
33:19–23	341
35:6	341

Leviticus

1:4	211
19	452
23:7–8	339
25:23	520

Numbers

11:25–26	325
11:29	325
14:11	349
14:22	349
15:19–30	383
15:30	383
19:4	422
27:18	210–211
27:23	210

Deuteronomy

4:12	21
4:29–30	353
4:32	250
4:34	349
5:8	422
6:22	349
8:5	520
13:5	206
13:7	249
13:8	249
14:1	520
23:7	520
24:17	296
24:19–22	296
26:5	520
27:19	296
28:49	249
28:64	249
30:4	249–250
32	363–364
32:6	520
32:39	202, 208
33:17	249
34:9	210

INDEX OF ANCIENT SOURCES   547

Judges
5:5	251
10:6–16	354
18:19	210

1 Samuel
2:10	249
4:1 (LXX)	34
7:4–17	315
10:1–6	312
10:6	325
10:10	325
16:13–14	312
16:13	317
19:23	325

2 Samuel
7	520
13:19	210
20:9–10	81
23:2	325

1 Kings
1:8	44
4:33 (LXX 5:13)	204
19:11	341
19:12–13	21
20:35	72

2 Kings
1:8	75, 312
2:3	72
2:5	72
2:7	72
2:15	72
4:1	72
4:38	72–73
5:11	211
5:22	72
6:1	72–73
6:32	73
9:1	72

2 Chronicles
25:8	73

Nehemiah
9:27	354

Job
4:16	21
5:18	202, 208
9:6	251
9:8b	342
9:11	341
28:24	249
31:27	210
37:3	249
38:13	249

Psalms
2	312, 317, 520, 532
2:1–3	423
2:6 (LXX)	532
2:7	420–421
2:8	249–250
18:7	251
19:6	250
22:27	249
33 (LXX)	510
33:2–34:16 (LXX)	405
33:8 (LXX)	509
34	530
34:9	509
42:7	357
45	312, 317
46:9	249
48:10	249
59:13	249
61:2	249
65:5	249
65:8	249
67:7	249
72	312, 317
72:8	249
77:14–15 (MT)	342
77:19–20 (MT)	342
89	312, 317
95	530
98:3	249
106 LXX	354
106:18 LXX	369
106:23–32 LXX	354
107	357, 359
107	354
107:6	354
107:13	354
107:18	369

Psalms (cont.)

107:19	354
107:23–32	354
107:28	354
107:10–16	353
107:29	357
110	312, 317
114:7	251
117	501
117 (LXX)	287, 515
117:22 (LXX)	502, 511–512
117:26 (LXX)	287
118	128, 287
118:22	502, 512
119:1 LXX	354
120:1	354
135:7	249
142:2 (LXX)	492
146:8	202, 208
147:3	202

Proverbs

17:24	249
30:4	249

Ecclesiastes

12:2	251

Isaiah

1:3	53
1:29	422
5:26	249
6	386
8:14	502, 511–512, 514
8:16	72
8:22	250
11:12	249
13:5	250
13:10	251, 315
13:13	251
24:16	249
24:23	251
26:17–19	361
28	503, 514
28:2	354
28:16	498, 502, 511–512, 514
28:17	354
29:5–6	360
29:6	354
30:30	354
34:4	315
38:1	206
38:10	369
40	21
40:3–5	21
40:3	13, 18, 21, 41
40:6–8 (LXX)	510
40:28	249
41:5	250
41:9	250
42:1	20, 319, 503, 514
42:7	353
42:10	250
42:24–25	307
43:6	250
45:22–23	255
45:22	250
48:9–11	306
48:20	250
49:6	250
50:2–3	315
52:5	306
52:10	250
56	290
56:7	290–291
56:10	290
56:11	290
59:21	325
62:11	250
66:19	255
66:23	255

Jeremiah

2:35 (LXX)	421
6:24	250
7	291
7:11	291
10:13	250
16:19	250
25:8–9	308
25:30	21
25:31	250
25:33	250
30:2	211
37:17	218
40:6 (LXX)	218
51:16	250
51:34	355

Lamentations
2:1	308
3:34	353

Ezekiel
1:12 (LXX)	47
1:25	21
6:4–13	422
7:2	249
8:10	422
11:5	325
13:10–16	354
21	308
32:7–8	251
34	203
34:4	203
34:16	203
34:23	203
36:20	305
38:15	249

Daniel
4:22	250
4:31	21
7:13–14	251
8:10	251
9:26	354
12:1–2	361
12:1	250, 354
21:1–2	361

Hosea
2:3 (MT)	513
2:23	501, 513
2:25 (LXX)	513
5:15	366
6:1–2	366
6:6	128
7:12	250
8:4–6	422
11:1	520

Joel
2:10	251, 315
2:18–26	360
2:26–29	312
2:28–29	325
2:30–31	312
2:31	251, 315
3:15	251
4:16–17	21

Amos
1:2	21
8:9	251, 315
9:5	251
9:11–15	360

Obadiah
12	250
14	250

Jonah
1:3	358
1:4–16	354
1:4–5	358
1:4	358
1:5	358
1:6	358
1:12	358
1:14	351
1:15	358
1:16	358
2:1–9	353
2:1 (LXX)	365
2:2–3	353
2:2 (MT 2:3)	365, 369
2:3 (MT 2:4)	357, 365
2:6 (MT 2:7)	369
2:9–10	353
2:9	354
3:5–6	351
4:6	351
4:9	351, 361

Micah
1:4	251
2:12	250
5:4	250
7:6	210

Nahum
1:5	251
1:7	250

Habakkuk
3:6	251
3:16	250

Zephaniah

1:3	354
1:14–18	354
1:15	250

Zechariah

2:6 (LXX)	249
2:10 (MT)	249
9–14	530
9:10	250
14:4–5	360
14:6–8	360

Malachi

2:10	520
3:1	21, 44, 54
4	315
4:5–6	312

Apocrypha

2 Esdras

5:5	251
7:26–44	361
7:39	251
9:1–13	361
9:3	360
13:11	354
13:37	354

Tobit

13:8–11	290
14:5–7	290

1 Maccabees

1:35	505
4:46	505
5:16	365
9:27	250

2 Maccabees

2:23	127
2:31	127
3:12	251
8:19	251
8:35	505
12:45	360

3 Maccabees

5:51	369–370
6:6–10	355
6:18–19	370

4 Maccabees

14:9	365
13:23	446
13:27	446
14:13	446
14:14	446
18:15	365

Wisdom of Solomon

7:20	204
8:7	506
8:12	210
11:22	251
16:13	369
16:15–16	354
17:19	251
18:24	251

Wisdom of Sirach

30:17	360
39:28–29	354

New Testament

Matthew

1:18–20	317
1:21	318
1:22–23	127
2:5–6	127
2:10	351
2:15	127, 530
2:17–18	127
2:23	127
3:1–12	22
3:1	51
3:2	22

3:3	13, 17, 21, 127	6:9	504
3:4–6	22	6:19–20	506
3:4	75	6:22–23	229
3:5	51, 75	6:24	379
3:7–10	51, 317	6:26	321
3:11–12	51	6:31	504
3:11	14, 19, 44, 75, 317	6:32	321
3:12	12	6:34	504
3:13–17	16, 18, 45, 52	7:1	506
3:14–15	52	7:12	504
3:14	22	7:14–15	382
3:16–17	18, 51–52, 316	7:20–22	382
3:17	76, 379	7:21–22	322
4:1–11	51	7:24–27	359, 370
4:1	318	8:5–13	139
4:4	127	8:15	361
4:6	127	8:17	127
4:7	127	8:18–22	359
4:10	127	8:22–23	359
4:11	161	8:23–27	6, 351, 358
4:12–17	14	8:23	358
4:12	161–162	8:24–25	358
4:14–16	127	8:24	358, 360–361
4:23	214	8:25–26	358, 361
5–7	36	8:25	358
5:1–48	78	8:26	358, 360
5:3–11	506	8:27	358
5:10–11	371	9:13	128
5:11	371	9:18–26	138
5:13	210	9:35	215
5:16	321	9:38	504
5:17–18	506	10	36, 216, 320
5:19	504	10:1–4	76
5:21–48	506	10:1	78, 216
5:21	127	10:6	504
5:23	504	10:7–8	320
5:24	40	10:8	217
5:27	127	10:17–20	320
5:31	127	10:21–22	327
5:33	127	10:23	242
5:38–42	273, 380	10:24–25	322
5:38	127	10:26	504
5:43	127	10:28	506
5:45	321	10:31	504
5:48	321, 504	10:32	320
6:1–18	321	10:34	506
6:1	40	10:35–36	128
6:2	504	11	321
6:8	504	11:2–6	11, 162, 319

Matthew (*cont.*)

11:7	105–106	14:22–33	346, 359
11:10	127	15:4	127
11:12	370	15:7–9	127
11:16–19	363	15:19	506
11:16	363	15:38	341
11:21	351	16:1–4	6, 351, 362
11:23	128	16:1	362
11:25–27	327	16:2–3	367
12	318–319	16:3	362
12:7	128	16:4	363, 368
12:10	214	16:11	371
12:17–18	319	16:13–20	6, 351, 367
12:18	313, 503	16:14–15	17
12:22–30	362	16:15–16	321
12:25–29	318	16:16	81, 102, 412
12:27	318	16:17–19	367
12:28	313	16:17	368
12:31–42	319	16:18	80, 369
12:38–42	6, 351, 361–362	16:19	370
12:38	362	16:21	369
12:39	363	16:22–23	81
12:40	127, 365, 369	16:22	369
12:41–45	319	16:24–26	371
12:41–42	363, 366	16:24–25	369
12:41	363	16:26	251, 379
12:42	250, 363	16:27–28	371
12:43–45	363	17:5	322
12:45	363	17:11–13	41
13	36	17:17	363
13:1–23	386	17:23	369
13:1	386	18	36
13:3	386	18:3	522
13:8	386	18:4	504
13:9	387	18:16	128
13:10	387	19:1	345
13:11	386–387	19:4–5	127
13:14–15	127	19:18–19	128
13:18	504	19:20	422
13:21	365	19:30	380
13:24–27	276	20:20–28	140
13:35	127	20:26	380
13:58	213	21:3	322
14:1–12	23	21:4–5	127
14:2	25, 361	21:9	128
14:3	505	21:12–17	140
14:5–12	45	21:13	127
14:13–21	346	21:16	127
14:21	341	21:18–22	138
		21:42	127, 502, 515

INDEX OF ANCIENT SOURCES 553

22:9	504	26:24–25	81
22:21	504	26:30–35	368
22:31–32	127	26:30–34	174
22:36–39	127	26:31	127
22:39–40	423	26:38–44	147
22:42	322	26:38	351, 361
22:43–44	127	26:47–49	80
22:43	322	26:48–49	80
23:3	504, 506	26:49–50	81
23:9	321	26:50	81
23:11	380	26:55b–56	38
23:13	370	26:58–75	368
23:29–36	363	26:58	166
23:31	155	26:63–65	128
23:35	351	26:64	128
23:36	363	26:67	178
23:39	128	26:69–74	82
24–25	36, 322	26:69	166
24:3–35	365	26:75	183
24:3	362	27:9–10	127
24:7	360	27:17–20	38
24:9–10	365	27:28	178
24:9	243, 365	27:29	178
24:14	243, 245, 248, 254	27:30	178
24:15	127	27:35	178
24:21	365	27:37	178
24:24	423	27:38	178
24:27–31	276	27:45	178
24:29–30	128	27:46	128, 178
24:29	365	27:48	178
24:30	362	27:50–51	322–323
24:31	249	27:51	179
24:32–35	126	27:52	360
24:34	363	27:54	179, 322–323, 361
24:36–39	354	27:57–58	182
24:36	210	27:60	179
25:13	504	27:64	361
25:32	243	27:65	179
25:36–44	215	28	138
25:36	216	28:1	144
25:39	216	28:2–3	179
25:43	216	28:2	183, 361
25:44	216	28:5	179
26:2	178	28:6	361
26:6–13	141	28:7	361
26:6	202	28:11	179
26:13	243, 251	28:13	179
26:14–16	80–81	28:18–20	50, 243, 412
26:17–20	142	28:19	323, 504

Mark

Reference	Pages
1–12	248
1–10	285
1–9	313
1:1	17, 245, 311
1:2	21, 44, 249
1:3	13, 17, 21
1:4–6	22
1:4	14, 53
1:5	75
1:6	44, 54, 75
1:7–8	16, 19
1:7	15
1:8	314
1:9–11	16, 18, 45, 52
1:10–11	18
1:10	52
1:11	17, 75–76, 379
1:12	312–313
1:13	161, 249, 315
1:14–20	85
1:14–15	14, 15, 246
1:14	14, 26, 161–162
1:14a	162
1:16–20	76
1:16–19	80
1:16–18	37
1:17	15, 54
1:24	313
1:25	313
1:29–31	37
1:31	213
1:38–39	248
2:5	294
2:13–17	349
2:14	76
2:18	79
2:22	168
2:23–27	349
3:1–6	213
3:1	213
3:5	213
3:11	17, 313
3:13–19	76
3:13	216
3:14–19	85
3:14	78
3:15	216
3:16–17	80
3:16	46
3:17	368
3:18	80
3:19–22	26
3:19	80
3:22–30	313
3:27	246
3:30	313
3:32–35	523
4:1–20	97, 386
4:1	387
4:2	387
4:3	387
4:9	387
4:11	386–387
4:13	387–388
4:20	387
4:28	246
4:34	79
4:35–8:26	337
4:35–41	344, 349
4:39	294
5:1–20	340, 344, 349
5:1	345
5:7	17, 313
5:21–43	138
5:21–23	344, 349
5:21	345
5:25–34	344, 349, 383
5:35–43	294, 344, 349
5:37	80
6:1–15	346
6:1–5	209
6:5	209, 210, 212–213, 217, 219
6:6	248
6:7	216, 314
6:14–16	23
6:15	17
6:16	23, 25
6:17–29	23
6:18	23
6:19–29	45
6:21	246
6:29	15
6:30–44	344, 346
6:34–44	344, 349
6:34	341
6:35	338

INDEX OF ANCIENT SOURCES 555

6:39	337–338	9:44	246
6:40	341	10:9	504
6:41	338	10:17–23	79
6:44	345	10:20	422
6:45	341, 344–345	10:21	380
6:45–52	341–342, 346	10:29	80, 246
6:45–51	344, 348–349	10:31	246
6:48	294, 341	10:33	246
6:49	341	10:35–45	140
6:50	341	10:36–44	80
6:53	344, 349	10:42	246
6:56	248	10:46–52	79
7:1–22	340	11–15	339
7:3–4	300	11–12	285–286, 297–299
7:21–22	506	11	285, 297
7:24–37	339	11:1–13:2	285–286, 297–298
7:24–30	79, 340	11:1–11	286–287
7:24b–30	344, 349	11:7	246
7:27	246	11:11–14	138
7:32–37	344, 349	11:12–21	288
8:1–21	341	11:12–14	286
8:1–10	338–339, 344, 349	11:15–19	140
8:3	339	11:15–18	286
8:11–21	348–349	11:17	290, 300, 340
8:14–21	338–339	11:18	294
8:17–21	338	11:19–25	138
8:22–26	344, 349	11:21–22	286
8:27–30	315	11:22–25	292
8:27	248, 340	11:23–25	286
8:29	80, 81, 102, 412	11:23	309
8:31–33	315	11:24	293
8:31–32	380	11:25	293
8:31	246, 294, 503	11:26–33	293
8:32–33	81	11:27–33	286
8:35	246	11:28	294
8:36	251	11:30–33	286
8:37	249	12:1–12	286, 294
8:38	249	12:6	17
9:1	242, 244	12:10	502, 515
9:2	80	12:12	294
9:5	80	12:13–37	286
9:7	17, 532	12:13–34	295
9:9	210	12:18	300
9:11	246	12:20	246
9:12	246	12:25	249
9:13	41, 44	12:28	79, 246
9:34–35	80	12:29–31	295
9:35	246	12:29	246
9:38–40	314	12:31–33	423

Mark (*cont.*)

12:31	219	14:51	315
12:35–44	296	14:55	155
12:35–37	296	14:56–58	315
12:36	314	14:56	155
12:43	79	14:59	155
13	104, 247, 285, 297, 314	14:61	17
13:1–2	286, 297–298	14:62–64	378
13:1	297	14:65	178
13:2	297	14:67–72	82
13:3–37	297–298	14:72	183
13:3	80, 297	15	314
13:4	217	15:10–11	38
13:6–13	246	15:17	178
13:7	246, 248	15:19	178
13:8	246, 360	15:24	178
13:9–10	245	15:25	143
13:9	245	15:26	178, 315
13:10	244–247, 249, 251, 300, 306	15:27	178
		15:32	315
13:13	246, 248	15:33	178
13:14–19	297	15:34	178
13:14	246	15:36	178
13:22	423	15:38	179
13:27	244–245, 249, 251	15:39	17, 179
13:28–31	126	15:42	300
13:30	242, 244	15:43	182
13:32	249	15:46	179
13:35	504	16:1–8	138, 182
13:37	251	16:1–2	144
14–15	286	16:3–4	179
14	338	16:4	179
14:1	178	16:5	179
14:3–9	141	16:8	181, 183, 245
14:3	202	16:9	246
14:9	244–246, 251, 300	16:15	244, 246
14:10–11	81	16:18	217
14:10	80		
14:12–18	142	**Luke**	
14:12	246	1:1–9:50	41
14:22	338	1–2	22, 41
14:26–30	174	1:1–18	38
14:31	246	1:1	151
14:33–36	146–147	1:3	46, 151–152
14:33	80	1:4	36
14:38	313	1:5–2:40	38
14:43–46	81	1:5	34
14:44–45	80	1:6–8	41
14:49–52	38	1:7	42
		1:15–25	41

INDEX OF ANCIENT SOURCES

1:15	42, 324	3:20	161
1:17	45, 324	3:21–22	16, 18, 51–52
1:26–38	41	3:22	76, 379
1:32	42	3:23	162
1:35	324	4:1–13	51
1:36	12	4:1	326
1:38	325	4:13	161
1:39–56	41	4:14	161, 326
1:41	42, 325	4:16–30	213
1:42–45	325	4:16–24	326
1:44	325	4:18–19	327
1:57–80	41	4:18	326
1:67	324	4:22	155, 327
1:69a	25	4:24	327
1:76	324	4:26	210
1:78b	25	4:27	210
2:1–40	41	4:28	327
2:25–27	325	4:34–35	126
2:32–35	326	4:38–39	37
2:41–52	377	5:11	37
3	23	6:7	214
3:1–3	43	6:12–16	76
3:1	43	6:29	506
3:2b–3a	51	6:30	506
3:2	43	6:31	219
3:3–18	22	6:37	506
3:3	43	7:1–10	37, 139
3:4–6	21	7:18–23	11
3:4	13, 17	7:24	105
3:7	44	7:36–50	37, 141
3:7–17	26	8:1–15	386
3:7–14	44, 326	8:1–3	387
3:7–9	51	8:3	377
3:8	504	8:4–8	387
3:11	23	8:10	386, 387
3:13	23	8:18	504
3:14	23	8:40–56	138
3:15–17	326	9:1	216
3:15–16	19	9:7–8	23
3:15	14, 19, 43	9:8	17
3:16–17	51	9:20	412
3:16	44, 75	9:22	503
3:16b–17	16	9:25	251
3:17	12	9:32	42
3:18–22	14	9:35	503
3:18–19	23	10	216
3:18	504	10:2	504
3:19–20	45	10:3–4	506
3:19	23, 162	10:7	506

Luke (cont.)		23:38	178
10:9	216	23:39–40	178
10:25–37	379	23:40–41	178
10:33–38	216	23:44	178
10:38–42	37, 141	23:46	328
11:13	327	23:47	179
11:31	250	23:50–52	182
11:35	504	23:55–24:3	144
12:8–12	327	24	138, 145
12:28–29	506	24:1–12	145
12:30	243	24:2	179
12:35–40	276	24:4	38, 179
12:54–56	367	24:12	145, 183
14:33	504	24:21–24a	145
17:18	210	24:24	145
17:25	503	24:36–49	37
17:26–27	354	24:36–43	423
17:30	243	24:39	423
18:17	522	24:45–49	412
18:19	210	24:46–47	243
18:21	422	24:47	249
19:12	101		
19:13	101	**John**	
19:14–15a	101	1–12	12, 56
19:15b–24	101	1	13, 27
19:27	101, 423	1:1–18	39
19:45–48	140	1:1–4	40
20:17	502, 515	1:1	40
21:11	360	1:5–8	39
21:17	504	1:5–7	40
21:24	243, 245, 249	1:6–8	40, 329
21:29–33	126	1:6	13, 41
22:1	178	1:7	13, 42, 155, 243
22:3	38	1:8–14	40
22:7–15	142	1:8	13, 155
22:40–42	147	1:9–14	40
22:42	48	1:12–13	522
22:44	48	1:14	42, 331
22:47–48	80	1:15–16	40
22:56–62	82	1:15	13, 16, 24, 26, 28, 31, 40–41, 155, 329
22:62	183		
23	178	1:16	40
23:4	38, 179	1:17	331
23:12	178	1:19–21:23	154
23:15	38	1:19–34	40
23:22	38	1:19–28	40
23:33	178	1:19–21	40
23:34	178	1:19	15, 44, 155, 329
23:35	504	1:20–21	17

INDEX OF ANCIENT SOURCES

1:20	44	3:16–17	243
1:21	45	3:16	427, 432
1:22–23	41	3:18	20
1:23	17, 21, 329	3:22	56
1:24–27	19	3:23–24	14
1:24	14–15	3:23	43, 163
1:25	15	3:24	14, 23, 160, 162, 163
1:25b	19	3:25–30	40
1:26–27	16	3:26	15, 22, 56, 155
1:26	20, 44	3:27–30	41
1:27	24, 26, 44	3:27	17
1:28	43, 345	3:28	17, 155
1:29–34	28, 52, 328–329	3:29–30	39
1:29–30	13, 31	3:29	17, 21, 30
1:29	15, 16, 24, 28, 40–41, 243	3:30	15, 17, 24, 26
		3:31	24
1:30	16, 24, 28	3:32	155
1:31	16, 18, 27, 29	3:33	24, 155
1:32–34	42, 45	4	13
1:32–33	41	4:1–15	28
1:32	16, 29, 155	4:1–2	22
1:33	16, 18, 28, 331	4:1	15, 56
1:33b	20	4:2	56
1:34	17, 20, 24, 155, 503	4:4–42	163
1:35–40	154	4:7–26	163
1:35	28	4:8	164
1:36	15, 16, 28, 31	4:9c	164
1:38	22	4:10–15	27–28
1:40–42	37	4:11	164
1:40–41	329	4:24	330
1:42	368	4:27a	164
1:48–51	28	4:28	165
1:49	20, 22	4:31–38	29
2–8	27	4:31–34	27–28
2:6	167	4:31	22
2:7	168	4:32–35	27
2:13–22	140	4:39	155
2:15–17	413	4:41	27
2:16	506	4:42	243
2:19–22	27	4:44	155
2:19–21	28	4:46–54	37
2:25	155	5	169
3	13, 429, 431	5:11	419
3:2	22	5:15	419
3:3–5	27, 30	5:23	243
3:3	413, 522	5:25	20–21
3:4	28	5:26–30	276
3:5	29, 413	5:28	21
3:11	155	5:31–37	329–330

John (*cont.*)

5:31	155	10:27	21, 30
5:32	155	10:30	330
5:33–37	13	10:36	20
5:33	14, 155, 331	10:40–42	14
5:34	155	10:40	14, 43
5:35	30	10:41	14
5:36	155, 330	11:1–2	141
5:37	21, 155	11:4	20
5:39	155	11:8	22
6	169	11:11–14	360
6:1–14	29	11:12	28
6:15	30, 346	11:19	243
6:25–59	29	11:27	20
6:25	22, 345	11:43	21
6:32–35	28	12:1–8	37, 141
6:33	243	12:2	252
6:51–53	27	12:9–10	142
6:51–52	28	12:17	155
6:63	333–334	12:23	332
7:7	155	12:27	147
7:33–36	27–28	12:28	21
7:37–39	331–332	12:30	21
7:53–8:11	45, 150	12:32	243
8:12	243	12:37	40
8:13	155	12:47–48	276
8:14	155	12:48	334
8:17–18	330	13:1–30	142
8:17	155	13:1–2	142
8:18	155	13:2	38
8:21–22	28	13:21	155
8:21	27	13:27	38
8:26	243	13:31	332
8:31–33	27	13:34	423
8:51–53	27–28	13:35	243
8:56–58	27–28	13:36	413
9:2	22	14:6	331
9:8–34	163, 166	14:12	330
9:35a	166	14:17	330, 332
10:2–4	30	14:26	331
10:3	21	14:31	243
10:4	21, 40	15	431
10:5	21	15:16	509
10:7–8	30	15:18–27	431
10:11–13	30	15:21	329
10:15–16	30	15:26–27	329
10:16	21	15:26	155, 330, 332
10:18	147	15:27	155
10:25	155, 330	16:7–15	330–331
		16:14	329

17:21	243	20:30	154
17:21–23	330	20:31	20, 169, 412
17:23	243	21	150
18:1–19:30	37	21:4–8	37
18	142	21:15–17	368
18:1–12	147	21:19	413
18:11	147	21:22–23	242
18:13	43	21:22	413
18:19–24	163, 166	21:23	156
18:19	43	21:24–25	149, 159
18:23	155	21:24	46, 154–155, 157, 163, 170
18:28	143, 167		
18:28–19:16a	163	21:25	154
18:36	30		
18:37	21, 155	**Acts**	
18:38	38	1–11	257
19:4	38	1:1–8:4	248
19:6	38	1:1–11	139
19:7	20	1:1	152
19:11	17	1:3	194
19:14	143	1:8	243, 249–250, 412
19:19	178	1:13	183, 415
19:24	178	2	50, 57, 63
19:29	178	2:1	183
19:30	332	2:10	247, 261
19:32–33	178	2:11	247, 261
19:34	332	2:17–20	312
19:35	154–155	2:36	505
19:38	182	2:37–42	50
20–21	138	2:38	475
20	30, 150	2:40	475
20:1–10	145	3–4	413
20:1	144, 179	3:1	415
20:2	144	3:12	415–416
20:8	15	3:15	424
20:9	15	3:18	424
20:11–18	163–164	3:19	505
20:12	38	4:1	415
20:15	164	4:2	415
20:17–18	165	4:5–7	415
20:17	165	4:6	43
20:18	165–166	4:8	415
20:19–31	150	4:10	424
20:19–29	37, 423	4:11	502, 515
20:21–22	332	4:17–18	416
20:21	332	4:19–20	416
20:22	29	4:23–31	532
20:29	18	5:42	412, 419
20:30–31	154	7:35–37	503

Acts (cont.)
7:58	505	10:48b	474
7:60	360	11	378
8	413	11:1	474
8:1	415	11:2	474
8:3–40	470	11:3	474–475, 488
8:4	257	11:4	474
8:14	415	11:5–10	474
8:16	192	11:11	474
8:22	505	11:12	473
8:25	415	11:12a	474
8:26–39	247, 470	11:13–14	474
8:27	261	11:15	474
9	257	11:16	474
9:22	412, 419	11:17	474, 490
9:29	257	11:18	471, 474, 476
9:30	258	11:19–26	257, 470
9:43	472	11:19–21	257
10–11	7, 257, 471, 475, 496	11:19	365
10	525	11:25–26	258
10:1–2	472	11:27–30	480
10:2	471	11:29–30	469
10:3–6	472	12:1	415
10:7–8	472	12:12	415
10:9–16	472	12:17	476
10:14	472	12:25	261, 415
10:15	472	13–28	247, 257
10:17–23a	472	13–14	257
10:19–20	474	13	257, 470
10:19b–20	473	13:1	261
10:23b–24a	472	13:5	415
10:23	474	13:13	415
10:24b–26	473	13:16–19	530
10:24b	473	13:25	15–16, 44
10:28–29	473	13:33	532
10:28	473, 484, 494	13:36	360
10:29–33	473	13:40	505
10:29b	473	13:47	243, 250
10:34–35	473	13:48	258
10:34	473	14:16	243
10:35	471	14:22	365
10:36–43	473	15	257, 378, 468–469, 478, 481
10:36	504	15:1	476
10:42	473	15:5	476
10:43	28, 473	15:8	475
10:44–46a	474	15:9	475
10:45	474	15:11	475, 490
10:47–48a	474	15:23–29	395, 469
10:47	474	15:37	261, 415

INDEX OF ANCIENT SOURCES

15:39	261	8:23	532
16–17	257	8:29–30	509
17:3	412, 419	8:33	509
18	50, 59	9–11	509
18:5	412, 419	9	509
18:15	59	9:6	509
18:24–19:7	14, 60	9:32	502, 515
18:25	49, 50, 59–61	9:33	504
18:28	412, 419	10:18	255
19	59, 257	11	509
19:1–7	25, 59	11:12	254
19:4	42	11:15	255
19:5	192	11:25	254
19:10	258	12:1	505, 508
20	257	12:9–21	506
20:23	365	12:9–19	500
21:17–22	188	13:10	505
28	257	13:12	242, 505
28:8–10	211	13:13	506
28:30–31	243	14:13	505
		14:16	505
Romans		14:19	505
1:5–15	253	15:19–28	253
1:5	252–253	15:19a	252, 254, 258
1:8	253, 504	15:20–21	248, 253
1:13	253	15:20	261
1:14	254, 261	15:23–24	248
1:15	247, 253, 256, 313	15:24	247, 253
1:18–32	506	15:24–32	258
2:17	420	15:25	195
3:3	493	15:26	195
3:5–6	493	15:27	194
3:19	251	15:28	247, 253
4:13	255	15:31	195
4:17–18	255	16:19	505
5:21	504	16:26	253, 255
6	58, 68–69	16:27	504
6:1–11	69		
6:3–11	2, 49, 58, 67–69	**1 Corinthians**	
6:5	68	1–4	59
6:7	68	1:10–4:21	59
6:8–9a	69	1:11–13	58
6:8	68	1:12	460
6:12–14	68	1:14–17	58–60
7:25	504	1:14–16	49
8	69	1:17	49, 58, 63
8:3	143	1:17a	58, 66
8:9–17	61	1:17b	58
8:15–17	521	1:23–24	509

1 Corinthians (cont.)

1:23	504
1:24	61
2	60
2:1	63
2:6–15	61
2:16	61
3	60
3:1	60
3:9	503
3:10–11	258
4:8	60, 505
4:16	505
5:7	143
5:10–11	506
6:2	195
6:9–10	506
7:17–31	66
7:26	242
7:39	360
9:4–6	195
9:5	191, 261
9:14	195
10:1–22	338
10:1–13	530
10:31	505
11:2–16	66
11:20	191
11:23–24	338
11:25–26	191
11:27–34	191
11:30	217, 360
11:32	191
12	60, 218–219
12:9–10	218
12:13	61, 65–66, 192
12:28	218
12:29–30	218
14	60
14:34	506
14:39	506
15	61, 64
15:3–11	424
15:3–5	526
15:5	261
15:6	360
15:7	261
15:8	194
15:9	192
15:12	61
15:18	360
15:20	360
15:29	49
15:29a	61
15:29b	61
15:42–50	62
15:51	360
16:1	195
16:21	190

2 Corinthians

2:14	467
5:19	255
6:6–7	506
8:4	195
8:14	194
8:24	505
9:1	195
9:12	195
11:26–31	253
12:9	218
12:20	506

Galatians

1–2	413, 416
1:1	504
1:4	424, 495
1:8–9	485, 487
1:10	494
1:13	192
1:15–17	477
1:15–17a	477
1:16	477
1:17	247, 258, 261
1:17b	477
1:18–19	416
1:18	413, 416, 477
1:19	191, 195, 416
1:21	258
2	481
2:1–10	416, 469, 483
2:1	417, 478–479
2:2	417, 424, 478–479
2:3	417, 424, 479, 487
2:4	479–480
2:5	479
2:6–9	471
2:6–8	479

2:6	478–480	3:28	64
2:7–9	255, 478, 494	4:6	66
2:7	416–417, 424, 478	4:13	217
2:8	416	4:14	218
2:9–11	425	4:25	248
2:9–10	479	5:1	505–506
2:9	408, 413, 416, 479	5:11	494, 504
2:10	195, 417, 425, 480	5:16	506
2:11–21	7, 460, 463, 468–469, 486	5:19–23	506
		6:10	505
2:11–14a	481	6:12–13	482
2:11	485–486	6:12	487
2:12	478, 481–482, 486	6:13	261
2:13	481	6:16	509
2:14–21	464, 486, 496		
2:14	482, 485, 487	**Ephesians**	
2:14b–21	481	1:3–14	509
2:14b	487, 488, 490	1:5	504
2:15–16	488, 490, 492	1:10	255
2:15	488–490, 492–493, 496	2:5–6	68
		2:11–3:10	509
2:16–17a	492	2:14–15	494
2:16	424, 486, 488–490, 492	2:19–20	503
		2:20	258, 502, 515
2:16a	489–490	3:13	365
2:16b	489	4:1	505
2:17	488, 490, 493–494	4:17	505
2:17ab	493	4:22	505
2:17a	492–493	4:25	505
2:17c	493	4:31	506
2:18	494–495	5:1	505
2:19–20	494–495	5:2	143
2:20	68, 424	5:3–7	506
2:21	495	5:7	505
2:21a	495–496	5:14	360
2:21b	495–496	5:15	505–506
2:21c	495	6:14–17	506
3	496	6:14	505
3:1–5	66		
3:1	495	**Philippians**	
3:8	255	1:11	504
3:13–14	495	1:14–18a	253
3:14	255	1:17	365
3:16–18	425	2:1–2	505
3:16	255	2:10–11	255
3:26–29	509	2:27	217
3:26–28	2, 49, 58, 64, 67–69	3:3	492
3:26	64, 522	3:4–6	490
3:27	64	3:6	422

Philippians (cont.)

3:7	490
4:5	242–243
4:8	506, 508

Colossians

1:5–6	255
1:6	251
1:7–8	256
1:23	248, 255
1:24–25	255
1:24	365
1:28	255
1:29	255
2:1	255
2:6	505
2:12	68
2:16	505
3:1–4	505
3:2	506
3:5–9	506
3:5	505
3:8	505
3:11	256, 261
3:12–14	506
3:12	505, 509
3:19	506
3:22–23	506
4:2–4	255
4:2	255
4:4	255
4:7–17	256
4:10	261

1 Thessalonians

1:4	509
1:8	258
1:9–10	471
2:9	506
3:3	509
3:13	195
4:1	505
4:13–17	360
5:6	505
5:9	509
5:10	360
5:14	218, 221

2 Thessalonians

2:1–2	242
2:15	505

1 Timothy

1:9–10	506
2:1	505
2:8	505
3:2–3	506
3:2	505
5:14	505
5:23	218
6:4–5	506
6:11	506

2 Timothy

1:8	505
1:17	247
2:1	505
2:6	255
2:10	509
2:21	505
3:2–5	506
3:16	255
4:11	261
4:20	218

Titus

1:1	509
1:7–8	506
3:1–3	506
3:5	522
3:6	504
3:14	506

Philemon

24	261

Hebrews

1:5	532
2:11–12	524
2:15	243
5:5	532
8:11	243
9:13	407
10:10	143
10:14	143
12:2	505
13:5	508

INDEX OF ANCIENT SOURCES   567

13:11–12	143	1:23	519
13:21	504	1:24–25	511
		1:25	500
James		2:1–10	7, 497, 499–500, 502, 515–516
1:10–12	406		
1:15	406	2:1–3	499, 500, 518, 528
1:16	406	2:1–2	499, 507, 511, 515
1:21	505	2:1	499, 505–506
1:22	506–507	2:2–3	511
2	452–453	2:2	506–507, 511, 519
2:5–10	451–452	2:3–10	515
2:8–10	452	2:3–6	511
2:14–26	490	2:3	499–500, 509–511
2:15	524	2:4–10	497–499, 502, 511
2:19–3:2	406	2:4–8	503, 511, 527–528
3:4–9	406	2:4–6	510
3:9	524	2:4–5	510, 511, 514–515
3:13–4:4	406	2:4	499, 500, 503, 510, 514
3:17	506	2:5	504, 508, 514, 519
4:9–5:1	406	2:6–8	503, 510
4:11	396	2:6	511–512, 514
5:13	397	2:7–10	511
5:14	218	2:7–8	499, 514
		2:7	499, 512, 514
1 Peter		2:8	504, 510, 512, 514
1:1–2	509, 527	2:9–10	499, 514–515, 528
1:3–2:3	518, 533	2:9	508, 509, 515, 528
1:3–12	519	2:10	501, 513, 515
1:3–9	527–528	2:11–12	529
1:3	413, 517, 519, 521, 528, 532, 534	2:13–17	529
		2:17	519
1:10–12	498, 502, 515–516, 527	2:18–25	527, 529
1:11–12	28	2:21	525
1:11	504, 508	3:1–7	529
1:12	519	3:8–12	511, 529
1:13–2:10	498	3:13–17	529
1:13	519, 527	3:15	528
1:14–2:3	519	3:18–22	413, 527–528
1:14–25	499	3:19	179, 182
1:14–16	518, 520, 528	3:21	507, 525
1:14	500	4:1–6	527, 529
1:15–16	511	4:1	505
1:16	520	4:3–4	506
1:17–21	518, 520, 527–528	4:3	506
1:17	504, 520	4:6	528
1:19	525	4:7–11	529
1:21	525	4:7	505
1:22–25	511, 518, 527–528	4:10–11	219
1:22	413, 506, 510	4:11	504

1 Peter (cont.)

4:12–19	527, 529
4:15	506
4:17	519
5:1–5	527, 529
5:1	505, 519, 529
5:2	413
5:6–11	529
5:6	505
5:9	519
5:13	400

2 Peter

1:5–8	506
1:16–21	526
1:17–18	532
1:18	532
3:4	242, 360
3:9	243

1 John

1:1–3	423
1:1	423
1:3	423
1:7	424
1:8	421
1:10	421
2	455, 457
2:1–2	454
2:2–7	455
2:2	251, 424–425
2:3–6	455
2:3–4	455
2:5–6	455
2:5	455
2:6	455
2:7–8	422
2:7	422, 455
2:8	422–423
2:9–11	422
2:18–23	418
2:18–19	418
2:18	422–423
2:19	420–421
2:22–23	421
2:22	412, 418–419, 423, 425
2:23	420
2:24	422–423
2:25	423
2:28–29	425
2:28	507
3:1	457, 524
3:4–10	457
3:9	457
3:11	422–423
3:15	457
3:16	454, 457
3:17	455
3:18	457
4:2	423
4:3	422–423
4:7–16	455
4:9–11	454
4:9–10	455
4:9	432
4:10	424
4:14	243, 432
4:20	457
4:21	432
5	457
5:1–3	457
5:1	424
5:5	424
5:19	243, 251
5:21	419, 421

2 John

1–9	406
7–8	404

Jude

1	524
8	506
15	243
16	506
25	504

Revelation

1:4	414
1:5–6	414
1:5	424
1:6	508
1:7	415, 425
1:9	414
1:18	370
2–3	259
2:1	414
2:7	414

2:10	365	11:13	360
2:11	414	11:19	360
2:17	414	12:5	243
2:29	414	12:17	524
3:5	524	14:8	243
3:6	414	15:4	243
3:13	414	16:18	360
3:22	414	17:14	509
4:15	425	18:3	243
4:17	425	18:23	243
5:9	243	20:6	508
5:10	508	21:8	506
6:8	370	21:24	243
6:12	360	21:26	243
7:1	249	22:2	243
7:9	243	22:11	415
7:14	365	22:12	415, 425
8:5	360	22:15	415, 506
9:1–11	370	22:20	190, 415, 425
9:20–21	506	22:22	243
11:7	370		

Q Source

Q		10	229, 231, 237
3	231	10:9	230
3:2–3	51	10:21	63
3:3	53	11:31–32	228
3:7–9	51, 53	11:49–51	227
3:16–17	51	12:6–7	229
3:16	54	12:8–12	229
3:21–22	51	12:8–9	229
4:1–4	51	12:11–12	229
4:5–8	51	12:21–33	228
4:9–12	51	12:42–46	190
4:13	51	13:25	191
6	229	13:28	229
6:46	190	13:29	229
7	51, 54, 57	13:34–35	227
7:18–19	51	14:27	231
7:19	54	17:20–21	230
7:22–30	51	17:24	191
7:24–28	51	17:26	191
7:29–30	51	17:30	191
7:31–35	51	19:12–26	190
7:35	63		

Old Testament Pseudepigrapha

1 En

9:2	370
18:2	250
39:6	20
40:5	20
45:3	20
45:4	20
48:6	20
49:2	20
49:4	20
51:3	20
51:5	20
52:6	20
52:9	20
53:6	20
55:4	20
56:8	369
57:2	251
61:5	20, 190
61:8	20
61:10	20
62:1	20
80:2	251
90:28–39	290
91	363
91:11–12	363
91:14–17	363
91:16	312, 360
93	363
93:9	363
93:10	363
99:11	369
102:11	369
103:7	369

2 Bar

10:18	370
25	250–251
25:1–4	364
27:7	360
53:7	354

3 Bar

11:1–2	370
16:3	354

4 Bar

4:4	370

4 Ezra

5:1–2	250–251
13:52	190

Apoc. Ab.

1:5	443
17:7	442, 445
27	308
30:8	360

Apoc. Sedr.

1:12–16	443
1:14	443–444

Aristob.

2:4	447
3:1	447
4:1	447
4:6	447

As. Mos.

10:4	360
10:5	251

Jos. Asen.

8:10	521
8:11	521
12:8	521
18:11	521

Jub.

1:9	315
1:23–25	520
7:29	369
8:19	315
22:22	369
23:11–14	364
23:14–21	364
23:14	364
23:18	354
23:22–25	364
23:26–31	364
23:27–31	360
24:31	369

49:19	338	3:752	360
49:23	340	3:796–807	364
		3:796–803	251
Let. Aris.		3:796–797	251
228	445	3:689–692	354
229	446	4:58–59	360
270	445	4:173	364
		8:204–205	354
Mart. Isa.			
9:16	194	*T. Benj.*	
		3:1–3	444, 449
Ps.-Orph.		4:1–3	444, 449
1:4–8	447		
2:1–5	447	*T. Gad.*	
3:3–7	447	6:1	442
Pss. Sol.		*T. Iss.*	
4:25	442	5:1–2	444, 448
6:6	442	5:2	442, 448
9:8	442		
10:3	442	*T. Jos.*	
16:2	369	10:5–6	449
18:3	442	11:1–2	449
Sib. Or.		*T. Levi.*	
1:296	442	4:1	251, 360
2:154–164	364, 366		
2:168–169	364	*T. Mos.*	
2:174–175	364	10:1	251
3:659–660	360	10:4–5	251
3:675–681	360		

New Testament Apocrypha

Acts of Peter		1:2	180
1:9–20	260	2:3–5a	175, 182
5	259	2:3	180
5:11–14	260	2:5	178
20	532	2:5b–6:22	174
		2:5b	183
Acts of Thomas		3:6	179–180
1:1	259	3:7	178–179
		3:8	178
Epistle to the Apostles		3:9	178, 180
30	259	3:10	178
		3:11	180
Gos. Pet.		4:10	180
1:1–2	174, 177	4:11	178

Gos. Pet. (cont.)

4:12	178
4:13	178, 180
4:14	178
5:15	178
5:16	178
5:18	178
5:19	178, 180
5:20	179
6:21	180
6:23–24	175
6:24	180
7:25	174, 176
7:26–27	175, 183
8:28	176, 179
8:28–9:34	174
8:30	179
8:32	179
9:35–10:42	175
9:35	179–180, 191
9:36	179, 183
9:37	179
10:41	179
11:43–44	175, 183
11:45–49	175
11:45	179
11:46	180
11:47	179
12:50–13:57	175, 183
12:50	180
13:57	183
14:58–59	175, 183
14:58	183
14:60	175, 183

Gos. Thom.

3	230
37	507
65–66	502, 515

The Letter of Peter to Philip

134:18–26	260
140:7–15	260
140:23–27	260

Qumran Documents

1QH

6:25–27	498
6:25	503
7:17	503
10:27–28	354
11:13–18	354
11:16–18	370
11:17	369
11:26–28	370
14:22–24	354, 357
14:23	357

1QS

3:20–21	187
4:2–14	506
4:20–23	55, 63
5:1–2	187
5:5	503
8:4–6	498
8:5–10	503
8:8	502
8:17	503
9:3–5	498

1QpHab

2:6–7	365
7:1	365

1Q20

20:29	211
22:32	191

1Q28b (1QS^b)

3:7	365

4Q397

14–21 7	187

4QFlor

1:6–7	498

4QpIsa^d

frg. 1	498

4QpPs 37

2:16	503

11QTª (11Q19)	
29:7–10	290
46:17–18	201

CD	
1:12–2:1	365
3:19–4:3	498

Early Jewish Writings

Josephus
Ag. Ap.

1.1	34
1.50	132

Ant.

1.8	34
1.147	262
3.99	35
6.5.4	74
8.2.5	204
8.13.7	74
9.2.2	74
9.3.1	74
9.4.4	74
9.6.1	74
10.9.1	74
13.10.5	74
15.1.1	74
18.2.1–2	43
18.116–119	14
18.116	161
18.117	53–54

J.W.

1.5	262
1.10–12	309
1.10	309
1.99	262
1.143	262
1.397	262
1.672	262
2.119–161	54
2.8.7 (136)	205
2.363	262
2.374	262
2.382	262
2.385	262
6.9.3	338
6.410–411	309
7.90	262
7.117–159	303
7.157	304
7.358–360	308

Life

2	74–75
38–39	74
430	34

Philo
Contempl.

2.1	205
11.83	205

Hypoth.

11.13	205

Opif.

134	62
135	62
2.205	34

Prob.

84	54

Spec.

2.145	340

Virt.

179	521

Rabbinic Writings

Mishnah

m. Taʿan. 2:4	356
m. Taʿan. 3:8	76
m. Ketub. 5:6	77
m. Pesaḥ. 5:1	143
m. Soṭah 9:15	365

Talmuds

b. Ber. 5b	213
b. Giṭ. 61a	208
b. Ketub. 96a	73
b. Ketub. 112b	365
b. Metziʾa 30b	206

Talmuds (cont.)
b. Metzi'a 30bz	206
b. Ned. 39b	206, 208
b. Ned. 40a	207
b. Qamma 100a	206
b. Sanh. 43a	80
b. Sanh. 97a–98a	365
b. Sotah 14a	206
b. Yebam. 46a	507
b. Yebam. 47ab	507
b. Yebam. 62b	83
y. B.M. 2:12–13, 8d	83
y. Ḥag. 77d	211

Targums
Tg. Neophyti Num 27:23	211

Tosefta
t. Ber. 7:18	65
t. Ketub. 5:6	77
t. Pe'ah. 4:6	79
t. Pe'ah. 4:18b	79

Other
Gen. Rab. 8:13	206
Gen. Rab. 306.7	211
Midr. Ps 73:11	213
Koh. Rab. 4b	211
Midr. Rab. Sir 7:1	252

Greco-Roman Writings

Appian
Bell. civ.
1.2.1	246

Aristides, frg.
2.10–11	210

Aristotle
Pol.
1264b5	204
1324^{b}10	246

Cassius Dio
40.55.1–4	139

Cicero
Att.
5.21	146
13.29	123
16.6	123

Cluentius
178	201

Fam.
10.28.1	123
12.4.1	123

Diogenes Laertius
Lives
1.33	65
2.60	115
2.61	115
2.62	111, 121
5.92	115
8.54	118
8.55	118
8.56	118
8.57–58	119

Epictetus
Disc.
1.8	113

Euripides
Phoen.
1439	210

Hadrian
Digestes
3.2.21	158
222.5.3	158

Homer
Iliad
4.223–421	347

INDEX OF ANCIENT SOURCES 575

10.17–179	347
23.257–897	347

Odyssey

1.125–148	347–348
14	347

Herodotus
Hist.

1.101	246
9.106	246

Artic.

47.39–40	210

Isocrates
Evag.

37–39	40

Lucian
How to Write History

55	142

Martial
Epigrams

1.66	111, 116, 126

Plato
Rep.

3.405a	200
420b	246
514a–521d	385
555c	379

Laws

743a	379
762e	380
776d	246

Apol.

20e	378–379
21b	379

Crito

49b	380

Alc.

2.141c	379

Pliny the Elder
N.H.

preface 21–22	117
preface 23	111, 118
2.79	143

Pliny the Younger
Ep.

10.96–97	420
10.97.2	157

Plutarch
Lives

Alex. 1.2–3	137
Ant. 12.6	140
Brut. 33.4	146
Caes. 7.4–8.2	144
Caes. 48.2	146
Caes. 60.3–5	140
Caes. 61.1–5	140
Cato Min. 22.3–23.3	144
Cato Min. 29.3–4	138
Cato Min. 48. 4	139
Cic. 15.1–4	144
Cic. 20.3–21.4	144
Crass. 13.3	144
Luc. 37.1–4	138
Nic. 1.5	137
Pomp. 8.7	137
Pomp. 55.5	139
Pomp. 80.5–6	146

Mor.

943A	62

Polybius
Hist.

9.2.1	118

Ptolemy V
C. Ord. Ptol.

31,1.12	124

Quintilian
Inst. Proem.

7	113

Seneca the Elder
Declamations

vol. 2: *Suasoriae* 2.19	119
vol. 2: *Suasoriae* 3.6–7	119
vol. 2: *Suasoriae* 3.7	120
vol. 2: *Controversiae* 10.4.21	119

Seneca the Younger
Ep.

79.6	121, 123
84	125
84.5	120
84.6–7	121
84.7–8	121
84.8	120–121
84.9	121
85	129

Suetonius
Claud.

25.4	420

Tacitus
Ann.

15.44.2–5	420

Valerius Maximus

6.2.5	139

Virgil
Donat. Vit. Verg.

46	122

Vitruvius
Arch.

7.preface.3	116–117
7.preface.4	117
7.preface.5	117
7.preface.7	117

Early Christian Writings

1 Clem.

1:1	504
13:1	505
21:1	507
22:3	507
30:6	507
35:5	506
42:1–4	259
43:2	505
50:7	504
58:2	504
59:3	504

Acts Pet.

5	259
20	532

Acts Pet. 12 Apos.

1:9–20	260
5:11–14	260

Acts Thom.

1:1	259

Athanasius
Ep. Fest.

39.5	399

Augustine
Harmony.

2.4	33
3	48

Barn.

2:8	507
6:2–4	502, 515
16:6–10	502, 515
19–20	506

Cassiodorus
De institutione divinarum literarum

1.8.4	402

Clement of Alexandria
Strom.

4.15.97	395
6.5.43	259
6.648	259

Cyril of Jerusalem
Catech.

4.36	399

Myst. Cat.

2.2	507

Procat.

4	507

Did.

1:4	507
1:5	507
5:1	506
7	14
9:4	504
9:5	192
10:6	190
14:1	191
15:3	507

Didascalia Apostolorum

13	191
23	260

Diogn.

5:1–5	261

Ep. Apos.

30	259

Ep. Pet. Phil.

134:18–26	260
140:7–15	260
140:23–27	260

Eusebius
Hist. eccl.

2.16.2	220
2.17.3	220
2.17.4	220
2.17.24	220
2.23	398
2.23.24–25	396, 398
3.1.1	260
3.3.5	398
3.25	398
3.25.1–5	397–398
3.39.15–16	132
3.39.15	85
4.22.7	193
4.23.1	395
5.15.5	394–395
5.18.14	259
6.14.1	401
6.25.5	395, 400
6.25.6	32
6.25.8	401
6.25.9	401

Firmicus Maternus
Err prof. rel.

19.1	30

Fragments of Polycarp

a. 5–12	260

Hippolytus
Apos. Trad.

21.3	507
21.9–10	507

De antichristo.

59	359

Haer.

9.13.2	193

Ign.
Magn.

5:2	504
8:2	504
9:1	191
10:2	507

Eph.

4:2	504
9:1	502, 515

Tral.

7:1	507

Irenaeus
Haer.

1.3.2	194
1.30.14	194
2.22.5	414
3	404
3.1.1–2	414
3.1.1	32–33, 414
3.1.2	47
3.3.4	414
3.11.1–2	414
3.11.8–9	47
3.11.8	47, 404
3.14.1	33
3.16.5–8	404
4.4	306
4.9.2	404

Jerome
adv. Pel.

3.2	52

Commentaire Sur S. Matthieu
   1:163 — 360
Ep.
   107, ch. 2 — 29
Fab.
   19 — 507
   77 — 201
Vir. ill.
   1–2 — 400

Justin Martyr
1 Apol.
   61.4–5 — 48
   66.3 — 45
   67.3 — 45
Dial.
   103.8 — 45
   103.56–58 — 48
   106.3 — 46

Pol.
Phil.
   1:3 — 504
   2:2 — 506
   4:3 — 506

Leontius,
De Sectis
   act 2.4 — 395

Mart. Pol.
   13:2 — 505
   18:2 — 505

Herm.
Vis.
   3 — 502, 515
   3.7.3 — 192

Origen
Cels.
   2.12 — 82
Comm. Jo.
   1.22.137 — 395
   2.23.149 — 395
   6.35.175 — 395
   19:6 — 401

Comm. Jn.
   1.138 — 400
   2.149 — 400
   6.175.9 — 400
   19.23.152 — 401
Comm. Rom.
   4:1 — 401
   4:8 — 401
   9:24 — 401
Hom. Exod.
   3:3 — 401
   8:4 — 401
Hom. Lev.
   2:4 — 401

Origen, *Hom. Job*
   7:1 — 401
Sel. Ps.
   31:5 — 401
Fr. Jo.
   126 — 401

Papias
frg.
   15 — 35
   16 — 36

Photius, *Bibliotheca Photii Patriarchae*
   cod. 109 — 402

Pre. Pet.
   3a — 259
   3b — 259

Ps-Clement
Hom.
   2.24 — 57
Rec.
   2.8 — 57

Tertullian
Cult. Fem.
   1.3.1–3 — 402
De baptismo
   12 — 359
Scorp.
   12.2 — 402

INDEX OF ANCIENT SOURCES

Papyri and Inscriptions

Papyri

P.Ant. 1.12 (P. Antinoopolis 12)	406–407
P.Cairo 10759	173
P.Oxy. XLI 2949	173
P.Oxy. LX 4009	173
P.Vindob. G 2325	173–174
𝔓⁵	406
𝔓²⁰	406
𝔓²³	406
𝔓⁴⁵	48
𝔓⁶⁶	503
𝔓⁷²	405–406
𝔓⁷⁵	33, 503
𝔓¹⁰⁰	406
Taylor-Schechter Misc. 35.87	194
Taylor-Schechter Misc. 35.88	194

Inscriptions

Ditt. Syll. 814.31	251
Ditt. Or. 458.40	251
Inscriptiones Graecae IV2 1, no. 126	212
OGIS 90.17	246